CARL SAGAN

CARL SAGAN

a life in the cosmos

William Poundstone

Henry Holt and Company   New York

Henry Holt and Company, LLC
Publishers since 1866
115 West 18th Street
New York, New York 10011

Henry Holt ® is a registered
trademark of Henry Holt and Company, LLC.

Published in Canada by Fitzhenry & Whiteside, Ltd.,
195 Allstate Parkway, Markham, Ontario L3R 4T8.

Library of Congress Cataloging-in-Publication Data
Poundstone, William.
Carl Sagan: a life in the cosmos / by William Poundstone.
p. cm.
Includes bibliographical references and index.
ISBN 0–8050–5766–8
1. Sagan, Carl, 1934–   . 2. Astronomers—United States—
Biography. I. Title.
QB36.S15P68   1999
520'.92—dc21   99-14615
[B]   CIP

Designed by Paula Russell Szafranski

Printed in the United States of America
1   3   5   7   9   10   8   6   4   2

To Arthur Flannigan Saint-Aubin

For what are Stars but Asterisks
To point a human Life?

EMILY DICKINSON

Contents

Foreword   xiii

Brooklyn   1934–48   3
The River Bug—Samuel and Rachel—Reality Check—Carl and Carol.

Rahway   1948–51   11
High School—Chemistry Set—Carnegie Hall—Knights of Columbus.

Chicago   1951–60   16
Hermann Muller—A Vial with Nonvirgins—Curious Pest— Flying Saucers—The Fermi Question—Harold Urey—Ice Bath—Gerard Kuiper—House of Cards—Lynn Alexander— Peddling Without a License—Newspaper of Record— Marriage—Joshua Lederberg—Sputnik—Dorion—NASA— Greenhouse Effect—Life on Jupiter, Scientist Says.

Berkeley   1960–63   45
A Non-Reputable Game—Mariner and Apollo—A Trip to Oz— Frank Drake—Green Bank—Drake Equation—Dolphin

Man—IQ Test—Wax and Wigglers—Symbiosis—Cover Story—Kaleidoscope—Firefly Tails.

Cambridge   1963–68   71
Talking Horse—Projects of the Space Cadets—"The Prey Runs to the Hunter"—My So-called Coauthor—Isaac Asimov—Escalation Clause—Flooded House—Linda Salzman—The Dead Planet—James Pollack—Winds of Mars—CTA-102—Project Blue Book—Expert Witness—Antarctica—Lester Grinspoon—Mr. X—The Numinous—Bell Curves—2001—Wheel of Fortune—As Cities Burned—Tommy Gold—Little Green Men—A Jewish Wedding.

Ithaca   1968–76   113
Town Without Bad Taste—Astronomy 101—Timothy Leary—Student Radical—Back Contamination—Andromeda Strain—Massachusetts General—Moon Dust—A Flying Saucer with Rivets—Alien Abduction—Folie à Deux—Message in a Bottle—Pornography in Space—Viva Zapata—Viking—Shoes for Shklovskii—Hurtling Moons of Barsoom—Fortune Cookie—Smokey the Bear—Condensation Theory—Wild Card—Armenian Breakfast—Life with the !Kung—Golden Age—Boy Scouts—Earth Prime—Mediums and Messages—A Storm on Mars—Down the Zambesi—Lightning in a Bottle—Early Faint Sun Paradox—Going North—Quicksand—Der Führer—Big Bird—Bora Bora—Mentor and Nemesis—The Guatemalan Poet—Rolling Stone—"Too Down to Mars"—Great Reckless Solo—Death of an Exobiologist—Polar Bears—Bruce Murray—Pet Shop—Ann Druyan—Proxy ET—"Let's Do It"—Cockeyed Optimists—Defection—Suicide Chess—Countdown—Life in the Clouds.

Pasadena   1976   197
Embassy of Mars—Cosmic Ice Hockey—Touchdown—Oasis—Rules of the Game—Pink Skies—Just Add Water—Super Curve—Important, Unique, and Exciting Things—Scavenger Theory—Normal Science—Utopia—Subrock Sample—Hard-Shell Bugs—Sudden Death.

Ithaca   1977–78   224
Double Squirt—Bitter End—Carbon Chauvinist—One-Sigma

Difference—Rocket Scientist—Time Capsule—A Lack of Historical Determinism—"Moscow Nights"—"Johnny B. Goode" Photo Album—Anatomy Lesson—World's Meanest Hyenas— Protocol—June 1st—Open Mike—String of Firecrackers— "Danny Boy"—Circle Line—Launch—Yellow Pad—Mosquito Nets—Existence Theorem—Metronome—The Pulitzer.

Los Angeles   1978–81   255
Two Mettlesome Horses—Special Effects—Director's Revenge—Pop Star—Popularization and Academia—Down to a Sunless Sea—Clouds of Titan—Loophole—Soap on a Rope— Malevolent or Hungry—Golden Fleece—The Perfect Zoo—A Still More Fatal Weapon—Muskrats, Drunkards, Extraterrestrials—Wedding.

Ithaca   1981–95   280
Take No Prisoners—Annie Effect—Home Life—Switzerland— Bait and Switch—A Paper a Month—Good Works— Nucleus—Nuclear Winter—Cornell West—Dust Storms and Dinosaurs—Appendicitis—Star Wars—Peer Review—Halloween Before 1984—Understanding TTAPS—Doomsday Machine—The World Turned Strangely Jewish—Through the Looking Glass—Asymmetry of Perception—$\infty = \infty$— C-Minus—Saber-Tooth—Without a Trace—Carl and Dorion— Roman à Clef—SETI-in-a-Suitcase—Throwing the Switch— Mysterious Uranian Gunk—Edward Teller—Who's Afraid of Autumn?—Burning Forests—Nuremberg Trial—Reagan in the Kremlin—900 Number—Chapter and Verse—Pale Blue Dot—Monsoon—Postmortem—Things That Go Bump in the Night—Great Martian Chase—Remodeling—Genealogy— National Academy—Freak Accident—Again with the Alien Abductions—Karmic Boomerang—Sagan Versus Apple Computer—The "I Touched Carl Sagan" Contest—Birthday Party—Conference Call.

Seattle   1995–96   370
Biohazard—An Isolated Experiment—Pirates—Zeno's Paradox—Postcard from the Titanic—X Rays—Martian Meteorite—Death.

Afterword   383

Notes   389

Bibliography   433

Acknowledgments   448

Index   451

\|

Foreword

ONE MORNING WHEN Carl Sagan was not yet five, his parents bundled him up and trudged to the Eighty-sixth Street elevated rail station. Carl was still young enough to ride piggyback on father Samuel's shoulders; to be more reassured than inhibited by mother Rachel's watchful presence. When the train arrived, the family embarked on a complicated journey through Brooklyn and Queens. When it was over, they were in a place called Corona, New York. Glinting in the brisk morning air before them was the city of the future.

Promoter Grover Whalen drained great tracts of Long Island marshland to build the 1939 New York World's Fair. Its theme was *time—future time*. Its message was the great credo of the twentieth century: that the future would be different from the past, and that science would be the primary agent of change.

It was "a day that powerfully influenced my thinking," as Sagan remembered it toward the end of his life. Fair goers gazed upon "a perfect future made possible by science" here rendered concrete in steel and glass. The great towers of Manhattan, slumbering in dreary 1939, paled by comparison.

In novelty the 1939 fair exceeded the Tomorrowlands and EPCOTs it inspired. Whalen was showman enough to blend edification with entertainment. A 280-acre amusement park had roller coasters, bobsled rides, and a 250-foot parachute jump. Such daring customers as Tallulah Bankhead and Admiral Byrd paid forty cents to experience the latter's breathtaking ten-second plunge. The fair midway impressed visitors as clean, modern, and tasteful. "The freak shows boast no overpowering monsters," reported one newsweekly (finding only the usual pygmies and two-headed cows). For dads there were enticements of another sort. Beautiful half-clothed women could be viewed in a dizzying variety of tableaux: "Arctic Girls" frozen inside cakes of ice; "Amazons" brandishing bows and arrows; "Crystal Lassies" undulating in a hall of mirrors, flesh and body stockings reflected to infinity.

*   *   *

The nudes and freaks, like the past, were prologue. The visitor then crossed a sweeping bridge into Whalen's "World of Tomorrow." Dominating the central plaza were the Perisphere and Trylon, a pearl-white sphere and streamlined obelisk. Around them spread a model city of tree-lined avenues, fountains, and calculated effects of color, lighting, and scale. The visibly creeping shadow of the world's largest sundial (its gnomon piercing eighty feet of air) reminded visitors of their own one-way trip into the future.

Defying worldwide depression and rumblings of war, sixty nations vied with America's corporations to sponsor the most dazzling displays of technology, art, and imagination. Of the world's largest and richest nations, only China and Hitler's Germany were absent. Stalin's cash-strapped Soviet Union (home to the Sagans' forebears) scraped together $4 million for a pavilion. This bought a great map of the motherland with every city and town picked out in jewels and semiprecious stones. A red porphyry pylon held a monumental statue of a Russian worker raising a five-pointed red star to the heavens. The Italian pavilion soft-pedaled Mussolini in favor of Italian arts and industries. It was easy to ignore the writing on the wall, which in this case read *Credere! Obbedire! Combattere!* (Believe! Obey! Fight!).

The U.S. presence was best seen in the corporate exhibits. There the shape of things to come was shaped by those paying the bills. In General Motors's popular Futurama, foot-weary visitors plunked down into comfy armchairs as a moving platform carried them relentlessly into the world of the year 1960. Revealed was a spread-out, suburbanized America of fourteen-lane freeways. The 1960 model cars would be teardrop shaped, drive themselves automatically, and sell for $200. Visitors exiting the exhibit got a button that said, "I have seen the future."

Several of the showcased technologies would have special significance in Carl's own future. The Transportation Zone offered a simulated rocket trip—to London. Visitors assembled at a "rocketport" to be loaded into a giant cannon that propelled an imaginary rocket through space. Details of the "landing" were vague. "Rocket flight is at present impossible," conceded the fair's science director, "but the problem is almost wholly limited to the invention of a proper fuel."

Television made its American debut at the fair. On opening day President Franklin Delano Roosevelt, standing and steadying himself with handles concealed in his podium, officially dedicated the fair to all humankind. His image flickered on TV receivers stationed throughout the fairgrounds. RCA's model had a seven-inch black-and-pale-green picture tube (the company preferred to call it "black and white"). The tube pointed skyward, and a built-in mirror reflected it horizontally for easier viewing. Television was already appreciated as a technology to be reckoned with. RCA executives were confident the TV receivers would work and produce acceptable pictures, said one magazine; "beyond that they know nothing."

One thing that particularly impressed Carl was the fair's time capsule. The Westinghouse Corporation buried a capsule intended to be dug up in the year 6939(!). This capsule was at the bottom of a fifty-foot well. The Sagan family saw only a duplicate. It was seven and a half feet long and streamlined like a rocket at both ends. Inside, an inert nitrogen atmosphere preserved objects held to be representative of the culture that produced it, including: a dictionary, a copy of Margaret Mitchell's *Gone with the Wind*, an assortment of publications on microfilm, a newsreel of Jesse Owens winning the 100-meter dash at the Berlin Olympics, instructions on how to *make* a newsreel projector, "a woman's hat, razor, can opener, fountain pen, pencil, tobacco pouch with zipper, pipe, tobacco, cigarets, camera, eyeglasses, toothbrush; cosmetics, textiles, metals and alloys, coal, building materials, synthetic plastics, seeds . . ."

The Westinghouse people showed more imagination in their attempts to ensure that people of 6939 would be able to find the capsule. They printed *A Book of Record of the Time Capsule* pinpointing the capsule's position to within an inch. Each book told when to open the capsule, using the Gregorian, Jewish, Muslim, Chinese, and Shinto calendars and (should none be in use 5,000 years hence) astronomical reckoning. Westinghouse sent copies of the book to the world's great libraries, museums, and convents. There the books still sit awaiting unborn readers, testament to the ebullient optimism of 1939 America.

*   *   *

Carl Sagan grew up to become as much a popular icon of science as the 1939 World's Fair had been to its public. Starting from a Brooklyn tenement, he achieved fame and influence unsurpassed by any living scientist. Like many an American success story, Sagan prospered by selling the public something it didn't know it needed or wanted. The linchpin of his success was a "high concept" no other scientist, no matter how brilliant, could match. Of all the scientific questions of the busily inquisitive twentieth century, nothing fired the public imagination so much as life on other planets.

According to one childhood friend, Carl Sagan's defining attribute was *clarity of purpose*: from an early age Carl was seized with the fabulous mission of searching for life on other worlds. During one discussion, Carl soberly calculated that he would not travel to the moon or Mars. He would be too old by the time it happened. Carl was then ten years old.

Over thirty years later, a Viking mission colleague told journalist Henry S. F. Cooper, Jr., that "Sagan desperately wants to find life someplace, anyplace—on Mars, on Titan, in the solar system or outside of it. In all the divergent things he does, that is the unifying thread. I don't know why, but if you read his papers or listen to his speeches, even though they are on a wide variety of seemingly unrelated topics, there is always the question, 'Is this or that phenomenon related to life?' People say, what a varied career he has had, but everything he has done has had this one underlying purpose."

Extraterrestrial life was the maguffin of Sagan's life and career. He staked out *exobiology*—the would-be study of alien life—as his own turf. The subject lay in the foreground or background of most of Sagan's 300 scientific articles. It is no exaggeration to say that Sagan's ability to capitalize on the topic's broad appeal made him rich and famous.

To colleagues unsympathetic or unimaginative, this worldly success was an enigma. There was something of Herman Melville's shape-shifting Confidence Man about Sagan, or Raymond Chandler's inventor of neon signs ("There's a boy who really made something out of nothing"). The *nothing* being extraterrestrial life—for of course Sagan never found the thing he spent much of his career looking for.

*　　*　　*

The Viking mission's failure to find life on Mars hardly dented Sagan's enthusiasm for exobiology, but it did force a reassessment of what he could expect to achieve in the field. With the encouragement of his third wife, Ann Druyan, Sagan reinvented himself as a politically engaged scientist-popularizer. His books were models of lucid exposition; his *Cosmos* TV series, seen by half a billion people, made him the first great "media scientist."

With Sagan's celebrity came political clout. Sagan's influence on the space program's planning and funding was unequaled. His opinions on pseudoscience, the environment, science education, women's rights, and racism were widely disseminated. Above all, Sagan was concerned with nuclear war. As a scientist he recognized it as the greatest threat to human existence (and even managed to see in it an unexpected connection to the subject of extraterrestrial life). Sagan believed that only radical reduction of nuclear stockpiles by all nations could preserve human civilization. This view was at the heart of Sagan's most politicized science, the "nuclear winter" articles he wrote with four colleagues. In this work Sagan played a complex, still bitterly controversial role in shaping the public and governmental attitudes that led to the end of the cold war.

As anyone who watches TV or movies knows, extraterrestrial life is our society's primary myth. This is not to trivialize its standing as a scientific conjecture but to recognize that certain scientific ideas can have broad and unpredictable cultural influence. Homer located sorceresses and monsters on Western islands because he could plausibly do so. In our own time, the credible frontier of fantastic beings has receded from the Earth to the planets to the distant stars. Today's credible myth maker may well be a scientist who appears on television.

Myths are more than stories told for diversion. Homer spoke to the spiritual concerns of a Greek world in which old gods were being discarded and the future was uncertain. In the twentieth century, science displaced many an old god and threw our survival as a species into question. Anyone seeking to understand our time would do well to ponder why extraterrestrial life has cast such a powerful spell over the intellectual and popular imaginations. For that they must turn to the poet of exobiology, Carl Sagan of Ithaca.

CARL SAGAN

BROOKLYN
1934–48

IN A MATTER of personal honor, and using only his bare hands, Leib Gruber killed a man in the village of Sasov. Gruber was Carl Sagan's grandfather. According to family tradition, the killing forced Gruber's hasty emigration to the New World. Had it not been for Gruber's fervid sense of honor, Carl Sagan would likely have never been born, nor would his family line have been elevated, in the space of two generations, from desperate poverty in the eastern European shtetl to the privileged circumstances of America's most prominent astronomer.

The River Bug

In Leib Gruber's time the village of Sasov was part of the Austro-Hungarian crownland of Galicia. Today it falls within the Ukraine. Too small to appear in most atlases, the town is a little to the northeast of Lvov, on the Bug River.

That river was Gruber's bread and butter. The Bug is shallow enough to wade across. In the absence of bridges or ferryboats, young men such as Leib hired themselves for passage, carrying passengers piggyback to the far shore.

With the law on his trail, Leib had to get out of the country. He did not have enough money for both his and his wife's passage. The cost of lower-cabin passage to America was about $30 (U.S.), a princely sum in the shtetl. In 1904 Gruber sailed alone to New York (by one account, disguised in women's clothing!). He promised his wife, Chaya, that he would send for her after he earned the money for her passage. This he did with scarcely a penny to spare. In late 1905 Chaya set sail from Hamburg on the *Batavia*. Required to declare how much money she had for the ship's manifest, she answered one dollar.

Chaya was detained at Ellis Island for a "valvular disease of heart." This was not judged serious enough to declare her an undesirable and send her back. She rejoined her husband in the New World. It must have been an ardent reunion, for Chaya conceived a child within weeks of her arrival.

The Grubers lived at 230 East Seventh Street in the bustling Lower East Side of Manhattan. There was a strong pressure to fit into American life. Chaya anglicized her name to Clara. She gave her new baby a good American name, Rachel Molly Gruber. This Rachel would be Carl Sagan's mother.

A few years later, Clara bore a second daughter, Tobi. The stress of childbirth was too much for Clara's weak heart. Within a month of Tobi's birth, she died of what official records called cardiac failure due to chronic endocarditis. Clara was thirty-three years old.

Leib Gruber now found himself alone again in a strange land. He could hardly raise two infant daughters and hold a job. He put Tobi in an orphanage and Rachel on an eastbound ship. Rachel's ship must have been uncrowded, compared to the teeming steerages of the westbound ships it passed. Upon arrival in Europe, Rachel was directed to the care of Leib's sisters in Austria.

Had Rachel spent her life in central Europe, she well might not have survived the Holocaust. Fortunately, Gruber took a second wife, a younger woman named Rose Klinghofer. The couple recalled Rachel, still only about four years old, to raise her in the United States.

As Rachel arrived back in New York, her hair was infected with lice from the filthy conditions of the ship. Leib took to calling her by a Yiddish nickname meaning "lice head"—a joke that must have proved irritating for a growing girl. It was a changed and somehow alien family that Rachel rejoined. Leib's attention was now directed to his new wife and her children. Leib informed Rachel that Rosie was her mother now. Rachel viewed Rosie as an impostor, a pod-person who had replaced her real mother. She refused to act as the others did, as if nothing had changed.

Samuel and Rachel

Samuel Sagan was born in Kamenets-Podolsk—only about 120 miles to the southeast of Sasov—to Louis Sagan and Etta Lisenbaum. As Carl told it, Sagan was a Jewish title of nobility derived from the name of Akkadian king Sargon of the twenty-fourth century B.C. "In modern Hebrew," Carl once explained, " 'Sagan' means 'lieutenant'—an illustration of the deterioration of titles of nobility with time."

The Sagan family's nobility was indeed at a low ebb. At about the age of five, Samuel Sagan left his impoverished parents behind to come to the United States with his siblings, sponsored by his uncle George. George was himself only about seventeen.

This waifish family contended not only against the prejudices of Anglo-Americans but against those of New York's established Jews, who feared that poor, uneducated arrivals like the Sagans could only inspire American anti-Semitism. Samuel determined to make something of himself. He set his sights on college and a pharmacy degree. At Columbia University he was known for his skills at the pool table. As he explained it, he could not afford to lose money gambling, so he had to be good enough to beat the sort of students who *could* afford to lose money at pool. This picaresque career carried him two years. Finally, the depression forced him to drop out and take a real job.

Samuel was a slender man of undistinguished features save for a head of flaming red hair. "Red" and "Lucky" were his nicknames. At a party he met the glamorous Rachel Gruber. It was love at first sight. They married in Brooklyn on March 4, 1933. As far as their children could determine, Samuel and Rachel never tired of each other throughout their long marriage. They were a case of temperamental opposites attracting.

One family member's "defining memory" of the couple took place at the dinner table. Rachel brought a new dish to the table and anxiously asked Samuel how he liked it. Samuel took a meager bite. Scarcely allowing himself the luxury of swallowing, he announced, "It's fine."

"YOU HAVEN'T EVEN *TASTED* IT!" Rachel shrieked.

Rachel was a "screamer." An intelligent, ambitious woman, she seemed limited by the four walls of her Brooklyn apartment. Her razor-sharp wit was famous throughout her circle of family and friends. People saved her letters. They sparkled with a dishy, almost Jane Austen delight at people's failing to live up to what society expects of them.

Rachel had a competitive nature. From childhood on, she was always trying to top the accomplishments of Rosie's children. She took it as an affront when one half sister gave birth to a daughter with flaming red hair (as if this were reason to question the fidelity of "Red," or "Lucky," Sagan). In the years to come, her half sisters would be kept well apprised of the successes of Rachel's son.

Samuel was less passionate than Rachel, though perhaps more *compassionate*. He was a "mensch"; a great kidder rather than a great wit; a man capable of quiet sacrifices. He had to do some compromising in his time. He worked as an usher in a movie theater, then took a job with George Sagan's business, the New York Girls' and Women's Coat Company. Samuel started as a cutter. He wielded a power saw, a machine-age marvel as efficient and hazardous as anything in *Modern Times*. The machine cut dozens of layers of cloth at once to any desired pattern. Bolts of cut cloth were then passed on to rows of efficient women sitting at sewing machines. It was a sweatshop, by today's standards. One perk was that the female side of the Sagan family never wanted for coats.

Samuel and Rachel lived in Bensonhurst, Brooklyn, successively occupying apartments on Bay Thirty-seventh Street and Bay Parkway. It was a tidy neighborhood of working-class Jewish and Italian families. There was still enough open space that some of the Italians operated truck farms on vacant lots.

Although there was not a lot of "house" to keep, Rachel made sure it was clean and well ordered. She was determined that the family have healthful, appealing, and kosher meals. A favorite Sagan family menu was broiled or baked fish, spinach prepared with eggs, and vegetables dripping with butter. To top off the meal, there would be generous helpings of chocolate pudding.

The depression taught Rachel to watch every penny. She never lost the habit of thrift. On a trip to Europe toward the end of her life, she confessed that she was finally able to spend without guilt because the foreign currency looked like play money.

On November 9, 1934, Rachel gave birth to a son, Carl Edward Sagan. Two explanations for the name Carl are extant. One is that he was named for Rachel's grandfather Kalonymous—Carl being a reasonable American equivalent. Another is that he was given a name similar to that of Rachel's mother, Chaya. The Edward came from Britain's Edward, Duke of Windsor.

The boy was bright, handsome, and personable almost from infancy. Rachel doted on him. She worried that he did not walk unassisted until he was thirteen months old. Ever afterward, she worried that he was too thin.

Rachel "followed prescriptions on childhood nutrition recommended by the U.S. Department of Agriculture as if they had been handed down from Mount Sinai," Carl later wrote. "Our government book on children's health had been repeatedly taped together as its pages fell out. The corners were tattered. Key advice was underlined." These government manuals convinced Samuel and Rachel to give up smoking—not for *their* health (cigarettes were still touted as a healthful alternative to sweets) but so that they could put the pennies saved toward vitamin supplements for Carl.

Samuel and Rachel likewise created opportunities to nourish Carl's mind. The family made trips to Manhattan's American Museum of Natural History and the Hayden Planetarium. Carl liked the planetarium's tricked-up scales showing how much one would weigh on other worlds. There was something comforting to the forty-pound boy in stepping onto the Jupiter scale and seeing the needle register a good, solid 100 pounds.

Reality Check

Carl remained slender, for all the vitamins and pudding. He was shy enough that Samuel was probably more pleased than angry when he got into a fight with a neighborhood kid. Carl thrust his fist through the plate glass window of Schechter's drugstore and needed two stitches. He was aware of having a dual nature. On the one hand, Carl liked to withdraw and spend time on the subjects that interested him. Opposing this was a strong competitive streak like his mother's. He strove to excel in the urban street games of stickball, handball, and basketball. (As a spectator he and Samuel followed the Yankees, their Brooklyn residence notwithstanding.)

By the time Carl entered Brooklyn's P.S. 101, his interests skewed broadly toward *fantasy*: comic books, Greek myths, stars, dinosaurs, big numbers, magic. At age five, Samuel told his son that there is no biggest number. "You can always add one," he explained. Hearing this, Carl determined to write down all the numbers from 1 to 1,000. Thrifty Samuel offered him a stack of old shirt cardboards. They were an unbleached gray a little *less* dark than the mark a soft pencil made on them. Carl began writing eagerly. Eventually Rachel insisted that it was time for his bath. He had not made it to 200 yet. Samuel offered to continue writing numbers if Carl took his bath. By the time Carl got out of the bath, his father was nearly up to 900. Carl took over and made it to 1,000 that night, only a little beyond his bedtime.

This numerical fascination informed Carl's hobby of stamp collecting. A prize acquisition was a stamp issued during the 1923 German hyperinflation, in the amount of 50 trillion deutsche marks.

*   *   *

Stars puzzled Carl. "I could see them at whatever time bedtime was in winter, and they just didn't seem to belong in Brooklyn." When he asked what stars were, people told him they were just lights in the sky. "Just small hovering lamps?" he wondered. "What ever for?" The *uselessness* of these lamps, way up in the lonely night air, invoked a sense of melancholy.

Carl went to the Eighty-fifth Street library and demanded a book on stars. The librarian gave him one on the likes of Clark Gable and Jean Harlow. He protested and got the right kind of book. It opened a world of enchantment.

The thing that hooked him was the statement that stars are suns—as big and bright as our own sun, diminished to twinkling pinpoints by the gulfs of light-years and the atmospheric phenomenon of scintillation. The hugeness of the universe, and the consequent insignificance of everything in the human realm, stunned him.

Carl encountered the concept of life on other planets no later than age eight, when he precociously deduced that other stars must have planets like our sun. (He almost surely was exposed to the idea in some form before that. He avidly read and collected comic books, including *Superman*—who is after all an extraterrestrial.)

At nine or so, Carl discovered Edgar Rice Burroughs's now-campy science-fiction novels of Mars. He devoured such titles as *Thuvia, Maid of Mars*, *The Chessmen of Mars*, and *The Warlords of Mars*. These had been written around the turn of the century, when eccentric American astronomer Percival Lowell was busily mapping the canals of Mars. In Burroughs's imagination, extraterrestrial life entailed herds of eight-legged beasts and Amazon-like women. His illustrators often supplied the latter with generous cleavage. The people who lived on Mars called the planet Barsoom. Carl liked the phrase "the hurtling moons of Barsoom."

At just about the time that his interest in astronomy began, Carl saw the original (1940) release of Disney's *Fantasia*. The movie was his first extended exposure to classical music, to prehistoric animals, and to mythology. All became subjects of absorbing interest. He learned from his astronomy books that there were centaurs and mythologic heroes in the night sky. He taught himself to identify the constellations and pointed them out to his family. In so doing, he absorbed much of the body of Greco-Roman myth.

It was by way of myth that Carl's academic gifts were first recognized. One day the students were required to give impromptu talks on a subject of their choosing. Carl chose Greek and Roman mythology. He fluently spun myth after myth, drawing astute connections and diagramming them on the blackboards. The boy's knowledge seemed endless. He filled all the room's blackboards.

Afterward, the school informed Samuel and Rachel that their son was gifted and might benefit from attending a private school. The Sagans decided against this—whether because of cost or as a matter of principle is uncertain. Carl stayed in public schools. Because of his exceptional ability, he was permitted to skip several grades.

Carl was intrigued by the sometimes thin line separating reality and fantasy. Burroughs's hero was a Virginia gentleman named John Carter who was able to travel to Mars just by looking at the planet in the sky and wishing himself there. Carl tried that one night in a vacant Brooklyn lot. There was a magician in the comic strips, Zatara, who could perform magic by saying commands *backward*. Carl tried to levitate stones by saying "esir, enots."

A reality check of a different kind came at a family gathering a few years later. Grandfather Leib asked Carl what he wanted to be when he grew up. An astronomer, Carl answered confidently. Leib's reaction was "Yes, but how will you make a living?"

The cold waters of the River Bug had disabused Leib of any illusions about making a living. Carl could not dismiss the patriarch's stern words. Thereafter his daydreams of an astronomy career had to acknowledge a daily grind in the garment trade or as a door-to-door salesman. Carl would save his pocket change and buy a telescope. Then he would spend nights in diligent observations as a gentleman astronomer.

Carl and Carol

The year Carl turned seven, Rachel gave birth to a daughter. Carl studied the matter and decided that his new sister should have a name as similar to his as possible. *Carol*, he determined, was the girl's name closest to *Carl*. Rachel named her daughter Carol Mae Sagan.

Carol's earliest memory of Carl began with a friend daring her to ride her tricycle down a too-steep Brooklyn street. Carol took the challenge, fell off the trike, and was seriously injured. Her brother appeared out of nowhere. Carl gently picked her up, as unconcerned about getting her blood over himself as he was about the shared letters of their names. He carried her home. Carl seemed to Carol strong and brave, almost a grown-up. He could not have been more than about twelve.

*   *   *

Rachel was a difficult mother for Carol. She made little attempt to conceal her favoritism for Carl, and for the male sex generally. Carol was a beautiful child who grew into a somewhat awkward adolescent. Rachel treated this as if it were a cardinal sin. She had little regard for unattractive women.

In Rachel's view, it was a woman's duty to be beautiful, popular, witty, and appealing—to men. Rachel dyed her hair a stylish blond. Each day, before Samuel got home from work, she would dress and make up her face. Each night, before going to bed, she put cold cream on her face. (Carl was once puzzled to find a beer in the bathroom. It was the "secret ingredient" in a beauty treatment for Rachel's hair.)

Fortunately, Samuel loved both his children equally. ("I am sane because of my father," Carol says today.) Samuel was perpetually in the position of being Rachel's "spin doctor," offering excuses for the behavior of the wife that, indeed, he deeply loved.

Many of the stories that family members tell about Rachel show she had a flair for creative engineering of the truth. When young Carl took it into his head not to eat mushrooms—for he could not stomach that mushy-sounding name—Rachel began telling him that they were onions. For quite some time mushrooms were known as onions in the Sagan household. Carl wised up only when he innocently ordered "onions" in a restaurant.

One day while the children were at school, Carol's canary died. Rachel rushed out, bought an identical bird, and replaced it for the dead one in its cage. Convinced that the family would never know, she said nothing. That evening, Carol reached into the cage to feed her beloved Petey. The strange bird flitted in terror.

If Rachel was no feminist, she was in some respects open-minded. In junior high, Carl got permission to bring a friend home for dinner. Rachel was surprised when the friend arrived. He was black, as were many of Carl's Brooklyn schoolmates. Afterward, she asked Carl why he hadn't mentioned the child's race. Carl said it hadn't occurred to him; it didn't seem important. While Rachel marveled at this as a token of the boy's otherworldly nature, she also found it laudable.

*   *   *

One afternoon in the apartment, Rachel gazed out the window at their view of Gravesend Bay and announced, "There are people fighting out there, killing each other."

"I know," Carl lied. "I can see them."

"No, you can't," Rachel corrected. "They're too far away." Before the fighting was over, the Nazis had exterminated the Jewish population of Sasov by firing squad and set their homes ablaze. Today almost nothing remains of the town's Jewish past.

RAHWAY
1948-51

SAMUEL SAGAN WAS moving up in the world. The coat company opened a new plant in Perth Amboy, New Jersey. Samuel became the new factory manager. With the promotion, he and Rachel decided it was time to get out of Brooklyn. In 1948 they moved to Rahway, New Jersey.

The town is a middle-class community about nine miles southwest of Newark Airport. To the Sagans, it must have seemed spacious, verdant, and exotically American. George Washington himself ate ham and eggs in Rahway's Merchants and Drovers Tavern, which still stands today. The Rahway scenery, claimed a booster of the 1930s, "has interested landscape artists because of vistas reminiscent of Italy." By the 1940s, the town's economy rested on the sturdy tripod of Wheatena, Three-in-One Oil, and the Merck Company, whose Rahway facility was one of the largest drug plants anywhere.

The new Sagan home stood at 576 Bryant Street. It had a backyard and room for dogs. The family spent money a little more freely than they had. They sent Carl to summer camp and took day trips to the nearby Jersey shore. Samuel and Rachel splurged on their first television set, a Dumont with an impressively crafted cabinet.

High School

Carl attended Rahway High School. The principal's name was Conway. Carl called the school CCC—Conway's Concentration Camp—rather pointed black humor for the time. In retrospect, Sagan felt he "wasted a lot of time" in high school. The teachers were poorly grounded in science, and Carl learned relatively little.

Much of what Carl did learn in his high school years came through his own reading. He graduated from Burroughs to more contemporary fantasies in *Astounding Science Fiction* magazine. One day Carl came across an advertisement for a book called *Interplanetary Flight*. The idea of a whole book on the subject was thrilling to him. Carl sent his money and waited impatiently for the book to arrive in the mail. It lived up to his expectations. He pored over the book's final two sentences:

> The challenge of the great spaces between the worlds is a stupendous one; but if we fail to meet it, the story of our race will be drawing to its close. Humanity will have turned its back upon the still-untrodden heights and will be descending again the long slope that stretches, across a thousand million years of time, down to the shores of the primeval sea.

The author of the book had a distinguished British name: Arthur C. Clarke. Sagan credited the book as being a "turning point" for him. It reinforced the still-novel idea that rockets to the planets would revolutionize the science of astronomy.

On a more practical level, it was a wake-up call about the importance of math. Carl had been an unenthusiastic math student. Calculus seemed gratuitous, invented by high school teachers for intimidation purposes. The Clarke book contained technical appendixes invoking calculus to compute interplanetary trajectories. Carl now realized that calculus was good for something.

Fired by the Clarke book, he discovered the then-flourishing British school of scientist-popularizers (most of whom were of a liberal political bent): Sir Arthur Eddington, Sir James Jeans, J. B. S. Haldane, and Julian Huxley. Carl absorbed their works, along with those of such Americans as George Gamow, Willy Ley, Rachel Carson, and Simon Newcomb. Newcomb's *Astronomy for Everybody* informed him that "there appears to be life on the planet Mars. A few years ago this statement was commonly regarded as fantastic. Now it is commonly accepted."

*   *   *

Carl simultaneously received a religious education. Rachel believed in God and in the importance of going to temple. Samuel was an agnostic who valued the Jewish cultural tradition—or parts of it, anyway. He adored ham and eggs, a dish he could consume only outside of Rachel's kosher kitchen. He was, as in almost everything else, tolerant of Rachel's sincere beliefs.

So Carl had a proper bar mitzvah in Brooklyn, and in Rahway, the family attended Temple Beth Torah, a Conservative congregation. Carl was sent to the Temple's Hebrew school. He was known as a troublemaker, easily bored and already skeptical of the Jewish faith—and every kind of faith. One teacher's trick for dealing with him was to give him exceptionally hard assignments. This played to his competitive instinct. Carl would immerse himself in the work to prove he could master it and would, without realizing it, "behave."

Chemistry Set

Carl's adolescence was not all about study. He discovered the female sex, which became just as abiding an interest as astronomy.

Rachel had already lined up a potential bride for Carl. She was Lu Nahemow, an intelligent and attractive girl who was the daughter of Rachel's best friend. Carl had a crush on Lu. Lu liked Carl—*as a person*.

As boys obsessed with science tend to be, Carl was a gangly teen of somewhat limited social skills. Recalls Lu, "Girls want boys to be interested in *them*, and most of us just weren't interested in space travel."

The lack of chemistry between Carl and Lu did not keep them from seeing each other. On one visit, in fact, they played around with a chemistry set Carl had been given. Lu's mother, a chemist, took a look at the set and warned Rachel that it was an *advanced* set, containing *dangerous* chemicals. It was not appropriate for Carl's age group.

Following instructions in the set's manual, Carl and Lu performed an experiment involving the "chlorine ring." It blew up, making a mess of the room. Lu's sister narrowly escaped injury. Rachel refused to punish Carl. She surveyed the devastation and then announced simply, "These things happen when scientists do experiments."

*   *   *

Rachel was not only tolerant of Carl's missteps but proud of the most minor of his achievements. When Carl was in a high school play called *The Goose*

Hangs High, Rachel threw a cast party and contrived to bake a cake in the shape of a goose. (Rarely did Carol's achievements merit that kind of recognition.) The goose's head broke off before the party. Rachel artfully turned the head so that the goose appeared to be preening itself. She concealed the neck fracture with a beautiful ribbon.

Carnegie Hall

During a science class in Carl's sophomore year, the subject of astronomers came up. Carl elicited from the teacher the admission that famous astronomers, people like Harlow Shapley at Harvard, got paid *just to be astronomers*. That undid the trauma of his grandfather's comment. One could make a living at it after all.

Carl wrote letters to a handful of prominent astronomers, care of Mount Wilson, Mount Palomar, or the other mythic aeries where astronomers were to be found. He was delighted when a few wrote back polite replies.

Neither of Carl's parents was entirely sold on an astronomy career. Samuel nursed the idea that Carl might succeed him in the garment business. Rachel wondered whether her son had the makings of a great concert pianist.

The Sagans bought Carl a piano, no casual purchase in view of Rachel's attitude toward money. Carl threw himself into his lessons. He played beautifully, according to family friends. There is a home movie in which Carl strikes a wrong note, grimaces, then recovers with the careless aplomb of a true performer. Carl came closer to achieving Rachel's ambitions for him than one might imagine. While still in his teens, he gave a student recital at Carnegie Hall.

*   *   *

As graduation approached, Carl began looking at colleges. Despite his excellent grades, his accelerated education was more hindrance than help. Carl would be sixteen as the 1951–52 academic year started. Most colleges were reluctant to take someone so young.

One of the few schools that *would* was the University of Chicago. Under Chancellor Robert Hutchins, Chicago was structured as an ideal meritocracy. The university had no age requirement; it did not even demand a high school diploma. To get in, students had only to pass an examination. Graduation was based solely on passing another exam.

Chicago employed a handful of the nation's greatest scientists, among them physicists Enrico Fermi and Edward Teller and chemist Harold Urey. It operated a famous observatory, Yerkes, whose credit line was familiar to any reader of illustrated astronomy books. Carl was favorably impressed by a university brochure promising a mediocre football team and no wild fraternity life, but a superb and broad education.

Rachel thought her son too young to be off on his own in another city. But Carl settled on Chicago. He did not have many other options.

Knights of Columbus

Toward the end of high school, Carl entered an essay contest sponsored by the Knights of Columbus. Taking up the theme of "Columbus," he posed the question of whether human contact with technologically advanced extraterrestrials would be as disastrous as contact with Europeans had been for Native Americans. It was an original tangent, to say the least.

At that time, and in the Knights of Columbus particularly, Christopher Columbus had an approval rating comparable to that of the Virgin Mary. By insinuating that the great Genoese navigator's voyage had not been a boon to Native Americans, Carl was skating on thin ice. The judges were nonetheless won over by his rhetorical skill. They awarded him first prize.

Carl's grades put him in line to be valedictorian. His classmates voted him "Most Likely to Succeed." A couplet in the Rahway High yearbook predicted, "Astronomy research is Carl's main aim / An excellent student, he should achieve fame."

At the last minute, a faction stepped in and blocked Carl from being valedictorian. The reason was the Knights of Columbus essay. It convinced some people in the high school that he was *too* full of crazy ideas. This would not be the last time that Carl Sagan's penchant for speculation offended the wrong person at a crucial moment.

CHICAGO
1951-60

SAGAN LIVED IN the University of Chicago's Linn House. It was a handsome neo-Gothic dormitory: all male, no female visitors allowed. He had his own room. Ronald Blum, who lived a few doors away, said the thing that most impressed him about Sagan's room was his wall of science-fiction books. "We'd all read science fiction," Blum explains. "We'd gotten over it. This was the room of someone who *hadn't*."

Sagan's reading interests were even then undergoing a broadening. The university was in the thrall of the "Great Books" program. All students took a mandatory liberal arts program. Sagan flourished under this system. It was, he said, "like moving from a desert to the Garden of Eden."

He was exposed to a broad, almost completely Eurocentric curriculum of Greek playwrights and architecture, Freud and music, anthropology and Russian novels. At the end, the student who passed a daylong examination was awarded "a B.A. in nothing," as Sagan put it, "which serves you for absolutely nothing afterwards, except that you are declared educated (and to a surprising degree you finally were)."

In college Sagan learned to burn the midnight oil. He claimed that the hours between 10 P.M. and 5 A.M. were the best for concentrated work. Ronald Blum worked part-time in a hospital for $1.50 an hour and told Carl he might be able to get him some work, too. Without a moment's hesitation, Carl replied, "My time is worth more than that."

Sagan maintained a busy schedule of extracurricular activities. He was in

16

the science-fiction club and the astronomy club (which Sagan founded with Tobias Owen, another astronomer-to-be). Sagan also captained a championship intramural basketball team. He now stood over six feet tall. He "had no visible musculature" as if this were "irrelevant to him," but was "known for the sharpness of his elbows." He was an agile and expert rebounder.

This competitive spirit extended to late-night debates in the dorm. "He argued propositions the way Jack Dempsey fought fights," recalls Blum. "He had a killer instinct."

Cut loose from Rachel's apron strings, Sagan began dating with new-found freedom. When his mother learned of Carl's first serious girlfriend in college, she pronounced her most unsuitable. The girl was not Jewish. Samuel didn't care. Carl's choice of conversational topics could still be a dating drawback. As he later told it, "Uncles of girl friends, at dinner, would say, 'Fly to the moon? Buck Rogers stuff?' And then they would advise the girl to leave me alone: I was obviously crazy."

By far the most remarkable phase of Sagan's career at Chicago was his acquisition of a trio of influential mentors: Hermann J. Muller, Harold C. Urey, and Joshua Lederberg. Sagan's fortune in befriending them is little short of astounding. Muller and Urey were Nobel laureates, and Lederberg soon would be. Each was a revered figure in his field with little time to devote to every green upstart with an idea or two. None of these mentors was an astronomer, and only Urey was then at the University of Chicago. All three shared Sagan's interest in the possibility of extraterrestrial life.

Hermann Muller

Sagan met Muller through sheer serendipity. During his freshman year he went back to Rahway on Christmas break. One day, as he was going out to play basketball, Rachel stopped him.

> There I have my sneakers on, basketball under my arm, walking out the door, and my mother says to me that she has a friend in town whose nephew is a scientist. Wouldn't I talk to him? And I say, "Oh, Mother, there's all kinds of scientists, and I don't want to go." And she said, "Look, he's probably an interesting guy; do it for me." I said, "All right, I'll see him later." And I went out to play basketball, came back, went to see this guy.

The guy was Seymour Abrahamson. He was a graduate student in genetics at Indiana University, working under Hermann Muller. The two budding scientists found they had a lot to talk about. They began a correspondence. Abrahamson then arranged for Carl to visit him on-campus at Indiana during the 1952 spring break. On this visit, he introduced Sagan to Muller.

By the time Sagan met him, Muller was sixty-two and not a well man. He was only five foot three (hoop-playing Sagan towered a head above him) and had a balding, Milquetoast appearance. His great work was long behind him.

"Impatient" with the slow mutation rate of laboratory fruit flies, Muller found he could speed things up by zapping flies with X rays. This led him to conclude, in 1926, that radiation causes mutations and is a mainspring of evolution. Muller should have gotten the Nobel Prize promptly. Instead he had to wait nearly twenty years.

The likely reason was Muller's politically incorrect support of eugenics. He wanted to breed better people using the latest genetic techniques. While the notion was not so outré in the United States at the time (in early speeches Hitler cited *America*'s enlightened support of eugenics), it was, to say the least, controversial.

By 1931 the climate became so uncomfortable that Muller left the country for Germany. He worked there until the Nazis closed down his institute, and then in the Soviet Union until he came afoul of Lysenkoism—and of Trofim Lysenko himself.

Muller ended up in Bloomington, Indiana. He was a dedicated communist until the day he died. His brittle perfectionism was legendary. At least two of Muller's grad students had nervous breakdowns within a few years of the time Sagan met him. One Sunday morning around nine Muller came into his lab to look for a grad student who had gotten married the previous day. The student wasn't there. Muller looked at the others and fumed, "Doesn't he know his weekends aren't *sacred*?"

A Vial with Nonvirgins

Muller took an instant liking to Sagan. They went out to dinner with Abrahamson, and Muller asked Sagan if he'd like to work in his lab. Sagan said yes and spent that summer and the next working for the great Hermann Muller.

Sagan was assigned the most menial job in the lab. Muller was still working with fruit flies, his scientific first love. Owing to their conveniently brief life cycle, the tiny insects that buzz around rotted produce are indispensable for genetic studies. It was Sagan's job to raise and sort these fruit flies so that others could perform the actual experiments.

It was a job with zero upside potential and unlimited opportunities for screwing up. The experiments demanded precisely known pedigrees. The flies Sagan turned over to the researchers had to be virgins.

The only practical way to make sure a fly is a virgin is to separate the sexes soon after birth. The flies were raised in glass vials, usually pint milk bottles, containing a dab of nutrient syrup. Every twelve hours, Sagan had to open the bottles, flush out all the adult flies, and reseal them. During the next twelve hours, the maggoty pupae in the syrup would mature into baby fruit flies, still too young to mate. Sagan would again open the bottle and remove the fruit flies, knocking them unconscious with ether. Then he put the anesthetized flies under a low-power binocular microscope. Taking a fine camel's-hair brush, he flicked males to one side, females to the other. The sexes came to be cloistered in separate vials.

The job's twelve-hour cycle was as incompatible with a *human* sexual life as a fly's. Like Cinderella, a technician who opened vials and sorted at noon would have to return to the lab by midnight, come hell or high water. There was no room for error. A single male that got missorted would tirelessly impregnate every female in the bottle. Muller made no secret of his contempt for sloppiness. "Oh, he wasn't very good," Muller once said of a former student who had achieved great renown. "He once gave me a vial with nonvirgins in it."

Curious Pest

Sagan, itching to prove himself, felt he was spinning his wheels. About the only way a lowly technician *might* distinguish himself was by discovering a new mutation. One day, Sagan found a population of weird-looking flies in one of his bottles. It was not a typical mutation; it was a *macromutation*. This was the nexus of a raging controversy. Biologist Richard Goldschmidt theorized that evolutionary changes sometimes came in great leaps: macromutations. Muller thought this idea was totally crazy. No one had ever seen a macromutation.

Suspecting that he had discovered something that would revolutionize genetics, Sagan rushed to Muller's office. He found Muller in near-darkness, peering into a microscope. Sagan explained his discovery.

"Extraordinary," Muller said blandly. "I don't suppose they're colored black, have four wings, and long fuzzy antennae?"

That was right. It was a curious pest of genetics labs, Muller explained. The creature was a moth that had learned the trick of infesting the laboratory vials. The female moth managed to lay its eggs in the syrup during the brief time the vials were unstopped. Of its offspring, those most likely to survive were those that could also sniff out an opened vial and lay their eggs before being brushed away by a lab assistant.

The humbling incident impressed Sagan with one of the facts of scientific life: that astounding results are almost always a mistake.

Flying Saucers

Muller and Sagan became very close. As different as they were, a freemasonry united them. It was this business of life on other planets. The subject's status in the scientific world of the 1950s was like that of sex in Victoria's England. It was *thought* about a lot, obviously, but it was somehow naughty to talk about it.

Muller read science fiction avidly. He delighted in swapping speculations with Sagan. They had long discussions about the origins of life on Earth, about how different extraterrestrial life might be from that on Earth, and about the possibility of intelligent extraterrestrial life. In later life, Sagan credited these discussions with Muller as being "the critical event. If not for meeting Muller I might possibly have bowed under the weight of conventional opinion that *all* these subjects were nonsense."

*   *   *

"Carl was a real pain in the ass," recalls roommate Abrahamson. "He never cleaned up; he expected us to cook for him; he was just a brat. We would ultimately clean up the apartment once every couple of weeks, but he was never around to help. We just let the dirt accumulate under his bed."

Unencumbered by trivialities, Sagan could devote extra time to his more speculative interests. One of them was UFOs. "Flying saucers" had became a media event in June 1947 (Sagan was twelve), when private pilot Kenneth Arnold reported seeing a string of hovering objects near Mount Rainier. The ensuing barrage of UFO reports seemed proof positive of Sagan's belief in life on other worlds. By the summer in Bloomington, Sagan sincerely believed in UFOs—not as swamp gas, not as mass hysteria, but as alien spacecraft visiting the Earth.

There was nothing Sagan wanted more than to see a UFO himself. He did not think it wise to leave that to chance. All summer long, Abrahamson would drag himself into the apartment after a long day's work and Sagan would bug him to go out and look for UFOs. Abrahamson acquiesced once or twice. They saw nothing more than a few shooting stars.

To Sagan the great mystery was why other people didn't take flying saucers as seriously as he did. "Not a single adult I knew was preoccupied with UFOs," he later wrote. "I couldn't figure out why not."

On August 3, 1952, Sagan took a sheet of Indiana University stationery and wrote Secretary of State Dean Acheson. He asked what the State Department planned to do "if the unidentified aerial objects sobriqueted 'flying saucers' were conclusively proved to be extraterrestrial vehicles investigating the progress of the United States and other nations in the fields of astronautics and nuclear physics, in order to prevent our expansion into space at the present time." He wanted to know whether the United States had plans to communicate with the aliens and/or to pool defenses against "the common enemy." He gave his return address as H. J. Muller's Laboratory.

A State Department underling wrote back tersely, "Under the circumstances of a purely hypothetical situation, the Department has no comment to make on the questions you asked."

*   *   *

One Sunday morning toward the end of summer, Abrahamson, his fiancée, and Sagan were washing the car the couple had been given as an engagement present. Sagan propounded a new theory: that Moses, Jesus, and all the great religious figures of ages past were really extraterrestrial beings. The miracles of the Bible had all happened as described. Moses parted the Red Sea, Jesus turned water into wine, and so forth. They used advanced technology that was perfectly ordinary on *their* planet—but which we earthlings could take only as proof of divinity.

Abrahamson good-naturedly challenged him. Sagan refused to budge. He was either serious or *acting* as if he was serious. With Sagan, it was hard to tell which.

That afternoon, Abrahamson took his fiancée and Sagan out to dinner at what was, for Bloomington in the 1950s, a very posh establishment. It was "the kind of restaurant where people went after church." In the middle of dinner, without any warning, Sagan slammed his fist on the table, sending the dishes rattling. He looked Abrahamson in the eye and bellowed, "I tell you, Jesus Christ *is* extraterrestrial!"

The restaurant fell silent. It took a subjective eternity for conversations to resume with something of their former spontaneity. Abrahamson and his fiancée wanted to crawl under the table.

The Fermi Question

Sagan was not the only one given to dinner-table outbursts about extraterrestrials. This may be the place to introduce another University of Chicago legend, the "Fermi question."

A couple of summers previously, in 1950, Chicago's Enrico Fermi was working at Los Alamos National Laboratory. One day, he walked to lunch in the company of Edward Teller, Emil Konopinski, and Herbert York. Somehow the subject of flying saucers came up. Konopinski mentioned a cartoon he'd seen in the *New Yorker*. There had, it seems, been a spate of thefts of New York City trash containers. The cartoon showed a flying saucer, just landed on an alien planet. Out were pouring little green men, each lugging a New York City trash container.

Flying saucers were not a subject that any of the four physicists took seriously. Interstellar voyagers would have to travel faster than the speed of light to get anywhere in a reasonable time. Einstein's special relativity said that faster-than-light travel was impossible.

"Edward, what do you think?" Fermi asked puckishly. "How probable is it that within the next ten years we shall have clear evidence of a material object moving faster than light?"

Teller guessed "10^{-6}"—1 in 1 *million*.

"This is much too low," Fermi countered. "The probability is more like ten percent."

The subject was dropped, and the group had lunch at Fuller Lodge. As Teller remembered it, the lunch conversation

> had nothing to do with astronomy or with extraterrestrial beings. I think it was some down-to-earth topic. Then, in the middle of this conversation, Fermi came out with the quite unexpected question, "Where is everybody?". . . The result . . . was general laughter because of the strange fact that in spite of Fermi's question coming from the clear blue, everybody around the table seemed to understand at once that he was talking about extraterrestrial life.

Fermi followed with some quick computations. He estimated that there must be many planets with intelligent life. Some would be far more advanced than us. Surely, Fermi felt, they would devise practical ways of navigating among the stars. They *would* visit the Earth. So: where is everybody?

This "famous and possibly even apocryphal question," as Sagan later called it, dogged Sagan for much of his professional life. To Sagan and many of his generation of exobiologists, the Fermi question held a central importance not unlike medieval scholars' questions about God's intangible nature.

Sagan, of course, soon enough recognized the weakness of the UFO evidence. Anyone less "sold" on the idea of extraterrestrial life has to wonder just why Sagan was so convinced there was life on other worlds. The answer has a lot to do with an extraordinary experiment conducted at the University of Chicago.

Harold Urey

A twist of fate directed Sagan toward that experiment and its authors. It was Muller's doing. He sent Sagan back to Chicago in fall 1952 with a letter introducing him to the no less renowned Harold Clayton Urey.

Urey was the son of an Indiana preacher. His father died when Harold was six, leaving the family in poverty. Urey become a country schoolteacher in his home state and Montana, then took a degree in zoology at the University of Montana. The First World War needed chemists more than zoologists, so he switched fields—with considerable success. In 1934 Urey won the Nobel Prize in chemistry for the discovery of deuterium, or "heavy hydrogen."

During World War II, Urey devised the uranium hexafluoride diffusion process that produced the uranium 235 for the first atomic bomb. Like many others on the Manhattan Project, Urey became a critic of nuclear weaponry. He foresaw the arms race and the proliferation of nuclear weapons to smaller, less stable parties. Urey believed a world government was the only political solution to a world in a which nuclear weapons existed. As liberal as Sagan, Urey believed scientists had an obligation to end poverty. He spoke out fervently against Joseph McCarthy and the execution of Julius and Ethel Rosenberg.

Urey was blunt-spoken and unpretentious. About the only visible difference the Nobel Prize made in his conduct was that he took to driving around in a car whose license number was the atomic weight of deuterium (the term "vanity plate" hardly applies). He was so devoted to his experiments that he often slept on a cot in his lab. He was so undeterred by the fact that he worked with such virulent poisons that he once used caged canaries to warn of a leak.

Sagan might never have met Urey if the Nobel laureate had not shifted focus late in his career. Urey never lost his early interest in biology. "I don't like rocks," he once said. "I like life." And as Muller knew, Urey had recently become interested in the chemistry of the planets, particularly as it related to the origins of life.

At the time Sagan met him, Urey was fifty-nine. He had square shoulders and a round face; his hair was turning white. Urey listened courteously to Sagan's ideas, then advised him to look up a grad student of his who was doing an interesting experiment. The grad student's name was Stanley Miller.

The Miller-Urey experiment, as it has come to be called, was then unknown outside Chicago's chemistry department. It was an attempt to simulate some of the chemical processes that may have led to the origin of life. In the first half of the twentieth century, British geneticist J. B. S. Haldane and Soviet biochemist Aleksandr Oparin separately advanced the doctrine of "chemical evolution." They proposed that ultraviolet light, lightning, or other energy sources on the early Earth had transmuted simple compounds into more complex organic compounds. These organic compounds then somehow formed the first living units. ("Organic compounds" is a confusing term. To a chemist, it denotes complex compounds of carbon. Such compounds are found in living organisms—and also in aspirin, gasoline, plastic, and other nonliving matter.)

There was no hard evidence for this idea. It was a challenge to imagine how it could be tested, even in principle. The first important attempt to do so took place at Berkeley. Melvin Calvin and colleagues zapped a mixture of carbon dioxide and water with ionizing radiation from the Crocker Lab's sixty-inch cyclotron. The zapping produced no visible result in the clear, seltzer-water mixture. However, the Berkeley group's careful analysis showed that tiny traces of formaldehyde and formic acid had been created.

These two simple compounds are conventionally called "organic." Neither, however, has bonds *between* carbon atoms, which are the true basis of the endlessly varied chemistry of life. That, and the minuscule yields, were disheartening. The production of these two nominally organic compounds did little to support the idea of chemical evolution.

Harold Urey thought that *he* knew what was wrong. At a November 1951 chemistry department seminar (the month after Calvin's article on the experiment appeared), Urey mentioned his belief that the Earth's early atmosphere would be "reducing." That is a chemical term meaning, in this context, that the gases would be richer in hydrogen. Urey believed that the Earth's original atmosphere would have consisted of gases like methane, ammonia, water vapor, and hydrogen. He proposed that *this* mixture be sealed in a glass tube and exposed to electrical discharges. Stanley Miller took up that suggestion in August 1952, shortly before Sagan's meeting with Urey.

Urey was once asked what he expected the experiment to produce. His famous reply was "Beilstein." Friedrich Beilstein is the author of a thick handbook on organic chemistry. Urey meant, *everything in the book.* He expected it to produce a cornucopia of organic compounds, not the paltry traces Calvin had managed.

Miller's results were almost instantly visible. After Urey's gas mixture was sparked, the insides of his glass tubes were lacquered with brown polymers. *Something* was happening.

The difficult part of the experiment was analyzing the polymers that had been produced. The results were a sensation. Not only had carbon-to-carbon bonds formed, but the mixture contained several of the amino acids that form proteins in living things. Glycine, the simplest amino acid, was produced in surprising quantity (about 2 percent yield).

Sagan attended a colloquium Miller gave on the experiment. There were, not unreasonably, skeptical questions from the audience. Urey himself rose to Miller's defense. After the talk, Sagan introduced himself to Miller. He was almost as protective of the result as if it had been his own. He earnestly told Miller he felt the audience had failed to grasp the work's true significance.

Sagan certainly *did* grasp the significance. The experiment had preferentially produced some of the important compounds of life. Prior to that, no one knew why proteins (as opposed to anything else out of the universe of imaginable polymers) figured in life. The experiment suggested the answer: that amino acids are readily produced from random interactions of simpler compounds.

Nothing in Miller's experiment was unique to the Earth. The gases he used are found throughout the universe. The laws of chemistry (surely) are the same throughout the universe. The experiment therefore implied that the first steps toward life would take place on *any* planet with suitable conditions. This cast a powerful spell over Sagan. The Miller-Urey experiment would become the wellspring of the new field of exobiology.

Ice Bath

In 1954 Sagan acquired his A.B. "in nothing." His grades were high enough for him to graduate with honors. But first, Sagan had to write a special thesis.

Still enraptured by the implications of the Miller-Urey experiment, Sagan wrote his thesis on the origins of life. He asked Urey to take a look it. Urey returned the manuscript awash in marginal notes, each painstakingly pointing out a serious error or omission. The sight of the marked-up thesis "was like a plunge into an ice bath."

Sagan carefully redid the thesis, earning his A.B. with honors. Under Chicago's system, this presented Sagan, finally, with the choice of a major. Just as he was being permitted to focus on one thing, Sagan's interests were ranging wider than ever. He loved astronomy, he had done genetics with Muller, Urey and Miller were chemists, and he was interested in biology, too.

He chose physics. It was a logical undergraduate major for an astronomer—plus, it kept his options open. Physics was and is often held to be at the top of the pecking order in scientific prestige. With youthful enthusiasm, Sagan talked himself into believing that his University of Chicago physics major linked him to Enrico Fermi. (The great Fermi was about as accessible to the average undergraduate as Sagan himself would be in his later years at Cornell.)

Sagan had a love-hate affair with the major. He was a talented student, as demonstrated by the scholarships he received (an Alexander White scholarship for 1954–55, a National Science Foundation predoctoral fellowship for 1956–57). His A grades did not come easily, however, and Sagan realized that his true interests were elsewhere. Sagan took an S.B. in 1955 and an S.M. the following year.

Toward the end of the spring 1956 semester, Sagan submitted his first scientific article (he was twenty-one). Titled "Radiation and the Origin of the Gene," it addressed the same subject matter as his thesis and appeared in the March 1957 issue of *Evolution*, a journal of biology. Sagan had written a review, a critical analysis of other articles rather than a presentation of new data. He cited an eclectic mix of authors, among them Urey and Miller, Watson and Crick, Oparin, Muller, Haldane, Schrödinger, Fox, and Calvin. There is a great deal of "hand-waving"; some of it reads like a windy answer to an essay test.

"It is difficult," writes Sagan, "to escape the conclusion that the design of the organism is merely to provide for gene multiplication and survival." This is a favored way of looking at things today. For Sagan to have been saying this in 1956—even if he was paraphrasing one or another of his celebrated teachers—shows prescient insight. Characteristic of the later Sagan is the lyric tone of the article's last sentence: "The cytoplasm may select the instruments, but it is the gene which plays the tune of life."

Gerard Kuiper

Sagan decided to do his postgraduate work in astronomy. But as he confessed, "I had only a vague idea what an astronomer does." He tried to remedy that by getting some observatory experience. He spent part of the summer at the McDonald Observatory in Fort Davis, Texas, working with Gerard Kuiper.

Kuiper was then the only important, full-time planetary astronomer in North America. Of Dutch birth, he came to the United States in 1933. Kuiper had worked under the legendary Percival Lowell (who was then in disrepute). He moved to the University of Chicago in 1936.

Kuiper and Urey had a long-standing feud of uncertain origin. In 1952

Urey published a well-received book titled *The Planets*. Kuiper might have felt that the last thing he needed was a high-powered *chemist* muscling in on his territory. Mutual slights had escalated. To Sagan's relief, neither Urey nor Kuiper forbid him to have anything to do with the other. That was about the limit of their civility. They were barely on speaking terms.

The summer of 1956 was one of the periodic witching hours for Mars studies. The planet was at opposition, meaning that the sun, Earth, and Mars were arrayed in a line. Mars was a mere 35 million miles away, closer than it had been in thirty-two years. It glowered in the night sky from dusk to dawn.

At McDonald Sagan got his first chance to view Mars under favorable conditions in a big (eighty-two-inch reflecting) telescope. The sight was disappointing. Mars's disk was *tiny*. It was a washed-out yellow, not a rich red. The darker surface markings were barely visible. To call them green (as some did) was an absurdity. There was even less to see as the summer wore on. In August a Martian dust storm, kicked up by the planet's close approach to the sun, obliterated its features.

Gerard Kuiper believed that the dark areas on Mars were vegetation growing on a clement planet of melting polar caps and seasonal renewal. Sagan, his intellectual heir, was at once the great defender and dismantler of this mind-set. The Kuiper-era belief in Martian life is so crucial to Sagan's later career that it is worth sketching here.

House of Cards

Planetary astronomy had never recovered from the realization that the canals Lowell so meticulously charted were illusions at best, delusions at worst. With Lowell's head on a post, so to speak, astronomers were determined never again to build grandiose theories on insubstantial foundations— *least of all,* theories about Martian life.

That is exactly what the generation of astronomers before Sagan did. They were seduced not just by the romance of the idea but by technology. *Their* findings used state-of-the-art technology. They couldn't be mistaken, not like Lowell, who had only looked through a telescope.

The case for Martian life was a house of cards. It was founded on a series of difficult observations and indirect estimates. The significance of the observations, and the accuracy of the estimates, were absolutely dependent on those that came before them. If one point was wrong, the whole conclusion was in trouble.

In a key observation, Kuiper directed the light coming from Mars through a prism. This produced a spectrum. By comparing this spectrum to that of moonlight (the moon is airless, of course), he hoped to deduce what gases were absorbing sunlight on Mars. In 1947 Kuiper (correctly) identified carbon dioxide in Mars's atmosphere on the basis of some infrared absorption bands.

This was the first hard fact ever established about the chemistry of Mars. Nothing else, not even water, was *known* to exist on Mars.

Kuiper followed this up with a colossal blunder. He estimated the pressure of carbon dioxide on Mars. He did not have enough information to do this with any accuracy. The result he got was 0.35 millibar. As it turned out, that was too low by a factor of about 16.

Kuiper had enough confidence in his wrong figure to miss out on a major coup. Since he had found carbon dioxide, not water, in Mars's atmosphere, he might well have concluded (correctly) that the polar caps of Mars are made mainly of carbon dioxide, not water.

Kuiper *considered* that possibility. Then he talked himself out of it. If the pressure of carbon dioxide was as low as he estimated, there wouldn't be enough of the gas to account for the polar caps. Kuiper instead seconded the conventional wisdom that the polar caps were made of water ice.

French astronomer Audouin Dollfus then tried to confirm that the polar caps were water ice by studying the polarization of light coming off them. His polarometer was cutting-edge technology for the time. The Martian polarization results were distinctly different from those of ice, snow, and frost here on Earth—which should have told him something. Instead Dollfus convinced himself the readings were close enough, and it must be water ice on Mars. He did not bother to check the polarization of carbon dioxide ice.

Hard data being at a premium, astronomers were quick to parlay any new fact—or "fact"—into new surmises. Frozen water in the visibly growing and shrinking polar caps implied water vapor in the Martian air. In another leap of faith, many astronomers were ready to assume that Mars's atmosphere was mostly nitrogen. Nitrogen had not been detected on Mars, any more than water had.

This assumption was again based on Kuiper's way-too-low estimate of the carbon dioxide pressure. Since Kuiper's claimed 0.35 millibars of carbon dioxide pressure was far, far less than estimates of the total atmospheric pressure on Mars—not that there was any good way of determining the total pressure, either—it followed that there had to be something else in the atmosphere. Nitrogen was the popular guess. It was a guess that, like the water ice polar caps, made Mars more Earth-like. Nitrogen is the main component of *our* atmosphere and is essential for earthly life.

And presumably there was a *lot* of nitrogen on Mars. There would have to be if the guesses about the total atmospheric pressure were right. Gerard

De Vaucouleurs's widely accepted 1954 estimate put the total pressure at 85 millibars. (That was way off the mark, too, over ten times too high.)

*   *   *

Satisfied that there was water on Mars, Kuiper turned his attention to the dark areas. These regions were reported to change with the Martian seasons. Observers saw the markings get darker or bigger in summer and paler or smaller in winter.

Percival Lowell had had no trouble understanding *that*. It was proof that the clever Martians' canals worked. But with intelligent Martians out of the picture, the seasonal changes demanded a new explanation. Various nonbiological explanations were floated. One was that the surface contained substances that got darker when they absorbed water vapor, roughly the way a paper towel gets darker when dampened.

This explanation was rebutted by Estonian-British astronomer Ernst Öpik. In 1950, he argued that Mars's well-known dust storms would cover the dark surface with dust. That the dark areas always reappeared on this planet of dust, Öpik believed, was powerful evidence for "regenerative" powers. And by "regenerative" he meant—well, go figure it yourself.

*   *   *

Starting in 1947, Kuiper sought to establish that these regenerative dark areas were acres upon acres of living vegetation. Forty years earlier, astronomers at Lowell's observatory had attempted to identify chlorophyll on Mars by examining the planet's spectrum. They decided that it couldn't be done; there wasn't enough light to work with. Kuiper had succeeded in identifying carbon dioxide with spectroscopy and now wanted to revisit the chlorophyll issue using the (somewhat) more advanced technology at his disposal. He determined to produce a spectrum of *just the dark areas* of Mars and compare that to the spectra of plants on Earth.

Producing a usable spectrum was still next to impossible. Rather than a full spectrum, Kuiper had to settle for measurements at four wavelengths. He reported that the light reflected from Mars was different from that reflected from ordinary green, leafy plants on Earth. However, Kuiper said, his Martian results *were* consistent with those of lichens and dry mosses.

Lichens are crusty growths (sometimes green or gray) that thrive on rocks in some of Earth's coldest and driest places. Kuiper was sophisticated enough about biology to know that any Martian life would be the product of a distinct evolutionary path. *Actual* lichens would no more exist on Mars than crabapples. But Mars might have acres of living, neutral-colored ground cover changing with the seasons.

As a pop paradigm, Kuiper's "lichens" were an instant success. The idea was trumpeted in the press and perpetuated in textbooks for years. There was not much data standing behind the lichen idea, though. Basically, what Kuiper found was that chlorophyll *could not be detected at all* in infrared observation of lichens and dry mosses. They have a nearly flat spectrum at the sampled frequencies. Likewise, Kuiper could not detect chlorophyll at all on Mars—just a nearly flat spectrum at the sampled frequencies. That was *it*. His talk of a "match" was almost like saying the air of Mars is too thin for flying creatures—and therefore proposing the planet must be populated by penguins.

Kuiper recognized the iffy nature of his result. Then once again, someone stepped in with an impressive confirmation of Kuiper's *error*.

In 1958, Harvard's William M. Sinton secured permission to use the 200-inch telescope at Mount Palomar to study Mars. (Such was the status of planetary studies that Sinton had to use the telescope during twilight, when it wasn't much good for anything else.) He reported finding infrared absorption bands similar to those of organic compounds in the dark areas of Mars, and only in the dark areas. He was now matching an actual spectral feature, not just the absence of a feature.

That added the final story to the house of cards. Buttressed by everything else, the "Sinton bands" seemed reasonably good evidence for life on Mars—possibly the strongest evidence one could expect, short of going to Mars itself. By the late 1950s, the conventional and sober picture of Mars was of a "lichen"-clad planet, changing with the seasons as humid breezes carried water vapor from the distant melting polar caps. This was the Mars, so soon to vanish forever, that Sagan inherited from his predecessors.

Lynn Alexander

The summer of 1956 was a busy, optimistic time in Sagan's personal life. When not occupied at McDonald Observatory, he spent much of the time on the road. He bought a blue-and-white Nash-Hudson station wagon for just over two thousand dollars and drove out West, stopping at Lowell Observatory, the Grand Canyon, and Los Angeles. There he checked out Caltech and UCLA and met Linus Pauling and Norman Horowitz. But Sagan reported that the smog in L.A. hurt his eyes. He suspected that, to do his best work, he needed the stimulus of cold weather.

Carl also had a new girlfriend. One day he was crossing the steps of Eckhart Hall, Chicago's math building, when he literally bumped into a precocious liberal arts student. Lynn Alexander looked too young to be a college student, and by the usual standards, she was. Having enrolled at fifteen, she was now just sixteen.

Lynn was the oldest of four daughters of Morris Alexander and Leone Wise. Morris was a liberal Chicago attorney-turned-businessman. He owned a company called Permaline that made a durable plastic used to create lane markings on highways. He and Leone argued a lot. The Alexanders lived on the South Side, within a stone's throw of the tenements.

Like Carl, Lynn was intellectually curious from early childhood. She read avidly, kept diaries, and took part-time jobs for pin money. She adored nature—not just the obvious, beautiful things but the tough, gritty things that survived in Jackson Park and along the Midway. She studied ant-hills and weeds. For Lynn, a dandelion gone to seed could be a thing of fascination.

Lynn felt deprived if a whole day went by without her writing *something*. She wrote plays, which she produced in the basement of her apartment building. Supporting roles were doled out to her younger sisters (which gave Lynn an excuse to boss them around); the lead she invariably reserved for herself.

Lynn was self-assured enough to leave her well-regarded middle school and switch to a notoriously dangerous public high school—a place where even the nice girls carried razor blades in their garters. Lynn thought there would be a better selection of potential boyfriends there. She did not bother to inform her parents of the switch.

Lynn aced her classes in high school and after her sophomore year passed the entrance exam to the University of Chicago. She jumped at the chance to put space between herself and her parents' bickering. She sought "something better"—and to meet interesting men.

Carl seemed to qualify. He impressed her as tall, handsome, and articulate. His enthusiasm for science inspired Lynn's own. Between the influence of Carl and the "Great Books" readings, she decided to pursue a career in biology.

It was a high-maintenance relationship. Carl and Lynn fought perpetually (one of Lynn's sisters remembers one argument when Lynn rammed her hand through a window). They broke up and dated other people; they made up and decided they ought to get married; they quarreled some more. When the relationship was on, they would take trips together. On the 1955 spring break, they shared driving duties on a trip to New Jersey. Carl wanted to visit his parents, and Lynn wanted to see Princeton. While in Princeton, Lynn looked up J. Robert Oppenheimer in the phone book, showed up at his home unannounced, and spent the morning with him and his family. She had just written a term paper on him ("Not 'Whether or Not?' but 'How?': J. R. Oppenheimer and the Decision to Drop the Bomb.")

Oppie fascinated Lynn. She liked his melancholy blue eyes and wondered if she could ever lose herself in morally ambiguous science the way he did. But Kitty Oppenheimer seemed crabby; maybe it was not such a good thing to be the wife of a famous scientist.

*   *   *

By July 1956, marriage plans were well under way. In one of his letters, Carl told "Lynnie" that he wanted four or five babies, preferably healthy geniuses of assorted genders. By fast-tracking the births at one per eighteen months, Lynn would soon be free to resume her doctoral work. Carl emphasized that he wanted Lynn to pursue her scientific career; he desired intellectual as well as physical companionship in a wife. Carl felt that Lynn's interests, then described as "bio-anthropology," were a perfect complement to his own. They could make an extraordinary scientific team.

At that time, Lynn was doing anthropological fieldwork in a village in Mexico. Carl drove down and spent two weeks with her. It was a miserable experience. Lynn was trying to fit into the culture (the locals had already pegged her with a name that meant "nose in a book"). She was mortified when Carl roared into town, driving his big American station wagon across the village's centuries-old cobbles. They argued throughout the visit and parted badly. Lynn sent Carl a letter breaking off the relationship. If the time in Mexico had been a taste of what married life would be like, she said, then they should call the whole thing off.

Carl countered that maybe they should forget about marriage and sex for the time being but continue to see each other. A letter of Carl's, dated September 12, enthusiastically assessed the pros and cons for life on Mars; then midway in the letter, almost as an aside, Carl mentioned that he had been dating two Latinas in Texas—both named Maria.

The more significant attachment seems to have been Maria Calderon. She was a political science major Carl met at a resort near the observatory. Her father had been killed during the Spanish Civil War for being an anarchist. In bed with Maria, Carl occasionally forgot that he was not with Lynn. He sometimes called Maria "Lynn"—or "Leen" in his attempt at a Spanish accent. Maria pretended not to notice. But once Carl found Maria crying. She would not tell him why.

By mid-September Carl and Lynn's relationship was on again. By October, there had been still another spat, and Carl was asking for just one more chance.

Lynn found it hard to get along with Carl's mother, too. During one visit, Lynn told Rachel that her mother, Leone, had suffered a nervous breakdown. Rachel threw a tantrum at this news. She ran up to her room, closed the door, and cried, lamenting that her future grandchildren might inherit the taint of an unstable temperament.

As the relationship with Carl continued this halting course, Lynn tried to talk sense into herself. She made herself a tape-recording to listen to whenever she weakened. It enumerated the reasons why marrying Carl Sagan would be an act of self-destruction.

Peddling Without a License

The fall of 1956 temporarily separated Lynn and Carl. Sagan began work at the University of Chicago's astronomy school in Williams Bay, Wisconsin. This is the home of the Yerkes Observatory. Completed in 1897, the forty-inch Yerkes refractor was housed in a brick-and-terra-cotta domed building. It was by then a storied relic.

Williams Bay had a population of barely 1,000. For city-bred Sagan, it presented a culture shock. For the first time in his life, Sagan encountered anti-Semitism. He also ran into trouble with the law. He attempted to raise funds for the Democratic party, asking householders for a dollar each. As Sagan told it,

> I spent all morning going door to door. And I got the most amazing responses: "The what party?" or "Shh! the master will hear!" or "Wait right here, young fellow, and I'll get my shotgun." Finally I was arrested by the sheriff, who had had innumerable complaints, on the grounds of peddling without a license. They figured I was peddling receipts at a dollar each. And I was remanded to the custody of the observatory director, who I don't think understood anything about it, but just said to me, "Be a good boy."

The Yerkes Observatory was the professional home of astrophysicist Subrahmanyan Chandrasekhar. Kuiper and Chandrasekhar represented the opposite poles of astronomy. Chandrasekhar was a true mathematical genius. His work was steeped in the exciting new physics of relativity and quantum theory. In 1930, Chandra, as he was almost always called, had computed that white dwarf stars about 1.2 times the mass of the sun would collapse under their own gravity. This laid the groundwork for the theory of neutron stars and black holes.

Most of the important discoveries in astronomy were being made in astrophysics or cosmology. Sagan found himself pressured to study stars, galaxies, cosmology—anything but planets. "There was a kind of view that the seriousness of astronomy was proportional to the distance of the object," Sagan recalled. The planets were too close.

Sagan took classes with Chandra, finding his reputations for brilliance and aloofness fully justified. "Frivolous questions from people who did not appear to have studied the material thoroughly were dealt with in the manner of a summary execution," Sagan recalled. Students literally crossed to the other side of the street when they saw Chandra coming; Sagan made it a point to take the observatory stairway that *didn't* go by Chandra's office. Sagan once invited Chandra to give a talk for his astronomy club and gave him an appreciative introduction. Afterward, Chandra's main comment was that Carl really should have worn a suit and tie to introduce a faculty member.

Sagan attended a colloquium in which Chandra filled the lecture room's blackboards with his neatly printed equations. The important results were numbered and boxed, as if they might be photographed and printed in a journal. During the question-and-answer period, someone said, "Professor Chandrasekhar, on blackboard . . . let's see, . . . 8, line 11, I believe you've made an error in sign."

Chandra fell silent. He did not dignify the comment by turning around to look at the questioned equation. When it became clear that *someone* had to break the silence, the chairman piped in, "Professor Chandrasekhar, do you have an answer to this question?"

"It was not a question; it was a statement," Chandra replied. "And it is mistaken." He never turned around.

Newspaper of Record

Kuiper's approach to math had more lasting relevance to Sagan. His forte was the "order-of-magnitude estimate," common in physics but less so in 1950s astronomy. Confronted with a new hypothesis, Kuiper would make a quick, simplified calculation of its consequences. If the answer was reasonable, then the hypothesis might merit further attention. If it wasn't, then something was wrong, and that something needed to be understood before time was wasted on a detailed calculation. In a field so full of uncertainties and conjectures as planetary astronomy, it was a valuable strategy.

Kuiper also had an unintentional role in initiating Sagan into the perils of dealing with the media. In December 1956, both Kuiper and Sagan presented papers on Mars at the American Association for the Advancement of Science meeting in New York. Kuiper focused on his "lichens." Sagan advanced an alternate idea.

Telescopic observers reported that the dark areas of Mars could "regenerate" quickly, *regardless of the season*. This struck Sagan as odd. He did not see how lichens could grow that quickly, even in the off-season. Sagan had a simpler explanation. What if there were no lichens at all, just dark rock covered with light-colored sand? The dark rock might be solidified lava. Seasonal winds would blow the sand around, uncovering patches of bare rock in some places and covering them elsewhere. The planet's dust storms ought to have a particularly dramatic effect. No sooner would the atmosphere clear than "new" bare dark areas ought to appear—just as was observed.

It was an impressive piece of scientific skepticism, all the more so because it cut against Sagan's desire for there to be life on Mars. He could hardly have expected to ingratiate himself with Kuiper this way, either.

The *New York Times* reported the meeting, headlining it "Mars' Dark Spots Held to Be Lava." But in an embarrassing slip, the article attributed everything Sagan had said to Kuiper, and vice versa.

Kuiper said nothing about it. At least one colleague did see it and remarked archly to Sagan, "I've been following your career in the *New York Times*." The implication was that serious scientists avoided being quoted in the press.

Sagan's propensity for the spotlight was already becoming evident. He was a campus legend, the sort of person everyone knew or knew *of*. It was rumored that one of the nation's leading scientists called Sagan once a day just to ask, "What are you thinking about now?" In 1957 Sagan started a university lecture series modestly titled "The Creation of Life and the Universe." Dubious faculty members called it "Sagan's circus." Sagan got physicist and science popularizer George Gamow to give one of the lectures. Another prominent speaker was Carl Sagan.

Marriage

The marriage was finally "on." Carl and Lynn set the date for June 16, 1957, a week after Lynn got her own A.B. (Lynn was now quite determined to pursue her study of genetics.) Leone Alexander spared neither time nor expense in arranging a wedding. Peter Pesch, a friend from Yerkes, was Carl's best man.

Privately, not everyone was rejoicing. Morris Alexander thought Carl was arrogant. He questioned his capacity to be a good husband or father. Leone tended to forgive this on the grounds that Carl would be a good provider.

Rachel Sagan could not understand what her son saw in that *scientist*. One scholar in the household seemed plenty. She complained to friends that Lynn was not attractive enough for Carl. (Rachel was famous for gratuitous advice on female beauty. She was once heard deriding the sagging breasts of African women in a *National Geographic*.)

To anyone *else's* eyes, Lynn made a resplendent nineteen-year-old bride.

(Carl was twenty-two.) The day of the wedding, Lynn received a telegram. It was from Rachel, who attended the wedding and could certainly have delivered any message in person. The telegram read: FROM A BACHELOR TO A MRS. IN ONLY ONE WEEK.

Joshua Lederberg

Carl and Lynn spent the summer of 1957 at the University of Colorado. He studied chemistry and nuclear physics under Edward Condon; she took courses in ecology and plant physiology. That fall Lynn began graduate studies in cell biology and genetics at the University of Wisconsin in Madison.

Carl refused to be trapped in Williams Bay. He and Lynn set up house in Madison. (They lived at 134 East Johnson Street and then at 116 Craig Avenue.) There was much more to do, more interesting people to meet, in Madison than in Williams Bay. That justified Sagan's ninety-minute commute to the observatory.

In Madison Sagan met the man who would have perhaps the profoundest influence of all his mentors: Joshua Lederberg. The son of a rabbi, Lederberg was nine years older than Sagan. From childhood, Lederberg too had been fascinated by the possibility of life on other planets. At thirteen he heard Orson Welles's *War of the Worlds* broadcast. He knew it was fiction. In fact, he believed the following news reports of a panicked American public were themselves part of the Mercury Players' ingenious hoax.

Lederberg became a premed student at Columbia, then turned to genetic research at Yale. He showed that the common bacterium *Escherichia coli* is able to exchange genetic information—"that bacteria have a sex life of a sort," as one popular magazine explained. Lederberg was a short, robust, balding man everyone regarded as a genius. He was married to, and worked with, a woman who was herself a brilliant geneticist.

Sagan and Lederberg were kindred spirits. They both appreciated that advances in rocketry would soon take extraterrestrial life from the realm of speculation to that of positive science. Lederberg did not know much about rocketry and astronomy. Sagan began tutoring him, aware of the irony in a twenty-three-year-old postgrad tutoring a Nobel-caliber genius.

Sagan likewise learned much from Lederberg, of course. Lederberg further impressed Sagan with the value to biology of finding an extraterrestrial life-form. To the zoo goer, the Earth's life is astonishingly varied; to the geneticist or biochemist, however, it is monotonous. All known life shares the basic architecture of proteins and nucleic acids. Biologists have no way of telling whether this architecture is necessary and universal or merely contingent, an accident of the way life got started on Earth. Would a Martian have DNA? Studying a Martian life-form, if such exists, would expand the horizons of biology as nothing else has. It would not have to be much of a life-form, either. The merest microbe would do.

These discussions were almost a hail and farewell. At the time Sagan met Lederberg, the geneticist was already preparing to leave Wisconsin and move to the West Coast. He would be making a trip to Stockholm, too, to pick up the 1958 Nobel Prize in medicine.

Sputnik

At a campus party, Sagan bet a friend that the United States would reach the moon by 1970. The stake was a case of chocolate bars (for chocoholic Sagan, this was enough to make things interesting). Shortly after the wager, the odds shifted abruptly in Sagan's favor. On October 4, 1957, the Soviet Union launched Sputnik.

It was possible to see the satellite glide across the twilight sky, a star full of portent. "The Soviet Union no longer is a peasant country," Nikita Khrushchev announced. In the United States, enthusiasm for the dawn of a new age of exploration was muted by inescapable military implications. America's pundits charged that the Soviets had placed the satellite's orbit at a sixty-five-degree angle to the equator so it might exult "in Red Triumph—over nearly all of the inhabited earth." Americans looked up at the point of light in the heavens and grimly calculated that it might carry an atomic bomb from Soviet soil in sixteen minutes.

The launch was held to demonstrate the need for better science education—and for better rockets. "By all odds," said American engineer Theodore von Kármán, "the most important job America now faces is to create an earth satellite—otherwise we leave ourselves open to naked inspection."

Meanwhile, sources inside the Soviet Union were already talking of sending humans to Mars by putting them in a "coma." On November 3, again without notice, the Soviets launched a second and bigger Sputnik. This one had a dog inside. After several days aloft, the Soviet press fell silent on the dog. "Laika" 's trip had been one-way. Its oxygen supply spent, the dog was allowed to asphyxiate.

*   *   *

Three days after the second Sputnik launch, Joshua Lederberg arrived in Calcutta to pay a visit to J. B. S. Haldane. There was a lunar eclipse that night. At dinner, Haldane remarked that it was also the fortieth anniversary of the October Revolution. What if the Soviets were to celebrate by putting a red star on the moon? By "red star," Haldane meant a hydrogen bomb.

Haldane and Lederberg (with dismay at the very thought) made some rough calculations. They concluded that a hydrogen bomb, exploded on the eclipsed, or dark-side, moon might indeed be visible from Earth. They stayed up to watch the eclipse. There was no red star.

This strange dinner conversation preyed on Lederberg's mind. He returned to Madison with a new mission. He quickly composed two one-page mimeographed memos and distributed them to Sagan and a few other colleagues he thought might be receptive. "I am deeply concerned over the incipient despoilment of an opportunity for biological exploration unique in our time," Lederberg wrote.

Nations would soon be sending rockets to the moon and other planets. Lederberg's concern was that these rockets would carry terrestrial microbes, spores, and organic molecules. Any native lunar microbes or spores would be difficult to identify after "the first rocket perhaps carrying casual dirt, pigment or even a dog is sent to crash spectacularly on the lunar surface." It would be necessary, Lederberg said, to forbid such recklessness and to sterilize any spacecraft that might land or crash on another planet.

Sagan fully concurred. Order-of-magnitude estimates convinced both men that the problem was real. Sacrificial canines being of topical interest, Lederberg made the macabre computation that a single space-faring dog or chimp, evenly splattered over the moon's surface, would make it impossible to detect any lunar life.

Dorion

One day, while Lynn was in her biology lab pipetting a solution of amoebas, she fainted. When she came to, she was on the floor, the pipette still in her mouth. She instantly knew she must be pregnant.

The baby was coming at a time when the couple's finances were at low ebb. Sagan had enjoyed an unbroken string of scholarships and fellowships from 1951 on. Then, in 1958, an NSF predoctoral fellowship in astronomy expired, and there was nothing to take its place.

Lynn had a fellowship waiting, but it had to be deferred until the baby arrived. The couple's main source of income was Sagan's part-time work. In 1958 he took a post as assistant physicist with Armour Research Foundation of Chicago. This was mainly paperwork that Sagan could do in Madison and mail in. The job paid $3 an hour and amounted to about $260 a month.

The baby, a boy, arrived in 1959. They named him Dorion Solomon Sagan. They found "Dorion" in a baby-name book. It suggested Wilde's *The*

Picture of Dorian Gray, which both parents admired, and the celestial epigram "D'Orion"—of Orion.

NASA

The post-Sputnik years were a time when ambitious space scientists could quickly make names for themselves. Kuiper being the only planetary astronomer in the United States, his students were in great demand. The scientists who designed NASA experiments tended to be young, and in a single mission they could eclipse the patient work of elders who headed observatories or academic departments. Sagan was quick to recognize this new fact of life. He began to consult with the space agency even before he had his Ph.D.

That was mainly Lederberg's doing. Lederberg's views on planetary contamination, and the broader prospects of detecting life on other planets, got a sympathetic hearing at the nation's new National Aeronautics and Space Administration. One of the first actions of NASA administrator Hugh Dryden was to request that the National Academy of Sciences set up a Space Sciences Board. This was to be a blue-ribbon group of academic experts advising the agency. Lederberg became head of the Space Sciences Board's exobiology panel.

Sagan's long association with NASA began with a letter from Lederberg to the space agency's Robert Jastrow, dated March 4, 1959. Lederberg raises the question of "a NASA contract to do some spadework, mainly consultation, on the generalities of biological probes. Our phone and travel bills are bound to mount, and also I would like to get some help from a young astronomer at Yerkes—Madison (name Carl Sagan) who is well informed and deeply interested in planetary biology."

Lederberg had just settled into his new surroundings at Stanford Medical School (where he was organizing a new genetics department). One of his initial goals for the exobiology panel was the publication of a "Handbook of Planetary Biology." "This really is a substantial job," Lederberg wrote, "and there is some problem in finding a sufficiently informed enthusiast to do the work. Fortunately Mr. Carl Sagan may be available for some months this summer, and perhaps again after he completes his dissertation in astronomy (planetary atmospheres) at the Yerkes Observatory."

In view of the geographic spread of talent, Lederberg suggested that the exobiology panel have two ongoing discussion groups, one on the East Coast ("Eastex") and the other on the West Coast ("Westex"). He proposed that "Mr. Sagan might have several functions: a) in the preparation of the consolidated reports of Westex (and, with their approval) Eastex for, perhaps, journal publication; b) as an advisor to Westex, particularly in the review of the existing literature, and c) in the preparation of the more extensive handbook." Lederberg asked for a part-time salary for Sagan of $4,000 per year.

*   *   *

Sagan was soon at work. "I sort of glided effortlessly between some kind of bull sessions late at night to advising the government." He pursued Lederberg's planetary contamination idea in two 1959 papers presented before the National Academy of Sciences. The obvious rebuttal to Lederberg's argument was that the moon, where rockets would be going first, was surely barren of life. What did it matter if we contaminated the moon?

Sagan's answer was that there might be organic molecules on the moon, buried under meteoric dust, and thus protected from the ultraviolet light that would otherwise destroy them. This organic material (itself of great scientific interest) would be vulnerable to contamination. It was possible, Sagan argued, to imagine a *single* earthly bacterium, transported to the moon by a crashed probe, multiplying by feeding off these organic molecules and underground caches of ice.

Also, Sagan thought it was conceivable that life had started on the moon. There might be fossils or even extant life. The idea "must not be dismissed in as cavalier a manner as it has been in the past."

*   *   *

Lederberg and Sagan's views held sway at NASA. The great unknown was whether and how the Soviets were sterilizing *their* space probes. In November 1959, while attending a meeting, Sagan managed to grill the Soviet Academy of Sciences' G. F. Gause on the subject. Gause insisted that Lunik 2 (the first spacecraft to crash onto another world) had been fully sterilized—both the instrument package and the final-stage carrier rocket. Sagan pressed for details. Gause coyly replied that the methods were known to every grad student in microbiology—and to every manufacturer of canned foods. He would say no more, posing the capitalist analogy that Chicago's Abbott Laboratories would not divulge its trade secrets to competing pharmaceutical firms.

But this is a matter for cooperation, not competition, Sagan parried. Gause did not see it that way. He did, however, take lunar biology at least as seriously as Sagan did. Gause spoke enthusiastically of using extraterrestrial microbes to prepare new types of antibiotics.

Greenhouse Effect

Sagan's analysis of lunar contamination became part of his Ph.D. thesis. Titled "Physical Studies of Planets," it was a highly unusual thesis—and highly characteristic of Sagan. It was one of the rare instances in which doctoral work is of capital importance, for it contained the first statement of Sagan's hypothesis of a greenhouse effect on Venus. But as if he could not bring himself to focus on one thing, Sagan's dissertation was an anthology of four minidissertations. The four parts were titled "Indigenous Organic Matter on the Moon," "Biological Contamination of the Moon," "The Radiation Balance of Venus," and "Production of Organic Molecules in Planetary Atmospheres: A Preliminary Report."

These topics were united by a theme not even hinted at in the title: life on other planets. Getting a doctorate in exobiology (it was virtually that) took ingenuity. Sagan was not allowed to take graduate courses in molecular biology. Getting a biologist to sit on his thesis committee was also a hassle. One Kimball C. Atwood finally agreed. He had trained as a gynecologist.

The section on Venus was by far the most influential. It too bore on exobiology—at least, it did at the time. Venus was still considered a possible abode for life. The planet is eternally covered with clouds, and no one could see the surface. Who knew what lay beneath the clouds?

"Everything on Venus is dripping wet," Svante Arrhenius wrote in 1918. "A very great part of the surface is no doubt covered with swamps." This quaint view of Venus had not been resoundingly refuted. One problem with it was that (just as with Mars) no water had been detected in Venus's atmosphere, only carbon dioxide.

Harold Urey believed that the *absence* of water was key to understanding Venus. He looked at things from a chemist's perspective. On Earth, water and carbon dioxide react with silicate rocks to form carbonate rocks (such as limestone) and silica (sand). On bone-dry Venus, the outgassed carbon dioxide simply accumulated, Urey proposed.

Harvard's Donald Menzel and Fred Whipple countered with almost the opposite idea. They suggested that the planet was entirely covered with an ocean. This prevented the carbon dioxide in the atmosphere from reacting easily with the underlying silicate rocks.

Cambridge astronomer Fred Hoyle had still another idea. He theorized that Venus had begun with far more hydrocarbons than water. Over eons, the hydrocarbons reacted with the oxygen of the water, producing carbon dioxide and hydrogen. Ultimately, this left the planet without a trace of water. Instead, there were great oceans of petroleum and clouds of smog.

Sagan remarked that anyone planning a piloted mission to the planet would not know whether to send a botanist, a mineralogist, a petroleum geologist, or a deep-sea diver. His thesis swept aside all these views.

He drew on puzzling new data. In the mid-1950s the Naval Research Laboratory in Washington, D.C., built a radio telescope on its roof for use in secret military operations. Cornell H. Mayer and his associates pointed the dish at Venus. They found that the planet radiated strongly at microwave frequencies.

Microwave energy is heat energy (hence its use in electronic ovens). Any hot object gives off microwaves, and it is possible to estimate the temperature of an object from the spectrum of microwaves produced. When Mayer and his colleagues did that with Venus, they got a shock. The microwaves implied Venus was scorching hot—something like 600° K on the physicists' Kelvin scale, or about 620° F.

This finding was met with disbelief. The disbelief had both a scientific and (as Sagan later asserted) an emotional component. Emotionally, people were reluctant to give up the appealing pictures of Venus with oceans and not-too-un-Earth-like temperatures. Scientifically, it was hard to see how Venus could be that hot. Venus is closer to the sun than the Earth is and receives about twice the sunlight. But the dazzling, pole-to-pole cloud cover bounces 70 percent of the sunlight back into space. These factors could not account for anything like 600° temperatures.

A great deal of attention therefore focused on some microwave observations at lower frequencies. They implied a much lower temperature: about 350° Kelvin or 110° F. That sounded more believable. The 600° K readings might then be due to a "hot" region in the planet's ionosphere or a Van Allen–like radiation belt around the planet.

Sagan (again) seized on the simple interpretation as most likely to be right. He argued that the planet's surface really was as hot as it seemed. His thesis was the first to offer a quantitative explanation for the high temperatures as a result of a "greenhouse" effect. A greenhouse grows warm on cold sunny days because the glass admits light but traps the warm air produced by the light. Gases like carbon dioxide in a planet's atmosphere produce an analogous effect. They trap the infrared light given off by a warm planet, lessening the normal radiation of heat into space. That keeps the planet warmer than it would be otherwise.

Sagan computed that carbon dioxide alone could not account for the high temperatures on Venus. The gas allows infrared light of certain frequencies to leak out into space. Water vapor, however, is also a greenhouse gas. It absorbs infrared light at some of the frequencies that carbon dioxide does not, and vice versa. Sagan therefore proposed that it was the combination of carbon dioxide and water vapor that created a powerful greenhouse effect on Venus.

This was speculative, for evidence for water vapor was still lacking. The greenhouse model was almost immediately taken seriously, however, and did much to make Sagan's reputation at the very outset of his career. Nor was the greenhouse effect merely an ad hoc explanation for one unpleasantly hot planet. Greenhouse warming is now recognized as a property of many planetary atmospheres, including the Earth's. Later work (by Sagan and many others) on the ancient climate of Mars, the so-called early faint sun paradox, global warming, and nuclear winter all drew on this key concept.

Sagan would spend much of the 1960s refining his models of Venus and attempting to rule out competing theories. However, he seems to have been convinced from the beginning of the essential rightness of the greenhouse model. Venus was hellishly hot and surely lifeless. In that regard, the planet was less interesting to him.

*   *   *

As his doctoral work drew to a close, Sagan began planning his future. In late 1959, he applied for an NSF postdoctoral fellowship at the Meudon Observatory in Paris. That was where Audouin Dollfus worked, another of the small club of planetary astronomers. Sagan had enough high school French to get by. It would be a big and difficult move for a two-career family. Lynn was nearing completion of a master's degree in zoology and genetics. She was also expecting another child.

At about the same time, Lederberg nominated Sagan for a Miller fellowship at Berkeley. Kuiper strongly encouraged him to take the Berkeley offer. Sagan's immediate research plans were for spectroscopy of planetary atmospheres. Kuiper told him that spectroscopy was not done at Meudon. Sagan agreed; Berkeley it would be.

During the preliminary questioning for his doctorate, Sagan was asked to describe all the principal forms of astronomical instrumentation. He forgot to mention the spectrophotometer, an odd omission considering his plans. He overcame this gaffe, of course, and in June 1960, the University of Chicago awarded Sagan his Ph.D. in astronomy and astrophysics. Along with it he acquired the lifetime bragging right of being "the only astronomer in the history of the world to have on his thesis committee a professor of obstetrics and gynecology."

Life on Jupiter, Scientist Says

The final part of Sagan's doctoral thesis concerned the production of organic molecules in other planets' atmospheres. "For a long while he had been completely devoted to Venus," explained NASA's Gerald Soffen in a 1963 piece on Sagan. "I can see that a new planet is coming into his thoughts—Jupiter! Whereas, this planet is so far beyond most of our imaginations that we haven't even thought about it, Carl is already talking about the biosphere of Jupiter. In short, Jupiter is becoming his new hero!"

"Hero" or not, Sagan gave Jupiter a lot of thought. At that time, it was common to suppose that the atmosphere of Jupiter contained large amounts of ammonia, methane, water, and hydrogen. It was not lost on Sagan that these were the gases in the Miller-Urey experiment.

In May 1960 Sagan presented this part of his doctoral work at a meeting of the Radiation Research Society in San Francisco. He spoke of the likelihood of organic compounds being formed in Jupiter's atmosphere. No one knew what Jupiter was like inside. Sagan speculated that there might be oceans—and if oceans, maybe life. The colorful idea of Jovian life merited a single sentence in the published article, where Sagan rated the possibility of life on Jupiter greater than that of life on Venus. Since Sagan believed Venus to be an inferno, that was not in itself a strong endorsement.

The society asked Sagan to give a press conference. Though still skittish from the *New York Times* mix-up, he agreed. "Look," he warned the reporters, "I'm talking about organic molecules, not life. I'm not saying that there's life on Jupiter. I'd be very unhappy if any of you wrote that I said 'life on Jupiter.' "

As Sagan remembered it, the very next day a San Francisco newspaper reported: "Life on Jupiter, scientist says."

BERKELEY

1960-63

THE MOVE WEST opened new horizons. Sagan's title at Berkeley was Miller Research Fellow in the University of California's Department of Astronomy, Institute for Basic Research in Science, and Space Sciences Laboratory. Though this post did not require him to teach, he insisted on teaching a class for the experience. He was known for his originality of thought. One day in Berkeley, Sagan told Ronald Blum (he had moved west, too) that he was worried about the carbon dioxide in the air. The burning of fuel was creating more carbon dioxide. This would increase the Earth's greenhouse effect and warm the globe with disastrous consequences. At the time, that was an incredible if not crazy thing to say. It could not have been later than 1963.

A Non-Reputable Game

The years at Berkeley were halcyon days for the new field of exobiology. The space program burgeoned. With it came funding for exobiology, both basic research and instrumentation. Studies on the chemical precursors of life continued to lend credibility to the idea of life on other planets. Claims of the discovery of lifelike forms in meteorites further spurred interest in the field. A pioneer attempt to search for *intelligent* extraterrestrial life commanded headlines. Sagan made it his business to be involved in each of these developments. Of all the talented people drawn into exobiology at the dawn of the space age, he alone spanned the field in all its diverse aspects.

One welcome advantage of the move was that Sagan could resume his close relationship with Joshua Lederberg. It was Lederberg who coined the term "exobiology." In his discussions with Sagan and others, "extraterrestrial biology" got to be too much of a mouthful. In academia, protective of departmental boundaries, words count for much. Invoking the name of a new science was an audacious move, not the least because exobiologists had nothing to study. A commitment to exobiology was a risky career move, a plunge into the abyss.

Lederberg was a special case. He had already won his Nobel Prize. He credited the Nobel with giving him the luxury "to stay in a non-reputable game. Not disreputable, mind you, but non-reputable. It might have been very, very difficult otherwise and it would [have been] very hard for a capable young scientist who's had a lot of risks to take in his career to hitch it to something as uncertain as exobiology."

No capable young scientist risked more on exobiology than Sagan did. Even his exobiology-friendly mentors tried to warn him of the hazards of focusing on a field where solid results may be unattainable. Typical is Harold Urey's Dutch-uncle advice when asked to comment on Sagan's work on lunar organic compounds:

> My principal criticism of your paper on the moon is simply this. I think it is an enormously wordy discussion on a subject that can be discussed very briefly as far as anything we know. . . . I think a young man such as you would do well to put your efforts on a subject in which definitive things can be secured rather than writing long papers on such doubtful subjects.

Doubtful subjects need not remain doubtful forever. As a young scientist with a long career ahead of him, Sagan was already anticipating the exploration of the moon and Mars. And in the early 1960s, the chances of finding life on Mars looked promising. Lederberg inclined to the view that Sinton's findings constituted "virtually conclusive evidence for 'vegetation'" on Mars. Urey himself endorsed the prospect of detecting life beyond the Earth as "surely one of the most marvelous feats of 20th-century science." In a 1959 article with Miller, Urey wrote, "All the projected space flights and the high costs of such developments would be fully justified if they were able to establish the existence of life on either Mars or Venus."

Sagan's own convictions are recorded in his first book. He and the Rand Corporation's William W. Kellogg edited *The Atmospheres of Mars and*

Venus, a compilation of scientific articles published by the National Academy of Sciences and the National Research Council in 1961. The two editors wrote a large amount of text, and Sagan's writing skills were already evident to Kellogg. A section titled "The Question of Life on Mars" concludes:

> The evidence taken as a whole is suggestive of life on Mars. In particular, the response to the availability of water vapor is just what is to be expected on a planet which is now relatively arid, but which once probably had much more surface water. The limited evidence we have is directly relevant only to the presence of microorganisms; there are no valid data for or against the existence of larger organisms and motile animals. . . . The ancient and exciting question of the possible existence of life on Mars will probably be answered in the next decade.

Carl and Lynn's second child, Jeremy Ethan Sagan, arrived in October 1960. The family moved into a house on Grizzly Peak Boulevard, Berkeley, with an impressive view of the Golden Gate. Neither the new baby nor the new home improved an increasingly troubled marriage.

As one visitor remembers it, Dorion, in another room, would scream at the top of his lungs. Lynn would bolt to see what was the matter. Carl would finish his sentence, unperturbed. Carl spoke of being impressed with the fact that Winston Churchill had never dressed himself in his entire life. He expected Lynn to handle all the duties of a 1950s housewife, from washing dishes to paying the household bills. Unlike most housewives, Lynn was trying to juggle two infants and a demanding husband with getting a doctorate.

Every waking hour of the day, Carl had an excruciating need for attention. He had been the apple of his mother's eye. That Lynn had other demands on her time and energy was an affront. He was even jealous of the attention Lynn lavished on the children. The couple argued like the parents Lynn had dreamed of escaping. Lynn now describes the marriage as like "a torture chamber shared with children."

For Lynn, the new baby took on a special significance. She told herself she would put off leaving Carl—until Jeremy was old enough to walk.

Mariner and Apollo

In 1960 Sagan got his first job as a NASA experimenter on Mariner, a Venus probe that was the first U.S. mission to another planet. Sagan's doctoral work had given him the imprimatur of an expert on the planet. Better yet, he was an expert with a theory to test.

It was hoped that Mariner would decide definitively whether the planet's surface was as hot as the microwave readings suggested. Sagan was a member of the team planning the probe's infrared radiometer, a compact device (it fit into a five-inch cube) capable of mapping the temperature distribution of the planet's clouds.

But Sagan had to watch helplessly as Mariner 1 malfunctioned just after launch and NASA controllers sent a command causing it to self-destruct. The Soviets' Venera 1 flew by Venus in 1961. It became the first craft to reach another planet. Scientifically, it too was a dud.

The second U.S. craft, Mariner 2, was launched in 1962. It performed almost flawlessly. Its observation of the solar wind was hailed as the first really important scientific discovery made by a space probe. Sagan's instrument returned encouraging results, too.

Absurdly primitive by today's standards, the infrared radiometer made just three scans of the planet. One swept across the daylight half, another across the night half, and a third across the terminator, the line of dawn and dusk dividing the two. The device found that the heat radiation was stronger at the center of Venus's disk than at its edge. That was what would be expected if the ground was hot, and thus in line with Sagan's hypothesized greenhouse effect.

The Mariner data could not say what was causing the high temperatures. Other explanations besides the greenhouse effect were advanced. Ernst Öpik proposed an "aeolosphere" model in which furious, dust-laden winds eternally scoured the planet's surface, heating it to near-red heat through friction.

While this idea struck many as far-fetched, Sagan's greenhouse model had gaps of its own—notably the gaps in the carbon dioxide absorption spectrum. Sagan conjectured a water level in Venus's atmosphere far above what was judged consistent with observations. Öpik sarcastically referred to one of Sagan's publications on the greenhouse effect as a "very stimulating and imaginative article."

*   *   *

Others in the exobiology community were already designing robotic devices to detect life on other planets. At one of the first Eastex meetings, astronomer Thomas Gold chided biologists for not having such a device. What they needed, Gold said, was a black box. Put something alive in that box, and it would beep *yes*. Put something *not* alive in it and it would beep *no*.

This call inspired a number of scientists to begin building "life-detectors." At Stanford, Lederberg and Elliott Levinthal began working with such devices. Sagan would come in the lab and kibitz. He was not by nature an engineer. (Samuel Sagan, as capable with a hammer as a pool cue, once complained that his son was "incompetent with his hands.")

The most famous of the early life-detectors was built by Wolf Vishniac, a Stanford-educated biologist then at Yale. Vishniac was the son of biologist Roman Vishniac, also known as photographer of the Warsaw ghetto. Sagan came to know Wolf Vishniac quite well. The world of exobiology was small enough that they were always running into each other at meetings.

Vishniac, as well as Lederberg and Levinthal, believed there would be microbes on any planet supporting larger life forms. Vishniac's Wolf Trap was designed to detect these microbes. It was a box with a pneumatically operated pickup arm. A whoosh of compressed gas pulled some dust into the box and into an internal growth chamber supplied with water and nutrients. If microbes multiplied in the liquid medium, they would almost certainly change the opacity and/or acidity of the water. The instrument monitored both. A change would be suggestive; an exponentially growing change would strongly imply life.

*   *   *

NASA was not so fixated on detecting extraterrestrial life as Sagan, Lederberg, and Vishniac were. On May 25, 1961, President John F. Kennedy spoke to a joint session of Congress, vowing to put an American man on the moon. Sagan described himself as "dazzled": "As a newly minted Ph.D., I actually thought all this had something centrally to do with science."

The Apollo program was a political response to Sputnik and all it implied. Few inside NASA or the executive branch were happy admitting that. It was presented to the public as a scientific mission. Though Sagan is best remembered as a critic of piloted spaceflight, he was at the time caught up in the general enthusiasm surrounding Apollo. He was certainly pragmatic enough to realize that any lunar mission would have great scientific value. Its cost-effectiveness (with Congress and the public enthusiastically supporting it) did not weigh heavily on him.

In May 1962 Sagan drew up a very preliminary, and very ambitious, scientific program for the Apollo mission. The astronauts, he hoped, would have backgrounds in organic chemistry or microbiology. They would carry a lightweight drill that would allow them to dig a core sample tens of meters below the surface. They would inspect these cores for fossils with a microscope and for organic compounds with a gas chromatograph. Then they would pack the samples in sterile containers and bring them back to Earth.

In a 1963 interview, Sagan even maintained that "there are certain times when only a man can serve the purpose—for example, in the detection of extraterrestrial life. I feel that until we send men, we are not going to be at all sure that we have characterized even the major kinds of life that may be there to find."

A Trip to Oz

By then a quite different idea for detecting extraterrestrial life had captured Sagan's interest. In September 1959, *Nature* published an article by Cornell physicists Giuseppe Cocconi and Philip Morrison. They maintained that the current generation of radio telescopes might be able to detect radio signals from intelligent beings in nearby star systems. They suggested tuning receivers to the twenty-one-centimeter line of neutral hydrogen. The article concludes:

> The reader may seek to consign these speculations wholly to the domain of science fiction. We submit, rather, that the forgoing line of argument demonstrates that the presence of interstellar signals is entirely consistent with all we now know, and that if signals are present the means of detecting them is now at hand. . . . The probability of success is difficult to estimate; but if we never search, the chance of success is zero.

The article made a sensation, nowhere more than in Green Bank, West Virginia. Astronomer Frank Drake had been planning just such a search with the new radio telescope at the National Radio Astronomy Observatory. The observatory director, Otto Struve, was incensed that Cornell was getting all the glory for an idea *they* had had. Struve immediately announced the search plans.

The search was called "Ozma" after L. Frank Baum's Oz books, which were to Drake what Burroughs's Barsoom tales were to Sagan. The Ozma project ran six hours a day, April through July 1960. It examined two nearby stars, Tau Ceti and Epsilon Eridani. Drake and colleagues listened through a loudspeaker and inspected a nervous seismograph trace on a rolling spool of paper. At that time they thought the most likely signals might be pulses beeping out prime numbers or digits of pi. They heard only static; saw only scribbles. As the project came to an end, Drake concluded that there were no communicating civilizations on the two stars, but looked forward to future searches with better equipment. "In a way we're like Dorothy making a trip to Oz," he told the press. "After we get there and back, we'll never be the same."

Frank Drake

Sagan viewed Drake's pioneering achievement from a distance with intense interest and surely some envy. Sagan knew Drake by phone and mail. Drake was one of the people making the microwave observations of Venus that Sagan was trying to fit into his radiation balance models.

Drake, four years older than Sagan, had been raised in Chicago. His parents were strict Baptists. Each week they sent him to Sunday school. His Sunday school teachers took him on field trips to the Oriental Institute's museum, whose silent rows of mummies and pot sherds were held to constitute proof of the literal truth of the Bible. The young Drake failed to see the connection. (Once, when asked to account for his interest in extraterrestrial intelligence, Drake wryly cited early exposure to fundamentalist religion.)

Drake settled on an astronomy career at Cornell. He enlisted in the navy during the Korean War and found the navy electronics course superior to Cornell's. Discharged in 1955, Drake took his Ph.D. at Harvard. While working late one night on his thesis, he came across a narrowband radio emission, apparently coming from the Pleiades star cluster. It was clearly an intelligent signal.

"What I felt," Drake said, "was not a normal emotion. It was probably the sensation people have when they see what to them is a miracle: You know that the world is going to be a quite different place—and you are the only one who knows."

To test the signal, Drake moved the telescope. He reasoned that the signal would vanish if it was really coming from the Pleiades. Instead, the signal remained. It was interference, coming from Earth. Soon after the experience, Drake's hair turned white.

It was genetics. By age thirty, Drake's hair was completely white. From late youth, he was prematurely cast in a paternal role. The white hair combined with the glasses and the gruff, no-nonsense air of an old navy man to striking effect.

Drake was, like Sagan, an accomplished piano player. At various times in his life, Drake also played the accordion, hunted, skin-dived, ground his own telescope lenses, made jewelry and wine, explored caves, rescued people from caves, fixed up old cars, raised orchids. Unlike Sagan, he had an almost magical knack for fixing equipment with his hands. He was able to fix souls as well as solenoids. Radio astronomy uproots talented, sometimes introverted people and sets them down in remote locales often lacking in support networks. In his career as senior radio astronomer, Drake was often a crisis counselor. In one case he talked a troubled colleague into surrendering a loaded gun.

Green Bank

Sagan met Drake in person the year after Ozma, at the now-famous Green Bank meeting. The meeting was the idea of J. Peter Pearman, an Oxford-accented biologist who was staff officer on the National Academy of Sciences's Space Science Board. Pearman had followed news of the Ozma project and was trying to build support in government for searching for extraterrestrial intelligence.

Drake was delighted with Pearman's idea for a meeting, and they began tossing out names of people to invite. They began with Cocconi and Morrison; and of course Struve, for it was his observatory. Sagan's name was soon mentioned. Pearman knew him from the Exobiology Committee, and Drake thought Sagan "knew more about biology than any astronomer I'd ever met."

Melvin Calvin, whom Sagan had now met at Berkeley, was added. Besides his pioneer work on the origins of life, Calvin was engaged in studies of organic molecules in meteorites.

Drake thought they should invite two electronics experts: Dana Atchley, president of a firm called Microwave Associates, who donated vital equipment for the Ozma project; and Bernard Oliver, vice president of research at Hewlett-Packard. (Oliver had read about Ozma in *Time* magazine and had flown in by private plane to check it out for himself.)

Looking down the list, Drake jokingly said that, with all these experts, the only thing missing was someone who'd actually spoken with extraterrestrials.

"John C. Lilly," Pearman replied, with hardly a pause. Lilly was a medical doctor and psychoanalyst known for his studies of dolphin behavior. He was trying to communicate with dolphins—alien intelligences on our own planet.

As soon as he got off the phone with Pearman, Drake told Struve about the meeting—hoping he wouldn't veto the whole idea. Struve approved and added another name to the guest list. This was Su Shu Huang, a Chinese-born former student who had just taken a job with NASA. Huang had worked with Struve on a subject relevant to the meeting, that of determining which types of stars were likely to have planets.

They ended up with a list of eleven. They were not trying to be exclusive; that was all the people they knew who were seriously interested in the topic. Searching for life on Mars was one thing, for intelligent life elsewhere in the galaxy quite another. Even Lederberg was dubious about that.

Sagan flew in from Berkeley on October 31. At twenty-six, he was the youngest person there. (He was getting a reputation for being the youngest at high-powered meetings.) He found Green Bank to be in a picturesque valley of abandoned farms. A prime attraction was the eighty-five-foot dish Drake had used for Ozma. It creaked mightily but was said to have a curve accurate to within a quarter of an inch.

Sagan coined the acronym for the subject under discussion: CETI, for Communication with Extraterrestrial Intelligence. Plus, Tau Ceti was one of the stars in Drake's search, *and* it was in the constellation Cetus, the Whale—an intelligent being on our own planet. ("CETI" stuck for a decade, then was modified to the more modest "SETI," or *Search* for Extraterrestrial Intelligence.)

Belying his white hair, Drake was next to youngest at thirty-one. The others were mostly in their forties and fifties, except for Struve, well into his sixties.

Otto Struve was the scion of a dynasty of European astronomers. He had lived a splendid, aristocratic life in Europe and elsewhere, the details of which he did not care to share with the Green Bank astronomers. Hints of his past were to be had in his military bearing and colorful afflictions. The hepatitis that flared up erratically had been contracted in a Turkish prison. Struve had one trick eye that pointed in a different direction from the other. Talking to him was unnerving; it was hard to know which eye to look at.

Struve was not the type to "go native," no matter that he was spending this part of his life in hillbilly country. He was never seen without a suit and tie of good cut. Incredibly, he never introduced his wife to the other astronomers—which was like not introducing a fellow castaway on a desert isle. Mrs. Struve would be seen, from a great distance, silently walking dusty back roads in her tasteful gowns.

Melvin Calvin was fifty and nearly bald, his conversation punctuated with bursts of laughter. There was a buzz that he was going to get the Nobel Prize for his work on photosynthesis. He could not have failed to hear these rumors, but like the gracious victim-to-be of a surprise party, he didn't let on.

Philip Morrison, stooped with a childhood attack of polio, walked with a cane and spoke so rapidly that it was hard to keep up with him. Cocconi was not with him; he had wired his regrets from Switzerland. Pearman looked as British as he sounded. He seemed to be the one who best understood Huang's heavily accented English.

Lilly was an unknown quantity, invited in the hope that he would fit in and mingle. He turned out to be the life of the party. Lilly, recalled Drake, "didn't look at all like the kind of man who had secluded himself in isolation tanks and pounded electrodes into his own head to find out what parts of the brain were centers for pleasure and for pain." Lilly had *done* that. He believed it was important to probe what he held to be the two taboo subjects of science: fear and love. Lilly also had a philosophy that you shouldn't do an experiment unless you were willing to do it on *yourself*. No matter what he had pounded into his head, Lilly was no geek. He had movie-star good looks.

Of the technical contingent, Oliver was a robust and worldly man of business. Atchley was the prototype of a ham radio buff, his Harvard education notwithstanding. Atchley's goal in life was to make shortwave contact with as many people in as many remote locales as possible. When he did make contact, he would talk mainly about how high his antenna was and how well the signal propagated. To Atchley, searching for extraterrestrial signals was extreme ham radio.

Drake Equation

The Green Bank meeting convened on the day after Halloween 1961. No one there thought of it as a historic event. No one taped the discussions; no one even took snapshots. The meeting was in fact held in semisecret, for fear of being mobbed by press.

Struve, stiffly regal as always, welcomed the group in the small conference room. He turned the meeting over to Frank Drake. Drake went to the chalkboard and started writing an equation. As he wrote, he said that arguments about the likelihood or abundance of intelligent extraterrestrials really depended on seven factors. These could be strung together in an equation. As chalk snapped across the blackboard, an approving murmur arose behind him. The equation was an immediate hit.

The "Drake equation" attempts to estimate the number of extraterrestrial civilizations in the Galaxy from a string of guesstimated values. Drake called N the number of communicating extraterrestrial civilizations in our Galaxy. That number is expressed as the product of seven factors: the rate of star formation; the fraction of stars that have planets; the average number of planets suitable for life in a planetary system; the fraction of such planets that actually do develop life; the fraction of life-bearing planets that develop *intelligent* life; the fraction of intelligent species that attempt to communicate across interstellar distances by radio; and, finally, the lifetime of such communicating civilizations.

The first and last terms may need explanation. It is the rate of formation of stars that, ultimately, sets into motion the evolutionary processes that lead to new civilizations. The longer the average lifetime of civilizations, the more civilizations there ought to be. The first factor is like the flow of water entering a tub; the last, the rate at which it drains out. Together the two determine the level of water in the tub.

Much of the meeting consisted of debating the values of the seven factors. The rate of star formation was not a value astrophysicists had on the tips of their tongues. The group figured they could estimate it by taking the number of stars in the galaxy and dividing it by the age of the galaxy. There are several hundred billion stars in the Milky Way galaxy, of which they estimated that about 10 billion were sunlike. By coincidence, the Galaxy is also about 10 billion years old. The big numbers cancel out, equaling 1. Drake wrote 1 as the value of the first factor. Of course, it was only an order-of-magnitude estimate, as all the estimates would have to be.

The second factor, the fraction of stars having planets, was Struve's territory. It was not known directly. Telescopes were incapable of detecting *any* planets of other stars. Struve, however, had measured the rotation rates of stars using slight shifts in the lines of their spectra. He found a surprising discontinuity. Large blue stars rotated quickly, while stars about the size of the sun and smaller rotated much more slowly. This was curious, for all stars are believed to result from the contraction of rotating clouds of gas. The angular momentum (tendency to keep spinning) of such clouds cannot disappear into space. It must be either retained in the star's own rotation or transferred to other objects such as planets. In our own solar system, the planets (particularly Jupiter) have most of the angular momentum.

This finding boosted hopes of there being planets and life outside the solar system. Struve told the group firmly that he believed *all* solar-type stars either had planets *or* were parts of multiple star systems. Since about half the solar-type stars were known to be parts of multiple star systems, he proposed that one out of two stars had planets.

Philip Morrison felt that estimate was high, favoring one out of five stars.

The third factor was the average number of habitable planets per star. Struve had wanted Huang to attend because he had done a study on this issue. Huang computed that each star had around it a "habitable zone" where temperatures were suitable for life. The zone was biggest around large, hot stars, but these stars have lives too short for the evolution of intelligent life. For small stars, the zone is so narrow it might not contain any planets. Huang thought our solar system was fairly typical and suggested the value was about 1.

Sagan thought this value was too conservative. He suspected there *was* life elsewhere in our solar system—on Mars, perhaps on Jupiter, or on the satellites of the big planets. He pointed out that the greenhouse effect could warm planets (or satellites large enough to have atmospheres) much farther from the sun than the Earth was. He felt that 5 might be about right.

The next factor was the fraction of planets "suitable" for life that in fact evolve life. Sagan eloquently insisted the value was 1. *Every* suitable planet evolved life. The laws of physics and chemistry were the same everywhere. There was no reason to think that the early Earth's chemical composition was unusual. In the Miller-Urey experiment, common gases subjected to common forms of energy produced the chemical building blocks of life—and did so quickly. Similar reactions would occur, with the inevitability of a chemical reaction, on any suitable planet.

Calvin seconded this. Then it was time to break for lunch.

Dolphin Man

After lunch, the group discussed the next factor: the fraction of planets with life that develop intelligent life. John Lilly dominated this discussion. Where the others were virgins in interspecies communication, Lilly had done it. Or said he had done it. Lilly regaled the group with tales of dolphin intelligence, humor, derring-do, and romance (dolphins are crazy about sex).

All of this was relevant—theoretically—because if dolphins qualify as intelligent, then intelligence evolved at least twice on Earth. That would support the idea that intelligence is a common adaptation of life and not unique to the Earth.

Lilly brought along tapes of dolphin calls. When certain vocalizations were slowed down, they sounded something like human speech. Lilly thought he was beginning to understand some of the calls. In times of distress, a dolphin would make a rising, then descending, crescendo. Other dolphins would recognize this as a call for help. Lilly himself was able to imitate some of these calls.

This being an all-male gathering, Lilly did not neglect to mention the male dolphin's fantastic endowments. The dolphin penis normally resides inside a slit. It becomes visible only when erect. A dolphin may go from total flaccidity to full erection in three seconds. These erections are voluntary, Lilly insisted—*acts of will*. He had trained a dolphin named Elvar to play a novel game of fetch. Lilly would toss a ring; when Elvar caught sight of it, the dolphin's penis would bolt out smartly; the dolphin would then *catch* the ring on his member and return it, quick as any dog.

Lilly (whose research had been supported by the navy and air force) sketched plans for the military applications of dolphins. They could rescue pilots at sea, ferry atomic bombs into enemy harbors, recover missile nose cones. Lilly conceded the possibility of defection. He wondered how patriotic these wily denizens of the deep would be, whether they would respect the boundaries drawn by the nations of the land—or whether they would prove to be irredeemable pacifists.

Philip Morrison, fearing they were straying, made the pleasantry that dolphins, intelligent as they were, would have a hard time building telescopes with their flippers. He agreed that the parallel examples of dolphins and humans suggested the survival value of intelligence.

Still under the spell of Lilly's dolphins, the group voted for a factor of 1. Virtually *all* planets with life would evolve intelligence eventually. That ended the first of the meeting's three days.

*   *   *

At breakfast the next morning, Melvin Calvin was paged for a phone call. It was his wife. An NBC news reporter had just called the house to ask how it felt to win the Nobel Prize.

The 1961 Nobel Prize in chemistry was worth $48,300. Soon phone calls and telegrams funneled into Green Bank. In a crazy way it seemed as if the Nobel legitimized the subject of the conference. The group broke out the champagne and got noisily drunk.

Struve gave the most memorable toast. "With Elvar's permission," he said, "I wish to appoint Dr. Calvin an Honorary Dolphin!" Exactly how that added to Calvin's laurels was unclear. In a fit of camaraderie, the group formed a club, the Order of the Dolphin. They swore eternal friendship; they vowed to meet again, to discuss regularly the fascinating subject of extraterrestrial intelligence. It would be a club limited to those present— and Elvar.

By midmorning, it fell upon the new Nobelist to insist on getting back to business. There were two factors to go in the equation. They were the most difficult to estimate, grounded more in sociology than physics.

They needed to know what fraction of planets with intelligent species evolved a technological civilization able and willing to communicate across interstellar distances. It was, as Morrison said, possible to imagine brainy species without technology. And technology could take many forms. Would all technological societies know about radio waves? Calvin said that electromagnetic radiation (of which radio is one form) is crucial to the evolution of life. A curious, technological civilization would want to explore the full spectrum of radiation. They would learn about radio waves sooner or later.

How many such technological civilizations would *choose* to communicate with others? That was tougher. Human civilization in 1961 could not be counted as an example. Ozma had listened but made no effort to transmit. TV and radio transmission might be detectable by alien civilizations but only with advanced instruments.

After much debate, and with less confidence than before, the group's estimates fell in the range of 1/5 to 1/10.

The last factor was the one designated L on the chalkboard—the average lifetime of a communicating civilization. The group was surprised by a curious thing. Of the first six factors, all had been pegged at 1 or within a power of 10 of 1. Sagan's "optimistic" guess of five planets suitable for life tended to balance the two factors that were fractions less than one. So the first six factors multiplied together to equal (very approximately) 1. That meant the equation boiled down to a simplified form: the *number* of civilizations, N, approximately equals L.

Drake assumed that extrasolar civilizations, like everything else, have a finite life span. L is most properly understood to be the lifetime in a communicative phase. It might be that, after a flush of youthful exploration, civilizations lose interest in communicating and go on to something else. Only the lifetime as a communicating civilization would count.

There were grimmer prospects. It was suggested that all technological civilizations blow themselves up. Philip Morrison, by then an arms control advocate, had worked on the Manhattan Project. He had personally armed the bomb that leveled Nagasaki. He was aware of how short the sixteen years of relative peace since Nagasaki were in the cosmic scheme of things. A civilization that keeps inventing ever more powerful weapons must surely annihilate itself.

Sagan, warming to this apocalyptic mood, pointed out that there were other possible catastrophes that could destroy a civilization. A planet might use up its nonreplaceable resources and revert to a pretechnological stage. In the long run, there were asteroid collisions (a novel idea for the time). Though the chance of impact is small in any given year, eventually a collision would destroy civilization, if not life itself.

They came to no consensus. It appeared equally possible to imagine that communicative civilizations had an average lifetime of, say, less than 1,000 years—*or* that they avoided planetary holocaust and survived for geological eons, hundreds of millions of years.

By the premise that lifetime in years equals number of civilizations, Drake announced that their conclusion was that there are anywhere from 1,000 to 100 million advanced extraterrestrial civilizations in the galaxy.

*   *   *

The meeting touched on a shared nagging fear, that an alien message would be impossible to decipher. The linear B script of the Minoans had defeated generations of attempts to understand it. Egyptian writing had been deciphered only via the fortuitous discovery of the Rosetta stone. These were human languages. If it was, in general, impossible to understand an unknown human language stripped of its context, what hope was there for understanding a vastly more alien language from the stars?

Lilly said that in his experience with dolphins, it was necessary to hear a two-way conversation. He had to observe the *effect* of one dolphin's vocalization on others to understand what it meant.

It was tough to imagine doing the equivalent with extraterrestrials. Calvin tried; he suggested glumly that we might have to find two extraterrestrial civilizations whose communications beam happened to pass right through the Earth. No one even tried to calculate the odds of *that*.

Though the subject of the conference was literally out of this world, it took on a social dimension. Everything hinged on *L*. It seemed that finding (or not finding) extraterrestrial intelligence would say something about our own chances for survival. Sagan particularly took this to heart.

One last bottle of champagne remained. They opened it for a final toast. "To the value of *L*," Struve said. "May it prove to be a very large number."

IQ Test

Shortly after Green Bank, Sagan received a gift from Melvin Calvin. It was a silver tie tack made from a reproduction of a 300 B.C. coin from the western Greek colony of Tarentum. The coin showed a boy riding a dolphin. Calvin had one made for each of the others. They became the Order of the Dolphin's official membership badges.

For the next year or two, Sagan served as the order's club secretary. He inducted a few new members: Freeman Dyson, J. B. S. Haldane, and I. S. Shklovskii. Haldane wrote Sagan that an organization with no dues, meetings, or responsibilities was the kind he appreciated.

About six months after the Green Bank meeting, Sagan got a letter from Frank Drake. It contained a typed sheet of paper headed "An Example of a Message That Might Be Received from Another Civilization in Space." This was followed by a long string of 0s and 1s, "random" to casual gaze. The "message" went:

```
111100001010010000110010000000100000101001000001
100101100111110000011000011010000000100000100001
000010001010100001000000000000000000010001000000
000010110000000000000000001000111011010110101000100
000000000000000010010000111010101010100000000000101
```

0101010000000001110101010101110101100000001000000
0000000000100000000000001000100111111100000111010
0000101100000111000000010000000000100000000100000
0011111000000101100010111010000000011001011111010
1111100010011111001000000000000111110000001011000
1111111000001000001100000110000100001100000000110
0010100100011110010111

The sheet ended: "A total of 551 0's and 1's. What does it tell us?"

Drake had mischievously sent this brainteaser to all the other Order of the Dolphin members, knowing that nine high-powered egos were at stake. To make things interesting, Drake also sent it to several other noted scientists, including physicist Richard Feynman.

Sagan did not solve it. None of the scientists did. The lone solver was Bernard Oliver—a man in private industry. (Feynman wrote Drake back saying he had entertained the idea that it said something about the fine-structure constant or the quantum numbers of electrons in the iron atom. These physical results are the same across the universe, and their numerical values do not depend on units of measure. Both were good, but wrong, guesses.)

*   *   *

Drake's encoding was a picture, a single frame of black-and-white television. The challenge in sending a picture across the Galaxy was that television uses an encoding scheme that is known to sender and recipient (or in practice, it's built into the circuitry of TV sets so people don't have to know the encoding scheme). An extraterrestrial who didn't know how many scan lines there are supposed to be, or how pixel values are encoded, would be out of luck.

The number 551 was a clue. It's a prime number ($551 = 19 \times 29$); that is, 19 and 29 are the only positive whole numbers (aside from 1 and 551) that can be multiplied together to get 551. Drake hoped that extraterrestrials would share our math, understand this clue, and conclude that the message must be a picture of nineteen rows of twenty-nine dots—or twenty-nine rows of nineteen dots.

The first format produces a jumble. The second produces a jaggy picture of a bow-legged being and a diagram of a planetary system.

The picture could of course be as big as desired, and therefore as detailed, by choosing larger prime numbers. Color information might be sent by repeating suitably designed frames. In fact, regular moving-picture television was possible by sending serial frames.

Drake's puzzle was a milestone in SETI thinking. You can learn a lot from pictures, or better, moving pictures. Here was a way to send visual imagery without any preexisting protocol. This eased worries that an ET message would be as indecipherable as Minoan or, almost as bad, that it would natter endlessly on mathematical arcana, incapable of saying anything about "real life" on Planet X.

Oliver replied to Drake with style, sending him another 0s-and-1s message in Drake's own diabolical "code." When Drake unscrambled Oliver's reply, he found a picture of a martini glass.

Wax and Wigglers

The year of Green Bank saw another provocative development for exobiology. It came in the form of "Wax and Wigglers: Life in Space?" as a *Life* magazine headline put it. Melvin Calvin was one of a number of chemists studying the organic chemistry of meteorites. "Organic," again, does not necessarily imply life. A group in New York including Fordham University chemist Bartholomew Nagy found peculiar waxy matter in the Orgueil meteorite, which fell in France in 1864. They likened the substance's chemical structure to butter and cholesterol. The *New York Times* quoted one of the researchers: "We believe that wherever this meteorite originated something lived."

In short order it was reported that another researcher, Frederick Sisler, had found *living* organisms in a meteorite. Sisler was *growing* the alien bugs—or whatever they were.

Soon Nagy and others were finding a plethora of "organized elements"— that is to say, alleged fossils or spores—in meteorites. They were said to look like mushrooms or umbrellas, "beautiful little buttons" or "crud." The most impressive were the "type five organized elements," which were hexagonal with tubes projecting from three sides. At least two investigators enjoyed the short-lived honor of naming the first "extraterrestrial species." Both took the traditional prerogative of naming the species after themselves.

The meteorite controversy became Harold Urey's pet retirement project. Here—*finally!*—was exobiology you could take to the lab. Urey was not at all sure the claims could be believed, but as he neared his seventieth year, he was old enough to do as he pleased. It pleased him to solicit expert opinions on pollen grains and to organize conferences on the meteorite findings.

Sagan was involved both directly and indirectly. Most meteorites were believed to come from the asteroid belt. One of the first questions skeptics asked was how there could be fossils (or living spores?) in pieces of rock that came from small bodies lacking an atmosphere or oceans. In reply, Nagy cited Sagan's thesis work on possible lunar habitats. If it was possible to conceive of life on the moon, it was possible to conceive of life on the asteroids.

A more pressing question was whether the organized elements were really extraterrestrial. Or were they pollen or some other kind of earthly contamination? Sagan and other nonexperts played amateur pollen detective. By comparing pollen samples, Sagan tentatively proposed that the type five elements were pollen from the evening primrose. University of Chicago's Edward Anders favored ragweed.

At Urey's behest, Sagan met with Swedish pollen expert Gunnar Erdtman in Tucson, Arizona, on May 11, 1962. Sagan showed Erdtman slides of the meteorite structures that had been prepared by Nagy and a colleague. Erdtman was adamant. The structures were *not* evening primrose pollen, nor ragweed pollen, nor *any* kind of terrestrial pollen, contemporary or fossil. He hedged only that there might be rare spores or fungi that he would not recognize.

This expert opinion made an impression on Sagan and Urey. In a July letter to Sagan, Urey wrote, "Anders is still arguing for his ragweed pollen, but I find it simply amazing that the outstanding pollen expert of the world would not recognize ragweed pollen. Why should he go out on a limb for these unknown men in New York?"

That summer of 1962, it seemed that the establishment of life beyond the Earth was at hand. Then the bubble burst. In 1963 Anders and a Chicago coworker, Frank Fitch, reported that when ragweed pollen was stained the way Nagy had stained his specimens, it was *then* indistinguishable from the type five elements. Nagy, who obviously did not know he was dealing with pollen, had used a different staining technique than pollen experts like Erdtman did.

Nagy pressed his case for some time. At a May 1964 symposium in La Jolla, California, he reported a new finding. Many of the compounds of life, such as amino acids and sugars, exist in two forms that are mirror images of each other. Both forms occur when the compounds are synthesized chemically, but only one of the two forms exists in life on Earth. Nagy was able to show, from the way that beams of light were rotated in passing through solutions of meteoritic compounds, that they contained more of one mirror-image form than the other. Furthermore, he got the *opposite* result when he did the experiment with earthly pollen grains. Nagy felt this argued for extraterrestrial biology.

Sagan came up with a clever rebuttal. Suppose, he said, that the meteorite contained both forms of the compounds but had been contaminated by terrestrial bacteria. They would eat the molecules they could digest, leaving a residue of the opposite-handed molecules. A similar technique is used to produce the uncommon isomers in the laboratory. This idea impressed Urey.

The controversy died, as so many scientific controversies do, with a whimper rather than a bang. The meteoritic fossil advocates ran out of things to try and had still not convinced anyone but themselves. It was Edward Anders who wrote the controversy's epitaph. The only connection between meteorites and life, he said, was "that an article on meteorites appeared in a magazine called *Life*."

Symbiosis

Work of far greater ultimate importance was going on in Sagan's own home. Despite the two infants and the incessant arguments, Lynn was quietly pursuing an idea that would revolutionize biology.

One of Lynn's professors at the University of Wisconsin, Hans Ris, had examined chloroplasts under an electron microscope. (Chloroplasts are the bodies within plant cells that contain green chlorophyll.) Ris found that the chloroplasts looked remarkably like cells of blue-green bacteria (or algae, as they were then called). Lynn interpreted this as evidence that chloroplasts *were* bacteria that had evolved to live symbiotically inside so-called higher plant cells.

The idea was not new, but it was long out of favor. Lynn wanted to follow it up by looking for DNA within chloroplasts. All bacteria had DNA. If chloroplasts were really bacteria, they might retain their own DNA, distinct from that in the cell nucleus. Lynn's professor Gunther Stent told her not to bother—this would be like looking for Father Christmas.

Lynn persisted. While at Berkeley she was able to show that there *was* DNA in chloroplasts. She became convinced that not only chloroplasts but mitochondria (responsible for oxygen respiration) were the descendants of former free-living bacteria that had either infected or been eaten by the host cells in which they now resided. Instead of being destroyed, both cell lines survived.

Lynn's idea was dubbed the *serial endosymbiosis theory*. Both Carl and Joshua Lederberg encouraged her. One of the theory's many important consequences was that the merging of cell lines, and not just the accumulation of mutations, was a driving force in evolution.

For Lynn, the Sagan household was not a congenial place to continue this work, or to raise children. Soon after Jeremy Sagan took his first tentative steps, his mother gathered him and his brother up and walked out the door. She vowed never to return.

Carl wrote heartfelt letters asking for a reconciliation. He visited Chicago and tried to lobby Lynn's sisters to his cause. One rambling, funny, brutally honest letter to Lynn (dated August 12, 1962) tells of Carl's experimentation with commercial erotica. On a trip to Chicago, he ducked into an "art film" establishment. He entered a booth, put a quarter in a slot, and viewed pornography. From this experience he concluded that it was love, not sex, that he desired. He left and called Lynn, hoping for an emotional lift. The phone call degenerated into another argument that left Lynn in tears. Carl reiterated that it was not too late to make up. He still hoped to live with Lynn, in love and mutual respect, for decades to come.

Cover Story

One spring day in 1962, Sagan got a call from an air force general, a specialist on aviation medicine, whom he had met several times. The general said he was in Los Angeles with three Soviet scientists. One of them was Alexander Imshenetsky, who led the Soviet effort to develop devices for detecting extraterrestrial life. Would Sagan like to meet the Soviets? Sagan of course said yes and took the first plane to Los Angeles.

He arrived May 8 and took a taxi to the home of a UCLA brain scientist. There were the general, the Soviets, and a translator from the Library of Congress—although all three Soviets spoke fine English. They had drinks, then packed themselves into two cars to drive to the airport and have dinner before the Soviets caught their plane. Sagan rode in the same car with Imshenetsky. Though the translator was in the other car, he had no trouble carrying on a fruitful conversation on life detection and sterilization of planetary probes.

Imshenetsky agreed with Sagan on the importance of sterilization. There were those who argued that the hard radiation of space would kill anything. No, Imshenetsky said, even the smoothest metal surface would be rough enough to shelter microbes lodging in the shade of surface flaws. The Russian commiserated with Sagan about the difficulties of convincing engineers of this—particularly regarding the moon. He observed, half jokingly, that cooperation between nations would be easier than cooperation between scientific disciplines.

Imshenetsky was more open than Gause had been two years earlier. He revealed that Lunik 2 had been sterilized by subjecting it to a mixture of formaldehyde and superheated steam. This was, apparently, the first time the "secret" of the Soviet space program's sterilization measures had been divulged to a Westerner.

They arrived at LAX and checked the bags. The Soviets excused themselves to go to the rest room. Sagan found himself alone a moment with the translator. The translator asked him what he'd found out.

Sagan innocently recounted the conversation in the car. The translator said it was good work. He asked Sagan who he worked for. Slightly mystified, Sagan answered, the University of California at Berkeley.

No, the translator said, not the "cover." It dawned on Sagan that the translator was a spy. Sagan was outraged. He idealistically insisted he would never spy on a fellow scientist. This remark was cut short when the Soviets returned from the rest room.

Sagan was now so upset that he refused to discuss any more science with Imshenetsky during dinner. They spoke of American movies and Soviet poets. Imshenetsky had quite a few drinks. He announced that, in his humble opinion, the greatest Russian poet was William Shakespeare. He also thought that American cowboy films were too violent.

The next day, back in Berkeley, Sagan looked up the Central Intelligence Agency in the San Francisco phone book. He called, and a voice answered by reciting the number he had just dialed. Sagan said he had a complaint to file. Another employee came on the line and Sagan started to explain, but the CIA man stopped him, saying it was unwise to discuss such things over the phone. He made an appointment to meet at Sagan's Berkeley office.

At the appointed time, two neatly dressed CIA agents showed up. Sagan purposely took his time in examining their credentials. He then told them his story. The agents assured Sagan that no one in the agency would act in the extremely uncouth manner that this "translator" had. They agreed to investigate, asking Sagan to keep quiet about the matter for the time being. He agreed.

A week later, one of the agents called back. He told Sagan that "the party in question" did not work for "our organization" under the name he had used with Sagan. It had taken a week just to check the personnel roster, which Sagan concluded must have been very long or very secret.

On May 15, Sagan sent a one-page write-up of his conversation with Imshenetsky to Lederberg.

A few days later, Sagan was informed that the translator did not work for the agency under *any* name. While no less guarded about what he could say on the phone, the agent now sounded concerned. He assured Sagan that the "company" was curious to know who the translator *did* work for.

A week after that, the same two agents appeared in Sagan's office. They had determined that the translator *was* employed by the Library of Congress. This was only a cover, of course. He was really an air force intelligence agent.

*   *   *

Two years later, in May 1964, Sagan and Wolf Vishniac attended a meeting of the Committee on Space Research (COSPAR) in Florence. COSPAR was attempting to set standards for the sterilization of space probes. One Soviet was there: Imshenetsky, now so ill he could barely participate. The Uffizi Gallery was kept open one evening for the delegates' viewing. Sagan and Imshenetsky toured it together. They stepped into one immense, hushed gallery hung with Botticellis. As they drank in the view, Sagan perceived that the room was not quite empty. At the far corner was a lone man.

"Isn't that the fellow who was with us in Los Angeles?" Imshenetsky whispered. It was the "translator" again, now disguised with a beard. "Very stupid fellow," Imshenetsky added.

Kaleidoscope

Sagan's years at Berkeley were a time of personal growth. He began to believe that there was more to life than science. He met new people, his political consciousness grew, and he was more open to new experiences.

One of these new experiences was using marijuana. Sagan ran across the drug from time to time at parties. He was reluctant to try it at first. He was concerned that it was addictive. From observation of his friends, he concluded that it was not, so he gave it a try.

The marijuana had little effect. He decided it was a placebo, that the claimed effects were a cultural construct. About the sixth time he tried it, Sagan learned that his placebo theory was wrong.

He was smoking a joint while lying on a couch in a friend's living room. As he idly gazed at the shadows cast on the ceiling by the leaves of a houseplant, the shadows resolved into a detailed picture of a Volkswagen Beetle. He could make out the chrome trim, the hubcaps, the license plate, even the oddly placed handle used to open the trunk.

When he closed his eyes, he found that movies were playing on the insides of his eyelids. A yellow path cut through green fields to a red farmhouse in a cartoon landscape. Beyond was a blue sky dotted with clouds. In a flash, the scene's colors shifted. The house turned orange, the sky brown, the clouds red, the fields violet . . . the path still yellow. Another flash, and the colors changed again. The scintillations matched the beating of his heart. Every pulse brought a new change of palette, and with every change the colors were exquisite and harmonious.

The experience was not frightening. Throughout he retained the knowledge that these were illusions caused by the drug and subject to his own creative manipulation. Sagan found himself acting simultaneously as intuitive creator of imagery and as a logical observer and appreciater of that imagery.

In his use of the drug, Sagan discovered that the creative part of himself worked best when supplied with ambiguous images: shadows, flames, kaleidoscopes. Looking at a fire though a kaleidoscope, the flames multiplying in its mirrors, was a moving experience for him. Another of his earliest hallucinatory experiences took place while gazing at a simple candle flame. Deep within the heart of the flame—magnificently indifferent to it all—stood a man in a black cape. Sagan recognized him as the Latin gentleman pictured on the bottle of Sandeman port wine.

Firefly Tails

Nineteen sixty-two was a nexus in Sagan's career. Harvard University offered him a position as assistant professor of astronomy. He would simultaneously hold a post at the Smithsonian Astrophysical Observatory in Cambridge, Massachusetts. Sagan was enthusiastic about taking the offer. He regarded Harvard as the pinnacle of American astronomy. At the observatory he would work under director Fred Whipple, one of the great astronomers of the time.

The dual Harvard and Smithsonian posts would mean settling down and committing to astronomy. It would likely be a more conventional brand of astronomy than what Sagan had been pursuing in Lederberg's West Coast exobiology circle. Sagan's interests had been edging in the direction of biology. Lederberg suspects that Carl must have contemplated switching fields.

For in California, Sagan had forged a unique reputation. Far from being in Lederberg's shadow, the twenty-eight-year-old Sagan was hailed as the exemplar of the new field of exobiology. He gave interviews on the topic to reporters with some regularity. (Lynn had tried to discourage this, without effect.) In 1961 Sagan made his network TV debut on a CBS news show on space exploration. "Carl has created a new field—one bridging the gap between astronomy and biology," stated Stanford medical school's Elie Shneour. "He is essentially alone in this field. He is, I believe, the only really fully cognizant scientist who is capable of bridging these two disciplines on a professional level."

These words may sound extreme coming from a man who worked with Lederberg and was fully cognizant of all he had done. Shneour was not alone in rushing to equate Sagan with exobiology. Sagan straddled disciplines more visibly and fully than did Lederberg. His youth was an asset, too. Only a young scientist could hope to realize exobiology's potential.

*   *   *

Sagan accepted the Harvard offer but delayed taking up his duties in Cambridge until February 1963. In the meantime, Lederberg had Sagan appointed visiting assistant professor of genetics at Stanford University School of Medicine. "Stanford was a pretty loose ship in those days," explains Elliott Levinthal. Even so, it was unusual for one of the nation's most competitive med schools to take on an astronomer.

Sagan was already a confirmed theorist. In a brief collaboration with Stanley Miller, Miller had to nag Sagan to pull his weight in the lab. (They sparked gases similar to those believed to exist on Jupiter, producing a rich yield of organic compounds.) Apparently recognizing this deficiency, Sagan wanted to get some lab experience before leaving for Harvard. One of his last projects on the West Coast was a collaboration with Cyril Ponnamperuma. It was an education in more ways than one.

Of Sri Lankan extraction, Ponnamperuma had worked in Melvin Calvin's lab. He was a talented researcher who shared Sagan's intensity of purpose. By this time NASA had a full-fledged Exobiology Division at its newly inaugurated NASA Ames Research Center. Ponnamperuma became its lead researcher on the origins of life.

Much of his work attempted to follow up the Miller-Urey experiment. Miller had made it look so *easy* to produce biologically interesting compounds. There followed a land rush in which researchers such as Ponnamperuma vied to be the first to synthesize a particular compound under "primordial" conditions.

Ponnamperuma had little tolerance for failure. Should he not get the results he expected, he instinctively concluded that the technique had been sloppy; the experiment would have to be repeated until it did produce the "right" result. He was somewhat in awe of Sagan. He briefed those in his lab beforehand so they would know who Sagan was and appreciate the chance to work with him. This reputation mostly rendered Carl immune from Ponnamperuma's demands. The main share of the physical work fell on Ruth Mariner, a young lab assistant. Sagan sat around in the lab, observing Mariner go through the procedures Ponnamperuma dictated. Mariner found Ponnamperuma difficult. Sagan, while charming, simply made her nervous.

The three were attempting to synthesize adenosine triphosphate (ATP) under conditions comparable to those on the early Earth. ATP is life's fundamental energy-storage compound. Its energy-rich phosphate bonds fuel the bound of the kangaroo, the wiggle of the sperm cell, the glow of the fire-fly. To show that ATP could be formed *easily* from simple gases and energy would go a long way toward explaining why this molecule, and not any other, was the universal currency of energy. This is what Ponnamperuma was set on doing.

Sagan was a logical collaborator because he had already sketched a theoretical basis for the significance of ATP. The adenine molecule (which is part of ATP) can absorb ultraviolet light. Sagan theorized that it did so on the early Earth and (somehow) channeled this energy into the synthesis of complete ATP molecules. It would be "photosynthesis without life." The photochemically produced ATP might have provided a ready energy source for the first organisms.

ATP consists of an adenine molecule attached in a certain precise way to a sugar molecule called ribose connected in another precise way to a chain of three linked phosphoric acid molecules. Ponnamperuma had already managed to produce adenine and ribose from simpler compounds. Small amounts of phosphoric acid would exist in nature. For this experiment, Ponnamperuma, Sagan, and Mariner (mainly Mariner!) sealed adenine, ribose, and phosphoric acid in a glass tube and exposed it to the light from four ultraviolet lamps. It was like pouring the three ingredients into a hat and taking out a cake—the ultraviolet light serving as a magic wand.

They found that ultraviolet light indeed caused adenine and ribose to link. This was a significant finding in itself. One particular combination of the two molecules is adenosine, and adenosine is one of the four basic components of DNA.

They also found that the reaction occurred *only* in the presence of phosphoric acid. That hints at why phosphoric acid is incorporated in the DNA and ATP molecules.

The grand prize was elusive. Try as Mariner might, she couldn't get one iota of ATP. To some, that would be a negative result; to Ponnamperuma, it was unacceptable.

Ponnamperuma had Mariner repeat the experiment with ethyl metaphosphate instead of phosphoric acid. Ethyl metaphosphate is a syrupy compound used for synthesis in chemical labs. It already contains the high-energy phosphate-to-phosphate bonds that exist in ATP. Using it in *this* experiment was a little like putting batteries in a perpetual motion machine. There was no reason to think that this exotic reagent was lying around in primordial times. If it *did* work, it would be unclear whether the ATP had formed by capture of the ultraviolet light's energy, as Sagan theorized, or merely from the chemical energy already existing in the metaphosphate syrup.

The metaphosphate did give Ponnamperuma the result he decreed. The experiment now produced ATP and other adenosine phosphates. The work was published to some acclaim in *Nature*. It was Sagan's first appearance in that prestigious journal's pages.

The work was nonetheless clouded with ambiguities. There are many ways of joining the component molecules of ATP. Only one form is found in living organisms. It was hard to say how much, if any, of that had been produced.

Ponnamperuma, Sagan, and Mariner were aware of this problem but were only partly able to address it with the primitive analysis techniques then available. In their most unusual test, they used dehydrated firefly tails. (There was a scientific supply house that sold them by the box.) The reasoning was that only the "correct," biological form of ATP would be likely to work in a biological system. This experiment may not have been definitive, but the result was positive. Supplied with their freshly synthesized ATP, the dead insects' lanterns lit up like tiny Christmas lights.

*   *   *

The impending move prodded Carl to attempt a reconciliation with his wife. Lynn and the boys were living in Port Richmond, California, sharing a place with another young mother. Carl pleaded with Lynn to give him another chance.

In early January 1963, Lynn's answer was a firm no. "Carl, you are a beautiful person," she wrote. "I have watched you grow and I feel you have the potentiality for true and mature love. Just not with me. You know that." She advised, "It will be easy for you to find many women who will derive immense pleasure from your professional and social success; perhaps it is my eternal tragedy that I can't gratify my ego through your progress. You must look for that in a wife."

Carl continued his entreaties. Shortly after he arrived at Harvard, he convinced Lynn to join him. It was a move of convenience. Lynn decided she had no desire to live on the West Coast permanently. Nor could she see herself returning to the stifling Midwest. Massachusetts had possibilities. She therefore accepted Carl's invitation to move east—vowing to keep her eye on the exit door.

CAMBRIDGE
1963-68

LYNN, DORION, AND Jeremy moved into an apartment with Carl in Watertown, Massachusetts, a few miles west of Cambridge. Carl's hopes were tempered by his awareness of Lynn's ambivalence. He told Leone Alexander that he wanted a wife, not a roommate. He feared it was a roommate he was getting.

Lynn, for her part, knew it would not last. She would not be able to tolerate life with Carl for more than a few more months. Then it would be over. She would be rid of him forever. Knowing this made her happy in her new home.

Talking Horse

This precarious domestic arrangement was not the only thing unusual about Harvard's new astronomy lecturer. Brash and outspoken, Carl was a minor sensation from the day he drove into Cambridge in his ramshackle car. He seemed to live in turtleneck sweaters. One friend improbably likened Sagan to the star of a then-popular sitcom: "Meeting Carl for the first time is something like encountering a talking horse. It's novel, but after the first impact, it matters only if the horse has something important to say! Carl Sagan always has something important to say."

The *way* he said things was unmistakable. Dorion described it best: his father's "bass voice (I heard it in the womb), perfect diction, encyclopedic memory, um-less speech, and a preternatural (if to me privately aggravating) way of orating reasoned paragraphs . . . made other people's speech sound like illogical jabberwocky."

As a teacher, Sagan was quickly recognized as one of the university's best. "He brought to the class three ingredients you really didn't get from the other professors," said Richard Berendzen, Sagan's first teaching assistant. "One was a broader perspective. The class wasn't just planetary astronomy. He would link it to physics, to chemistry, to biology, to history. He also had a great emphasis on what we now call 'diversity.' From the earliest days I knew Carl, he was stressing the role of women and ethnic minorities. Harvard has a bigger point of view than almost any other place I know, but Carl had a *very* broad perspective.

"Two, he was *funny*. He had this sort of deadpan humor that was quite disarming. At first you weren't entirely sure he *was* joking. He wouldn't smile, he would say something flat that was really quite witty.

"Third, he would occasionally say things with more poetry than any other professor would. You know how it normally was in the physical sciences: 'We take the double integral . . .' Carl would wrap that in, really, a literary phrase. He was not alone in doing that. Harvard had the wonderful tradition of Harlow Shapley, who said beautiful poetic statements—but Sagan whipped them off all the time."

Sagan possessed a strong sense of scientific destiny. At the beginning of his Harvard career, he was quoted, "I feel that I'm remarkably lucky to be alive at this particular moment in history, because I'm doing precisely what I would have wanted to do at any time." Had he lived a couple of generations earlier, he said, or a couple later, he could not have participated in the exploration of the solar system and the search for the origins of life. This was no offhand comment. Sagan makes nearly the same point, in strikingly similar words, a decade later in his book *The Cosmic Connection*. It was the credo of Sagan's scientific career.

The sense of having a mission, combined with an awareness of his talents and personal charm, made Sagan self-absorbed (at least) and obnoxiously egotistical (to many, not just Morris Alexander). He was a poor Jewish kid from Bensonhurst who now found himself in the heart of WASP academia, with Nobel laureates and the press hanging on his words. It was difficult not to feel some insecurity and to let early successes go to his head. Carl's own sister, Cari (as Carol was known in adult life), found him a "snob" at this stage in his life.

Snobbery is not rated as much of a sin at Harvard. Still, something in Sagan's manner rubbed some people the wrong way, even if they couldn't quite put their finger on it. "He is too quick," complained one colleague. "I doubt that he has ever been faced with a difficult (for him) problem and been compelled to struggle to solve it. Perhaps he should have been."

Sagan avoided wearing a watch and was infuriatingly casual about appointments. During a meeting in Spain, Sagan was supposed to meet Wolf Vishniac and his wife, Helen, at their hotel. Sagan never showed up, nor did he ever apologize or even mention that he had forgotten the meeting.

Sagan had a way of appropriating everyone's ideas without going through the full ritual of genuflection. When quoted in the press, he would often be paraphrasing the ideas of Lederberg, Urey, or Muller. Coming from the mouth of someone so young, this seemed faintly disreputable. When Sagan was called to introduce a speaker who had an exciting and original finding to report, he often could not resist revealing the "punch line" in his introduction—and outlining its broader implications.

Confronted with those he regarded as intellectual inferiors (Lynn identifies this as "most people") Sagan could be merciless. Like his mother, he was quick to voice the cruel truths that others only thought.

Sagan sat on a committee vetting experiments for NASA's "bio-satellite." The satellite was to launch living things into space. (The Soviets had dogs in space; there was an animals-in-space gap to be closed.) Since the satellite had little real scientific value, NASA had a problem attracting first-rate biologists. One earnest young scientist was describing an earnest experiment with beetles. The scientist wanted to see what would happen to beetles subjected to . . . *zero gravity.*

Sagan, in his black turtleneck phase, listened with his feet on the desk, his back to the beetle scientist. At the end of the pitch, Sagan turned to NASA's Orr Reynolds. "You know, Orr," he said, "we're hearing this proposal from a guy who probably feels *lucky* to get $10,000 to do an experiment. And he's proposing to spend several hundred thousand dollars on this beetle experiment. You know, I can tell him how he can change the gravitational effect by a factor of 2 at almost no cost."

The beetle guy eagerly asked how.

"Just turn them on their ass!" Sagan said.

*   *   *

There were many who found Carl a real "character," a rare soul with a refreshing commitment to the truth. Carl was never boring. There was also a genuine charisma (a quality that rarely exists without a healthy self-esteem). It was easy to be swept up by the charm that Sagan was equally capable of exhibiting. Even Lynn allows that Carl's "extraordinary self-centeredness" was "charming to strangers." In an almost breathless profile written at the time of Sagan's move to Harvard, journalist Shirley Thomas predicted:

If the odds of probability are applied to Sagan's future, it seems likely that he will substantially advance science. The elements in his favor are numerous—his own brains, imagination, and youth, plus the incalculable opportunities of the Space Age. Meanwhile, he continues his role as stimulator—and shocker!

Projects of the Space Cadets

Fred Whipple was an Iowa farm boy who became the world's great comet and meteor man. He had made an exact science out of those poetic phantasms and in the process had become head of Harvard's small but elite astronomy department. Whipple took a fond, fatherly interest in Sagan. He had no great problem with Sagan's exobiology interests. He did, however, do his best to steer Sagan into areas where hard results could more certainly be obtained than in exobiology.

With his Harvard appointment, Sagan was already starting to provide fatherly advice to his own group of grad students. His Harvard students included James Pollack, David Morrison, and Clark Chapman, all of whom became leading planetary astronomers. These students were full collaborators with Sagan and were often remarkably productive in their postgraduate years. Chapman attributed this fertile environment to Sagan's talent for putting an unexpected twist on any scientific question. Sagan asked questions that no one else would. This encouraged his students to look at problems from novel perspectives.

There was also a tonic sense of urgency. With other professors, the doctoral time would drag on for years. "With Carl," said Berendzen, "it would move faster: let's get on with life."

*   *   *

Sagan inaugurated his own research career at Harvard by publishing an article saying that one of the university's Nobel laureates was dead wrong. Harvard's Edward Purcell had won the Nobel Prize in physics for discovery of the twenty-one-centimeter line of hydrogen (which was, coincidentally, so central to the search for extraterrestrial intelligence). Purcell was even something of a SETI advocate. What he thought absurd was interstellar *travel*.

In science fiction (then and now), people are *always* zipping to Alpha Centauri and back. This was implicit in the UFO mythos as well. More seriously, with inter*planetary* travel on the horizon, several people had begun taking serious looks at inter*stellar* travel.

In a much-quoted 1960 speech at Brookhaven National Laboratory, Purcell considered "the projects of the space cadets," as he called them. To get to other stars in a reasonable time, he reasoned, you would have to travel at nearly the speed of light. The energy required to achieve those speeds would be stupendous.

Purcell computed that a trip to a star twelve light-years away would demand 400,000 tons of fuel (half of that *antimatter*). Purcell concluded: "All this stuff about traveling around the universe in space suits—except for local exploration which I have not discussed—belongs back where it came from, on the cereal box."

*   *   *

Sagan believed that interstellar travel was part of the human race's destiny and that "other civilizations, aeons more advanced than ours, must today be plying the spaces between the stars." So he said to an appreciative audience in Los Angeles, the American Rocketry Society, on November 15, 1962. This talk and the 1963 article came to a conclusion diametrically opposed to Purcell's. This disparity says a lot about the way science reflects personal preconceptions (and why the public is so often bewildered by dueling scientific experts).

Both Purcell and Sagan had good points. Purcell assumed it was obvious to everyone that the computed energy requirements would forever be prohibitive. It was not obvious to Sagan. He assumed that aeons-more-advanced civilizations would find a way around any difficulty that was short of a flat-out physical impossibility.

Sagan shopped around for an interstellar rocket design "as he might . . . for a new sports car," in one journalist's words. He was ultimately sold on the Bussard ramjet, an interstellar propulsion system proposed in 1960 by a Los Alamos physicist. This would scoop up interstellar gases and use them as fuel. Rockets would not have to lug around all the needed fuel. Like cross-country drivers, they would refuel as they went along. The Bussard ramjet was a few years away from production, to say the least.

Invoking the time-warping physics of relativity, Sagan computed that interstellar travelers could reach the galactic center in twenty-one years as measured on the spaceship. When and if they returned to Earth, they would find that tens of thousands of years had passed. (He termed this leap into the future a "bonus adventure.")

There is probably not much incentive for a civilization to finance expeditions that will return tens of millennia in the future by the stay-at-home reckoning. Shorter trips could be completed in exponentially shorter time. Sagan argued that extraterrestrial civilizations might be willing to use relativistic space travel to span the distance to the nearest neighboring civilizations. Using some optimistic ballpark figures, he computed that the Earth might well have been visited by aliens as many as 10,000 times in the Earth's history. "It is not out of the question that artifacts of these visits still exist, or even that some kind of base is maintained (possibly automatically) within the solar system to provide continuity for successive expeditions." Sagan dryly concluded that "contact with such a base would, of course, provide the most direct check on the conclusions of the present paper."

"The Prey Runs to the Hunter"

The interstellar rocket paper led to one of Sagan's most important collaborations. In 1962 he became aware of a Soviet scientist who had a peculiar theory about dinosaurs. I. S. Shklovskii was an astrophysicist who loved theorizing about catastrophes.

Shklovskii and Valerian Krasovsky theorized that a supernova had exploded in the sun's galactic neighborhood about 80 million years ago. It flooded the heavens with deadly cosmic rays, exterminating the hapless races of dinosaurs.

The idea was colorful enough to rate mention in the science sections of newspapers and popular magazines. Sagan sensed that Shklovskii might be receptive to his own paper on interstellar travel. He sent Shklovskii a letter and a preprint, hoping that a letter mailed from Cambridge could reach an astrophysicist far behind the Iron Curtain.

Much quicker than Sagan imagined, he got a reply from Shklovskii. It began, "The prey runs to the hunter."

When Shklovskii had received Sagan's letter, he had pen in hand and was about to begin a new chapter in a book he was writing about communication with extraterrestrial intelligence. The subject of the chapter was communication by interstellar rockets.

This extraordinary coincidence—Shklovskii could only describe it in the Russian proverb he used to open his reply to Sagan—transformed both men's lives. Shklovskii (who spoke and wrote English well) was impressed with Sagan's letter and paper. The most compelling thing about the paper may have been Sagan's discussion of the Drake equation. It was likely Shklovskii's first exposure to it.

When he learned of Shklovskii's book, Sagan offered to arrange for its translation into English. Shklovskii agreed, and they began corresponding regularly. Shklovskii's enthusiasm for extraterrestrial life was such that Sagan must have wondered whether he was corresponding with a doppelgänger. Actually, Shklovskii was a generation older and had had a much harsher life.

*   *   *

Iosif Shmuelovich Shklovskii was born on July 1, 1916, a year before the Russian Revolution. He came from the Ukraine, as did Sagan's ancestors; like Lederberg, he was a rabbi's son.

The young Shklovskii felt he was an artist by calling. Although his family could not afford art supplies, he taught himself to draw using chalk or bits of brick. Poverty forced him to drop out of high school and take a job on a Siberian railroad construction crew. During this time Shklovskii came across a magazine article on the discovery of the neutron. He resolved to become a scientist.

The war interrupted his graduate studies in Moscow. As the Nazis plunged eastward in 1941, Shklovskii and many of the nation's most brilliant scientific minds (among them Andrey Sakharov) were packed into railroad cars. Not exactly prisoners, they were shipped to a relocation camp in central Asia, realizing that they might never return. There, on the chill and barren steppes of Ashkhabad, they awaited word of the outcome of the Nazi invasion.

After the war, Shklovskii embarked on a brilliant scientific career at Moscow University's Shternberg Institute. In what he considered his best work, Shklovskii demonstrated that the Crab Nebula produces its visible light not by ordinary fusion but by the effects of electrons skittering in intense magnetic fields. This work established Shklovskii as a first-rate scientist and attracted the notice of Western astrophysicists.

Shklovskii's activities extended to fields that were not spoken of in the West. He seems to have invented a technique or device of military significance. (A radar system was Sagan's guess.) Whatever Shklovskii had done or invented, it must have been important. A charmed bubble surrounded him. Shklovskii was freely critical of the Soviet Union, seemingly with impunity. He waged a crusade against anti-Semitism in Soviet academia. Shklovskii was no less critical of the United States. He knew a great deal about the U.S. military and what it was doing in secret (another hint of a more than casual link to the Soviet defense establishment).

The official tolerance had its limits. In Shklovskii's case, those limits were conterminous with the Iron Curtain. For twenty years, he was refused permission to travel beyond eastern Europe. When he did travel, he was accompanied by watchers, the Soviet counterparts of the "translator" who had offended Sagan. At least once, the question of why he couldn't attend an upcoming conference was put to Shklovskii directly. Shklovskii turned to his

watcher and replied, "Because the sons of bitches know that if I went, I'd
never come back!"

My So-called Coauthor

Like much that Shklovskii said, that was calculated more to provoke a
reaction than to express the literal truth. The Soviet Union was home for
Shklovskii, a sincere Marxist.

In October 1961 a Soviet official requested monographs to commemorate the fifth anniversary of Sputnik. Shklovskii offered to finish a book he
was writing on extraterrestrial intelligence. It was a bluff. He had not written a word. Shklovskii knew he could write the book quickly and suspected
he would be the only one of his colleagues to make the deadline. That would
give it a better chance of getting past the censors.

Censors were very much an issue. Writing about life on other worlds
meant dancing around the theories of Lysenko and Oparin (who, notwithstanding his wide influence in the West, was a follower of Lysenko's). It was
still difficult for a Soviet to obtain a textbook on evolution or genetics.

Shklovskii's book, completed in August 1962, sailed past the censors
with no serious problems. Moscow's Nauka Press published it a few months
later. The Russian title literally meant "Universe—Life—Intelligence."

The first printing of 50,000 copies sold out in a few hours. It went
through five editions. The book created a sensation without overly upsetting
the powers that be. Most upset was Oparin. Shklovskii wrote him a polite
letter about the book. It was returned, ripped to pieces, in the same
envelope.

Certainly, Shklovskii's book was a success before Sagan had much of anything to do with it. Shklovskii was, however, conscious of his sketchy background in contemporary biology, and so he invited Sagan to "make any
additions he wished to the American edition."

Sagan interpreted this request broadly. He believed the subject of extraterrestrial intelligence deserved a wider audience than Shklovskii had contemplated. Making the book intelligible to a diverse audience meant adding
a great deal of background. In Sagan's hands, Shklovskii's narrowly conceived treatise became a book about life, the universe, and everything. The
project occupied much of Sagan's first years at Harvard. At the end of the
writing, Sagan counted up his contributions and found that he had approximately doubled the book's length.

Although the American version of the book, titled *Intelligent Life in the
Universe*, was always called a collaboration between Shklovskii and Sagan,
Shklovskii's posthumously published memoirs reveal that he was not aware

that a "collaboration" was going on until after the fact. Shklovskii writes with prickly amusement of his surprise at receiving "an elegantly produced fat volume entitled *Intelligent Life in the Universe*. The size had doubled and on the cover were crammed the names of two authors: Shklovsky and Sagan. I should say that Sagan showed a certain integrity; he left my text unchanged and set off his with little triangles." He refers to Sagan as his American "coauthor"—in scare quotes. (He adds: "I have no grievance against this businesslike, cheerful, and congenial American.")

Those triangles delimiting Sagan's text made Shklovskii's life easier. Not all of Sagan's views were congenial to the Soviets. Sagan did some censoring of his own. Shklovskii's original Russian brims with what Americans less liberal than Carl Sagan might have called commie propaganda. A nuclear holocaust is likely, Shklovskii wrote, until and unless capitalism can be expunged from the planet. He confidently predicted that the enlightened and peaceful societies of the Galaxy would be found to be based on the principles of Karl Marx and Vladimir Lenin.

Isaac Asimov

Extraterrestrial intelligence was of course a staple of science fiction. This work brought Sagan into contact with several prominent science-fiction writers. Sagan corresponded with Isaac Asimov; he even tried his hand at writing some science fiction of his own. None of these early attempts were published. Sagan penned one tale in which the aliens looked exactly like humans—except for the absence of a navel.

Asimov was nominally on the biochemistry faculty of Boston University and lived nearby. Now that Sagan was in town, they resolved to do lunch. They met on February 19, 1963.

"I visualized him as an elderly person (the stereotype of the astronomer at his telescope)," Asimov, then forty-three, wrote, "but what I found him to be was a twenty-seven-year-old, handsome young man; tall, dark, articulate, and absolutely incredibly intelligent."

Asimov had claimed that there was only one person whom he would readily admit was more intelligent than he was, and that was Marvin Minsky (the MIT computer scientist). Upon meeting Sagan, he had to amend that claim to *two* people. The second was Carl Sagan.

Asimov's background was not unlike Sagan's. Of Russian Jewish stock, he grew up in Brooklyn dreaming of stars and life out there. Whatever the merit of Frank Drake's theory about the influence of fundamentalist religion on SETI, it is striking how much of twentieth-century ideation about life in the universe—scientific and science-fictional—has its roots in the eastern

European Jewish experience. Being a relative outsider may have encouraged an openness to the idea of the ultimate "other." For Asimov and Sagan, and perhaps no less for Shklovskii, Lederberg, and Vishniac, life in space was a dream that held particular resonance, a galactic empire of their own.

Shortly after the lunch, Asimov put a sheet of paper in his typewriter and began an essay on the search for extraterrestrial intelligence. The piece was quickly finished, as Asimov pieces generally were. The essay was for Asimov's monthly column in the *Magazine of Fantasy and Science Fiction*. Like most of these essays, it started with a personal anecdote, in this case, Asimov's meeting with Sagan. Asimov showed the piece to Sagan, who was uncomfortable with the anecdote. Though it said nothing unflattering about Sagan, he asked Asimov to delete it. Asimov courteously rewrote the introduction. Sagan was starting to hear criticism from colleagues that he was too interested in self-promotion and sensational subjects. A personality profile in a science-fiction magazine would be like a red flag to a bull.

*   *   *

In 1964 Sagan met Arthur C. Clarke, who of course wrote science fiction as well as rocketry treatises. Together they went to the 1964 New York World's Fair. Impulsively, they ducked inside a free exhibit sponsored by the Moody Bible Institute. It was a film claiming that nature is so ingeniously constructed that it can only be the result of divine creation. The filmmakers chose as their unlikely object lesson the sex life of the grunion.

A few minutes of this, and Sagan was fuming. Wasn't it *obvious* that natural selection was a simpler, more satisfactory answer? He could not contain himself. He grabbed the nearest usher and launched into a lecture on evolution, Occam's razor, et cetera, et cetera—as the object of his tirade squirmed like a trapped bear. Clarke was mortified at Sagan's "American" behavior. He whispered, "It's not as if we had paid admission."

Escalation Clause

Just a few months after moving to Watertown, Lynn informed Carl that they were getting a divorce. It was nonnegotiable, a fait accompli. She kicked him out of the apartment.

Carl moved into a place on Franklin Street, Cambridge. They began negotiating the terms of divorce. The agreement provided that Carl pay $75 per child per month in support. Lynn's attorney father suggested that there be an escalation clause. Carl was likely to be making a lot more money in the future, Morris Alexander observed; there could be a provision for the child support to increase in step with the father's income. Carl "went through the roof" and vetoed that idea.

Lynn raised the boys on a scant $150 a month from their father. In the years afterward, as Carl's reputation and income *did* increase, Lynn was often asked how she could have left him. Her answer was that "I was unable to do what 10,000 in an auditorium had difficulty doing for him—satisfying the incessant need for full attention."

*   *   *

The divorce, granted in 1964, was probably a greater success than the marriage. Lynn reports she has never been unhappy since. It was a relatively civilized separation. At a Harvard New Year's Eve party, both Carl and Lynn showed up with dates. Carl went into therapy in hopes that it would help him understand how Lynn could have rejected him. He believed the therapy did help, a little.

Carl and Lu Nahemow had a postmortem analysis of the marriage at Tavern on the Green in New York. Carl admitted he was disappointed with himself and recognized that he bore the greater share of the blame. He was sad about losing Lynn. Significantly, Nahemow noticed, he said nothing about the boys.

*   *   *

Lynn had not yet filed her Ph.D. thesis. She took part-time work creating science-teaching materials and teaching undergraduates at Brandeis University. Nights and weekends, she continued to work on her serial endosymbiosis theory. She outlined the theory and mailed mimeographs of it to a number of scientists she thought might be receptive. Most weren't.

She was told that she was crazy or dabbling out of her field. One returned the mimeograph, having corrected her grammar. The exception was J. D. Bernal, the British crystallographer. He wrote a long letter congratulating her for solving the "problem of the origin of the nucleated cell." Coming at that time, the encouragement was welcome.

Lynn got her Ph.D. the year after the divorce. Her serial endosymbiosis theory was published in 1966. Fifteen journals had rejected it or not even replied to her submission. This central work of modern biology finally appeared in the *Journal of Theoretical Biology* under the name Lynn Sagan.

In 1967 Lynn married crystallographer Thomas Margulis. It is by the name Lynn Margulis that she is known today as one of the world's most influential and controversial biologists. For years after the divorce, though, Carl persisted in writing his ex-wife's name as Lynn Sagan Margulis—to Lynn's exasperation.

Flooded House

John Lilly ran dolphin research facilities in Saint Thomas, U.S. Virgin Islands, and Coral Gables, Florida. In the years after Green Bank, Sagan often visited on winter vacations. This allowed him to combine his love of snorkeling with his continuing interest in Lilly's attempts to communicate with these "alien" intelligences.

Marine mammals were a pop-culture phenomenon. There was a TV show, *Flipper*, about a dolphin as anthropomorphic as those in Lilly's tales— though a good deal less overtly sexual. Lilly advised *Flipper*'s producer, Ivan Tors, and two of Lilly's dolphins appeared in a movie version of *Flipper*. Lilly's books on dolphins became best-sellers. His example must have been on Sagan's mind as he forged his own writing career.

In winter 1963 Sagan met Elvar. Elvar with the voluntary erections. Lilly took Sagan into a room with a large tank of seawater. Elvar poked his head above the water.

"Carl, this is Elvar," Lilly announced. "Elvar, this is Carl."

Elvar expertly smacked his head against the water surface. A neat spray of water nailed Sagan in the forehead.

Lilly left Sagan and Elvar alone. The dolphin lolled in the water like a happy dog. Soon Sagan was scratching his belly. The dolphin would periodically dive, swim to the opposite end of the tank, and return for more scratching. Sagan tired of this before the dolphin did. Elvar reared up out of the water, balancing a moment on tail flukes, and emitted a single word: "More!"

At least, it *sounded* like "more." It was a high-pitched monosyllabic squeak.

Sagan went and found Lilly attending some electronic equipment. He informed him, excitedly, that Elvar had said "more."

"Was it in context?" Lilly wanted to know.

"Yes, it was in context."

"Good," Lilly said. "That's one of the words he knows."

*   *   *

Lilly believed his dolphins could speak English—not well, of course, and their vocabulary was limited. Sagan was not so sure. He was fascinated by all he saw in Lilly's finny kingdom. But it was never clear what was "real" and what was anthropomorphizing. Lilly sometimes seemed unmotivated to make these distinctions.

Lilly would talk about the great experiments he was going to do. Then another year would go by, Sagan would see him the next winter, and it would turn out that the actual, controlled experiment still had not been done. Lilly would spin another colorful tale. They had been trying out the concept when *the dolphin did the damnedest thing* . . . One year, some of the captive dolphins committed suicide—or such was Lilly's understanding. Lilly gallantly set the surviving dolphins free. These anecdotes were what made Lilly's books on the dolphin so engaging. But "the really critical scientific tests were somehow never performed," Sagan complained.

Sagan tried to nudge Lilly along. He outlined specific experiments and controls that would actually *prove* something. It had not even been established that dolphins can communicate arbitrary information to other dolphins. Until that was proved, everything else Lilly did would rest on shaky ground.

Sagan suggested a Bach-versus-Beatles experiment. They would teach a dolphin to distinguish between the music of Bach and the Beatles (dolphins have excellent hearing). The dolphin would be rewarded with tasty fish every time it tapped a fish dispenser that was playing Beatles music underwater (say) but never when it tapped an identical dispenser playing Bach.

Then they would introduce a new dolphin that knew nothing about music and how the fish dispensers worked. A barrier would now prevent the "educated" dolphin from tapping the fish dispensers. Only the uneducated dolphin would be free to do that. Every time the uneducated dolphin hit the "right" dispenser, both dolphins would get food. The educated dolphin would then have an incentive to "instruct" the new dolphin on the way to get food. If dolphins communicate, that would be demonstrable (in many tests, with many pairs of dolphins) by the greater slopes of the learning curves.

*   *   *

Lilly never performed this experiment. He suspected that if dolphins were to learn human speech, it would have to be through "total immersion," through being isolated from other dolphins and living with a human, hearing only human speech.

This naturally entailed "total immersion" for the human, too. Lilly envisioned a *flooded house*. It would be a home with the comforts of middle-class suburbia, only there would be water in it. Dolphins would glide freely among the human occupants' legs. In such a house dolphins might learn human language. It could even, Lilly speculated, be the foundation of a future utopia in which humans and dolphins would coexist as equal partners.

A frustrated romance of Sagan's played a small role in Lilly's most famous dolphin study. One night in Saint Thomas, Sagan dined at a remote mountaintop restaurant. The hostess caught his eye. She was an attractive

young woman with dark hair and a healthy, tomboyish quality. Her name
was Margaret Howe. She told Sagan that she was bored. Her job as a hostess
was evenings only. She wanted something else to occupy her on the island.

Sagan tried to get Howe into bed. Howe rebuffed him, but the meeting
had one result: Sagan introduced Howe to anthropologist Gregory Bateson,
who was then running the Saint Thomas facility. This led to a job and
plunged Howe into one of the most unusual experiments of the 1960s.

In the summer of 1965, Howe lived in the company of Peter, a male dolphin, twenty-four hours a day, six days a week in a simplified flooded house.
There are surreal photographs of Howe working efficiently at a desk or chat-
ting on the telephone, eyed curiously by a dolphin as her whole environment is sopping in twenty-four inches of water.

"A dolphin is more like a shadow than a roommate," Howe said. The
thing would stay by her all day and never leave. She could talk on the phone
for hours. The dolphin wouldn't get bored. He wouldn't leave. As weeks
passed, Howe was subject to depression and crying jags. "I have found that
during the day I will find any excuse to get out of the flooded room," she
wrote in her diary. (Lilly meanwhile was contemplating a flooded car for the
future bispecies society.)

Peter began exhibiting courting behavior. He lightly nibbled Howe's
legs, getting erections, and rubbing against her ardently. As a matter of
expediency, Howe took to giving the dolphin hand jobs. Peter would "reach
some sort of orgasm, mouth open, eyes closed, body shaking, then his penis
would relax and withdraw." Dolphin libidos being what they are, this had to
be repeated two or three times; then, *finally*, the dolphin could concentrate
on its lessons.

That made for a pretty good conversation stopper. Otherwise the experiment's results were debatable. It seemed that Peter learned to say "hello"
and "ball" and parrot consonant sounds. But when Howe asked Peter to get
the ball, he would often get the cloth.

*   *   *

After this experiment, Sagan visited Saint Thomas and played a game of
catch with Peter. Sagan threw the ball to Peter, and Peter dove under it and
batted it back with his snout. His aim was as accurate as a human's. Then,
after a few volleys, the dolphin began returning the ball far to the side of
Sagan. Peter was toying with Sagan, performing an "experiment" of his own.
Figuring that two can play that game, Sagan retrieved the ball one last time
and held it, treading water.

For about a minute, both mammals stood their ground. Peter gave in. He
swam into Sagan's side of the tank, circling him, repeatedly brushing past

him. This puzzled Sagan. It didn't seem as if the dolphin's tail flukes had brushed him. Then he realized the dolphin had a hard-on.

The frustrated triangle of Sagan, Howe, and Peter was worthy of Sartre. There was a further twist. Peter was one of Lilly's ex-actor dolphins. Sagan had been propositioned by Flipper.

* * *

By the mid-1960s, Lilly's interests had shifted to human consciousness. He was experimenting with the isolation tanks he had invented and with the then-new drug known as LSD-25. The Sandoz Company hoped to find a commercial use for the drug, and the Defense Department was said to be particularly interested. In a research proposal, Lilly requested the drug "to see its effects on dolphins."

Sagan and Lilly drifted apart. While he admired Lilly as a visionary, Sagan believed that Lilly was veering farther and farther from science. As for LSD, Sagan felt it was an entirely different matter from marijuana. It was a new and unknown chemical that had not been "tested" by centuries of cultural practice. Sagan reasoned that LSD is hazardous because its dosage is so minute and its effect is delayed. Users cannot tell they have consumed too much until it is too late.

Linda Salzman

Back in Cambridge, Carl was one of the town's most eligible bachelors. He would be seen attending lectures on "sexual freedom" or some such topic—generally in the company of a striking young woman.

One of these young women was Linda Salzman. She was an artist who studied at the School of the Museum of Fine Arts, Boston. There she honed a masterful academic ability to render the human figure. Linda was "extraordinarily attractive"—in the discerning estimation of Isaac Asimov. She had curly black hair that looked perpetually wind tossed and an attractive figure that she dressed in avant-garde 1960s fashions.

Linda was soft-spoken, shy, intuitive. That she was *not* a scientist might have been a welcome change for Carl after his tumultuous experience with Lynn. Linda was quietly pursuing a career doing figurative paintings in bold, fauve/psychedelic colors.

Shortly after she met Carl, Linda fell ill. Carl wanted to come visit. Linda tried to turn him away. She was vomiting; she did not look or feel well enough to see a new boyfriend. Carl said that was nonsense. He insisted on nursing her back to health.

This gesture helped cement the relationship. They started dating steadily. Linda became a particular favorite of Asimov's. He first met her at a dinner in early 1966. Asimov found Linda "quite obviously in love with Carl." The ostensible purpose of the dinner was for Asimov to get Sagan's comments on the manuscript of his book *The Universe*.

"I haven't had time to look it over yet, Isaac," Carl said. "I've been awfully busy."

Asimov replied: "Of what importance is your work, Carl, compared with my manuscript?"

"You're joking, Isaac—except that you're not *really* joking, are you?"

"No Carl, I guess I'm not joking."

The Dead Planet

On Bastille Day 1965, Mariner 4 flew by Mars. It sent back twenty-one photos, and part of a twenty-second, that forever destroyed the planet of Lowell and Burroughs. The photos went a long way toward destroying the planet of Lederberg and Sagan.

Expectations had been high. Exobiology had received much press, both popular and scientific. Walter Sullivan's best-selling 1964 book, *We Are Not Alone*, introduced the subject—and Carl Sagan—to a wide audience. Geologist Bruce Murray had prepared for the Mariner mission by studying photographs of folded oceanic sediments. He had to be primed to spot evidence of the ancient oceans of Mars. Aware of public expectations, NASA's press department warned that Mariner could hardly detect any signs of life. That disavowal was of course far from neutral. One spin was to suggest that Mariner "may answer long standing questions about the 'canals' of the red planet."

As imaged by Mariner 4, Mars looked almost like the *moon*. Craters pocked its surface. There did not seem to have been much erosion on Mars for billions of years.

As Mariner 4 slipped behind Mars, the planet's atmosphere refracted its radio beam just before the planet's bulk eclipsed it. This finally made it possible to deduce the atmospheric pressure accurately. The results were shockingly low—4 to 7 millibars. That is only about 1/200 the sea level pressure of Earth.

That changed everything. Liquid water could not exist at such pressures *at any temperature*. It would either boil or freeze. Without even the *possibility* of liquid water, it was hard to imagine life. In fact, the watery nutrient in Vishniac's Wolf Trap device would boil or freeze if it ever got to Mars.

Earth-based observations had already revealed the error of Kuiper's too-low estimate of the carbon dioxide pressure. Applying that to the new findings, the Mariner team was able to deduce (now correctly) that Mars's atmosphere is almost all carbon dioxide. Caltech's Robert Leighton and Bruce Murray soon concluded that the polar caps must be solid carbon dioxide, *not* water ice.

That same year, another key piece of evidence for life on Mars fell out of the picture. A group of Berkeley chemists demonstrated that most of Sinton's absorption bands better fit heavy water than organic molecules. It later became apparent that the heavy water was not even on Mars. Sinton's results had been confused by heavy water in the Earth's own atmosphere. Sinton gracefully conceded the error.

In short, most of the evidence or assumptions propping up the idea of Martian life fell away by the end of 1965. Obituaries for exobiology were already being written. The *New York Times* eulogized "The Dead Planet." President Lyndon Johnson told a NASA group, "As a member of a generation that Orson Welles scared out of its wits, I must confess that I'm a little bit relieved that your photographs didn't show more signs of life out there." The *New York Times* noted that the new data "seem to refute the thesis of the National Academy of Sciences panel which last April argued it was 'entirely reasonable' to believe that Mars had 'living organisms. . . .' Mars, it now appears, is a desolate world of a strangeness beyond imagination."

Sagan took the "dead planet" talk as an almost personal affront, too deep to be forgotten. Eight years later, he was able to quote, almost verbatim, President Johnson's pleasantry about the Orson Welles broadcast. In his 1975 book, *Other Worlds*, he reproduced the *New York Times*'s "Dead Planet" editorial next to a bold headline of his own, "Better Red Than Dead."

James Pollack

With polar caps of dry ice, air pressure too low for liquid water, and spectroscopic evidence of "lichens" ignominiously refuted, there remained only one observation supporting life on Mars. That was the color changes, seasonal and long-term, in the dark areas.

Sagan's personal disappointment did not prevent him from making the most of the Mariner 4 data. The new information supported Sagan's idea that dust, and not vegetation, was the cause of the seasonal changes on Mars. Sagan developed that theory using the new pictures, new technology, and a new collaborator.

This was James B. Pollack, Sagan's first graduate student. Pollack quickly became a major collaborator. In 1967 alone, Sagan published eight articles in collaboration with Pollack. Sagan and Pollack were complementary opposites. Where Sagan was glib and mercurial, Pollack spoke and acted deliberately. As an infant, he had been so slow in learning to speak that the family worried he was retarded. A psychologist told the family that the child's thoughts were so rapid that spoken words could not keep up with them.

Pollack spoke slowly for the rest of his life. In conversation Pollack insisted on backtracking until he understood everything. It was said that if you couldn't explain an idea to Jim Pollack, you probably didn't understand it, and it was probably wrong. Pollack would often, through a few incisive questions, spot a fatal error and demolish everything the speaker had done. (Sagan, in contrast, would most typically reply with a letter "ninety degrees off from everything you thought of.") Even in basketball, a sport he shared with Sagan, Pollack was deliberative. He took his time; he usually made the basket.

Pollack's doctoral thesis was on the Venus greenhouse effect, building on Sagan's own work. Pollack was such a rising star that his oral examinations at Harvard turned into a series of recruitment pitches by professors hoping to lure him away from Sagan. In a backhanded way, that was a tribute to Sagan. A better tribute was that Pollack stayed with Sagan.

*   *   *

Jim Pollack was gay. A handsome man of masculine appearance, he was adored by women and men alike. Carl was at once tolerant of Jim and conflicted about homosexuality in general. His family background may have played a factor in this. Rachel disapproved of homosexuality. She had a gay half brother who was given a lobotomy and spent his life in a mental institution. Rachel kept this brother's existence from Carl for her entire life.

Dorion remembers attending a meeting with his father around 1967 at which a very obviously gay science enthusiast told Carl how much he admired his work. Carl "turned to emotional ice."

Linda's artistic background gave her a different perspective. In art school, she had unknowingly fallen in with a lesbian social set. Though heterosexual herself, she grew to be comfortable around gays. Linda became good friends with Pollack's boyfriend, Bill Gile. Carl and Linda freely socialized with Jim and Bill, something that was not so common at the time, even in liberal academic circles. (For the most part, Carl would talk shop with Jim while Linda would talk with Bill, a theater major.) Carl once became quite angry when a university health service emergency room balked at treating Bill for a minor accident. He insisted on making sure that his colleague's lover got prompt attention.

There were misgivings nonetheless. In high school, Dorion became friends with a gay classmate. A worried Carl sat him down and lectured him that homosexuality was not the way the species propagates itself. He invoked natural selection, rather than Leviticus, as the basis for his disapproval (this to the son named in homage to Oscar Wilde!).

Winds of Mars

In no visible way did Pollack's homosexuality impede Sagan's long and productive collaboration with him. Pollack was seemingly without pettiness, a valuable attribute in working with the increasingly celebrated Sagan.

With the mounting evidence that Mars was not at all like the Earth, Sagan and Pollack developed the dust idea further using a new technology, Doppler radar spectroscopy.

It had long been assumed that the bright areas of Mars were higher than the dark areas. This was a throwback to the days of the canals and even before, when the dark areas were mapped as seas and lakes. Radar showed that this conventional "relief map" of Mars was upside down. The dark areas were *highlands* rising above the light areas.

Not all dark areas changed color. The radar studies showed that those areas that *did* change color were lower and flatter than the permanent dark regions. Furthermore, the color-changing dark regions were invariably "peninsulas" or "islands" surrounded by bright areas.

This fit neatly into Sagan's theory. Sagan and Pollack argued that Martian winds blow the light-colored dust onto the nearby dark foothills, making them lighter. Opposite winds scour the dark regions of dust, "regenerating" their dark color. Not much dust gets carried into distant, dark highlands, which consequently show little color change.

Sagan was far from giving up on Martian life, however. One of the articles on seasonal darkening, published two years after Mariner 4, ends with the caveat: "Both the biological and the dust models are consistent with the above statistical analysis of the seasonal-darkening phenomenon, and a choice between these models must be made on other grounds." That was a modest way of concluding an article that presented an impressively reasoned refutation of the biological model.

Sagan did another study where he concluded, with satisfaction, that a photographic survey at Mariner's resolution would have been unlikely to find a single unambiguous sign of life on Earth. That was further reason to doubt that mere telescopic observations of Mars could have seen vegetal growth. Conversely, it implied that the question of Martian life must remain open.

Sagan and Pollack also tackled the question of the Martian "canals." Mariner 4 found no canals and nothing that *looked* like canals. Most everyone else was muttering how Lowell must have been crazy. Sagan realized there was a genuine puzzle. The canals had been mapped, with some consistency, not only by Lowell but by his skeptics. Evidently the canals are some kind of illusion, but why doesn't the same illusion occur when looking at the moon?

Again using the radar findings, Sagan and Pollack proposed that the light regions are the "ocean basins" of Mars, filled with dust, not water. The Earth's undersea topography is crisscrossed with midocean ridges and island arcs. Analogous structures on Mars, poking up through the dust, may create the broken linear detail the eye merges into straight lines.

*   *   *

In 1966 Sagan published twenty-four scientific articles and abstracts, an average of a scholarly publication every two weeks. He would match that record (in 1972) but never beat it. Sagan was confident enough that the rival ionospheric model of Venus had been disproved that he could title a paper (written with G. Russell Walker) "The Ionospheric Model of the Venus Microwave Emission: An Obituary." More dramatic confirmation came in 1967. In October the Soviet Venera 4 sent a probe into the atmosphere of Venus, and the U.S. Mariner 5 flew by the planet. Their instruments confirmed that the temperature near the surface was nearly 900° F.

Not only had Sagan been right about Venus temperatures and the Martian seasonal changes, but the proof that he was right came early in his career. Writing a few years later, British journalist Ian Ridpath spoke of Sagan's "habit of extrapolating adventurously from limited data—and being infuriatingly right."

CTA-102

Sagan never met Shklovskii during the time he worked on *Intelligent Life in the Universe*. Like a game between reclusive and patient chess masters, the work was carried out through the mail. Shklovskii's letters would often arrive in Cambridge blazoned with the censor's stamp. Once Shklovskii wrote to Sagan, "The probability of our meeting is unlikely to be smaller than the probability of a visit to the Earth by an extraterrestrial cosmonaut."

Sagan would occasionally run across traveling Soviet scientists and ask about his unseen coauthor. "Fifty percent of what Shklovskii does is brilliant," one Soviet astronomer told Sagan. "But no one can tell which fifty percent it is."

Supporting that statement was an incident that occurred as Sagan was completing work on the American book. In 1965 a Soviet astronomer named Evgeny Sholomitsky discovered an apparent signal from space. It was coming from or near a point source of radio emissions called CTA-102. Sholomitsky told several associates about it, and soon Shklovskii was in on the secret, too.

The Soviet group followed the "signal" for several months. It varied in intensity slowly, over a period of about 100 days. They theorized that it was a beacon, a way of calling attention to the senders from across the universe. They could find no information in the 100-day cycle. They worried that it might be transmitting a message with inhuman slowness. If it took 100 days to send a 0 or 1 bit, it would take *years* to transmit a word. Everyone alive would grow old and die before a single alien *concept* could be deciphered.

The finding leaked to the press, and Sholomitsky hastily called a press conference at Shternberg Institute. The institute's courtyard filled with luxury cars of foreign correspondents. Shklovskii got up and said the announcements had been premature. Sholomitsky, too, was guarded. Others were more optimistic, and the press clamored for their opinions. Caught up in the moment, Shklovskii joined in and reversed his position, endorsing the finding.

He regretted it. Among the congratulatory letters and telegrams was one from Caltech. "CTA-102" means the 102nd object in Caltech Catalog A. The Caltech group insisted that the variation was a natural phenomenon, and they were, of course, right. CTA-102 is what we now call a quasar, a prodigiously energetic young galaxy.

*   *   *

The American edition of *Intelligent Life in the Universe* appeared in 1966. Sagan sent galleys to Harold Urey, apparently hoping for a favorable blurb. Urey replied that he had not had time to read the entire book. "One just cannot read all the things that come to one's desk." Urey seems to have felt that a book on intelligent life in the universe should be like a joke book on the wit and wisdom of Calvin Coolidge—a slim volume whose covers enclose nothing at all. "What is needed, I think, is to abbreviate the discussion to a point where people could find time to read it instead of expanding it into a book of this size."

Philip Morrison was a good deal more sympathetic. In a review, he acknowledged (with some self-deprecation!) the attitude of people like Urey toward the subject matter: "Here is a body of literature whose ratio of results/papers is lower than any other."

Translations of Russian scientific treatises are not usually hot sellers. In 1966 the name Carl Sagan meant about as much to American book buyers as Iosif Shmuelovich Shklovskii did. But sales were brisk, and most reviews were favorable. The book went through fourteen printings by 1975. *Intelligent Life in the Universe* demonstrated Sagan's skill as a writer to a new public. The book still has a quasi-mystic status in his oeuvre. More than one person I've spoken with in the writing of this book has cited *Intelligent Life in the Universe* as Sagan's best book. It was a chance to write at length on his most personal and passionate subject. A milestone in twentieth-century intellectual history, *Intelligent Life* is both a technical work and a popularization (a difficult balancing act that even Sagan never managed again).

Project Blue Book

In the spring of 1966, Sagan's attention again turned to UFOs. This came about through Edward Condon, the University of Colorado physicist Sagan had worked with the summer after his wedding. Condon was asked to direct a scientific investigation of the air force's Project Blue Book.

Blue Book was a classified study of sightings of strange lights in the sky, dating back to 1948. By the early 1950s, a group of the air force's own investigators apparently believed that some UFOs were extraterrestrial spaceships. Others privy to Blue Book did not take this conclusion seriously. By June 1965, Blue Book had 9,265 reports, of which 663 were held to be unexplained. With (correct) rumors of a cover-up flying, the air force felt pressure to make the Blue Book data public. It was decided to turn the data over to a committee of civilian scientists for review and publication.

Condon was well aware of Sagan's interest in UFOs and invited him to serve on this committee. Sagan accepted and became the youngest of the six scientists, engineers, and psychologists on Condon's Ad Hoc Committee to Review Project Blue Book.

Blue Book was based at Wright-Patterson Air Force Base, Ohio. Sagan called up files on the base's mechanical file retrieval system, and a mechanical rack, like that in a dry cleaner's, brought dossiers to him. The committee examined hundreds of reports, including a case where a UFO turned out to be a firefly trapped between two panes of glass in an airplane cockpit window. The cases that lacked such a neat physical explanation fell into two categories: "unexplained lights in the sky" that were often puzzling though not necessarily extraterrestrial; and reports of incontrovertible spaceships and aliens. It seemed an absolute rule that the latter sightings could never be substantiated by a group of credible witnesses or by compelling physical evidence.

Sagan surmised that the governmental secrecy on UFOs had roots closer to home. Wright-Patterson's *real* function was keeping tabs on new Soviet aircraft and military technology. With cold-war defense predicated on deterring a first strike, it was deemed necessary to check how quickly the U.S. early warning defense systems could detect a Soviet nuclear bomber—and how quickly the Soviets could detect a U.S. bomber. In an exercise called "spoofing," each side occasionally sent high-performance jet fighters into enemy territory—or into its own territory—to see how long it would take for someone to notice and raise an alarm. Many of the "unexplained lights" sightings may have been average folks understandably befuddled to see classified Soviet hardware zipping under the radar and over their rooftops. The air force had reason both to collect these reports and to keep quiet about what was really going on.

In March 1966, the Ad Hoc Committee produced a short report recommending that the Blue Book files be made available to the scientific community and public. This was followed in 1969 by the publication of the book-length report *Scientific Study of Unidentified Flying Objects*. Despite the fact that Condon's committee was supposedly privy to all the government's files, the publication suffered some censorship. A small but bizarre example is in the book's Appendix U. The phrase "the Director" (referring to the CIA's director) was repeatedly excised, apparently on CIA orders. Years after the fact, the CIA did not want to acknowledge that its director had attended certain meetings.

*   *   *

Sagan did realize his college dream of seeing a UFO. He gave a popular lecture at Harvard. There were several questions on UFOs in the question-and-answer period. Sagan gave the standard reply that the vast majority were natural phenomena misinterpreted. As he left the lecture hall to meet friends for dinner, Sagan saw two policemen pointing up at the sky. They were pointing at a UFO.

Not caring to be confronted by his audience, Sagan hurried along to dinner. The UFO was still there when he arrived at the restaurant. He ducked in and told his friends to come out and take a look. Their interest was contagious. The whole restaurant emptied onto the sidewalk to get a look.

The UFO was a bright light, waxing and waning in intensity as it glided across the sky. At times they heard a faint drone from it. Sagan was close enough to home to fetch his binoculars before the object vanished. The binoculars resolved the object as two steady white lights and two blinking lights. It was an airplane; as it later turned out, a NASA weather plane. The disappointment was acute.

Had Sagan not told people in the restaurant there was something extraordinary in the sky, few would have noticed. Had it not been for the binoculars, everyone would have gone home with a UFO story. Had the sighting been reported to authorities, it would have been impossible to identify from eyewitness accounts. Many of the witnesses likely would have been scornful of the suggestion that they had seen only an airplane.

Expert Witness

Sagan's UFO exploits also figured in his most famous classroom "routine," a rollicking story said to have had "jaded ex-preppies shrieking and crying with laughter." It had begun when the astronomy department received a telegram from a district attorney in Nebraska. The DA was prosecuting a con artist who claimed to have been aboard a flying saucer. He had been using that story to fleece well-to-do Midwesterners. The attorney wondered if anyone would be willing to testify as an expert witness. One young astronomer jumped at the chance.

Plump and sixtyish, the defendant was glib and somehow attractive to women of a certain age. He claimed that he had been minding his own business when he ran across a flying saucer parked beside a Nebraska highway. Inside were aliens of both sexes who looked exactly like humans except that they dressed in flowing robes. They spoke a language called *Hochdeutsch*. So, it happened, did the defendant. The saucer people were from the planet Saturn.

The defendant took several spins in the saucer. During one of these voyages, the aliens remarked that they had instruments capable of detecting mineral deposits. They knew of rich veins of gold, platinum, and uranium, unknown to earthlings. They also knew of a vein of cancer-curing quartz in California. Another time the Saturnians took the defendant to the Great Pyramid of Giza. He and the saucer people mingled with a tour group—for they looked just like humans, except for the robes. The tour wended its way through the pyramid's *interior*. At a certain point, the aliens pulled the defendant aside and led him into a secret chamber. Inside were an old, beat-up flying saucer, a wooden cross, and a crown of thorns. Oh, yes, they explained. One of their agents had been sent to Earth two thousand years ago.

UFO cultists paid the man's way to conventions, took him in as a houseguest, and invested in the cancer-curing quartz mine. Many of his patrons were lonely women to whom the defendant made proposals romantic as well as financial. Money had changed hands. It was hard to say how much had been given as gifts, how much as loans, and how much as investment principal.

What *was* clear was that the man was married; he had sold shares, adding up to more than 100 percent ownership, in a quartz mine he did not own; and there could be no humanoids on Saturn. It was Sagan's job to testify on that last point.

The assistant district attorney established Sagan's credentials, then asked him how likely it was, scientifically speaking, that there were people on Saturn. Sagan said it wasn't very likely at all, mentioning the extremely low temperatures, the noxious gases, the lack of oxygen, and so forth. He generously added that he did not rule out *some* form of life there—but definitely no humanoids in robes.

The cross-examination began. "Dr. Sagan, I don't mean to be disrespectful," said the defense attorney, "but isn't it a fact that four or five hundred years ago, university scientists like yourself were maintaining that the Earth was . . . *flat*?"

The DA objected. The judge overruled.

The defense attorney knew that the first rule of examining expert witnesses is to ask a simple question whose answer will be too complicated for the jury to follow. He confessed that one part of Sagan's testimony had puzzled him: the spectroscopic tests used to determine that Saturn's atmosphere contained the poisonous gas ammonia. Hadn't Sagan kept an important fact from the jury—namely, that *all* these results were based on the *assumption* that the laws of physics were the same on Saturn as on Earth?

Sagan replied that it was highly unlikely that the complex patterns of absorption lines seen in the spectra of Saturn would match those of ammonia on Earth if the laws of nature were completely different. He glanced at the jury box. The seed of doubt had been planted.

How do we know, asked the defense attorney, that the fantastically low temperature readings aren't coming from high clouds, while the surface is much warmer?

He had done his homework; he was throwing the Venus microwave controversy back in Sagan's face. "But these are indirect arguments, aren't they?" the attorney demanded. "You don't really *know* there's no oxygen on Saturn?"

Sagan conceded that *all* astronomy is based on indirect evidence. With that, the attorney dismissed the witness.

The next major exhibit was a movie, so the jurors paid rapt attention. It documented the Saturnians' adventures with the defendant. Since the defendant had not had a camera handy when the actual events occurred, he had filmed a reenactment with human actors. He had promised some of his investors roles in the film.

The jury found the defendant guilty of fraud.

Antarctica

With authentic extraterrestrials so hard to come by, the exobiologists of the 1960s spent much time and effort investigating the sparse life of Antarctica. The southern continent has dry valleys, bare of ice or snow, that are the coldest and most arid to be found on Earth. Many were thinking of these dry valleys as Earth's little patch of Mars and thus as a bellwether for exobiology. If life could survive *there*, that strengthened the case for life on Mars. The converse was true as well.

NASA sent Roy Cameron to Antarctica to collect soil samples. These samples were distributed to scientists designing devices for detecting life on Mars. They were the subject of a particularly determined study by Caltech's Norman Horowitz.

Horowitz is credited with one of the crucial insights of modern biology: that each gene encodes the structure of a single enzyme. Raised in Pittsburgh, he was a member of the tribe that produced so many exobiologists. His interest in extraterrestrial life was as long-standing as Sagan's. A journalist once described Horowitz as looking a little like a fox terrier. It could be said that Horowitz possessed handsome and neatly groomed features, an alert expression, and a scrappy disposition. Of all the exobiologists, Horowitz was the vocal skeptic on Martian life. The finding that the atmospheric pressure on Mars was too low to permit liquid water weighed on him more than it did Sagan and Lederberg. The Antarctic findings further downsized his expectations.

In a 1967 article, Horowitz and Cameron reported the unprecedented discovery of *sterile soil*. They claimed that some of the Antarctic samples had not a *single* viable spore or bacterium that could be cultured into growth.

This caused a sensation. It is a maxim among microbiologists that *nothing* in nature is sterile. To Horowitz, at least, the message was clear: no liquid water equals no life. Profligate evolution had bred the dolphin and the tumbleweed; velociraptors, smallpox, and chimney swifts. The icy seas around Antarctica were teeming with life. But not the dry valleys. Desiccation raised a barrier that ever-mutable life could not breach, not even at the microscopic level.

The findings also bore on Sagan and Lederberg's sterilization issue. If our *own* microbes can't hack it in Antarctica, Horowitz asked, how in the world were they going to colonize Mars (in comparison to which Antarctica was sheer *paradise*)?

Sterilization of spacecraft was an expensive nuisance. For the most part, the geologists and engineers working on NASA projects wished the sterilization requirement would go away. Sagan had done elaborate risk-benefit calculations that were used to develop a stringent sterilization protocol. This called for heating components of Martian landers to about 300° F. After that, a hermetic seal was put in place and could not be removed until the craft was beyond the Earth's atmosphere.

The sterilization temperature limited the types of materials that could be used. It was impossible to use low-melting solder or certain color filters in the imaging cameras. If anything in a craft had to be repaired or changed, that meant breaking the seal and going through the sterilization process again.

There was also the Soviet question. No one believed the Soviets were as scrupulous about sterilization as the Americans. Horowitz and Bruce Murray argued that this made the whole contamination issue academic. Were there any realistic possibility of terrestrial microbes contaminating Mars, it had already happened. The Russians had spoiled it for everyone— so why couldn't we relax our sterilization measures?

Sagan did not lack for counterarguments. Some were ingenious proposals whereby liquid water (and life) might yet exist on Mars, if only sporadically or deep underground. Ultimately, Sagan's most compelling rebuttal was the simple recourse to ignorance. With our experience limited to one planet, he argued, it was premature to be dogmatic about Mars.

Regarding the Soviet crashes, Sagan, Elliott Levinthal, and Lederberg wrote in a March 1968 *Science* article:

> An analogy that has been useful in discussing such steril-
> ization issues concerns a dry forest in tinderbox conditions.
> If the individual in front of us throws a lighted match into
> the forest, it does not follow that we may throw large num-
> bers of lighted matches as well, particularly if we are seek-
> ing out the driest parts of the forest. His match might not
> ignite the forest; ours might. Also, if we are cautious with
> matches, the need for caution and the method of achieving
> it might be grasped by our companion.

As well reasoned as this was, it got less compelling with every errant Soviet probe crashing into Mars. After it became clear they would not win the moon "race," the Soviets made Mars a top priority. By 1976 the Soviet Union would send at least thirteen spacecraft to Mars (it acknowledged only eight).

Mars 1 missed the planet entirely and vanished into space. Zond 2 probably crashed into the Martian surface. It contained a bust of Lenin to commemorate the first Mars "landing."

Mars 2 achieved orbit in the midst of the planetwide dust storm that would plague Mariner 9, a U.S. probe of Mars. There was no way for the Russians to reprogram it. Its computers automatically released a lander into the swirling deluge. The lander crashed. The official spin was it succeeded in delivering a Soviet pennant onto the sands of Mars.

Mars 3, braving the same dust storm, achieved the first soft landing on another planet. It sent back twenty seconds of coded TV data from the surface, then went silent. Sagan's theory was that the craft's parachute, caught like an umbrella in the raging storm, dragged the craft horizontally until it hit something. Something was wrong with the twenty seconds of TV data, too. The Soviets could never decipher it.

Mars 4's braking engine misfired. It too missed the planet. Mars 5 achieved orbit and sent back a relatively meager sixty photos. It and the lost Mars 4 were apparently intended to serve as communications relays for the next two probes. Mars 6 had no orbital module and was designed solely to make a soft landing. It crashed. Mars 7's lander separated incorrectly and missed the planet. Lederberg's 1957 prophecy of a reckless attitude toward space, spurred by considerations of national prestige, ended up being right on the mark.

Lester Grinspoon

Sagan took a keen interest in another matter of national prestige, the evolving war in Southeast Asia. On lunch hours, he inveighed against the troop deployments, the nuclear arms race, and the huge sums spent on military hardware. In 1965 Sagan resigned from an Air Force Scientific Advisory Board to protest the war. Sagan also supported the civil rights movement and African-American educational causes. From 1963 through 1972 he was a visiting lecturer at Alabama's predominantly black Tuskegee University, something unusual for a Harvard astronomer. (It is Sagan's doing that there is now a crater on Mars called Tuskegee.)

At one Cambridge party in the mid-1960s, Sagan found himself outnumbered on Vietnam. Almost everyone supported the war. Like oil and water, the two factions separated. Sagan found himself backed into a corner with, virtually, the only other person present who agreed with him. They introduced themselves.

The other man was Lester Grinspoon. He was an affable Harvard Medical School psychiatrist with a Boston accent. Although Grinspoon had trained in psychoanalysis, he was working on a study asserting that antipsychotic drugs help schizophrenics more than Freud's talking cure does. Sagan was impressed with Grinspoon's integrity in accepting this finding.

*   *   *

Carl and Lester soon became best friends. Thereafter, Carl's visits with his two sons were often at the Grinspoons' house. Whatever his shortcomings as a father, Carl had a natural rapport with children. To Lester's son David, "Uncle Carl" was an almost magical figure. "When you're a kid," he explains, "a lot of adults are boring. They're *just* adults. Carl was the kind of adult that made you want to read and think about intellectual things. There was something really exciting about the way he'd talk to you as if you could understand complex things."

At night Carl told Dorion, Jeremy, and the Grinspoon boys bedtime stories about neutron stars, black holes, and time travel. These were often complex serials continued from visit to visit. Dorion particularly remembers one story that was unusual in that it was *not* about black holes and such, although the characters in the story were named Europa, Ganymede, Callisto, and Io. They came across a row of four identical trees in a line. The significance of *that*, Carl promised, would become clear—at a later point in the story.

He never mentioned the four trees in a row again. Either he had forgotten, as absentee dads do, or he had never intended to explain the trees at all. They had served the purpose of keeping the boys listening. In this experimentation with the bedtime serials, Dorion suspects, were the beginnings of his father's career as a science popularizer.

*   *   *

One thing Sagan and Grinspoon had in common was marijuana, though from quite divergent viewpoints. Sagan was part of the diverse spectrum of mostly young people then using the drug. Grinspoon was alarmed by that phenomenon. He recognized that there was a credibility gap. He had the idea of assembling a truly scientific case against marijuana and publishing it so that young people, suspicious of the "establishment," would recognize the dangers.

In 1967, with his work on the schizophrenia study complete, Grinspoon began his study of the "marijuana problem." As he began to search the literature, Grinspoon found that there had been almost no scientific study of the drug. He also found that its reputation as a dangerous drug was of recent origin.

Cannabis had been in use as a medicinal and recreational drug for thousands of years, mostly in non-Western cultures but also to a degree in the West. George Washington grew cannabis on his estate, and a note in his journals seemed to imply he was growing it for the drug as well as the hemp fiber. Queen Victoria's physicians prescribed her cannabis tinctures. Marijuana cigarettes had been legal in most U.S. states.

This pattern of acceptance changed in the 1920s. Marijuana became popular among Mexican laborers and jazz musicians in the South. Southern newspapers began playing up the marijuana angle whenever a user committed a crime. It made good copy to imply that a not too well known drug used mainly by poor nonwhites drove them to commit horrible deeds. Like most tabloid stories, this was not based on any controlled scientific study. Some people who smoke tobacco commit horrible crimes; the question has to be: does the drug cause them to commit crimes? But in the 1930s, with this question unaddressed, the Federal Bureau of Narcotics stepped in with an "education campaign" to inform the public of marijuana's dangers. A shift in public opinion led to the 1937 Marijuana Tax Act and then to prohibition.

Ever on Grinspoon's mind was his friend Carl Sagan. Carl was the embodiment of the work ethic and of hardheaded, rational thought—everything a pot smoker was *not* supposed to be.

Mr. X

Grinspoon's research ultimately led him to conclude that marijuana is less dangerous than alcohol and tobacco are. It is not without risk, for no drug is. But marijuana is not addictive, and the likelihood of an overdose is very low.

Grinspoon therefore felt that marijuana should be legalized. He argued that the trauma and risk caused by arresting Americans for marijuana possession outweighed such hazards as it did pose. This was a radical point of view even in the 1960s. Timothy Leary still cast a long shadow over Harvard (he left in 1963) and over any Harvard doctor saying that presently illegal drugs may not be so bad.

Grinspoon published his research in his 1971 book, *Marihuana Reconsidered*. Never while he was writing the book did Grinspoon try the drug he was writing about. He anticipated that, after the book's publication, he would be called to testify about the drug and that (ironically!) any personal experience with marijuana would be used by foes to discredit him. Sagan's experiences with cannabis thus played an unusually important role in shaping Grinspoon's book.

One chapter of *Marihuana Reconsidered* consists of excerpts of literary figures' accounts of experiences with marijuana. Grinspoon thought that Sagan ought to contribute a piece on his own experiences. Sagan agreed on the condition that it be published anonymously.

Grinspoon wrote,

The following biography is approximately accurate. Mr. X is a professor at one of the top-ranking American universities, head of an organization producing important new research results, and is widely acknowledged as one of the leaders in his specialty. In his early forties, X has lectured at virtually every major American university, and his scientific and popular books have been bestsellers of their kind. His productivity has steadily increased over the last decade. He has won many awards and prizes given by government, university, and private groups, is happily married, has a wife and children, and asks that his anonymity be respected.

There followed Sagan's seven-page essay on his experiences with marijuana. Whatever one thinks of marijuana or Sagan, it is a strikingly candid and analytic piece.

"My high is always reflective, peaceable, intellectually exciting, and sociable, unlike most alcohol highs, and there is never a hangover," Sagan wrote. By this time, he required only a single joint to get high. Once, he got high just by breathing the smoke in a movie theater where someone was smoking. He could test for a high by closing his eyes. If he saw flashes of color or cartoonlike images, the drug was taking effect. These closed-eye images appeared before the onset of hallucinations with his eyes open. "I would guess this is a signal-to-noise problem," he wrote, "the visual noise level being very low with my eyes closed."

Sagan likewise proposed an "information-theoretical" reason for the cartoonlike quality of the flashed closed-eye images. Because they existed for a moment, they were only as detailed as could be apprehended in that moment: cartoons rather than fully detailed pictures.

The imagery of his hallucinations had become more complex over time. Initially the imagery had been inanimate or, if human, mute like the man on the port label. Now there was often human interaction and multiple levels of meaning. In one hallucination, he saw two people talking. As they spoke, their words appeared around their heads in yellow letters. An occasional word appeared in red. The red words fit the conversation perfectly; but Sagan found that if he strung together *just* the red words, he got a new and different message that turned out to be a brilliantly devastating critique of the two people and what they were saying.

Once high, Sagan found he was sated and did not feel an inclination to smoke more. He proposed a mathematical ratio to measure the abuse potential of a recreational drug. This he defined as the time required for a dose of drug to take effect divided by the length of time it would take to consume a dangerous dosage. For marijuana, this ratio is low, insofar as a puff on a cigarette "kicks in" almost immediately and it would take many cigarettes for a user to become ill. A low ratio is a prerequisite for a safe recreational drug, Sagan reasoned.

"When cannabis is legalized," wrote Sagan, "I hope to see this ratio as one of the parameters printed on the pack. I hope that time isn't too distant; the illegality of cannabis is outrageous, an impediment to full utilization of a drug which helps produce the serenity and insight, sensitivity and fellowship so desperately needed in this increasingly mad and dangerous world."

The Numinous

Sagan felt that the drug enhanced all forms of sensory experience. Mundane experiences such as eating a baked potato could become magical under the drug's spell. This was the result not of hallucination but of a state of consciousness in which he was aware of usually ignored undertones and overtones of perceptions.

Listening to classical music while high, Sagan was able, for the first time, to hear the distinct parts of three-part harmony and to appreciate counterpoint fully. These insights remained when he was *not* on the drug. He also spent much time looking at reproductions of art. As intrigued with other worlds as Sagan was, he felt an affinity for the paintings of French surrealist Yves Tanguy, the eerie landscapes of rocks and shards piled on a grayish beach, rising to a grayish sky with no horizon.

Sagan made the natural experiment of having sex under the drug's influence. He reported that "cannabis also enhances the enjoyment of sex—on the one hand it gives an exquisite sensitivity, but on the other hand it postpones orgasm: in part by distracting me with the profusion of images passing before my eyes." Orgasm itself was greatly lengthened, or so it seemed.

During his winter vacations in the Caribbean, Sagan would sometimes get high before immersing himself in the kaleidoscopic beauty of the reef. One such experience culminated in a long, purposely exhausting swim. Sagan dragged himself out of the blood-warm water and collapsed. All around him were antlers and oddments of coral snapped off in storms and tossed onto the shore. With the magnified perception of cannabis, this scene took on profound dimensions. He was able to perceive that he was *in* a Tanguy painting, a lucent world of pastel coral shards.

Sagan's drug experiences were often of a numinous character. "I do not consider myself a religious person in the usual sense," he wrote, "but there is a religious aspect to some highs. The heightened sensitivity in all areas gives me a feeling of communion with my surroundings, both animate and inanimate. Sometimes a kind of existential perception of the absurd comes over me and I see with awful certainty the hypocrisies and posturing of myself and my fellow men."

Bell Curves

The most singular of Sagan's cannabis experiences was doing science. "I have made a conscious effort to think of a few particularly difficult current problems in my field when high," he wrote. "It works, at least to a degree. I find I can bring to bear, for example, a range of relevant experimental facts which appear to be mutually inconsistent." Sagan cited a "very bizarre possibility, one that I'm sure I would never have thought of down" that he mentioned in a scientific article.

Grinspoon affirms that Sagan truly believed he got many of his scientific inspirations under the influence of the drug. After *Marihuana Reconsidered* appeared, people sent Grinspoon unsolicited gifts of marijuana. One time someone sent a particularly potent batch. "You've got to give that to me," Sagan told Grinspoon, only half-jokingly. "I've got some work to do."

The use of drugs to enhance the creative process is not uncommon in the arts. Writers ranging from Allen Ginsberg to Stephen Sondheim have credited cannabis as inspiring some of their best work. In the hard sciences, though, this is rare. It is probably fair to assume that the drug could only amplify talents already present in Sagan's makeup, notably his much-commented-upon ability to look at problems from novel perspectives. Sagan used the high for generating "crazy" ideas, then sober reason for skeptically examining and winnowing. Of course, scientific ideas are further winnowed by their ability to account for evidence better than competing theories. A verified hypothesis is independent of its source.

The inspirations were not limited to astronomy. Once while taking a shower, high, Sagan was struck with a profound insight into the origins of racism. It was an elegant refutation of the racist mentality. The insight was *mathematical* in nature. It had something to do with Gaussian distribution curves.

Sagan thought it imperative that he remember and disseminate the idea. He knew from experience that he had to write the idea down, or he would forget it. There was nothing to write with in the shower. He grabbed a bar of soap and frantically drew bell curves in soap on the shower wall.

Out of the shower, he set out to put his great insight into the logical, linear form that his "down" self could apprehend. As his words took shape on paper, other, equally brilliant ideas competed for attention. At the end of a feverish hour, he had written eleven short essays addressing many of the world's great social, political, and philosophical problems. Sagan reread the essays in the cold, clear light of the next day. He believed that most of the ideas held up. As the weeks passed, Sagan mentioned some of these ideas to colleagues. Their reactions were favorable. Over time, he used many of the ideas in his lectures and in his books.

*   *   *

Sagan gave serious attention to how he might best preserve drug-induced insights and translate them to his usual frame of consciousness. He needed hard copy, and a minicassette tape recorder seemed to work best. In a group of people, he would excuse himself and step off to a quiet corner to record his thoughts.

There was a self-acknowledged Dr. Jekyll and Mr. Hyde quality to this passing of notes. "I had a very accurate sense that these feelings and perceptions, written down casually, would not stand the usual critical scrutiny that is my stock in trade as a scientist," Sagan wrote. "If I find in the morning a message from myself the night before informing me that there is a world around us which we barely sense, or that we can become one with the universe, or even that certain politicians are desperately frightened men, I may tend to disbelieve; but when I'm high I know about this disbelief."

The high Sagan consequently had to convince the straight Sagan that he knew what he was talking about. Feats of memory were proof of the high Sagan's mental prowess. With cannabis, Sagan could reconstruct childhood events that he had only partly understood at the time, recall the name of a long-forgotten schoolmate, or describe in detail the typography and binding of a book in another room. These recollections, recorded in the notes, could be checked and generally proved accurate.

When this logic failed, there remained intimidation. One tape berated his workaday self: "Listen closely, you sonofabitch of the morning! This stuff is real!"

*   *   *

The first letter Grinspoon received from a reader of his book began, "You dirty Harvard Jew!" *Marihuana Reconsidered* was better received by the academic community, though of course many Americans were uncomfortable with its thesis. The book is today regarded as the bible of the legalize-marijuana movement, and Grinspoon is best known for his ever controversial advocacy of that movement.

As the years passed, it became evident that the late 1960s had been a high-water mark of American tolerance of cannabis and recreational drugs. Grinspoon kept his promise to keep "Mr. X" 's identity secret throughout Sagan's life. However much Sagan believed that adults have the right to use a drug that makes them feel good, he was aware of how this was at odds with the views of most other Americans. Grinspoon once wrote an article for the *New York Times* in which he commented that marijuana was used by people in all walks of life. The sentence trailed on with a long string of professions. Among them was *astronomers*. Sagan was upset even at that mention. He was circumspect about disposing of the drug. Once, toward the end of a South Pacific cruise with the Grinspoons, Carl insisted that all traces of the drug be thrown overboard—weighted down with a cruise line ashtray.

2001

On the less controversial (?) subject of extraterrestrial life, Sagan was becoming quite visible in the media. He gave more print and electronic interviews. He consulted on the 1966 book *Planets*, one volume in a series of illustrated science books put out by Time-Life. He wrote a skeptical piece on flying saucers for the *Saturday Review* (August 6, 1966) and a December 1967 feature on Mars for *National Geographic*. Both are engaging articles already in Sagan's mature style. Sagan was, as one journalist had it, the scientific community's "collective unconscious," ever willing to speak out on the taboo subject of alien life.

The *National Geographic* piece ran an artist's conception of Martian life. Credited to artist Douglas Chaffee "in consultation with the author," it's a document of what Sagan must have hoped or imagined the Vikings might find a decade later. One of the depicted creatures looks like a froth of gelatinous bubbles sprouting tentacles on the bottom. The caption explained that the bubbles are a "glassy shell" protecting the creature from ultraviolet light. It was already apparent that the merciless ultraviolet radiation was a formidable impediment to Martians of any kind. The bubble creature grazes on "mossy ground cover"—moss had replaced lichens, it seems. Other plants grow perfect crystal spheres around them like those in Bosch's *Garden of Earthly Delights*. Also shown are large, artichokelike plants that "have developed an ultraviolet tolerance."

One consequence of all this was that Sagan became, to the media and the world at large, the primary expert on extraterrestrial life. Since he was also a friend of Arthur C. Clarke's, Clarke asked Sagan for advice on the production of *2001: A Space Odyssey*.

Sagan met with Clarke and director Stanley Kubrick in Kubrick's New York penthouse. The film was already in production, though they were still trying to decide on an ending. Kubrick showed Sagan what they had. There was footage of a space vehicle approaching one of the moons of Jupiter. As it approached, it was revealed that the moon was not a natural satellite but an artificial structure. There was a neat hole in the moon, with stars visible through it. The moon was actually a gateway to another part of the universe. The space vehicle zoomed through the hole and ended up in an alien solar system.

That was as far as Clarke and Kubrick had gotten. They knew they wanted the humans to meet the aliens. They weren't sure what would happen then. They also weren't sure what the aliens should look like. They wanted Sagan's opinion on that.

Sagan replied that they *wouldn't* look like humans in makeup. Anything he or Kubrick or a makeup designer imagined would be wrong. It would look too much like earthly life of some kind.

The Zenlike tone of this answer suggests why movie directors rarely consult with scientists. Kubrick elected *not* to show the aliens—either because Sagan convinced him or because he ran out of money. Both explanations are part of the film's folklore. Kubrick did experiment with, then reject, such imaginative depictions of extraterrestrials as a dancer in black tights with white polka dots filmed against a black background.

To lend the film credence, the producers shot interviews with several prominent scientists for a promotional clip. When they asked Sagan to participate, he asked how much money they were paying. The movie people said they weren't paying anything. Sagan refused to be interviewed.

(With UFO sightings in the news, Kubrick tried to get Lloyd's of London to insure him against the possibility that real aliens would be discovered and render his film obsolete. Lloyd's passed. Sagan was convinced the insurance syndicate missed a good bet.)

Wheel of Fortune

Sagan's increasingly public career did not go unnoticed at Harvard. "There was a sort of a rumble among the senior astronomers, and among a few of the grad students as well," recalled Berendzen. "Carl was much younger and much more outspoken than the other faculty, and he was dealing with much more controversial things. Not that it was all negative—it was just that the subject matter was so *unusual*. We were accustomed to studying galactic structure, stellar interiors, that kind of thing. This was much more speculative. It was on the edge."

By far Sagan's edgiest interest was exobiology. The field had its critics, and many of them happened to be at Harvard. The most famous put-down was that exobiology was a science about nothing, a field that may have an empty set as its experimental objects. Harvard paleontologist George Gaylord Simpson carped that he could not share the euphoria of "certain biologists (some of them now ex-biologists converted to exobiologists)" for finding life beyond the Earth. Harvard astronomer David Layzer said of exobiology: "Its speculations cannot be confirmed by observations or experiments and so it is not a science; it has no data. It only sounds like science."

Strong as these words were, pro- and con-exobiology factions coexisted in the Harvard community like a big, happily quarreling family. Simpson was the father-in-law of Wolf Vishniac. Layzer was on neighborly terms with both Carl and Lynn; his kids played with Dorion and Jeremy.

For his part, Fred Whipple was eager to have Sagan made a full professor. In the mid-1960s, Harvard's astronomy department had only about seven full professors. Three of them were Whipple, Donald Menzel, and Bart Bok, all famous astronomers. Nontenured professors expected to wait seven or eight years before being considered for tenure. Few achieved full professorship much shy of their fortieth birthday. At thirty-two, Sagan was on the fast track.

*   *   *

Then one day the wheel of fortune turned, suddenly and inexplicably. Whipple was silent on the details. Sagan was given to understand only that he could no longer expect tenure at Harvard. Sagan was so humbled— and mystified—by the matter that he scarcely discussed it with such close friends as Berendzen and Grinspoon. Others noticed, belatedly, that Whipple no longer spoke of Sagan's advancement at faculty meetings, and wondered what had happened to his former protégé.

An academic who is denied tenure is "damaged goods." The stigma is so great that those who suspect they will *not* get tenure sometimes leave of their own accord to avoid the disgrace of a denial. Sagan, it should be emphasized, had not been turned down for tenure. His nomination had not even progressed that far. As a man of intense ambition, though, he could not remain at Harvard. By March 1967 he was putting out feelers for jobs elsewhere.

MIT was an obvious choice. It was within walking distance of where he (and Linda Salzman) already lived. MIT was also the professional home of his friend Philip Morrison. Though MIT did not have an astronomy department per se, its Earth and planetary sciences programs were first-rate. An MIT physicist, Bruno Rossi, had founded the field of X-ray astronomy.

Then, just as suddenly and mysteriously, MIT's interest in Sagan cooled. Whatever evil star dogged him shone over both ends of Cambridge.

As Cities Burned

There was more bad news. Sagan was a consultant on NASA's ambitious Mars lander mission, which went by the name Voyager. It was supposed to carry the robotically controlled biology experiments that people like Vishniac and Lederberg were working on. It would also have a rover to explore the Martian terrain. The price was put at $2.4 billion.

In the summer of 1967, Congress debated Voyager appropriations. Racial tensions and antiwar sentiments led to violent demonstrations in sixty-seven U.S. cities. Grandiose space programs looked irrelevant as inner cities went up in flames and campuses exploded in confrontations. Polls showed the public was no longer interested in costly space programs. "What will it profit this country," asked Detroit's mayor, Jerome P. Cavanaugh, "if we . . . put our man on the moon by 1970 and at the same time you can't walk down Woodward Avenue in this city without some fear of violence?"

Voyager might yet have escaped the chopping block had it not been for some supremely bad timing. As cities burned, NASA asked its contractors for proposals for *piloted* missions to Mars and Venus. Congress was outraged. It appeared to some that Voyager had been a dry run for putting people on Mars—and on frying-pan-hot Venus. Congress refused to vote any further funding for Voyager, killing the program.

The termination put Sagan out of a consulting job and left NASA without any planetary missions in the planning stages. Congress's reluctance to get behind new missions persisted for years afterward. For Sagan, who had bet so much on a mission to find life on Mars, it was an anxious time.

Tommy Gold

The job search continued. Cornell University was then assembling a first-rate astronomy department under Thomas Gold. Gold knew Sagan from space and exobiology meetings and had always been impressed with him.

The Vienna-born Gold was a dapper man who "wears his renown as correctly as he wears his British tweeds." His speech was an amalgam of Vienna, Cambridge, and the United States. In 1959 Gold moved to Cornell to oversee the construction of the Arecibo radio observatory and to handpick an astronomy faculty.

Famously egotistic, Gold was known to everyone as "Tommy." "In choosing a hypothesis," ran one of Gold's maxims, "there isn't any virtue in being timid." He favored high-risk science: novel, dramatic ideas that were probably wrong and certain to be branded crazy. But *if* they were right, they would be of first-rate importance.

Gold first made a name for himself as coauthor of just such an idea, the steady-state theory. Advanced in opposition to the big bang theory, it was the most famous *wrong* cosmological theory of the century.

Gold shared Sagan's interest in extraterrestrial life. In the particular field of SETI, Cornell was shaping up as a center, if by accident. Cocconi and Morrison had been at Cornell when they wrote their classic article. Frank Drake was then at Cornell and was as determined as Gold to recruit Sagan.

Like Sagan, Gold was a media scientist. During the Apollo era, he too was a familiar figure on TV space coverage, often seen brandishing a vial of simulated moon dust. The dust was the color of cocoa and so fine the grains were invisible. Gold boldly theorized that the moon was covered with fine dust like that, in some places a mile deep. Astronauts who dared step out onto the lunar surface might fall into freeze-dried quicksand, never to be seen again. When Gold shook his vial, the ersatz dust sloshed like a liquid.

*   *   *

Having heard that Sagan was open to leaving Harvard, Gold approached Dale Corson, Cornell's provost. He touted Sagan as a brilliant planetary astronomer on the way up, a rare find. There was only one catch, Gold added. The astronomy department didn't have the money to hire him.

This was a familiar routine to Corson. He knew that department heads preferred to plead poverty and spend someone else's money—preserving department funds for things the university might not approve so quickly. Gold in turn knew that Sagan was valuable enough that Cornell *would* come up with the money if pressed. He promised Corson, "You won't regret it."

*   *   *

With credit line in hand, Gold invited Sagan to Cornell to have a look around. He took him to Treman State Park, a favorite spot of Gold's that proved just as enchanting to Sagan. It was as beautiful as a national park. Nothing in Cambridge was that green and that close to the city.

Gold told Sagan that Cornell could start him off as an associate professor. He'd have tenure in a couple of years. Sagan, a tough and imaginative negotiator himself, said he wanted to continue his experiments on the origin of life and to hire associates from Harvard. He asked for his own laboratory.

None of Cornell's other astronomers had a laboratory. The type of work Sagan was doing was usually done by chemists or biologists. Gold didn't let that stand in the way. The deal was closed, and Sagan got his lab. It was called the Laboratory for Planetary Studies, with Sagan effectively being director for life.

Little Green Men

In February 1968, as Sagan was completing his work at Harvard, there was another spurious detection of alien "signals." Jocelyn Bell, a Cambridge grad student, was doing a thesis on interplanetary scintillation. Her chart recorders showed a regular, inexplicable pulse, once every 1.3 seconds. Other, similar sources were soon found. Cambridge astronomers took to calling the sources LGM, for *little green men*. When speaking to the press, they were careful to add that LGM was a *joke*.

It was not a joke to Sagan. He believed it possible that the pulses were intelligent signals. The pulses were amazingly regular. Rotation and revolution of celestial bodies show just such regularity. But revolutions of celestial bodies characteristically take *years*; rotations take *days*. For a once-a-second pulsing star to stay in sync, it would have to be compact enough for signals, traveling at the speed of light, to cross its diameter in a second. Otherwise one end of the object would have no way of staying in phase with the other end. The sources would therefore have to be smaller than a light-second across (186,000 miles), probably much, much smaller—that is, smaller than the smallest stars, smaller than a planet. One thing that would fit that requirement is an alien broadcasting station.

One reason astronomers were reluctant to believe they had detected extraterrestrial signals was that other LGM sources were found. The whole sky couldn't be full of extraterrestrial signals, they thought. Sagan, aware of the generous numbers predicted by the Drake equation, did not find that to be much of an objection.

Nor did Frank Drake, who was the victim of particularly cruel irony. He was then director of Arecibo, the world's biggest and best radio telescope, in the hills of Puerto Rico. But Arecibo was not able to receive the sources' frequency. The LGM pulses were in the band reserved for television transmissions. Drake drove to a Puerto Rican Sears and bought the biggest TV antenna they had. It cost $30. He charged it, drove back to the observatory, and hooked it up to the great dish.

Tommy Gold agreed that anything pulsing once a second had to be very small. But Gold suspected the sources were *neutron stars*, a theoretical idea first proposed by Chandrasekhar. Neutron stars would be so small and dim that no one expected to observe them. What, Gold asked, if small, rapidly rotating neutron stars emitted powerful radio waves from certain points on their surfaces? Then radio pulses might be detected once a second, each time the star rotated. It was as crazy as any idea Gold had ever come up with. It was also correct.

A *Jewish Wedding*

On New Year's Eve, Linda gave Carl an ultimatum: Marry her, or move out of the apartment they shared. Carl opted for marriage. They picked April 6, 1968, for their wedding. Linda was adamant about wanting a traditional Jewish ceremony. Carl preferred something as *un*religious as possible.

Ronald Blum finds a paradox in that Sagan was an "intensely Jewish character"—straight out of Brooklyn, with his love of the word and of disputation—yet "I don't recall him saying one single thing relating to his Jewishness. He was a black hole on that." Sagan's background seemingly helped shape his dedication to work, his choice of wives, and perhaps even his science fiction. (Sagan's unnaveled humanoids are more easily read as a metaphor for the Jew than as plausible extraterrestrials. His later novel, *Contact*, analogizes the Jewish immigrant experience to extraterrestrial contact.) Yet Sagan's ethnicity was something he generally kept low-key. Even at the height of his fame, some of Sagan's Jewish readers were surprised to learn of his Jewish ancestry.

As a compromise, Carl and Linda got a rabbi to perform their wedding service in the MIT chapel, a modernistic Eero Saarinen cylinder that is non-denominational with a vengeance. In the center of the cylinder is a marble cube and a weird abstract metal screen loosely suggesting the *Star Trek* transporters.

The rabbi proposed reading a passage from Genesis during the ceremony. Sagan tried to talk the rabbi into mentioning the big bang.

Lester Grinspoon was best man. Isaac Asimov served as the required official witness who knew Sagan's father's Hebrew name. Carl and Linda exchanged vows in front of the *Star Trek* screen. The rabbi's speech quoted Genesis, *not* mentioning the big bang.

The reception was held around the pool at the Grinspoons' house. Rachel Sagan greeted Isaac Asimov by asking, "And how are your grandchildren, Dr. Asimov?"

Asimov was forty-eight, and his vanity about age was not entirely an act. "I am *not* a grandfather," he answered.

"There's nothing wrong with being a grandfather," Rachel said.

"Undoubtedly. I just happen not to be one."

"Mr. Sagan and I have never been so happy as since we've had grandchildren."

"Look," Asimov blurted, "be delirious with happiness for all I care, but I am not a grandfather!" His wife, Gertrude, then had the good sense to pull him away.

*   *   *

Carl and Linda honeymooned in Portugal, then moved to Ithaca. They left Cambridge still not knowing why Carl had been passed over for Harvard tenure. Carl had one theory. He had advised the Harvard chapter of the Students for a Democratic Society. He asked Lester Grinspoon if he thought that might have something to do with it. Lester thought it unlikely.

As years passed and Sagan's fame increased, a mythology grew up to explain this kink in Sagan's résumé—without much help from Sagan, who at first was as puzzled as anyone and, later, silent by choice. It was alleged that Sagan was too "flamboyant" for Harvard. A Mozart-Salieri relationship was imputed between the charismatic young Sagan and the stodgier old dons, squinting through their telescope eyepieces. It was charged that Sagan was a martyr to exobiology. One magazine reported a rumor that Sagan himself suspected that David Layzer had blocked his tenure (along with Layzer's firm denial). Layzer was indeed as surprised as everyone else at what had happened.

For years afterward, Fred Whipple debated whether to tell Sagan the reason for his downfall at Harvard. He felt it best to keep quiet. But Whipple's wife, Babette, thought it would be better to tell Carl—so that Carl would understand that it wasn't the doing of anyone at Harvard.

ITHACA
1968-76

CORNELL IS ROUTINELY, and without much contest, called the most scenic of Ivy League schools. Located in Ithaca, near the New York Finger Lakes wine country, the university rests on a slope dramatically overlooking Lake Cayuga. It is a campus of picturesque Victorian and Romanesque and Gothic revival buildings; of gardens, stately trees, statuary, and unleashed dogs (reputedly, an eccentric millionaire's benefaction was contingent on the right of canines to roam free for all time). The signature building, pictured on postcards and mugs, is the Uris Library bell tower, whose carillon plays a concert three times a day. This often ends on the naggingly familiar "Far Above Cayuga's Waters," the alma mater that has been shamelessly stolen by schools nationwide.

Town Without Bad Taste

Ithaca is a town without bad taste. The visitor is struck by the eerie, Swiss-like perfection of the place. It seems that everyone's house has just been painted, every lawn mowed and weeded. No one has a rusted recreational vehicle in their front yard. Neither poverty nor ostentatious display of wealth is much in evidence. Billing itself as "America's Most Enlightened City," it has almost no industry aside from higher education and supporting those in higher education. Minimum-wage jobs are done by Cornell students. Those who run restaurants or dry cleaners or gas stations seem themselves to be scholars without portfolio, drawn by the intellectual climate.

Draw a ten-mile-radius circle around downtown Ithaca, and it will enclose 150 waterfalls. The area concentrates such a diversity of sights in a small compass that there was a short-lived attempt to create a motion-picture industry in Ithaca in the 1910s. Francis X. Bushman and Lionel Barrymore shot films there, and some of Cornell's frat houses are former mansions of silent film stars.

Sagan (who spent most of his adult life there) found Ithaca to be "centrally isolated." "A lot of people aren't just casually dropping in," Sagan told one local journalist, adding that "if I didn't do a fair amount of traveling I might get stir crazy." It is a town with a lot of quiet time, reputedly a salubrious place for writers.

If there is a drawback, it is the weather—although the point is enthusiastically argued both ways. The region has glorious, leafy Junes and long winters where the sun may hide behind clouds for weeks. "Ithaca, thankfully, isn't in the snowbelt," insists a brochure for Cornell students, which locates the snowbelt way off around Buffalo. Campus lore holds the suicide rate to be one of the highest, with the splendid and lethal gorges offering ample opportunities for dramatic exits. In Cornell's astronomy department, the prerogative of wintering at tropic Arecibo is a prize perk.

*   *   *

Carl and Linda established themselves in a rented house at 1013 Triphammer Road, in a pleasantly wooded area north of the campus. Linda and Pollack's friend, Bill Gile, decorated the Sagan home in "comfortable modern" furnishings, mostly bought on excursions to Bloomingdale's in New York.

The Sagans were ardently in love and physically demonstrative. In the time that could be spared from love and work, they appreciated good food. Their cupboards were perpetually full of costly or unusual items bought on whim. To Carl, stoves and dishwashers were "foreign objects," but Linda prepared ambitious gourmet recipes as well as stick-to-the-ribs fare like veal roast and chocolate cake. Chocolate was certainly a favorite. The couple's cleaning man recalled finding chocolate-chip cookie crumbs all over the house, even in bed.

Linda's attitude toward housekeeping was of a piece with Carl's: let someone else do it. Both left personal effects all over the house. Periodically a cleaning man sorted through the chaos. An especially vigorous cleaning campaign preceded each visit of Carl's parents. Linda arranged special meals to impress Samuel and Rachel. One plate of toasted sandwiches impressed Rachel as inedible. "If I'd ordered these in a restaurant," she told her daughter-in-law, "I'd have sent them right back." The toast was a little too dark.

Sagan now tooled around town in a Corvair Monza Spyder convertible with turbo-charged engine. "It *flew*," one Cornell student remembers. This allowed him to make the most of Ithaca's blend of natural splendor, small-town living, and first-rate intellectual company. The couple entertained an eclectic mixture of astronomers, science-fiction writers, academics in both of the "two cultures," and other hangers-on. Tommy Gold was a frequent visitor; Isaac Asimov would get tipsy on Linda's punch. According to a local newspaper's profile, Sagan

> likes to walk in the flower garden across from the soccer field at Cornell, to shop in the open air of the Ithaca Commons, to stop at Marion's roadside stand on Route 79, to take his son to the animal exhibits at Pyramid Mall.
>
> Sagan is a small-town boy, he said, from Rahway, N.J. Although Rahway and Ithaca are about the same size, Ithaca offers more of the good life, he said, particularly when it comes to good restaurants. He particularly likes the Japanese food at Utage and the French cuisine at L'Auberge du Cochon Rouge. And if he could change just one thing about this almost perfect environment, what would it be?
>
> "I would move Ithaca to the Caribbean," he said with a mischievous smile.

Astronomy 101

Sagan's influence as a Cornell teacher was immense. Over the years, a large fraction of the nation's best planetary scientists funneled through his classes. He got students jobs working on NASA's planetary missions, and this often led to important publications at an early age. Sagan's lab was one of the few places to launch a career in origins of life studies. In addition to high-powered courses, Sagan taught Astronomy 101 and 102.

Sagan could shift gears quickly. He had an uncanny sense of when students were following him and when they weren't. He told one suspiciously silent graduate class, "No one was born with Fourier transforms in their head; you must ask and learn."

One rule Sagan instilled in his students was to avoid becoming emotionally attached to one's own theories. At first sight, this may seem surprising advice coming from Sagan. Most likely, Sagan recognized the need to check emotional involvement in himself and thus was better able to articulate the problem than someone less prone to it.

"If a scientist identifies his self-esteem too closely with theories he proposes, then, when the theory is demolished—as many theories are—the person is also demolished," Sagan said. "This is scientific suicide. The theory and the person are not the same."

Sagan's prescription was to make it a habit to come up with as many different hypotheses as possible. Should a favored hypothesis be proved wrong, it is then easier to discard it and move on, rather than digging in one's heels for an unprofitable battle against the evidence.

Busy as he was, Sagan read and responded to letters from students interested in astronomy. He regarded this as an obligation. One of his many success stories was Princeton astrophysicist Neil deGrasse Tyson. As an African-American high school student in the Bronx, Tyson wrote Sagan a letter. Sagan invited him to Cornell, discussed astronomy careers with him, and even drove Tyson back to the Ithaca bus station and gave him his home phone number in case the snow kept the buses from running and he needed a place to stay.

*   *   *

In his research, Sagan remained a quintessential theorist. He preferred devising theories to conducting observations, and he was happier coming up with twenty new ideas for theories than following one through to completion on his own. He preferred to work on many projects simultaneously, with many collaborators. There were those who slighted him for this, but it was behind his broad influence.

In his collaborative efforts, Sagan was aided by an impressive memory. When he met people at scientific conferences, he could instantly recall what they had talked about the last time they met and could resume the conversation from where it had ended, over a gap of months or years. Taking a leaf from Kuiper, Sagan memorized scores of useful physical and astronomical constants and made a veritable art form out of stunning, off-the-cuff calculations.

This showmanship aside, Sagan lacked the truly first-rate mathematical insight of a Chandrasekhar. Sagan's more densely mathematical articles (and there were a fair number) were done in collaboration with more mathematically inclined colleagues. "When it came to the mathematics," said colleague William I. Newman candidly, "he did not have much to add." Sagan was instead a "catalyst," Newman explained, someone who never lost the "latent ten-year-old," the sense of wonder that was necessary in posing good questions.

Grad students were inclined to liken Sagan to a great fertile oak tree, shedding acorns from which great theories would grow. "He was someone who had more ideas than he could possibly handle himself," said Steven Squyres. "If you just hung around him, the ideas would fall off of him." Sagan "would take your new result and spin back twenty different logical consequences of it," says David Grinspoon. (Lester's son became a planetary astronomer, at least partly inspired by "Uncle Carl.")

The esteem in which Sagan was held can be judged by the number of Harvard colleagues who joined him at Cornell. Jim Pollack carefully slid a board underneath the mountain of papers and books littering his Harvard desk, then wrapped and shipped the whole pile to Ithaca, so that he could resume work without the delay of cleaning his desk off. Sagan also recruited Bishun Khare, Joseph Veverka, and Peter Gierasch from Harvard. Their relationship with Sagan was mutually beneficial. "Some people have a tendency to surround themselves with people who are less competent and can't function on their own," Veverka observed. "Carl always looked for the best people and the most independent people. He wasn't looking for a bunch of flunkies."

*   *   *

In 1970 Cornell made good on its promise to grant Sagan tenure. This was followed by an endowed chair, the David Duncan Professor of Astronomy and Space Sciences. Sagan's influence far transcended Cornell. One reason was his editorship of a then-new journal of planetary science called *Icarus*.

When Sagan took over the journal, at the start of 1969, *Icarus* was not even peer-reviewed. Sagan brought its editorial practices into line with other journals and talked the best planetary scientists into contributing. Prominent among the contributors, of course, were Sagan and his grad students. *Icarus* further became known for publishing speculative articles, on extraterrestrial life and other topics, that might not have been published elsewhere.

For many scientists, editing a journal is a chore. Sagan relished the job; he even liked assembling the tables of contents. Too impatient to correspond with authors by mail, Sagan phoned long distance to the Soviet Union and elsewhere. His phone bills regularly astounded the journal's publisher.

*   *   *

In the classroom and in his personal life, Sagan had a mischievous sense of humor. A technical problem with a lecture slide would effortlessly inspire a dry quip, then another, and then, without missing a beat, a devastating capper that would bring down the house. It was like a well-written farce, the more amazing for being improvised before the class's eyes.

"When people first meet him," said NASA scientist Gerald Soffen, "they are not sure how much of what he says is tongue-in-cheek." A favorite mode of performance for Sagan was advancing a crazy idea totally deadpan to provoke a reaction. (There was, perhaps, a parallel to the way he did science.) For many years, a map of Mars was posted outside Sagan's Cornell office. On closer inspection, it proved to be a map of the Mars of Edgar Rice Burroughs, supplied with canals, monsters, and an "atmosphere-generating station."

Timothy Leary

In a similar spirit of put-on, Sagan and Frank Drake paid a visit to Timothy Leary. This began when Leary wrote Sagan a letter saying he had become interested in space travel. Would Sagan be willing to meet and discuss an idea Leary had? If so, Sagan would have to go to Leary, not vice versa. Leary was in the California State Medical Facility at Vacaville. This was the kind of institution whose name used to end in the words "for the Criminally Insane." Charles Manson was in Vacaville. Leary had been put there because he escaped from a lower-security institution. He had originally been sentenced for a minor count of marijuana possession.

As it happened, Sagan and Drake had to attend a meeting in California. They wrote the prison and made the necessary arrangements. Once at the facility, they presented their IDs, went through a metal detector, and submitted to a guard slapping his hands against their bodies for any non-metallic weapons. Finally, they were taken into a bare room with a few chairs. One guard kept watch through a window—just in case someone tried something—while another brought in Leary.

The first thing they noticed was that Leary looked . . . *great*. He had been exercising behind bars. He radiated energy. Leary began running in a circle around the two astronomers. He offered no explanation—it was exercise, maybe. As he ran he talked excitedly, never getting winded.

The first thing Leary said was that he had been framed. The powers that be had planted drugs on him. They did that because they knew he was going to run for governor of California and that if he *did* run, he would win.

Sagan asked how "they" managed to be so *sure* that Leary would win.

Leary said he would get the hippie vote, the freak vote, and the drug vote. In California, that's all you need.

Leary then came to the reason he had asked them there. He believed that nuclear war would soon wipe out the human race. His plan was to build a cosmic Noah's ark. Three hundred of the Earth's most worthy people would go into the space ark and blast off for a nearby star system, there to continue the human species. Money was not a consideration in this plan. Leary had wealthy friends who would finance everything. What he wanted from Sagan and Drake was technical know-how. What star, not too far away, is most likely to have a planet where people could live?

Sagan and Drake looked at each other a moment. They gave the standard scientific reply. No, they couldn't recommend a star. They didn't know of *any* other star that definitely had planets. But that was beside the point. You couldn't just write a check and have someone build you a space ark. The technology didn't exist.

Leary, still jogging, drank this in. "All right, not today," Leary said. "In ten years then?"

No, no, no, they said, not in ten years, not in anyone's lifetime. Drake (less sold on the Bussard ramjet than Sagan) tried to explain about the energy costs. To accelerate a spacecraft, big enough to carry *hundreds* of people, to anywhere near the speed of light would require more fuel than had been produced since the Industrial Revolution. It was just plain impossible.

Leary wanted to know how Drake could be *sure* it was impossible if (as they had just said) the technology hadn't yet been invented.

Sagan and Drake left, passing through a gift shop selling items made by inmates. Among the most popular pieces were ceramic sculptures of psychedelic mushrooms. They seem to have scarcely subdued Leary's enthusiasm. Leary called up Lester Grinspoon (they knew each other slightly from Harvard) and asked him for help. He wanted Lester to convince his friend Carl to serve as *captain* of the space ark.

Student Radical

As an emblem of the 1960s youth culture, Leary likely both fascinated and disturbed Sagan. Sagan identified with the liberal social values of the time, but he was distressed by "a drift away from science" among college-age people. He chafed at the cultural stereotyping that led many to assume that, as a scientist, *he* must be stodgy, politically conservative, and "irrelevant."

One of Sagan's first grad students at Cornell was Steven Soter. Soter attended Students for a Democratic Society (SDS) meetings but looked so "straight" that the SDS members suspected he was an FBI spy. One day in the fall of 1968, Sagan commented that he'd like to meet an authentic student radical. (Soter apparently didn't qualify.) Soter arranged a meeting with Deane Rink, a literature grad student and cofounder of Cornell's SDS chapter.

Rink was a hippie. He showed up at the Sagans' door in full 1960s regalia. Linda let him in. The three had a somewhat formal dinner, then Rink and Carl went to the living room to talk. Rink *seriously* doubted that a scientist would be capable of understanding the immorality of the Vietnam War. Rink offered Sagan a joint, as one might offer a vampire a cross. Sagan took one polite puff. Rink then launched into a long, earnest antiwar diatribe. Before it was over, he learned that his views were not so different, nor so original. Rink stayed till the early morning. When he left, he felt he had made a new friend.

*   *   *

The world, and academia with it, was changing. During a trip back to the University of Wisconsin, Sagan had to flee a cloud of tear gas. With no intentional irony, police had used the toxic gas to disperse a student demonstration against the manufacture of napalm.

In April 1969 Carl and Linda went to London, where Carl was narrating a film for the BBC. It was a tumultuous month in Ithaca. A little before 3 A.M. on April 18, a brick flew through the window of Wari House, a coed, mostly African-American dormitory at Cornell. The residents awoke to discover a burning cross on their front porch steps.

The wood used in the cross was traced to the Cornell campus store, where it was sold for art classes. Early on the morning of the nineteenth, a group of about 100 black students entered Willard Straight Hall with wire, chains, and rope. It was "parents' weekend" at Cornell, and the hall was occupied mainly by sleeping parents. The students hurried the parents out of the building. They secured the entrances and exits and held control of the building in a tense, five-day standoff. The students demanded amnesty and a separate housing system for blacks.

There were rumors (probably all false) of a bomb in Willard Straight Hall, of drunken carloads of white students with guns, and of a sniper in the library tower, sighting among the carillon bells. The black students armed themselves, fearful that the campus police would not protect them. The occupation ended in a divisive faculty vote acceding to the students' demands. Footage of gun-carrying students leaving the building made an indelible impression on the national news. In many ways, it was a different Cornell after Sagan's return from London (the film he had been narrating was titled *The Violent Universe*).

The takeover abandoned the nonviolent, color-blind ideal of 1960s liberals for a new, often separatist, ethos in which change was achieved by any means necessary. It was a time of ambivalence for liberals like Sagan, one of hope mixed with paranoia. Youthful protest would usher in a new utopia— or else a repressive totalitarian regime. It was hard to tell which.

Shortly after the Kent State massacre, Sagan took Jim Pollack and Bill

Gile on a ride into the countryside around Ithaca. Sagan drove alongside a picture-perfect barn with a windmill beside it. He asked if they noticed anything *unusual* about the barn.

Gile, who grew up in farm country, recognized that the windmill was too close to the barn.

Sagan maintained that the "barn" was no barn at all. It was a *holding facility*. The city of Ithaca had a tiny jail. The "barn" was built to be ready for the coming mass arrests of student radicals and protesters. Sagan feared this might really happen, and that gay rights protesters might be targeted, too. The trip was a warning to Pollack, not to be too visible with his gay rights advocacy.

*   *   *

Actually, Pollack was as low-key in his homosexuality as in everything else. (Carl drove the flamboyant muscle car; Jim had a sensible Volvo.) But Pollack was active in the Stonewall-era gay rights movement. He brought gay and lesbian activists to speak in Ithaca and often helped out with their travel expenses.

In at least one case, Pollack talked Sagan into adding gay rights to his roster of liberal causes. Gay activist Frank Kameny had studied astronomy at Harvard (not with Sagan) and was later fired from a government job because of his sexual orientation. He filed a landmark lawsuit attempting to assert the right of gays to hold government jobs. This lawsuit left Kameny low on funds and in need of work. At Pollack's urging, Sagan hired Kameny to do some freelance research examining photos of Mars at NASA's Washington headquarters. Kameny's lawsuit had particular relevance for Pollack, who had, with trepidation, passed a NASA-mandated security check while sharing a one-bedroom apartment with another man.

Back Contamination

In 1969 Mariners 6 and 7 entered Martian orbit. Mariner 7 flew over the polar caps with instruments designed to check whether they were carbon dioxide or water ice. It confirmed that the caps were indeed carbon dioxide.

The latest Mariners had better cameras than Mariner 4 had. Thanks to the sharper imagery, it was possible to see that the craters had been softened and rounded slightly. Mars had once had a thicker atmosphere capable of weathering. Visible in these photos—but scarcely noted at the time—were streaky features looking like drainage channels.

Sagan spent much of 1969 preoccupied with the Apollo 11 mission. His most visible role was as lobbyist for the crew's quarantine upon return. The new buzzword was "back contamination." This was the opposite of the "forward contamination" that had initially worried Lederberg and Sagan. If there were microbes on the moon, it could be dangerous to bring them back to Earth and release them into the environment.

By 1969 Sagan did not believe there was much chance of life on the moon, much less of lunar life that could also thrive in the utterly different environment of Earth. His position was that even a remote chance had to be taken seriously when, potentially, the safety of the whole world was at stake. "Where we are profoundly ignorant should we not err on the side of safety?" he liked to ask.

A recurring motif in Sagan's public career is his preoccupation with very small risks of very great catastrophes. There was, according to Lester Grinspoon, a slightly "paranoid" component to Sagan's personality—not in the clinical sense, of course, but in the common and informal way people use the term "paranoid" in discussing friends. One of Sagan's favorite sayings was that, in America today, if you're not a little paranoid you're out of your mind. Sagan could be fretful of his health; worried about, yet on some level fascinated by, covert machinations of the CIA, the Defense Department, and the "establishment."

The most common means of coping with small risks of great catastrophes is to deny they exist. It was Sagan's character to take these imponderable hazards seriously. That may be called paranoid; with equal justice, it may be called actuarial, as Sagan did. An insurance company sets rates by multiplying probabilities and costs. With only money at stake, it is easy and necessary to be dispassionate. Sagan was, or felt he was, able to do a parallel kind of emotional math, multiplying fantastic improbabilities and global dooms.

Sagan's philosophy on back contamination prevailed for most of the Apollo era. In 1964 the Space Sciences Board organized the Interagency Committee on Back Contamination, a colorfully disparate group of experts that included not only a well-known exobiologist (Wolf Vishniac) but people from the Public Health Service, the Department of Agriculture, the Fish and Wildlife Service, and the biological warfare unit of the U.S. Army. The committee convinced NASA of the need to sequester the returning astronauts until they could be given a clean bill of health. Congress approved funds to build an $8.5 million quarantine facility in Houston, the Lunar Receiving Laboratory. One of the committee's reports stated, in classic bureaucratese, that

> the existence of life on the moon or planets cannot . . . rationally be precluded. At the very least, present evidence is not inconsistent with its presence. . . . Negative data will

not prove that extraterrestrial life does not exist; they will
merely mean that it has not been found.

This caused one NASA reviewer to pencil in the margin, "Like witches."

Certainly, many people working on Apollo grumbled that astronaut quarantine, like sterilization of unpiloted craft, was an expensive boondoggle.
They believed it *was* possible to be sure there was no life on the moon (no
air! no water! etc.). The University of Chicago's Edward Anders offered
to *eat* moon dust to prove its safety. Sagan's response to Anders was "Fine,
but he will have to eat it *on the moon.* It will be too late if he eats it down
here. If he is wrong and gasps and dies, then whatever killed him is already
among us."

Even Lederberg disagreed with Sagan on this issue. In a July 1969 letter
to the *New York Times*, Lederberg blasted "the absurdity of the efforts now
programmed as if they were intended to protect the earth from a tangible
risk of global infection by lunar microbes. In fact, no responsible official or
scientific advisor believes there is such a risk. If there were, the response
would have to be the cancellation of the entire manned lunar program.
We would have to be able to destroy the 'contraband' or send it back, measures which we do not contemplate for national heroes having accomplished
an arduous and courageous feat."

Like many a political compromise, the lunar quarantine grafted two reasonable but antithetic philosophies to produce a wildly illogical chimera. A
bona fide quarantine raised grim ethical dilemmas that NASA never faced
up to. "Suppose something goes wrong," Elliott Levinthal said at one briefing headed by an astronaut trainee. "You're inside the quarantine facility,
and whatever goes wrong makes you want to get the hell out. Who on this
NASA site is authorized to shoot you?"

The question was of course rhetorical. NASA's quarantine would operate on the honor system. Indeed, NASA ruled that the quarantine was
not absolute. It could be suspended—in the event of a life-threatening
emergency.

*   *   *

In previous spaceflights, the returning capsule had been opened in midocean. This posed obvious risks, should there be lunar microbes. NASA
and the back contamination committee devised a protocol in which the
sealed capsule would be recovered from the ocean by helicopter, shipped to
Houston, and placed inside a sealed lab. Only then would the capsule be
opened and the astronauts permitted to emerge. The crew would greet their
wives and children through high-impact thicknesses of glass. Moon dust

would be tested on sterile mice, delivered by cesarean section, for ill effects. Reduced air pressure inside the lab would prevent dust particles from finding their way into the outside world. Even the astronauts' bodily wastes would be rigorously sterilized before entering Houston's sewage system.

Andromeda Strain

The back contamination committee considered everything except a sense of drama. That may have been its undoing. The astronauts were to be treated as biohazards, not heroes. Armstrong, Aldrin, and Collins balked. *If* they got back, they said, they were not about to spend more time in that sealed capsule. Not only was this uncomfortable and inglorious, it posed a real risk to the astronauts. The plan was to hoist the sealed capsule up by helicopter or crane and set it down softly on ship deck. That was easier said than done. The capsule was heavy, suspended like a pendulum above a ship so much more massive that it would effectively be an immovable object. A gust of wind or a heaving ocean could slam the capsule onto the ship with the force of a head-on freeway collision.

With a near-mutiny on its hands, NASA had little choice but to accede to their demands. So in May 1969 NASA announced a revised quarantine procedure. This was a stranger chimera yet. The space agency could hardly back off from its widely publicized vow to protect the world from any lunar pathogens.

Under the new plan, a navy frogman would crack the Apollo capsule hatch in midocean. He would toss in three "Biological Isolation Garments," then slam the hatch shut again. The astronauts would emerge only after donning the garments. The frogman would then swab them down with Betadine, the rust-hued disinfectant favored by surgeons and obsessive-compulsives.

Sagan was alarmed by the new plan. "Maybe it's sure to 99% that Apollo 11 will not bring back lunar organisms," he told *Time* magazine, "but even that one-percent uncertainty is too large to be complacent about." He had an unexpected ally on the best-seller lists. Michael Crichton's recently published novel, *The Andromeda Strain*, concerned a plague brought back from space. NASA received thousands of well-meaning letters from people who read the novel and were worried. The space agency felt obliged to answer each letter.

Massachusetts General

NASA stuck to the new quarantine plan. For twenty-one days before launch, the astronauts were isolated. NASA did not want them catching something on Earth, knowing that the merest cold would raise fears that they had caught a lunar bug. But it was Sagan, not the astronauts, who fell ill.

From his adolescence onward, Carl had a chronic medical problem called achalasia, in which the walls of the esophagus lose their ability to contract normally and move food down into the stomach. As with a stomach ulcer, the condition usually lacks any obvious cause and flares up unpredictably with inflammation and bleeding. While in college, Carl had gone to the Mayo Clinic for a gruesome treatment that consisted of forcing steel weights down the throat to tear the ligaments of the esophagus. In mid-June 1969, just after Carl had briefed the Apollo astronauts, the condition became serious enough that he admitted himself to Massachusetts General Hospital for surgery. He was to have a modified Heller myotomy, in which the esophageal sphincter muscle is cut. His surgeon was considered one of the best in such surgery.

On the eighteenth, Isaac and Gertrude Asimov visited Carl and Linda in the hospital. All joked genially about the ill timing of what they took to be a minor bout of illness. They made plans to have dinner as soon as Carl got out.

The condition was more serious than they imagined. Lester Grinspoon saw an alarming X ray of Carl's chest. The esophagus had ballooned out like a second stomach.

Carl bled profusely during surgery, needing ten or eleven units of blood. Asimov tried to calm Linda. Almost immediately afterward, it was clear that something was wrong. Though Carl was being given oxygen, his complexion took on an ominous blue cast. The oxygen wasn't getting into his bloodstream. His lungs were filling up with fluid. The lack of oxygen affected his mind. Carl became genuinely paranoid. He decided that the doctors at Massachusetts General were plotting to kill him.

That was of course not true, but unfortunately Carl's surgeon had left town immediately after the operation. He left instructions for a nurse to lift Carl up every twenty minutes, allowing the fluids to drain from his lungs. Carl was a big man, and the nurse was hardly able to raise him. Both Lester and Carl were afraid that Carl would suffocate before a nurse knew what was happening.

Lester sat up with Carl, periodically lifting him up, forcing the chest to rise and fall, acting as a human iron lung machine. Every now and then

Linda would look in to see how they were doing. She was either unaware of the gravity of the situation or unable to deal with it.

Lester remained in the hospital, with barely catnaps to sustain him, for forty-eight hours. His back was killing him (he already had a ruptured disk), and he missed his anniversary with his wife, Betsy. At length, Carl's color and mental outlook improved to the point where both men felt it was okay for Lester to leave. Ever after, Carl credited him with saving his life.

Lester dutifully went into his office. He had been there a short while when the phone rang. It was the hospital. Carl wanted his opinion on his doctors' orders.

Carl remained suspicious of his doctors for the rest of his visit. He routinely refused orders, medication, or procedures *until* they could be cleared with Lester. Nurses, new on the shift, would be told to "check it with Dr. Grinspoon"—and were perhaps not so surprised to find that this "Dr. Grinspoon" was a psychiatrist.

Moon Dust

Carl was in this less than totally lucid state when Neil Armstrong bounded onto the lunar surface on July 20. He watched on a black-and-white TV in his hospital room. "There were these two strangely garbed figures, as in a dream, skipping into the air and falling back to the ground impossibly slowly," Carl later recalled. "And it just perfectly flowed out of the dream state. It took me a couple of minutes to figure out what was happening—exultation! . . . It was a triumph for the species."

And a minor triumph for Carl Sagan. He had won his candy bar wager, with five months to spare.

The return was no triumph for the back contamination committee, though. The astronauts emerged in midocean. Whatever else the "Biological Isolation Garments" accomplished, they made the astronauts *look* like alien invaders. A helicopter ferried them in a wire cage twelve miles to the USS *Hornet*, a navy aircraft carrier.

Once the helicopter landed, the astronauts—now stifled by the greenhouse effect of their isolation suits—paid no heed to a brass band playing as they walked to a customized Airstream trailer. Sealed inside the trailer, they showered, put on fresh clothes, and greeted President Richard Nixon through a window. (Had the astronauts gotten ill, the president would have already been on his way back to safety.)

The quarantine itself became a comedy of errors—fortunately not a tragedy. A glove used for handling moon rocks imploded, mixing lunar gases with the outside air. Photo developer Terry Slezak touched a film magazine with moon dust on it and used his notoriety to promote a bar he owned. Heather Owens, described as an attractive twenty-three-year-old brunette, entered the all-male confines after she was splattered with blood droplets from a test mouse. It was said that a cockroach had been seen crawling out of the lab—and then crawled back inside. One of the back contamination committee members, Cornell microbiologist Martin Alexander, overheard NASA staffers saying the quarantine was a "sham" and that "the public needs to be comforted, and the quarantine serves that function."

* * *

Carl got out of Massachusetts General in late July. He had spent seven weeks in the hospital. The surgery left him with scars over much of his abdomen. He pressed Lester Grinspoon into a curious documentation project, insisting that Lester photograph the scars from all angles. Grinspoon himself is uncertain of Carl's motivations. He proposes only that Carl had a strong sense of his personal history and wanted to have a photographic record.

* * *

The astronauts left quarantine on August 10. They were in the pink of health. Lunar dust had been sprinkled on potted plants, fed to mice and Japanese pheasants, without so much as a mutation. NASA began parceling out lunar samples to scientists nationwide.

The first moon rocks were prizes rarer than sapphires. They were the ultimate scientific status symbol. A career-making discovery might lurk in the tiniest crystal or vesicle. Carl Sagan was not on the list of scientists who were supposed to get a lunar sample, but his boss, Tommy Gold, was.

Apollo 11 had offered little support for Gold's more dramatic ideas about lunar dust. When Neil Armstrong stepped onto the lunar surface, he reported that his boots sank "maybe an eighth of an inch." That was a dig at Gold, or so the press thought. Gold had helped design a James Bond–style camera for the astronauts. It was a "gun" they pointed at the ground to take close-up pictures of the lunar surface. To Gold's annoyance, Neil Armstrong used it as a walking stick.

These photos were not nearly as detailed as those that could be made on Earth. Gold intended to examine his sample under the most powerful microscope available. Although Cornell did not have a suitable microscope, there was one at the Corning glassworks, about an hour's drive from Ithaca.

Sagan insisted on accompanying Gold to the glassworks and seeing the first images. It wasn't enough for him to see the photos after Gold did; he wanted to be there, in the same room, seeing the photos at the same time Gold did. As Gold scrutinized the photos for evidence of the moon's geologic history, Sagan scanned them for spores, bacteria, fossils, *anything* that might bear on the question of life. Sagan found nothing. Gold determined that the dust was virtually indistinguishable from the fake dust in his famous vial.

*   *   *

In a couple of ways, Sagan was vindicated by the Apollo findings. Gas chromatography identified trace amounts of organic compounds in the lunar samples. NASA continued the quarantine procedure through Apollo 14. That mission brought back a drill sample of the lunar crust (as Sagan had proposed in 1962; but it was not the much deeper one Sagan wanted). The sample was "dead as doornail," Sagan conceded. That was enough for NASA; it dispensed with the quarantine thereafter.

Apollo 12 brought back a piece of Surveyor 3, an unpiloted probe that landed in 1967. NASA scientists discovered *Streptoccocus mitus* bacteria inside a foam insulation board. Possibly someone had sneezed near the Surveyor's TV camera, all precautions aside. The bacteria had survived two and a half years on the moon. "Probably," admitted Apollo 12 commander Pete Conrad, "the quarantine was a damn good idea."

A Flying Saucer with Rivets

The matter-of-fact reality of space travel did nothing to dim public interest in UFOs. The year of Apollo was also the year of the Condon report's publication. It of course concluded that the Blue Book files provided no reason to believe that the Earth was being visited by extraterrestrials. It was probably naive to think that the report would close the book once and for all on UFOs. Even some scientists weren't so sure about the report. Harold Urey, of all people, was quoted in the press as saying that the Condon report was wrong and UFOs were "real." Donald Menzel, a prominent skeptic, asked Urey what in the world he meant by saying that. Urey replied that he simply meant he had seen *lots* of UFOs and didn't know what they were; so they were real.

The Condon report's publication provided the occasion for a scientific debate on UFOs. Ever concerned with the antirationalist trends in American society, Sagan believed that a scientific examination of the UFO question would have didactic value, not only in showing the poor quality of evidence for extraterrestrial spaceships but in demonstrating how science works. In 1968 Sagan and Wesleyan University astronomer Thornton Page pitched the idea to the American Association for the Advancement of

Science (AAAS). The AAAS board approved and scheduled the symposium for its December 1969 meeting, so that participants would have had time to digest the Condon report.

The meeting was attacked for a variety of reasons. Linda tried her best to talk Carl out of it. She was relatively open to "new age" beliefs—relative to Carl, anyway—and did not think that anything was to be gained by attacking UFO believers. Many scientists hated the symposium for almost the opposite reason. They were mystified at why Sagan would think patent nonsense worthy of a symposium—no matter that millions of average folks believed in UFOs. Some threw up their hands and asked what's next, an *astrology* symposium? (Sagan didn't think that was necessarily such a bad idea.) One scientist threatened to report Sagan to vice president Spiro Agnew.

Sagan conceived the symposium as a moot court, with both sides being argued before a scientific jury. At that time, the most distinguished American scientist who was vocal about believing in UFOs as spaceships was probably James E. McDonald. McDonald was a tall, sandy-haired University of Arizona atmospheric physicist of about fifty. His specialty was clouds. A member of the National Academy of Sciences, McDonald had testified on UFOs before Congress. He complained that the scientific community laughed at the matter, while the government seemed to have a vested interest in "debunking" the phenomenon. When Sagan asked McDonald to present his case, he agreed.

McDonald conceded that the "signal-to-noise" ratio of UFO sightings was small. Many reports *could* be explained in conventional ways. There were outright fabrications, too. But McDonald believed that Sagan, the Condon committee, and the scientific community in general were being too hasty in discounting the "signal" because of the "noise."

McDonald focused on a "hard core" of well-attested and distinctly unusual sightings. As preparation for the symposium, Sagan and Philip Morrison investigated a number of UFO sightings, including some of McDonald's most credible cases. They found that it would often be the least reliable and/or most excitable witness who would report a UFO. When other witnesses were contacted, they would corroborate the story *up to a point*. Yes, they had seen *something*, but not the specific details that had made the first story so compelling.

One report looked particularly good on paper. It looked good because it contained a detailed mechanical drawing of the flying saucer a woman had seen. The UFO was made out of sheet metal riveted together. It was an Ed Wood flying saucer. Sagan and Morrison soon discovered that the drawing had been done by the witness's husband, a professional draftsman. He had not seen the flying saucer himself. He worked for a naval shipyard, drawing ships made out of . . . sheet metal and rivets. His wife had never claimed to see rivets on the flying saucer, not in so many words. The man had drawn what his wife *must have seen*.

Alien Abduction

By this time there was a new twist to the UFO literature: alien abductions with vaguely sexual "experimentation." This started with the celebrated case of Betty and Barney Hill, who claimed under hypnosis to have been abducted in 1961. A book about the recovered memory, *The Interrupted Journey*, became a best-seller. The story had everything: UFOs, sex, and race, for the Hills were an interracial couple. The Hills' story was considered powerful evidence for alien visitation in much of the UFO community—though not for James McDonald. He thought that people who said they had actually been onboard flying saucers were *noise*.

Lester Grinspoon knew the Hills' hypnotist, Benjamin Simon. He asked for and got permission to play the audiotapes of the Hills' hypnosis sessions for Sagan and McDonald.

The Hills' story was that, on the night of September 19–20, 1961, they saw a bright, starlike UFO during a drive through the White Mountains of New Hampshire. Upon arriving home, they were surprised to find the trip had taken two hours longer than they expected.

Betty read a book on UFOs and began having nightmares about being abducted by aliens. Soon both Barney and Betty were describing the UFO they had seen as looking not like a point of light but like a flying saucer—with little men glaring out the windows at them. They began seeing Simon, a Boston hypnotherapist. Using hypnosis, he elicited similar stories from Betty and Barney in separate sessions. They claimed that during the "missing" time, they had been paralyzed, taken aboard the flying saucer, and examined. Tiny gray aliens inserted a long needle into Betty's navel. The Hills seemingly had little to gain from telling their fantastic story. Barney worried that it would compromise his work with the NAACP.

In listening to the tapes, Sagan was struck by "the absolute terror" in Barney's voice. One feature of the story particularly commanded his attention.

At the time of Sholomitsky and Shklovskii's notorious 1966 news conference, the *New York Times* ran a map locating the (invisible to naked eye) radio source CTA-102 against the stars of the constellation Pegasus. Betty Hill saw that map. It reminded her of a similar map she had seen during her alien abduction. As Betty told it, she found herself alone in a room on the flying saucer with the head alien she called Leader. They had a strange conversation that was, one might say, Saganesque.

Betty asked Leader where the aliens came from. How much did *she* know about the universe? Leader asked. She admitted not much. She had once met the astronomer Harlow Shapley, who had written a wonderful book on the universe. "I had seen photographs that he had taken of millions and millions of stars in the universe."

Leader said he wished she knew more about the universe. A wall opened up and a three-dimensional map appeared. It was, by Betty's description, a random field of "stars" of various sizes, some connected by lines. Leader said the lines represented "trade routes" or "expeditions."

He asked Betty where *she* was on the map. After she admitted she didn't know, Leader grew curt. "If you don't know where you are, then there isn't any point of my telling where I am from," he said. He snapped the map away, back into wherever it had come from. When Betty asked him to show her the map again, he laughed sardonically.

Folie à Deux

A common skeptical position on "recovered memories" is that they are the result of a therapist cueing a compliant subject. Simon did not seem to fit that pattern. He was oddly noncommittal about the whole story. Grinspoon suggested that the Hills were a case of *folie à deux*; that is, one partner "goes along with" a fantasy concocted by the other. This acceptance reinforces the belief, and ultimately, both take the fantasy seriously.

Simon denied it was *folie à deux*. Yet he did not endorse the objective reality of the Hills' statements. Maybe, he proposed, it was only a "dream" (but not *folie à deux*!).

The symposium was held at the AAAS meeting in Boston, December 26 and 27, 1969. Participants included Donald Menzel, Philip Morrison, Frank Drake, UFO investigator J. Allen Hynek, and Walter Sullivan of the *New York Times*.

James McDonald's case amounted to the Sherlock Holmes maxim "Eliminate the impossible and whatever remains, however improbable, must be true." He believed he had exhausted all possible earthly explanations for his best cases. The "UFO problem," as he called it, could have only an improbable, and likely extraterrestrial, explanation. "I am enough of a realist," he said, "to sense that, unless this AAAS Symposium succeeds in making the scientific community aware of the seriousness of the UFO problem, little response to any call for new investigation is likely to appear."

Sagan found the appeal of the extraterrestrial hypothesis to be partly "religious."

> I think it is pretty clear that over the last few centuries science has systematically expropriated ideas which are the traditional concerns of religion. . . . At the same time, traditional forms of religion have been a very firm portion of nearly every culture of mankind; it is unlikely that the needs for belief in the gods, whether valid or not, can be destroyed so easily. In a scientific age what is a more reasonable and acceptable disguise for the classic religious mythos than the idea that we are being visited by messengers of a powerful, wise, and benign advanced civilization?

Much of what he said could apply equally to the appeal of Sagan's more scientifically legitimate conjectures about extraterrestrial life. In that sense, his words are a prophetic analysis of Sagan's own pop-culture celebrity of a few years hence.

Grinspoon and Alan D. Persky gave a presentation on the psychiatric aspects of UFOs, which were, after all, more likely to be germane than the astronomical ones. Grinspoon remarked that a widely publicized UFO sighting (one he was not at liberty to identify, for reasons of confidentiality) could best be understood as a case of *folie à deux*.

*　　*　　*

The symposium demonstrated that the emotions behind the UFO phenomenon were all too real. For people like James McDonald and Betty Hill, the aliens were a dream, or a nightmare, from which they would never wake. By the time the symposium's proceedings appeared in 1972 (as *UFO's—A Scientific Debate*), the debate had turned tragic.

A massive power blackout threw the northeastern United States into darkness. McDonald speculated that it had been caused by UFOs. In the vacuum of information, that statement received wide publicity. McDonald was subjected to sometimes merciless ridicule. When he testified before Congress on unrelated scientific matters, political opponents would bring up the fact that he believed in UFOs. There was a private despondency as well. In June 1971, McDonald went out into the Arizona desert, put a .38 revolver to his head, and pulled the trigger.

Message in a Bottle

As 1969 ended, NASA was readying Pioneer 10 for a flyby of the asteroid belt and Jupiter. As a side effect of the encounter with Jupiter, the craft would accelerate enough to escape the sun's gravity altogether. It would become the first human artifact to leave the solar system.

Eric Burgess, a writer for the *Christian Science Monitor*, and Richard Hoagland, a freelance writer, approached Sagan with the idea of putting a symbolic message on Pioneer—a greeting for any extraterrestrials who might find it. They figured Sagan would be the one capable of selling the idea to NASA. They were right. Sagan loved the idea, and NASA quickly approved it.

No one, least of all Sagan, thought it likely that anyone or anything would ever recover such a message. Pioneer was not headed for a nearby star. Orbital mechanics would fling it in what amounts to a random direction, and stars are scattered so thinly that the craft could wander through space for a time much greater than the age of the universe without ever encountering a star, much less an inhabited solar system. If you even wanted to *fantasize* about ETs finding the message (as Sagan did in his writings about the message), you would have to imagine that the ETs had technology capable of detecting and retrieving alien artifacts in deep space.

Sagan was put in charge of designing the message. He conceived it as an etched metal plaque. Because any physical object would affect the spacecraft's center of gravity, the probe design couldn't be finalized until NASA had the finished plaque in hand. That meant they needed it almost immediately.

After the NASA meeting in Washington, Sagan flew to San Juan for the December 1969 meeting of the American Astronomical Society. During a ten-minute coffee break, Sagan buttonholed Frank Drake in the hotel corridor and told him about the message. Sagan asked Drake what he thought they should put on the plaque. They quickly came to a consensus. They needed pictures of human beings, a diagram of the solar system, and a location map showing where the solar system was situated in the galaxy.

The location map was the tricky part. Imagine sketching a map of North America on a cocktail napkin, pinpointing your house so precisely that someone could drive there. Worse—since we scarcely know what our galaxy looks like as seen from afar—imagine doing this back when maps showed the Northwest Passage cutting across Canada and California as an island. Still worse, imagine the map will not be used for a billion years, at which time continental drift will have totally altered the globe's appearance.

Sagan suggested a star map showing the Big Dipper and other constellations as seen from Earth. Although the aliens wouldn't recognize our constellations (which themselves change over millennia), it was conceivable that they would maintain a great database of the positions of all the stars in the Galaxy. They might be able to plug in the map and surmise just when and where you had to be to see the Big Dipper.

Drake improved on that. He had become quite an expert on LGM—later identified as neutron stars, or pulsars (Drake himself coined the latter term). Pulsars are easily detected throughout the Galaxy, and their frequency slows with time. A pulsar map specifying the current frequencies would allow the ETs to pinpoint us in time and space—again, assuming that they kept very good astronomical records.

Sagan asked Drake if he could deliver the pulsar map almost immediately. Drake said he could, and so the content of the message was settled by the end of the coffee break.

Linda produced the plaque's drawing of a nude man and woman. As diversity conscious as her husband, she attempted to draw figures of composite ethnicities. Her sketch for the woman blended Asian and European features. The man was a mix of African and European. The translation to the medium of etched gold made the figures look more Caucasian. The woman's hair, conceived as black but shown only in outline, looked blond; the man's Afro looked more like curly Mediterranean hair.

Pornography in Space

Two six-by-nine-inch flight plaques were produced, made of gold-anodized aluminum. In March 1972, the first was launched toward Jupiter aboard Pioneer 10. Another followed on Pioneer 11. Whatever the odds of the plaque achieving its nominal aim, it was extensively deciphered and deconstructed by humans. The Pioneer plaque became an iconic image, the subject of cartoons, graffiti, and unauthorized commercial reproductions in such media as tapestry and silver medals.

Some people thought that Linda Sagan's demure nudes were pornographic. Among them was the caretaker of Cornell's Space Sciences Building. The *Philadelphia Inquirer* erased the woman's nipples and the man's genitals from its illustration. "A family newspaper must uphold community standards," explained one of its editors. The *Chicago Sun Times* printed an unexpurgated picture, then thought better of it. From one edition to the next, the male figure's genitals mysteriously vanished. The *Catholic Review* thought that the plaque should have had a picture of praying hands rather than nudes. The *Los Angeles Times* printed the plaque daringly complete, for which it received an irate letter:

I must say I was shocked by the blatant display of both male and female sex organs on the front page of the *Times*. . . . Isn't it enough that we must tolerate the bombardment of pornography through the media of film and smut magazines? Isn't it bad enough that our own space agency officials have found it necessary to spread this filth even beyond our own solar system?

As usual, the *New York Daily News* had the definitive headline: "Nudes and Map Tell about Earth to Other Worlds."

*   *   *

There was a feminist critique of the plaque. Some objected that the woman's posture indicated subservience to the male. They wanted to know why the man's hand was raised, but not the woman's. The most blatant phallocentrism was to be found in the absence of the woman's vaginal slit.

This led to a story that NASA had censored the plaque. Sagan denied any pressure on the part of NASA but admitted some *self*-censorship. He and Linda kept the drawing unprovocative in order to ensure that NASA would have no objections. "In retrospect," Sagan wrote, "we may have judged NASA's scientific-political hierarchy as more puritanical than it is." He claimed that Linda had based the figure partly on ancient Greek sculpture and that such sculpture did not conventionally have a slit for the vagina.

It also appeared that Linda's composite figures had the uncanny quality of being perceived as the viewer's own ethnicity. A Nigerian newspaper speculated on why NASA had depicted Africans. Asians saw them as Asian. The *Berkeley Barb* captioned a picture of the plaque "Hello. We're from Orange County"—implying the figures to be particularly square Caucasians.

Viva Zapata

Carl and Linda conceived a child at just about the time they were conceiving the Pioneer message. In September 1970 Linda gave birth by cesarean section. It was a boy. The couple devised a name epitomizing the sensibilities of the age: Nicholas Julian Zapata Sagan. *Nicholas* was Greek for "victory," as in *victory for the people*; Julian stood for civil rights leader Julian Bond and also for Julian the Apostate, the Roman emperor who renounced Christianity; and Zapata, for Emiliano Zapata, the Mexican revolutionary.

In one letter, Rachel Sagan carefully typed out the full name, allowing each name a separate line as if it were a strange poem. "As the hard-hats say," she wrote to Cari, "you better believe it."

Rachel had no problem with the name's owner. Almost from the moment of his portentous birth, Nick showed signs of remarkable verbal abilities. A family friend jostling the nine-month-old infant crooned *"Up and . . ."* Nick chimed in *"down!"* It was apparently his first word—and it was in context. Exposed to *Sesame Street*, he had absorbed not only the sounds of words but the concept of opposites.

Within a short time he was speaking as well as a much older child. He was able to discourse on his preverbal existence, recalling, for instance, the time he realized that (still-nameless) colors differed from one another. Incredibly, these memories extended all the way back to his surgically assisted birth. He remembered the experience as *red* and then *cold*.

Viking

The moon landing accomplished, NASA suffered a lack of direction. The agency's future depended on capturing the public imagination with a mission as appealing as Apollo—though much less expensive. Had Carl Sagan not existed, the space agency would have done well to invent him (it might have lacked the imagination to do so). It was Sagan more than anyone who framed the robotic exploration of the solar system as a quest for life. Sagan made it possible for NASA to enter the next, and scientifically most productive, phase of its existence.

NASA was again planning a lander mission to Mars. Called Viking, it was approved in 1968, a year after Congress pulled the plug on the more costly Voyager. Viking would be the first craft to do real science from the surface of Mars. Prominent among its goals was a search for life.

For Sagan, Viking was an irresistible gamble. He and about 100 other scientists staked some of their most productive years on a mission whose success would yield immense payoffs. But if Viking crashed or malfunctioned, the mission's scientists were out of luck. The only insurance policy was that there were *two* Vikings.

Sagan was, with some justification, christened the "guiding spirit" of the Viking project by the press. More concretely, he played two main roles. He was one of four original experimenters on the Viking lander imagery team, the group in charge of what the press called Viking's "television cameras." Taking ground-level pictures of Mars was, arguably, the most important of all Viking's scientific duties. Thomas ("Tim") Mutch, a geologist at Brown University, headed the imaging team. By the time of the landing, the team had increased to seven, including Jim Pollack and Stanford's Elliott Levinthal.

Sagan was not directly involved in the design of Viking's biology experiments. Two distinct biology teams handled that. Joshua Lederberg and Wolf Vishniac were on the "active biology" team; Melvin Calvin, Harold Urey, and Leslie Orgel were on the "molecular analysis" team.

Sagan's other main role was as one of a dozen or so scientists advising on the selection of places to land the two Viking craft. The landing site deliberations are well documented, for Sagan (characteristically) had insisted on it. Minutes were kept, and Sagan often showed up with written memos that were, so to speak, read into the record. His memos were well reasoned and lucid; to some, he must have come off like the kid who always does the extra-credit homework.

This landing site working group met for the first time on September 2, 1970, at MIT. The meeting was a brainstorming session in which A. Thomas Young, Viking's "science integration manager," urged the group to verbalize what they wanted in a landing site, without worrying about practicality for the time being. That being Sagan's forte, he dominated the discussion. He observed that biologists, meteorologists, and geologists each had different things they wanted to see on Mars. Biologists wanted to land where the chances of life would be greatest, in the warmest, moistest regions of Mars. Meteorologists wanted to land where they might see clouds, fog, or dust devils. They wanted to watch the seasons change in the dark areas and/or at the polar caps. Geologists wanted to see a variety of features and, with luck, experience a Mars quake.

By the December 2–3, 1970, meeting, Sagan already had a list of six favorite landing spots and a memo outlining a *philosophy* of site selection. The philosophy was based on the need to balance science with "survivability." Sagan concurred with team member Alan Binder's sentiment that "a crashed lander is not very useful even if it did crash in the most interesting part of the planet."

Sagan therefore maintained that Viking 1's site should be chosen with great weight placed on safety. *If* Viking 1 landed without incident, then a more interesting, higher-risk site might be in order for Viking 2. It was agreed all around that the team lacked the information to make any final decision. They needed better photographs of Mars. That would come with Mariners 8 and 9 and with the Vikings' own photography as they approached the planet.

*   *   *

In 1970 Sagan lost a valued collaborator at Cornell. Jim Pollack accepted an offer to move west, to NASA Ames Research Center. The scientific relationship between Sagan and Pollack was so close and so complementary that some likened it to the left and right sides of the brain. The analogy was not always in Sagan's favor. When one MIT scientist heard of the move, he remarked that the *thinking* side of the brain had moved to California.

Shoes for Shklovskii

Sagan finally got to *meet* another of his collaborators: I. S. Shklovskii. A welcome thaw in the Soviet Union allowed Shklovskii to travel to the West.

He was just past fifty, a bespectacled man who could, by turns, look distinguished or flash an infectious, Alfred E. Neuman grin. Shklovskii would arrive in the United States dressed for Russian winter, an exuberant tourist insisting on seeing Disneyland, the Brooklyn Bridge, Mount Palomar, burlesque shows, kosher restaurants, the Statue of Liberty, any museum with paintings by El Greco, and the site of the Kennedy assassination. Shklovskii took the liberty of making a personal investigation into JFK's death. His conclusion: a single marksman stationed in the book depository.

Shklovskii's English was fluent enough to permit displays of wit. (When he had something funny to say, he would grab Sagan by the elbow or poke him about the lapel—anything to keep him from missing the joke.) He was entranced by Western consumer goods. Shklovskii once stopped dead in his tracks in front of a window display of *shoes*. He could see that the workmanship was *excellent*. He went in and bought a pair, explaining that Russian shoes were junk.

No Western good delighted Shklovskii more than a pack of pornographic playing cards he found in Berkeley. He particularly liked the way there was a *different* girlie picture on each card. Shklovskii told Sagan that the deck would make fifty-two presents for friends back in the Soviet Union.

On the same trip, he bought a slogan button of the sort popular in the 1960s, saying "Pray for Sex." "In your country," Shklovskii explained, "this slogan is offensive for one reason. In my country, two reasons."

Shklovskii's American spending binges were restrained by the fact that traveling Soviet scientists were not permitted much walking-around money. During one visit, Shklovskii didn't have enough money to pay for lunch. His American companions joked that Shklovskii ought to be *rich* by now.

"How's that—rich?" Shklovskii asked.

"Come on, your book with Sagan came out in paperback. That's worth tens of thousands of dollars!"

Shklovskii had to explain that the Soviet Union had not signed international copyright agreements. The book's publisher, Fred Murphy at Holden-Day, was not legally obligated to pay him anything—and he had *not* paid him anything.

When this story got back to Sagan, he contacted Murphy (a friend of his from Chicago) and insisted he pay Shklovskii. In due course, Holden-Day sent Shklovskii a royalty check, handsome by American standards and phenomenal by Russian ones. Shklovskii never cashed it. He feared it would get him in trouble with the KGB.

Hurtling Moons of Barsoom

One of Shklovskii's pet notions, discussed in *Intelligent Life in the Universe*, was that Phobos and Deimos, Mars's two unusually small moons, were space stations built by intelligent Martians. The two moons were just pinpoints of light in the biggest telescopes, and no one knew much about them. Shklovskii observed that some reported anomalies in Phobos's orbit could be explained with the assumption that Phobos was *hollow*. Moons don't get hollow by themselves. Therefore, someone must have hollowed it out.

How much Shklovskii believed this theory is hard to say. One colleague downplayed it as something Shklovskii mentioned when he gave popular lectures and had to grab a jaded public's attention. But Shklovskii insisted his space stations "weren't just a joke."

Dangling this idea in front of Sagan was like teasing a dog with meat. This is not to say that he believed it, either. But early in the mission planning for Mariners 8 and 9, Sagan noticed that the craft would pass by both of Mars's moons. He began looking at ways to take the first detailed photos of the moons.

All it would take, he determined, was to move a scan platform. Sagan floated his idea at the Jet Propulsion Laboratory (JPL) and found the staff receptive. Then he took the plan to NASA. The agency management shot it down. There was a mission plan, they said, a thick book detailing what the mission was about. Phobos and Deimos were not mentioned in that book. That meant they couldn't be photographed.

Sagan bounced back with a new argument. Forget about Shklovskii's idea; the moons are very likely captured asteroids. In that case, photographing them with the Mariners would be like a free trip to the asteroid belt. It would, yes, *save NASA money*—to the tune of $200 million, which Sagan pegged as the cost of mounting an asteroid belt mission. This argument got a somewhat more sympathetic hearing.

The plan was for Mariner 8 to map the planet, while Mariner 9 would concentrate on the dark areas and their seasonal changes. That plan changed abruptly after Mariner 8's liftoff on May 8, 1971. The Centaur rocket engine conked out unexpectedly. Rocket and probe fell into the ocean. Mariner 9 lifted off on May 30. It was now a solo mission.

Fortune Cookie

Even as Sagan was busy with Mariner and Viking, he was publishing actively. A series of lectures at the University of Oregon was issued in book form as *Planetary Exploration* (1970). Sagan was coeditor of proceedings on *Planetary Atmospheres* (1971), *Space Research* (1971), and the aforementioned *UFOs—A Scientific Debate* (1972), which was revised and brought out by the commercial publisher W. W. Norton in 1974. Sagan also had a small advisory role in a volume on *The Air War in Indochina* (1971). He was such an expert on life, terrestrial and otherwise, that he was commissioned to write the *Encyclopaedia Britannica* entry on "Life."

Sagan's expanding career as a writer caught the attention of Jerome Agel. Agel was a so-called book packager, someone in the business of spotting trends and up-and-coming people and arranging to have books written by or about them. Sagan met with Agel at a Polynesian restaurant in Boston. Agel told Sagan that he ought to write a popular book. Sagan agreed. They tossed around ideas for an informal book that would discuss the search for life beyond the Earth and what contact with extraterrestrial intelligence might mean.

Sagan vowed to give it a try. At the end of the meal, he opened a fortune cookie that read, "You will shortly be called upon to decipher an important message."

Smokey the Bear

Sagan took a leave of absence for the 1971–72 academic year. He and Linda spent most of the year in California, where Sagan was working at JPL during Mariner 9's encounter with Mars. They gave up their rented house in Ithaca and put their furniture in storage. They had, meanwhile, begun construction on a new house on a lot with an impressive view of Lake Cayuga.

A couple of months before Mariner reached Mars, Sagan realized a dream he had nursed since about 1967: a truly international conference on extraterrestrial intelligence.

Sagan had proposed the idea to Soviet astrophysicist Nikolai Kardashev, a student of Shklovskii's. Kardashev had wanted to be an astronomer ever since age five, when his mother took him to a show at the Moscow Planetarium. Beneath the darkened dome of artificial night, costumed actors portrayed vignettes from the lives of the great astronomers. Kardashev began his study by asking his mother how many points the stars in the sky had. Her answer was five; the stars in the heavens could be no different from those on the Soviet flag.

Kardashev started building support for the conference in the Soviet bureaucracy. Czech astronomer Rudolf Pesek was also brought in on the planning. He offered to host the meeting; for a while, it looked as if the meeting would take place in Czechoslovakia. Then Soviet tanks rolled into Prague. One thing led to another, and the meeting was moved to the Byurakan Astrophysical Observatory in Soviet Armenia. It took place September 5–11, 1971.

Although not so well known as Green Bank, the Byurakan meeting had a much bigger and more diverse group of participants. It was Sagan's most glittering scientific salon. By design, Byurakan was no Trekkie convention. They invited brilliant people who were not "true believers" in extraterrestrial intelligence. Thus it had real debates. Sagan had insisted on this broadly multidisciplinary group against the objections of Kardashev, who maintained that anyone who was not an astronomer or radio physicist was a "philosopher," which is to say, a *windbag*.

The group of over fifty included biologists, archaeologists, cryptographers, linguists, anthropologists, historians, and philosophers. SETI had become a humanist (though still pretty much a white male) pursuit. On hand were Philip Morrison and Frank Drake (they sat on the American organizing committee with Sagan), Francis Crick, Freeman Dyson, Thomas Gold, David Hubel, Marvin Minsky, Leslie Orgel, Charles Townes, and William McNeill. Absent was John Lilly; playing a somewhat analogous role was ethnographer Richard Lee, who was at any rate full of entrancing stories. Lee had lived with baboons. "The main thing," he told Shklovskii, "is not to look full-grown males in the eye."

*   *   *

Byurakan, a windswept village of unpaved streets and free-ranging livestock, sits over a mile above sea level. The brilliant blue water of nearby Lake Sevan nestles among mountains as bare and treeless as Nevada. Also visible from the village (though across the border in Turkey) is Mount Ararat, the legendary peak where Noah's ark is said to have come to rest.

The observatory lies at the base of another peak, Mount Aragatz. It is a good place for an observatory. At night, the surroundings are eerily dark, a grim consequence of the Armenian genocide.

Sagan's cochair on the Soviet organizing committee was Viktor Ambartsumian, autocratic director of the Byurakan observatory. He was a great lumbering bear of a man, and the observatory was his Xanadu. In this barren corner of the world he had decreed a showplace of technology and a garden paradise. He lived in a big house close to the telescopes. Fruit orchards and manicured beds of flowers (coaxed into November bloom) covered the grounds. Observatory phones were linked to the outside world via laser beam. A jittery red pinpoint of light was a laser shot from Erevan, fifteen miles distant, and capable of carrying twenty-four simultaneous conversations with crystal clarity.

Ambartsumian was the local hero, a fervently patriotic Armenian who had made good in the Soviet system. The Russians felt he looked down on them as barbarians. The Americans felt that Ambartsumian looked like Smokey the Bear. They communicated the joke to Shklovskii, who was unfamiliar with the forest-fire-fighting cartoon bear, but who concurred that Ambartsumian did look like *a* bear. Shklovskii took to calling Ambartsumian Ursa Major.

*   *   *

By American standards, the meeting was rife with tourism horror stories. Customs lines were interminable and required even after flight segments within the Soviet Union. It seemed to be the practice to search luggage when it was loaded onto a plane *and* when it was taken off again. After a twenty-minute wait in a stalled customs line, a Soviet official took mercy on the irate Americans, granting them the rare privilege of bypassing customs. They were instructed to climb onto the luggage delivery racks and crawl backward on their hands and knees, dragging their baggage—*quickly*, before anyone noticed.

Sagan convinced NASA to pay for a stenotypist so that the proceedings could be recorded and published. (The book, gracefully edited by Sagan, was published by MIT Press in 1973 as *Communication with Extraterrestrial Intelligence (CETI)*.) The stenotype machine almost didn't make it through customs. The Soviet authorities suspected it was a *Xerox machine*. They had heard about those Xerox machines, capable of making thousands of copies of official state documents. While it was plain that the stenotype machine was *not* a Xerox machine, the Russians feared that, by pushing some concealed button, it might be switched to Xerox machine mode.

Attendees had to bribe Soviet officials to obtain taxis, then run half a mile in driving rain and darkness to get to where the black-market taxis were. Philip and Phylis Morrison were talked into looking after some other people's luggage—a mistake, given how much they'd be lugging it themselves, and in what weather.

The rigors of travel to Ambartsumian's Shangri-la of flowers and telescopes made for an informal meeting. There were few ties and jackets. Sagan wore sport shirts, open at the collar, the sleeves rolled up. Spirits were high. Marvin Minsky brought along some great ice breakers: Frisbees and toy rockets. The Soviets, who had never seen Frisbees before, were dumbfounded.

And Shklovskii was . . . Shklovskii. One long-winded Soviet astronomer spoke on a theory that all the great scientific accomplishments—of Newton, Darwin, Einstein, and so forth—were conceived during periods when sunspots were most active. Shklovskii's eyes met Sagan's. Yes, Shklovskii said, but *this* theory must have been conceived in a year when there were *no* sunspots. It was characteristic of Shklovskii that he said this loud enough that everyone in the room could hear.

Condensation Theory

The participants met each day in a conference room at the observatory, more spacious and comfortable than the one at Green Bank. Once again, the Drake equation provided a framework for discussion. As emcee, Sagan began with a recap of the equation, then introduced speakers who had expertise on specific factors.

Tommy Gold spoke first on the formation of solar systems and Earth-like planets. He showed computer models of hypothetical solar systems. They seemed to imply that our own solar system's design, with small rocky planets near the sun and bigger, gaseous ones farther out, was a common one.

Ambartsumian objected that this computer modeling stuff was all *too* hypothetical. They ought to stick to *real* findings about *real* stars. He went on for some time about flare stars. They had not been mentioned until then, and their relevance was hard to discern. Philip Morrison diplomatically asked Ambartsumian a question about flare stars. After Ambartsumian's answer, Gold said that he was *glad* Ambartsumian had given that *background material . . .* and tried to drag the discussion back to the formation of planets.

A short while later, Ambartsumian commented that he was "slightly skeptical of the condensation theory."

Gold had been talking about how planets condense out of disks of gas. That was how virtually *every* late-twentieth-century astronomer believed planets were formed. Ambartsumian's comment was like a biologist being "slightly skeptical of evolution."

None of the astronomers dared touch the remark. It took David Hubel, a neurologist, to confess ignorance. Hubel allowed that probably all the *astronomers* there knew what Ambartsumian was talking about, but speaking as a *non*astronomer: what, exactly, was Ambartsumian talking about? Other than condensation, what possibilities were there?

"The disintegration of superdense bodies," Ambartsumian replied. There had been *articles* written on it, he added. No one else seemed to have read those articles.

The discussion turned to Barnard's star, a nearby red dwarf star. Weak evidence suggested that it might have planets. Sagan warned of "G star chauvinism." There was a tendency to think that *only* stars like our sun could support life. Sagan believed that planets of small red stars, such as Barnard's star, might support life as well. Red dwarfs have long, stable lives, measured in tens of billions of years.

Ambartsumian contended that there was an article saying that many red stars were actually quite young. Especially *flare stars*. Sagan gingerly asked if that article applied to Barnard's star.

It was only a "statistical calculation," shrugged Ambartsumian.

Wild Card

The quality of debate improved with the next discussion. Ambartsumian was mostly silent; Sagan, and SETI itself, were on the hot seat.

The discussion treated the likelihood of life originating on a planet. Sagan served as the first speaker. He remained the optimist. The experiments of Miller and Urey, Ponnamperuma, Fox, Orgel—and Sagan's own experiments—had produced all the principal amino acids, sugars, and nucleotides present in life today. Life-as-we-know-it evolved out of the very molecules most likely to form.

Sagan conceded that we cannot estimate the probability of life evolving from statistics (we know of only one planet that has life) or from a deep understanding of the mechanisms involved (which we lack). In estimating the chance of life developing, Sagan said that we had to use something he called "subjective probability." This is the "probability" of gut instincts and educated guesses.

Sagan put the subjective probability of life arising on a suitable planet at virtually 100 percent.

His main adversary was none other than Francis Crick. Crick of course owned a 50 percent share in the greatest biological discovery of the century. He was naturally conscious of his scientific contributions and ever defensive about his portrayal in James Watson's *The Double Helix*. (Watson had all but painted his colleague as an amiable doofus who got lucky.) There was, in any event, another side to Crick, that of a skilled and unyielding debater. Crick did not think much of Sagan's subjective probability.

No one, he observed, had ever sealed a glass tube full of chemicals and shocked it into producing anything *living*. Crick said that in order to display the difference between my position and Professor Sagan's, I have to make an analogy and I am sorry it is so conventional. Consider a man who has been dealt a hand of playing cards. The character of his hand is that he has to have one particular sequence, one particular combination of cards. We know that this is a rare event and it is not reasonable to try to estimate the probability of the event simply because it has happened to us. Professor Sagan's argument is that there are plenty of playing cards. But we have only a unique event and strict probability theory says that we are not allowed to deduce probability in that way.

Sagan replied:

Professor Crick and I are playing different card games. In his interesting playing card analogy, I do not believe there is only one sequence of cards which wins. My expectation is that there are many paths to the origin of life, and that the joint probability that one of them has been taken on a suitable planet over billions of years is rather high.

The best evidence for Sagan's case was the fossil record. He mentioned that the oldest fossils then known, of blue-green algae, were about 3.2 billion years old, and that they were not likely to be the oldest that would ever be found. (He was right; the current oldest-known fossils are 3.9 billion years old.) That meant that life had started early, within the first third of the Earth's existence. Considering that the *very* early Earth must have been too hot or unstable for life, the time it took for life to evolve must have been only a few hundred million years or less. "This, to me, speaks rather persuasively for a rapid origin of life on the primitive earth." And if life formed rapidly, that suggested that it was not such a rare thing.

*   *   *

Crick made the telling point that they had to be concerned not only with the *values* of the Drake equation factors but with the *uncertainties* in those values.

The Green Bank group of ten years earlier had been perfectly aware that their estimates carried large and impossible-to-evaluate uncertainties. Sagan himself sometimes called the Drake formula an "entertainment." It is harmless fun to plug in numbers, just as long as you realize they are liable to be off by orders of magnitude. Still, SETI optimists always had an over-stuffed cushion to fall back on: the unimaginably huge scale of the universe. Sagan maintained that it is difficult to argue ETI out of existence by plugging "pessimistic" estimates into the Drake equation. There are orders of magnitude to spare.

Or are there? Crick's fear was garbage in, garbage out. If just one of the factors in the Drake equation was a wild card, *impossible to evaluate at all* with our present knowledge, then that *total uncertainty* would be transmitted to the final result. The Drake equation would fail. It would give a number that wouldn't mean anything.

If the chance of life getting started on a suitable planet were 1 in 1 million (instead of Sagan's 1 in 1), then we might expect to find we were alone in the Galaxy. Sagan's confidence in communicative life in the Galaxy would be unwarranted. Crick was not saying that life *was* so unlikely an occurrence. He was saying, rather, that we had no reason to be confident it wasn't unlikely.

The discussion ended with this difference between Sagan and Crick unresolved. Philip Morrison, a great gentleman and diplomat of science, concluded: "If there is anything more to be said about these probability arguments, it can be said by the probability theorists; it is a complicated problem and I think they can handle it themselves. It seems to me that eloquent proponents of both positions have had their say."

Armenian Breakfast

Harvard's David Hubel gave a presentation on the evolution of intelligence. (He apologized in advance if his talk was unclear, citing jet lag and "Academician Ambartsumian who insisted that we have an Armenian breakfast complete with cognac.") Hubel confessed that he did not know why or how intelligence evolved. There are successful life-forms like insects that have been around for hundreds of millions of years, filling diverse niches, and (in some cases) living in highly organized social groups with "language" of a sort—yet never evolving what we would call intelligence. "I have not the slightest idea what it is that has caused one group of animals to evolve along a direction leading to high intelligence and others to go the direction of the insect, ending in a sort of evolutionary cul de sac."

Crick's hand-of-cards analogy was perhaps more relevant here than for the origin of life. Sagan could not cite the fossil record in defense. Intelligence evolved very late in the Earth's history, on the morning of December 31 by Sagan's cosmic-calendar analogy.

Life with the !Kung

This discussion was followed by Richard Lee's talk on the evolution of technology. (Lee had lived with the !Kung Bushmen of the Kalahari desert for several years, learning their language and sharing their way of life. He was so comfortable living out in the open that he alarmed the Soviets by spending one night outdoors in Byurakan, the better to appreciate the sunrise.) Lee's thesis was that intelligence is synonymous with language—but neither necessarily implies technology. Lee praised the oral culture of the !Kung. The stories they tell around their campfires are full of wit, irony, metaphor, symbolism, and everything else we associate with the literature, theater, or cinema of an "advanced" culture. But the !Kung have never taken up agriculture, have few tools or material possessions, and no domestic animals save the dog.

It was, then, a mystery to Lee why technology arose in some societies and not in others. But Lee did not believe it an unlikely event. He thought it would happen sooner or later, once an intelligent species with language existed.

*   *   *

William McNeill, a University of Chicago historian, had a complaint to lodge. The Drake equation always struck him as arbitrary. He didn't see why there were 3 factors representing the chance of a technological civilization developing. Why not 4 or 5 or 6 factors? And if you did put in more factors, each less than 1, that would make the final answer smaller, wouldn't it?

Sagan agreed that the particular form of the equation *was* arbitrary. You could break it down further and make a formula with *100* factors in it.

At least, McNeill said.

Or *1,000* factors in it, Sagan continued. But the final answer would be the same.

McNeill didn't see how that was possible.

Shklovskii, mystified at what they were even talking about, asked McNeill to restate his problem.

Sagan and Leslie Orgel then valiantly collaborated on an analogy that kept getting longer and longer. Suppose, Orgel said, you were traveling from Cambridge to Erevan. You might break the trip down into *three* stages: from Cambridge to London, from London to Moscow, and Moscow to Erevan. The chances of making any one of these short trips would be larger than those of making the full Cambridge-to-Erevan trip; but, multiplying the three probabilities together, you would get the same result. And if there was *another* way you could get to Erevan via Budapest, *that* probability would have to be added in. . . .

"If someone managed with great difficulty to accomplish the Budapest-Erevan flight," continued Sagan, "he might conclude it is almost impossible to reach Erevan. But the pathway via Moscow makes arrival in Erevan much more likely."

"So, that is why it doesn't make any difference how many [factors] we have," Orgel concluded triumphantly.

Still baffled, McNeill gave up.

Golden Age

What would aliens look like? has long been a favored question of journalists. While Sagan thought it was unanswerable, Frank Drake preferred to conjure the memorable image that "if you saw them from a distance of a hundred yards in the twilight you might think they were human." At Byurakan, Marvin Minsky cited an article by Isaac Asimov (who was not present) in which Asimov had reasoned that a plausible intelligent alien would be bilaterally symmetrical and would have sense organs concentrated near the brain to minimize reaction time. In other words, aliens would have *faces*.

Tommy Gold agreed that aliens would have eyes more or less like our own. He mentioned the octopus and squid. They live in an environment as different from dry land as another planet would be different from the Earth, yet they have (independently of vertebrates) evolved eyes with a pupil, iris, and retina. Gold maintained that this basic eye design was dictated by the physics of light. It was not a caprice of evolution but something that might be expected of an active creature on any planet.

This view was itself partly in the eye of the beholder. Neurologist Hubel objected that octopus eyes are not all that similar to ours. Their receptor cells *de*polarize in light, he said. Ours *hyper*polarize.

*   *   *

I. S. Shklovskii's aliens would have neither eyes nor faces. He was the next speaker, and his nominal topic was the most speculative of all. It was the average lifetime of an advanced civilization. He did not attempt to estimate this; rather, he tried to imagine how an advanced extraterrestrial civilization might be different from our own. Shklovskii proposed that the most advanced civilizations in the Galaxy would not be biological. They would be computers, robots, something of that order.

Gunther Stent (the Berkeley virologist who had tried to discourage Lynn Margulis's chloroplast DNA research) took up this speculative bent from an opposite perspective. Stent predicted that human society was about to undergo a profound transformation. The new condition of the human race he called the Golden Age.

In the Golden Age creativity would be obsolete. This had allegedly happened in Tang dynasty China, where (in Stent's analysis) a broad cultural fluorescence achieved such an unprecedented level of security and comfort as to enervate all subsequent creative impulses. It had happened in Polynesia, where (again, in Stent's understanding) the luxuriant natural environment eradicated the will to dominate nature. Polynesians sought *harmony* with nature. Creativity in the arts and sciences was pointless and ceased to exist.

Our own society, of course, was different, said Stent. We are a "Faustian" society in which Nietzsche's "will to power" is inculcated in every infant. Stent believed nonetheless that the global, technological culture was soon to enter its own Golden Age. Things would get so comfortable that people would cease to innovate.

Stent believed that similar Golden Ages would overtake extraterrestrial societies. Paradise was inevitable. Perfect societies, the "galactic Polynesian archipelago," would focus on their inhabitants' inner tranquillity. And they would have better things to do than communicate with galactic civilizations.

* * *

This vision of Nirvana, of unsurpassable cosmic harmony, was a great provocation to certain people from MIT.

Surely, asked Bernard Burke (an MIT physicist), there would be *some* room in Stent's "soft Apocalypse" for rare creative genius? The great pinnacles of art and science were the achievements of a relative few. In our own, imperfect age, when most people produced useful goods, there was still a place for "a few academics to discuss abstruse subjects."

Stent apologized for not making himself more clear. It was not that the Golden Age would *forbid* creativity. In the future, the *desire* to innovate would be absent, even in the nominally creative minority.

Marvin Minsky would have none of "the horrifying Golden Age of Doctor Stent." He seconded, and elaborated on, Shklovskii's vision of post-biological society.

Minsky allowed "a sentimental attachment to one's biological shell." However, the advantages to becoming mechanical were too great to pass up. A truly advanced society would have the sense to transmute itself into a species of small and powerful robots durable enough for interstellar travel or whatever adventures brave technologic posterity might offer.

"I will simply have to play poker with you," Minsky confided, "and say that I have here in my hand some evidence that artificial intelligence exists."

It was no bluff. The evidence was the doctoral dissertation of MIT student Terry Winograd. Winograd had developed a program that could discourse in complex and relatively natural-sounding language about a "universe" of toylike colored blocks arrayed on a tabletop. It was a signal breakthrough for AI, and at that moment, no one could say how far its momentum would carry the field. Minsky claimed that Winograd's program represented a significant fraction of human intelligence.

What fraction? Philip Morrison wanted to know. Minsky put it at somewhere between 1 part in 10 and 1 part in 1 million. It was another of those order-of-magnitude estimates.

Tommy Gold spoke up. Had they considered the virtues of "very large and powerful machines . . . machines of enormous size and power"?

He entranced the group—or rather a subset of it—with the most flagrant technophilia. Our present machines, said Gold, were still scaled to the hands and minds of mere biologic mortals. Some day, *machines* would build *machines* . . . and machines would *design* machines. Very likely, they would grow to enormous proportions.

Gold's fantasy turned subterranean. The big machines would dig for ores, more efficiently than human miners, providing the cheap raw materials for the production of even more gargantuan machines. There would be a *feedback loop*. Gold boldly prophesied that big machines would burrow sixty kilometers under the Earth for ore, reroute the Mississippi River to California, manufacture artificial foods.

"I believe huge change should be contemplated," Gold said. "In fact, I don't understand why we haven't moved in that direction yet."

Minsky, heartened by these remarks, bid the group not to neglect the possibilities of *small* machines. His laboratory was working on them, too. The potential of this nanotechnology was fantastic. He affirmed, in short, that the problems of the world were best handled "by an aggressive technological expansion."

Boy Scouts

Not the least remarkable thing about Sagan was his synthesis of these two great and seemingly antithetical streams of Western thought. Sagan spoke next on the Drake equation's final result, the number of advanced civilizations in the galaxy. Encapsulating and, where necessary, reconciling all that had been said, Sagan came to a conclusion that was less optimistic than Green Bank's by a factor of 10. The "streamlined version" of the equation now set the number of advanced civilizations in the Galaxy at about one-tenth of the average lifetime (in years) of such civilizations.

Shklovskii had not advanced a figure for the lifetime. Sagan proposed 10 million years. He argued that perhaps only 1 percent of civilizations avoid planetary holocaust, but those that did would achieve a peaceful steady state and last for geologically long times. The latter group would raise the average lifetime, even if 99 percent of civilizations quickly destroyed themselves.

This estimate in turn led to a value of 1 million for the number of civilizations in the Galaxy. The nearest would then likely be a few hundred light-years away. But Sagan warned that "if we assumed a pessimistic scenario, as reading the daily newspaper does not always discourage us from doing," the average lifetime could be in decades—in which case we could be alone in the Galaxy, with no one to talk to but ourselves.

*   *   *

The discussion turned to the labyrinthine difficulties of contacting an extraterrestrial civilization. In this task, as in so much else, technologic "progress" was a double-edged sword.

Many shared Philip Morrison's worry that advanced civilizations would communicate not with radio waves but with some means that has yet to be invented on Earth. Would "advanced" civilizations even *want* to communicate with us? That concerned Sagan: "I therefore raise the possibility that a horizon in communications interest exists in the evolution of technological societies, and that a civilization very much more advanced than we will be engaged in a busy communications traffic with its peers; but not with us, and not via technologies accessible to us. We may be like the inhabitants of the valleys of New Guinea who may communicate via runner or the drum, but who are ignorant of the vast international radio and cable traffic passing over, around and through them."

This of course would make SETI much more difficult than the Drake equation implied. One possible remedy received much attention at Byurakan.

It had to do with a seemingly crazy idea that Sagan's co-organizer, Nikolai Kardashev, had been espousing since the early 1960s. Fully sharing the technological optimism of Gold and Minsky, Kardashev projected that the amount of energy available to civilizations would grow exponentially, as it had since our own Industrial Revolution. In a few centuries, almost *anything* would be possible. Kardashev therefore suggested that some extraterrestrial civilizations might be altruistic enough to make things easy for us. They might expend incredible amounts of energy on interstellar communication, allowing us to pick up their signals with relative ease.

Kardashev divided these hypothetical supercivilizations into three types. Type I were those willing to devote a planet's worth of power to SETI. Type

II were those expending a star's worth of power. And Type III would have a galaxy's worth of power. There was no mention of a Type IV (willing to devote all the energy in the universe?!?). There was no *need* for Type IV. Kardashev computed that a Type III signal would be detectable anywhere across the known universe.

Even a Type II civilization's signal would be easily detectable anywhere in our galaxy or in nearby galaxies. It was the Type I signal that was a challenge. It could be detected only from relatively nearby stars.

Shklovskii was sympathetic to these ideas. Kardashev's supercivilizations were very much on the Soviets' minds during the CTA-102 debacle. The notion that something with the energy of a quasar might be an alien signal did not appear nearly so impossible to the Soviets as it did to their American counterparts.

Starting in 1963, Shklovskii had been trying to convince people to search for signals in the Andromeda galaxy. Such a signal would have to be Type II. (A Type I signal would be too weak to pick up. Were there a Type III signal in Andromeda, we wouldn't see the galaxy because all the starlight would have been transmuted into signal!) The advantage of this idea is that Andromeda occupies a small patch of the sky. If there were a Type II civilization *anywhere* in Andromeda, it could be found in a few days' search. An exhaustive survey of our own galaxy would have to cover the entire sky and would take years.

The Shklovskii-Sagan book publicized Kardashev's ideas in the West. Gradually, the Americans were warming to them. At Byurakan, Frank Drake offered some calculations along this line. He showed that the most readily detectable ET signals were likely to be very powerful but distant. This was analogous to the brightness of stars in the nighttime. Most visible stars are not especially close. They are exceptionally *bright* stars, visible in spite of their great distance. So it might be with ETI signals.

For SETI to succeed, Sagan concluded, we must hope that certain advanced civilizations *want* to communicate with us and purposely use "antique communication modes" such as radio to do so. "The best search mode," he said, "is to examine other galaxies for the few very advanced civilizations there rather than to examine our immediate neighborhood for civilizations nearly as dumb as we."

Leslie Orgel warned that the only people using antiquated communication modes on Earth were Boy Scouts and ham radio operators. "It seems to me that we should watch out that it is neither of these classes that we contact when we meet our first Type II civilization."

Earth Prime

The discussion now turned to the question of whether we would be able to understand an alien message. "If a lion could talk," Wittgenstein claimed, "we would not be able to understand him."

That was roughly the position of the Soviet Academy of Sciences' B. I. Panovkin. He gave a presentation on understanding an extraterrestrial message—something he thought was unlikely given the absence of a shared culture and its common points of reference. Panovkin held that the only hope of communication, and it was not *much* of a hope, was to be found in parallel evolution. We would have to locate a planet whose history coincidentally paralleled our own, a bizarro world different yet eerily similar. Panovkin called this planet "Earth prime."

Both Panovkin and McNeill doubted that even mathematics was truly universal. "The confidence that I know mathematicians and natural scientists have," said McNeill, "that they have a universal language seems to me a case of chauvinism, to use our favorite term."

But Sagan believed that math chauvinism was one kind of chauvinism that *was* justified. He, Morrison, and Drake therefore believed that Drake's prime number scheme for sending TV pictures had pretty much resolved worries that extraterrestrial messages would defy decryption. They expected the ETs to send a multimedia dictionary, complete with (in Morrison's words) "a very rich three-dimensional, moving, carefully scaled cinema."

Y. I. Kuznetzov of Moscow's Institute of Energetics described his own interstellar television scheme, seemingly less elegant than Drake's. Kuznetzov showed how it would be possible to send a picture of a cat into space. He admitted that, on a planet with a different refractive index, "the picture would be distorted; distorted cats would be received." But he assured the group that the topological structure of the cat would be preserved. This led Sagan to suggest that they might be better off transmitting the cat's genetic code. Let the aliens clone their own cats.

In the face of such abstractions, some tried their hand at the more tangible task of deciphering *Armenian*. The neon signs of Byurakan sizzled in an entrancing, elegant script, as "alien" to the Russians as to the Americans. Morrison and Freeman Dyson succeeded in mapping the Armenian alphabet onto its Roman equivalents. They proved their triumph by determining that the movie playing at the local theater was *Oliver*.

(Shklovskii too had his doubts about the decipherment problem. His favorite response was an anecdote. At a previous conference, also in Byurakan, he and Kardashev had taken a walk through the village. They came across a donkey cropping grass beside the road. At the sight of a young girl, the donkey developed an erection. Said Kardashev: "And you doubt the possibility of establishing contact with civilizations on other planets.")

Mediums and Messages

Philip Morrison spoke on the social consequences of the reception of an ET message. In place of Sagan's analogy of Native Americans versus Europeans, Morrison posed the more hopeful metaphor of the rediscovery of Greek antiquity.

He computed that everything we know about ancient Greek culture—every word of surviving text; every statue, ruin, and painted vase—came to no more than 10^{12} bits of information. This is a one-way message. Homer still speaks to us today, but we can't get so much as a word back to Homer. The message of Greek antiquity is one we are still "deciphering."

Even Sagan's optimistic estimates put the nearest civilizations hundreds of light-years away. It would take centuries to send a message and receive a reply. Conversations would be impossible. An extraterrestrial radio message would have to be one-way. It would be a civilization's grand soliloquy, sent out for the benefit of whoever might receive it. Morrison maintained that such messages would likely contain much art and literature—or whatever corresponds to them on the ETs' world—for these expressions, unlike science or mathematics, would be unique. (Frank Drake wasn't crazy about that; he wanted the ETs to send plans for a tachyon telescope.) The message would not be something that could be "translated" and then printed in the next morning's newspaper. To understand it would be to reconstruct the web of shared points of reference of an alien culture. That would be monumentally difficult but not, Morrison thought, impossible. The project of understanding an ET message would be "a discipline rather than a headline or an oracle."

"It seems to me," said J. R. Platt of the Michigan Mental Health Center, "that Morrison is saying that the medium is the message."

"Is it a joke?" asked Shklovskii (for whom Marshall McLuhan was not a shared cultural reference).

"No, no joke," Platt said.

Shklovskii asked Platt to rephrase what he'd said.

"The medium is television. It brings the message that there are television stations."

Morrison's message was getting a little garbled. McNeill spoke up. He said he had been listening to Morrison's remarks with special concern—concern about whether *any* skepticism about extraterrestrial communication would be expressed. He regretted to report that it had *not* been.

"Unless my reading of history is radically wrong," McNeill said, "contact between men has shown that those who had the power used it. Athens was a brutal master."

Morrison demurred. Pericles "was a tyrant in life; but once in Thucydides and dead 2000 years he was only a moral example!"

Morrison's point was that we could expect alien encyclopedias, not conquistadors. Relativity's speed-of-light limit would make interstellar conquest forever impractical. (But the SETI community has had divergent views on this business of interstellar travel; witness Sagan's 1963 article, as well as more speculative talk of faster-than-light travel.)

McNeill allowed that *if* extraterrestrial conquest could be ruled out, and *if* the message could be deciphered, then SETI would be a worthwhile activity. He doubted both premises. He said that in listening to the proceedings, he detected the beginnings of "a pseudo or scientific religion." "I remain, I fear, an agnostic, not only in traditional religion but also in this new one."

Bernard Oliver in turn said he found McNeill's remarks *interesting* "because they reflect opinions that we are apt to encounter in the educated person who is not intimately acquainted with science." He hinted darkly that they had "political significance."

Then Pesek—either refuting McNeill's claim of a new religion or illustrating it—said he believed that SETI would help solve the Earth's problems and prevent us from destroying ourselves. Shklovskii held that the best statement on the risks and benefits of SETI came from Andrey Sakharov, who did not attend but sent an opinion of fortune-cookie concision: "To an intelligent and good person contact will be useful; to a stupid and bad one, harmful."

*   *   *

There was a sense of melancholy as the conference ended. In his concluding remarks, Sagan made a plea for international cooperation in SETI. On the final night, the group feasted on tables overlooking Lake Sevan and an eighth-century island monastery. Toasts rang out in Russian, English, !Kung, and Armenian.

A Storm on Mars

Sagan jetted back to the United States and, with scarcely time to unpack, was off to another high-powered conference. This time the venue was Pasadena and the subject was "Mars and the Mind of Man." The other participants were Ray Bradbury, Arthur C. Clarke, Walter Sullivan, and Bruce Murray.

Murray was cast as the "heavy" in this crowd. He was as contentious as some of the Byurakan people had been, if for different reasons. Murray called the search for life on Mars "a modern version of the pursuit of the Golden Fleece." He lamented that the Mars of Edgar Rice Burroughs and Percival Lowell still influenced the public and even, yes, the scientific community. "I think the observations will have to become so unambiguous and so compelling that finally we are forced to recognize the real Mars." It was a sad commentary on things that "the most advanced society in the world" still found it necessary to go through the pointless ritual of sterilizing the entire Viking lander. Quoting his Caltech colleague Norman Horowitz, Murray called sterilization "a monument to a Mars that never existed."

*   *   *

As the red planet generated a certain amount of hot air in Pasadena, a storm was brewing on Mars. On September 22, 1971, a bright yellow-white smudge appeared over the desert plain Noachis. It was a dust storm of unprecedented ferocity. Telescopic observers watched the whitish region grow day by day. By early October, the cloud had engulfed nearly the entire planet. All the familiar telescopic features of Mars, even the brilliant white slice at the south pole, were erased.

On November 8, Mariner 9 sent back its first photos of Mars. They showed nothing, a blank disk. The view was scarcely better when Mariner entered orbit on November 14. Its cameras could barely make out the south polar cap and four dark spots. All other detail was lost. It was the stuff of gallows humor. Sagan said the planet was about as interesting as a tennis ball—but without the seams. Someone cracked that maybe they had sent the craft to *Venus*.

In a way, the storm was a victory for Sagan and Pollack. No longer was it possible to doubt that storms moved dust planetwide. Analysis of the photos would ultimately provide impressive confirmation for their theory of the seasonal and long-term changes on Mars.

Another victory was that NASA's leadership decided that Sagan's idea about observing the moons wasn't so bad after all.

*   *   *

On Mariner's twenty-fifth revolution around Mars, it took the first photo of Deimos, the smaller moon. Sagan and Joseph Veverka watched the data come in pixel by pixel. It was hard to tell much. Because Deimos is smaller and more distant from Mars than Phobos, its image was small. The raw data displayed on the monitors showed a low-contrast disk with many data errors.

On November 30, Mariner took the first decent photograph of Phobos.

This was the moment of truth. This time the raw image was distinctly misshapen.

That alone did not rule out Shklovskii's idea. Artificial satellites of a long-extinct civilization would presumably be in ruins, subject to cratering as natural satellites are.

Sagan and Veverka worked long into the night. They had JPL's Image Processing Laboratory enhance the image contrast and clean up the data errors. The contrast-enhancement software spit out lines of pixels at a leisurely pace. As the picture scanned down, a dark round region appeared. A single point of light glistened in the middle. For a moment, Sagan suspected he was seeing *through* the moon, to the stars beyond . . . or that he was seeing an artificial light.

Sagan and Veverka then had the software remove single-bit errors. The point of light vanished. It was a glitch.

They became the first people to see the real face of Phobos. It was of course a natural object. The dark area was a huge crater, marking nearly the largest possible impact that would stop short of blowing the satellite to bits. In all, Sagan likened the satellite's irregular and cratered form to a "diseased potato."

Down the Zambesi

The dust storm took its time in clearing. There was slight improvement after Thanksgiving; then it seemed that things stayed the way they were, with no further improvement until after the new year. Everyone at JPL was anxious to find ways to keep themselves and Mariner busy. Sagan and Pollack tried to answer the question of the moment: how long would it take for the dust clouds to clear?

They used Mariner's infrared interferometric spectrometer. Unimpeded by the dust, this was able to measure the temperature at various heights in the Martian atmosphere. Sagan and Pollack determined that the dust storm was heating the high atmosphere while cooling the ground. This was not surprising. Since a lot of sunlight was being absorbed by particles high in the atmosphere, the high atmosphere was warmer than usual. That same sunlight *didn't* make it to the ground, so the surface was cooler.

They reasoned that the temperature difference might allow them to estimate how much dust was in the atmosphere, and that, in turn, would lead to an estimate of how long it would take to fall out. They created some preliminary models. Then the storm itself answered the question.

By March 1972 the dust was largely settled and the planet revealed to Mariner's cameras. Mariner 9's 7,300 photographs captured a Mars unlike that of the previous Mariners. For the first time in a quite a while, Mars had become a *more* interesting place. It was definitely not the moon.

The four dark spots they had seen were the peaks of titanic volcanoes poking up through the dust clouds. One volcano, christened Olympus Mons, was over 300 miles across. A spectacular canyon, Vallis Marineris (named for the spacecraft), was far deeper than the Grand Canyon and nearly as wide as the conterminous United States. Like everyone else, Sagan was inspired and delighted. He compared the excitement to that of traveling down the Zambesi for the first time.

Of life there was not a trace. There were hints of water, past and present. The photographs showed sinuous channels, looking like dry riverbeds or gullies carved by flash floods in deserts. While Sagan believed they were water channels, others were not so sure. "If it were not Mars," admitted geologist Hal Masursky, "and if water weren't so hard to come by there, we would think that these were water channels." Bruce Murray suspected that lava had carved the channels.

Helping Sagan's case was Mariner 9's news about the polar caps. Its instruments suggested that the "summer polar cap," the small residue that remains throughout the year, contains some water ice in addition to carbon dioxide. Even more intriguing, photos revealed the polar caps to have a complex layered structure, similar to some of the Earth's polar ice. Like the growth rings of a tree, this suggested that Mars's climate had varied over time.

*   *   *

Hal Masursky, the head of Mariner 9's imaging team, was a geologist with the U.S. Geological Survey. His most prominent feature was his glasses; their huge lenses magnified his eyes with disconcerting effect. During one meeting, Masursky proposed to let Mariner go out with a bang. The craft had performed almost flawlessly, and they were getting all the planned photographs. Why not send the probe into a lower orbit, permitting even-higher-resolution pictures?

Lederberg turned ashen. A lower orbit would increase atmospheric drag. The craft would slowly spiral inward and crash into Mars. Mariner 9 had not been sterilized for a landing. In an emotional confrontation, Lederberg and Sagan insisted that the craft remain in high orbit. The Mariner 9 photos had boosted their hopes of finding life on Mars. They were not about to give up the contamination battle yet, and once again, they prevailed.

*   *   *

With the mission complete, the Sagans returned to Ithaca. The cross-country drive afforded Carl time to concentrate on the book he was writing for Agel. He bounced ideas off Linda and ended up dictating much of the text in the car. Nick's verbal skills were no less astounding. He began mumbling words from road signs. He had taught himself to read, three months shy of his second birthday.

This literate toddler act was a shock to those outside the family. At an airport, Nick once read aloud a sign. An onlooker glared at Linda, indignant, as if this were some kind of cheap parlor trick.

Nick also showed his father's knack for looking at problems from unusual perspectives. He was given an alphabet book in which one page had the letter *M* and a picture of a melon. Nick pointed at the picture and said, "Watermelon!"

"No, *M* as in 'melon,' " his parents corrected.

Nick turned the book upside down, transforming the *M* into a *W*. "*W* as in 'watermelon'!" he said.

*   *   *

The new house was still a long way from being finished. The Sagans spent the next few years in a succession of temporary residences. Linda turned her artistic talents toward customizing their surroundings. In one apartment, where they knew the landlord, Linda painted the cabinets and Formica surfaces in bold, bright colors—several times, for she could not decide what color looked best.

Carl had copies of all 7,300 Mariner 9 photos installed close at hand in a small room of the Space Sciences Building. For years afterward, he would dip into the photos at odd moments, studying them, hoping to find something no one else had noticed. "My idea of heaven," Sagan once confessed to a visitor, "would be to be able to shut myself up in here for a month."

Lightning in a Bottle

The Apollo era drew to a close in December 1972 with the nighttime launch of Apollo 17. Sagan watched from Cape Kennedy. A dolphin frolicked in the nighttime lagoon as the dramatically lighted Saturn booster took off.

Nineteen seventy-two was also a year of auspicious beginnings. The outer planets were conveniently lining up in their orbits, something that had not happened since Thomas Jefferson was president, as Sagan noted. A single probe might fly by Jupiter, Saturn, Uranus, and Neptune. That made it possible to promote such a probe as a cost-effective mission suitable for the post-Apollo era. Congress agreed and approved funding—at least as far as Jupiter and Saturn. The mission recycled the old name Voyager. The understanding was that if it performed well, the mission might be extended to Uranus and Neptune.

As he looked forward to Voyager, Sagan was doing some of his best work in the lab. One might imagine that the Laboratory for Planetary Studies occupied its own building on the Cornell campus. In fact, it occupied an office and a basement room, each of modest dimensions. The grand-sounding name showed Sagan's flair for self-promotion as well as science; but a great deal of science was done in that small space. That would not have been possible without Bishun Khare.

While at Harvard, Sagan ran an ad in *Physics Today* looking for a collaborator skilled in lab work. This led to his hiring of Khare, an expert in working with gases and vacuums. Khare moved to Cornell with Sagan and collaborated with him for the rest of Sagan's career.

Viewers of *Cosmos* may remember Khare as a glowering, white-coated east Indian man experimenting with electrical discharges. Khare was presented as the Frankensteinian antithesis of Sagan's blissful philosopher in corduroys. In one expressionistic shot, Khare's face scowls in distorted reflection from a glass tube.

The real Khare was a gentle man, never too busy with his primordial gases to dispense some *helium* for toy balloons—to the delight of Sagan's children, whenever they visited the lab. Khare's work *did* have a whiff of Frankenstein to it, though. He and Sagan were trying to see how life might be created with sparks, shocks, and weird glows.

Sagan and Khare became the first to produce the sulfur-containing amino acids cysteine and cystine in Miller-Urey-style experiments with simple gas mixtures. They achieved this result by adding hydrogen sulfide and ethane to the gas mixture and irradiating it with long-wavelength ultraviolet light. In these experiments (much more elegant than the early work with Ponnamperuma), the hydrogen sulfide was able to absorb the ultraviolet light and initiate chemical synthesis.

Other experiments used shock waves (such as might be produced by an incoming meteor or asteroid). The yield of amino acids in these experiments was often amazingly high. As left-wing as his politics were, Sagan had a strong entrepreneurial streak. He reasoned that here was a dirt-cheap way of making amino acids. Chemical or pharmaceutical companies might be interested in that. Also, amino acids are the components of protein, and protein is food. Ergo, synthetic *meat* from *light*.

U.S. Patent 3,756,934, "Production of Amino Acids from Gaseous Mixtures Using Ultraviolet Light," was awarded to Sagan and Khare in 1973. (A related patent, 3,652,434, went to Sagan and two other colleagues the previous year.) It was not much of a get-rich-quick scheme. Sagan and Khare assigned their patent to Cornell. Like most patents, it went nowhere commercially and quietly expired.

Early Faint Sun Paradox

In 1972 Sagan and George Mullen, then of Cornell, published an article in *Science* titled "Earth and Mars: Evolution of Atmospheres and Surface Temperatures." It is now recognized as one of Sagan's most original and influential articles.

It brought to general attention a tantalizing puzzle generally called the "early faint sun paradox." Since the 1950s astrophysicists had accepted that stars burn hotter and brighter as they age. Therefore, our sun must have been about 30 percent *less* bright at the time the Earth's oldest rocks were formed. That's a *huge* difference. All other things being equal, the Earth's oceans should have been frozen solid.

There is strong geological evidence that this was *not* so, that the Earth has always had liquid water. Ancient rocks show mud cracks, ripple marks, and the "pillow lava" formed when the sea quenches molten rock. As Sagan mentioned at Byurakan, the fossil record itself goes back over 3 billion years. The earliest fossils include photosynthetic bacteria, which live in water.

Sagan was not the first to realize there was a contradiction. But as a rare straddler of fields, he was the first to pursue the issue seriously. The Sagan-Mullen article identifies the greenhouse effect as the most plausible way of resolving the paradox. If the ancient Earth had a pronounced greenhouse effect, and if that effect slowly lessened with time, it could have counterbalanced the effect of the sun's increasing luminosity.

Sagan and Mullen considered all the likely greenhouse gases, including the familiar carbon dioxide. For various reasons, they ruled out carbon dioxide and argued that the likeliest candidate was ammonia.

There is virtually no ammonia in the atmosphere today. But most scientists believed there were more substantial amounts of ammonia in the Earth's original atmosphere. Ammonia is a potent greenhouse gas. Sagan computed that as little as a few parts per million in the early Earth's atmosphere would have created a greenhouse effect big enough to explain the paradox.

The early faint sun paradox has reverberated throughout the community of scientists investigating the origins of life. Whatever its source, the (approximate) dovetailing of the greenhouse effect's lessening with the sun's brightening seems almost magical. This could mean that the Earth's ever temperate climate has been the result of an unlikely coincidence. In that case, the Earth's long evolutionary history, and the consequent evolution of intelligence, may be a relative oddity.

Alternatively, the "magical" fit may mean that unknown feedback mechanisms act to maintain clement temperatures. The most widely publicized of all such theories has been promulgated by Sagan's first wife. It is the most notable way in which the scientific interests of Dorion's "Earth mother and space father" have overlapped.

Starting in 1972, Lynn Margulis worked on an idea originally advanced by British chemist and inventor James E. Lovelock: the Gaia hypothesis. Gaia is the Greek goddess corresponding to Mother Earth. The hypothesis named for her holds that the Earth's biota—the aggregate of all the planet's living matter—is able through growth, metabolism, and chemical interaction to maintain the planet's temperature and atmospheric composition at levels suitable for life. In this view, the explanation for the early faint sun paradox is conceptually simple: over billions of years, life itself has produced the greenhouse gases needed to keep temperatures comfortable.

Gaia's holistic, Earth-mother vibe has made for countless popular articles—many of them distortions, Margulis complains. (Like Sagan's theorizing about extraterrestrial intelligence, Gaia has been viewed with suspicion by some in the scientific community because of its very popularity.) One point that is clear is that any full explanation of the early faint sun paradox must account for the actions of life itself. All agree that the Earth's oxygen is the result of life, of the photosynthesis of cyanobacteria and plants. This oxygen would have quickly destroyed any ammonia that was present. By Sagan and Mullen's model, that would have reduced the greenhouse effect and cooled the Earth—even as the sun was, over the long term, getting hotter and brighter.

Insofar as the Gaia hypothesis purports to explain the activities of the planet's biosphere over 3 billion years, it defies any single, direct experimental test. The proper test of Gaia, or of Sagan and Mullen's model, would be to follow two identical planets, one with life and one without, over the eons. Lacking that, Sagan gave a lot of thought to the examples of Venus and Mars. He proposed that Venus was victim of a "runaway greenhouse" effect and Mars of an insufficient greenhouse effect. The Sagan-Mullen article held that the ancient Mars had a thicker atmosphere and an enhanced greenhouse effect. This would account for the evidence of ancient water on Mars. Over time, Mars lost most of its atmosphere and hence its greenhouse warming.

One point where ex-husband and wife differed almost 180 degrees was on the question of life on Mars. Margulis tended to agree with Lovelock (who had consulted with NASA on Martian biology experiments) that the presence or absence of life on a planet could be inferred from its atmosphere. Oxygen, a reactive gas that must be replenished constantly, betrays the presence of life on Earth. In contrast, Mars's carbon dioxide–nitrogen atmosphere is chemically stable. It was not necessary to assume that any nongeologic agency was at work. Margulis believed that the Gaia hypothesis would be supported by having the Vikings land on Mars—and prove the planet lifeless.

Going North

Sagan of course was hoping for the opposite result. Consequently, he and Joshua Lederberg did a lot of worrying about the water on Mars.

It had originally been their intention to select a landing site for Viking on the basis of water. Where water was most likely to be found, they reasoned, life would be most likely to be found. The planet was not cooperating. The low atmospheric pressure meant there was not a drop of liquid water anywhere on its surface. At most, the landing site team could choose a spot where water *had been* (in some remote geologic epoch) or where it *would be* if the pressure and temperature were higher than they were. Were such criteria still worthwhile?

Instruments showed that such water (vapor and ice) as there was on Mars existed mainly at the poles. This further threw Sagan and Lederberg's reasoning into disarray. They had been looking for a relatively warm, wet place. Now it appeared that the wettest places were all cold, the warmest places all dry.

Lederberg spoke by conference call to the August 5, 1972, meeting of the Viking landing site group. He proposed going north. They should consider sending one of the two Viking craft to a northern region that had just been uncovered by the retreating polar cap.

This was a new way of thinking. The discussion of landing sites had concentrated on a zone within 30° of the equator. That zone, the warmest part of the planet, had been assumed best for life. It also maximized power for Viking's solar cells. But that "optimal" zone, Lederberg warned, might actually be the *least* promising for life. Maybe the water vapor issuing from the ice, and not the higher temperatures, was crucial.

Following Sagan's philosophy, Lederberg advocated the "polar option" for the second Viking only, and then only if all went well with the first. In any event, Lederberg argued, this plan would allow a look at two very different places on Mars. That could only help the chances of finding life.

*   *   *

Lederberg's proposal split the committee for the next few months. It forced Sagan and everyone else to reevaluate what they were really looking for on Mars.

There had been a time when Sagan and Lederberg and everyone else had wanted to land in a dark region—deep in the lichen country of Kuiper. In the orbital photos, the telescopic light and dark areas were scarcely discernible. More important, Sagan and Pollack had established that the dark regions were highlands. Landing there would be risky. The altitude implied an even lower air pressure. With the biological explanation of the dark regions discarded, life was generally assumed most likely to favor regions where the pressure was higher.

By "Earth chauvinistic" standards, Mars was profoundly inhospitable. Mariner's instruments measured the temperatures in the polar region at about −190° F (−123° C). The ultraviolet radiation alone was enough to kill terrestrial microbes in seconds. At this remove it is easy to see why people like Norman Horowitz and Lynn Margulis were ready to rule out life on Mars. It may be harder to understand why Sagan and Lederberg clung so tenaciously to the possibility.

In a series of articles Sagan and others argued—speculatively though often quantitatively—that the Martian environment was not so incompatible with life as it might seem. In a 1962 article Lederberg and Sagan wrote that Mars might have microenvironments where conditions were more hospitable. Volcanoes produce hot springs in Iceland; maybe there were areas where Martian volcanoes melted permafrost and yielded liquid water.

This plausible idea fell into trouble as estimates of the air pressure became more accurate. Permafrost or not, there could be no liquid water on the surface of Mars. Sagan then suggested that the melting took place underground, where the pressure of overlying rock might permit liquid water to exist.

There was also talk of puddles of natural antifreeze. There is a salty pond in Antarctica, its bitter water saturated with calcium chloride, whose freezing point has been measured at −60° F. The minerals would also inhibit boiling under low pressure. Were there such ponds on Mars, it was reasoned, they might be habitats for life. However, even a calcium chloride–saturated pond would not be proof against the thirsty air of Mars. The pond in Antarctica is sterile or nearly so.

There remained the photographic evidence of drainage channels on Mars. It became increasingly hard to argue they were created by anything but water. In 1971 Sagan advanced a theory whereby the Martian climate would cycle between a "long winter" (now) and brief clement periods.

Robert Leighton and Bruce Murray computed that Mars's axis of rotation changes with a 50,000-year cycle. At the midpoints of the cycle, Sagan theorized, the water in the polar caps might be released into the atmosphere. That would increase the air pressure and (through a greenhouse effect) the temperatures as well. Surface water would become possible.

In his popular writings, Sagan promoted this idea with the full poetic treatment: "Twelve thousand years ago may have been a time on Mars of balmy temperatures, soft nights, and the trickle of liquid water down innumerable streams and rivulets, rushing out to join mighty, gushing rivers." Martian life might then be like desert wildflowers, springing up after the rare rain, living out an accelerated life cycle, and producing seeds to wait out the next long dry spell.

Viking would be landing in the depth of a dry spell. That might still allow Viking's biology experiments to coax seed or spores into renewed growth. Linda wryly suggested that the recipe for finding life on Mars might be: *add water.* That is roughly what two of Viking's biology experiments did.

Sagan and Pollack tackled the ultraviolet radiation question in a 1974 article. They computed that Martian life could escape ultraviolet radiation by inhabiting a layer about a centimeter below the surface. At this depth, nearly all the ultraviolet light would be blocked, yet enough visible light might filter through the sand grains to permit photosynthesis.

It seemed, in short, that Sagan could outargue any impediment Mars had to offer. Not everyone was convinced, but the landing team's geologists had no compelling alternative criteria to offer in choosing a landing site. It would have been great to see a volcano close-up or to straddle a canyon precipice. But the places most interesting to the geologists were dangerous. Sagan's water-and-life criteria prevailed.

*   *   *

The split over Lederberg's polar option was not along "party lines," however. Sagan opposed it. He felt the poles were just too cold. Wolf Vishniac, who had impressed Sagan with his cultures of terrestrial bacteria under extreme conditions, reported that he could not get *any* bacteria to grow at temperatures much below 10° F (−12° C). It would be much, much colder than *that* at the Martian pole. Sagan was concerned that Viking's robotic arm would scrape helplessly against the solidly frozen surface.

Sagan was also worried about a safe landing. There was no radar coverage of the polar regions. That was a technical limitation they had to live with. The radar was one of the ways they had of identifying rough terrain. No radar meant more risk of a crashed lander. Sagan computed that the chance of a safe landing in the polar regions was less than 50 percent. So there was a greater-than-50-percent chance of losing one lander, whose value Sagan pegged at $200 million, or about the cost of a mission to Jupiter and Saturn. "When I total up the pros and cons," he wrote in a memo, "I find that the scientific advantage of a polar landing site, while real, is far outweighed by the risks."

Sagan's opposition struck Lederberg as "out of character." Feeling he was losing the battle, Lederberg met with NASA administrator James C. Fletcher and complained that the "engineers" weren't giving the idea a fair hearing—though in this case that pejorative (?) term included one exobiologist. Fletcher simply ruled that no decision should be made until they had heard from all the science team leaders.

Some of the geologists admired the drama of Lederberg's idea. "It's not that different from any other polar journey," said Thomas Mutch. "You equip yourself as best you can. You set some intermediate goals, and if all goes well you make a dash for the pole."

*   *   *

On April 2, Lederberg conceded defeat. A polar site was not the best bet. The group struck a compromise. The second site would be in the middle north latitudes, where the temperature would be roughly at Vishniac's limit for terrestrial bacterial growth.

A set of sites and alternates was announced to the press on May 7, 1973. If all went according to plan, Viking 1 would land in Chryse, a plain at the mouth of the "Martian Grand Canyon." Viking 2's main site was Cydonia, 44° above the equator. Both sites had low elevations and relatively high atmospheric pressures. Viking 1 would be landing in summer in the Martian tropics. That meant the temperature might barely surpass that of an ice cube.

Quicksand

This announcement actually settled nothing. The maxim "Work expands to occupy the time available for it" applied fully to the Viking site selection. With so much at stake, no new datum could go ignored. The landing site group pondered and agonized over every detail. Sagan was a master worrier.

The Vikings could not, of course, be targeted to the inch. They would fall out of the sky and hit the ground at a random point within a large, elliptical swath. If a craft landed on top of a boulder, it would tumble and probably be destroyed. Even a small rock could tilt the lander so that its robotic arm would plunge uselessly skyward.

There were two ways of judging a site: by photos and by radar. Both techniques had their partisans.

Photos were easy for anyone to understand. The trouble was that the photographs taken from orbit showed, at best, "Rose Bowl size hazards" 100 meters or more across. They were not nearly detailed enough to reveal the features they had to worry about.

There were, nonetheless, geologists who believed that by examining the photographs they could gain a sense of how rough the terrain was at smaller scales. It was a matter of instinct. How well skills gained on Earth translated to Mars was anyone's guess. Sagan's guess was that the photos could not be trusted.

Unlike many of the geologists, Sagan was comfortable with radar. Radar had been indispensable in his work on the seasonal changes. The radar people, led by G. Leonard Tyler of Stanford, used the Arecibo, Goldstone, and Haystack radio telescopes. They aimed their beams at that pinprick in the sky called Mars and listened for an echo.

What they got back was a jittery graph, not a picture. Interpreting these data was a black art. The radar people spoke of how the radar "feels" boulders and slopes a meter across or less.

Not that the radar could detect individual rocks. In the hands of capable practitioners—and assuming that these practitioners' assumptions were correct—the radar could gauge the *average* roughness of the surface. Should the radar find an area with 0 percent average slope, that would be a safe place to land. Such a finding would, theoretically, be more valuable than a photograph of smooth terrain, for such terrain could still be littered with boulders too small to resolve.

Sagan thought the radar was likely to be more useful than all the photos they would have. He was less certain of how correctly the radar people were interpreting their data. Radar observations were equivocal; several different models could account for a given echo.

One of the things that had Sagan worried was "quicksand." On Mars, this obviously wouldn't be *wet* quicksand but a dry dust. It would be something like Tommy Gold's old idea about lunar dust. A Soviet space program official had suggested that the failed Mars 3 might have become mired in Martian quicksand.

There were areas on Mars that looked smooth in the photographs and had low reflectivity in the radar. The geologists said these areas were fields of sand dunes. The low radar reflectivity was assumed to be a result of scattering by the sand. Some of them had been judged safe landing sites. But Sagan suspected that the radar measurement might indicate absorption by a deep layer of dust or "quicksand." If so, a lander might plummet through the dry ooze, its cameras never returning a picture of the Martian surface.

Der Führer

By March 1973, Sagan's radar worries prodded Viking project leader Jim Martin into action.

Martin did not look like a scientist—media or otherwise—and he was not the sort of man to hold forth on Eastern religions in *Rolling Stone* magazine (Sagan was doing that, at about this time). For twenty-two years Martin had been a defense aerospace engineer, building missiles and fighter planes. He had a strong jaw and blue-gray hair trimmed almost to a crew cut. Martin said that NASA had hired him because he looked like a contractor.

Martin was the General Leslie Groves of the Viking mission, a man who successfully marshaled a disparate group of scientists, some of whom lacked the people skills for such intensive collaboration. Martin was more respected than liked. Some of the scientists called him "Der Führer," the "Prussian General," or the "Great White Chief."

As different as their personalities were, Martin and Sagan were united in the bond of worry. Both fretted endlessly about Viking. Martin compiled two books on the subject of what might go wrong with Viking. Volume 1 was about the things that might go wrong but could be fixed—and how to fix them. Volume 2 was about the things that might go wrong and couldn't be fixed. Each volume was roughly the size of the Manhattan phone book.

Viking's Führer was ready to take cover in a bunker, should it come to that. Under Martin's contingency plan for nuclear war, key Viking officials were required to maintain up-to-date passports at all times. In the event of a nuclear confrontation, they were to abandon Pasadena and set up base in Madrid or Canberra, Australia. If they did not make it, people in Madrid or Canberra were authorized to open emergency manuals and carry on with the mission of retrieving data from Mars.

When Sagan said there *might* be quicksand on Mars and that neither photos nor the radar interpretation could be relied upon to assess the risk, Martin was in his element. It was another contingency to prepare for. Martin formed a radar study team, headed by Len Tyler. He adopted Sagan's suggestion to make new and better radar observations, particularly at Arecibo after its upgrading. The report of Tyler's group, on November 4, 1974, was disconcerting. They found that Mars's radar reflectivity varied greatly, and that these variations did not correspond much to anything they saw in the Mariner photographs. The radar was seeing a totally different Mars.

Big Bird

In 1973 the International Astronomical Union met in Sydney, Australia. Between sessions, a man introduced himself to Sagan and Frank Drake. His name was Yury Pariisky. He was a Soviet who looked something like Bob Newhart, although with not quite so much hair. Pariisky, director of radio astronomy at Leningrad's Pulkova Observatory, was yet another student of Shklovskii's. He suggested that they take a walk.

As they strolled through the streets of Sydney, past a theater playing *Last Tango in Paris*, Pariisky announced that he'd detected what seemed to be extraterrestrial signals. For several months, he had been receiving a series of pulses once a day. They were broadband, like noise (and like the CTA-102 "signal"). *These* pulses had to be artificial. Each day, they beeped out the same series: 1 pulse, 2 pulses, 7 pulses, 9 pulses.

He couldn't make sense of that. Had they been *prime numbers*, that would be one thing. Another weird thing was the *daily* repetition. How could extraterrestrials know that the Earth turned every twenty-four hours? Pariisky had of course considered terrestrial or satellite interference. He asked members of the Soviet military if the signals came from one of their satellites or from a U.S. satellite. They said they knew nothing about them.

Naturally he didn't want to announce the findings and repeat the CTA-102 fiasco. Neither did he want to sit on the matter forever. He said he had wanted to write Sagan or Drake for advice but hadn't dared. His mail would be read. The penalties for sending sensitive information to the West were severe.

Sagan told Pariisky that anyone who believed what the Soviet military said, about Soviet *or* U.S. operations, was *crazy*. Both Sagan and Drake thought it unlikely the signals were extraterrestrial.

In the weeks after the meeting, Sagan investigated Pariisky's signals. Dealing with a somewhat more open military establishment, he traced them to a secret U.S. reconnaissance satellite code-named Big Bird. The satellite's passes over the Soviet Union matched the times when Pariisky had detected the signals.

Bora Bora

On their way back to the States from Australia, Carl and Frank stopped off in French Polynesia. They both wanted to do some snorkeling, and Sagan wanted to try out an underwater camera he'd bought.

They stayed on Bora Bora, an emerald-green, volcanic island sitting in the middle of a lagoon enclosed by a circular atoll. The hotel was on the mountainous island. The lagoon was rich with colorful undersea life.

The hotel had outrigger canoes on the beach for the use of the guests. One day, Sagan commented that the Pacific had been settled by Polynesians using such canoes. He and Drake decided it would be fun to make a minivoyage of their own, to travel to one of the low sandy islets of the atoll.

They got in a canoe and began paddling. They traveled some distance when they noticed that the canoe was sitting low in the water. It was taking on water. They continued until the canoe was entirely submerged. Both men sat chest-high in the water.

Sagan thought *that* would make a great photograph. He snapped pictures of them sitting there, seemingly in the middle of the ocean.

They asked each other what they should do. They could continue paddling or abandon the canoe and swim. Either way, they could go for the sandy islet (uninhabited as far as they knew) or return to the main island.

There were sharks in the lagoon. They had seen them while snorkeling. That was a reason to stay in the canoe; it would provide some shark protection, at least on the outrigger side. The sharks, and their fatigue, were reasons to head for the islet. It was much closer than the hotel.

So they resumed rowing for the sandy islet. With the hull now completely underwater, it was like rowing through molasses. They had to hold the paddles way up to dip in the water from above. By the time they got to the islet, their muscles were in knots. They pulled the canoe and themselves safely on shore and collapsed.

Rats were skittering everywhere on the island. This was not a place they wanted to spend the night. It was already late afternoon. They had told no one in the world where they were going. Sagan and Drake made mental estimates of how long it would take before anyone knew they were missing . . . anticipated the reaction of a belated search party to their remains, two distinguished scientists who had been too *stupid* to get out of this mess. Here they were, two "Professors" on Gilligan's Island; there had to be a "logical" way out.

They explored the island. It had rats, coconuts, and palm trees. The only thing that seemed to bear on the problem was the coconuts. They could use the coconut shells as bailers. Sagan and Drake gathered the best-shaped coconut shells, put them in the canoe, and set off for the main island. This time one paddled as the other bailed with the coconut shells. With this stratagem, the two daring men escaped the island of the rats and returned safely home to Ithaca.

Mentor and Nemesis

Fred Whipple was scheduled to give a lecture at Cornell shortly after Sagan's return from the South Pacific. The trip stirred up anew the question of whether to tell Sagan about the tenure matter at Harvard. The issue was settled unexpectedly when Sagan met Whipple in Ithaca and announced, "You know, I've had the strangest letter from Harold Urey . . ."

Harvard uses the "ad hoc committee" system for tenure. Opinions on a candidate for tenured professor are solicited from a group of leading experts in the candidate's field. In view of Sagan's interests and his personal relationship with Urey, Whipple had quite naturally selected Urey for the committee.

Urey responded with a scathingly negative two-paragraph report on Sagan. Whipple was aghast. He had no reason to think that Urey was anything but an enthusiastic booster of Sagan's.

A scorched-earth letter, even from a Nobel laureate, does not automatically derail tenure. In Sagan's case, it upset delicate calculations about departmental politics. Sagan was young and his emphasis on exobiology controversial. Whipple expected opposition from within Harvard. He also expected to prevail. For that, he was counting on glowing endorsements from Sagan's celebrated mentors.

The Urey review could not even be swept under the rug. Harvard's rules forbid that. The review went directly to the dean. It was so negative, Whipple thought, that it was useless to proceed any further.

The scenario replayed at MIT. After Sagan made his interest known, Bruno Rossi solicited an opinion from . . . Harold Urey.

Urey's attitude toward Sagan is puzzling. In his personal dealings with Sagan he was often blunt in his criticism—and no less frank in his praise. Urey's letter to Bruno Rossi begins by citing a 1967 *Astrophysical Journal* article, "Thermodynamic Equilibria in Planetary Atmospheres," in which Sagan had been one (the last) of four coauthors. It reported a NASA-funded study that attempted to determine whether the observed atmospheres of Venus, Earth, Mars, and Jupiter were in chemical equilibrium. The subject was of interest to Sagan because it tied into the idea that life may be inferred from an atmosphere in chemical disequilibrium.

Urey, who refereed the article, judged it weak. The authors restricted their attention to atmospheres. They stated that the Earth's nitrogen-oxygen atmosphere is in chemical equilibrium; that is, the nitrogen and oxygen will not normally react with each other. That is strictly correct. Urey made the reasonable objection that the atmosphere is *not* in equilibrium when the oceans are taken into account. Nitrogen *will* react with oxygen and water to form nitric acid. (And does; but the nitrates formed foster photosynthesis, producing more oxygen.)

The four coauthors addressed this point only in a footnote, where they said they would take the oceans into account in a future article.

Urey wrote Rossi:

> This article illustrates to me the sort of activity that Carl Sagan has been engaged in for years—very long, wordy, voluminous papers that have comparatively little value. . . . Many many words, oftentimes quite useless. . . . Some time ago Sagan published a paper discussing the oxides of nitrogen on Mars. I think he took 17 pages to do this; I believe the subject was worth a few sentences.

The 1965 "Nitrogen Oxides on Mars" article was a different story. There Sagan was the lead author, and there Urey agreed with the article's conclusion. The article was written in response to C. C. Kiess's off-the-wall idea that the polar caps, dust clouds, and other features of Mars were made of nitrogen oxides. (As evidence, Kiess cited those ever ambiguous Sinton bands!) Hardly anyone took Kiess's idea seriously. Kiess further claimed that nitrogen oxides, being toxic, rule out life on Mars.

Well, those were fighting words to Sagan. He let Kiess have it with both barrels. The article ("only" sixteen pages!) has somewhat the quality of killing a gnat with a very large mallet. That was Urey's complaint. Still, as the article mentions, George Gaylord Simpson *did* take Kiess's claims seriously and cited them as grounds for not wasting any more money on a search for Martian life. Sagan therefore felt a rebuttal of Kiess was in order.

"Wordy" as the paper might have been, it is not without gems of brevity. "A typical value for the abundance of NO_2 over the city of Los Angeles exceeds the corresponding value for Mars," noted Sagan. "Life in Los Angeles may be difficult, but it is not yet impossible. The same goes for Mars."

The arguable faults of these articles cannot account for the tone of Urey's letter to Rossi. Urey chose to focus on "pet peeves" about two relatively obscure articles rather than on Sagan's widely recognized work on Venus and Mars. He saw in the two articles an emblem of broader and more serious misgivings. Urey concluded:

> Sagan has dashed all over the field of the planets—life, origin of life, atmospheres, all sorts of things. Personally I mistrust his work right from the beginning. He is a smart fellow and he is interesting to talk to. Perhaps he will be a

valuable professor at your institution. But for years I have been disturbed by this sort of thing illustrated by the paper I have discussed here in detail.

Such a damning assessment was impossible to ignore.

*   *   *

And then, sometime between 1967 and 1973, Urey changed his mind. Sagan ran into Urey at the Sydney meeting. Still innocent of all this, he must have flattered his old mentor. This prompted the strange letter Sagan mentioned to Whipple. Urey wrote Sagan (September 17, 1973):

> You embarrass me enormously by the remarks that you made in Sydney that I had been so nice to you. As a matter of fact, I have not always been nice to you, and I have tried my best to catch you alone and tell you so, and in addition tell you that I have been completely wrong. I admire the things you do and the viguor [sic] with which you attack them. I just wanted to say this. . . . Please forgive my past unkindnesses to you, and accept me as a good friend today.

Catching the drift of these words, though still not knowing any details, Sagan tactfully replied: "I've thought as carefully as I can, and I can't recall a single instance of unkindness from you. If you are thinking of some anonymous activity—such as refereeing a paper or giving your opinion on promotion—it is no unkindness to express a candid view under such circumstances. But whatever the incident was, I cannot believe that your motive was other than the best interest of science."

What convinced Urey that he had been "completely wrong"? This too is unclear. Many close colleagues (such as Stanley Miller) were unaware that Urey had ever held such negative opinions of Sagan. Miller conjectures that Sagan's work on the early faint sun paradox (a topic that intrigued Urey) may have been at least partly behind the change of heart.

Still, Sagan had done much important work by 1967. The flip-flop seems more akin to the perceptual shifts of the face/vase illusion, an abrupt reversal that is occasionally to be found in human relationships as well. Urey seems to have conceived a new way of looking at Sagan, a way to appreciate him for who he was rather than faulting him for what he wasn't.

The Guatemalan Poet

With that nagging mystery of his past explained, Sagan was embarking on a new phase of his life. In 1973 he published his first truly popular book (*The Cosmic Connection*) and appeared on the *Tonight Show* for the first and second time. To many colleagues, it was a mystery how Carl Sagan, a gifted practitioner of a somewhat rarefied field, became the world's best-known living scientist. The answer involves both the message and the messenger.

By his late thirties, Sagan stood six feet two inches tall and weighed about 190 pounds. It was a commonplace among those who knew him that he got better looking as he entered middle age. He shed his geeky horn-rims and nerdy sport shirts; discarded an experimental mustache. He was a darkly handsome man who retained an adolescent charm. He wore his hair long, though neatly trimmed, the part sweeping at an artistic angle across his high forehead. This managed to convey both intellect and an affinity for youth culture. His most striking feature was his eyes, touched with green, and set so deeply that they were often in slight shadow.

He had a charisma that people struggled to put into words. A 1975 profile in *New York* magazine claimed that Sagan looked "like a Colombian novelist—the peer of Gabriel Garcia Marquez, Julio Cortazar, and Mario Vargas Llosa." A friend compared Sagan's "presence" to that of a "Guatemalan poet." Whatever these people were driving at, it's not the sort of thing that is said of very many scientists. There was about Sagan a hint of mystery—or maybe the term should be "magic-realism."

Sagan sometimes seemed at pains to demonstrate that he was *not* like the other scientists with the bad haircuts. He complained that he got *bored* by the company of scientists. His wife was an *artist*. He surrounded himself with writers, liberal intellectuals, and celebrities. He drove an orange Porsche 914 with the vanity plate PHOBOS. (He had really wanted BARSOOM. Six letters was the maximum.) In some cases, all this alienated Sagan from the pocket-protector crowd.

Sagan's flawless extemporizing was uniquely suited to the demands of the television medium. He was a master of the sound bite. Even his self-caricatural "punching" of syllables commanded attention in a medium ruled by short attention spans. Above all, Sagan had a high concept. Extraterrestrial life was one of the few scientific questions that could dependably pull in TV viewers. Anyone who read comic books knew what extraterrestrial life was, and no Nobel laureate could say the subject was unimportant.

As an example of how Sagan fit the needs of the media, consider *Time* magazine's 1971 feature story, "Is There Life on Mars—or Beyond?" Sagan was so patently the most frank and accessible of the scientists polled that the article opened with a statement from him and quoted him liberally throughout. With evident editorial delight in finding a "live one," *Time*'s writer called Sagan "exobiology's most energetic and articulate spokesman." Sagan was the only scientist pictured in the piece.

Rolling Stone

Sagan's prose also began appearing regularly in the counterculture press. He wrote essays for *The Whole Earth Catalogue* and was interviewed by *Rolling Stone*. This was a natural outgrowth of his earlier attempts to reconcile science and the youth culture. At a time when science was suspect among much of the population, this coverage forged a reputation for Sagan as a socially conscious, iconoclastic scientist.

The 1973 *Rolling Stone* piece came about through the suggestion of Timothy Ferris. Ferris was what was then known as a "new journalist." One of his interests was astronomy. He was working on a book called *The Red Limit*. Scientists were not normally featured in *Rolling Stone*, but Ferris sensed, correctly, that Sagan would make a good interviewee.

The two men got along well and soon became friends. Ferris was young, bright, good-looking, and funny; a Manhattan bon vivant who knew people like Jann Wenner, Hunter S. Thompson, and Diana Vreeland. Some of Ferris's questions for Sagan were a real mouthful. "Is the scientific method changing from a purely deductive, rational method to a more creative activity which tests itself against coherent data? And is our conception of the universe changing from seeing it as entropic and random to a view that it is essentially unified, and that the things science treats are only part of a greater unity? Is that actually going on?" (Sagan's answer, basically, was no.)

A sizable fraction of *Rolling Stone*'s 1973 readership used recreational drugs. In his interview Sagan did not endorse drug use, nor speak of his own experiences, but he did allude to the drug culture knowingly. He termed the possible discovery of extraterrestrial life a "mind-expanding experience." Most interesting was Sagan's rumination on the objective validity of mystic insights. He observed that the perception of being "one with the universe" is common to the drug experience and to the mysticism of Eastern religions and Christianity. The phrase, an unsatisfactory attempt to express a nonverbal experience, carries with it the perception of revealed truth. Sagan complained, however, that he hadn't found anyone who was able to test objectively a mystic revelation. He gave as an example of a testable revelation having a vision of an experiment involving shooting deuterons into a vanadium target and producing a specific, unexpected result. *If* the revelation predicted a result at odds with what the experts believed, and *if* the experiment were done and the revelation was right, that would establish the validity of the mystic revelation. That had never happened. "So while not at all taking away from the ecstasy of such an experience," Sagan told Ferris, "I'm skeptical about whether it really makes contact with the way in which the universe is put together. I think it makes contact with the way our skulls are put together, which is a different thing."

"Too Down to Mars"

Recreational drugs were so broadly accepted in the early 1970s that they could figure in the marketing of popular science books. The book that Sagan wrote for Agel was originally titled *The Cosmic Perspective*. An editor at Doubleday observed that the recent movie *The French Connection* (a thriller about drug smuggling) had inspired a spate of similar-sounding titles and tag lines. Maybe *The Cosmic Connection* would be hipper? That title may not have aged gracefully, but it succeeded in marketing the book to a wide audience of 1973 college kids and their elders.

The Cosmic Connection contains Sagan's most explicit statement of what he saw as his manifest destiny.

> Even today, there are moments when what I do seems to me like an improbable, if unusually pleasant dream: To be involved in the exploration of Venus, Mars, Jupiter, and Saturn . . . to land instruments on Mars to search there for life; and perhaps to be engaged in a serious effort to communicate with other intelligent beings, if such there be, out there in the dark of the night sky.
>
> Had I been born fifty years earlier, I could have pursued none of these activities. They were all then figments of the speculative imagination. Had I been born fifty years later I also could not have been involved in these efforts, except possibly the last. . . . I think myself extraordinarily fortunate to be alive at the one moment in the history of mankind when such ventures are being undertaken.

In keeping with its accessible approach, the book was heavily illustrated. Much of the art was supplied by an artist who became another good friend of Sagan's, Jon Lomberg.

Born in Philadelphia, Lomberg was then living in Toronto, juggling a double career as a radio correspondent for the CBC and a specialist in the field of astronomical illustration. Astronomical illustration is the uniquely twentieth-century trade of supplying "artist's conceptions" of planets, galaxies, space stations, and colonization projects for NASA, space museums, book illustrations, and so forth. Like wildlife art of ducks or deer, astronomical art is a specialized field with a specialized constituency. (It irks *astronomical* artists when people confuse them with *science-fiction* artists.)

At that point in his career, Lomberg's particular niche was as the Peter Max of astronomical illustration. Eschewing the meticulous old-master technique of Chesley Bonestell's followers as "too down to Mars," Lomberg painted planets and galaxies in a style loosely inspired by psychedelic posters and album covers. If the combination of hard science and pop sensibility sounds unlikely, it was one that Sagan, of all people, could appreciate. Recognizing this, Lomberg sent Sagan a letter. Sagan wrote back, saying they ought to meet. Thus began a lifelong collaboration.

Great Reckless Solo

Celebrity no less than science may be a matter of being in the right place at the right time. Sagan-the-celebrity's biggest break was his November 30, 1973, appearance on the *Tonight Show*.

With *The Cosmic Connection* coming out, Doubleday's publicity department was trying to book Sagan on talk shows. Johnny Carson, then the longtime host of the *Tonight Show*, happened to tune in to a TV special on UFOs hosted by his talk show rival, Dick Cavett. Sagan was one of the experts on the special. Carson was immediately sold. He told his staff, "I want that guy."

Sagan was slotted into the last fifteen minutes of a ninety-minute show. He appeared after a pair of harmonica-playing hillbilly twins and a mute crow whose owner *swore* the bird could talk—all the excitement must have spooked it.

Carson stumbled over the pronunciation of Sagan's name, unsure whether it was *Sigh*-gen or *Say*-*gone*. Then Sagan, without a trace of unease, suavely fielded questions on UFOs and extraterrestrial life. "He was passionate about astronomy and science in general," Carson recalls, "and was able to convey that passion to the general public without sounding condescending." So Carson took the rare step of inviting Sagan back just three weeks later and allotting him the show's final half hour. *New York* magazine's Stuart Baur wrote:

> Sagan launched into a cosmological crash course for adults. It was one of the great reckless solos of late-night television. . . . When Sagan finished and settled back into the eye of the hush that he had generated, one was willing to

bet that if a million teen-agers had been watching, at least a hundred thousand vowed on the spot to become full-time astronomers.

The *Tonight Show* exposure helped send *The Cosmic Connection* through twenty printings in hardcover and paperback. It sold over 500,000 copies. Talent bookers recognized Sagan as a dependable performer. NASA's planetary missions provided a steady stream of new material. So did the inexhaustible fount of popular delusions.

On Dick Cavett's talk show, the topic turned to the Bermuda Triangle. Sagan ticked off the usual counterarguments: that some of the most-cited cases were known fabrications; that the number of ships and airplanes lost in this vast and heavily traveled swath of the Earth's surface was not statistically remarkable; that *any* disaster occurring in midocean could be expected to cause a craft to sink and "vanish without a trace." How odd, Sagan commented, that ships and planes "disappear mysteriously" but never trains.

"I can see you've never waited for the Long Island Railroad," Cavett said.

In one daft juxtaposition, Sagan and Viking experimenter Gil Levin joined Hermione Gingold on the *Today Show*. Levin droned on as scientists tend to do in front of TV cameras. Sagan spoke eloquently of the philosophical implications of searching for life on Mars. After this, Miss Gingold could only ask the host, "What am *I* doing here?"

For the first time Sagan became known to the entire Cornell student body. In the mid-1970s, one campus newspaper's parody issue ran a fake interview with Sagan. Practically every other word was in italics or boldface. ("It captured his speaking style perfectly," thought one undergraduate.) People recognized Sagan on the streets of Ithaca. Within a few years, Sagan became one of the few instantly recognizable scientists of his time.

Those closest to Sagan were often the best able to accept his fame and, on occasion, put him gently in his place. Discussing his still-new fame with Lederberg, Sagan once commented, "You know, if I went to every meeting I'm asked to, I could spend all my time going to meetings."

"That's nothing," Lederberg countered. "If I spent my time just *answering* all the invitations to go to meetings, I could spend all my time doing nothing else."

One who never lost perspective was Sagan's mother. Rachel happened to be present at one big gathering when Carl started to hold forth on some new scheme. "You know what I ought to do . . . ," he said.

"No, *what* are you going to do, Mr. Big Carl Sagan?" Rachel asked. Her delivery was perfect, just the way she must have addressed the three-year-old Carl when he was being particularly cute.

Death of an Exobiologist

Ten days after Sagan's *Tonight Show* debut, Wolf Vishniac fell to his death in Antarctica.

Vishniac could not accept Horowitz and Cameron's reports of sterile soil in Antarctica—and with it the implications that Mars was lifeless and spacecraft sterilization unnecessary. He was dealing with a more personal disappointment, too. NASA determined that there would be room on Viking for only three biology experiments, not four. The one they dropped was Vishniac's "Wolf Trap." It was the "wettest" of the biology experiments, the only one that required that Martian microbes be able to grow in a liquid water medium. That cost-paring move threw out a decade of Vishniac's lifework.

Vishniac responded to these setbacks by going to Antarctica himself. He was determined to prove that there were microbes Horowitz and Cameron had missed. For Vishniac this was an act of almost foolhardy bravado. Childhood polio had stunted his right arm. Having failed a physical required of those going to Antarctica, he got a senator to pull some strings for him. He also had himself excused from taking the navy survival course normally demanded of scientists doing Antarctic fieldwork.

In November 1973, Vishniac and a geologist took a helicopter from McMurdo Station on the Ross Ice Shelf to a dry valley near Mount Baldr. He set out his instruments and sets of simple glass slides, which he had found useful in culturing soil microbes. A month later, he began retrieving his samples.

On December 10, Vishniac wandered off alone into the insomniac summer night of Antarctica. He said he was going to retrieve some samples and would return in twelve hours. The last entry in his logbook records picking up samples at 10:30 P.M. The air temperature was then $-16°$ F.

The hours of nominal night passed. Another Antarctic day began. When Vishniac failed to return, a search party set out. They found his body in an area well off the marked trails, in a region that had never before known a human tread. Vishniac had fallen off a 500-foot cliff and tumbled several times on a sheer slope. He was found near the base of Mount Baldr and Mount Thor, named for the gods of the Vikings.

Polar Bears

Vishniac's death at fifty-one was a blow to the entire Viking group. It was sharply felt at Cornell. Sagan eulogized Vishniac as "the first person since Giordano Bruno to lose his life in the pursuit of extraterrestrial life." Sagan pored over the maps of Mars, found an unnamed crater at the same far-southern latitude where Vishniac had died, and had it named Vishniac. Thomas Gold deemed himself responsible for Vishniac's death (solely because it was his comment that had led to the invention of the Wolf Trap). Twenty-four years later, sitting at his kitchen table in Ithaca—with Sagan too now gone—Gold told me he *still* considers himself responsible.

With so much effort, and now a human life, sacrificed to the search for life on Mars, it was natural to reassess the odds. How likely was it that the Vikings would find life? In public, Sagan was often evasive, like the child not daring to lay odds on finding the pony under the Christmas tree. Pressed by one journalist in the long days of anticipation before the landing, Sagan could only turn the tables. "What do *you* say?" he asked the reporter. "One in ten thousand? One in a hundred thousand? One in a million?"

The reporter said "one in a million" sounded about right.

"O.K.," said Sagan, "here's my penny. Now where's your money?"

Others on the Viking team tried their own hands at subjective probability. Harold Klein, head of Viking's biology team (he had been brought in after Vishniac's death) went public with a guesstimate of a 1 in 50 chance of finding life. Klein used "Drake equation"–like math to arrive at that figure. Vance Oyama, designer of one of Viking's biology experiments, put the chance of life at 50 percent; Norman Horowitz, designer of another, put the chances at "not quite zero." Bruce Murray told one journalist, "I'm an honest-to-God, card-carrying geologist, and none of us expects to find life on Mars."

Privately, Sagan told Clark Chapman that he believed the chances of finding life on Mars were 50 percent. Sagan's rationale was simple agnosticism: there were two possibilities (life and no life) and no basis for favoring one over the other.

Chapman believed the odds were much less. Sagan was willing to put his penny where his mouth was. He bet Chapman the Vikings would photograph "polar bears" on Mars. Loser would buy the winner a drink.

"Polar bears"? This was one of Sagan's pet ideas. As Sagan argued, polar bears are big, active creatures that live in what we think of as a hostile and impoverished environment. Grass cannot live on the Arctic ice, nor can mice. A mouse is so small that it would quickly freeze into a solid lump of mouse meat. Polar bears survive because their ponderous bulk insulates them against frigid winds and long stretches between meals.

Nineteenth-century biologist Karl George Bergmann noticed that related species tend to be *bigger* in *colder* climates—on Earth, anyway. Apply "Bergmann's rule" to Mars, which is *really* cold, and Sagan semiseriously concluded the animals there ought to be *huge*. There could be "polar bears"—meaning large life-forms whose size would protect against cold, dry, and perhaps ultraviolet as well.

Sagan promoted his "polar bears" idea widely. It figured in his next popular book, *Other Worlds*. Agel wanted Sagan to write a dumbed-down version of *Cosmic Connection* (itself more or less a dumbed-down *Intelligent Life in the Universe*). *Other Worlds* was it; a paperback original with lots of pictures and cartoons and just enough text to allow perusal in a single sitting. Its sans serif text overprinted on black-and-white photos must have embodied some '70s book designer's most "advanced" concepts. One two-page spread is more legible than many. The text is printed on a photograph of a polar bear in the snow.

Maybe it should therefore be emphasized that Sagan did not envision Martian "polar bears" as looking like real polar bears. In more sober discussion Sagan favored the term "macrobe"—opposite of "microbe"—for these life-forms big enough to see. He and Lederberg imagined a bestiary of possible Martian macrobes. *Crystophages* (ice eaters) might tap the permafrost for water. *Petrophages* would derive water from a diet of rocks, after the model of desert kangaroo rats that manufacture needed water from desert seeds. JPL commissioned illustrations of these ideas, and *Time* magazine published several just before the Viking landing. The artist's crystophage looked unconvincing, more like futuristic airport seating than something alive. The petrophage rendering stands up better, a blossom-topped octopus sprawling among rocks and sand.

Bruce Murray

Despite this genuine enthusiasm, it would be a distortion to say that Sagan *believed* in his "polar bears." The very term is playful. It was a way of turning the tables on Horowitz and Murray; showing that arguments from the Earth's polar biology could cut *both* ways.

What Sagan *did* believe was that Viking should be designed to detect the widest possible range of potential Martian organisms—not excluding large and/or mobile organisms. It was *this* conviction that often brought Sagan into conflict with Viking's engineers and geologists.

In the media, Sagan's opposition was often embodied in the person of geologist and JPL director Bruce Murray. The press presented Sagan's conflicts with Murray as a scientific morality play: the visionary versus the regular guy. Whenever Murray and Sagan appeared together, the contrast was striking. Sagan had the undeniable poise of someone born for the TV cameras. Murray looked like a stocky corporate type who'd never been told not to wear striped jackets on TV. When asked to justify space exploration, Murray would speak unabashedly of patriotism. Sagan would rattle off five reasons and underscore the opportunities for international cooperation. (Toward the end of his four-decade relationship with Sagan, Murray confessed to feeling "like an odd pair of siblings joined at their navels.")

In his way, Murray was as passionate about geology as Sagan was about exobiology. As an MIT undergraduate, Murray had entertained thoughts of becoming a biologist. He changed his mind after visiting a biologist's office and finding it to be a *wunderkammer* of formaldehyde-filled jars of specimens. The place gave Murray the creeps. Geology promised a healthier, more outdoorsy type of work.

Like much scientific debate, that over Martian life was rooted in personal predispositions. Shortly before Viking landed, Sagan was asked why the prospect of life on Mars held such meaning. "I think it's because we human beings love to be alive," he replied, "and we have an emotional resonance with something else alive, rather than with a molybdenum atom."

But to Bruce Murray, Mars was just fine the way it was in the Mariner photos. It had volcanoes and canyons, dust storms, craters, and icecaps. Mars didn't need life to be interesting. And he couldn't understand why Sagan was so preoccupied with life.

Pet Shop

Sagan had many ideas about how to maximize the necessarily imponderable chances of detecting life. One of them was a "flashlight." "I keep having this recurring fantasy," Sagan said, "that we'll wake up some morning and see on the photographs footprints all around Viking that were made during the night, but we'll never get to see the creature that made them because it is nocturnal."

Lederberg had doubts about this. He expected that any polar bears would be sound asleep, conserving their warmth through the frigid Martian night. But imaging team leader Thomas Mutch backed Sagan on the flashlight because he believed that it would allow them to watch frost forming.

Engineering realities tabled the idea. Viking's power came from two thirty-five-watt generators—barely adequate to power the undersized lightbulb in the back of a refrigerator. They couldn't divert more than a fraction of the total power to a flashlight, and it probably wouldn't be bright enough to show much.

Another of Sagan's rejected ideas showed ingenious economy of means: edible paint. He suggested that they paint the Viking lander with various types of nutrients. This "bait" might draw any mobile Martian life, increasing the chance that the cameras would see something alive. By using zones of different nutrients (for instance, right- and left-handed amino acids) it would be possible to see if some attracted (or poisoned?) Martians more than others. This test might reveal something of Martian biochemistry. Even the biology experiments were not designed to do that.

As a member of the imaging team, Sagan was most closely concerned with Viking's cameras. Viking did not carry conventional TV cameras. A real-time video feed from Mars would require too much bandwidth. Early in mission planning, there had been thought of storing images on videotape and letting cached data dribble back to Earth. Once again sterilization posed a problem. The necessary temperatures destroyed videotape.

They settled instead on a lightweight electronic camera invented by ITEK, a Lexington, Massachusetts, firm. The ITEK camera took only still images. It did not "snap" a picture instantly as today's digital cameras do. It was essentially a fax machine. A fluttering mirror scanned the Martian landscape one vertical line at a time and "faxed" it to Earth, where the lines of data were fitted together to form a panoramic picture. Each lander had two cameras, spaced some distance apart. This made it possible to take 3-D pictures that could be viewed with special glasses.

The camera's unusual design concerned Sagan. As Sagan saw it, the camera was a biology experiment—the one least dependent on preconceptions of alien biochemistry. "A silicon-based giraffe," he told an interviewer for PBS's *Nova* series, "would be detectable if it walked by the Viking camera." But while documents don't move during the time it takes to fax them, a Martian giraffe *might* move faster than the Viking cameras scanned. This could distort its image oddly. *Quickly* moving creatures would be as invisible as pedestrians in a time exposure of city streets.

*   *   *

Imaging team leader Thomas Mutch was not greatly worried about quick-moving Martians. Mutch was a seasoned geologist, a man with a great passion for mountains. (It was a mountain that would kill him one day: he died during a climb in the Himalayas in 1980.) Mutch had a henpecked look and a dry sense of humor founded on understatement. "I don't think the engineers are wallowing in ignorance about what we want to do, Carl," he would say. This seemed to be the right approach in mediating disputes. Mutch was a man almost everyone admired. One geologist said he admired Mutch for not *shooting* Carl Sagan.

Mutch's biggest concern was that Viking's fax-machine camera was being invented as it was built. It might not even *work*. Mutch kept bugging the ITEK people to let him see it in action.

Permission wasn't granted until August 1974, when it was too late to do much of anything if a defect were to be found. The design was frozen, and several cameras had already been shipped to Martin Marietta's Denver plant for incorporation in Viking.

As the manufacturer saw it, the cameras were like new cars. Every mile on the odometer counted. The imaging team had to be content with testing some "factory seconds" that *weren't* going to Mars. The scientists wanted to take the cameras to some place out in the desert. They were told that was impossible. The cameras (the flawed surplus cameras) were too fragile to be transported on the highway. Mutch wanted to know how these fragile cameras were going to survive being put in a rocket and blasted to Mars.

After some initial tests just outside the Martin Marietta plant, a company honcho did an about-face. He decided that maybe it would be okay to take the camera somewhere that *really* looked like Mars. The imaging team agreed to meet the following day at Great Sand Dunes National Monument, an arid region of Colorado. Along the way, Sagan stopped off at a pet shop. He obtained a garter snake, a chameleon, and two tortoises.

The next morning, the group began taking pictures. The camera performed flawlessly. With the routine tests out of the way, it was time for Sagan's circus. Sagan placed his surrogate Martians, successively, on the sand in front of the lander. The tortoise was the most photogenic species. When it moved in the direction of the scanning, its image morphed into a weird tortoiseshell river. Head and limbs were not apparent. When moving in the opposite direction, it was compressed.

Snake and chameleon were too fast altogether. They flitted into thin air, leaving not so much as a pixel on the scanner photo. The imager could capture only their tracks in the sand.

Sagan made his point. *Knowing* what a turtle is, you might not recognize it from the distorted pictures. The problem of recognizing an alien creature of unknown appearance and movements would be formidable. Fast creatures were invisible.

At that point, the only possible fixes were in software. The camera could be programmed to freeze its horizontal tracking and scan a single vertical line repeatedly. This mode, like looking through a crack in a door, was a sensitive motion detector. Changes in the brightness values on that line would indicate that something in the scene is moving. It would not show what that something looked like. These single-line scans were programmed at Sagan's insistence.

Spirits were high enough that the group ended the day with a trick photo. The camera took about ten minutes to produce a panoramic group portrait. The scientists "cloned" themselves by posing motionless, leapfrogging ahead of the scanner, and posing again, and again, forming a crowd of virtual Carl Sagans and Thomas Mutches and the others, all assembled in the midst of the American desert.

Ann Druyan

Sagan began staying at Timothy Ferris's apartment on his trips to New York City. As a *Rolling Stone* editor, Ferris usually had a stack of invitations to glamorous events. On occasion Sagan would tag along.

In autumn 1974 writer Nora Ephron threw a buffet supper at her Manhattan apartment. Ephron was a friend of Ferris's and knew Sagan as well. At a lecture sponsored by the *Washington Post*, Sagan had warmed up the room by asking a question to test the scientific literacy of those present. Only one person in the room got the correct answer: Ephron.

So Ephron invited Carl and Linda; Timothy and his fiancée, Ann Druyan; film producer David Obst and his wife, Lynda, a writer; theater critic Frank Rich; historian Taylor Branch.

Timothy's girlfriend, Annie (as everyone called her), was an aspiring novelist. She was twenty-five, tall, chic, and spectacularly beautiful. If she did not look "bookish," she had a great love of books. As a girl in Queens, New York, she read Mark Twain's works with a flashlight under her covers at night. She studied literature at NYU, somewhat distractedly as it was the height of the 1960s. Then she worked a string of day jobs while writing a novel in her Upper West Side apartment. The book, *A Famous Broken Heart,* was a comic fantasy about literary characters in limbo, waiting to be "cast" in novels. This allowed her to use characters like Willy Loman and Miss Havisham (the title's "broken heart").

Well read as she was, Druyan had never heard of Carl Sagan. Ephron assured her that he was a fascinating person, not like the typical scientist. When Annie arrived at the party, she found a man sprawled on the floor, laughing almost hysterically at something someone must have just said. This was Carl.

Annie and Carl hit it off immediately. Carl was impressed with her knowledge of the history of baseball. Annie could rattle off stats and trivia about the major, minor, and Negro leagues. She had traveled to Cooperstown for Hall of Fame inductions. They also spoke about capitalism and Leon Trotsky, who had written a mordantly funny *History of the Russian Revolution* before Bolshevik assassins bashed in his head with a hammer.

Annie decided that Carl, with his shirtsleeves rolled up and his warm smile, was indeed not at all like the typical scientist.

Proxy ET

In autumn 1974 another "message to extraterrestrials" was sent into space. Cornell's Arecibo observatory was upgrading its radio telescope with a half-million-watt transmitter and a new reflector surface. To celebrate, Frank Drake wanted to *send*, rather than listen for, a message.

The message would be a bigger version of the puzzle picture that had stumped the Order of the Dolphin, a string of 1,679 bits that could be assembled—only one way—into a picture. The picture, seventy-three scan lines of twenty-three pixels, would be a cosmic diagram packed with suitable information.

Drake sent a memo to the National Astronomy and Ionospheric Center (NAIC) staff, asking for suggestions about message content. Sagan, who was not affiliated with NAIC, did not get the memo. Instead, Drake planned to use Sagan as proxy extraterrestrial.

This took place during a long lunch at the Cornell faculty club. Without saying a word, Drake placed his cosmic diagram in front of Sagan, and Sagan tried to decrypt the picture.

Sagan did a great deal better on this "test" than the first one. To the average viewer, there is only one obvious part of the diagram, a stick-figure human. Nearly as obvious to an astronomer are the blocky sketches of the Arecibo radar dish and the solar system. Sagan got that, information on our genetic code, and a binary number system used to give size information. Both Sagan and Drake were pleased.

On November 16, 1974, at 1 P.M., about 250 people gathered under a party tent at Arecibo for the dedication. The message was beamed in the direction of the M13 globular cluster, nearly overhead at the time. M13 is a city of stars, about 300,000 suns packed into an area of the sky about the size of the full moon. This increased the chance that there would be an intelligent species somewhere within the beam's coverage. M13 is 25,000 light-years away, meaning that any response would take 50,000 years to come.

No one knew how fast to run through the message. Drake decided simply to connect the transmission to the public address system and play it at a rate that would sound good. Transmitted at ten bits a second, it produced an intelligible *dih-dih-da-dih-da.* . . . For those in attendance the transmission was an emotional experience, no less so than rocket launches are for rocket scientists and families. There were tears and sighs. An engineer in the control room noticed that the first six bits tapped out *HI* in Morse code.

"Let's Do It"

The upgrade of Arecibo's telescope motivated Sagan to conduct one of the most audacious scientific observations of his time. Its negative result temporarily devastated even him.

It began with Shklovskii and Kardashev's idea about observing nearby galaxies for extraterrestrial signals. Shklovskii had long hinted that the Soviets were about to conduct such a search. There had been one halfhearted effort. In 1968, during a survey of nearby stars, V. S. Troitsky of Gorky State University turned his dish to the Andromeda galaxy. He found nothing. But Troitsky had been using a 50-foot dish, even smaller than the one Drake used for Ozma. Arecibo had a *1,000-foot* dish.

So Sagan was eager to use Arecibo to listen for extragalactic signals. He would call up Drake and say, "Let's do it." Or they would run into each other at Cornell. "Let's do it."

For a time, the upgrading of the telescope got in the way. The dish would be so much more capable afterward, Drake maintained, that they might as well wait. With the upgrade complete, they wrote a proposal and in 1975 finally gave it a try.

*   *   *

Arecibo's location was chosen by sliding a quarter around on a map of Puerto Rico. At the scale of the map, the quarter represented the 1,000-foot-wide dish they needed to build. The coin came to rest on a natural hollow approximating the size and shape of the planned dish.

This divination put the observatory in the middle of nowhere. First-time visitors to Arecibo are shocked to learn that the telescope is almost a day's drive from the San Juan airport. How can *anything* be a day's drive in Puerto Rico? The answer is, narrow, two-lane mountain roads with no passing and a few slow trucks.

Arecibo is a place of spectacular sunsets, majestic thunderstorms, and nightly serenades of the *coqui*—tiny, unseen frogs whose name is onomatopoeic. It can be a very "colonial" outpost. American radio astronomers do not always speak Spanish, and Arecibo's are notorious for failing to learn the language and culture. Puerto Rican nationalists suspect that "El Radar," as it is called locally, has something to do with nefarious military operations. There have been threats of sabotage.

Amenities are few. In the mid-1970s, there was not even a television set. During the Watergate hearings, Cornell's James Cordes secretly rigged an antenna to the observatory's video screen in order to use it as a TV set and watch reruns of each day's hearings. Cordes never told Sagan that he was borrowing the same video display that Sagan used for his SETI work.

Cockeyed Optimists

When Sagan came to Arecibo, he was like the movie star cowboy who can't ride a horse. The world's most visible proponent of searching for extraterrestrial intelligence, Sagan had never done a SETI study.

As eager as he must have been to earn his spurs, this was no ego trip. Sagan made a real effort to steep himself in the technology. He and Drake were doing something that had never properly been done before, something that might finally succeed in detecting intelligent life in the universe. "It was a big trip, here was the world's largest telescope, and we had the finest computers in the world," Drake told me. "I think Carl really thought we were, within one day or so, going to detect radio signals."

Sagan and Drake stayed at a small beach-front hotel patronized by vacationers. Each night an aged hotel attendant awakened them at 4 A.M. Shrugging off sleep, they piled into a car. Drake drove, dodging chickens and toads. Sagan, half-awake, chewed leftover garlic bread for breakfast. By the time they arrived at the observatory, dawn streaked the Caribbean sky. Telescope time slots, not darkness, dictate the schedule of a radio astronomer.

The plan was to observe four nearby galaxies on the 1420 MHz emission frequency of neutral hydrogen. The obvious choice was M31, the Great Nebula in Andromeda. It is the biggest of nearby galaxies. Unfortunately, Andromeda rides high in the northern sky and Arecibo is in the tropics. Unlike an amateur telescope, the great dish had limited steering. Cranked to its northernmost setting, the telescope's beam sliced across the galaxy's southern reaches. They could not cover the entire galaxy. This was freakish luck, for the galaxy is, in angular extent, only about the size of a quarter held at arm's length.

Nonetheless, they resolved to try the part of the Andromeda galaxy the telescope *could* reach, including its two small satellite galaxies, M32 and NGC 205. These two galaxies are each compact enough to fit within a single beam setting of the telescope. They also searched M33, a spiral galaxy in the constellation Triangulum.

Their receiver sampled 1,008 frequency channels at once. (Ozma sampled just one at a time.) That was a great convenience, even though they were theoretically tuning into a single frequency. The motion of the Earth, as well as that of the presumed transmitting planet, would shift the frequencies. It is necessary to search on a wide range of frequencies near 1420 MHz to be reasonably sure of receiving a nominal 1420 MHz signal.

The results were displayed on an oscilloscope. An electron gun painted the screen with green pinpoints of light: a radio spectrum. They believed that an artificial signal would appear as a point or points much higher than the rest of the spectrum. Sagan's body language made an indelible impression on Drake. For the first minutes, Sagan sat rigidly forward in his seat, his back almost at a forty-five-degree angle. He contrived to place his eyes as close to the green phosphors as possible. He was not about to blink at *history*.

The first spectrum was virtually a flat line. Nothing.

The dish shifted an imperceptible increment, and the process started anew. A new spectrum appeared on the screen five minutes later. Again Sagan bolted forward. Again there was nothing. As the search went on, Sagan's posture shifted. He leaned back in his seat, dispirited. There was nothing in all of the Triangulum galaxy.

They spent about 100 hours in observation. "All we saw were level, flat spectra," Drake said. "After two nights of that, it *does* get boring. But to Carl it was really disappointing. He really had this feeling that we would succeed almost within hours."

*   *   *

"It was an actual feeling of depression," Sagan said of his reaction, "not just disappointment: there was no one on any of those stars trying to reach us in the most obvious way." Sagan was too disheartened to publish the result properly (a negative result on so important a question would have been fitting for *Icarus*). Instead, he buried it in the *Arecibo Observatory Quarterly Report*. A single paragraph soft-pedaled the observation as a way of checking out the equipment. It read in full:

> A brief run on the night of March 24/25 served as the first shakedown of the new autocorrelator and a test of detection sensitivity. Normal terrestrial communication signals reflecting from the moon near 430 MHz were picked up with the Arecibo telescope and analyzed with the first 252 channel quadrant of the correlator. Later in the evening various galactic and extragalactic sources were observed at 1420 MHz. No non-terrestrial narrow-band signals were detected.

The significance of Sagan and Drake's negative result—or lack thereof—can be debated endlessly. This is the great occupational hazard of SETI, where *all* results (so far) are negative, and *no* negative result seems to be meaningful.

At the very least, the observation threw cold water on the most uninhibited theorizing of Green Bank and Byurakan. If there were *thousands* or *millions* of distinct superadvanced civilizations per galaxy, one might imagine that at least one would be interested enough in communicating to broadcast with a star's worth of power at 1420 MHz (or at a selection of frequencies including 1420 MHz, or at *all* possible frequencies). Sagan and Drake's study seems to have ruled that out.

It could not explain the negative result—that is, whether there was no intelligent life in the other galaxies, or whether there were advanced ETs but they had no interest in communicating with such primitives as us, or whether Kardashev's idea of a civilization channeling a star's power into extragalactic beacons was simply absurd. Most SETI people now tend to favor the third explanation. "The more you think about it, the less it means," William Newman says—and he does not believe that Sagan brooded too long about it afterward.

Nevertheless, the negative result had its effect even on stoic Drake. "If there were once cockeyed optimists, there aren't any more," he wrote shortly after the galaxy study. "In a way, I am glad. The priceless benefits of knowledge and experience that will come from interstellar contact should not come too easily. . . . I hope it is a cosmic rule: among civilizations there shall be no spoiled children. They must earn the right to their inheritance."

Defection

The Arecibo result was a particular disappointment to the Soviet SETI community. One Soviet who took it to heart was I. S. Shklovskii. He concluded that extraterrestrial intelligence either does not exist or is extremely rare; we are probably the only technological race currently existing in the local group of galaxies.

What about the Drake equation? At least one of the ballpark estimates had to be off—*way* off. Shklovskii suspected that the great error was the average lifetime of a communicating civilization. It alone was totally speculative. In Shklovskii's grim analysis, the lifetime was short because all technological civilizations blew themselves up.

It weighed on Shklovskii that all the ways an extraterrestrial species might call attention to itself on a cosmic scale—intergalactic beacons, interstellar rockets—entailed fabulous amounts of energy. To zip around the galaxy, a civilization would need to wield far more energy than that contained in all the nuclear weapons in the Earth's arsenals. Naturally, before this level of technology would be used for idealistic scientific enterprises, it would be used for weaponry, and that was the key to the mystery. Weapons that get built get used. It was apparently a law of nature that technological civilizations perish in a planetary holocaust before they get around to sending messages or spaceships across the galaxy.

Shklovskii published his new view of things in a 1976 article in the Russian journal *Voprosy Filosofii*. The article's title translates as "Could Intelligent Life in the Universe Be Unique?" News of Shklovskii's apostasy spread throughout the SETI community. It was a personal setback to Sagan. Shklovskii had been one of the first to share a dream that so many considered outlandish. Now—and for the remaining decade of Shklovskii's life— Sagan would spend their occasional meetings trying to reconvert Shklovskii. Sagan trotted out all the arguments: that the ETs were out there but had decided to let us alone for our own good; that they were trying to communicate using some alien modality uninvented on Earth; that we might yet pick up signals of nearby civilizations, not too much more advanced than ours. Never could Sagan change Shklovskii's mind. In Shklovskii's view Sagan and Drake had performed SETI's own Michelson-Morley experiment at Arecibo. The expected ethereal message was simply not there.

Suicide Chess

At long last, the Sagans' new house was finished. Carl, Linda, and Nicholas moved in for the 1975–76 academic year. A unique feature of the house was a three-dimensional model of a galaxy.

Jon Lomberg had conceived the idea of a galactic model consisting of many parallel, vertical panes of glass. Stars and nebula would be painted on one or another of the panes with fluorescent paint, creating a three-dimensional effect like that of the multiplane animation in Disney films. The model would then ideally be installed in a darkened room. Concealed "black lights" would make the painted stars glow. As the glass itself would be invisible, the stars would float eerily in space. It would be like the *Star Trek* holodeck—or like the famous "star map" Leader showed Betty Hill.

As soon as Sagan heard about this, he had to have one. He commissioned Lomberg to build it and installed it in a room where it could be displayed to visitors.

"I have two comments," Isaac Asimov said when he saw it. "One, I already invented this. Two, this dark room would be a great place to make out."

*   *   *

Growing up, Nick Sagan regarded his father and mother as complete opposites. His father was the embodiment of science, and his mother, the embodiment of art; antithetic muses sharing the same roof.

Linda's artistic interests now included filmmaking. Ithaca's film industry was not dead, as demonstrated by several documentary filmmakers working in the university's orbit. Linda produced the documentary *Two Ball Games* with Ithaca filmmaker David Gluck. She also did a drunk-driving film, narrated by Dick Cavett, that was shown to those arrested for DUI.

Carl meanwhile was attempting to learn the art of fatherhood. He was taken aback one day when he asked Nick what he wanted to be when he grew up. Nick's answer was "a daddy and a host." Host of a TV show.

Nick shared his father's interest in Greco-Roman mythology. "I'm Pan!" he would announce. Assuming the temporary identity of one pagan god or mortal, he would delight in telling how he was related to the other figures of classical myth.

Carl pressed Nick to read the books that had influenced him as a child, such as the Burroughs Mars novels and *The Count of Monte Cristo*. Once while Nick was happily immersed in a *Superman* comic book, Carl mentioned that there was *another* superman. He astutely compared and contrasted the Friedrich Nietzsche and DC Comics versions. Nick wished his father would just let him read the comic book.

One day at Nick's nursery school, the class art project was to have the children trace their bodies on large sheets of paper, cut the silhouettes out, and add a few markings for eyes, nose, and mouth. Nick brought his self-portrait home. His father took one look at it and decided that it looked amazingly like the Tassili frescoes. These ancient North African wall paintings of goggle-eyed beings had been taken by some as evidence for extraterrestrial visitation. Carl published Nick's drawing in *Other Worlds* as a refutation of the extraterrestrial hypothesis.

Carl bought a Ping-Pong table, and he and Nick played the game intensively. Carl's specialty was slams. Nick became expert at setting them up by putting backspin on the ball. There was a large poster of the moon on the wall beside the table. Nick creatively modified the rules to allow bank shots off the "moon."

*   *   *

Dorion and Jeremy were baseball nuts. Jeremy once mildly shocked his father when he referred to a Cornell cleaning woman as "Babe." She was wearing the name tag "Ruth," which Jeremy linked with baseball's Babe. Dorion insisted on teaching the sport to an unlikely pupil, his grandmother Rachel. Dorion apologized each time Rachel missed the ball, insisting that his pitching had been at fault.

Carl taught all three sons chess. The boys found regular chess a bit tame and amused themselves with invented variants: accelerated versions played against the clock, and "suicide chess," where the first player to lose all his pieces wins. The rules required that each player capture the other's pieces whenever possible. Observed Nick, "The queen is a very dangerous piece in this game."

The kids were naturally aware of their father's marijuana use. During a combined Sagan and Grinspoon family vacation in Trinidad, Dorion, Jeremy, and David Grinspoon decided it would be interesting to spy on one of their parents' pot parties. After being put to bed, they crept to their parents' cottage. The adults' laughter was so contagious that the boys had trouble remaining silent as they peered through the nighttime windows.

Countdown

Carl, Linda, and Nick spent much of August 1975 in Florida. They were there to watch the launch of Viking 1 to Mars. Two hours before the planned liftoff on August 11, workers discovered a corroded valve. It probably would have worked, but they dared not risk a half-trillion-dollar spacecraft on a cheap valve. Launch was moved up to August 14.

In the confusion of that postponement, someone turned a switch on and left it on, draining some batteries. When the problem was discovered, the batteries were putting out an anemic nine volts. They expected thirty-seven.

The Viking batteries could not be popped in and out. Technicians would have to open the sterilization shield, replace the batteries, and go through the sterilization process anew. Fortunately, there were *two* Vikings. They swapped them. The former Viking 2 became the new Viking 1.

The reconfigured rocket lifted off on August 20, 1975, at 5:22 P.M., Eastern Daylight Time. One project scientist called the launch "a screwed-up mess."

*   *   *

The delays meant that the Sagan family was holed up at the Cocoa Beach Ramada Inn, killing time and anxiously wondering whether to hold out a few more days or give up and go home. Lederberg was there, too, now striking a somewhat more pessimistic tone. It worried him, too, that there were no gases out of chemical equilibrium in Mars's atmosphere.

Carl filled the hours playing with Nick and the other children in the pool, sometimes giving impromptu science talks. Journalist Henry S. F. Cooper, Jr., recorded a snippet of one of these poolside talks, on the subject of the Viking lander:

> "What if it blows up?" the boy in red trunks asked.
> "That's one reason we have two of them," Sagan said.

"What if a leg falls off?" the girl with the ponytail asked. This had happened to the model that Sagan had in his hand. "Then it will have a limp—Viking will tilt," Sagan said. "What if a Martian cuts off an eye?" another boy asked. "That will be terrific! Then the other eye will see him." "What if the Martians have sophisticated weapons that blow it up?" another girl asked. "Then we'll have a blown-up lander," Sagan said. "And maybe the cameras will photograph the Martians doing these bad things. But the Martians probably won't be bad. They'll either be kindly or they won't care about us."

Life in the Clouds

As the Vikings set off to look for life on Mars, Sagan revisited an even more speculative theme: life on *Jupiter*.

The notion had necessarily changed a good deal since Sagan's first mention of it. At the time of Sagan's 1960 speech in San Francisco, some astronomers believed there might conceivably be oceans of liquid water on Jupiter. It was also thought that Jupiter's atmosphere contained large proportions of ammonia and methane.

Both ideas turned out to be wrong. Jupiter's atmosphere is mostly hydrogen and helium, like the sun's. (Sagan participated in a crucial determination of that, using observations of Jupiter's 1971 occultation of the star Beta Scorpii.) Ammonia, methane, and water are present as traces, which would scale back, though by no means eliminate, the production of organic molecules.

By current understanding, Jupiter is nearly all gas and lacks a solid surface. Notwithstanding the scales at the Hayden Planetarium, there is no place on Jupiter to stand and register your increased heft. A person or any solid mass would be in free fall.

Jupiter's atmosphere gets denser and warmer with depth. Deep inside the atmosphere the air is crushingly dense and blazingly hot. Between the icy heights and the hellish inferno, Sagan realized, there ought to be a layer with balmy, Earth-like temperatures. *This* layer might have everything necessary for life except a solid surface.

Sagan therefore conjectured balloonlike animals. "We can imagine organisms in the form of ballasted gas bags," he wrote in his portion of *Intelligent Life in the Universe*, "floating from level to level in the Jovian atmosphere, and incorporating pre-formed organic matter, much like the plankton-eating whales of the terrestrial oceans." The 1966 book *Planets* contained an "artist's conception" of dirigible-like creatures floating in the lemon-colored sky of a Jupiter-like planet.

Sagan's science-fiction writer friends loved this idea. Isaac Asimov mentioned Sagan's Jovian life-forms in his *Fantasy & Science Fiction* column. Arthur C. Clarke worked them into a story, "A Meeting with Medusa." Clarke's hero, valiantly piloting a hot-hydrogen balloon through Jupiter's atmosphere, is almost devoured by a floating Portuguese man of war. Life on Jupiter was a pretty original concept even by the standards of science fiction, where most writers confined their man-eating polyps to the good, solid ground of Ganymede or Callisto.

Most astronomers and biologists were less receptive to the idea. Clark Chapman once gave a talk at an astronomy conference where Sagan stood up and asked a difficult question. Chapman's mind raced for a quick, effective reply.

"Well, Carl," Chapman said from the podium, "you can't change the laws of physics . . . not as easily as you did with floating life on Jupiter."

Peals of laughter filled the room. No comeback was possible, not even for Sagan. A few of those present started to *applaud*.

Chapman was surprised by the force of the reaction. He had not meant to call Sagan's balloon animals childish. It was rumored that the Jovian gasbags haunted Sagan for the rest of his career; that the life-on-Jupiter idea cost Sagan grants, awards, and/or tenure.

There were those, like Norman Horowitz, who thought we already knew enough about Jupiter to be sure there can't be life there. The most fundamental objection was simple gravity. No matter how many billions of tons of organic molecules may have been produced, every last purine and amino acid must finally sink into Jupiter's hot zone and incinerate.

Sagan was unimpressed by the gravity argument. It is easy to make back-of-envelope calculations proving that hailstones can't exist and flying machines will never get off the ground. He believed no one could be certain about what can and can't have happened in Jupiter's immense and chaotic atmosphere.

Sagan had never published the life-on-Jupiter idea in full in a major scientific journal (a fact that, doubtless, was not surprising to his critics). Cornell had a brilliant mathematical astrophysicist who just happened to be an expert on Jupiter's interior, namely, Edwin E. Salpeter. Sagan—who could be science's Tom Sawyer, capable of convincing others that whitewashing *his* fence was the most fascinating of all possible demands on their time—convinced Salpeter to collaborate on an extended treatment of Jovian life. Together they produced one of the more singular scientific articles of the time, a quantitative analysis (with sixty equations) of life, love, and death in the air of Jupiter.

For a creature to survive on Jupiter, it would have to contend with some pretty relentless facts of life. Sagan and Salpeter concluded that a "sinker," an eternally falling creature, was conceivable. Jupiter's atmosphere is so huge that a falling mote or balloon could float downward for weeks before it reached the hellish lower depths. Sinkers would have to reproduce before they burned up. They would also need some way of getting their offspring back into the upper atmosphere to start the life cycle anew. They might, for instance, burst open like puffballs, releasing spores so minute that updrafts would carry a few of them back to the upper atmosphere.

Alternatively, Sagan and Salpeter proposed "floaters." Balloon creatures might acquire the ability to pump the helium out of their interiors. (We think of helium as a light gas, but it's the *heavier* of the two main gases in Jupiter's air.) The pumping would leave a lighter, hydrogen-rich gas inside the creatures. They could be as light as air and never have to sink.

Salpeter had surreal discussions with Sagan on how balloon creatures would mate. With buoyancy at a premium, it would make sense if male and female merged. But they were unable to imagine a convincing biological zipper for conjoining the genders. Similar logistics would apply to predator and prey. The article deadpans, "The distinction between hunting and mating under these conditions is not sharp."

*   *   *

"We are creatures who have fallen to great depths," says a Thomas Mann character who is actually living at the summit of *The Magic Mountain*. Sagan and Salpeter's article has somewhat the same oddly poetic paradox. They succeeded in demonstrating that you could *engineer* motes, balloons, or dirigibles that would stay aloft in Jupiter's atmosphere long enough to be consistent with plausible biological life cycles. In a broader sense, the article poses one of the deepest questions of exobiology. Is life such a richly abundant thing that it exists wherever it is conceivable, or are there potential environments for life that remain forever barren? That question confronted Sagan throughout 1976, the year of Viking.

PASADENA
1976

AT THE TIME of Viking, Sagan's second marriage was settling into a resigned middle age. As the physical ardor cooled, Carl and Linda were coming to realize what different people they were. It seemed to some friends that, in his two marriages, Carl had swung from a too-exclusive focus on brains to an equally extreme focus on body. A therapist told Carl that his problem was that he had to choose between his prick and his brain. Carl's sensible reply was, "Why can't I have both?"

Carl and Linda's personality differences expressed themselves in squabbles over trivia: who left stale food in the refrigerator; whether Carl needed to change his shirt for a TV interview; whether, in a game of Monopoly, Carl should lend Linda some play money so that she could stay in the game. (Carl refused. Didn't she know the whole point of Monopoly was to assume the role of ruthless and jackal-like real estate magnates? Linda sent board and plastic hotels flying.)

By mid-June 1976, this domestic drama was playing in Pasadena. Carl, Linda, and Nick shared an apartment with Dorion, who was studying nearby, Timothy Ferris, who was covering the Viking mission for *Rolling Stone*, and Ann Druyan.

"In a certain sense I spent a year on Mars," Sagan wrote. He at any rate spent half a year in Pasadena, and many more months in Ithaca preparing for the Viking mission. He boned up on geology. In 1975 he was made a member of Cornell's geology department. In name at least, Sagan was now a card-carrying geologist.

In the months before the landing, Jim Martin instituted drills for all the Viking teams. Each received simulated data and was required to deal with all readily imaginable contingencies. For the imaging team, Martin set up a studio simulation of Mars. It was a big sandbox with a functioning lander. One day the cameras revealed a fossil trilobite. The scientists had to analyze the fake pictures and present their findings to fake journalists, who then would pose obtuse questions. Occasionally Martin himself took a turn as ersatz journalist, doing what was said to be a fair imitation of the *Mary Tyler Moore Show*'s Ted Baxter.

Embassy of Mars

Sagan was meanwhile dealing with quite a few *real* journalists. Media demands grew exponentially as the landing approached. Deadline-conscious reporters learned to direct all manner of questions to Sagan, knowing that they'd get concise, lucid answers. (At the time of Viking, Sagan carried a suede satchel labeled "Embassy of Mars" in wine embossing.)

This made for some awkward tensions. To many Viking scientists and engineers, it appeared that Sagan was getting too much of the attention for their team effort. Sagan was aware of being disproportionately in the limelight. He used to complain about it to Timothy Ferris—"I don't think with complete sincerity," Ferris says. "But he would try to work other people's names into TV interviews, and the producers would cut those parts out. He once told me that he thought it was ridiculous that so much attention was being paid to him. But then, when I dropped him off at JPL, he went off searching for a Swedish television crew."

Not only did Sagan command much of the attention, but his statements on the prospects for finding life were often at odds with many of the other scientists' views. In a debate with Bruce Murray, Sagan once snapped, "You at Caltech live on the side of pessimism." Murray refrained from the obvious comeback that people at Cornell seem to live on the side of optimism.

Murray compared his and Sagan's approaches to science to the Napoleonic Code and English common law. Murray believed that ideas were wrong (or more exactly: *unworthy of anyone's serious attention*) until proven right by evidence. Sagan operated under the precept that attractive ideas were right (worthy of attention) until evidence proved them wrong.

This approach was expressed in his discourse. "Carl is a great one for posing a question in terms of, 'We have seen nothing that can rule this out,' " noted Viking's Harold Klein. "He's very clever—he doesn't promise anything."

The double negative is often encountered in scientific writing as a form of "scientific caution." Sagan turned this rhetorical convention upside down, using double negatives to advance new and provocative ideas. The double negatives were not so much weasel words as a way of exploring and structuring the great gaping universe of possibilities. When a *Time* magazine writer asked him about the double negatives, Sagan defended himself on the grounds that he uses them "to keep possibilities alive, which he feels is the essential nature of science."

Murray's complaint (Urey's, too, it seems) was that Sagan's speculation did not in itself produce the solid, if plodding, advance of knowledge normally expected of a scientist. "Carl serves an important function," Philip Morrison observed at the time of Viking—"at some risk to himself."

*   *   *

Some of the intramural rancor made it into a *New Yorker* profile of Sagan published in the days before the Viking landing. The writer, Henry S. F. Cooper, Jr., was a knowledgeable journalist with long-standing interest in the space program. His extensively researched article was informative and witty—if you were not the subject of the article, anyway.

"Carl's the greatest menace since the black plague," an unidentified geologist told Cooper. "He's charming, he's bright, but he's totally uncritical," claimed a "scientist." There were enough unattributed quotes of that tenor that Sagan must have watched his back ever afterward. After reading Cooper's article, Sagan told Ferris that he had once heard that a proper magazine profile was supposed to make its subject almost angry enough to sue the magazine—almost but not quite. By that definition, he thought the *New Yorker* piece was a successful article.

*   *   *

Most every day in Pasadena, Sagan would get up, down a chocolate milkshake for breakfast, and head for JPL. The Viking meetings were coming at an accelerating pace. The landing site team alone would meet forty-eight times before both Vikings rested on Martian regolith.

Sagan would enter Building 264, pass a guard checking for bombs (more of Jim Martin's contingency planning), and make his way to Room 461. This large, normally undistinguished conference room was then papered with photomosaics and maps of Mars. A globe of Mars, larger than any *terrestrial* globe most people had ever seen, dominated one corner. Folding tables formed a nearly continuous rectangle paralleling the walls. Inside the rectangle was a large empty space, affording everyone a view of everyone else. Sagan and the other committee members sat in chairs arranged around the outside of the tables. Citizen Martin sat at this table, too, in no way distinguished by his position.

*   *   *

Viking 1 achieved orbit on June 19, 1976. Two days later a maneuver tweaked the orbit so that the craft could take detailed photos of the Chryse landing site. The first photograph came in on the evening of June 22, in the midst of another theoretical discussion about extrapolating surface features from large-scale photographs.

The orbital photos brought good news and bad news. The good news was that the images were marvelously sharp and detailed. The bad news was that almost everything known about the chosen landing sites was wrong.

Viking revealed the "bland" terrain around Chryse as a deeply cut riverbed. There were teardrop-shaped "islands" within channels and disturbing hints of almost fractal detail. Sagan was, on the one hand, delighted. The pictures left little doubt that running water had existed on Mars. That helped the case for life. On the other hand, the chosen landing site was in the midst of a drainage basin with sharp contours and (the geologists guessed) large boulders carried by ancient floods. Viking 1 could not land there.

It appeared that the dust had never really settled during the Mariner 9 mission. It was the dust haze, not the surface, that looked so smooth and inviting.

*   *   *

There began an agonized struggle to find an acceptable place to land Viking on Mars. The landing site team became four dozen angry men, unable to come to a verdict as time ticked away and tempers flared.

The orbiter instruments never found any of the warmer, wetter "oases" that Sagan and Lederberg had hoped to find. There did not seem to be much difference in water vapor at a given latitude. So water, which had dominated the early discussions, became largely a nonissue.

Sagan's philosophy in the renewed deliberations was that a safe landing outruled everything else. In the ongoing photographs-versus-radar controversy, Sagan thought that the immediate issue wasn't which side was right. The issue was ensuring the best odds of a safe landing. Sagan argued that prudence dictated a site that looked good in the photographs *and* in the radar.

Although the logic of this argument won Sagan allies, it was easier said than done. It seemed that whenever a potential site looked really good in the photographs, the radar people insisted it was bad.

When Sagan believed there was insufficient information to make an informed decision on a site, he would abstain from voting on it. This irked Martin, whose management style set great store in conducting "straw votes" on candidate sites. Martin instituted a "Carl Sagan rule" whereby everyone had to vote or else explain their position.

"Carl," snapped Martin during one of these abstentions, "we have a *real* spacecraft orbiting the planet with explosives in bolts waiting to be detonated to release a *real* lander in the very near future. We need an unequivocal opinion."

Sagan named his choice. When Martin asked why he couldn't have done that right off, Sagan replied, "I don't vote, I *decide*."

(Levinthal later asked Sagan about the voting. Sagan explained, "Elliott, you don't believe that I counted all of those votes equally.")

Until a site with good photos and radar was found, it seemed logical to Sagan to abstain. He knew that NASA managers were not always perfectly logical—and feared that they were sold on a Fourth of July touchdown no matter what. He was pleasantly surprised when, late on June 26, Jim Martin decided that they would not be landing Viking 1 on the Fourth of July. The holiday worried Martin anyway, because he was afraid the landing would be lost among the coverage of the nation's Bicentennial festivities. Martin had NASA send out a press release announcing the postponement, just in time for TV anchors to cancel their flights to the West Coast for live coverage.

Cosmic Ice Hockey

The nation's 200th birthday passed without a suitable landing site. There was beginning to be a "timeline problem." Viking 2 was nearing Mars for an August 7 arrival. The Viking team, already the largest in NASA's history of planetary missions, could not handle two simultaneously active missions. They needed to have Viking 1 landed in time to deal with Viking 2.

Unfortunately, radar observations had a lead time. It would often be days before a new candidate site could be examined by radar. With time a-wasting, this raised the question of whether to forget about the new site, wait for the radar data (which might be bad), or consider landing without the radar data. The landing site team was getting punchy (they ate their meals at meetings and spent the time between meetings preparing for the next meeting). By July 7, the front-running candidate sites, narrowed down from earlier options, were designated A-1NW and WA-1NW. A-1NW had good photographs, bad radar, but no detailed photos were yet available. A straw vote went 23 to 12 in favor of A-1NW, bad radar notwithstanding. The group was shocked when it realized what it had done. What the group was really saying was that it was sick of deliberating.

*   *   *

They had moved the landing site progressively "downstream," into the middle of Chryse Planitia, the "Golden Plain." Hal Masursky wanted to land right in the middle of the plain. But the radar hinted that there was something funny about the middle of Chryse. There was a puzzling area where the radar signal dropped off so much, as Len Tyler put it, that it was almost like a hole through the planet. That worried Sagan. By July 12, they compromised on a site midway between the center of Chryse and the basin's rim. This region looked good in the radar and in photos.

Martin cut the meeting short. There were some more photos due to come in. They would adjourn, meet after the pictures arrived, and then decide. If they didn't decide *then*, he warned, they would meet again at 3 A.M.—and continue until they did come to a decision.

Because the craft could not be targeted with pinpoint precision, a landing site effectively took the form of an ellipse. By targeting the center of the ellipse, they could be reasonably confident that the craft would end up somewhere within the ellipse. It was necessary, then, to find elliptical regions as free as possible of hazards. Hal Masursky saw three possible landing areas, which he named Alpha, Beta, and Gamma. He moved ellipses around a photomosaic in what he called a game of "cosmic ice hockey." No matter where an ellipse was placed, it covered something that looked dangerous. There were small craters and objects ejected from them everywhere. Masursky counted the hazards within each ellipse and factored in the radar results. Alpha looked best.

One of Sagan's more inspired suggestions had been for JPL to recruit interns from local colleges, eager young students to perform such mind-numbing tasks as counting craters. The crater counters' results came in toward the end of the meeting. Alpha had 9 percent hazardous terrain. Beta and Gamma had 19 percent hazards.

Len Tyler reported that while all three sites had decent radar, Alpha's radar was actually the *least* good of the three.

They took a vote. It was unanimous for Alpha. Sagan, and even Tyler, raised their hands in favor. They adjourned the meeting at midnight.

Touchdown

Viking 1 was expected to touch down on July 20, early in the morning hours, Pasadena time. JPL's hillside campus was awash with light against the black mountains. NASA fitted out the Theodore von Kármán Auditorium as a press center and threw a big all-night party for an unusual mixture of journalists, scientists, bureaucrats, science-fiction writers, and the occasional Hollywood celebrity (the buzz was that Angie Dickinson was coming). It was a chance to see history made; conceivably, to find out whether there was life on Mars.

For most of the Viking team except for Sagan, "macrobes" were a touchy subject, easier to crack jokes about than discuss seriously. JPL was awash in office cartoons and T-shirts bearing cartoon depictions of "Martians." These were bug-eyed, tentacled, and generally intelligent. Even the more skeptical people recognized that they were confronting the sort of abject unknown that sometimes confounds expectations.

The plan was for the Viking lander to jettison its aeroshell at 19,000 feet above the surface. Its parachute would unfurl, its landing legs extend. At 4,000 feet it would fire retrorockets burning purified hydrazine (hydrocarbon-free, to avoid confusing the instruments that would be looking for organic molecules). Viking would detach its parachute and set down at a speed of less than six miles an hour.

Traveling at the speed of light, Viking's signals took eighteen minutes and eighteen seconds to reach Earth. This created a foreboding drama with no precedent in the moon missions. The nominal landing came just before 5 A.M. "It's on Mars, one way or another," someone said. There followed an eighteen-minute interval in which no one could know whether Viking had landed safely or crashed.

At 5:12 A.M., JPL's Dick Bender announced, "Touchdown, we have touchdown!" Signals confirmed the craft was stable and intact. Viking 1 had landed at 22.4° North, 47.5° West, in Chryse Planitia.

Oasis

Sagan was in front of the television cameras on Earth when the first picture came in from Mars. At 6:09 P.M., ABC's Jules Bergman announced, "Here's what appears to be the first picture coming in, Carl."

"Can I go take a look?" Sagan asked.

The imaging team had sweated every detail of the first two photographs. Since something might go wrong with Viking at any moment, each photo was planned as if it would be the last they would receive.

The first photograph was black and white (color requires more time to acquire and transmit). By tourist snapshot standards, its composition was bizarre. Viking pointed its camera down and took a picture of a strip of ground next to the lander, about five feet away from the camera mirror. This photo showed no horizon at all. The reasoning was that a close-up of the ground would show the surface in greatest detail, permitting resolution of features about one-tenth of an inch across.

"You would have believed that all the people in that room were ten years old," JPL's Gentry Lee said, "because we all got up and forty of us ran over to the scope and watched it come in line by line."

The first photograph from the Martian surface revealed a strip of small rocks and soil ("regolith" to purists, but most lapsed into calling it "soil"). Beautifully sharp and rich in contrast, it required no digital processing to be legible. Part of one of the spacecraft's footpads fell within the image. Sagan commented that he had never been so glad to see a rivet.

There was a ghostly reminder of Sagan's concerns about the scanning rate. An indistinct but perfectly vertical dark band appeared in the picture. Evidently, dust raised by the lander—or the parachute or a cloud—had obscured the sun while that part of the picture was being scanned.

The second photograph, taken minutes later, was a 300° panorama of the horizon, also black and white. For Sagan, this was the moment of truth. It would show nearly everything there was to see from the lander's position.

Once again Mars trashed expectations. The landing site team had imagined Chryse Planitia to be a smooth sandy desert, flecked with a few craters that they hoped to avoid. The second photo showed that the craft was resting in the midst of a reef of boulders. Many were big enough to have upturned Viking. The rocks stretched to a horizon believed to be two miles distant. There were small hills on the horizon, possibly the rims of far craters.

Everyone thought the thin air of Mars implied a near-black sky, maybe tinged blue near the horizon. But all the visible sky was light. Stark as the panorama was, the light sky gave it an oddly Earth-like ambience. It put viewers in mind of Arizona or a Hawaiian lava flow, *not* the moon.

*   *   *

"There was not a hint of life," Sagan conceded shortly after the first photos came in—"no bushes, no trees, no cactus, no giraffes, antelopes or rabbits." As disappointed as he must have been, Sagan was nonplussed. He spent about eighteen hours explaining what the photos meant on a succession of television shows.

That night, Sagan, Ferris, and Druyan stayed up in the Pasadena apartment, examining the photos more carefully. To anyone casually looking at that stark panorama, this might seem to be beating a dead horse. But they were looking for less-evident forms of life. They searched for holes that might be burrows; patches on rocks that might be something growing; tracks of swift and restless Martians invisible to the camera; structures with bilateral symmetry; top-heavy objects that seemed to defy gravity and entropy; and (as the landing team's publication in *Science* put it) "spoor."

Sagan taped together the sections of the photograph to assemble the full 300° panoramic view. He rolled the two-foot panorama into a near-complete cylinder and put his head in the middle. Sagan sat on the couch in the Pasadena apartment, for some twenty minutes, with the photo around his head, immersed in Mars. Ferris did likewise.

"Bring full concentration to it," he encouraged Ferris. "Try to imagine yourself there."

Sagan instructed Ferris to look at a rocky outcropping on the horizon, perhaps a quarter of a mile from the lander. He asked Ferris to describe what he saw.

Ferris looked closely and saw—*an oasis.* A Lilliputian oasis, as if things were smaller on the planet Mars. A tangle of mangrovelike trees grew from a shimmering lake. Off to one side stood a single "palm tree." Allowing for the distance, Ferris estimated that all this could not be larger than five feet across.

"I had," Sagan announced, "exactly the same hallucination."

Hallucination it was. In the light of morning, Sagan and Ferris both agreed that the "oasis" was a play of light and shadow on rocks, nothing more.

Mars was casting a strange spell on other Viking scientists, too. Gentry Lee found "chicken tracks" in one image. He ultimately concluded the tracks were made by pebbles blown outward by the lander's retrorockets.

Some of the rocks, it was noticed, were oddly shaped. A few of Viking's scientists informally called dibs on them—*I saw it first*—just in case one turned out to hold some significant secret. Sagan staked a claim on a rock near the lander that was spherical—maybe too spherical? There was also a cylindrical rock dubbed "Midas Muffler" and a "Dutch Shoe." One rock seemed to have the letter *B* scrawled on it. Grad student Alan Binder innocently mentioned this whimsy within earshot of a TV reporter. Stations soon cut in with news bulletins on the "Martian graffiti." It did not help that Binder's name began with a *B.* The *B* reminded Sagan of "Barsoom."

Mars invaded Sagan's dreams. On July 23, he dreamed *he* was on Mars. He was taking a stroll on the planet he now felt he knew. Even in the dream, the science was accurate. He bounded under the lower gravity, and he could see that the horizon was relatively near, as demanded by the geometry of a small planet. The landscape zoomed by as on a video game highway. Sagan came to some foothills and saw something in the rocks. One rock was segmented, divided into three. It was a trilobite.

Rules of the Game

The day after his "hallucination," Sagan was back at work. There was still Viking 2 to be landed.

An "undefinable pessimism" (Thomas Mutch's words) dogged the second Viking. Sagan's paranoia was catching. Suddenly everyone was brooding over what a failure might mean. The public jubilation over Viking might sour quickly.

Hal Masursky opened the meeting. "The rules of the game," he said, "were if we were successful with the first one, we'd be gutsy this time."

That was Sagan's rule, but now he was backing away from it. With Viking 1, Sagan warned, "we were reasonably lucky." ("It was hard work and perseverance," muttered Jim Martin.) Thirty percent of the Viking 1 landscape, chosen to be practically the safest on the planet, had boulders that would have upset Viking had it come down on top of them. That was not much of a mandate to strike out for a riskier site, Sagan believed. The trouble with a northern site was that they would have no radar coverage to guide them.

Gentry Lee did not think that the jagged Viking panorama was much of a testimonial to the rock-avoiding powers of radar. Wasn't Sagan trying to have it both ways: to claim the Viking 1 site is risky *and* credit radar for choosing such a safe site?

"Look," Sagan said. "I have this coin." He flipped a quarter. "It comes up heads once. May I then deduce I have an excellent chance that it will come up heads a second time?"

"It's your coin!" objected Lederberg. The general laughter undercut the point Sagan was making, which was fine with Lederberg because he still wanted to go as far north as practical. "If I were an organism and found myself at those latitudes," Lederberg said, "I would head north."

*   *   *

Ultimately, Sagan let himself be talked into Lederberg's idea of north. He voted with the majority, reconfirming the midnorthern region in Cydonia originally chosen. That meant no radar coverage. The understanding was they would redouble efforts to find the safest spot possible using the orbital photos.

The orbiter made an interesting find in Cydonia. It was a formation that looked a little like a face—enough so that everyone *called* it a face and joked about it. For years afterward, this Martian face was a familiar icon, appearing regularly in the *Weekly World News* and on the *X-Files*. (Not until 1998 did NASA's Global Surveyor return more detailed photos showing the "face" to be an unremarkable, and not very facelike, natural formation.)

Pink Skies

The lander's third, *color* image of Mars was eagerly awaited. For this, Viking 1's camera scanned the landscape through filters for red, green, and blue. Three infrared measurements were also taken. On Earth the data were converted into photographs by exposing a sheet of color film to modulated red, green, and blue laser beams, scanning exactly as the Viking imager had.

That was the idea anyway. NASA folklore holds that cameras always respond a little differently after spaceflight. Also, the color filters used on Viking did not exactly correspond to the laser beams used to produce the photos on Earth. The color imaging thus had to be recalibrated and tweaked.

When calibrated with the techniques that had been used in the test shots on Earth, the first color picture showed a bright red ground and a coral pink sky. Everyone thought that *couldn't* be right. The imaging team eyeballed a correction and came out with a second version in which the ground was a neutral brick red with bluish shadows and the sky was a smoggy Pasadena gray. It looked reasonable.

Within thirty minutes of receiving the data, this photo was broadcast on TV. Print media were clamoring for hard copy, and JPL released photographs within eight hours. In some of the printed reproductions, the cool gray sky edged toward the blue.

"Look at that sky—light blue sky—reddish hue," Mutch said proudly. "It's a very exciting thing to see this distinct reddish coloration to the surface. . . . Even in the deserts here on Earth the reds are not crayon reds as painted by a child."

Viking carried color calibration swatches. They provided the best way of gauging the accuracy of color images. A check of these color samples showed that the released pictures were wrong. On July 21, Jim Pollack announced the error. The ground of Mars was really a saturated brick red. The Martian sky was *pink*.

Pollack was *booed*. People thought the new Mars was aesthetically offensive. When Jim Martin sent a technician around to adjust the colors on JPL's video monitors, people balked. Biology experimenter Gil Levin's son, Ron, went around turning the monitors back to the blue-sky setting, incurring a gruff chewing-out from the Führer himself.

"The sort of boos given to Jim Pollack's pronouncement about a pink sky reflects our wish for Mars to be just like the Earth," Sagan scolded the next day. Reporters asked if the sky was going to turn *green* in the next photo. Then they went home and filed sidebars about scientific fallibility. Apparently the only one who had predicted a pink sky on Mars was a psychic quoted in the *National Enquirer.* In his *Tonight Show* monologue, Johnny Carson announced the discovery of the first gay planet.

Just Add Water

Viking's photographic mission was only beginning, of course. Throughout the mission, the Viking cameras took photographs under varied conditions of lighting and resolution. One photo was by general consent a "masterpiece"—"a real Ansel Adams picture" in Mutch's opinion. It was a black-and-white image of sand dunes dramatically backlighted by the setting sun of Mars. "You can't look at that picture," boasted Sagan, "—the gently rolling horizon, these drifts like a terrestrial desert, the ray of stones and boulders—without wishing you were in it."

In the absence of macrobes, it was proposed that the single-line scans be canceled. Sagan consented. (But when Clark Chapman genially reminded him about the polar bear bet, Sagan shrugged—and never paid up. Chapman charitably suggests that Sagan "would probably say that we *still* haven't explored Mars enough.")

Hopes for finding life on Mars now rested exclusively with microscopic life. Within the compass of a cubic foot, Viking packed a $50-million biology lab capable of performing three types of experiments. Each of the three had been chosen from a wide field of proposals and had survived a long and competitive cycle of refinement. All three experiments were based on detecting the metabolism of any Martian microbes.

*   *   *

Vance Oyama, designer of Viking's gas-exchange experiment, was a soil chemist at NASA Ames Research Center. He had the look of a cherub who had just tasted something sour—a cherub who favored stretchy plaid pants and short-sleeved shirts with ties. Oyama's experiment was conceptually simple, like holding a mirror to the nose of an unconscious man to see if he is alive.

Oyama's device spritzed a soil sample with what everyone was calling "chicken soup," a solution of amino acids and other nutrients. It then monitored the sample chamber for several common gases: carbon dioxide, carbon monoxide, oxygen, nitrogen, nitrous oxide, methane, hydrogen, and hydrogen sulfide. This seemed to cover a lot of bases.

Because Oyama's experiment cast its net so widely, it was judged unlikely to miss a pronounced metabolic reaction, were one transpiring. On the other hand, the experiment was held to be the most liable to return a false positive.

*   *   *

Gil Levin was a genial, round-faced man who got into exobiology by way of sanitary engineering. His Martian life-detector had started as a way to detect bacteria in drinking fountains and sewers. Its use of radioactive isotopes scared off customers—those planning to use it on *this* planet, at any rate. NASA was impressed with the technique's sensitivity.

Levin had known Sagan since the early 1960s. He was impressed enough with the young Sagan to offer him a job, which Sagan "was smart enough to turn down," jokes Levin. As used on Viking, Levin's instrument took a soil sample and dribbled a nutrient "soup" on it. The carbon in this experiment's soup was "tagged" with radioactive carbon 14. The radioactive carbon shouldn't interfere with any biologic reactions, but metabolic products containing the carbon 14 would be easily detectable by their radioactivity. Gases coming off the sample were sent to a miniature Geiger counter. By tallying the scintillations, it produced a quick, accurate account of how much nutrient had been taken up. In tests with Earth soils, this was a highly sensitive way of detecting microbes.

Both Oyama's and Levin's devices could be said to epitomize Linda Sagan's "just add water" philosophy. They presumed that Martian life is like a desert wildflower lying in wait for the thunderhead's rain. Of course, the picture of Mars had changed greatly between the time these experiments were conceived and the landings. Rain could never fall on Mars, and ice could never melt. For the two "wet" experiments to work at all, they had to be artificially heated and pressurized.

*   *   *

The third experiment was Norman Horowitz's pyrolytic-release experiment. To much of the biology team, Horowitz was an enigma. He was *so* skeptical about the prospects for finding life that they wondered why he had joined the group or remained with it. Adopting the standard boast of exobiology skeptics, Horowitz had said he would gladly *eat* a mouthful of Mars dust—*if* it would convince Sagan and Lederberg that there was no further need to sterilize Martian spacecraft.

Horowitz was dismissive of the two "wet" experiments. He reasoned that *if* there was life on Mars, the only fact we could know about it was that it survived under those miserable Martian conditions (no water, numbing cold, and scant atmospheric pressure). In his experiment, virtually nothing was added. The soil sample simply sat in a chamber filled with Martian atmosphere, under a xenon lightbulb simulating the Martian sun. Small amounts of carbon dioxide and carbon monoxide, both tagged with radioactive carbon 14, were added to the atmosphere.

Surely nothing could grow *quickly* under such austere conditions. The sample was therefore permitted to incubate for five days. Then the Martian atmosphere was flushed from the chamber. The soil was heated to kill any life and break down any organic compounds. Had any microbes incorporated the carbon 14, the gas produced in the cooking would be radioactive. A radiation counter told how much carbon had been incorporated.

The main deviations from Horowitz's ethos of total Martian "authenticity" were that the lightbulb did not put out the sterilizing ultraviolet rays of Mars and that the running temperature, intended to be local Martian temperature, was actually warmer because the device was jammed in the same cubic-foot box with the heated, pressurized experiments. By Sagan's thinking, Horowitz's device was liable to miss any spores awaiting "soft rains." They would simply remain dormant. But the experiment was carefully designed to distinguish between biological and nonbiological reactions. A positive result would have to be taken seriously.

There was, however, some uncertainty about just how high a reading constituted a "positive result." Similar ambiguities applied to the other experiments. NASA had intended to "calibrate" all three devices exhaustively by testing them on hundreds of samples of Earth soils, live and sterile. But the biology package malfunctioned in early tests and underwent major design changes almost until launch. Calibration tests were done, on duplicate instruments, even as the Vikings were en route.

*   *   *

Aside from the three biology experiments, there was a gas chromatography/ mass spectrometer experiment (GCMS). Its designer, MIT's Klaus Biemann, was a man apart in JPL's acres of rumpled polyester and T-shirts. He wore crisp seersucker suits, as if his Baedeker had pronounced them just the thing for tropic Pasadena. Biemann's experiment was a miniature chemistry lab that would check for organic compounds in the Martian soil. The chances of finding them seemed good. There were, after all, minuscule traces of organic compounds in the moon rocks.

If there *was* life on Mars, Biemann's device might take on additional importance. The three biology experiments were designed only to detect life—a yes-or-no answer. Biemann's device alone had the potential of revealing something about Martian biochemistry, of starting to address the questions that had obsessed Calvin, Lederberg, Urey, Sagan, and many others.

*   *   *

The ambitious search for Martian microbiology got off to a slow start. First Viking's robotic arm got stuck. The glitch solved, the arm plunged into the Martian surface on July 28. The first sample was apportioned between the three biology devices. The second went in the gas chromatography instrument. Or did it? Viking failed to send a signal confirming that the sample container was full.

JPL instructed Viking to pick up *another* scoop of soil and put it in the gas chromatography hopper. There was still no "full" signal. Viking used a thin wire to sense that the container was full. Maybe it had snapped. With Biemann fretting over this, JPL moved on and dug a fourth sample for an X-ray fluorescence experiment.

Some had imagined the Martian regolith to be as dry and fluid as the sand in an hourglass. Actually, the sampling arm left a trench with sharp, crumbly borders, like slightly damp sand. Caltech's Ronald Scott proclaimed that the soil was much like that in Los Angeles backyards. This statement turned out to be very wrong.

Super Curve

The first biology experiment to get a result was Gil Levin's. By the early evening hours of July 30, the labeled release device was detecting radioactive gas, far above the range of experimental error. Every sixteen minutes, the experiment made another measurement. Plotting the data points produced a "super curve."

Sagan was not there. No one had expected such quick results, and most people had left for the day. Gil Levin stayed late, and he was now convinced he had something. He sent out for a bottle of champagne. At 7:30 P.M., he ripped out the latest dot-matrix printout, then showing an impressive curve. At the top he wrote "Tonight!"—as in the Sondheim lyric from *West Side Story*—and the date and time. He passed it around for people to sign.

Sagan was enthusiastic when Levin showed him the curve. He requested the data so that he could look it over. Soon, Oyama's gas-exchange experiment was producing surprising results, too. Oyama's device had been programmed to humidify the sample chamber with water vapor before wetting it. Even the humidification was enough to get a rise out of the Martian soil. The instrument reported that the soil was producing oxygen and some carbon dioxide.

On Earth, oxygen is a product of photosynthesis. But Oyama's experiment was being done in a dark chamber. The production of oxygen seemed too fast for photosynthesis anyway.

Levin's instrument was insensitive to oxygen. It could measure only gases containing radioactively tagged carbon. This meant that both devices were reporting "positive" results for life, and they were *distinct* positive results.

Important, Unique, and Exciting Things

NASA's policy was to release results as they came in. So on July 31, Jim Martin and Harold Klein reported the big news. There were "important, unique, and exciting things," said Klein. Levin's device detected "a fairly high level of radioactivity which to a first approximation would look very much like a biological signal." Oyama's experiment was positive, too. Since Horowitz's experiment required a long incubation, its results were not in.

Klein qualified the results as "very much like biological activity"; something in the soil "may in fact mimic—let me emphasize that 'mimic'—in some respects biological activity."

For the most part, the media accepted these qualifications. On August 1, the *Los Angeles Times* ran the headline "2 Viking Labs Report Unusual Soil Findings." Undercutting this tone of restraint was the fact that the article ran next to the recently released photograph of the Martian "face."

*   *   *

Just hours before the first news conference on the biology data, Juan Oro, a chemist at the University of Houston, advanced a chemical explanation for the findings. He theorized that the ultraviolet light had broken down the water on Mars, producing hydrogen peroxide and hydrogen. The hydrogen peroxide might be absorbed by soil particles, creating a highly reactive soil. When the soil was exposed to water, it might fizz like an Alka-Seltzer tablet. This could explain the creation of oxygen in the gas-exchange experiment. If the peroxide reacted with the tagged carbon in Levin's experiment (as it would with formic acid, one of the supplied nutrients), it could produce radioactive carbon dioxide and account for that result, too.

Many variations on this idea were offered over the following days and weeks. If not hydrogen peroxide, then other reactive soil chemicals might be responsible. This line of thought seemed to be confirmed by the incoming biology experiment data. By August 1, gas production in Oyama's experiment had decreased. The device then saturated the same sample with soup. This caused the carbon dioxide production to rise again, briefly, then tail off. The oxygen production continued to diminish. Yeast can bubble as long as there's food; an Alka-Seltzer tablet has so much fizz and then it's gone. It was looking more like a chemical reaction.

On August 2, Levin announced that his instrument's readings no longer fit the exponential curve typical of growing organisms. The curve had tailed off. On the other hand, Levin said, it did not quite look like the expected curve for a chemical reaction either.

Sagan began presenting the biology data at scientific meetings. The findings were equivocal, and Sagan successively made good cases for the soil chemistry and biological hypotheses. As one possible explanation for Oyama's results, Sagan proposed that water was toxic to Martian life. Oyama's first oxygen peak might have been the death gasps of microbes *killed* by the water vapor. All were dead by the time of the second dose; hence there was no reaction.

As to Levin's experiment, Sagan found it suspicious that the amount of gas released was no greater than would be expected from the oxidation of a single nutrient. "Your superoxide, or whatever it is, oxidizes the formate, but it can't oxidize anything else!" he said in one debate. "That sounds funny, given a medium so rich in easily oxidized compounds! Could it instead be a finicky organism—one that is fussy about its food?"

There was naturally great anticipation for the results of Horowitz's "dry" experiment. Sagan was in Washington, D.C., proofreading the imaging team's article in *Science*, when Horowitz announced that his results were . . . positive.

Sagan took a plane back to California, miffed at having missed the excitement. Horowitz's experiment did not produce a curve as did the others. It returned just two numbers, a "first peak" figure that was normally ignored and a "second peak" figure that was supposed to indicate whether it had detected life. Based on the calibration tests that had been done, a second peak reading of 15 or higher was claimed to mean life. The value Horowitz got from Mars was 96.

"You could have knocked me over with one of those Martian cobbles," Horowitz said of that result. He and colleagues spent several hours trying to convince themselves something was wrong. They couldn't.

Ninety-six was not actually a high reading. Ordinary terrestrial soil registered in the thousands. A sample from the dry valleys of Antarctica had registered 106. For Mars, 96 seemed about right.

All three of Viking's biology experiments had now returned "positive" results. Many a former skeptic was ready to match Sagan's even odds on there being life on Mars. Not Horowitz, though. Although forced to concede the possibility that his result was biological, he was not breaking out the champagne. He was not sure what to think, except that he didn't like the press hanging on his every premature surmise or wondering-out-loud. "I want to emphasize," he said, "that if this were normal science, we wouldn't even be here—we'd be working in our laboratories for three more months— you wouldn't even know what was going on and at the end of the time we would come out and tell you the answer. Having to work in a fishbowl like this is an experience that none of us is used to."

*   *   *

For Sagan, one encouraging thing about Horowitz's results was that they could not easily be explained by the presumed soil oxidants. Horowitz's device was designed to detect only carbon that had been incorporated into organic molecules. Oxidants would destroy, not create, organic molecules.

Horowitz was acutely aware of that. He soon came up with a nonbiological explanation for his result. As mentioned, Horowitz's device did *not* subject its soil sample to hard ultraviolet light. In early tests, the xenon lamp's ultraviolet light had synthesized traces of organic compounds from the Mars-like atmosphere; the device was like a miniature Miller-Urey experiment. So Horowitz had to add an ultraviolet-blocking filter.

Horowitz now guessed that the filter had cracked or become dislodged. If so, *all* his results would be off. The device would be synthesizing the very compounds it was trying to detect.

Horowitz was so confident the results were not biological that he said he was a little worried about Sagan's spirits when the inevitable letdown came. For the time being, Sagan's spirits were fine. Sagan attempted to make the best of ambiguity, to stake out chemical reactions as a partial "victory" for his side.

"If it turns out that these signals are *not* biological," Sagan told one journalist, "it means that there are nonbiological processes simulating life just lying around on the soil . . . little metabolic cycles of oxidation and reduction are going on all the time by themselves." Even if the "less interesting alternative" were correct, Sagan said, it would have "deep implications for terrestrial life."

One thing was clear: the Viking team had failed to deliver Thomas Gold's black box, the magical life-detector guaranteed to give a yes-or-no answer. The very concept may have been unrealistic. "The only instrument I know capable of doing that," reflected Lederberg, "would be something like a divining rod."

Scavenger Theory

Klaus Biemann's gas chromatography experiment now took on greater significance. It would help the case for life on Mars if it were to establish that the soil contained organic compounds. So was there or was there not a soil sample in the device?

Biemann's team could either direct Viking to start the analysis in the hope that it did have a sample or try to pick up another sample. If they went ahead with the analysis, they risked wasting precious time and one of the experiment's two remaining "ovens" on an empty container. (Viking had just three ovens for this experiment, and one of them wasn't working.)

They decided to play it safe and take another soil sample. The robotic boom extended, picked up another sample, was in the process of retracting . . . and then jammed just before it could deposit it in the hopper.

There was nothing to do but send the command to start the gas chromatography analysis anyway, hoping there was a sample to analyze. The results came in on August 12. They surprised everyone.

The device found no organic compounds at all. Or as good as none. It detected traces of benzene and methyl chloride, two solvents that had been used to clean the device. Those traces confirmed that the device was working up to specs. The device also detected a small amount of water. That must have come from the soil. It implied that there was a soil sample after all.

This result was the single most devastating blow to all who hoped to find life on Mars. The test should have found organic compounds in any sample of Earth soil. Were the level of organic compounds on Mars only 1/100 of that in Sahara sand, it should have registered.

Everyone believed that meteorites deposited organic compounds on Mars. The result therefore implied that the Martian environment actively destroyed organic chemistry. That appeared to rule out not only life on Mars but even Sagan's "little metabolic cycles."

It further called into question Sagan and Lederberg's oases. Mars's planet-girdling, 200-mile-an-hour dust storms could be expected to sweep any organic compounds all over the planet. Absence of organics, even at one "boring" place on Mars, made it more difficult to argue for life *anywhere* on the planet's surface.

*   *   *

The gas chromatography finding met with some disbelief—by Sagan and many others. Gerry Soffen, Viking project manager (a youngish man whose goatee made him look more like a jazz musician than an M.D.-turned-exobiologist) suspected that the sampler *had* to be empty. He bet A. Thomas Young a dollar the second analysis would prove it.

Biemann had trouble accepting the results himself. His device easily found organic compounds in terrestrial soils because there is a great deal of dead organic matter relative to the amount of living matter. On Earth, *most* organic matter is "dead." Biemann wondered if things were different on Mars. "In harsh conditions, what could be more efficient than scavengers?" he asked. "They might live in a colony; whenever one died, it would be immediately devoured as food. That way, there would be too small an amount of organic matter left lying around for the GCMS to detect."

Gil Levin liked this theory. Horowitz hated it. ("You have to endow your bugs with special qualities to fit the facts!" he countered.) Sagan was more impressed with the sensitivity gap between Biemann's and Horowitz's instruments than with the scavenger idea per se. He noted that a positive result in Horowitz's experiment was not necessarily incompatible with the negative result in Biemann's experiment.

The amount of complex carbon compounds detected by Horowitz's experiment was minute, equivalent to the organic matter of 100 to 1,000 bacterial cells. Comparable amounts of organic matter would *not* have been detectable by Biemann's device. It was yet possible to imagine a fantastically sparse microbial biota where dead cells and their organic matter were quickly eliminated by cannibalism, oxidants, or other means. How *likely* this was was a matter of opinion. But as Sagan emphasized, it was a possibility that could not be excluded by the existing data.

Normal Science

After the excitement of the first biology results, the press quickly lost interest in Viking. Even Sagan was less visible. To a surprising extent, Horowitz and everyone else was permitted to conduct "normal science" without undue distraction.

Normal science means running controls. In mid-August, Levin and Horowitz repeated their experiments with an all-important difference. This time they first sterilized the soil by heating it to about 320° F for three hours. That would turn a loaf of bread into a hard rusk. Any microbes should have been killed.

Had the original positive results been biological, the results should be *negative* on the control. On the other hand, if the original results were due to soil chemistry, the heating might not have much effect.

They had their results on August 20. Levin's result was negative, and Horowitz's was borderline negative. Horowitz's second peak reading was only 15, strictly speaking the threshold for life, but far less than the original 96. Heat appeared to have "killed" whatever had caused the initial results.

Levin's result provoked debate about whether soil oxidants might be unstable enough to be destroyed by the heating. That possibility could not account for Horowitz's result. Significantly, the diminished reading on the control run established that the ultraviolet filter must have been intact after all.

Oyama did not run a control. He, and just about everyone else, was convinced that his initial burst of activity had to be a chemical reaction. After that, the readings had flatlined, as would happen when a fizzy chemical loses its fizz. Oyama judged it more valuable to let his experiment continue incubating with the original sample. He vowed to let his experiment run for 200 days uninterrupted. A sample of Antarctic soil had taken that long for its microbes to multiply enough to produce sufficient gas to register.

Sagan sounded heartened in an interview in the August 30 issue of *U.S. News and World Report*. He reminded the public that the landing site was chosen for its "blandness" and wondered "if there aren't far more exciting areas on Mars." He added, "I don't consider it out of the question that there are more-advanced organisms waiting to be discovered."

*   *   *

A scientific result is supposed to be repeatable. On August 25, Horowitz and Levin ran their experiments a third time, now using fresh, unsterilized soil. It was a repeat of the initial experiment, and they expected to get similar results.

They didn't. Levin got a *stronger* positive reading—about 50 percent more pronounced than the first. Horowitz got a *weaker* result. The second peak reading was 27, still considered positive but less than a third of the original result. No one knew what to make of that. Confusing the issue further was the fact that a computer glitch had caused Horowitz's experiment to be incubated several days at a higher temperature than planned.

Having now duplicated his original experiment, Levin tried something new. He gave the same sample a second injection of nutrients.

Levin expected that "hungry" bugs would gobble up the "second helping," producing more radioactive gas. The skeptics expected the second injection to have little effect. Whatever chemical had been responsible for the "super curve" would have been used up in the first reaction.

Again the results surprised everyone. The "super curve" developed a "fish hook" at the time of the second injection. The amount of gas *decreased* sharply, then curved back up.

The only reasonable explanation seemed to be that the rewetted sample absorbed about 20 percent of the gas that had already been produced. But if the soil was alive, why hadn't there been a new curve of gas production? Levin suggested that the Martian organisms had not taken to being pulled out of their natural environment and isolated in a box. Maybe they were all dead.

Utopia

Such ideas met with mixed reviews. A group of scientists including Lynn Margulis and Cyril Ponnamperuma visited JPL for a briefing on the biology results. Margulis did not share Sagan's and Levin's willingness to give Martian life the perpetual benefit of the doubt. She was particularly critical of Levin's presentation. His results were "trash," Margulis charged, designed for a planet with water.

Meanwhile, the landing site team had Viking 2 to worry about. Cydonia was out. Photographs revealed it to be pocked with craters and a polygonal network of cracks. Many of the biologists were still pressing for a northern site, say at 55° latitude. Sagan thought it important to find a place where the temperature goes above the freezing point of water.

They settled on a region called Utopia. ("That's gotta be the place!" someone said at first mention of the name.) It appeared to be covered with sand dunes of titanic proportions—but, they believed, few rocks. At a press conference, a reporter asked Jim Martin, "Do you call 155-foot-high sand dunes a better landing area?" Martin said the Viking could land on any sand dune that existed in the United States. "I would trade sand dunes for big rocks any day."

Viking 2 landed in Utopia at 3:58 P.M. PDT September 3, 1976. At touchdown the team broke out cases of champagne for a celebration that seemed at least as deeply felt as the first.

Lest anyone get overconfident, the first pictures showed that they were again profoundly wrong. Not one sand dune was to be seen. It was a *much* rockier place than the Viking 1 site. Viking 2 must have landed on a rock. One antenna was bent, and the spacecraft tilted 8°, throwing a crazy undulation in the panoramic pictures. Gazing at the first photos Sagan said, "If that's Utopia . . . " He never finished the thought.

"The next time I want you to find a landing site," Jim Martin told the landing site team, "I'll ask for one full of rocks!"

*   *   *

Sagan found the Viking 2 site disappointingly similar to the first. But Viking 2's biology experiments, all but ignored in the press, were indispensable for understanding what was going on in the soil of Mars.

Vance Oyama took the opportunity to repeat his experiment in Utopia.

The results were similar, though less gas was produced. That made sense. Utopia was a more humid locale, and its soil oxidants, partly quenched by the air, would have less fizz to release.

When Levin repeated his experiment in Utopia, he got the strongest reading yet. Maybe Martian life *did* favor the high latitudes, as Lederberg thought. And if there was less oxidant in Utopia's soil, that meant something *other* than oxidants was responsible for the enhanced result in Levin's experiment.

Norman Horowitz had a problem. The summer sun of Utopia was beating down on Viking 2, raising temperatures above what they had been at Chryse. So he couldn't repeat the experiment *exactly* in the new location. (Ambient temperatures didn't matter so much to the two "wet" experiments, which were electrically heated anyway.) JPL's engineers recommended that Horowitz switch off the xenon bulb in order to avoid overheating. He did so, reluctantly.

This time he got a reading of 23. It was lower but still positive. Whatever had caused the reading, it did not depend on light. It wasn't photosynthesis.

*   *   *

On October 1, Levin did a "cold sterilization." It was a second control experiment, only this time the soil was heated to a modest 122° F. That might kill a microbe adapted to frigid Mars, but it seemed unlikely to affect a chemical reaction. In fact it *did* "kill" the reaction, or most of it. That was a point in favor of biology. Levin termed this result "mind-boggling."

In one trial, Horowitz violated his own philosophy and spritzed his sample with water. The "bugs" or chemicals didn't like that at all. The reading was a 2, the lowest yet. It was much *less* than the reading with the control experiment's heat-sterilized soil.

That struck Horowitz as peculiar. The control reading was actually borderline (15). It had seemed low next to the original 96. But maybe, Horowitz reasoned, the control experiment's 15 was actually a *positive* reading. Then the reaction had survived heat sterilization after all. That was a point in favor of chemistry.

The one unambiguous experiment was Biemann's. In Utopia as well as Chryse, his device found not the slightest trace of organic chemistry. *Zip*. Gerry Soffen lost his bet with Young. "That's the ball game," he said of these findings. "No organics on Mars, no life on Mars."

Subrock Sample

Sagan was not yet ready to throw in the towel. Even if the chance of establishing life on Mars was now slim, it was crucial not to squander any opportunity to settle the issue one way or another. Sagan played an important role as gadfly, brainstorming a profusion of testable hypotheses of Martian life, circulating them in memos, and nagging and pleading with the biology team to test them in the precious time remaining.

It *was* a race against time. The Vikings were developing malfunctions; running out of pressurized gas or empty sample compartments. Horowitz's device on Viking 2 had a gas leak. Had that happened in his lab in Pasadena, he would have discarded the equipment and results and started anew. On Mars, he had to plug onward and try to make allowances.

One of Sagan's ideas was to have Viking dig a trench to collect soil a foot below the surface. The deep soil might contain more water, organic compounds, and/or microbes; *less* oxidants. The biology team and Biemann were sympathetic. (Biemann was understandably concerned that his state-of-the-art organic chemistry lab had been sent to a planet with nothing to analyze.) NASA's management was less convinced. Whenever Sagan or the other scientists proposed trying something new and different, Jim Martin and staff listened and went "Hmmm . . . ." This earned them the nickname "the hummers."

Still carrying the painful memory of the Viking 1 arm's jamming, the hummers thought that digging a deep trench was dicey. Then Sagan lucked out. While performing a routine operation, the Viking 2 arm accidentally moved a rock. This was a revelation. No one had imagined that the rocks on Mars were *loose*. Sagan seized the opportunity to talk up the virtues of a "subrock sample." The soil beneath a rock would be shielded from ultraviolet light and might have the same advantages.

Martin okayed the idea and assigned a team of engineers to puzzle out the logistics. Sagan tried to talk them into a "dark dig." He thought they should move the rock at night so that the soil would never be exposed to sunlight. The engineers vetoed that, for they suspected it was low temperatures that had caused the Viking 1 arm problem. The trench would have to be dug in the ultraviolet light of day.

A separate team of geologists decided which rock to move. They drew up a list of candidate rocks and voted for them on a beauty pageant–style ballot with weighted categories for gripability, accessibility, sampleability, and rollability.

The winning rock turned out to be *cemented* in place. When Viking's sampler arm pressed against it, it actually moved the spacecraft, not the rock. The geologists succeeded in moving two runner-up rocks. One sample went in Biemann's machine. The other was apportioned among all three biology experiments. Oyama, who had intended to do another 200-day incubation at Utopia, cut it short expressly to test Sagan's new, subrock sample.

After all that buildup, the subrock sample's readings were nothing special. Biemann again found no organic compounds whatsoever. Levin got another super curve. Oyama got a much-diminished release of gas. Horowitz's device had another negative result: a second peak value of 7.5.

Hard-Shell Bugs

Mars passed behind the sun in November. JPL put the Vikings into a resting mode and was unable to communicate with them for about a month. The forced hiatus was a time to reflect. On November 8, Sagan joined a group of Viking colleagues for a press conference in Washington, D.C.

Sagan had new ideas and most of the old enthusiasm. He believed that biology remained the simplest explanation for Horowitz's results. He was more inclined to discount Levin's and Oyama's findings as chemical. "Is it conceivable that all the biology experiment results are not biological?" Sagan asked the crowd. His answer: "Conceivable, but not likely."

Yet the biology results had to be squared with the utter failure to detect organic chemistry. Sagan outlined a new solution to that puzzle: *hard-shell bugs*. He asked his listeners to imagine small organisms armored against ultraviolet light and soil oxidants by a tough, silicate- and iron-rich shell. The shell would be semipermeable. "Say some of these bugs get shoveled into Biemann's GCMS," Sagan said. "They are heated to five hundred degrees during his pyrolysis. The heat can't break the silicate bonds. Biemann's instrument is full of bugs, and he's not registering any!"

Sagan showed how this might account for some of the anomalies of Horowitz's results. The bugs' shells would provide some immunity to heat. Maybe a few of the hardiest bugs had survived the heat sterilization in Horowitz's control experiment. That would account for the borderline reading of 15.

Sagan proposed (again) that it was *water* that was deadly to the bugs. He imagined that their semipermeable shells could absorb water but not excrete it. Perhaps that was never necessary in the Martian environment. So when Horowitz spritzed them with water they died (the 2 reading). Few if any lived in the more humid soil under a rock (the 7.5 reading).

This theory *did* account for a lot of the puzzling data. It had something to tweak everyone. Levin thought he'd detected life, while Horowitz was sure he hadn't; actually, Sagan was saying, it was just the other way around. Biemann's instrument had failed to do what it was supposed to do, and his "scavenger theory" was wrong. Linda was wrong. "Add water" was how to *kill* a Martian.

Horowitz blasted the hard-shell theory as ad hoc; a last-ditch attempt to salvage what Sagan wanted to believe. Levin offered a more colorful objection. When heated inside the gas chromatograph, wouldn't Sagan's hard-shell bugs explode like popcorn? The inside of Biemann's machine should have been splattered with Martian protoplasm.

Sudden Death

On December 16, with Mars out of radio eclipse, JPL beamed a signal causing the Vikings to "wake up." Oyama's and Levin's experiments had been left incubating during the communications blackout. The Vikings reported that nothing much had happened in the interim. There had been no population growth.

The first postblackout experiment was Horowitz's "sudden death" experiment. One point where Horowitz agreed with Sagan was that water destroyed whatever was responsible for his results. So he would "kill" Sagan's bugs *twice*—once by spritzing them with water and again by heating them. Then he would see if there was any activity. If Sagan was right, the answer would be no. All his bugs would be dead.

Horowitz expected there *would* be a reaction. His hunch was that the light from his xenon bulb was synthesizing small amounts of organic molecules—filter or no filter. The lightbulb could not be the whole story. But on the first run at Utopia, when the light had been *off*, Horowitz got a 23, while the first run at Chryse, with the light *on*, had given that never-matched 96. It looked to him like the lightbulb had something to do with it.

The sudden-death experiment, done at Chryse, returned a second-peak reading of 34. Whatever produced it had survived drowning and baking. That could not be Sagan's bugs, Horowitz was confident. On the other hand, the result was incompatible with most of the chemical explanations that had been advanced. The spritzing should have destroyed the oxidants.

*   *   *

Such puzzles remained as the year ended and JPL's visiting scientists began packing up and going home. Neither Sagan nor Horowitz had imagined it would be so hard to get a definite yes or no. It seemed that Mars was playing a shell game with them, confounding expectations whenever someone dared to think he had figured things out.

Sagan vented his frustrations in a tongue-in-cheek article for *Nature*'s Christmas 1976 issue. The piece is about the Loch Ness monster. Sagan mathematically computes the population of monster(s) consistent with alleged sightings and radar soundings in the Loch Ness. "Similar calculations of organism spacing and loading density could be made on other planets, were macro-organisms to be discovered there," Sagan writes, "—as, for example, on Mars . . ."

Norman Horowitz indulged in dry humor of his own. He posted on his office door *his* conception of a Martian macrobe. It was a ghostly visage superimposed on the orange and rust Martian landscape, the grinning face of Carl Sagan.

ITHACA
1977-78

SAGAN CELEBRATED THE new year by paying a visit to a witch. At a New Year's gathering back in Ithaca, someone suggested that they all pile in cars and go and see a witch who lived in nearby Enfield, New York. The group included Carl and Linda, Timothy and Annie, and Joseph Veverka and his wife, Joy. They arrived at a run-down house occupied by one witch and a great many cats.

The witch of Enfield told fortunes. "There's going to be an explosion in this group," she said, "that will take years to recover from. It's going to be *big!*" She also saw a wedding in the group's future and some news about life on Mars. Afterward, everyone played the game of trying to figure out what the prophecies meant. The "explosion" was easy to figure: Joe and Joy Veverka's marriage was on the rocks.

*   *   *

Back in Pasadena, JPL okayed Sagan's foot-deep dig. The subrock sample had been only inches below the surface. The hope was that a foot-deep sample would contain more water. With the biology results still inconclusive, the Viking team needed to try *something* different.

The dig was to take place at Chryse. In anticipation of hitting a water jackpot, the chosen spot of ground was nicknamed "Atlantic City."

But Viking 1 was showing its age. Its gas chromatograph went on the fritz. Biemann had to switch it off (by this point, few thought it was going to find anything). A more pressing problem was that the biology experiments' sample hopper was full. Once soil was in the hopper, it had to stay there or else funnel into one or more of the devices. It would therefore be necessary to sacrifice one of the biology experiments—to use it as a trash can for the old soil. That had to be Oyama's instrument, the one that clearly hadn't found life.

The stop-and-go telemetric dig took about a month. Just as the desired foot-deep sample was almost within reach, Viking 1's radio receiver developed problems. If they lost contact, they could not initiate any further experiments. Faced with this prospect, Horowitz and Levin decided that it was too risky to wait for the foot-deep sample. In March they sent commands to start their experiments immediately, using the old soil already in the hopper. Sagan's foot-deep trench, the greatest construction project ever made on the planet Mars, went for naught. So for that matter did Horowitz and Levin's capitulation. The radio link cleared up soon after the experiments had begun.

Double Squirt

Levin used his sample for the "double-squirt" experiment. This was to be the decisive test between soil chemistry and Sagan's "finicky bugs."

Sagan himself no longer had much use for finicky bugs—at least not regarding Levin's experiment. Oyama, working in his lab back at NASA Ames, had shown that the iron oxide mineral maghemite produces a curve much like Levin's when fed Levin's nutrients. Everyone had always believed the red of Mars owed itself to some kind of iron oxide. Viking carried a magnet, and photos showed grains of Martian soil clinging to it. Maghemite is magnetic. For Sagan that was a pretty convincing explanation for Levin's results.

Levin did not buy the maghemite hypothesis. With each run, save the control, his super curve had risen quickly and then leveled off. Did the curve level off because the active soil chemicals were used up, or because the bugs ran out of food? To find out, Levin gave his sample a double dose of nutrient solution all at once. If the limiting factor was depletion of a soil chemical, this shouldn't make much difference. If the bottleneck was depletion of a nutrient being consumed by microbes, then the result ought to be a super-super curve, perhaps twice as high.

Mars had not lost its ability to dash all reasonable expectations. This time there was *no* super curve. The sample produced only a slight reading.

Levin and colleague Patricia Straat blamed the "old" soil. The soil they were using had sat in the hopper for nearly five months. Like an idling car,

Viking was warmer than its surroundings. They claimed the heat had killed the bugs. However, it was also possible to argue (as most now did) that the heat had done something to the soil chemistry.

Strangely enough, the same stale soil was potent as ever in Horowitz's device. It rated a 33.

Since it had not been necessary to sacrifice Oyama's Chryse instrument after all, he alone was in a position to try out the foot-deep soil. With communications reestablished, a foot-deep sample was delivered to Oyama's instrument. But before the experiment could return a result, it went dead.

Bitter End

Experiments continued to the bitter end. In April, frigid temperatures mandated that the Utopia gas chromatograph be turned off lest cold crack the electrical insulation. Biemann was totally out of the game.

Sagan was now concerned about the (relatively) high temperatures under which all the experiments had been conducted. "It's as if the Martians sent equipment to Earth that detected life only at 200° Fahrenheit," he said. Horowitz agreed completely. He had always wanted to do a "cold incubation." That would mean switching off the heaters and letting the watery nutrient in Oyama's and Levin's experiments freeze solid like milk on a wintry doorstep. Then *his* device could operate the way it was intended, at ambient Martian temperature.

The biology team elected to let Horowitz do his cold incubation for the final experimental run at Utopia. As the sampler arm was delivering its final soil sample, *it* froze and could not be moved. Horowitz gave up.

Oyama and Levin pressed on, even though it was uncertain whether their instruments would be able to function. They dumped old soil from the hopper on top of already used samples. Levin now got little reaction. He interpreted this as a sign in favor of life, for he was again using, as he saw it, *old* soil that had been left standing too long.

At the end of May, all the remaining biology experiments were shut down for good. A NASA press release stated, "Biologists have not reached any final conclusions about the presence or absence of life on Mars."

Carbon Chauvinist

Sagan ultimately concluded that Viking's puzzling and equivocal biology results were inadequate to support so important a claim as the existence of life on Mars. In this, Sagan's views came into line with those of nearly all the other Viking scientists, with the notable exceptions of Gil Levin and Patricia Straat.

Sagan's conclusion was based on the totality of evidence. The biology results had to be judged in the context of the stark Viking photos and, especially, the uncompromisingly negative gas chromatography results. How can there be life without carbon-based organic chemistry? "I am, reluctantly, a self-confessed carbon chauvinist," Sagan said in this regard a few years later.

Sagan and everyone else agreed that Oyama's instant, quickly fizzling reaction was chemical. The other two biology experiments were more problematic.

There was a peculiar pattern to Horowitz's results. He had done nine experimental runs, six at Chryse and three in Utopia. The Chryse readings ran 96, 15, 27, 35, 34, 33; the Utopia readings, 23, 2.8, 7.5.

Each of these runs had been done under different conditions. Ignoring the details, two things stand out. First, in each location the *initial* reading was much higher than any that came after. Second, the Chryse readings were generally higher than those at Utopia.

Some theorized that exposure to the vacuum of space had done something to Horowitz's organic vapor trap, making it give inflated readings the first time it was used. Horowitz disputed this, but it seemed hard to account for the high initial readings otherwise. The lower readings at Utopia might have reflected a real difference in soil chemistry or only a difference in the equipment.

Sterilizing, spritzing, switching off the light, using a subrock sample, or using "old" soil did not appear to make any consistent or dramatic difference in Horowitz's experiment. Nothing that was *supposed* to matter did. That indifference was more characteristic of chemicals than organisms.

By 1977 Horowitz had flip-flopped on his interpretation of the first control experiment at Chryse. This was the trial where heat-sterilized soil produced a 15. Coming after the 96, the 15 had been taken as a negative. But now that it looked as if there was something funny about that 96, Horowitz decided to count the 15 as a positive, too. That would mean the reaction had survived the control run's test of fire, refuting a biological explanation.

The best case for life was probably Levin's results. He had a robust, repeatable response that was destroyed by even modest heating. It was consistent with a hypothetical microbe that could metabolize a watery nutrient but would not multiply in it. "Consistent with life" is not the same as saying it *was* life. There was mounting evidence that chemicals could produce similar reactions and show similar sensitivity to heat.

Oyama, Horowitz, Oro, and many others were busy in their labs, trying to duplicate the Martian results with inorganic mixtures. In 1977 Sagan, Owen Toon, and Jim Pollack published an article on the composition of the particles in the Martian dust storm of 1971–72. Based on Mariner 9 infrared spectra, they concluded that the dust contained montmorillonite and other clays. This conclusion was provocative, for clays have an active surface chemistry. They are capable of absorbing or emitting gases and catalyzing reactions. In separate studies, Horowitz found he was able to get results similar to those in his Viking experiments using iron-rich clays.

*   *   *

There was nonetheless no single, elegant refutation of the biological hypothesis. (Ironically, Wolf Vishniac's rejected experiment, designed to be sensitive to cellular *multiplication*, might have returned a valid negative.) Rarely if ever is a scientific idea refuted with black-and-white precision. There is always room to argue that the refuting data are somehow wrong. Knowing when to make such arguments and when to give up is a delicate judgment call.

Sagan never entirely rejected the possibility that life existed somewhere, or at some time, on Mars. The Viking results were inadequate to prove that negative, just as they were inadequate to prove the positive. But Sagan accepted that his advocacy of the biological explanation for the Viking results had served its role in the scientific conversation. It was time to move on. This is where Sagan and Levin parted ways.

Gil Levin had great faith in the instrument he built for Viking. He believed that its results alone were enough to sustain the hypothesis of life in the soil of Chryse and Utopia. As much as he wanted to share that opinion, Sagan could not.

One-Sigma Difference

Levin began examining the Viking lander photographs on his own, some 10,000 images. He knew that Sagan had already scrutinized the photos for any trace of life. But Sagan had been focused on macrobes. Conceivably, he might have missed something more subtle.

Levin was drawn to rocks that had patches of "green." *Green* in quotes, for their hue, in the imager's three-channel color data, is most accurately described as containing relatively more green than the other rocks. Levin concentrated on three rocks in the Viking 1 images. He called them "delta rock," "flat rock," and "patch rock."

One night, Levin compared a photo taken right after the landing with one taken 301 Martian days later. The illumination was effectively identical, allowing direct comparison. The "green" area on "patch rock" had *changed*! Too excited at this finding to continue working, Levin got in his car and drove up Angeles Crest Highway to compose himself among the nighttime pines of the San Gabriel Mountains.

Levin was not exactly saying that green equals life. But why would a green patch be changing? Levin imported rocks from the Maryland woods to see what they would look like when photographed by the Viking imaging system at JPL. The rocks were covered with *lichens*. At the distance of patch rock from the imager on Mars, no details smaller than one-fifth of an inch could be resolved. The pictures could not distinguish lichens from green slime from green rock.

Levin had a hard time convincing people of the significance of his discovery. Were the rocks even green? Levin took snapshots off the video screens and showed them to people. "Gil, that's ridiculous," Gerry Soffen said, "what are you looking at? That's just gray!" (Further complicating the issue was Levin's conviction that the imaging team had gotten the colors wrong. He believed that the original, cool-gray-sky images were closer to reality. That would make all the rocks bluer or greener.)

Levin believed that Sagan might be the only one willing to give his findings a fair shake. He contacted Sagan in December 1980. Levin then met with Sagan and Dave Pieri at Cornell. Sagan's initial reaction was the opposite of Soffen's. "It really looks like you've got something," he told Levin.

Sagan, Pieri, and Levin returned to JPL. They found a way to make Polaroids of the images, detailed enough to show each pixel. Comparing pixel to pixel, they concluded the data *did* show differences in the green channel. They made plans to publish the results. As discoverer, Levin would get first billing, and Sagan and Pieri would be coauthors. The article would carefully enumerate and critique all the possible explanations for the change (there were many, of course). It would take the position, simply, that a biological explanation *could not be excluded*. That alone would force a reassessment of the biology experiments.

They flew back east and began working. A couple of weeks later, Sagan called Levin with some bad news. He had decided to withdraw his name as coauthor.

Sagan said he'd calculated that the color changes were not of much statistical significance. They were only about one sigma. He didn't feel a one-sigma difference was enough to justify a scientific article.

Levin tried to wheedle him. A one-sigma difference still means the change is 68 percent likely to be real, he pointed out. Sagan had thought it worthwhile to face longer odds in trying to establish life on Mars. Levin proposed looking at clusters of pixels. Maybe they could squeeze a two-sigma difference out of it.

Sagan stood firm. The color change wasn't the extraordinary proof demanded of an extraordinary claim. Levin had to publish the article without him. Norman Horowitz believes that the loss of Sagan as an ally on this issue was Levin's greatest disappointment of the Viking project.

Rocket Scientist

Viking's failure to find life meant surrendering some of Sagan's own most cherished assumptions. His career had been built around the once-so-tantalizingly-plausible prospect of life on Mars. To some extent, a normal life as husband and father had been sacrificed to this goal, too. Now it was not to be.

During the year of Viking, Sagan worked closely with JPL's director of mission planning, B. Gentry Lee. Lee was not a typical rocket scientist. He was *smarter* than that. Lee was as comfortable with the engineering as with the science, and nearly as comfortable with great literature as with science. He read everything William Faulkner had written; also the works of Dostoyevsky and Camus.

Lee did not look much like a JPL manager, least of all like Jim Martin. Lee wore loud, floral-print shirts and had his hair long on the sides. Since his hair was thinning on top, this gave his head a distinctive, sphinxlike profile.

Lee shared Sagan's postmission depression. To them, even without the discovery of life, Viking was an incredible emotional peak. As far as the public was concerned, Mars might as well have been in *China*. "Here we had brought Mars right into people's backyards," Lee complained, "and yet it was as if no one had noticed."

Sagan and Lee had trouble understanding why that was. They decided that the problem was the media. After the initial flurry of interest—after it became clear that there was nothing to see but red rocks—the media forgot about Viking. And if the media didn't care about space, then the public wouldn't, and Congress wouldn't. It would be impossible to fund new missions.

Lee approached Sagan with an idea for starting a company to produce a TV series about astronomy. In 1976 they formed Carl Sagan Productions, Inc. The business plan was to sell the TV series (working title: *Man in the Cosmos*) and also to market Sagan, his writing, and science itself. They did not separate the goals of educating the public and making money. They expected that Carl Sagan Productions would do both.

*   *   *

Sagan and Lee were not the only ones thinking about an astronomy series. So was Greg Andorfer, a producer at Los Angeles public television station

KCET. Like almost everyone who works in public television, Andorfer had a case of Brit envy. Why did the British get to do all the great intellectual series? Why couldn't PBS do something of the kind rather than import it?

Andorfer pictured Ray Bradbury, Arthur C. Clarke, or Fred Hoyle as host of an astronomy series. He had not thought of Sagan. But when he heard that Sagan was trying to sell an astronomy show, he recognized that he would be the perfect host.

Sagan and Lee met with the KCET people and agreed to work together. They spoke with British producer Adrian Malone. Malone had done many of the BBC's acclaimed nonfiction series. Among them was *The Ascent of Man*, a philosophically toned science series built around physicist Jacob Bronowski. Having done that, Malone wasn't sure he wanted to do *another* science series. He agreed to fly to New York to meet with Sagan and Lee. "They said great things," Malone recalled. "But when I realized that the whole thing was not formed, and they didn't want me to come in and just put their ideas down on film, but wanted me to contribute, *then* I was taken with the idea."

Sagan and Lee were taken, too. They hired Malone in March 1977. The PBS series was announced in May 1977. Sagan, Lee, Malone, and Andorfer collaborated on a treatment for a thirteen-part series. Completed in August, it was detailed enough to compute a production budget.

The outline and budget put them in a position to meet with potential funders. They found two major underwriters, Arco and the Arthur Vining Davis Foundation. Arco, a big oil company headquartered in Los Angeles, had long been supportive of KCET productions. The Davis Foundation was a more unlikely patron. Arthur Vining Davis, a former Alcoa CEO, was a devoutly religious man who died in 1962, leaving a great deal of money and vague instructions about what to do with it. A share of the money went to support seminaries. The foundation had also gotten into supporting public television and had been looking for a worthy science program.

Sagan's celebrity had a lot to do with selling the show, of course, but Gentry Lee was a compelling pitchman in his own right. It was said half-jokingly that after hearing Lee's pitch for the series, the funders invariably had one question: would Lee be interested in working for *them*?

Time Capsule

As the TV show was moving forward, Sagan was consumed with yet another unusual project. In December 1976, John Casani, project manager for the Voyager mission, asked Sagan to devise another symbolic message to extraterrestrials. Like the Pioneers before them, the two Voyager spacecraft would be ejected out of the solar system. Casani thought the Voyagers ought to have a message, too. Sagan agreed.

Sagan quickly assembled a group of consultants, many from the Green Bank and Byurakan crowds. They included Frank Drake, Philip Morrison, Bernard Oliver, and Leslie Orgel; Harvard astronomer A. G. W. Cameron and University of Chicago philosopher Steven Toulmin; science-fiction writers Asimov, Clarke, and Robert Heinlein.

Morrison thought the new message should include a couple of well-known artworks, such as the famous Leonardo da Vinci drawing of human proportions. Oliver wanted to send a recording of Beethoven's Ninth Symphony (but there was concern that cosmic rays would scramble a magnetic tape).

During the January 1977 meeting of the American Astronomical Society in Honolulu, Sagan and Drake shared a cottage at the Kahala Hilton Hotel (it had a private pool inhabited by two dolphins). During spare moments, Drake and Sagan sketched the main part of the message.

Drake's brainstorm was sending a *phonograph record*. They knew that an etching on metal would last a long time. A phonograph record's grooves could therefore be etched into metal instead of vinyl. A phonograph record could include Beethoven's Ninth Symphony if that's what they wanted. In principle, it could also encode pictures or any kind of information, Drake said. Sagan liked the idea instantly. A record could contain an audiovisual "time capsule" of Earth.

They made back-of-the-envelope calculations about how much information they could pack onto an LP record. They figured there was room for about ten pictures and four pieces of music or sound. Drake outlined a table of contents. He envisioned sending biochemical data, human figures, and pictures of the Taj Mahal and Sydney Opera House (all of which ended up on the final record).

*   *   *

Sagan pitched the record idea to NASA. The agency approved it, and Sagan began assigning responsibilities. The assignments were utterly nepotistic—which is just as well, for NASA had little to nothing to pay. The core team was Carl, Linda, Timothy Ferris, and Ann Druyan. The four often "double-dated," and they had spoken of collaborating on some sort of project.

Ferris was named producer of the record's music selections. Druyan was creative director and was also put in charge of creating a sampler of natural and technological sounds.

Since the record was a greeting, they decided it should have recordings of people saying "hello" in the languages of the Earth. Linda's responsibility was to assemble the greetings.

Frank Drake and Sagan's artist friend, Jon Lomberg, were put in charge of the pictures. Wendy Gradison and Amahl Shakhashiri assisted them in finding photographs and getting permission to reproduce them. A staff photographer, Herman Eckelmann, took original pictures for the record and rephotographed existing photos.

Of all the assignments, the most significant in personal terms was Ann Druyan. In later life, Carl would say he fell in love with Annie the instant he met her; it just took several years for him to realize that.

One of Druyan's best friends was Lynda Obst, the writer (by then, *New York Times* editor) she also met at Nora Ephron's party. She confided to Lynda that she feared she was falling in love with Carl—feared because such an attraction was unthinkable. She had of course said nothing to Carl, or to Timothy.

While working on the Voyager record, Carl invited Annie and Timothy to Lester Grinspoon's place. It was obvious to Lester that Carl was taken with the young woman. Everything Carl said was directed at her. But Carl said nothing of this attraction to Lester.

Nor did he reveal his feelings to Annie. Shortly after the Viking landing, Carl passed through New York. He spent a day with Annie, touring museums. During dinner at the Russian Tea Room, Carl was bold enough to remark that the most stimulating conversations he had ever had with any woman had been with Annie.

"With any *woman*?" Annie asked. "Why not with any *human*?"

Carl said he had started to say that. Then he realized that, in all honesty, he had had a few better conversations—with Joshua Lederberg.

He added, "That's kind of a problem for me."

"Why?"

"Because you're a woman."

That comment was left hanging. The waiter arrived and the subject was dropped, not to be picked up again.

A Lack of Historical Determinism

From their experience with the Pioneer message, Sagan and Drake knew that any choices they made about what to put on the record would be second-guessed. There was not time to solicit everyone's opinion and address all criticisms. They decided to consult a small group of experts for advice, but otherwise, to keep a low profile with the record project.

Ferris had the idea of asking John Lennon to select the music. The project might appeal to the ex-Beatle, and Lennon and Yoko Ono's apartment was just blocks from where Ferris lived. Ferris contacted Lennon's people. He heard that the musician was interested, but he was then in tax exile.

Lennon had to establish residency outside the country in order to avoid being hit with U.S. income taxes. So Lennon had to pass. It was Ferris and Druyan who made the music selections, with some help from Sagan.

"Making the record," Druyan wrote, "became an oddly practical way of confronting some abstract questions about art and life on earth." Chief among them was whether it was possible for humans to create anything "universal" at all.

The challenge was to send something that could be understood by beings of a totally alien culture. While Sagan and Drake held that science and mathematics stood the best chance of being a universal language, they were, for that very reason, subjects on which we could have little to say that would be unique. Our biology, history, culture, art, and music ought to be more interesting to extraterrestrials. The "lack of historical determinism in the details of a civilization" guarantees that these would be unique to the human race.

The downside to this approach was that it was uncertain whether extraterrestrials would be able to understand messages that were largely cultural and aesthetic. The Voyager record contains a lot of music; the aliens might not have ears.

They wouldn't have phonographs anyway (it's getting hard to find them on Earth!). The record therefore was supplied with a gold-plated aluminum cover with a diagram showing how to play it and specifying the proper playing speed. Underneath the cover, next to the record, was a stylus, ready to play. The cover also had a diagram showing how to reconstruct the pictures. The ETs would have to supply their own equipment for that.

The LP format was normally played at 33⅓ revolutions a minute, which permitted 27 minutes of playing time per side. Sagan figured they'd put the music on one side, pictures and other information on the other.

Twenty-seven minutes isn't much for a world survey of music. They stuck with that limit, with increasing dissatisfaction, through March. Finally, they decided it just wasn't enough. Sagan and Ferris elected to record the record for replay at half of the normal LP speed, 16⅔ revolutions per minute. This gave them 108 minutes total, for music, pictures, and other content.

*   *   *

The record contained about 87½ minutes of music, comprising twenty pieces. Thanks to Rachel's insistence on piano lessons, Sagan had some grounding in classical music. He liked rock and reggae, particularly the music of Bob Dylan and Bob Marley. Two pieces he especially admired were Dylan's "Hey, Mr. Tambourine Man" and Debussy's "La Mer." Neither made it onto the Voyager record.

Sagan had the notion that at least some of the music ought to express "cosmic loneliness." One piece that was thought to do that was Beethoven's Cavatina, a favorite of Druyan's. There was also an attempt to select pieces whose abstract structure might be particularly interesting. Bach's densely mathematical counterpoint was felt to qualify. Sagan and the others earnestly debated whether it was okay to include recordings by Nazi sympathizers (a fair selection of the world's classical repertoire had been conducted by such) or pieces by Hitler's favorite composer, Richard Wagner.

Sagan was at any rate adamant that the selection should not just be dead white males. He wanted to represent the whole globe's musical traditions. They asked many of the (Western) world's most prominent musicologists for opinions. Most were in various degrees astonished by the nature of the request. A late-night call to Martin Williams, the Smithsonian Institution's curator of jazz, got the reaction: "Now, let's see if I got this straight. You're calling me up at home at eleven o'clock on a Sunday night to ask which jazz to send to the stars?"

Just because a piece of music was, in someone's learned opinion, one of the best ever created on this planet did not mean it was in print. Druyan had an arduous time tracking down a recording of an Indian raga, Surshri Kesar Bai Kerkar's "Jaat Kahan Ho." This piece rated number one on Berkeley musicologist Robert E. Brown's list, and he was positive that nothing else would do. Days before the deadline, Druyan found three pristine copies in a Lexington Avenue hardware store. She bought all three.

"Moscow Nights"

With Sagan's feelings about cooperation in space, there was one culture that *had* to be represented. Sagan asked Murry Sidlin, then conductor of the National Symphony Orchestra, to suggest a piece of Russian music. Sidlin touted a recording of "The Young Peddler," sung by Nicolai Gedda.

This is a lighthearted folk song about a capitalist Casanova who seduces young Russian working women. Were the jokes still funny in today's Soviet Union? Sagan wondered. Sagan sent a telegram to a colleague in Moscow explaining the record and saying that "The Young Peddler" had been proposed as a specimen of Russian music. Could he suggest anything more fitting?

This innocent request set in motion ponderous bureaucratic gears. The matter was taken out of the hands of the telegram's recipient. Sagan's request drifted upward to the leadership of the Soviet Academy of Sciences, and possibly to the Kremlin itself. There were (Sagan later heard) debates about the merits of prerevolutionary Russian music. Lenin was cited, for he had said that prerevolutionary culture, even its distinctly capitalist aspects, was part of the national heritage and worth preserving.

Days passed, and the deadline approached. There was no word from Moscow. In the meantime, musicologist Alan Lomax suggested another Soviet, or more exactly Georgian, work. It was a choral piece, "Tchakrulo," about peasants protesting a rich landowner. The Soviets couldn't object to *that*.

They found a Radio Moscow recording of "Tchakrulo" at virtually the last minute. They also found a native speaker of Georgian who came to the recording studio, listened to the piece, and certified its lyrics inoffensive. "Tchakrulo" went on the record.

The official Soviet reply to Sagan's telegram came many weeks later. The best, most worthy and representative work of Russian music, they announced, was a piece called "Moscow Nights."

"Moscow Nights"? Sagan played it. It was like Mantovani. Only worse, for at least Mantovani wasn't trying to rip-off someone so bland and dated as Mantovani. It was a relief that the record's deadline had passed, providing Sagan with an incontestable explanation for why it wasn't used.

"Johnny B. Goode"

One area where Sagan and company felt qualified to override the experts was rock and roll. Many of the experts felt the Voyager selection shouldn't have *any* rock. It wasn't a question of not liking rock (so they said). The musicologists objected that rock was a new and possibly ephemeral form of expression.

The Voyager team figured they could permit themselves *one* rock song. (Sagan rationalized that rock was the fusion of African and European musical traditions in an American setting.) If there was to be just one rock song, it had to be the Beatles, all agreed. They gave some thought to "Sgt. Pepper's Lonely Hearts Club Band" but settled on the cosmic imagery of "Here Comes the Sun."

All four Beatles thought it was a great idea. The problem was that the Beatles did not own the song. Northern Songs did, and it was notorious for demanding exorbitant fees. NASA had very little money to pay copyright holders. Northern Songs could not be persuaded a make an exception for the extraterrestrial market. The Beatles were out.

There was no consensus on who should replace the Beatles. Elvis Presley was mentioned without much enthusiasm. By this time the project's nominal secrecy had been breached, and articles on the Voyager record had begun appearing in the press. With the Beatles scratched, the members of the Jefferson Starship offered their music for free. The record team was in the uncomfortable position of saying thanks but no thanks.

Druyan and Ferris wanted to use Chuck Berry's "Johnny B. Goode." They played it for Sagan. He thought it was awful. They managed to convince him that Berry had had a broad influence on rock (and on the Beatles, particularly). Unlike Elvis, Berry had a claim to being an inventor of the rock idiom, and he composed his own material. Druyan liked "Johnny B. Goode" because it was good traveling music.

*   *   *

The final music selection ran: Bach's Brandenburg Concerto No. 2 in F; "Kinds of Flowers" (Javanese gamelan); a Senegalese percussion piece; a Pygmy girls' initiation song; "Morning Star" and "Devil Bird" (Australian horn and totem songs); "El Casabel" (Lorenzo Barcelata and the Mariachi México); "Johnny B. Goode" (Chuck Berry); a New Guinea men's house song; "Cranes in Their Nest" (Japanese bamboo flute); Bach's "Gavotte en rondeaux" from the Partita No. 3 in E Major for Violin; Mozart's "Queen of the Night" aria, No. 14, from *The Magic Flute*; "Tchakrulo" (Georgian chorus); a Peruvian panpipes and drum piece; "Melancholy Blues" (Louis Armstrong and his Hot Seven); "Ugam" (Azerbaijan bagpipes); Stravinsky's "Sacrificial Dance" from *The Rite of Spring*; Bach's Prelude and Fugue in C from *The Well-Tempered Clavier*, Book 2; Beethoven's Fifth Symphony, First Movement; "Izelel je Delyo Hagdutin" (Bulgarian bagpipes); Navajo "Night Chant"; Anthony Holborne's "The Fairy Round" (Renaissance music); Solomon Islands panpipes; a Peruvian wedding song; "Flowing Streams" (Chinese *ch'in*); "Jaat Kahan Ho" (sung by Surshri Kesar Bai Kerkar); "Dark Was the Night" (Blind Willie Johnson); Beethoven's Cavatina from the String Quartet No. 13 in B flat.

Of all the choices, the Berry piece drew the most attention. There were hidebound conservatives who objected to sending rock and roll into space, no matter that the piece was a golden oldie. It didn't help that Berry had a prison record and was being indicted on income tax charges (some very "creative" accounting sent him to prison in 1979). The controversy inspired a *Saturday Night Live* bit in which a four-word message was detected from space: SEND MORE CHUCK BERRY.

Photo Album

The Voyager record's encoded photographs posed the question of how universal a language pictures might be. Obviously, the finder would need a sense something like our vision. Philip Morrison and Robert Heinlein warned of a subtler problem: pictures are not a universal language, *even on Earth*. There were hunting-and-gathering cultures that never used pictures. They had to learn how to look at photographs and paintings and understand them as flat representations of what you might see somewhere else.

Sagan and Lomberg took this objection seriously. They made some effort to explain the concept of a picture—in pictures. On Morrison's suggestion, the first image is a circle. This would help reassure the finders that the translation from grooves to two-dimensional image was correct. The record's engraved cover also contains a circle near the diagram showing how to decode the pictures.

The second encoded picture combines Drake's pulsar map with a photo of the Andromeda galaxy. Both are asymmetrical images, allowing the ETs to confirm that they aren't decoding the pictures in mirror-image reversed format.

These were followed by diagrams explaining our number system and weights and measures; and then, a concise photograph album of Earth and its cultures.

They decided it was possible to send some photos in color. To do this, they included three consecutive black-and-white images of the same scene, each photographed with a red, green, and blue filter respectively. It was hoped that the finders would recognize that certain images are (nearly) repeated three times and interpret these as color separations. A color picture of a solar spectrum, streaked with the dark emission lines familiar to any science-literate alien, serves as a color calibration swatch.

* * *

The Voyager team sought expert advice for the record's visual content, too. Jon Lomberg got on the phone with quintessential modern designer Charles Eames in Santa Monica. Charles and Ray Eames were known for their interest in science education. With Philip and Phylis Morrison they did a classic film and book, *Powers of Ten*, which zooms from macrocosmos to microcosmos.

Lomberg explained the record. Eames *hated* the idea. If they were doing that, he said, they shouldn't be rushing it. The project should take *years*. It shouldn't be scientists deciding what goes on the record; it should be real experts in the arts. Eames refused to have anything to do with the project.

In the end most of the visual content was selected by Lomberg and Wendy Gradison with input from the others. They searched the Cornell and Ithaca libraries for picture books of all kinds: *Birds of North America, The History of Toys, Plant-Devouring Insects*; also, every issue of *National Geographic* back to 1958.

In photographs and diagrams, the record depicts the sun and planets;

DNA; dividing cells; human anatomy; the human reproductive cycle; geological diagrams; islands, seashores, rivers, mountains, deserts; forests and trees; flowers and insects; evolution; assorted animals; human beings of various ages, ethnicities, and occupations; human dwellings; transportation; science; and, finally, a string quartet and a photo of a violin with the score of Beethoven's Cavatina.

Anatomy Lesson

As with the Pioneer plaque, an essential illustration was a frankly biological portrait of human beings. Although NASA had not taken the "smut in space" reactions to the Pioneer drawing too seriously, a nude photograph is different from a nude drawing. Lomberg needed a photo revealing enough for curious aliens and tasteful enough for prudish earthlings.

There was debate about whether to show young, physically perfect humans—or to attempt an objective documentation of "real people." They took some test shots of models. Then Lomberg came across a textbook photo that seemed perfect. It was a standing nude man and woman, the woman pregnant.

Sagan liked it. It fit perfectly into a sequence of photos on the human reproductive cycle. No one could say it was a *Penthouse* centerfold.

They also wanted to show internal anatomy. Frank Drake remembered the acetate overlays of anatomies in children's encyclopedias. They contacted the *World Book Encyclopedia* and got permission to use its acetate diagrams.

There were two problems. Given the realities of Mississippi school boards, the diagrams had no sex organs. Also, the overlays contained dozens of small black numbers—keys to a legend that was in the encyclopedia but wasn't being used on the Voyager record. *World Book* had no version of the art without the keys.

So Lomberg had to draw diagrammatic male and female sex organs on one of the overlays. Linda expertly painted the legend numbers out. The work done, she set the acetates aside to dry. As the paint dried, it flaked cleanly off. The deadline nearing, the overlays had to be used with the encyclopedia numbers.

One diagram of human evolution has an in-joke at the expense of the Pioneer plaque's more humorless critics. *Homo sapiens* is represented by a close duplicate of the couple from the Pioneer plaque. This time, it's the *woman* who is raising her arm.

World's Meanest Hyenas

The record's sound essay started to take form one green May day in Ithaca. As insects chirped and buzzed, Ferris, Druyan, and Gradison joined Carl and Linda around their dining room table. They made a long list of sounds they might want to send. The next day Druyan returned to New York and started work.

Recordings of thunder vary as much as recordings of Bach, it seems. Druyan learned to rely on recommendations, much as she had with the music. *I understand you have a recording of the world's meanest hyenas*, she would begin. *We want to put it on a record and send it into outer space.*

Druyan was floored at how much money some commercial sound libraries wanted for practically nothing—a few seconds of *wind* or *footsteps*. One man (said to have superlative recordings of children playing) surmised that Annie, and skinflint NASA, were wasting his valuable time. He threw her out of his office, screaming that NASA "had some nerve sending a little girl to talk to a big soundman like me."

Fortunately, a few key people were entranced by the concept. A Warner executive offered all the sound effects of Electra Sound Archives for free.

Druyan and Ferris spent a day auditioning sounds in Washington, D.C. At the Library of Congress's Archive of Recorded Sound, they heard what was believed to be the first battlefield recording ever made. It was a ponderous lacquer disk recorded in France during World War I. They listened as an American soldier barked orders for a mustard gas attack, his voice "horribly cheerful and thoughtless, as mechanical a sound as the answering hiccup of the poison canister."

Druyan and Ferris couldn't get the recording out of their heads. That night they had dinner with the Sagans and Murry Sidlin and told them about the battlefield recording. This led to a discussion about whether to show the dark side of Earth: war, famine, crime, racism. Violence was as much a part of the human race as sex; wasn't it as "Victorian" to expurgate violence as to leave out sex? But Sagan was unconvinced. The record should properly have sex—but not violence.

*   *   *

The sound essay began with "Music of the Spheres," an experimental digital piece by composer Laurie Spiegel. This was followed by the sounds of a volcano, an earthquake, and a thunderstorm; wind, rain, and crashing waves; crickets, frogs, and birds; hyena, elephant, chimp, and dog calls; human footsteps, heartbeats, and laughter; making a fire and chipping flint into tools; domesticated animals; agriculture, Morse code, and an aural montage of transportation, from horse and cart to the liftoff of a Saturn 5; a kiss, a mother and child; and, finally, the recorded warbling of pulsar CP1133.

The record team did not license the recording of a kiss. They tried recording kisses in the studio, discovering that authentic kisses were often very quiet. Jimmy Iovine, a young sound engineer (today the Interscope Records mogul), insisted that he could produce the perfect kiss—by sucking his arm.

Druyan felt that wasn't "authentic" enough for a record that might last longer than any human artifact. They continued taping real kisses. Finally, Timothy pecked Annie lightly on the cheek. It recorded perfectly, and they used it.

Protocol

Sagan had a half-sensible, half-crazy idea about how to get the spoken greetings. He would hold an open mike session at the United Nations. The UN has a sound studio. Sagan would simply invite delegates to drop by at their convenience and say "hello" in their various languages.

When Sagan asked the U.S. delegation for help, the Americans begged off politely. A message to the universe was too important for them to act on their own.

Sagan knew several members of the UN's Outer Space Committee, and his next step was to ask them for help. Their excuse was that the Outer Space Committee could not initiate anything on its own. Only specific national delegations could do that.

Undeterred, Sagan went back to the U.S. delegation. The Americans now said they could act only if authorized by the State Department. Sagan was also firmly told that he had made a *big* mistake by going to the Outer Space Committee directly. As an American scientist, Sagan's very presence advertised that the record was an American project. There were nations that would oppose the project on that ground alone.

The U.S. delegation also told Sagan that an open recording session was politically unworkable. A diplomat who happened to be out of town that day might be insulted that a message had been sent to the stars without him. A more practical idea, they said, would be for each member of the Outer Space Committee to record a "hello."

For someone as diversity-conscious as Sagan, that was a disappointment. Because China did not sit on the Outer Space Committee, the language spoken by the most people on Earth would go unrepresented. And because the committee was nearly all male, females would be underrepresented.

In any event, the Outer Space Committee would first have to vote on whether it wanted to say "hello" to extraterrestrials. The next meeting was in late June. Sagan explained that that was too late. He was asked if the launch could be postponed.

The State Department was no more comforting. It said it could act only if NASA requested. Furthermore, if the State Department was going to go out on a limb and help, it needed an iron-clad guarantee that any greetings obtained would be sent into space. It could not risk having a delegate find out that his recording had not been used.

Sagan couldn't guarantee that, for indeed NASA had not guaranteed that the record would go on the spacecraft. The space agency retained a right of refusal in case something on the record threatened to be an embarrassment.

Sagan contacted NASA again. This time a diplomatically savvy administrator, Arnold Frutkin, knew the right strings to pull. He convinced the State Department to order the U.S. mission to cooperate. He also went directly to UN Secretary General Kurt Waldheim.

June 1st

Annie meanwhile was working on the daunting assignment of finding the one most "worthy" piece of music from 5,000 years of Chinese history. She called Columbia University's Chinese musicologist Chou Wen Chung. No sooner had she explained herself than she had an answer.

" 'Flowing Streams,' " he said. "Because it is a meditation on the human sense of affinity with the universe. Because all kinds of Chinese people, on every side of political divisions, would be moved by such a choice. And it must be the performance by the late virtuoso Kuan P'ing-Hu, the Heifetz of the *ch'in*."

Druyan found the Kuan P'ing-Hu recording, and it was as magnificent as promised. Sagan was then at a conference in Tucson. Pleased that she had found the Chinese piece, Annie called his hotel and left a message.

Carl returned her call. "I got back to my room and found a message that said, 'Annie called,' " he began. "And I asked myself, 'Why didn't she leave me that message ten years ago?' "

"Well," Annie replied. "I've been meaning to talk to you about that, Carl." Then: "Do you mean for keeps?"

"Yes, for keeps. Let's get married."

They had never had sex, never kissed, never acknowledged that an attraction existed. The phone call was short; Annie never mentioned the Chinese music. Moments after she put the phone down, it rang again. It was Carl: "I just want to make sure that really happened. We *are* getting married?"

This incredible proposal—the more incredible for having led to a durable, twenty-year union—took place on June 1, 1977. Late in the afternoon of that same day, Sagan got a call from NASA. The UN had okayed a recording session for members of the Outer Space Committee the following day.

Sagan called Ferris, the strangeness of the upcoming change in their relationship surely weighing on him. He asked Ferris to attend the UN recording session and make sure things went all right.

Annie called Lynda Obst with the big news. Lynda responded with the crucial question that must be asked whenever a woman falls in love with a married man: when was Carl going to tell his wife?

Open Mike

When Ferris arrived at the UN the next day, he found some of the committee members assembled and others missing without explanation. Politically, the *worst* nation to be left off the record would be the Soviet Union. The Soviet member was not there. Ferris assessed the balance of languages. It was pretty *un*balanced. Of the fifteen nations present, a third spoke English.

Ferris told the delegates to keep their greetings short because the space on the record was limited.

Nearly everyone had written a speech. Most started by identifying themselves and their great nations in overblown language. These *preambles* were longer than the entire greetings were supposed to be.

Sagan had not briefed the committee on the concept of extraterrestrial life. It had not seemed necessary, since the greetings were supposed to consist of *bonjour* or *hello from Earth* or the like. Some of the UN messages were bizarre. Australian member Ralph Harry gave his greeting in the "universal" language of Esperanto. Nigeria's Wallace R. T. Macaulay had the most memorable image: "My dear friends in outer space, as you probably know, my country is situated on the west coast of the continent of Africa, a land mass more or less in the shape of a question mark in the center of our planet."

Sagan and Ferris played back the tape and tried to decide what they had. By edict they had to use everyone's greeting or face an international incident. But there was no way they could use the full text of the greetings. They would have to excerpt. Some messages did not make much sense in their entirety. Some of the excerpts they used sounded as if the speaker got the vaudeville hook. One rambling contribution was hacked down to: ". . . and good luck. Sierra Leone is a member of the Committee on Outer Space and we believe this committee good for . . ."

* * *

The UN press office announced the recording session to the press. Someone hadn't heard that the record was supposed to be kept secret. That someone also hadn't known exactly who Timothy Ferris was. He was incorrectly identified as a NASA official.

Sagan was told that neither he nor his friends could speak for NASA. There was one pleasant surprise, though. The day after the ill-starred recording session, Sagan learned that Kurt Waldheim himself had independently recorded his own greeting. Miracle of miracles—*it made sense.* Waldheim's statement was lucid and concise; it struck no wrong notes. Sagan felt that Waldheim's message *had* to go on the record. (As Sagan fussed over sending Wagner, he had no way of knowing of Waldheim's still-secret Nazi past!)

Unfortunately, Waldheim's message triggered another diplomatic domino effect. Sagan figured he had to invite the U.S. president to record a message, too, since the United States was paying for Voyager. In a few days, word came back that President Jimmy Carter *did* want to provide a message.

Carter's message then got NASA worrying about the Constitution. The executive and legislative branches of government are supposed to be in balance. NASA maintained that Congress had to be represented on the record, too.

Five hundred thirty-five long-winded messages could fill up several records itself. Sagan bargained NASA into settling for a list of the names of everyone on every Senate and House committee that had anything to do with NASA appropriations. This typewritten list was photographed and incorporated as a picture. Somehow NASA consented to leave out the judicial branch.

* * *

After all this, the record still didn't have a reasonable representation of the world's languages. Linda looked to Cornell's renowned language and literature departments. Its faculty spoke a great many of the world's languages, living and extinct. With the help of Sagan's assistant, Shirley Arden, Linda arranged two recording sessions in Cornell's Administration Building on June 8 and 13. They ended up with short specimens of fifty-five languages, from Sumerian to Sinhalese, and including at least the two dozen with the greatest number of speakers. Nick Sagan delivered the English-language greeting, "Hello from the children of Planet Earth."

String of Firecrackers

The record's most unusual "message" is a recording of human brain activity. This was Druyan's idea. During a bout of encephalitis the previous year, she had been hooked to an electroencephalogram machine. Why not record someone's EEG traces and inscribe them on the record? The admittedly far-fetched idea was that somehow, some way, the ETs who found it might be able to reconstruct the traces as *thoughts*. Maybe they could reexperience those thoughts in mental virtual reality; understand what it was like to be human.

On June 3, Druyan went to a laboratory in Bellevue Hospital, New York. She was hooked up to a Honeywell computer that would record brain, heart, eye, and muscle data for one hour.

The techs left Annie alone in a lab room so that she could concentrate on a prepared list of things to think about. It was more or less a complete history of the world. She thought of the evolution of life on Earth, of the grand sweep of human history, of the crises in which we find ourselves, and of what it was like to be deeply in love.

The data were compressed so that the hour of internal dialogue consumed a mere minute. When the recording was through, an engineer played the compressed data on an audio speaker. It sounded like a string of firecrackers going off.

"Danny Boy"

Everything on the record now had to be cleared with NASA. A group of NASA administrators met with Sagan at the Manhattan studio of CBS Records to audition the music and greetings. The NASA executives were not world music fans. Most of the selections left them stonily unmoved. Chuck Berry got a nod of recognition. *They had heard that before.*

They pronounced the music acceptable.

The next day Sagan got a call from a NASA associate administrator. They'd made a mistake, the caller said; they forgot to put some Irish music on the record. Sagan drew a breath and launched into what was becoming a rote explanation. There were *many* cultures not represented on the record—no Italian opera, no Jewish folk songs, and so forth.

Tip O'Neill is Irish, the NASA administrator explained. They didn't want to offend the Speaker of the House. He asked if it was too late to include "Danny Boy."

Sagan talked him out of that. The pictorial content occupied another meeting. Sagan flew to Washington, D.C., with slides of each of the 120 pictures. When he came to the nude photo, the NASA people stopped him. There was no way they were sending a nude photo into space, they said. Sagan countered that the woman was pregnant. The picture was about the family.

The bureaucrats didn't buy it. If anything, the fact that it was a picture of a pregnant woman made it *worse*—and kind of *weird*.

NASA had other questions, too. Why weren't there any great works of art? Sagan said it was because there hadn't been time to assemble a team of art historians. Why weren't there any cathedrals, temples, or houses of worship? Sagan replied that there were dozens of major religions. Anyone whose religion had been left out would be offended, probably *more* offended than the people who thought their culture's music had been neglected.

The NASA people okayed everything except the nude photo. They offered the unavailing compromise that they would permit nude *statues*—Michelangelo's *David*, maybe. Just no nude people.

*   *   *

Sagan got on the phone to Lomberg and Drake. "There's a *little* problem," he began. He relayed the nude statue idea. They all hated that. It allowed odd misinterpretations, like *humans who take their clothes off turn to stone*.

They went back to NASA with a counteroffer to replace the nudes with silhouettes of the same two figures. This would allow Lomberg to diagram the fetus residing within the woman's abdomen, something that might not be obvious otherwise. NASA okayed that.

A few days later, a NASA staffer sent the team a memo pointing out that some people find nude photos of pregnant women extremely erotic.

Circle Line

Carl and Annie spent a day together in New York taking the Circle Line tour, a four-hour riverboat cruise around Manhattan. The tour offered the fresh air and privacy that they thought would be conducive to discussions of their future plans and their most immediate problem: how to break the news to Linda and Timothy.

Linda had a sharp temper when wronged. The divorce would mean giving up yet a third son. Carl and Annie made the idealistic vow, perhaps of little substance under the circumstances, that they would do all they could to keep Nick from being hurt.

On top of these concerns was another, more unusual one. They did not want to do anything to jeopardize the Voyager record. If NASA was worried about nude pictures, it might not like hearing that the Voyager project had caused a married man to abandon wife and family for another project employee. They feared that NASA might decide not to use the record at all.

They resolved to keep quiet about their relationship until after the Voyager launch. They also decided to inform Linda and Timothy simultaneously. Otherwise, people might get on the phone, and principals could hear about it from a third party. They vowed to break the news at 1 P.M. two days after the Voyager launch.

*　　*　　*

Frank Drake had a vexing, if less emotional, problem. A lot was riding on his assumption that pictures could be converted into phonograph record grooves. But no one in the television industry had heard of a device for putting pictures on an LP. They used videotape.

Drake was looking for a machine capable of converting high-frequency television signals into low-frequency audio signals. Once the audio signals were on tape, *any* recording studio could cut a record from it. Drake brought on a first-rate hardware hacker named Valentin Boriakoff. Boriakoff located a start-up company, Colorado Video, whose founders had the idea that people would someday want to send television pictures over phone lines. That meant converting TV signals to audio signals. They had recently built a device to do that, and they were willing to help with the record.

The day before they cut the record, another major crisis arose. Lomberg's photographic selections ran over the budgeted space on the record, to the tune of about ten minutes' recording time. Lomberg suggested that maybe they could cut some of the music.

Ferris insisted that no music could be cut. The music people had stuck to *their* time limit. After some phone calls to Honeywell, Drake determined that it was possible to use both stereo grooves to inscribe picture data. Then everything would fit on the record.

Sounds and pictures were inscribed onto two wax masters—one for each side of the final record—at CBS studios in New York. (Bruce Springsteen was making a record next door.) Ferris wanted to inscribe a handwritten message in the take-out grooves—which John Lennon, for one, often did with his own records. Ferris added the dedication "To the makers of music, all worlds, all times."

Ferris took the masters to Los Angeles, where copper versions were made. Two identical flight records were produced, one for each of the two Voyagers, plus several duplicates. Each record was one-twentieth of an inch thick and weighed one and a quarter pounds. Plated with gold, they ended up looking like industry-award "gold records."

Launch

Celestial mechanics decreed that Voyager 2, the second to arrive at Jupiter, would have to be launched two weeks earlier than Voyager 1. The Sagans, Drake, Ferris, Druyan, and Lomberg attended the Voyager 2 launch on August 20, 1977. To the end, NASA was oddly noncommittal about the record. When the copies of the record were delivered, a zealous inspector rejected them. The reason was that the specs said nothing about Ferris's last-minute inscription. After that was cleared up, Sagan and company held a press conference. They were assigned a room that seemed intentionally uncomfortable. A band playing next door drowned out what they had to say.

As the rocket lifted off, all were conscious of an awesomeness to the task they had completed. The Pioneer plaque, Sagan had calculated, would survive long after the Pyramids and all other earthly monuments had crumbled to dust. The Voyager record, supplied with its protective cover, could be expected to last longer yet.

A space-faring message would be immune to such hazards as looters and archaeologists; smog and nuclear annihilation. The major threat would be micrometeorites. Slamming into the record at fifteen kilometers a second, they might ultimately sandblast its lofty melodies into nothingness. The erosion would be most intense at journey's beginning, in the dust-strewn solar system. Sagan and JPL's Paul Penzo computed that, in the first light-year of travel, an unprotected record might find 10 percent of its outward surface pitted, making it impossible to play, barring some heroic act of extraterrestrial restoration.

For this reason the records were placed behind aluminum covers. That would reduce the expected pitting to 2 percent of the record's surface in the first light-year, and another 2 percent in the next 5,000 light-years, which would take about 100,000 years to traverse.

As further insurance, the first side of the record, designed to contain the more crucial information, was mounted inward, where it is buffered both by the other side of the record and the cover. The first side contains all the pictures, the greetings, the sound essay, and a third of the music. Sagan estimated an average lifetime of a billion years for the record as a whole. The inner side would survive a time comparable to the age of the universe itself.

Yellow Pad

Carl had told Lester Grinspoon about Annie. He and Lester decided it would be best for Carl to break the news to Linda when the Grinspoons were present for mutual support. They arranged for the two families to go to the Grinspoons' summer home on Cape Cod.

There, on August 22, Carl told Linda that he wanted a divorce. He was marrying Ann Druyan. Linda was incredulous, then furious. She still loved Carl. She still intended to honor her marriage vows.

Carl was undeterred. He sat out on the deck with Linda and drew up a list of the couple's assets on a yellow legal pad. They would split things right there, Carl said. Lester said that wasn't such a good idea; these things were for lawyers to handle. Carl ignored the advice. He wanted to get things over and done with.

Linda asked for item after item. For the most part, Carl okayed them. He took the position that he did not mean to hurt Linda or Nick.

All four stayed up until 4 A.M., recriminations flaring. Carl broke away to phone Annie. The urbane Ferris had taken the news as well as could be expected. He had been disappointed in love once before; he was able to be relatively philosophical about the cruel turns of love.

It was easier to return engagement presents than to undo nine years of marriage. One thing Linda wanted was not on the list. She said she wanted Carl to impregnate her again. She had always planned on having another child. Now she might not have another opportunity because of Carl's abandonment.

Carl and the Grinspoons did their best to talk her out of this idea. Linda was adamant. She vowed to entice Carl into bed, by devious means if necessary—to do whatever it took to conceive another child.

Mosquito Nets

Behind the rash threats was a deeply hurt woman whose life had been turned upside down by a husband and a friend she must have felt she no longer knew. (Two days before, Linda and Annie had cried like sisters as Carl stood proudly at their side, watching the rocket blast off for Jupiter.)

There followed the unpleasant task of informing Nick. He was not quite seven. The half-heard arguments in other rooms had alerted him that something was wrong. Even he was not precocious enough to anticipate the cause. When Carl and Linda told him they were splitting up, Nick responded with Chinese parables.

He had been reading a book of Chinese parables. He related one in which a man's aged parent was bedeviled nightly by mosquitoes and could not sleep. The noble son put his bed outside his parent's room, offering his flesh to the insects so they would not bother his esteemed parent.

"Don't think I'm going to do something like that," Nick announced, "not when there are mosquito nets and insect repellent."

Carl and Linda's guardedly optimistic interpretation of this was that Nick was not going to let himself suffer unnecessarily for their sake.

*   *   *

There is no safe or foolproof reaction to the news that a twice-married man has fallen in love with his friend's girlfriend. Jon Lomberg had suspected nothing. It seemed Carl spent more time with Tim than with Annie. "Are you sure she feels the same way about *you*?" Lomberg asked Carl.

That same August, Samuel and Rachel Sagan took title on a retirement condo in Florida. When Carl met with his father and told him he was leaving Linda for another woman, Samuel happened to be standing at the window, his back to Carl, engaged in the mundane act of closing venetian blinds.

"I hope it's Annie Druyan," Samuel said casually.

Samuel had met Annie only once or twice and had no more reason than anyone else to suspect a love affair. Somehow he knew.

Harry Druyan was, like Samuel Sagan, a veteran of the New York garment trade. Carl met Harry at Maxwell's Plum in New York to tell him he intended to divorce Linda and marry his daughter. Harry looked Carl in the eye and replied, "*Deeds*, my friend, not words. *Deeds*."

Existence Theorem

He had a point. An actuary of love could not have given the match much chance. With two wives cast aside, Carl's track record was unencouraging. By age and looks, Annie could be mistaken for the archetypical trophy wife.

Carl and Annie proved the doubters wrong. To those close to the couple, their love was one of the marvels of the romantic world. Lynda Obst took to calling Annie "Miss Bliss." "I was always in a state of normal ambivalence," Obst explains, "and she was always in a state of bliss." To Obst, the partnership was, in suitably brainy metaphor, an "existence theorem," a proof that true fulfillment in love is possible after all.

Alloyed with that was a sense of love's frailty. "I think Annie feared for Carl from the first moment she met him," Obst said. "There was a sense that she was so incredibly lucky to have the husband she was meant to have.

That kind of luck has with it a fear that it's temporary—that it can be taken away from you, that your fortune is too extreme."

*   *   *

Linda did not want Carl and Annie being seen around town. For the time being, Carl humored her. He and Annie traveled together but did not move in together until January. Their first home was in Slaterville Springs, a bucolic community several miles beyond the Ithaca city limits.

In the fall, Carl came down with a painful gall bladder attack in Vancouver. He went to Beth Israel Hospital in Boston to have the gall bladder removed. The doctors ran some tests and told him they had some very bad news. He had Hodgkin's disease.

Hodgkin's disease is a chronic condition producing inflammation and enlargement of the lymph nodes and spleen; sometimes the liver and kidney. It is usually fatal. For a day Carl, and with him Annie, looked death in the face. Then as suddenly as the bad news had come, his doctors granted a reprieve. They decided that he did not have Hodgkin's disease after all. There had been some puzzling findings . . . he seemed to be okay.

Metronome

Despite these tumultuous changes in his personal life, Sagan was doing some of his best writing ever. By the time of the Voyager launch, *The Dragons of Eden* was drawing impressive reviews for its accessible account of the evolution of the human brain. It was also making him wealthier than the average college professor. By early 1981, *The Dragons of Eden* had sold 200,000 hardcover and over 1 million paperback copies. This surprised Sagan as much as it did his publisher. The hardcover alone earned Sagan something like $250,000 in royalties.

In his popular writing, Sagan did not talk down to the reader, nor did he attempt to teach Astronomy 101. Sagan had a knack for identifying those aspects of science that hold appeal to the nonscientist. Once he identified those themes, he was able to chart a route from premise to conclusion permitting a minimum of extraneous detail.

There are people who have to recite the entire alphabet to tell you what letter comes after *R*. Much science writing is like that: in order to discuss a topic, the scientist thinks it's necessary to explain almost *everything* he or she learned prior to that topic. To someone who knows science, it is amazing how much Sagan leaves *out* of explanations. This is not dumbed-down science but the truest form of clarity. It is also a type of expository style that is not necessarily expected in a classroom or a research lab, and that is why not every scientist who turns to writing is another Carl Sagan.

Sagan avoided both the computer and the typewriter. His favored technology was the dictating machine. He would dictate copy into a tape recorder, sentence after sentence, paragraph after paragraph, of um-less prose without losing his train of thought or having to make a flurry of corrections. In summer he would often work outside, in a patio area set in a pine and oak forest dotted with wildflowers. As he would dictate, deer would sometimes approach curiously.

The dictation would be sent to a transcriber and returned as a typed manuscript. Sagan would make changes in the manuscript and repeat the process anew. A book would typically go through two dozen or more drafts.

One consequence of this procedure was that Sagan *heard* every word and phrase as he composed. This may have played a role in fostering the poetic quality of his writing. Sagan's exposure to poetry was substantial and adventurous. Sagan was friends with Cornell poet Diane Ackerman and invited her to view NASA launches. Swinburne, Blake, and Shakespeare were favorites of Sagan's. He once insisted on rereading *Moby Dick* aloud. Another book that impressed him was *Broken Spear*, a translation of Aztec poetry composed as the Spaniards were eradicating Aztec culture.

"When I try to express an emotion in prose," Sagan once told an interviewer, "I find that there's a little metronome inside of me which tries to convert it—at least as far as meter goes—into poetry. It's a means of expressing feelings. I think that science has been separated artificially from feelings."

Sagan's "poetry" is not merely "decorative" (as might be said of some who attempt to write in his vein). Like the best "real" poetry, it succeeds by wedding shock value to truth.

> It is always raining sulfuric acid on Venus, all over the planet, and not a drop ever reaches the surface.

> In the history of the world, more societies have advocated incest or infanticide than have taught that comets were benign, or even neutral.

> With his artificial nose of gold or brass, his entourage of dwarfs, his legendary drinking parties, and palatial island observatory, he was not your typical astronomer.

Sagan's writing enterprise became a well-oiled machine. Researchers and assistants helped with background research and fact-checking. (Sagan would have Xeroxed articles to read on planes, saving time.) Druyan became an important collaborator, sometimes as coauthor, otherwise as first editor. She conceived most of the titles of Sagan's later books. (A manuscript that started life as "The Alien and the Skeptic" became "The Demon-Haunted World.")

Like many scientist-popularizers, Sagan uses personal anecdotes. These often take on mythic dimensions. *The Dragons of Eden* has a real-life Zen parable about the "observer" of cannabis experiences. Sagan writes that his "informant" (conceivably Sagan himself?) became aware of the dispassionate and rational part of himself commenting on the kaleidoscopic imagery of the marijuana experience. "Who *are* you?" the informant asked. The reply was simply "Who wants to know?"

Coming on top of Sagan's visibility on the Viking and Voyager projects, *The Dragons of Eden* made Sagan one of the nation's best-known scientists. In December 1977 President Jimmy Carter invited Sagan to give a command performance. Carter, the first U.S. president to report seeing a UFO, was a space buff whose engineering background allowed him to follow current developments in astronomy. Carter asked Sagan to give a talk on astronomy for the president's and vice president's families.

The talk took place one frosty night on the grounds of the U.S. Naval Observatory. Recognizing that he had a responsibility to speak for the whole astronomical profession, Sagan was careful not to give undue weight to his own interests. But the president loved Mars—especially life on Mars. Were they *sure* the Vikings hadn't found life? Carter wanted to know. Why had they landed in such boring places? Hadn't they heard the old saying "Nothing ventured, nothing gained"?

"You know," Carter told Sagan, "you ought to write a few more books to really get people interested in planetary exploration. Then we could do some really exciting missions."

"But Mr. President," Sagan countered, "*you* only need write your name at the bottom of a single sheet of paper and we could have a rover mission to Mars."

The president just smiled.

The Pulitzer

The following spring, *The Dragons of Eden* won the 1978 Pulitzer Prize. This award came as a surprise. There are only three nonfiction book categories in the Pulitzer balloting. As "general nonfiction," *Dragons of Eden* competed against *all* nonfiction books, save history and biography, published that year.

You could retire on a Nobel Prize. The Pulitzer's cash award is more in the price range of new carpeting. Sagan received $1,000. In less mercenary terms, the prize was validation not only for Sagan's popular writing but for a genre of science books for a broad intelligent audience. *The Dragons of Eden* was the first real science book to win.

Dragons had its critics, though, mostly in the neurology profession. Some took the cheap shots that are the due of any academic daring to write out of his or her specialty. One perhaps apocryphal story has it that a well-known British brain researcher was visiting Caltech. Norman Horowitz mentioned that Carl Sagan had written a book on the brain and won the Pulitzer Prize.

"For fiction or nonfiction?" asked the neurologist.

The more substantiative part of the grousing had to do with the book's discussion of Paul MacLean's model of the "triune brain"—a somewhat fuzzy idea whose intellectual respectability peaked at about the time Sagan wrote his book. The model proposes that our brain is a composite of reptilian, mammalian, and uniquely human elements, each having a distinct effect on behavior. MacLean is a pioneering neurologist who prefers to call the triune brain a metaphor rather than a theory. Sagan uses similarly cautious language in *Dragons*. Still, his extended discussion of the triune brain implicitly endorses it as (at least) an interesting idea. That was what some neurologists found objectionable. "It's dismaying for people like us," complained Boyd Campbell of Walter Reed Army Medical Center, "to see Sagan come and swallow all that stuff, write *The Dragons of Eden*, and get a Pulitzer Prize for it."

Even as the theory/metaphor was taking its lumps, the popularized version of it was taking on a touchy-feely life of its own. A New Jersey elementary school structured its classes around the triune brain. Since learning was held to involve the mammalian brain, school officials created a "totally non-threatening environment" to prevent children from "downshifting" to their lower, reptilian centers. Sagan of course had nothing to do with the sometimes absurd excesses. It was, however, likely that most of the people perpetuating these excesses had heard about the triune brain by way of Sagan's marvelously well written best-seller. Such were the rewards, and occasional hazards, of popularization.

LOS ANGELES
1978-81

WITHIN A SHORT TIME, three generations of the Sagan family were living in a city where none had ever lived before—Los Angeles. This was the result of good and bad fortune.

The good fortune was Carl's PBS series, which began production in Los Angeles in mid-1978. This led to major changes in his lifestyle. Carl and Annie rented a big orange house in Hollywood at 1756 Sierra Bonita Avenue. Carl took a two-year hiatus from research and teaching; he relinquished editorship of *Icarus*. At his request, Shirley Arden and Steven Soter also moved from Ithaca to L.A. to work on the show.

The bad news came from Florida. Samuel Sagan had lung cancer. He grew frail and thin. It was ever more difficult for Rachel to get him to eat. She pleaded with friends in Delray Beach to make Samuel bacon, ham and eggs, *anything* that would appeal to his flagging appetite.

As time became precious, Carl had his parents move out to Los Angeles. With the TV show taking up so many hours of his day, this was about the only way he could arrange to spend time with them. It also gave Samuel and Rachel a chance to see their grandson, Nick. He and Linda were in Los Angeles, too.

In the divorce proceedings, both Linda and Carl had aggressive and expensive legal talent—in Carl's case, Los Angeles celebrity divorce attorney Marvin Mitchelson. As Grinspoon had feared, the schedule of assets

255

Sagan had drawn up on Cape Cod came back to haunt him. There was end-less argument over what he had or had not offered to give Linda.

One point of dispute was which state's divorce laws should apply. Linda had moved to Ithaca to be with Carl. With the marriage being dissolved, she felt she had no reason to stay there. She thought of moving to New York City, where her art or filmmaking career might be better pur-sued. Because of the TV show, Carl had become a California resident. In the ongoing game of divorce chess, that put him in a vulnerable position. Linda responded by moving to Los Angeles. Now that they were both Cali-fornia residents, the divorce would be governed by the state's community property laws.

Two Mettlesome Horses

Adrian Malone was married and having sex with a woman, not his wife, who worked on *Cosmos*. This parallel in their romantic lives did nothing to bond Malone and Sagan. Malone considered himself an expert in present-ing intelligent science programming to TV audiences. He did not initially appreciate that Sagan considered himself an expert in that very same field. "What it's been like on *Cosmos*," Malone said, "is having two fairly mettle-some horses put together to pull a carriage. We get going at a hell of a speed, but we're often out of step, and there's some danger the carriage may tip over."

Malone was a loose cannon. "Do you like children?" he once asked Carl, glancing at the visiting Dorion. "I hate them." Malone boasted of having screwed every secretary he ever had. He complained that KCET had forced him to hire a few "Hottentots." Talk like that appalled Sagan. At one gather-ing, Annie had a chance to meet Rita Bronowski, Jacob's widow. "He mur-dered my husband," Rita said of Malone. "Don't let him murder yours."

In the summer of 1978 Malone, Sagan, Druyan, and the rest of the show's staff sat around a big table at KCET in Los Angeles. They were com-mencing production on a thirteen-part series budgeted at $8.2 million. They were still about a million short.

Sagan insisted that everyone, from himself to the station gofer, give their ideas about what they thought the show ought to be. Malone thought that was a waste of time. It wasn't how they did things at the BBC. Sagan also insisted on giving the staff a two-week crash course in astronomy. He thought that the people who make a science show should understand its content.

From Malone's point of view, there were several ongoing problems.

Problem number one was Sagan's insistence on scientific accuracy. Every time Malone wanted to try something different, it seemed, Sagan would say it was scientifically wrong. He would refuse to allow it.

A second problem, as Malone saw it, was Druyan. Sagan listened to everything she said and wanted to implement most of her ideas. Druyan said the show's title, *Man in the Cosmos*, was sexist. Why not just call it *Cosmos*? Sagan agreed; Malone didn't see what was the big deal.

A third problem was the accompanying *Cosmos* book. Closely intertwined as book and TV series were, the book was a separate matter and commanded its own share of Sagan's time. Malone thought the TV show came first, and Sagan could finish the book later, whenever. Sagan and his publisher, Random House, had some shibboleth about the book being in stores when the TV series aired.

Malone had at least one problem that had nothing to do with Carl Sagan. KCET was a clip joint. Malone ordered a prop table—not even to appear on-camera—and was charged about four times what it would cost elsewhere. He also had to pay the station a "general and administrative" fee for overhead. In fiscal 1980, this came to 43 percent of the production budget. In effect, this was a way of siphoning money raised for *Cosmos* into the station's general till.

Special Effects

Star Wars preyed on Malone's mind. He feared that the PBS show's special effects would be compared to those of the George Lucas blockbuster film—no matter that this was television, and public television at that. Malone therefore hired some of the special-effects artists who had worked on *Star Wars* to design the show's visuals.

People who had seen *Star Wars* would not sit still for Sagan's voice over still photos of stars, Malone thought. They needed something more dynamic. In principle, Sagan agreed. All liked the concept of showing Sagan zipping through the universe in a spaceship. But the spaceship raised scientific qualms with Sagan. He had, after all, written articles on interstellar spaceflight.

A *real* interstellar spaceship would take a long time to get anywhere (even allowing for relativistic time dilation). Sagan felt the spaceship shouldn't be too literal. It should somehow suggest that this was a journey that could take place only in imagination.

Jon Lomberg (whom Sagan hired to supervise the art) suggested that the spaceship should resemble a dandelion seed. It was a crazy, Pre-Raphaelite notion, the opposite of the *Star Wars* sensibility. They'd show Sagan holding up a head of a spent dandelion, and then a floating seed would transmute into the spaceship.

After a short discussion, everyone was sold on the idea. What the spaceship would look like from the inside was still open. They ended up building a spare structure of plywood and Plexiglas at KCET, almost entirely free of hardware. (To some viewers, this was held to resemble a cathedral.)

Sagan also worried about the stars and galaxies seen through the spaceship's windows. Was it to be a generic view of a typical star field zooming by—roughly as you see on *Star Trek*—or was it to show a *specific* route through the universe with cartographic accuracy?

Sagan wanted cartographic accuracy. Lomberg's crew hit the celestial atlases. They couldn't just copy charts; they had to use trigonometry to visualize the universe in three dimensions. It was a lot of work.

When they showed Sagan the sketches, he said he thought they were great, and he wanted to swing by the Pleiades.

It's not on the route, Lomberg told him.

Sagan wanted the route changed, so that it did go by the Pleiades. The sketches were redone.

*   *   *

Shooting began in 1979. Sagan called the *Cosmos* shooting regimen "the toughest schedule I've ever had for a sustained period." Mounted for easy reference on his kitchen cabinet, the schedule broke up the days into thirds: mornings, afternoons, and evenings. Rarely was there a free slot, even on weekends or holidays. For the first time in his professional life, Sagan refused media interviews. What nominal free time he had was allocated largely to seeing to his dying father's needs.

"I don't like the acting part," Sagan complained. "You'll do 11 takes and they'll use take one." One article reported that Sagan's poise as a lecturer allowed many scenes to be shot in a single take. Sagan required only "a little light makeup to knock down the beard shadow."

For a production that was supposed to be a "British show" done in the United States, a lot of it was done elsewhere. Location shooting took the production to the Netherlands, Germany, Britain, Italy, Greece, India, Japan, Alaska, Hawaii, and Death Valley, which doubled for Mars. One of Sagan's favorite travel stories was about passing through Egyptian customs. Packed among the luggage was an incredibly realistic "Rosetta stone."

*   *   *

A boon for the show and for planetary astronomy was the impressive performance of the Voyagers. They skimmed through the Jupiter system around

March 5 and July 9, 1979, returning stunning images of the giant planet and its moons.

Lynda Obst had recently switched careers and coasts, taking a job with movie producer Peter Guber. She threw a party for the Voyager team and for Hollywood. Carl brought along the latest pictures of Jupiter from JPL. God, Carl, these are great, Bianca Jagger said; did you take them? Also present was Obst's college roommate, Marianne Williamson, a well-known "new age" author and speaker. Sagan and Williamson got into a prickly debate over predestination. Carl "took every single one of her arguments and, in the most incredibly brilliant Oxford debating form, annihilated them point by point," recalled Obst. The performance drew a crowd. At last, Williamson could only throw up her hands and say, "Well, you have to believe!"

*   *   *

Cosmos ran a year over schedule. A professor who exceeds Cornell's two-year limit on sabbaticals theoretically risks losing tenure. Yervant Terzian, then the head of Cornell's astronomy department, managed to turn a blind eye. The production also reportedly went $500,000 over budget. (Malone denied this, saying, "I've never been over budget in my life.")

KCET had financial responsibility for overruns. Sagan and Druyan met with Arco executives in their Los Angeles headquarters to ask for more money. There was a delicate problem. One of the show's segments dealt with the greenhouse effect, not just on Venus but on Earth. It presented a montage of smoggy cityscapes, smokestacks, and tailpipes as Sagan warned that the burning of fossil fuels threatened to warm the climate with unknown consequences. The Arco people listened to Sagan's pitch and approved the extra money on the spot. They didn't ask to see a cut of the show (and Sagan never heard a complaint from them about the greenhouse-effect montage).

*   *   *

Samuel Sagan did not live to see *Cosmos*. He died in Los Angeles on October 7, 1979. Carl was with him at the end. His last words to his father were "Take care."

The TV series exacted from Sagan a visible toll like that claimed of the presidency. One associate found Sagan a "gaunter, more somber individual" after the production than he had been at its outset.

Toward the end, Sagan could be as tough a taskmaster as Hermann Muller. Deane Rink, the Cornell SDS member, was hired for odd jobs. One was clearing permissions for the many photographs used in the *Cosmos* book. Rink aspired to continue in the TV field and got a network offer too good to refuse. It began just after the *Cosmos* deadline. He accepted. But the book work ran late. Sagan asked Rink to stay on until the book was finished. When Rink refused, Sagan acted "like a petulant child who was denied something he wanted and thought he deserved." Though Rink did most of the permissions work, he was not credited in the *Cosmos* book.

One day in 1980, Jeremy Sagan called his father from Pasadena and asked if he could stay with him for a while. Carl refused him, saying he was too busy. He undeniably *was* busy . . . but this was his own son. Lynn was angry when she found out. When she confronted Carl, he questioned whether Jeremy even *was* his biologic son. (Most observers would find Jeremy's physical resemblance to Carl prima facie evidence of paternity.) For a long time afterward, Jeremy was on the outs with his father.

Director's Revenge

Nor was Malone at his best. By the end of the production, *Cosmos*'s two mettlesome horses were barely on speaking terms. Malone left the production early, thereby cutting short the usual process of tweaking and refining in the editing studio.

One consequence of this was evident in the spaceship sequences. The special-effects firm responsible for creating the starry imagery visible from the windows of Sagan's spaceship was prompt at cashing the *Cosmos* production's checks but slow in delivering the work. Many of the effects sequences were never delivered. It was necessary to fill in somehow. Malone used "reaction shots" of Sagan beatifically pondering the universe.

Many viewers thought these shots were too long and made Sagan look kind of silly. A *Newsweek* reviewer likened Sagan's "perpetual expression of awe-struck reverence" to the little boy in the film *Close Encounters of the Third Kind*. At *Cosmos*'s generally well received premiere at American University, there was a murmur about there being "a lot of Carl and a little bit of cosmos."

It's hard to believe that the reaction shots were the *only* way of covering the missing sequences. (In fact, Sagan later reedited the spaceship sequences for a repeat showing and video releases.) Jon Lomberg's theory is Malone included these shots as director's revenge. "You don't want a director mad at you," he observes.

And despite the show's phenomenal success, Adrian Malone never again spoke with Sagan or Druyan.

Pop Star

Cosmos fell into a pleasant windfall. An actor's strike kept the networks in reruns well into the fall 1980 season. PBS wasn't affected and was getting favorable buzz for several new shows. In Los Angeles *Cosmos* got extra publicity in the form of an emergency KCET pledge drive, in which station spokespersons fingered the mega-dollar astronomy series for their cash-flow problems.

"If we get a high rating," Malone predicted, "it may move the networks to recognize something that has been staring them in the face for years: the audience out there does have an intelligence quotient above 70."

From its September 28, 1980, debut, *Cosmos* became the highest-rated series ever on public television. It would eventually be seen by half a billion people in sixty nations. For many viewers, Sagan's influence was like that of the more usual sort of TV celebrity. Even during the show's production, KCET had to fend off Sagan groupies—something that is not normally a PBS problem. Earnest women appeared at the studios demanding to see Sagan, convinced that the soulful astronomer had been speaking to them, personally, through their television sets.

Members of a New Orleans amateur astronomical society began dressing like Sagan, wearing turtlenecks and tan corduroy jackets. There was at least one dog, one cat, and one newborn boy named Sagan. People wrote to say that *Cosmos*'s stream of colorful images and hypnotic music entranced two-year-olds who couldn't understand Sagan's words. After a baby-sitter exposed one-year-old "Robbie" to repeated showings of *Cosmos*, the toddler pointed at the screen and said "Carl Sagan!" These were reputedly the child's first words.

"*Yes*, Robbie, that's *Carl Sagan!*" the baby-sitter reinforced. The child began bouncing up and down on the sofa, chanting "*Carl Sagan! Carl Sagan!*"

When the baby-sitter took Robbie outside to return him to his father, the child pointed at the moon. "Carl Sagan *moon*, da!" The baby-sitter announced, "*Yes*, Robbie, that's *Carl Sagan's moon.*"

*   *   *

Not everyone was delighted with the series. *Cosmos* was shown in Nick Sagan's science *and* history classes in Los Angeles. One schoolmate came up to Nick and informed him that his parents had made him watch *every* episode of *Cosmos*. It was not an expression of gratitude.

One critic found Sagan's voice "simultaneously nasal and throaty . . . an unlikely one for television." He also thought that Sagan's lifted chin made him look snobbish. Catholic educator William J. O'Malley panned the series and found Sagan "just plain snotty."

Cosmos drew a few surprisingly ungrateful comments from KCET. The issue was not its content but its cost. A year after the series aired, the very studios where *Cosmos* had been shot were put up for sale. KCET president James Loper vowed never again to do such an expensive series and blamed *Cosmos*'s poor foreign sales for the crisis.

But wasn't *Cosmos* a hit overseas? Well, yes, a KCET staffer admitted, *Cosmos*'s overseas sales "were actually quite good." Loper explained that by "foreign sales" he had really meant "foreign sales and domestic sales to schools and libraries." The show's school and library distributor then denied that sales had been disappointing.

The real problem was that the station had attempted to parlay *Cosmos*'s success by developing two other multimillion-dollar series. *Cosmos* partly subsidized KCET via the exorbitant overhead fees that bedeviled Malone. But when the federal government scaled back support for public television and *Cosmos* revenues underperformed the station's optimistic projections, KCET was unable to cover its bets. The two new series were canceled, and the station was left struggling to make its payroll.

*   *   *

Sagan was confident that the *Cosmos* book would be as successful as the TV series. He tried to convince Random House to increase the first printing. The publisher tactfully ignored him. The book consequently sold out and was unobtainable during the peak holiday buying season. Random House tried to scrounge extra copies from book clubs and the British edition to meet the demand. By early January 1981, *Cosmos* was reported to have 395,000 hardcover copies in print, with a fifth printing of 57,000 copies on order. This would have earned Sagan about $1.3 million in royalties, just on the American hardcover. The book stayed on the best-seller list for seventy weeks and sold more copies than any English-language science book ever published.

*   *   *

Cosmos established Sagan as the best-known scientist of his time. He wore that uncomfortable mantle for the rest of his life. Colleagues knew it was impossible to conduct normal business with Sagan in a restaurant. People would come up to the table every few minutes to tell Sagan how much his books or TV shows had meant to them. Out of self-preservation, Sagan took to seating himself facing the wall. Stories circulated about how "aloof" Sagan supposedly was. There are similar stories about Einstein—and about

Oprah Winfrey, and anyone who is famous. Sagan was the *only* celebrity in planetary astronomy, and in Ithaca, New York. In both small communities he was taken to task for the basic survival tactics of the famous.

Sagan took it in stride, for the most part, anyway. One thing that annoyed him was the *billions and billions* business. Johnny Carson began doing *Tonight Show* parodies of Sagan in which he used the phrase. Evidently Carson's writers *thought* Sagan had said that, or something like it. By the unfathomable logic of such things, the phrase became a meme. Suddenly it was in every professional and amateur jokester's repertoire. A Gary Larson cartoon had a boy and girl on a nighttime hillside, gazing up at the starry sky. "Look, Becky," the boy said. "There must be hundreds and hundreds of them up there!" The caption read: "Carl Sagan as a kid."

Sagan took the position that the offending words were like "Play it again, Sam," something he never actually said. In the mid-1980s Sagan reviewed the *Cosmos* series for a rerun showing and specifically checked to see if he ever said the phrase. He concluded that he did not. (For what it's worth, the phrase "billions upon billions of stars" appears in the *Cosmos* book.)

Sagan's patience wore thin. People would innocently ask him to write or say the phrase, and he'd refuse. At a 1981 speech for the Planetary Society, some audience members smirked expectantly every time he said "billions"—*hoping he would say it.* Sagan glared at them. Toward the end of his life, Sagan made enough peace with the phrase to use it as a book title. But *Billions and Billions* opens with the disclaimer: "I never said it. Honest."

Popularization and Academia

The most difficult part of Sagan's fame was the way it transformed colleagues' perceptions of him. "Parochial astronomers," wrote Clark Chapman, "unappreciative of Carl's multidisciplinary breadth, could not handle the mismatch between his fame . . . and his 'mere' A- achievements in planetary astronomy."

It was felt, in short, that Sagan's fame-to-accomplishment ratio was anomalously high. He was belittled as the "Joyce Brothers of astronomy." A Cornell provost complained that Sagan was *traveling* too much. He wasn't missing classes; he was just leaving town too often. "Many of his peers treated him like shit," publisher Stewart Brand said. "They wouldn't even listen to the content of ideas he had. It was *Carl Sagan's* idea—yuk, yuk."

Behind this sense of "mismatch" was academia's broad and deep suspicion of the source of Sagan's fame: popularization. "I don't know whether you have to sell science in the way he does it sometimes," Norman Horowitz told *Time* magazine. "It goes against all the instincts of professional scientists to exaggerate that way."

Why is popularization so unpopular? To anyone who is not a college professor, this may be a mystery. Several explanations have been advanced. Sagan sometimes cited mere envy. "A scientist who devotes his life to studying something arcane like the hyperfine structure of the molybdenum atom," he said, "and whose work is ignored by everyone except the world's three other experts on molybdenum, naturally is jealous and outraged to see reporters hanging on me for my latest pronouncement about the possibility of extraterrestrial life."

Doubtless this argument applies in some cases. It would be unfair, though, to think that everyone in academia secretly lusts to appear on the *Tonight Show*. The suspicion of popularization is deeper than that.

The one sweeping claim that can be made about the academic profession is that its members think very highly of what they are doing. With this goes a certain incomprehension of why anyone would want to do anything else. The near-universal sentiment is not that popularization is bad, but only that it is less important than doing original research. For a young and vigorous scientist to write popular books or TV shows is to show a suspicious lack of ambition. Or worse, the wrong kind of ambition. Whatever the actual motives, a popularizer is suspected of being more interested in the pursuit of fame and fortune than of knowledge.

Sagan's position, stated in his writings and interviews, was clear enough. He wrote popular books because it came easily and naturally to him. He likened it to being in love (with science) and wanting to express that love to the world. He further recognized the political need for popularization in an age when most science is expensive and must be funded by voters.

Not mentioned by Sagan was a desire for public adulation. Many of those close to him, such as Lynn Margulis and Timothy Ferris, would add this desire to any entirely candid list of reasons (with no slight intended; both are themselves popularizers of science).

An hour on *Nightline* is an hour not in the lab. Sagan occasionally struggled with this irrefutable equation. Clark Chapman recalls an early conversation with Sagan, shortly after his first *Tonight Show* appearances, in which Sagan said he would have to decide between research and popularization; he did not see how he could do both.

Sagan obviously changed his mind about that. He spent the rest of his career in contented denial of these time conflicts. To a surprising extent, Sagan managed to have his cake and eat it too.

Down to a Sunless Sea

For Sagan was doing science, even squeezing in a few articles during the busy *Cosmos* years. As his TV series geared into production, Sagan and Cornell's David Wallace advanced an ingenious solution to the puzzle of "riverbeds" on a planet whose air pressure cannot permit liquid water.

In a remarkable article that starts with a quote from Coleridge, Sagan poses a question no one else had seriously considered: what *would* happen to a body of water on Mars? Most vaguely assumed it would vanish into thin air. Sagan and Wallace's calculations showed that the vigorous evaporation from a Martian lake would quickly freeze its surface. Once its surface was sealed with ice, the rate of evaporation would drop greatly. An ice-covered Martian lake might persist for tens of thousands of years.

The only likely source for a body of water on Mars would be geothermal or impact melting of underground ice. Were an ice-covered lake to have a steady source (such as a geothermal spring), the water would have to spread outward, freezing at its surface as it contacted the air. In suitable terrain, there could be ice-covered rivers. Wallace and Sagan computed that these ice rivers could carve channels hundreds of miles long—then freeze-dry over tens of millennia, leaving only the dry channels.

Most of the Martian channels seem to be something like a billion years old, relics of a past age of greater geologic activity. By Wallace and Sagan's analysis, there is no need to assume the atmospheric pressure was much higher then. That gave the idea one advantage over many rival explanations, some by Sagan himself. In broad outline, the analysis suggested how liquid water might exist on other celestial bodies with little atmosphere. That notion was especially topical as Voyager revealed Jupiter's moons of ice.

*   *   *

In 1978 and 1979, Pioneer Venus provided further data supporting the greenhouse effect theory. Pioneer orbited the planet and sent four probes down into its atmosphere. The picture of Venus had changed a great deal since the early 1960s. Jim Pollack helped establish that the planet's clouds were composed of neither water nor dust but sulfuric acid. Venus truly is hell. (Only two of Pioneer's probes made it to the surface intact.)

Associated with the sulfuric acid rain is a trace of sulfur dioxide in the atmosphere. Small amounts of hydrogen chloride and carbon monoxide were also detected. All are greenhouse gases. Combined with the carbon dioxide and the small amounts of water detected by Pioneer Venus and the Soviet Veneras 11 and 12 craft, they were computed to produce greenhouse heating neatly matching the measured high temperatures. With that, the work begun in Sagan's doctoral thesis came to a satisfying resolution.

Clouds of Titan

The Voyagers passed Saturn on November 12, 1980, and August 25, 1981. Spectacular as the rings were, Sagan's absorbing interest was the planet's largest satellite. "In a way, I grew up with Titan," he recalled. Ever since Kuiper proved that Titan had an atmosphere, there had been speculations of complex organic chemistry or even life. Sagan suspected that a greenhouse effect might raise Titanian temperatures to almost balmy levels.

That proved wrong. Like Mars, Titan was much colder than its advance publicity: about −180° C. Another disappointment was that impenetrable orangish clouds shrouded the planet. It was impossible to see the surface.

The Voyagers revealed the outer solar system as a world of extravagant color: burnt orange and cream, maple candystripe and icy-cool celadon. What made the giant planets and their moons so colorful? Sagan came up with a clever idea building on Kuiper's spectroscopic studies. He, Bishun Khare, and associates cooked up organic polymers in Miller-Urey-type experiments and compared their reflection spectra to those of planets and moons. By varying the gases used, they attempted to create a mix of polymers whose spectra matched (say) the spectra of Titan. Then whatever was in the tube would be what was on Titan. The logic was not ironclad, but Sagan reasonably argued that the coloring in the outer solar system is likely to come from the molecules that are *easiest* to form.

The gas mixtures they started with were as transparent as air. Ten minutes of electrical discharge produced a viscous brown pigment filming the inside of the glass. As the experiment continued, this film condensed into droplets, then streaks, then a tarry gunk. Sagan looked up the Greek word for "mud." From that, he christened the stuff "tholin" in two 1979 articles. (The term ignited a minor turf war. Some chemists were miffed that astronomers had coined a chemical term.)

Tholins became the specialty of the house at the Laboratory for Planetary Studies. Voyager's instruments determined that Titan's orange-red atmosphere consisted largely of nitrogen, with some methane (which Kuiper had detected), traces of other simple hydrocarbons, and hydrogen cyanide. By irradiating such colorless gases, Sagan, Khare, and a group at Oak Ridge National Laboratory produced a reddish mixture with a spectrum approximating that of Titan. Boasted Sagan, "We claim to have bottled the clouds of Titan."

*   *   *

Harold Urey died in January 1981, shortly after the first Voyager's encounter with Saturn. Sagan provided an appreciative obituary for *Icarus*. "When I remember Urey the man I see a melange of images," Sagan wrote.

Among his recollections was Urey's "willingness to change his mind in a case where he blocked the advancement to tenure of a young scientist at another institution and then later asked to be forgiven." He did not say that the young scientist was Carl Sagan.

Loophole

Sagan's research competed for time with many other projects in the wake of *Cosmos*. Sagan was also cutting a movie deal, negotiating a million-dollar publishing contract, and launching a merchandising venture. To some scientific colleagues, it indeed seemed that he had gone Hollywood.

Now that Lynda Obst was in the movie business, she thought Sagan would be a natural to come up with a motion picture idea. She asked Carl if he had any ideas for science fiction. "You know," Sagan said, "I think I do."

Just as *Cosmos* reached millions who might never open a science book, a big-budget movie would reach millions who might never watch public television. Sagan, Druyan, Gentry Lee, and Obst got together and sketched a plot around the idea of what might happen if SETI actually succeeded. "It was the toughest thing I have ever done," Obst claimed. "I tried to translate the rules of screenplay drama to Carl, but he was so rigorous he wouldn't let me. He'd say, 'Is this an argument by authority or an argument of convention? Is this a priori?' "

Sagan went into the project with the notion, perhaps naive, that visual digressions on science could be woven painlessly into a Hollywood film. He spoke of "doing *Cosmos*-type effects on a large screen. That's very appealing to me. It's never been done."

Soon they had a 113-page treatment for a project they called *Contact*. Obst showed it to her boss, Peter Guber. He loved it and bought it. For a while, things moved quickly. The movie deal earned Sagan and Druyan "a very, very large sum" (their agent was contractually obligated not to say how much) and a share of the film's profits. Soon Guber had interest from Universal. As *Cosmos* debuted, Guber's PolyGram took out a congratulatory ad in the trades. "We are proud to be associated with Carl Sagan and Carl Sagan Productions in the making of the first motion picture Contact for Universal Pictures in 1981."

*   *   *

Sagan was so fired with the *Contact* idea that he thought of turning it into a novel. A novel would permit him to write the story exactly the way he wanted. There was also a financial reason for doing a novel.

Sagan was in the middle of a four-book deal with Random House. The first two books had been *The Dragons of Eden* and *Cosmos*. Random House, naturally, was delighted. Sagan's literary agent, Scott Meredith, was less ecstatic. The deal provided for a $250,000 total advance for all four books. That had seemed generous in 1976. But that was before the Pulitzer and before *Cosmos*. Sagan would never be hotter, yet Meredith had to sit on his hands and watch Sagan write his next two books for $62,500 advances. Were Sagan a free agent, the sky would be the limit.

There was, however, a loophole. According to Meredith, Sagan's Random House deal applied only to works of nonfiction. So Sagan was free to sell a *novel* to the highest bidder.

Meredith copied Sagan's outline for the novel and had it hand-delivered to editors at nine publishing houses on December 5, 1980. He gave the publishers two weeks to submit bids. He quickly heard from Random House. They were, in Meredith's words, "quite resentful."

A few days later Meredith met with Random House CEO Robert Bernstein, editorial director Jason Epstein, and Sagan's editor, Anne Freedgood. "We had a gentlemanly but not especially friendly get-together," Meredith told the *New York Times*. "They seemed surprised when I pointed out the contract called for four books of nonfiction. I think there was grave disappointment on Random House's part, and I understand it completely. But there was grave disappointment on my part that they didn't come up to snuff financially."

Clauses restricting a publishing contract or option to works of nonfiction are fairly common. But Random House denied that such a restriction existed. "It's Sagan's position that the contract applied only to books of nonfiction," Random House's Anthony M. Schulte stated. "It's not our position, but we chose not to argue it." The *New York Times* cited a "well-placed publishing source" as saying that the publisher feared that even a successful court fight would damage relations with one of their most valuable authors: "It goes back to the old saying about half a loaf being better than none."

Accounts of the bidding differ, too. Meredith said that Random House bid aggressively and remained in the bidding to the end. Schulte flatly denied that the publisher bid at all. Random House didn't get the book, at any rate. Simon and Schuster topped the bidding at $2 million. That was the biggest sum *ever* paid for a book that had yet to be written.

Like a lottery jackpot, the $2 million was to be paid in installments over a ten-year period. (Sagan gave Gentry Lee 15 percent for his role in shaping the plot.) Sagan contracted to deliver the completed manuscript in January 1982. Simon and Schuster optimistically announced that *Contact* would be available in stores in spring 1982. (It wasn't.)

There was another contractual point to clarify. In March 1975 Sagan had briefly collaborated with Francis Ford Coppola on an unsold TV movie project called *First Contact*. This was to have been an update of the *War of the Worlds* broadcast, in that the program would start with a fake news bulletin announcing that scientists had established radio contact with extraterrestrial intelligence. Over succeeding nights, it would follow humanity's reaction. In Sagan's deal with Coppola, he had agreed to split any royalties from a possible book version. The question was: was Sagan's novel *Contact* so similar to the old *First Contact* that the contract applied? Sagan called Coppola and informed him of his intention to write a book. Coppola okayed the novel. Aside from the broad similarity of theme, the plots and characters were different.

For both publisher and author, Sagan's $2-million novel was a gamble. It was hard to know how well Sagan's talent at science exposition would translate to fiction. (Asked Sagan: "What's the worst thing that could happen? That I'd write a crummy novel.") With a $2-million advance, a *great* novel could sit on the best-seller lists, sell hundreds of thousands of copies, and *still*, the publisher might lose a million dollars on the deal.

Soap on a Rope

Carl and Annie traveled to Japan for that nation's premiere of *Cosmos*. While there, an odd souvenir caught Annie's eye. It was a hemispherical bowl of thin metal. Printed on the inside of the bowl were the stars of the night sky. Sliding within the bowl was a mask with oval cutout. Rotating the cutout revealed which stars were visible at any time or season.

Annie, Carl, and Gentry Lee all thought this was a great idea, much better than the flat star finders sold in the United States. They decided to sell something like it in America. To do that, Carl Sagan Productions launched a new business called the Cosmos Store.

Sagan and Lee secured a $700,000 line of credit from Security Pacific National Bank. They set up shop as a publisher of popular science books, a manufacturer of science-themed gifts and toys, and a retail operation. They began producing Cosmospheres, as they called the star finder, at a suggested retail price of $19.95. The Cosmosphere had its name printed in the same typeface used in the book and TV show.

As a book publisher, the Cosmos Store's most impressive offering was a handsome coffee table book, *Visions of the Universe*. At $29.95, it was no bargain in 1981 dollars, but that bought a preface by Sagan, text by Isaac Asimov, and lush color illustrations by Japanese astronomical artist Kazuaki Iwasaki. A 1982 *Cosmic Calendar* ($7.95), inspired by Sagan's appealing analogy, was a fully functional calendar offering such novel experiences as entering one's next dental appointment on December 16—"first worms" in the cosmic scheme of things.

Sagan and Lee's business plan conjectured that they could do without salespeople. They planned to take out ads touting their products. *Cosmos* viewers would see the ads, go to their local bookstores, and demand their merchandise. The stores would be forced to stock the Cosmos Store's wares. The company would thereby pocket the money that conventional publishers spend on sales staff salaries.

They also planned a chain of their own retail outlets. The first (and only) Cosmos Store opened at 2409 Honolulu Avenue in the L.A. suburb of Montrose, a few minutes' drive from JPL. Underpinning the whole operation was an idealism expressed in a written store "credo." "Anything that does not teach science is not worth doing," Sagan explained. "The credo of The Cosmos Store explicitly says that we will forgo large amounts of money. It was written for new employees who wanted to know why we don't sell T-shirts or Sagan soap on a rope."

*   *   *

In retrospect, the Cosmos Store was a forerunner of the Nature Company stores, which sprung up like profitable mushrooms in malls nationwide. Leapfrogging salespeople to appeal to the public directly is the pitch of many an Internet start-up. Unfortunately, doing without salespeople in 1981 did not work as well as it had to do for the Cosmos Store to succeed.

The Cosmos Store had a booth at the May 1981 booksellers' convention in Atlanta. The booth's inexperienced attendants shooed away a woman in blue jeans (obviously looking for free samples!). She was a buyer for Waldenbooks, the nation's biggest book retailer.

Nineteen eighty-one was a tough time to be starting a business on borrowed capital. Interest rates surged. Soon Carl Sagan Productions was paying 23 percent on its bank loan.

Cosmos Store products appeared in many bookstores (including Waldenbooks) for the 1981 Christmas season. As the holiday season came to a close, Lee estimated they had sold $600,000 to $700,000 worth of merchandise. But they still had an L.A. warehouse piled high with unsold Cosmospheres.

"The economy is such that established businesses are failing left and right," Sagan said. "Considering that, we've done extremely well." He and Lee spoke hopefully of a postholiday reassessment and bringing in a new, professional manager.

In fact, the operation was quietly liquidated. "Businessmen are a special breed," Sagan announced. "It takes certain skills that even famous academics might not have."

Malevolent or Hungry

Cosmos popularized not only the nuts and bolts of astronomy but its more imaginative aspects. Prominent among them was SETI. The field's increasing visibility brought increasing criticism, from within and without the scientific community.

Drake's Arecibo message to M13 caused Sir Martin Ryle, astronomer royal of England, to object that aliens might be malevolent—or hungry. It was dangerous to let them know we were here. In December 1982, a *New York Times* editorial revisited the extraterrestrial cannibalism issue (as the author called it; another species eating *us* would be carnivory). The *Times*'s interest was piqued by a National Academy of Sciences report containing the alarming statement that ET contact "could have a dramatic effect on human affairs, as did contact between the native people of the New World and the technologically more advanced peoples of Europe." The *Times* wondered what dramatic effect the NAS was thinking about (being put on reservations?). "What if these high-tech aliens are unpleasant, mean, or even cannibalistic?" the editorial asked. "Contact with an extraterrestrial civilization could have its hazards."

Sagan quickly fired back. "Even if human beings were a famous interstellar delicacy," he wrote, "the freightage would be prohibitively high." He was less successful in guaranteeing the benign intentions of ETI. Sagan pointed out that "all major radioastronomical SETI programs are intended to listen, not to transmit." That was true enough, but Sagan and Drake's well-publicized "symbolic" messages demonstrated that there wasn't really any kind of ethos forbidding transmissions.

Sagan ended with what had become his (and Drake's) favored comeback to the hostile-alien-cannibals issue. TV networks and military radar were already announcing our location to the universe.

Golden Fleece

Within the scientific community, a more common objection to SETI was that then espoused by Shklovskii—that the failure of SETI to date furnished evidence that ETI doesn't exist.

One who felt that way was Tulane University astrophysicist Frank Tipler.

Tipler is a proponent of the "anthropic principle," a metaphysical claim that the laws of nature have been fine-tuned for the existence of life. This was Tipler's personal crusade, as much as extraterrestrial intelligence was for Sagan. In Tipler's view, it was unlikely that both ideas were right.

In the late 1970s, Tipler wrote an article titled "Extraterrestrial Beings Do Not Exist" and submitted it to *Science*. The journal sent it to the leading expert in the field of extraterrestrial life. Sagan rejected it.

Tipler revised the article and resubmitted it. *Science* sent it back, saying it was no longer interested. The journal did not forward the revised article to Sagan.

Tipler next submitted the paper to *Icarus* (which Sagan was then still editing). According to William I. Newman, Sagan played fair with the Tipler paper. He did not summarily reject it; he sent it to peer reviewers who found it faulty and recommended rejection. Tipler's story is that Sagan refereed the paper himself and sent the identical criticisms he had offered for the first version of the paper. "I feel," Tipler said, "as if I have become involved in a theological debate."

Tipler contacted Wisconsin senator William Proxmire. Proxmire had been in the habit of announcing a monthly "Golden Fleece Award." This was a booby prize for what he held to be the most ridiculous waste of taxpayers' money. Some of Proxmire's targets deserved his ridicule. To many scientists, however, Proxmire was an ogre because he did not seem to have much understanding of what made one scientific project worthwhile and another one flaky. Should someone's legitimate, government-funded research happen to involve *sex among baboons*, Proxmire was a man to be feared.

Tipler told Proxmire that he ought to look into the money NASA was spending for contacting aliens in outer space. The space agency was funding a modest SETI study. Proxmire called a news conference on February 16, 1978, and awarded the study the latest golden fleece. Proxmire suggested that the study be postponed—postponed for "a few million light-years," that is.

As that suggests, Proxmire did not know much about astronomy. But Tipler did, and he was of the opinion that extraterrestrials do not exist. One thing that Proxmire *had* learned was that interstellar signals would take centuries to reach Earth. "If we intercept messages sent from them," Proxmire complained, "they could have been sent not only before Columbus discovered America or the birth of Christ, but before the Earth itself existed. The overwhelming odds are that such civilizations, even if they once existed, are now dead and gone."

NASA requested $2 million a year for SETI beginning with the 1982 fiscal year. Proxmire was by then chairman of the Senate Appropriations Committee, in part because of his reputation as a fighter of government waste. *Intelligent life in space?* Proxmire asked; why, it was hard enough finding intelligent life in *Washington*. Proxmire drafted an amendment forbidding NASA from spending a penny "to support the definition and development of techniques to analyze extraterrestrial radio signals for patterns that may be generated by intelligent sources."

Sagan contacted Proxmire's office and arranged a meeting. He met with the senator and explained that a centuries-old ET message would be a fascinating and worthwhile thing—not at all "out of date." He argued that finding evidence of extraterrestrial intelligence would demonstrate it was possible for societies to live with the problems of technology and war. This seemed to have an effect: "I could see a light going on upstairs" in Proxmire's head, Sagan reported to a colleague.

Senator Proxmire made no public recantation. The next year, corrective legislation was introduced, restoring the SETI funding. Proxmire did not object, and it was passed.

*   *   *

Meanwhile, in 1980 Tipler succeeded in having his paper published in the *Quarterly Journal of the Royal Astronomical Society*. There Tipler updates the reasoning imputed to Enrico Fermi, plugging in some figures.

Tipler cites so-called von Neumann machines, which are sometimes mentioned as part of the "Fermi question" legend. John von Neumann, a mathematician who also spent time at Los Alamos, demonstrated that machines could be designed to build copies of themselves. This seemed to Tipler the perfect vehicle for interstellar reconnaissance. An ET civilization could program self-reproducing automata to colonize the Galaxy and send back reports of anything interesting.

If there was advanced intelligent life anywhere in the Galaxy, Tipler reasoned, eventually these von Neumann machines would get built. (Tipler cited Sagan's own proposals for robotic Mars probes as "a step in the direction of a von Neumann machine.") They would be set loose, reproduce exponentially, and take over the whole Galaxy. Tipler computed that this would take about 300 million years (still a "short" time compared to the age of the Earth or Galaxy). There would then be machines in every solar system, including ours. Since there is no sign of these machines in our solar system, that proves that there is no ET intelligence *anywhere*, claimed Tipler.

The Perfect Zoo

A perpetual problem with SETI is that such issues can be argued either way by well-informed and imaginative people. In a somewhat similar vein, Shklovskii spoke of "cosmic miracles." He imagined that advanced galactic civilizations would engineer monuments or public works projects of stupendous scale. A galactic civilization's counterpart to the Great Pyramid or Hoover Dam might be light-years across and visible to us in the night sky. There would be vast, "astrophysical" phenomena that are clearly artificial. But of course, no one has ever found anything like that. This absence of "miracles" argues against ETI, Shklovskii maintained.

One of Sagan's rebuttals to this argument was to suggest that ET "wonders of the world" could be so beyond our comprehension as to elude us altogether. There must have been ants crawling over the Colossus of Rhodes, Sagan said. They could not have dreamed that they were crawling over something artificial and extraordinary. So Sagan argued in 1973; in a 1974 publication, he noted that there *are* enigmatic astrophysical phenomena that, for all we know, could be "miracles" of extraterrestrial engineering.

The quintessential idea of this kind, published in *Icarus* (under Sagan the journal became a sounding box for these lively musings), is the "zoo hypothesis" of John A. Ball. Maybe we don't see evidence of extraterrestrials, Ball suggested, because we are in a zoo run by those extraterrestrials. Ball proposed that the Galaxy had been explored and colonized long ago by technologically advanced species. They resolved to set aside much of the Galaxy as a nature preserve. "The perfect zoo (or wilderness area or sanctuary) would be one in which the fauna inside do not interact with, and are unaware of, their zookeepers," Ball wrote. *Our* zoos' inhabitants are confined by moats or hedges or sheer hillsides, all of which are designed to appear natural. There are zoos in the middle of bustling cities, and sometimes it is necessary to use a wall of fake boulders or painted backdrops to screen the traffic from view. So maybe when *we* look out at the starry universe, we see only what the zookeepers want us to see. Some of it may not be real.

A Still More Fatal Weapon

Ideas like Ball's are fun to mull over . . . but are they science? Is SETI itself, after all the failures, science?

People have been trying to "tune in" to ETs for decades now. Never has anyone succeeded, and (Shklovskii being the major exception) hardly ever has any "true believer" given up or lost enthusiasm. All echo one of Sagan's favorite truisms (usually credited to cosmologist Martin Rees): "Absence of evidence is not evidence of absence."

Shouldn't they have detected signals by now, assuming there are signals to be detected? The answer is, only if the broadcasters were incredibly powerful or incredibly nearby. There remains a vastly greater "search space" of potential signals that are undetectable with current technology.

The difficulties of maintaining enthusiasm for a search that may take lifetimes and whose outcome is uncertain certainly weighed on Sagan. In a couple of places in his later writings, he quoted lines from one of Kafka's *Parables*:

> *Now the Sirens have a still more fatal weapon*
> *than their song, namely their silence . . .*
> *Someone might possibly have escaped from their singing;*
> *but from their silence, certainly never.*

Sagan wasn't ready to give up the search. But he who lives by Occam's razor is apt to get nicked. To some critics, extraterrestrial intelligence seemed close to being an *unfalsifiable* hypothesis. Philosopher Karl Popper maintained that a useful theory must allow its own disproof. A theory that does *not* do this is unfalsifiable. It is easy to imagine the kind of evidence that would prove ETI exists. It is less clear how many and what kind of failed searches could convince us that ETI does not exist.

* * *

In 1982 Sagan published in *Science* a petition of scientists favoring an international SETI effort. The petition's wording was carefully inclusive. "We represent a wide variety of opinion on the abundance of extraterrestrials, on the ease of establishing contact, and on the validity of arguments of the sort summarized in the first sentence of the previous paragraph"—the latter including the absence of extraterrestrial colonists or engineering. The petition's sixty-nine signers included not only the usual SETI suspects (a fraternity now coed with the inclusion of Jill Tarter) but many distinguished astronomers and biologists who were not particularly known as SETI enthusiasts. Among them was Sagan's former teacher at Williams Bay, Chandrasekhar; David Baltimore, Francis Crick, Stephen Jay Gould, Stephen Hawking, Fred Hoyle, Paul MacLean, Bruce Murray, Linus Pauling, Cyril Ponnamperuma, Lewis Thomas, Kip S. Thorne, and Edward O. Wilson. There were seven Nobel laureates at the time of publication; Chandra would later pick up a Nobel in physics. By prodigal son criteria, Sagan's greatest coup may have been Shklovskii's signature—provided out of affection for Sagan and covered under the "wide variety of opinion" clause.

Muskrats, Drunkards, Extraterrestrials

Sagan also did his own analysis of the Fermi question. Written with William I. Newman, a former Cornell student then at the Institute for Advanced Study, Princeton, it was titled "Galactic Civilizations: Population Dynamics and Interstellar Diffusion" and published in *Icarus*. Like the Jovian life article, it is conventionally considered an eccentric footnote to Sagan's scientific career, a stalwart attempt to peek a little farther into the cosmic mysteries than present knowledge permits.

The originality of the article lies in its use of "potential theory" to analyze the Fermi question. A time-honored classroom analogy is the "drunkard's walk." A drunk man starts at a lamppost and tries to make his way home. He walks a few paces in a random direction (since he has no idea where his home is), then collapses. A little while later, he revives, gets up, and heads off in another, random direction. Repeated many times, the man's erratic movements may not get him closer to home but do tend to take him farther and farther from the lamppost. A mathematical formula can give the average distance of the man from the lamppost with time.

Similar mathematical treatments can model the erratic movements of gas molecules and many biological phenomena. In the 1930s R. A. Fisher published pioneering biological models in now-forgotten journals with names like *Annals of Eugenics*. (Sagan had heard of Fisher by way of Muller.) The life cycle of the muskrat, for instance, is much like the fictitious drunkard. Young muskrats leave the nest and head out in a random direction to mate, give birth, and die. The next generation sets out from *that* nest in random directions. This behavior prevents inbreeding. It also allows the muskrat to colonize new territories. The muskrat (which is American) was introduced into Europe in 1905. Potential theory was successful in accounting for its rate of spread.

Like drunkards or muskrats, then, an extraterrestrial civilization would start on one planet and send out colonists in all directions. The colonists would establish new bases on new planets. Ultimately these new outposts would send out their own colonial expeditions.

In the SETI literature, it was often assumed that the speed of colonization would be only somewhat less than the speed of the spaceships used. This implied that a single civilization, with near-light-speed spaceships, might colonize the whole Galaxy in as little as 100,000 years. What Newman and Sagan found (Newman, since he did the tricky math, got first billing) was that, in a wide range of plausible models, outward expansion or "colonization" is much slower than the top speed of the spaceships involved. " 'Rome was not built in a day,' " the authors wrote, "although one can cross it on foot in a few hours."

Newman and Sagan computed a typical outward velocity for a wave of ET colonization at about forty kilometers a second. That is surprisingly slow and is actually *less* than the terminal speed of the Pioneer and Voyager spacecraft. This counterintuitive result can be understood by imagining the Galaxy as consisting of concentric shells around the Earth (or any ETI's home planet). Each shell contains many worlds, and it takes many generations to settle them. Then, when a shell is fully populated, its worlds muster expeditions to colonize the worlds in the next shell out. Settling a shell takes much longer than crossing it in a spaceship.

The article concluded, in fact, that spaceship speed is relatively unimportant to the speed of colonization. This is a convenient finding, for no one really knows how fast ETIs might travel. Modern science insists that the speed of light is the cosmic speed limit. Modern science *fiction* is no less adamant that faster-than-light travel will be a cinch a few centuries hence. According to Newman and Sagan's analysis, even ETIs with warp drive would not colonize the Galaxy much faster. They could of course zip to a *particular* planet on the far side of the Galaxy, were there some reason to do so. But there are billions of planets, and the Earth is unlikely to command special interest. We would probably have to wait for the general wave of colonization to reach us, and that would advance slowly.

*   *   *

Newman and Sagan did their best to expand this mathematical result into a theory of galactic history. They estimated that even the nearest ETI would likely require tens of millions of years to colonize a sphere of stars large enough to include the sun. That is much longer than had been imagined. Even so, it is short compared to the lifetime of the Galaxy.

Sagan argued that galactic empire building has a short lifetime. The empire-building instinct is likely to be associated with instincts for territoriality, war, and self-destruction. Sagan now partly sided with Shklovskii that "a strong commitment to territoriality is probably inconsistent with survival after the advent of weapons of mass destruction."

Sagan further claimed that advanced civilizations were likely to have very low or zero population growth. The speed of colonization is more sensitive to the rate of population growth than to spaceship speed. Low population growth would greatly slow the colonization.

From these necessarily speculative arguments, Newman and Sagan concluded that most galactic empires last much less than the tens of millions of years it would take the nearest empire to reach the Earth. It's unlikely that *any* aliens have *ever* made it to Earth. Since two active waves of colonization hardly ever meet, Newman and Sagan deduced that "star wars" are unlikely, too. (Sagan whimsically insisted on using that term, which struck Newman as unusual "for a guy willing, in a millisecond, to give a detailed critique of that movie.")

This work took place simultaneously with the *Cosmos* production. Newman was slightly "horrified" when Sagan told him he was planning on using their interstellar diffusion model in one episode. Newman's position at the Institute for Advanced Study was temporary, and he was looking for a job. He wasn't sure it would help his prospects to have his crazy fling of an article with Sagan suddenly get prime-time publicity.

"Not to worry," Sagan reassured him. "In Hollywood we can do anything."

Wedding

The Sagans' divorce dragged on interminably. Linda repeatedly changed her mind about what was and wasn't acceptable. Aside from a thoroughgoing bitterness that colored every detail, there was the imponderable issue of how much Carl Sagan was worth. The division of assets came at the most difficult possible time. Much of Sagan's net worth was in future income streams from books, TV, and movies and in spin-offs like the Cosmos Store. The value of these assets depended on the marketability of Carl Sagan himself, and that seemed to be increasing exponentially. With Sagan's stock rising from one month to the next, there was little incentive for Linda or her attorneys to settle anything quickly. The divorce was granted, and the community property split, in May 1981.

Carl and Annie married on June 1, the fourth anniversary of their declaration of love. Carl's third and last wedding was a spare-no-expense production of cinematic proportions. He and Annie arranged to hold it at the Hotel Bel-Air, one of Los Angeles's most beautiful, secluded, and expensive hotels, amid verdant gardens and swan-filled pools. Hollywood hair and makeup artists were brought in to do free makeovers of the female members of the wedding party. Afterward, the newlyweds left for a romantic honeymoon in Venice and Sardinia.

Lester Grinspoon again served as best man. Lynda Obst helped Annie pick out the wedding dress. Rachel *liked* Annie. She struck her half sister's pretty daughter from the guest list, the better to ensure that Carl's bride would be the fairest of all.

Among the guests there was a general note of relief that after four years as a couple, Carl and Annie were finally free to marry. Annie's "improving" effect on Carl was already the stuff of comment. In his toast to the couple, Annie's brother, Les, remarked that he didn't know Carl before Annie met him, but if what everyone was saying was true . . . he was glad he *didn't* know Carl then.

ITHACA

1981-95

THE HOUSE THAT Cornell students generally point out as "Carl Sagan's house" is one of Ithaca's strangest and most imposing buildings. It is a pseudo-Egyptian temple perched high above Fall Creek Gorge in the village of Cayuga Heights. Before it became "Sagan's house," it was known to locals as Sphinx House or simply *That House*. Stories about its origins are contradictory. A hard-to-credit tradition says that it was originally someone's tomb. Another legend, apparently inspired by the waterfall, holds it was a power plant. In fact, the building was once the meeting place of Cornell's Sphinx Head Society. It was one of those places, still to be found on some venerable campuses, where a fraternity's members repair for secret rites behind locked doors and windowless walls. One account says it was built in 1890; another says 1925.

In the course of time, the society became defunct, its holy of holies mere real estate. Sagan was not the first Cornell professor to get the "clever" idea of fixing up the place and living in it. Since the 1960s, two professors in succession had lived there. One, a nuclear physicist with an artistic bent, used it as a sculpture studio. The owner immediately previous to the Sagans was a design professor who spent years renovating it before he departed for Manhattan. The house's notoriety was trying. Shortly before leaving in 1981, the latter professor confessed, "I've lost my identity to this building."

Sphinx House was thus on the market when Carl and Annie returned to Ithaca and began house shopping. The place reminded them of the

Alexandria Library (which had been featured in *Cosmos*). The hillside lot also had a separate contemporary house. They decided they could live in the modern house and use the Egyptian "temple" for offices. They bought the place and moved in.

Like Sagan himself, Sphinx House was visible and flamboyant—and also remote and unapproachable, or so it was perceived by some of the Cornell community. Its spectacular seclusion drew looky-loos who might otherwise not have cared where Carl Sagan lived. Sagan's "Graceland" had a security system worthy of its Memphis counterpart. An iron gate slammed behind visitors. Surveillance cameras silently scanned visitors' movements. In lieu of a moat, the 200-foot plunge to the gorge acted as guarantor of privacy.

No such protection was possible for Sagan's car, now an environmentally sensitive VW Rabbit with a plain New York license plate. "His security problems at Cornell are not that serious," one campus newspaper reported, "just occasional vandalism to his car—which he takes in stride as 'a kind of tax I pay.'"

When a college town's most famous citizen lives in a stone fortress on a hill, you can expect the fortress and its occupant to figure in the local folklore. Across the gorge from Sphinx House is Cornell's Fraternity Row. One fraternity had a Saturday night ritual of going over to Sagan's house and smashing the driveway's circular traffic mirror. The financial damage was not great, but it was done with some consistency. One of Ithaca's (true!) "urban legends" runs that the men of Alpha Sigma Phi sent the Sagans a neighborly dinner invitation. Suspecting that the frat house was behind the vandalism, Sagan declined, suggesting that they contact his lecture agent. Alpha Sigma Phi retaliated for the rebuff by stringing their house's Christmas lights to spell out "Carl Sagan Sucks."

Take No Prisoners

Such tales show the ambivalence of the Cornell community toward its best-known faculty member. It is no paradox (other than the paradox of human nature) that people's assessments of Sagan as a person differed widely. Much of the discourse continued to turn on Sagan's self-image. The perception that Sagan was "arrogant" was so newsworthy, it seems, that in 1985 a *New York Times* journalist felt justified in baldly asking Sagan about it. (Sagan's answer: the *Cosmos* series's "interminable close-ups of me looking awed" created the *impression* that he was arrogant.)

"On a personal level," maintains Dorion, his father "was positively handicapped by his ego." Carl would send back orders in restaurants; send a gofer to three delis in succession until he got a "perfect" sandwich; get upset when a waiter gave him one order of salad dressing (he had ordered *two*). This behavior caused Jill Tarter to playfully refer to him as "King Carl." She is quick to add that "King Carl" could "be the most considerate, compassionate and generous of individuals."

Timothy Ferris calls the "arrogant" label "a crock." As the word was applied to Carl, he explains, it simply "means you know what you're after and you insist on getting there." People lacking Sagan's drive were apt to label it arrogance. (Ferris ended up on cordial terms with both Carl and Annie.)

Druyan will go so far as to grant that her husband could be a man who did not suffer fools gladly. "He had a take no prisoners approach to life," says Lynda Obst. "Carl was sort of shot out of a cannon to succeed from the University of Chicago. He could be relentless in his ability to destroy somebody's argument or in his ruthless assessment of reality."

Cannon shots make for rocky landings. "Carl had a Jekyll and Hyde personality," believes astronomer Tobias Owen, who knew him from the same University of Chicago. "I saw too much of the Hyde part of him."

Annie Effect

The above remarks may suggest how some people saw Carl, but how he saw himself is something else again. The central fact of Carl's inner life would appear to be his contented and unconflicted zest for life. Particularly in the third marriage, he struck associates as the living embodiment of Freud's prescription for happiness. He loved what he was doing, and he loved his wife, both with a passion of almost otherworldly depth. Carl arose each day full of enthusiasm, seemingly immune to depression or self-doubt. In that regard he was an object of amazement.

Much of this was credited to Annie. To sympathetic observers, she made him into a "complete person"; "the best possible version of himself." "Annie was aware of the effect that Carl had on others," Obst explains. "She was the person who could say to Carl, 'you're going too far, you're going too fast, you're being too tough.'"

Carl was the relatively rare sort of person who takes a probing, philosophical interest in ethics. He was willing to change his behavior, even in midlife, based on ethical arguments from Annie or others. Grad student Peter Wilson once asked Carl how he justified the killing of animals to make the beloved leather jacket he wore. He couldn't justify it, so he stopped wearing the jacket.

At the dinner table Carl would amuse himself and family by posing a question for discussion, such as: is it ethical to keep pets? Through this sort of self-analysis, he exorcised the last vestiges of his early sexism; pulled his views on gays into line with those of other American liberals. In *The Demon-Haunted World* Carl poses a thought experiment in the ethical sphere: How do we know that the behavior we consider to be ethical today will be so regarded by future ages? Are there any absolutes in ethics? He muses that posterity may judge us immoral for "eating animals and jailing chimpanzees; or criminalizing the use of euphoriants by adults; or allowing our children to grow up ignorant."

In disputes with others, Carl would often advance the sort of ethical arguments that might convince himself. In many cases, this cool logic was more infuriating than the more usually encountered screaming. A striking phrase that Annie uses in describing Carl is "not an alpha male." Communi-   •
ties of chimpanzees and baboons (and humans?) are dominated by high-ranking "alpha males" to whom the others show deference. In Annie's view, at least, her husband was the *opposite* of this—a Carl who would *not* be king—the seeming forerunner of a new, noncompetitive, cooperative male.

*   *   *

Unlike Linda, Annie took a keen interest in the details of Carl's science. Unlike Lynn, she was willing to provide the undivided commitment that seems to have been one of Carl's deepest needs. This made Annie a full partner, personally and professionally.

The perfection of the match sometimes bordered on the uncanny. Asked a question by a journalist, Carl would occasionally turn to Annie and ask, "What do we think about that?" The marriage was so close that Carl took it personally even when Annie and Lynda Obst excluded him from their "girl talk." He didn't see why *he* couldn't participate.

"Carl," Richard Berendzen said at one gathering, "I miss your turtle-necks, but you look terrific in your pinstripes tonight." Carl was wearing a handsome pinstripe suit. Annie was also wearing a pinstripe suit.

"Well," Carl replied quietly, "I don't know, I wear this kind of thing sometimes."

Annie leaned to Berendzen and whispered, "You know, I think his pin-stripe suit, maybe, is my influence."

There were a few dissenters in this marital paradise. Gentry Lee found it difficult to work with Carl after Annie came into his life and became such an integral part of that life. He was unhappy to find himself with two business partners, as he saw it. In 1982, Lee decided he wanted out of Carl Sagan Productions. Sagan paid Lee his 15 percent of *Contact* out of the first advances, and Lee agreed to relinquish any further claims to the property. This business divorce ended up being nearly as contentious as the personal one Carl had gone through. Ultimately, not even the friendship survived. To some it seemed that Annie's love had erected a protective wall around Carl, and this could be a formidable thing.

*   *   *

Two substantial changes were due to Annie and/or to the time of life Carl shared with Annie. One was a new emphasis on social activism. There is a big difference between talking politics on the lunch hour and doing something about it. Annie nudged Carl toward more active engagement—a gentle shove he would not likely have gotten from his astronomy colleagues.

A second change was that Carl found the time to be a more proper husband and father. Annie made a real effort to get Carl to improve his relationships with his three sons. This had mixed success with Dorion and Jeremy (now adults); more with teenage Nick.

To his wife, Carl was not only indulgent but creatively romantic. Shown a dress that Annie had bought, Carl would ask how much it cost, and add: Did it come in other colors? You should have gotten six of them. More impressive, Carl spent six months arranging an elaborate celebration for Annie's fortieth birthday. He located friends and relatives and brought them together for a seagoing reunion. All boarded a yacht for a four-day cruise of Long Island Sound, stopping at places that had been significant in Annie's life, dining on foods that had been significant in Annie's life. Flapping in the wind, the ship's nautical flags spelled out an encoded birthday greeting.

Home Life

Carl began most mornings of this contented third marriage with a substantial breakfast. When time permitted, he favored omelets and a leisurely reading of the morning's *New York Times*. He drank tea occasionally but not coffee. Lunch could be substantial, too. There was a period when he favored egg salad. Chocolate remained a favorite. These cholesterol-laden meals were not without their effect. Cornell students who knew him from TV were often surprised to find how heavy he was.

Friends kidded him about his lack of exercise (Annie once replied that Carl enjoyed *one* form of exercise). The kidding got Carl to buy a treadmill. He fell off it; it did not get much use.

Carl was as unhandy as Jewish husbands are alleged to be. He did not like shopping for clothes. Annie would pull him into a clothing store, and he would suddenly announce he was tired. That was a complaint otherwise rarely heard.

The Sagan home contained shelf after shelf of books on seemingly all possible subjects. Carl read mostly nonfiction. He liked some mysteries and, from time to time, revisited science fiction. A movie that made an impression on him was *Lawrence of Arabia*, particularly Peter O'Toole's enigmatic Lawrence. He admired Coppola's *Godfather I* and *II*, though not *III*. He liked the TV production of *Brideshead Revisited*; the series *All in the Family*, *Hill Street Blues*, and *L.A. Law*.

Carl preserved but did not much augment his childhood stamp collection. He had an impressive group of scientific and literary manuscripts, mostly gifts from Annie. Displayed in his home were framed letters by Frederick Douglass and Gandhi and a crazily meticulous page from Einstein's doomed unified field theory. There were prints by Rembrandt, M. C. Escher, and David Hockney (a gift from the artist); two Mirós, Le Corbusier furniture, and a mixture of genuine and fake antiquities (including the replica of the Rosetta stone). Annie favored American folk and commercial art. A red steel Pegasus logo, salvaged from a Mobil gas station, decorated one wall.

More unusual than this conventional "good taste" was the collection of astronomical art. The Sagans were major patrons. They owned the original paintings by Chesley Bonestell, the very Giotto of the field, that had been used to illustrate Willy Ley and Wernher von Braun's classic *The Conquest of Space*. Carl made it a point to buy astronomical paintings commissioned for his books. Don Davis (who painted the cover for the hardcover edition of *The Dragons of Eden*) judged Carl his most demanding and perceptive patron.

*   *   *

Carl's Cornell assistants had the daunting, at times unenviable, task of handling his mail and phone calls. Of all the world's scientists, he alone was familiar from television and Sunday supplements, seemingly as accessible as the local Wal-Mart. He received hate mail from UFO believers, anti-Semites, political foes, antiabortionists, and religious folk who could hardly be called "Christian." There were death threats.

There was also a much greater volume of the harmlessly outlandish. Carl saved a subset of this mail in a file cabinet in his home that, since Linda's time, had been given the label "Fissured Ceramics"—as in "crackpot." Into this file went letters from earnest citizens convinced that they had discovered grand new theories of the universe or been abducted by aliens; solved the world's most intractable problems; invented spaceships, time warps, ray guns, or perpetual motion machines that they were pretty sure would work. Through the sampling effect, the writers' concerns paralleled Sagan's, if in a grotesque, fun-house mirror sort of way.

Many writers believed that extraterrestrial life has already made itself manifest on Earth and thought that Sagan ought to know about it. The inhabitants of Venus spoke to one writer through her shower head. Other people picked up extraterrestrial signals on their dental fillings. Many writers were concerned with time, with getting someone to believe them before it was too late. "Images will pop into my head that *I did not put there*," complained one letter. "If I finally go psychotic from all this pressure—or have another heart attack—there goes your last sure evidence that there is life in space."

Switzerland

Annie was solicitous of Nick, conscious that he had become an unwitting martyr to her present happiness—mosquito nets or not. In the wake of the divorce, Nick was the one person in the family on good terms with Linda and Annie. He had resolved to be "Switzerland" in the Linda versus Carl and Annie war.

Nick Sagan was now old enough to have interests that his father did not understand. He avidly played Dungeons and Dragons, the role-playing game that had many a 1980s parent alarmed. He wanted to see movies like the animated *Heavy Metal*. As the digital revolution hit, Nick became immersed in the first generation of networked computer adventure games. He would play dozens of games simultaneously.

Carl worried that there was a dark/gothic/escapist tone to all this. He wondered if the divorce had something to do with it. One summer he and Nick saw a family counselor in Rochester. Nick thought the most therapeutic part of the experience was the drive, a couple of hours' enforced quality time with his ever busy father.

*   *   *

Rachel Sagan accepted Annie as she had neither Lynn nor Linda. (She gave Annie her favorite Jewish cookbook, inscribing it: "To the only true daughter-in-law that I ever had.") She did not have long to enjoy that daughter-in-law. At Beth Israel Hospital, Boston, Rachel was diagnosed with pancreatic cancer. She, Carl, and Annie went back to their hotel suite and made a fire. Struggling to find something to take Rachel's mind off the diagnosis, Carl announced that he and Annie had some good news about their TV series—of course, it was supposed to be a *secret*. . . .

"Don't worry, darling," Rachel said. "I'll take it to my grave."

*   *   *

Rachel spent her last days with Carl and Annie. Shortly before her death, Carl, Annie, and Cari went to the hospital to see her. They were warned she was unconscious, her body bloated by her failing metabolism. Annie, assuming the role of emotional midwife, went in first to make sure that the sight was not too disturbing. Rachel died in February 1982. She was deeply mourned by her son.

In an essay on hallucinations, written shortly before his own death, Sagan remarked that he occasionally heard his dead parents call out his name, in a conversational tone of voice.

A number of family members believe that Rachel influenced Carl's career ambitions. She had to be tough to survive, and passed on some of that toughness to her brilliant son. Carl realized the worldly success his mother could not. Of all possible arenas for that success, he chose the starry heavens—so far from Brooklyn.

Annie and Carl's first child was born in November 1982. They named her Alexandra Rachel Druyan Sagan.

Bait and Switch

Carl Sagan was a powerful draw in attracting students, faculty, research grants, and media attention to Cornell. Reportedly, the question most commonly asked by visitors to the Cornell campus was "Where is Carl Sagan's office?" (It was Room 302 of the Space Sciences Building, no bigger than the other offices.) Sagan's name was often featured prominently in recruiters' pitches, a practice that perhaps bordered on bait and switch. "High-powered faculty members aren't sequestered away from undergraduate classrooms," read one Cornell brochure. "The shoulder rubbing and coffee drinking that go on at Cornell among professors, advanced students, and undergraduates create a true university—a community of scholars. Ezra Cornell wouldn't have it any other way."

Any undergraduate expecting to rub shoulders with Carl Sagan had another thing coming. Freshmen learned that Sagan was rarely seen by any but a small clique of grad students and coworkers. After *Cosmos*, Sagan complained that he found it impossible to teach his introductory astronomy classes. The "words of *Cosmos* would be echoing in my ears," he said. In a typical year of his late career, Sagan taught one class open to undergraduates. Enrollment was limited to 25. One year, 300 signed up. That's a 12:1 cut. (In comparison, Cornell is considered highly competitive because it has about six applications for every space in its freshman class.) It was reported that Sagan sifted through the 300 applications for this class and that both ability and diversity counted.

This bred a certain defensiveness about Sagan's on-campus presence. "I feel that he should be accessible to the undergraduates . . . as he is," a campus newspaper quoted astronomy department head Yervant Terzian, significant ellipsis and all. It was explained that "many people do not realize that Sagan is only a half-time employee, teaching only one of two semesters."

At social gatherings, Sagan's grad students would be pressed as to whether they ever saw Sagan. Of course, the answer was yes, though sometimes this took a bit of planning. Owen Brian Toon found Sagan easiest to catch in the elevators. Between the third and ground floors of the Space Sciences Building, there was time for a concise caucus.

Among the nonscience faculty, Sagan was often resented (and envied) for remaining on the faculty with the barest minimum of commitments. Few of Cornell's scientists felt that way. Sagan's esteem among much of the astronomy faculty was and is little short of startling. Many of those under thirty freely admit that Sagan was at least partly responsible for their being in astronomy, at Cornell, or both.

A Paper a Month

Even as his career as writer and TV personality expanded, Sagan continued to make time for research. The widely presumed drop-off in Sagan's scientific output with celebrity is hard to discern. Only four scientific papers appeared in 1980, the year *Cosmos* aired. Afterward, Sagan's scientific output returned to nearly his peak levels. As late as 1989, Sagan published 20 professional articles, which is good for any scientist at any age. In all, Sagan published about 300 scientific articles in his career. Adding abstracts (short descriptions of ongoing research) would swell the total to about 500. This amounts to a paper-a-month clip sustained over four decades, an impressive achievement by any standards.

It may be suspected that these figures were "inflated" through Sagan putting his name on articles done by others in his lab. Sagan was a theorist, someone who comes up with ideas for others to test. (He never acquired the skill or patience for doing complex experiments by himself.) Because Sagan was prolific with ideas while (usually) not directly involved in time-consuming research, he had his hand in more projects than would have been possible otherwise. But "he was unfailingly scrupulous about authorship," former Cornell grad student Christopher Chyba says. "If he had not made major contributions to the research, he would not be a coauthor, and if he had not been responsible for the majority of the ideas in the paper, he would not be first author."

Besides Chyba, important collaborators of Sagan's late career included Khare and Veverka; Steven Squyres, Stanley Dermott, Dave Pieri, E. T.

Arakawa, Gene McDonald, Peter Wilson, Laurence Soderblom, and W. Reid Thompson.

Most of Sagan's best scientific work was done young, before he was a celebrity. He was twenty-six when he did his thesis on the Venus greenhouse effect; a bit over thirty when he and Pollack explained the Martian seasonal changes; turning thirty-eight when he published the early faint sun paradox article. This does not imply that Sagan's science fell victim to celebrity. *Most* truly great scientific work is done early. In mathematics and physics, thirty is said to be the cutoff point for achieving anything of the first rank. Astronomy is more forgiving (the instruments keep getting better over an astronomer's career). Still, the tendency toward front-loaded careers remains. There is, then, nothing too unusual about the general curve of Sagan's scientific achievement, aside from the fact that he was also turning out books and TV shows in the latter part of it.

Good Works

Sagan also took on a *third* career as activist and statesman of science. He found time to give speeches and lobby in Washington, D.C., for environmental, antiwar, and human rights causes. He sat on advisory boards for such august institutions as the American Civil Liberties Union (1981–96); the Smithsonian Institution (1975–85); the National Book Awards (1975); the American Heritage Dictionary (1976–82; 1987–96); the National Women's Hall of Fame (1981–86); Mothers Embracing Nuclear Disarmament (1986–90); Consumers Union (1986–96); the Nature Conservancy (1991–96); Literacy Volunteers of America (1994–96). Druyan was secretary of the Federation of American Scientists; she sat on the board of the National Organization to Reform Marijuana Legislation.

That ardent Marxist I. S. Shklovskii deemed Sagan to be "a very progressive millionaire." Sagan believed there should be a redistribution of wealth, caps on income, and a national health plan. Since he was a hardworking millionaire, Sagan's radical convictions can in no way be called self-serving. Neither did they visibly inhibit him from enjoying the finer things in life. Dorion wryly notes that Carl and Annie "would hold court on the top floor of the Ritz Carlton, carrying on about Marxism as they ordered room service and left the lights on when they left the room. Capitalism for him and Annie was something dirty done by corporate executives and unenlightened Republicans."

Sagan's sons were more conservative on many issues. Nick debated his father on capital punishment. Carl categorically opposed it; Nick found it justified on occasion.

*   *   *

Sagan was a founder of organizations. During the Voyager flyby of Jupiter, he commiserated with Bruce Murray over the difficulty of funding new space missions. In response they founded a nonprofit organization to stir up support for space exploration, the Planetary Society. (Sagan nixed the suggestion that the society's name have "cosmos" in it. He took an almost proprietary attitude toward that word.)

The unlikely pairing of the planetary science community's yin and yang worked. Murray lent a no-nonsense probity to Sagan's celebrity pull. Paul Newman (who was intrigued with SETI) contributed $10,000 to the organization, while Gene Roddenberry signed an open letter encouraging all *Star Trek* fans to join.

The society bolstered Sagan's influence as Washington lobbyist for space funding. Unlike most of the academics testifying on Capitol Hill, Sagan could point to a constituency. In time the Planetary Society grew to have 100,000 members. The membership was always a number that Sagan could quote.

Sagan also played a role in founding the Committee for Scientific Investigation of Claims of the Paranormal (CSICOP). The Buffalo, New York–based organization attempts to examine sensational popular claims with scientific rigor. Sagan, Isaac Asimov, Martin Gardner, and James Randi signed on as founding members. CSICOP's publication, *The Skeptical Inquirer,* deals in "tabloid" subject matter—UFOs, ghosts, repressed memories, religious miracles, alternative medicine. Inevitably, the great majority of its subjects end up being properly "debunked." But CSICOP's stated goal, much in the spirit of Sagan, is to dismiss nothing out of hand.

*   *   *

Sagan gave speeches for these and many other causes. His talks were so articulate and well organized that people were often astounded to find how little he had prepared for them. He would have *thought* about what he was going to say beforehand, but notes would be limited to a few words written on a card or napkin. Absent this ability, Sagan could hardly have kept up his staggering lecture schedule.

He would often remove his jacket at the start of a talk, and cuff his shirtsleeves two turns. He would warm the room with a pleasantry, then launch into his topic. He was particularly adept at question-and-answer sessions. Anyone who saw him speak much must admire how he handled hostile questions—of which he got quite a few, the number increasing in proportion to his fame and political involvement.

Sagan didn't make things easy for himself. He strove to answer every question when it was possible, and when it wasn't, he would scan the house for a final question, demanding, "Whose need is greatest?" (a tactic that stacks the deck in favor of zealots of all stripes).

A complaint Sagan heard more than once was, roughly, "You've debunked everything that makes us think we're worthwhile. What do we do now?" Sagan's reply was "Go do something worthwhile. That is your answer."

*   ⋆   ⋆

Sagan was a prolific corespondent with scientific heavyweights and unknown students alike. The letters were often handwritten. He visited prisons and spoke at naturalization ceremonies for new citizens. He showed up for jury duty.

Part of the Sagan legend was his massive curriculum vitae, "kind of a work of art for him," in Timothy Ferris's assessment. It ran 261 printed pages at his death but for the sake of the rain forests was available on two floppy disks. It covered not only Sagan's scientific, literary, and social work, which are prodigious, but also press coverage of his career, which was even more prodigious. The CV documents, for instance, the date when the *Lima* (Ohio) *News* reprinted a *Staten Island* (New York) *Advance* article reporting on a conference that Sagan attended in Colorado Springs, April 5, 1989.

Why Sagan did so many *minor* good deeds is something of an enigma. The causes were worthy but not always, seemingly, the best use of his time and talent—even when you make allowances for the fact that Sagan's off-the-cuff speeches were a way of road-testing material for future articles and books. A friend once asked why Sagan had driven five hours to accept a relatively minor honor (the "Fifth Annual New Jersey Literary Hall of Fame Award"). Sagan replied it was so his kids could see the nearby science museum. One guesses that can't be the whole story. There must have been a restless, compulsive drive to keep moving.

Nucleus

Adrian Malone's optimistic prediction had come true. *Cosmos*'s impressive ratings *had* convinced the commercial networks that there was an audience with 70+ IQs. Sagan, Druyan, and Steve Soter began outlining a new TV series to be called *Nucleus*.

One inspiration was Lester Grinspoon's interest in the emotional denial of nuclear war—the necessary way that people go about their lives, mostly

oblivious to the omnipresent risk of annihilation. Grinspoon and Sagan convened meetings with defense experts such as Richard Garwin and George
Kistiakowsky. By 1982, Sagan, Druyan, and Soter had written a treatment.

The six-part series would be about nuclear physics and, even more,
about uncertainty: how the strange indeterministic nature of the quantum
had changed our view of reality and how the nuclear arms race had created a
world whose continued existence was itself uncertain. It would be as visu-
ally innovative as *Cosmos*. It would also be challenging in ways that *Cosmos*
was not.

Nucleus would trace the moral and political history of the arms race,
skewering the hypocrisy (as its authors saw it) of many of the principals. It
would be critical of the U.S. bombing of Nagasaki, particularly—an action
difficult to justify with the ethical and strategic arguments often advanced
for Hiroshima. The series would argue that it was most often the United
States that had initiated cycles of nuclear arsenal–building, despite protesta-
tions that the nation only wanted to maintain a balance of power. Nor would
scientists be spared. The series would note how few Manhattan Project scientists left promptly after Germany's defeat, despite the rationale that they
were building the bomb only to protect the planet from Hitler. In view of
the subject matter, Sagan felt that the series must be shown in the Soviet
Union as well as in the United States. He traveled to Moscow to pitch the
series.

In the United States, ABC bought the treatment. It was a brave move. In
format, intelligence level, and political slant, *Nucleus* was a PBS-style series.
ABC was then doing *The Day After*, a TV movie dramatizing the aftermath
of a nuclear war. That movie was already a lightning rod for conservative
critics, and Sagan's series promised more of the same. As one network
executive warned Sagan, they did not want people to start thinking of ABC
as the Moscow Broadcasting Company.

Nuclear Winter

Nuclear war was becoming a major theme of Sagan's scientific and political work. In the mid-1980s, Sagan was the central player in the "nuclear
winter" controversy, one of the most troubling demonstrations of the so-
called relativity of scientific truth. When Sagan came to write his 1990
account of nuclear winter, he asserted that "the central thesis of nuclear winter seems more valid today than ever before." By then, that statement flew
in the face of most public opinion.

The public, at any rate, was confused. Sagan was the vocal spokesman for a group of distinguished scientists and policy makers saying one thing, while another, equally distinguished group said almost the opposite. Unfortunately, nuclear winter was no aberration. Today's public policy decisions increasingly involve science, whose proclamations are provisional, sometimes equivocal, and often subject to political spins. In the new mingling of science and politics, activist scientists such as Sagan play a powerful and misunderstood part.

Sagan had the much-noted ability to see connections between things that others thought weren't related at all. Nuclear winter drew on subjects as diverse as Martian dust storms, dinosaurs, volcanoes, and the history of warfare. If there was one theme lofty enough to compete with extraterrestrial life in Sagan's imagination, it was the end of the world. This was a windmill he tilted against repeatedly over the years; to continue the quixotic metaphor, he often found that his view of things differed from that of those around him. This had to do not only with objective "truth" but with Sagan's personal philosophy of risk. Most people live their lives in denial of remote risks of doom. Sagan, with his amalgam of rationality and "paranoia," took naturally to the task of assessing small risks of the very greatest of catastrophes.

Any attempt to tell the tangled history of the nuclear winter affair must start by qualifying the extent of Sagan's involvement. The science of nuclear winter was developed at NASA Ames Research Center, in part by students of Sagan's. The prime movers behind the original nuclear winter study were Richard Turco and Owen Brian Toon. They used an aerosol model earlier developed by Jim Pollack and themselves. The support of Pollack, as senior scientist at NASA Ames, was crucial to this work. Sagan joined the team after most of the scientific work had been done. His role was that of strategist and publicist—a role that in this case was anything but incidental.

Cornell West

Hardly known to the public, NASA Ames Research Center is situated in Mountain View, California, the heart of Silicon Valley. Rising above the complex is a visionary dome built not for rockets but for dirigibles, relic of a bygone admiral's scheme for a dirigible base. Most of the other buildings look like a high school in a town that voted to cut taxes to the bone. Interior space is dissected ruthlessly into Dilbert cubicles.

Ames is nonetheless a place that has traditionally handled much of NASA's most provocative research. So many of Sagan's students have worked at NASA Ames that there is talk of a pipeline between Ithaca and

Ames, or "Cornell West." The greatest of Sagan's students at Ames, and some say the center's most distinguished scientist without qualification, was James Pollack.

When Pollack first came to Ames he had again been concerned about security clearances for a gay man. The space agency's policy seemed to be don't ask, don't tell. Pollack had a tempestuous relationship with another Ames employee (and Cornell graduate), who became one of the early AIDS casualties. At Ames Pollack was known as a gentle, somewhat absentminded man with a sense of humor, a niece he adored in Long Island, and a willingness to help other people with their problems. There was often a line of people seeking help outside Pollack's Ames office. He never made these visitors feel rushed, recalls one frequent visitor.

The clutter that had been confined mostly to Pollack's desk now took over his entire office. File cabinets lined the walls; stalagmites of stacked folders, papers, and books grew from available surfaces. An obsessive streak had become pronounced. While talking on the phone, Pollack would tear off strips of Scotch tape and stick them on his desk. His desk became laminated with cellophane. Whenever Pollack got out of his car, he walked completely around it, studying it from every angle. Brian Toon once asked him why. Jim replied that he had once left his lights on. The battery went dead.

Pollack was an enthusiastic subscriber to the San Francisco Opera, applying the same intellectual spirit of adventure present in his science. He liked Wagner, *Turandot*, and anything unusual, obscure, or rarely performed. When he had seen a good performance, one colleague noted, he would radiate sheer delight for days. In Pollack's honor, one of NASA Ames's computer stations was named Tosca.

Dust Storms and Dinosaurs

Pollack did not write or say much about the germination of nuclear winter or its antecedents. In the early 1970s, he and Bill Gile took a cross-country drive. Pollack insisted on stopping in Arizona to see the famous Barringer meteor crater. He was moved by this natural spectacle. There by the side of the highway was graphic evidence that cosmic cataclysms could occur on Earth.

That drive would have been about the time of Mariner 9 and its dust storm. Sagan and Pollack's computations about the Mariner 9 dust storm used many of the mathematical tools that would later figure in the nuclear winter work.

Sagan and Pollack first applied these mathematical models to volcanoes. It was known that big volcanic eruptions, such as the 1815 eruption of

Tambora, threw enough dust in the upper atmosphere to cool the climate by a few degrees. The year 1816, coming after Tambora, was known as "the year without a summer." After Mariner, a group consisting of Pollack, Sagan, Brian Toon, Audrey Summers, Betty Baldwin, and Warren Van Camp tried to see if the Martian dust model could account for the observed cooling from volcanic eruptions. In two articles published in 1976 they reported that it did.

The group was then joined by Richard Turco, who worked for R&D Associates, a Defense Department think tank consulting on nuclear war. From 1975 on, Turco, Toon, and Pollack developed a general computer model to study the effects of aerosols (suspended particles) in the air. One question they posed was whether the exhaust from supersonic aircraft would affect the climate. Some environmentalists feared it would. Using their model, Turco, Toon, and Pollack concluded that the effect was insignificant.

*   *   *

Then in 1980, Luis and Walter Alvarez published their celebrated article proposing that the dinosaurs had been killed by an asteroid hitting the Earth. The asteroid would have thrown great masses of dust into the air, wreaking havoc on climate and the ecosystem. As evidence, the Alvarez team showed that there were enhanced amounts of trace elements such as iridium in the geological layer marking the demise of the dinosaurs. Iridium is more common in meteorites than in normal Earth sediments.

Many questioned whether an asteroid impact, even a cataclysmic one, could kill dinosaurs on the other side of the globe. What was needed was a quantitative model of how impact-generated dust would affect the climate. Pollack realized that his group at Ames already had the type of model needed. With Toon, Turco, and others, Pollack examined the dinosaur extinction question. They determined that an asteroid about ten kilometers wide impacting the Earth would create a worldwide pall of dust. At its worst, it would be pitch black at noon and freezing cold. Photosynthesis would be impossible. The dust would, however, clear in a matter of months. The climate would return to normal.

This conclusion was just about right for the Alvarezes' hypothesis. It suggested why large animals would die, while a few small, warm-blooded scavengers (the early mammals) might survive.

*   *   *

Sagan did not participate in the asteroid study. He was tied up with *Cosmos* and other projects. He was already thinking about the connection between nuclear war and climate, though. One segment of *Cosmos* was devoted largely to nuclear war, that ever present threat to the last factor in the Drake equation. In the *Cosmos* book, Sagan wrote presciently that a nuclear war's dust would "cool the Earth a little. Even a little cooling can have disastrous agricultural consequences." He had spoken of collaborating with Pollack and Toon on a study of the issue, and the planned *Nucleus* series was to tackle the subject more directly.

On October 19–22, 1981, the Geological Society of America met in Snowbird, Utah, to discuss the Alvarezes' idea and asteroid impacts in general. Toon gave a talk on the Ames group's work. Among those present were a retired admiral, William Moran, and Lee Hunt, who sat with Moran on the National Research Council. Hearing Toon's talk got them to wondering about the effect of dust raised by nuclear explosions. They requested that the Ames group study the matter.

Recognizing the importance of such a study, the Ames group set about applying the "dinosaur" model to the dust created by a nuclear war. The scientific team at this point consisted of Pollack, Toon, Turco, and a new Ames employee, Thomas Ackerman. Turco's expertise was invaluable, for he had access to detailed information on the sizes of dust particles thrown up by nuclear tests.

Plugged into the existing model, this data implied a significant cooling. This was surprising because a 1975 National Research Council study, *Long-Term Worldwide Effects of Multiple Nuclear-Weapon Detonations*, had found no great climatic effects.

Meanwhile Hunt and Moran scheduled a special National Academy of Sciences (NAS) meeting on climatic effects of nuclear war for April 6, 1982. Turco was slated to present the latest Ames findings. A couple of weeks before that meeting, Turco made a momentous discovery.

He was attending a defense workshop in Santa Barbara. There National Oceanic and Atmospheric Administration scientist Fred Fehsenfeld told Turco of a new study then in press. Two atmospheric scientists, Paul Crutzen of the Max Planck Institute and John Birks of the University of Colorado, had studied the effect of *smoke* after a nuclear war.

Hiroshima and Nagasaki set off firestorms. Vastly more powerful hydrogen bombs would set cities, petroleum stockpiles, forests, and fields ablaze. Crutzen and Birks computed that the burning would create so much smoke as to turn day into a hellish twilight. The Crutzen and Birks article, to be published in a Swedish environmental studies journal, *Ambio*, was in fact titled "The Atmosphere After a Nuclear War: Twilight at Noon."

The Ames group had been beaten to the punch—partly, anyway. Crutzen and Birks stated that the reduction of light would make agriculture difficult or impossible. They raised the possibility of climatic change. But lacking a sophisticated computer model, Crutzen and Birks came to no firm conclusion. They acknowledged that the gloom would tend to make things cooler. At the same time, the increase in carbon dioxide and destruction of the ozone layer might work in the *opposite* direction, making things warmer. They could not tell which effect would dominate.

Sagan independently heard of the Crutzen and Birks article from the University of London's Joseph Rotblat. He discussed the article with Pollack and Toon at a meeting at NASA Ames on the origins of life. All three concurred that *smoke* needed to be taken into account along with *dust*. The issue justified a new, more complete study for publication in a major journal. Pollack arranged to use Ames's Cray supercomputer to run the mathematical models.

*   *   *

The general press ignored the Crutzen and Birks article. Turco mentioned the article at the April NAS meeting, and the Ames group sent a letter to academy president Frank Press outlining the importance of the issue. They proposed cooperating with the Defense Department on a study. Nothing much came of that letter.

Coincidentally, in June 1982 two foundation executives (Robert W. Scrivner of the Rockefeller Family Fund and Robert Allen of the Henry P. Kendall Foundation) and the president of the National Audubon Society, Russell W. Peterson, decided to organize a conference on the biological effects of nuclear war. The Conference on the World After Nuclear War, as it was called, formed a steering committee of environmentally liberal scientists.

Sagan was one of the first scientists they contacted. He briefed the group on the work being conducted at Ames. With characteristic persuasiveness, Sagan all but commandeered the conference. The preliminary Ames results were so unexpected and so horrific, he said, that they were impossible to ignore. The Ames study would change everything anyone would have to say about the aftermath of a nuclear war. The conference's sponsors were impressed. From that point on, the conference was planned around the presentation of the Ames results.

During the summer, the Ames group began to feel political pressure from NASA. A talk on the ongoing research was scheduled for the American Geophysical Union's fall 1982 meeting in San Francisco. The day before the meeting, NASA Ames's upper management pressured Pollack to cancel the talk.

Clarence Cyvertson, Ames's director, and his assistant, Angelo Gustafero, told Pollack that they were concerned because the research had not been fully reviewed. They were candid enough to admit that they were also worried about the study's political implications. To say that almost any likely nuclear war could have catastrophic effects on climate (as the models seemed to indicate) was to take on the Defense Department. In a time of cutbacks, they did not want the Reagan administration to get the idea that NASA Ames was unfriendly to its interests. "Two weeks ago," Cyvertson explained, "some nut tried to blow up the Washington Monument; last week the Senate killed the MX missile; and this week you want me to be responsible for telling the President that his whole nuclear strategy is wrong?"

Pollack, as slow to anger as he was to speak, conceded the point that the research had not been reviewed. He agreed not to speak on the study until it had been properly reviewed and published.

*   *   *

This development prodded Sagan into action. He reasoned that if NASA wouldn't let Pollack discuss the findings because they hadn't been reviewed, then the agency could hardly prevent him or the other Ames employees from participating in a review. Sagan therefore proposed holding a special "peer review" meeting.

Normally "peer review" describes a drawn-out process conducted through the mail. A scientific article submitted for publication is copied and sent to other scientists for comments. Sagan's peer review meeting was to work more like an oral examination for a doctorate. The Ames work would be presented to a large group of scientists, subjected to questions, defended, and then put to a vote. Only if the study passed would they proceed with the planned public conference.

They set the peer review meeting for April 1983. That winter, the California group started feeling heat all the way from Washington, D.C. Wary NASA officials cut the Ames group's research funds by $40,000. The NASA hierarchy objected that a study of nuclear war was outside the space agency's field. Fortunately, most of the work had already been done. In this case, Ames management was sympathetic enough to allow some internal funds to be diverted to the study.

*   *   *

Sagan recognized that it was important, politically and scientifically, to have a Soviet scientist on the peer review panel. Had Soviet scientists no opportunity to inspect the Ames work and present criticisms, their leaders could not be expected to base policy on it. Americans, in turn, were unlikely to make policy changes unless they could be assured the Soviets were doing so. In the time that it might take for Soviet science to get up to speed on the issue, precious momentum could be lost.

This was an astute perception, for it turned out that the Soviet scientific establishment was unaware of the Crutzen and Birks article. It had been censored by their government. Early in 1983, Sagan met with Yevgeny P. Velikhov, vice president of the Soviet Academy of Sciences and a confidant of Gorbachev's. As Sagan knew, it normally took about a year for the KGB to permit a Soviet scientist to travel to the West. Sagan explained the situation and asked if it would be possible to get a Soviet expert on short notice. He mentioned several scientists he had in mind.

Velikhov said *he* knew just the right person: Vladimir Alexandrov. The name meant nothing to Sagan. Alexandrov is an expert on computer modeling of climate, Velikhov explained. The meeting ended with the understanding that Velikhov would do what he could.

Sagan called around to see what he could find out about Vladimir Alexandrov. It turned out that he was well known in the United States. He had spent time at the University of Oregon and the National Center for Atmospheric Research (NCAR) in Colorado. He had been the houseguest of his American hosts (a stringent test), and the reports were positive.

Alexandrov was described as a likable, outgoing guy of forty-five. He headed the Climate Research Laboratory at the Computing Center of the Soviet Academy of Sciences. Russian to the core, he spoke excellent English and had a keen appreciation of American pop culture. Alexandrov loved hamburgers and barbecue. He read novels like *Gorky Park* and watched James Bond movies. He had dressed up as Santa Claus for an Oregon nursery school. Alexandrov was a devoted family man. His wife, Alya, had been allowed to travel to Oregon with Vladimir. *That* was almost unheard of in the old Soviet Union, where the family back home were traditionally hostages against defection. Alexandrov spoke fondly of their daughter, a chubby, asthmatic girl with ambitions of becoming a ballerina. In short, Alexandrov seemed perfect for the peer review meeting, if they could get him.

Appendicitis

In March 1983, Carl came down with appendicitis. He had an appendectomy—a botched appendectomy by one account. This was followed by another flare-up of his esophagus disorder. A doctor in Ithaca told Annie there was no chance Carl would survive, but he was too famous to die in their little hospital. They moved Carl to a hospital in Syracuse. Grinspoon dutifully flew in to Syracuse. He was pleased to find that Annie was a capable patient advocate.

The doctors in Syracuse did not consider the situation quite so hopeless. They recommended an experimental procedure called a jejunal interposition. They would remove a section of the small intestine and use it to replace the damaged esophagus. Carl spent ten hours on the operating table. Bleeding was so copious that he almost died. Afterward, he was white as a napkin. Recuperation demanded that his chest be kept open to allow fluids to drain and permit the physicians to make sure that all was healing properly. Like one of the more gruesome martyrs, Carl spent long days in the hospital, his ribs spread apart to expose the replaced esophagus.

Paired with Carl's ever fragile health was a robust drive and energy. Not only did this expedite his recovery, it also manifested itself in a near-mythic resistance to anesthesia. Several incidents defied what experienced physicians thought possible. During the long operation, with his chest opened, Carl came to. He raised up on the operating table. People dropped their instruments; this was like a resurrection. "Fellows," Carl asked his doctors, "can you give me a break here? I have to rest."

Afterward, the doctors told Annie that Carl had been given so much anesthesia and painkiller that he would be unconscious for twenty-four hours. Friends pleaded with her to go back to her hotel and get some rest. Well before the twenty-four hours were up, Annie returned to the hospital. She found that Carl had roused himself and had managed to write a note to his nurses. It was a childish scrawl asking, "Is Annie okay?"

Star Wars

At least one friend thought that this brush with death increased Sagan's concern with making time count. Sagan's heightened urgency was evident even in his hospital bed. On March 23, President Reagan gave his famous speech on the Strategic Defense Initiative (SDI). (In this case, it was the media, not Reagan, that insisted on the label "Star Wars.") The president proposed a system of lasers and other high-tech innovations that would zap intercontinental missiles before they could reach targets in the United States. Reagan and his advisers knew it was a visionary plan, something on the order of Kennedy's pledge to go to the moon. A lot of technology would have to be invented. Whether, and how easily, this could be done was a matter of divergent opinion.

Annie made the "huge mistake" of telling Carl about the speech while he was in intensive care. From what could have been his deathbed, he insisted on organizing a petition against SDI. Though Carl was alert enough to insist that every day counted and the petition had to get out before Congress acted, he remained physically incapacitated. Annie had to do all the work of phoning offices of potential signers and taking down Carl's dictation of the petition, draft by draft.

Sagan firmly believed that Reagan's plan was unworkable because it required a level of reliability unrealistic in space navigation. NASA's string

Carl at age four
Courtesy of Lynn Margulis

Sagan's childhood visit to the 1939 New York World's Fair was a pivotal influence. The "Perisphere" contained exhibits of "a perfect future made possible by science."
Corbis/Underwood & Underwood

Carl's mother, Rachel
Courtesy of Cari Sagan Greene

Clowning with Lynn at the wedding
Courtesy of Lynn Margulis

Leone Alexander, Carl, and Lynn
Courtesy of Lynn Margulis

Carl and Dorion at Madison,
Wisconsin, home
Courtesy of Lynn Margulis

Herman Muller was the first of Sagan's Nobel-laureate mentors. Sagan had a summer job raising the object of Muller's scrutiny—fruit flies. *Courtesy of the Lilly Library, Indiana University, Bloomington*

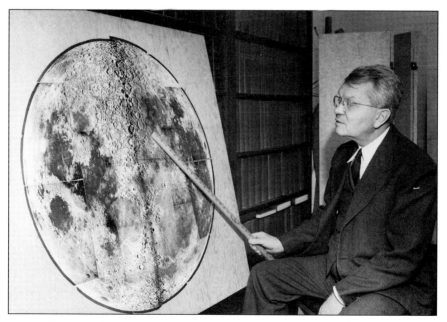

Muller introduced Sagan to Harold Urey, a chemist interested in the planets and the origins of life. *Corbis/Bettmann*

Sagan met Joshua Lederberg, then at the University of Wisconsin, while doing graduate work at Yerkes Observatory.
Corbis/Hulton-Deutsch Collection

Subrahmanyan Chandrasekhar, Gerard Kuiper, and Otto Struve at Yerkes Observatory. "Chandra" looks sprightly in this photograph, but he was such a terror to grad students that Sagan went out of his way to avoid him. Kuiper was the only planetary astronomer of his time.
Yerkes Observatory

Jeremy Sagan *(right)* with Carl and David Grinspoon
Courtesy of Lester Grinspoon

Lester Grinspoon
Courtesy of Lester Grinspoon

Carl reading a bedtime story to
Lester's son Peter
Courtesy of Lester Grinspoon

Linda Salzman and Carl at their wedding
Courtesy of Lester Grinspoon

A group portrait taken while "stoned": Lester Grinspoon, Linda, Betsy Grinspoon, and Carl
Courtesy of Lester Grinspoon

Carl, Nick, and Linda
Courtesy of Lester Grinspoon

Jim Pollack
Courtesy of Bill Gile

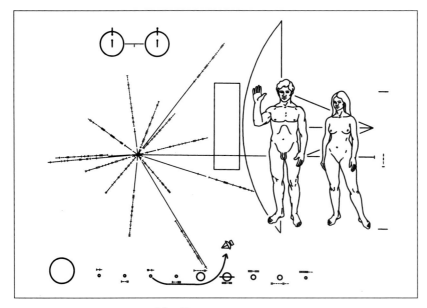

The Pioneer message
JPL

Frank Drake
University of California, Santa Cruz

A JPL artist's 1975 illustration of a Martian "petrophage," based loosely on Sagan and Lederberg's "The Prospects for Life on Mars: A Pre-Viking Assessment"
JPL

Jim Martin and Gerry Soffen
Hans Biemann

Gentry Lee
Hans Biemann

Vance Oyama
Hans Biemann

Norman Horowitz
Hans Biemann

Gil Levin
Hans Biemann

Klaus Biemann
Hans Biemann

Sagan and Hal Masursky *(right)* examine possible landing sites for Viking.
Hans Biemann

Viking 1's first panorama of Mars. Inset shows the outcropping that Sagan
and Timothy Ferris briefly took for an "oasis."
JPL

Thomas Mutch sharing a laugh with Sagan, 1976. Mutch died just four years later while climbing the Himalayas.
Hans Biemann

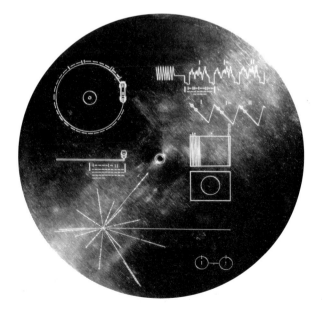

Cover of the Voyager record
JPL

Carl and Ann Druyan at JPL

JPL

Carl and Annie awaiting booking at Nevada Test Site protest
Courtesy of Lester Grinspoon

Three generations of Sagans at the sixtieth-birthday symposium: Alexandra, Carl, Annie, Lynn Margulis, Tonio, and Nick
Cornell University

A Cornell campus contest
The Cornell Review

of successes was founded on the fact that its craft were intended only to return *information*. If one of two Mariners succeeds in getting to Mars, that's a success. The criterion of success is necessarily much more stringent for a defense system. A system that destroys 99 percent of 1,000 incoming missiles would allow ten American targets to be nuked.

Worse, Sagan believed the system could only step up the arms race. An SDI capable of destroying most incoming missiles would motivate the Soviets to build all the more missiles in order to maintain a balance of power. The still-unpublished Ames study was suggesting that even a small nuclear exchange could wreak climatic havoc. Sagan therefore saw SDI as disastrously ill conceived.

Proofreading one of Annie's drafts of the petition from his hospital bed, Carl snapped, "You spelled 'cislunar' wrong!"

Annie wanted to deck him.

Peer Review

Sagan's agent, for one, was relieved that Sagan pulled through. On April 12, Scott Meredith struck a new deal with Random House. It was a four-book contract for $4 million, or sixteen times the money of Sagan's previous four-book deal.

Once Sagan was out of the hospital, he invited Turco and Toon to his home in Ithaca to prepare for the peer review meeting. Though he was still recuperating, his energy was impressive. Turco, a much younger man, left the meeting "exhausted by the pace Carl had set."

On April 22–26, 1983, about forty physical and ten biological scientists met at the American Academy of Arts and Sciences, Cambridge, Massachusetts, for Sagan's peer review. The meeting was closed to the press. As Sagan stated in the invitation letter,

> We are, of course, keenly aware that the public has a significant right to know about this issue, but are concerned that the premature discussion of these results before they are critically reviewed may lead to misinterpretations and misuse. We therefore ask you to exercise all reasonable precautions against general release of the contents of this paper.

Like Joyce's *Ulysses*, the prepublication study was bound in a plain blue cover and had a cachet of exclusivity. Only about 150 copies were distributed. The authors were listed as Turco, Toon, Ackerman, Pollack, and Sagan.

At this meeting, the article was christened "TTAPS" from the authors' initials, entering the acronymic sphere of MAD, MIRV, and ICBM. (Sagan noted that "TTAPS" was also evocative of the military bugle call played at lights-out and funerals.)

TTAPS used two mathematical models that can be thought of as two idealized planets. Each planet was a near-twin of the Earth: precisely the same size as the Earth, orbiting at the same distance from the sun, and possessing an atmosphere like the Earth's. One planet was a water world of pole-to-pole oceans. The other planet was a land world without a drop of surface water.

The advantage of these models was that the behavior of the atmosphere on all-water or all-land worlds is much simpler to compute than that on the continent-dappled Earth. Of course an all-water planet (inhabited, if at all, by pacifist dolphins!) is an unlikely theater of war. There would be no cities or forests to burn. TTAPS therefore estimated the smoke and dust produced by various (earthly) nuclear war scenarios and assumed that it all suddenly materialized in the northern hemispheres of the water and land planets. The researchers then used the laws of physics to track the consequences.

On TTAPS's two featureless planets, the movement of smoke and dust particles east and west, and north and south, would be irrelevant. By the very symmetry of things, any particles drifting east ought to balance any drifting west, and so forth. The important movements would be up and down. TTAPS focused on these vertical movements exclusively. This made it a "one-dimensional" model. In effect, TTAPS broke the atmosphere into infinitely thin vertical columns of air.

This was a "simplifying assumption." Such assumptions are used all the time in science. In calculating the moon's orbit, astronomers usually pretend that the moon and Earth are perfect spheres. They're not, but it makes the calculation much easier, and the results using that assumption are extremely close to the reality. The TTAPS authors believed that the one-dimensional model was a decent first-order approximation to the three-dimensional reality.

The study's main conclusion was that smoke and dust from a nuclear war would compromise the Earth's greenhouse effect. This statement can be confusing. We are used to hearing about the "greenhouse effect" as a bad thing, something caused by our technology and leading to unwanted "global warming." But the Earth has a *natural* greenhouse effect. Were there no greenhouse effect at all, the Earth's temperature would be cooler by some 45° C. Everything would be frozen; life as we know it could not exist.

TTAPS's models implied that the smoke and dust of a nuclear war would tend to absorb sunlight above the atmospheric layers mainly responsible for the greenhouse effect. This would greatly diminish the natural greenhouse warming.

At the same time (and as Crutzen and Birks had mentioned), carbon dioxide created in nuclear firestorms would have the *opposite* effect, enhancing the greenhouse effect. However, TTAPS's computations were now able to show the latter effect was much smaller than the former. The net effect would be to reduce the greenhouse effect and cool the planet.

In the case of the water planet, the net cooling effect was always quite modest. The oceans are such great reservoirs of heat that even the worst-case nuclear scenarios cooled the water planet only a few degrees.

For the land planet, the effect was often staggering. In the TTAPS "base-line scenario"—one projection of how much smoke and dust might be released in a plausible nuclear war—the land planet's temperature dropped by as much as 35° C, enough to cause hard freezes in midsummer.

The pressing question was: what would happen on the *real* planet we live on? That could not be directly addressed with the one-dimensional models. The TTAPS authors reasoned that the two idealized planets should bracket what might be expected on the Earth. The actual cooling would be more than on the water planet, less than on the land planet. Presumably, the cooling in places like Bermuda and Hawaii might approximate that of the water planet (which is to say, there would be hardly any cooling). Places like the Dakotas and Mongolia might approach the deep freeze of the land planet.

The good news was that all the projected effects were temporary. Over periods measured in months, the temperatures would return to normal. That was not as comforting at it might seem. The TTAPS authors believed that, even in a modest nuclear war, the cooling would be severe enough, last long enough, and be accompanied by enough gloom, to make agriculture impossible. A missing growing season's worth of food could mean mass starvation.

*   *   *

These findings were received with a great deal of interest and a great deal of skepticism. The general tone of the meeting was that the TTAPS one-dimensional models had been properly implemented. The criticisms clustered around two foci.

One was "garbage in, garbage out." The TTAPS authors had to "plug in" a lot of dicey guesstimates. How much smoke would be produced in the burning of the world's great cities? How high would it rise in the atmosphere? No one knew that. TTAPS's cooling figures could be no more accurate than the numbers plugged in—and the numbers plugged in were often only guesses.

The other major criticism was that it was hard to be sure how the one-dimensional models related to the real, three-dimensional atmosphere. There was a huge gap between the water-planet and land-planet predictions. On the one hand, we live on a "water planet." On the other hand, everyone lives on the land part of our water planet.

Many reviewers looked forward to seeing three-dimensional models. One was Vladimir Alexandrov, whom the Soviets *had* permitted to attend. Alexandrov remarked that in a three-dimensional climate model (he assumed that was the next step), it was always necessary to tweak the parameters to get the model to agree with the real climate. But with the "shockingly different" conditions of postnuclear climate, there could be no measured values to work from. Many different three-dimensional models would be possible, Alexandrov thought, and it would be impossible to know which one to believe.

This was, roughly, one reason why the Ames group had used a one-dimensional model. In the absence of any information for calibration, they believed the existing three-dimensional modeling techniques introduced more uncertainties than they eliminated. It was better to do the definitive one-dimensional model than to attempt an overambitious and half-baked three-dimensional model. (There was something of Pollack's scientific personality in that.)

Not everyone agreed with Alexandrov. Three-dimensional models had been used successfully for the atmospheres of other planets, it was pointed out. (Of course, there were observational data about other planets; none about the postnuclear Earth.) There was general enthusiasm for a three-dimensional model, and Sagan spoke of this as the next step.

The reviewers agreed that TTAPS's weaknesses were inevitable under the circumstances and not a reason for rejecting the work. The magnitude of the cooling in the land-planet model was so great as to make a serious case for climatic disaster following a nuclear war. At the very least, it showed the need for more research. The reviewers approved the article.

*   *   *

Sagan found Vladimir Alexandrov to be as likable as promised. After the Cambridge meeting, Sagan pressed Alexandrov to do his own study of nuclear cooling. It would be helpful, he said, to have a corroborating Soviet study available at the time of the public announcement of TTAPS. Alexandrov concurred. He spoke wistfully of doing the first *three-dimensional* model of the problem. This seemed a long shot. The public conference was set for Washington, D.C., in October. Queues for Soviet computers were like the fabled ones in Russian department stores—even for someone of Alexandrov's stature. At the Soviet Academy of Sciences, Alexandrov used such computers as the BESM-6, regarded as a joke in the West. The BESM-6 had about as much RAM as an IBM PC of the time. It was said to be 500 times slower than the Ames Cray.

*   *   *

On August 4, 1983, the TTAPS article was submitted to *Science*. The journal's editors put the article through its own, more conventional, peer review.

After the article had been submitted, NASA suffered another attack of the jitters. It ruled that the terms "nuclear war" and "nuclear weapons" must not appear in the article's title. The agency did not want to advertise that it was doing nuclear war studies. Since NASA Ames was paying three of the authors' paychecks, they complied by choosing the title "Nuclear Winter: Global Consequences of Multiple Nuclear Explosions."

The poetic term "nuclear winter"—coined by Richard Turco, not Sagan—did a lot to sell a highly complex idea. It granted Sagan (especially) the license to broaden the concept beyond the cold and the dark. Many other consequences of nuclear war, most known prior to TTAPS, would occur simultaneously. The best known was radioactive fallout, a worry since the days of fallout shelters. More recently appreciated, and not so well known, were the merely chemical hazards that would be loosed by the burning of modern cities: noxious clouds of toxins from burning plastics; dispersed asbestos; nitrogen oxides that would deplete the ozone layer and increase ultraviolet radiation. These and other environmental insults might combine to create effects greater than the sum of their parts. The scope of these "synergistic" effects was impossible to predict, however.

Emotionally, all these projections were a "hard sell." The plumes of smoke visiting nuclear winter on the land would be rising from the ashes of New York and Moscow, Paris and Beijing. Most people have trouble worrying about catastrophes piled on top of catastrophes. It was, at any rate, the ability to put numbers to the catastrophe of thermonuclear war that TTAPS promised. Only if those numbers were reasonably accurate could TTAPS qualify as good science. Only if TTAPS was good science could it be expected to be taken seriously by world leaders who might not like what it said.

*   *   *

The Sagans were not popular people in the Reagan White House. Ron and Nancy Reagan (whose conjugal mind-meld was not so entirely unlike Carl and Annie's) had been willing to overlook the political gulf between themselves and the Sagans. Three times the Reagans invited the Sagans to dinner at the White House. Each time the Sagans declined. "You are out of your minds!" a White House social secretary informed them.

Sagan had an idiosyncratic attitude toward the corridors of power. He could not bear to be co-opted. He would avoid any job or social relationship that might inhibit him from saying exactly what he thought. He felt it would be hypocritical to have dinner with the Reagans and not tell them what he thought of their defense policy. But if he did that, it would insult the president, and you don't insult someone who's invited you to his house for dinner.

As much as this made sense within Sagan's frame of reference, it was liable to be interpreted as rudeness or pomposity. So the Reagans seem to have taken it. Some time later, a White House helicopter pilot told Sagan that "you wouldn't believe how often those guys were talking about you"—*not* in flattering terms.

It was even rumored that the Reagan administration wanted ABC to drop Sagan's *Nucleus* show. In September 1983, during a meeting at the network, a note was passed to ABC's Richard Wald. As he scanned it, his expression changed suddenly. He abruptly excused himself and left the room.

Carl and Annie soon found out the cause. Korean Air Liner 007 had been shot down by the Soviets for violating their air space. In this case at least, Reagan's "evil empire" was living up to its billing.

This international incident seems to have been the straw that broke the camel's back. ABC put *Nucleus* on the far-back burner and never brought it forward again. The project collapsed, as did the idea for a book. As with *Cosmos*, the *Nucleus* book was to have been so closely integrated with the series and its visuals that it seemed unthinkable as an independent project.

Halloween Before 1984

The following month, the Conference on the World After Nuclear War took place at the Sheraton Washington Hotel. The TTAPS article, accepted by *Science*, was still in press and would not appear until the December 23 issue. The conference was essentially a prepublication presentation to the press and public. Its proceedings, published as *The Cold and the Dark*, received wide dissemination the following year.

There was an unmistakable political tilt. The thirty-one sponsoring organizations were a cross section of liberal and "green" do-gooders: Common Cause, the Environmental Defense Fund, the Federation of American Scientists, the Audubon Society, Planned Parenthood, the Sierra Club, the Smithsonian Institution, Union of Concerned Scientists, several United Nations agencies, and Zero Population Growth.

The conference's scientific advisory board was impressive, including David Baltimore, Hans Bethe, Francis Crick, Jared Diamond, Paul Ehrlich, Stephen Jay Gould, Edward Purcell, Abdus Salam, Jonas Salk, Lewis Thomas, Victor Weisskopf, Jerome Weisner, and Edward O. Wilson. Conspicuously absent from the meeting were Pollack, Toon, and Ackerman. NASA had pressured them not to attend.

*   *   *

"It is the Halloween preceding 1984," Sagan began, "and I deeply wish that what I am about to tell you were only a ghost story, only something invented to frighten children for a day."

The subject matter notwithstanding, the conference had a Woodstock-like zeitgeist. Lewis Thomas felt that TTAPS and related studies might turn out to be "the most important research findings in the long history of science." Butler University's Thomas Malone said that posterity would view the conference as nothing less than "the turning point in the affairs of humankind."

These were not just American reactions. Participating via a video link in Moscow, Yevgeny Velikhov said:

> We see that no military or psychological arguments—and there are many of them—can refute these results. I think the only conclusion possible is that our nuclear devices are not and cannot be used as weapons of war or tools of war; nor can they be a tool of politics. They are simply tools of suicide.

If the conference had a mantra, it would have to be *robustness*. (Either that or *consensus*.) This robustness was central to Sagan's argument. It goes without saying that no one can predict the details of a nuclear war. Sagan claimed that the predicted cold and dark were robust in the sense that they were not strongly dependent on a particular set of assumptions. Cold and dark would obtain in almost any plausible nuclear war above a certain fuzzy threshold. Despite the myriad uncertainties, Sagan insisted, there was consensus about the reality of nuclear winter.

"How could that be?" was something that a few people were heard asking.

An answer, if a partial one, was to be had in the other research presented. Alexandrov attended in person. He had managed to get the computer time and had run a three-dimensional model. This he printed in English and distributed, bound in blue paper.

So there was Soviet corroboration, of a sort. Some of Alexandrov's predictions were unsettlingly at odds with those of TTAPS. In some parts of the globe, Alexandrov's model predicted even colder temperatures than TTAPS had. In the Himalayas and Rockies, however, Alexandrov predicted that the temperatures would be *warmer*, not cooler. He said that this was due to the suspended particles heating the upper atmosphere. "This would cause the mountain snow and mountain glaciers to melt," warned Alexandrov, "and would probably result in floods of continental size—I repeat, for emphasis, of continental size."

At the conference, no one seemed to make too much of this difference. Some nontechnical observers were impressed with Alexandrov's work. U.S. vice admiral John Lyons called Alexandrov's model "a quantum jump in detail over the work of Sagan and his colleagues."

Sagan was less sold. It seemed that Alexandrov's 3D model had fallen victim to the very problem he had mentioned at the peer review meeting. After the meeting, Sagan privately asked Alexandrov how his model derived the mountain warming effect.

"It's what the computer tells us," Alexandrov shrugged.

Understanding TTAPS

What exactly did TTAPS say? This question vexed the press and public for a long time afterward.

TTAPS represented the new digital science, something still unfamiliar in 1983. Sagan made the point that nuclear winter involved no new physics or chemistry—in principle it could have been discovered twenty years previously. Certainly the *idea* of smoke-induced cooling might have occurred to someone long before TTAPS. But TTAPS had taken all the number-crunching power of a then-state-of-the-art Cray computer. The TTAPS model was the product of generations of successive calculations and refinements. Without the ease of testing and tweaking afforded by the computer, TTAPS could no more have existed than could the digital dinosaurs in the film *Jurassic Park*.

The polymorphic nature of computer modeling was one of the things that made the nuclear winter controversy so hard for the average person to understand. The impatient and practical mind does not want an infinite ensemble of predictions (which is what models like TTAPS produce) but a single figure. How cold would it get? How many would die? Neither TTAPS, nor any study easily conceived, is geared to answer such questions directly.

TTAPS's model, and the later models that would challenge it, are complex mathematical functions. You must "plug in" assumptions about the production of smoke and dust. Then the computer model produces, in effect, a graph showing how temperatures dip and return to normal in the weeks and months after a nuclear war.

The *Science* article presented ten scenarios, ranging from a relatively modest 100-megaton attack to a "future war" of 25,000 megatons (nearly twice the total nuclear arsenal existing in 1983). For most average folks, the ten scenarios were information overload. By default, the case that got the most attention was the so-called baseline exchange.

The authors held this to be a reasonable vision of a nuclear war between the United States and USSR. It assumed that 5,000 megatons of nuclear bombs were detonated, 20 percent exploding in urban or industrial areas where they might start smoky fires. At the time of TTAPS, the combined nuclear arsenal of the United States and Soviet Union was put at 15,000 megatons. Five thousand megatons might represent a "moderate" war in which "restraint" was shown; or perhaps more realistically, an all-out Armageddon in which many missiles were destroyed in their silos, others malfunctioned, and others did not get launched because of loss of command.

In this and most of the other scenarios, a graph of the temperatures looks like a reversed and recumbent question mark. Temperatures plummet in the weeks after the war, reach a minimum, then turn around and return, ever more slowly, to normal temperatures.

In the quest for a single number, it was natural to focus on the land-planet model. That alone had dramatic cooling. It was also natural to focus on the minimum temperature reached. The most-quoted number, the "bottom line" that got most of the attention, was the *minimum cooling* of the *land-planet* model in the *baseline scenario*. TTAPS put this at 36° C (65° F) *less than normal*.

*   *   *

It must be remembered that the minimum is a momentary value. Temperatures would not remain near the minimum very long. It must also be remembered that this applies to the land planet, a Mars-like globe whose temperature swings would be greater than on Earth. The pressing question, once again, is what would happen on Earth.

The TTAPS article did not have a good answer. It estimated that "actual temperature decreases in continental interiors might be roughly 30 percent smaller than predicted here [in the land-planet model], and along coastlines 70 percent smaller." This was not much more than an educated guess.

Accepting these corrections, the baseline scenario maximum cooling would be around 10° C near coasts and 25° C in the middle of continents. Most people live near the coasts. For any postnuclear survivors there, an 18° F cold snap might seem to be the least of their problems. But the world's breadbaskets tend to be in the middle of the big northern continents. There, a predicted 45° F cooling would be a knockout blow. There would be frost on the July corn.

*   *   *

This was alarming enough, but much of the press on nuclear winter cited the more extreme land-planet predictions. The TTAPS article did not do much to clear up the confusion.

The article largely presents the land-planet data. While the distinction between the land-planet model and the real Earth is concisely made, anyone skimming the article can easily miss it. The article has just one graph of cooling curves, and that presents the uncorrected land-planet data. This graph's caption says that "temperatures generally apply to the interior of continental land masses"—a "your mileage may differ" disclaimer that is not quite what the article says elsewhere.

For the cooling depicted in the graph is, according to the article's own estimates, more than triple that predicted for the coastal regions where the world's population concentrates. That point was easy for even *Science*'s technically adept readers to miss. For many a mere journalist, plugging through a technical article and then coming upon that graph, the "disclaimer" might as well have been in fine print.

There were scientific reasons for focusing on the raw land-planet data. TTAPS was reporting the results of a digital simulation, not of a real-world experiment. The connection between TTAPS's virtual planets and the real world was the most tentative link in the argument. There was something to be said for presenting the raw simulation data rather than confusing things by imposing a still-conjectural "correction."

"Our estimates of the physical and chemical impacts of nuclear war are necessarily uncertain," the TTAPS authors wrote, "because we have used one-dimensional models, because the data base is incomplete, and because the problem is not amenable to experimental investigation. . . . Nevertheless, the magnitudes of the first-order effects are so large, and the implications so serious, that we hope the scientific issues raised here will be vigorously and critically examined."

Doomsday Machine

This was a sound way of prefacing what was, indeed, a preliminary study. But by the time the *Science* article appeared, nuclear winter was already much more than a scientific question for Sagan. It was the political import of the Ames study that first drew Sagan to it. During the investigation and subsequent controversy, it was never a matter of indifference to Sagan whether nuclear winter was right or wrong. His commitment to the idea was comparable to his commitment to the idea of life on other planets.

Strange as it may sound, Sagan perceived a real link between the question of extraterrestrial intelligence and our own world's nuclear dilemma. In a 1983 article (one volley in the Sagan versus Frank Tipler feud), Sagan and William Newman wrote:

> Weapons of mass destruction force upon every emerging society a behavioural discontinuity: if they were not aggressive they probably would not have developed such weapons; if they do not quickly learn how to control that aggression they rapidly self-destruct. . . . Civilizations that do not self-destruct are pre-adapted to live with other groups in mutual respect. This adaptation must apply not only to the average state or individual, but, with very high precision, to every state and individual within the civilization. . . . The required changes might take thousands of years or more, if the society does not destroy itself first. They might involve major new departures in rearing the young, in education, in the structuring of adult society, or even in prosthetic or biological intervention. Perhaps— although we consider this unlikely—very few societies succeed in such a programme.

Long before TTAPS, Sagan believed that nuclear arms were such a threat to world civilization as to override the traditional concerns of national sovereignty. This view was in sympathy with those of Oppenheimer, Urey, Morrison, and many of the other scientists who built the first nuclear weapons. It never gained much ground with the American public (and even less with the defense establishment). People worried about the bomb and wished that the arms race could be stopped. But year after year, most Americans were more comforted by incrementing, rather than dismantling, their nuclear arsenal.

Sagan had seen two generations grow up with the bomb. The public had become inured to an escalating threat whose consequences (dwarfing those of Hiroshima) no one had ever witnessed. To someone as accustomed to looking at the long term as Sagan, the absence of a nuclear war in four decades was little comfort. History showed that weapons that got built eventually got used.

With nuclear winter, Sagan hoped that a scientific finding could provide the political leverage needed to end the nuclear arms race. In this he was an optimist as far as both science and human nature were concerned. It was a risk to found a political crusade on freshly minted science, at least in such an uncertainty-riddled field as climate prediction. And assuming TTAPS was correct, it could inspire disparate reactions.

Sagan believed that, faced with the possibility of annihilation, people would take the politically difficult actions necessary to avoid it. In that sense, the worse nuclear winter was, the better it augured for the future of humanity. A pessimist could argue the opposite, of course.

It could also be maintained that nuclear winter would only reinforce people's preexisting convictions. Hawks are hawks because they believe a strong defense is the best way to minimize chances of a nuclear war—and nuclear winter, if there is such a thing. Why should nuclear winter change anyone's thinking?

Sagan attempted to address these questions in a much-quoted article in *Foreign Affairs*. He offered three major conclusions: "There is a real danger of the extinction of humanity. A threshold exists at which the climatic catastrophe could be triggered. . . . A major first strike may be an act of national suicide, even if no retaliation occurs." In these claims Sagan was stepping beyond the scientific content of TTAPS—and beyond what could be demonstrated to the satisfaction of skeptical but open-minded critics. (This may be said of most articles in *Foreign Affairs*.)

Sagan was not alone in his apocalyptic thinking. The previous year, *The Fate of the Earth*, Jonathan Schell's book on the effects of a contemporary nuclear war, had raised the specter of human extinction—and this was prior to TTAPS's claims of climatic effects. Predictably, liberals embraced Schell's claims and conservatives dismissed them.

Sagan had somewhat more science with which to make his case. Immediately following TTAPS in the pages of *Science* was an article titled "Long-Term Biological Consequences of Nuclear Wars." Sagan, but none of the others in the TTAPS group, was among the twenty coauthors. This article cataloged the many other terrors and inconveniences a nuclear war would bring and raised the possibility that they might combine synergistically.

Sagan used this and other publications to paint a picture of a dark, frozen world where survivors could neither get water from wells nor bury the dead. Most compelling was the analysis of postnuclear agriculture or the absence thereof. A couple of degrees' cooling could nearly wipe out the Canadian wheat crop. There would almost certainly be a season without normal agriculture—even assuming that the postnuclear survivors went about their plowing and planting, unperturbed.

In most U.S. cities, there is only about a week's worth of food on hand. Something like a year's worth of stored grain exists in silos, but it is hard to imagine this being efficiently distributed in a cold, dark, radioactive world.

There was still a great deal of hand-waving in making the leap from that to the *extinction* of humanity. The "Long-Term Biological Consequences" article ends with the statement that "the possibility of the extinction of *Homo sapiens* cannot be excluded." That epitomizes Sagan's philosophy of risk, whereby even a very small chance of annihilation demands action.

That philosophy was not universally shared. "If you believe the threat of the end of the world will change thinking in Washington or Moscow," one prominent nuclear strategist told Sagan and Turco, "you have never spent any time in either of those places."

*   ⋆   ⋆

Sagan's "threshold" was probably the most controversial and misunderstood of his claims about nuclear winter. He asserted that there must be a certain minimum amount of smoke, X, that would produce catastrophic global cooling. Consequently, it was vital for everyone to make sure that X amount of smoke was never released.

Sagan realized (as some in the press did not) that this threshold would be a fuzzy, inexact thing. He estimated that the burning of 100 major cities (caused by anywhere from 500 to 2,000 nuclear warheads with a combined power of 100 megatons) could produce threshold smoke and thus global catastrophe. However, a war where most bombs hit missile silos—more plausible by most strategists' thinking—would require a much larger number of detonations to create the threshold smoke.

One point that no one contested was that 100 megatons was a trifle. Even that theoretical construct, a "limited" nuclear war, would probably involve hundreds of megatons.

Sagan advocated cutting the world's store of nuclear arms to the point where the simultaneous detonation of every bomb would not produce the threshold level of smoke.

> The Chernobyl and Challenger disasters remind us that highly visible technological systems in which enormous national prestige had been invested can nevertheless experience catastrophic failures. And Hitler and Stalin remind us that madmen can achieve control of modern industrial states and that leaders can become mad in office. The only prudent response, it seems to me, is to arrange a world in which the worst cannot happen even after some unlikely concatenation of technological malfunctions, human error and madness in high office—that is, to reduce the global nuclear arsenals below the level at which nuclear winter could conceivably occur.

Such a response would entail reducing U.S. and Soviet arsenals to less than 1 percent of what existed. At the time, talk of cutting nuclear arsenals in *half* was held to be a starry-eyed fantasy.

Since the dawn of the nuclear age, theorists have worried about sneak attacks or "first strikes." Such attacks would logically target the other side's missile silos, crippling its ability to retaliate. As the scenario went, the aggressor might gain world dominion without suffering a retaliatory attack. Conceivably, it might not cause too many casualties in the targeted nation, for missile silos tend to be in remote areas.

While hardly any defense expert thought this fantasy likely to play out as neatly as sketched, the necessity of *deterring* such an attack was a cornerstone of both superpowers' defense thinking.

Defense theorist Herman Kahn wrote of a "doomsday machine." It was an indestructible machine designed to destroy all life on Earth, if and when someone launched a nuclear attack. If such a machine existed—and if everyone *knew* it existed and acted rationally—then no one would ever start a nuclear war. Kahn did not go so far as to recommend building a doomsday machine. He too recognized that machines can fail, and people are not always rational.

Sagan claimed that nuclear winter would itself constitute a doomsday machine. To destroy a superpower's nuclear arsenal would take something like 3,000 megatons. That is well over the presumed nuclear winter threshold. A first strike would therefore be suicidal and thus self-deterred. "The incidence of armed robbery," Sagan wrote, "would decline dramatically if firearms routinely blew up in the faces of those who use them."

Needless to say, this required that everyone believe in the catastrophic climatic effects predicted by TTAPS.

The World Turned Strangely Jewish

Not long after the conference, ABC aired *The Day After*. The film was indeed grim but did not show "nuclear winter" cooling (to which its Midwest setting might have been particularly vulnerable). Sagan appeared in a panel discussion the network aired after the movie. The guest list was in the TV tradition of putting a variety of incompatible dogs in the same kennel to see what happens. Other panelists were William F. Buckley, Jr., Henry Kissinger, Robert McNamara, Brent Scowcroft, and Elie Wiesel—all moderated by Ted Koppel.

The show began with a remote feed of Secretary of State George Shultz. He recapitulated President Reagan's position and mildly insisted that reduction of the nuclear arsenal "has been at the top of his list."

Sagan looked haggard. He seemed to have aged ten years since the coverage of the 1981 Voyager Saturn encounter. In his first words, Sagan observed that the United States had been asleep during the past thirty-eight years, and that "the reality is much worse than has been portrayed in the movie."

Sagan recycled one of his favorite analogies. The United States and the Soviet Union, he said, were like two mortal enemies. One is armed with 9,000 matches, the other with 7,000 matches. Both stand in a room flooded with gasoline.

The one *cheerful* face on the panel was that of William F. Buckley, Jr. He said that what Sagan was saying was good news. It meant that the Soviets would not launch a first strike.

Henry Kissinger could not share that optimism. He was deeply upset over the TV movie, "a very simple-minded notion of the nuclear problem." Were they aware that he had written a *book* on the matter thirty years ago? Kissinger did not see that there was any cause to "engage in an orgy of demonstrating how terrible the casualties of a nuclear war would be, and translating into pictures statistics that have been known for *years*—and then to have Mr. Sagan say it's even *worse* than this."

Wiesel, agonized over what he had seen and heard, was the easiest to identify with. He admitted he was not an expert on nuclear war like the others. The movie was oddly familiar; it reminded him of the Holocaust. "Maybe," he said, "the whole world, strangely, has turned Jewish."

*   *   *

Whatever else it did, nuclear winter succeeded in getting a large public to contemplate the specter of atomic warfare. Hoboken, New Jersey, declared itself a nuclear-free zone. Ann Arbor contemplated a similar measure, then voted against it. Students at Brown University and Colorado University pressed their campus health centers to stock cyanide pills to be dispensed in the event of a nuclear war. Columbia University offered future physicians a course in which they could plan their role in treating the post-nuclear survivors who hadn't taken cyanide pills. The American Psychiatric Association held a symposium (organized by Lester Grinspoon) on the psychological aspects of nuclear winter. A survey claimed American teenagers worried about nuclear war more than anything except losing a parent. TV preacher Jerry Falwell espoused an "Armageddon ideology" holding nuclear annihilation of the human species to be a fulfillment of biblical prophecy. When President Reagan guardedly endorsed the idea (he was not about to come out *against* biblical prophecy), a *New York Times* editorialist simply refused to believe that the president had meant what he said.

Through the Looking Glass

The publication of the *Science* article essentially disbanded the TTAPS group. Pollack found the prospect of studying nuclear war distasteful. After the article's publication, he went back to his regular scientific pursuits. Turco and Toon managed to continue research bearing on nuclear winter. Sagan, often accompanied by Turco, set off on a globe-trotting campaign to educate policy makers and the public about nuclear winter.

Sagan briefed heads of state in Canada, Mexico, Argentina, France, Sweden, Greece, Tanzania, and New Zealand. He spoke at each of the U.S. service academies; to the Joint Chiefs of Staff, the CIA, and a closed session of Congress. These talks took place under circumstances ranging from collegial to just plain weird. Sagan recalled cases in which officials hid behind a one-way mirror, lest it be known they had attended the briefing.

One nuclear strategist insisted privately that nuclear winter could never happen because Sagan had published the "threshold." The prudent strategists of both sides would be forced to keep the megatonnage below it. He added that, game-theoretically speaking, it was a big mistake to have published that threshold.

Sagan thought he got a warmer hearing with career military officers than with civilian appointees. Despite the liberals' stereotypes, the officers were polite and open to new ideas. Civilians in the Defense Department tended not to want to hear anything that challenged their political views. When U.S. military experts criticized TTAPS, it was often on the grounds that the "scenarios" used were unrealistic. The Pentagon's Richard DeLauer objected that targeting of cities (in TTAPS's baseline scenario, for instance) was neither "credible" nor "moral." Needless to say, Sagan was not endorsing targeting of cities. His point was that the incredible and the immoral were neither unthinkable nor unprecedented.

Asymmetry of Perception

To defense conservatives, nuclear winter (or, more exactly, Sagan's policy conclusion that nuclear weapons must never be used) was a destabilizing doctrine. It threatened to undermine the deterrence that had prevented a nuclear war over four decades. Conservatives' great fear was not that nuclear winter was right (gloomy though the prospect might be) nor that it would be generally believed, right or wrong. Who wouldn't welcome a theory that scared everyone out of launching a nuclear war?

The underlying fear of people like Buckley and Kissinger went by the label "asymmetry of perception." They were concerned that nuclear winter would be an easier "sell" in the United States than in the Soviet Union. The U.S. defense establishment has to listen to the voters—after a fashion, anyway—and these voters are influenced by media-savvy people like Sagan, exercising their right to free speech. The Soviet military leadership was a great deal more independent of the Soviet people, whose sources of information were more restricted. The Soviets, furthermore, had greater conventional forces than the United States did. If nuclear weapons were suddenly out of the picture, the Soviet military position would be enhanced.

Some suspected an asymmetry of *sincerity*, too. Conservatives worried that Americans *really* believed in nuclear winter while the Soviets only *pretended* to do so. It was this asymmetry that created nuclear winter's least likely celebrity of the moment: Vladimir Alexandrov.

People sympathetic to Sagan's cause realized that Alexandrov had unique political value. There, in the flesh, was proof the Soviets believed in nuclear winter. Alexandrov agreed not only with the basic science but, at least in outline, with Sagan's policy conclusions. The superpowers would have to agree to substantial arms reductions.

Alexandrov was paraded like a noble captive though the West's halls of power. He appeared on American TV with Sagan. He spoke to the U.S. Senate at the behest of Senators Edward Kennedy and Mark Hatfield. In January 1984, Sagan, Alexandrov, Stephen Jay Gould, and fifteen other scientists spent a three-day retreat in the Vatican, preparing a report on nuclear winter. As Sagan presented the report to Pope John Paul II, Alexandrov was at his side.

Was Alexandrov "for real"? Fringe publications such as *New Solidarity*, distributed in airports by supporters of right-wing presidential candidate Lyndon Larouche, took up this question. One article blasted Alexandrov's congressional testimony on nuclear winter as a "KGB Road Show" now playing the U.S. Senate. Another claimed, "The nuclear winter lie was given wide currency by the Soviets, who used it to foster illusions in U.S. military and policy-making circles that nuclear war was unwinnable and therefore unthinkable."

$$\infty = \infty$$

Sagan played a somewhat comparable role in the Soviet Union. He lobbied many of the Soviet Union's leaders. He asked one scientific adviser to the Soviet government why they thought it necessary to match the U.S. nuclear arsenal, when a much smaller number of bombs would suffice to wipe out all of America's cities several times over. The scientist responded by writing an equation in a notebook: $\infty = \infty$. Infinity equals infinity—too many bombs are not enough.

Sagan's greatest coup was his 1986 briefing of the Soviet Central Committee on nuclear winter. Several who were present have said that the effect of Sagan's talk on Soviet military thinking was profound. Cosmonaut and General Alexei Leonov reported that, after Sagan left the room, a dozen men on the Soviet General Staff looked at each other and agreed that the nuclear arms race was over. It would have to end; the threat of massive retaliation wasn't credible anymore.

These reverberations were felt throughout the remaining days of the Soviet Union. Major General Boris Trofimovich Surikov of the Soviet General Staff said nuclear winter was often discussed in the Soviet Defense Ministry and convinced them of the need for major arms reductions. Gorbachev personally told Sagan that he had read all of Sagan's nuclear winter research and that the Soviet Union saw itself as implementing his foreign policy. After the fall of the Soviet Union, physicist Roald Sagdeev and Alexei Leonov went so far as to credit Sagan with ending the cold war.

Some of these testimonials may be colored by friendship, but they are no longer subject to suspicion as political dissimulations. Sagan had a unique status in the Soviet Union. His ancestors came from Russian soil, he had real friends in Moscow, and he was one of the few scientists consistently encouraging East-West dialogue throughout the long cold war. This gave him a credibility in Moscow that very few other American scientists had.

C-Minus

Perhaps it was more surprising, all things considered, that Sagan was making inroads with President Ronald Reagan. Reagan's words in a February 1985 interview with the *New York Times* were virtually cribbed from Sagan:

> A great many reputable scientists are telling us that such a [nuclear] war could just end up in no victory for anyone because we could wipe out the Earth as we know it. And if you think back to a couple of natural calamities—back in the last century, in the 1800's, just natural phenomena from earthquakes, or, I mean, volcanoes—we saw the weather so changed that there was snow in July in many temperate countries. And they called it "the year in which there was no summer." Now if one volcano can do that,

what are we talking about with the whole nuclear exchange, the nuclear winter that scientists have been talking about?

The administration's provisional acceptance of Sagan's science did not extend to his policy recommendations. The following month, Sagan clashed with the Pentagon's Richard N. Perle on the floor of the House of Representatives. "We are persuaded that a nuclear war would be a terrible thing," Perle said, "but we believe that what we are doing with respect to strategic nuclear modernization and arms control is sound and we believe it is made no less sound by the nuclear winter phenomenon."

Worst of all from Sagan's perspective was that TTAPS was being cited as demonstrating the need for SDI. "You would have to be really loony tunes to bet the survival of the world" on SDI, Sagan said. He told Congress that if the Defense Department's report had been submitted to him at Cornell, "it would get a D, maybe a C-minus if I was in a friendly mood." Perle retorted that he would give Sagan an F on his understanding of the issue.

Of this exchange, William F. Buckley, Jr., wrote that "Sagan gave a performance so arrogant he might have been confused with, well, me."

Saber-Tooth

In March 1985 Sagan lost two Soviet friends under very different circumstances.

I. S. Shklovskii developed an embolism in his leg. Protesting that he felt fine, he was hospitalized for surgery. The blood clot broke loose and went to the brain, causing a massive stroke. As Shklovskii lay in a coma, the Soviet Academy placed a call to Frank Press of the U.S. National Academy of Sciences, asking for medical assistance. It was too late to do anything. Shklovskii died in Moscow on March 5, 1985. Sagan eulogized, "We are all diminished by his death."

Sagan's last meeting with Shklovskii had been in Graz, Austria, the previous summer, prior to a meeting on Soviet-U.S. cooperation in space. Sagan was excited by the idea of a joint Soviet-U.S. mission to Mars. Shklovskii had been resolutely pessimistic about the Soviet Union. Nothing could change in the next fifty years, he prophesied.

At that meeting Sagan made his final pitch to reclaim SETI's strayed sheep. Shklovskii would have none of it. He spoke of the saber-toothed cat. Generation after generation, it evolved ever longer curved tusks in order to compete with the other saber-tooths and *their* longer tusks. Finally the teeth were *too* long. The cat was ill suited to catch its prey, and the species died out.

Shklovskii's point was that intelligence is a freak of evolution that quickly burns itself out. We will burn ourselves out with hydrogen bombs or the weapons that we devise after that. And that is why there was no one signaling in Andromeda, why the universe is empty, or will be after our spark grows cold.

Without a Trace

In the days after Shklovskii's death, Vladimir Alexandrov found himself in a hall of mirrors worthy of the spy fiction he so enjoyed. He fell afoul of someone in power. That much is reasonably certain. Little else is.

No one ever duplicated Alexandrov's prediction of melting Himalayan glaciers. Sagan and colleagues came to realize that Alexandrov's science was not all it might have been. Richard Turco rated Alexandrov's climate model "a very weak piece of work, crude and seriously flawed." It had been copied from a 1970s climatic model created in the United States.

When Alexandrov requested permission to use the more powerful computers at the Institute for Cosmic Research for further nuclear winter studies, he was turned down. Had someone decided that nuclear winter studies were not in the Soviet interest? By January 1985, the United States had also barred Alexandrov from its supercomputers. Someone wrote on Alexandrov's visa: "Not permitted direct or indirect access to the supercomputers in the United States." The obvious surmise is that someone suspected Alexandrov of trying to steal supercomputer technology for the Soviets.

*　　*　　*

If someone were going to do that, nuclear winter might provide an excellent cover story. The climatic models used in nuclear winter studies demanded the most powerful computers available.

The distinction between spy and visiting scientist was not absolute in the Soviet Union. It was well known that Soviet scientists whose work allowed them to glimpse cutting-edge Western technology would be debriefed on their return. It was also known that much Soviet military technology was "reverse-engineered" from its American counterparts. The question is whether Alexandrov used American supercomputers in ways unknown to his American hosts—stealing technology or running programs (of defense significance?) that could not be run so quickly, if at all, in the Soviet Union.

Scientists at Oregon and NCAR insisted that Alexandrov was never permitted to operate the computer alone. Nevertheless, Alexandrov learned how to use a Cray-1A at NCAR and spent a known 120 hours on the machine.

Some faulted Alexandrov for being a glib promoter who did little real science. (Some faulted Sagan on similar grounds.) "It is hard to tell the difference between [Soviet] scientific workers and propagandists," stated a Pentagon report released March 1. "The primary atmospheric circulation model used by the Soviets in the case of the widely publicized study by Soviet researchers V. Alexandrov and G. Stenchikov is based on a borrowed, obsolete, U.S. model. . . . Time after time their presentations contain exaggerated claims, which are criticized by their foreign colleagues . . . but subsequent presentations do not reflect any change, even though in private the Soviets acknowledge the exaggeration." That last clause must have raised eyebrows in Moscow.

*   *   *

On March 29, 1985, Alexandrov arrived at the Madrid airport for a meeting in Córdoba, Spain. Soviet officials intercepted his driver and insisted that *they* were supposed to drive him to the Soviet embassy in Madrid. This they did, with the driver following. Alexandrov spent a half hour or so inside the embassy. When he came out, he was a man who needed a good stiff drink.

He demanded that his driver take him to a bar, any bar. The driver complied. When Alexandrov came out, he was falling-down drunk.

The driver took him to Córdoba, arriving in early evening. Later that night, Córdoba police found Alexandrov lying unconscious in the Jewish quarter. They drove him back to the university where he was staying.

Alexandrov spoke at 10 A.M. the next morning. He was "sullen and gray-looking, almost ghostlike," according to another speaker. He missed a presentation that night, evidently to go on another drinking binge. He showed up in a taxi at 3 A.M. Some conference organizers were still up, working, and observed that Alexandrov was so drunk that he tried to pay his driver with an American $50 bill. One of his colleagues stepped in and paid the driver. It took Alexandrov a while even to understand that the fare had been paid.

To those who knew how penurious the Soviets were, it was a mystery how a traveling scientist came by a bill that large, much less one *not* in the local currency.

On March 31, another driver took Alexandrov back to Madrid. Every time they passed a place that looked as if it sold alcohol, Alexandrov announced, "Restaurant. Stop." The driver ignored him.

This driver took Alexandrov not to the airport but to the Soviet embassy—an unwelcome change of plans. According to one report, Alexandrov wrenched open the car door so forcefully he broke the handle and tried to make a run for it. An embassy employee caught him. Strangely, however, Alexandrov was then taken to the nearby Hotel Habana, checked into Room 614, and left there, *alone*.

At about 11 P.M., he was seen leaving the hotel, drunk, and trying to get into the place next door, a closed bingo parlor. Magnificently indifferent to it all, he demanded Spanish wine. That was the last that anyone saw of Vladimir Alexandrov.

*   *   *

Alexandrov "was a guy who disappeared a lot," Brian Toon told me—speaking as if this were part of his very character. Toon once saw Alexandrov onto a Seattle-bound plane. Alexandrov failed to show up. It turned out that the plane had been forced down in Oregon. Alexandrov rented a car and drove to Seattle, without telling anyone of the change of plans. Such habits led some Americans to hope that Alexandrov would yet again turn up safe with a colorful excuse.

On the morning of April 1, Soviet embassy representatives showed up at the Hotel Habana to pick up Alexandrov. He was not there. It was said the Soviets found his passport and wallet (with money) in his hotel room; also that the wallet, passport, and airline tickets were discovered in a trash can, either in the room or somewhere nearby.

No body was ever found. That makes it hard to believe that Alexandrov was a victim of accident, suicide, or casual murder. Within months of his vanishing, Alexandrov was an unperson in the Soviet Union. This was underscored by the publication of *The Night After . . . : Climatic and Biological Consequences of a Nuclear War*, a Soviet-published (but English language) book drawing heavily on Alexandrov's research. Nowhere was Alexandrov's name mentioned. That was the usual treatment of Soviets who had defected.

Sagan was alarmed at the loss of a friend and crucial colleague. In trying to make sense of what happened, he ran up against disquieting stonewalling. Sagan was told that no agency of the United States or Soviet Union was holding Alexandrov or knew anything of his whereabouts. "Vladimir had a promising career," one Soviet official told Sagan, "and anyway the Soviet Union hasn't assassinated one of its people abroad since Trotsky."

For some time Alexandrov's name did not appear in Soviet publications. Then, just as mysteriously, it again became acceptable to mention him. Sagan's theory was that the Soviets finally concluded that Alexandrov had *not* defected.

*   ★   *

The minor paradoxes of Alexandrov now took on disturbing dimensions. Where Shklovskii hadn't beer money, Alexandrov was able to save his allowance and buy a VCR. This he shipped home along with a tape of *Doctor Zhivago* (a film that moved him to tears) and Jane Fonda's *Workout* tape for his would-be ballerina daughter.

Few Americans were ready to believe that their government would abduct (and kill?) a high-profile Soviet national. There was speculation about a midlife crisis or nervous breakdown. It was easier to believe that Alexandrov had become a liability to his government. The Soviets were concerned about his drinking or the direction of his research, and what he might say under the influence of wine or truth.

It was theorized that Alexandrov had been ordered to promote the idea that a nuclear war would be suicidal while, really, the Kremlin pursued plans based on a "survivable level" of environmental consequences. Perhaps Alexandrov had initially been unaware of the duplicity, had discovered it, and had intended to speak out—forcing the Soviets to silence him.

Or maybe he committed a blunder Moscow could not forgive. "He prided himself on what he knew about the Cray," said Jerry Potter of Lawrence Livermore Laboratory. "He would name-drop." One of Alexandrov's boasts was that he could hack into the Livermore's Cray X-MP.

The Cray X-MP was the Lamborghini of computers. It was likely this kind of loose talk that caused the United States to deny Alexandrov access to supercomputers. For in February 1985, someone tried to log on to the Livermore Cray X-MP. The phone call was traced to Moscow.

Carl and Dorion

In November 1984 Sagan's travels took him to Bellagio, Italy, for an international conference on nuclear disarmament. He stayed in a monastery. One night around 3 A.M. he was awakened by heavy pounding on his door. Opening it, he was told, "Your grandfather has died."

Sagan's grandfathers were long dead. In the morning, Sagan learned the real message: that he had *become* a grandfather.

It was Dorion's child, a boy named Tonio Jerome Sagan. Dorion's wife, Marjorie, had wanted to name the baby Dorion, Jr. (contrary to the practice of Jewish families). They settled instead on Tonio, from the Thomas Mann story "Tonio Krueger." That evening in Bellagio, an international crowd, with delegates from both of the nuclear superpowers, drank to the boy's health.

*   *   *

Carl's relationship with Dorion was the most difficult of all his relationships with his children. Dorion grew up bitter at his father's abandonment, conscious of the mixed blessings of being a famous man's son. In the mid-1980s, Dorion and Lynn Margulis wrote a book on bacteria titled *Microcosmos*. Carl thought the title was a rip-off. He was afraid *his* readers would see *Cosmos* and *Sagan* on the book's cover and buy it by mistake.

"I never felt close enough to him to criticize him and be assured of his love," Dorion explained; "therefore I was always on my guard, and our emotional arguments took the form of intellectual ones." Dorion tried to get Carl to read Derrida and judged him naive for his almost "religious" faith in science. Having thus drawn up sides, father and son played out their emotional conflicts in an uneasy chess game.

Dorion took up magic as a teen. One of Dorion's good memories of his father is of Carl being entranced by his sleight-of-hand tricks. As an adult, he moved to Fort Lauderdale and began performing magic professionally. The year after his son was born, an intruder entered his home and nearly bludgeoned him to death in his sleep.

When Carl heard of the attack, he flew to Florida. The injuries were so serious that Dorion's doctors planned brain surgery to forestall meningitis. During one hospital visit, Carl found his son in a state of paranoid delirium. Dorion rambled about the Godhead splintering into separate selves as in Hindu cosmology—each self no longer bored—because of the *illusion* of death.

Carl replied that there was nothing *unusual* about such thoughts. The question of whether God could commit suicide had been long debated by theologians.

Dorion pulled through. His father's support led to a thaw in their relationship. Things were improved enough that Dorion felt able to communicate more honestly with his father, to express the love, and the anger, he felt. Carl told Dorion that his grad students sometimes continued conversations in letters, and he might want to do the same. Dorion vented his rage in an impassioned letter that he hesitated to send. A friend of his looked at the letter and told him: don't.

There followed a phase in which the relationship's axis tilted back to an icy but placid equilibrium point. Carl noticed that something had changed. The relationship had improved. He asked Dorion if he knew why.

I gave up on you, Dorion said. Carl asked if there was anything he could do to improve the relationship. No, Dorion said, not really. It's a Zen thing. Just accept it.

Roman à Clef

Fall of 1985 found two Carl Sagan books on the best-seller lists. Simon and Schuster published the much-anticipated *Contact* in October. A month later, Random House released *Comet*. "We have a dream," Scott Meredith told the *New York Times*, "that one day soon we'll find that 'Contact' is No. 1 on the fiction best-seller list and 'Comet' is No. 1 on the *nonfiction* list."

The books did not quite achieve that, but no one was complaining. *Comet* was more than an attempt to cash in on the return of Halley's comet. It reported on an area of research that was becoming quite active in Sagan's lab and elsewhere: the possible role of comets in the origin of life. The book was more of a success than the comet, which was poorly placed for viewing from the Northern Hemisphere. The book was also the first public recognition of the role Druyan was playing in Sagan's writing enterprise. She got equal billing as coauthor.

Contact was commercial science fiction in the vein of Michael Crichton (which is what a publisher paying $2 million wants). Unusual for sci-fi, it was a roman à clef. Before the book came out, Carl and Annie pulled Jill Tarter aside at a gathering. Carl announced that he was writing a novel. Well of course Tarter knew that; reports of the $2-million advance had not gone unnoticed at Cornell. Carl coyly said that Jill particularly should read the book.

Tarter did not know what to make of that. She couldn't think the book would be "about" her, for Sagan didn't know her that well. When she got the book, she was startled to find that the heroine "Ellie" was in some respects closely modeled on her. The book described her relationship with her father and had an accurate bit about a male colleague who took credit for her work. It turned out that Sagan had done some detective work and used elements of Tarter's life for verisimilitude.

*   *   *

As the manuscript of *Contact* neared completion, Sagan called Caltech's Kip Thorne, one of the greatest relativity physicists. He asked Thorne to take a look at the manuscript to make sure he had the general relativity right.

The manuscript had people hopping across the Galaxy by ducking into black holes. Thorne recommended that Sagan change that to wormholes. Black holes are real (so Thorne and everyone else in the field think). No one could go down a black hole and survive. Wormholes are a theoretical construct, permitted by Einstein's equations, but perhaps not really existing. It was less clear that you couldn't travel down a wormhole; Sagan would be on safer ground there. (A novel set in Atlantis is less open to factual nit-picking than one set in Paris.)

Sagan's plot also involved time travel. He asked Thorne if there was any way that an "infinitely advanced civilization" might use general relativity to travel in time. This was not the sort of question physicists were accustomed to ask. (Thorne dubbed it a "Sagan-type question.") It inspired Thorne and a number of colleagues to begin playing around with schemes for time travel.

They soon decided that *if* an "infinitely advanced civilization" could keep a wormhole open long enough to travel through it, then time travel *would* be possible. That was good news for Sagan's plotting. His voyagers could spend a day across the Galaxy somewhere, then return a split second after they left.

But the scheme would also permit them to return *before* they left and meet themselves. It would allow *all* the classic time travel paradoxes. That seemed so preposterous that Thorne suspected there must be something wrong with the idea of navigable wormholes.

Thorne and grad student Mike Morris published their results in 1988 (*Contact* was already out in paperback). The effect of their paper's bold title—"Wormholes in spacetime and their use for interstellar travel"—was undercut by the subtitle: "a tool for teaching general relativity." They soft-pedaled the work as a classroom diversion to show they hadn't *totally* gone off the edge.

The work was taken seriously by Stephen Hawking, for one. He was confident that time travel was impossible. There was too much experimental evidence against it: we haven't been mobbed by tourists from the future. Hawking proposed a "Chronology Protection Conjecture" holding that the laws of physics "conspire" to prevent paradoxical time travel, be it accomplished with wormholes or anything else.

These questions have inspired a number of papers, and work on resolving them continues. The subject is by no means as frivolous as it may sound. Were someone to demonstrate that the theory of relativity "breaks down" in certain contexts, that would be a stunning development. Already Sagan's role as "stimulator and shocker" has been highly unusual. You might have to go back to Simon Newcomb's measurement of the precession of Mercury to find another case of a planetary astronomer influencing theoretical physics.

*   *   *

Thorne's heady theorizing in Pasadena was of little account in Hollywood, where the *Contact* script was going through changes of its own.

In 1982 Peter Guber moved to Warner Brothers, taking *Contact* with him. After the novel came out, Guber decided that the original movie treatment of *Contact* contained cinematic elements not in the novel. He had a meeting with Gentry Lee, liked his ideas, and hired him as coproducer. As Lee was then on rocky terms with Sagan, his hiring did little to improve relations between Sagan and the studio. Lee worked with screenwriters as Guber commissioned script after script. They added a Native American astronaut. They added a teenage stowaway. Guber was keen on the stow-away angle; it would be Ellie's estranged teenage son. "I thought it lent a tremendous element to the picture," Guber explained. "Here was a woman consumed with the idea that there was something out there worth listening to, but the one thing she could never make contact with was her own child."

Sagan and Druyan were somewhere between amused and appalled. *Lost in Space*'s Dr. Smith notwithstanding, a stowaway on a small and precisely engineered spacecraft defied plausibility. Guber shrugged off technical objections. As Sagan learned, he would not have the same degree of control over a Hollywood movie as over a PBS series.

SETI-in-a-Suitcase

At about the time of *Contact*'s publication, Sagan became involved in a new, vastly more sophisticated SETI program, Project META. (META stood for Million-channel Extra-Terrestrial Assay.) META's origins go back to 1981, when Jill Tarter, then at NASA Ames, invited a young Harvard physicist to spend some time at the center. The physicist was Paul Horowitz. He is probably best known today as coauthor of the classic text *The Art of Electronics*. Horowitz had become hooked on SETI when his Harvard roommate took a class from Sagan. While at Ames, Horowitz and Ivan Linscott designed their own SETI machine.

Their design made use of the power and miniaturization of the new microprocessors. It was a desktop SETI machine, half-jokingly called SETI-in-a-suitcase. They did not build the device, though. That would cost about $20,000, and they didn't have it.

Horowitz gave a talk on the design. Tom McDonough, a Planetary Society member, happened to hear it and was impressed. When Sagan learned of the system, he was equally enthusiastic. The Planetary Society arranged joint funding with Ames in a mere thirty days' time. In six months Horowitz had a working prototype.

To make use of the device, Horowitz needed a radio telescope that could be devoted to SETI for months or years on end. That was a tall order, and it required more money.

Annie had the idea of asking a man who had made a lot of money from extraterrestrials: Steven Spielberg. Sagan had somewhat mixed feelings. He had judged *Close Encounters of the Third Kind* "pretentious" and faulted it for endorsing UFOs as extraterrestrial spaceships. (He insisted that the film's Cornell sweatshirted scientist couldn't be *him*.) In any event, Annie coaxed both Sagan and Spielberg into a meeting. Spielberg liked Sagan's pitch enough to write a check for $100,000.

Throwing the Switch

META used Harvard's Oak Ridge Observatory, an eighty-four-foot dish in the small town of Harvard, Massachusetts (an hour's drive from Harvard University in Cambridge). The September 1985 dedication took place just after the dregs of a hurricane had passed through Massachusetts, uprooting trees but not the Harvard dish. Sagan, Horowitz, and Spielberg were all in attendance. So was Spielberg's infant son, Maxwell, himself a budding celebrity. As had been reported in the popular press, the child's mother was actress Amy Irving, and the couple had chosen not to marry.

Horowitz decided that the occasion called for a switch to pull. He found a huge knife switch (real mad-scientist stuff) and rigged it to complete a circuit initiating the search hardware and software. When Sagan saw the switch, he casually placed his hand across the open circuit. *You could have killed yourself!* Horowitz gasped—adding that, fortunately, he had the switch on a low voltage line.

"I knew you'd do that," Sagan replied.

The switch was thrown, and Project META was in business. Horowitz's mother, who lacked none of Rachel Sagan's chutzpah, introduced herself to Spielberg at the reception. She graciously offered three words of advice: "Marry the woman."

The META search covered the entire sky visible from Massachusetts. For the most part, the dish was kept motionless, letting its beam drift across the heavens as the Earth rotated. Each day the dish tilted a bit farther south so that the telescope beam swept a new strip of sky, covering the heavens like an apple peeler. Over the course of years, it swept the whole sky several times over.

This approach meant that the outcome would not depend on anyone's guess of where to look—on such imponderables as which stars might harbor life, or whether at least one spendthrift civilization might budget the energy for an intergalactic beacon. This maximized the chances of success. It also made it somewhat harder to discount a failure. No longer was SETI a purely symbolic effort.

Mysterious Uranian Gunk

The success of Voyager at Jupiter and Saturn convinced Congress to extend the mission. On January 24, 1986, Voyager 2 passed by Uranus, beaming back 7,000 images of the planet, its rings, and satellites. Some of the photos of Uranus's satellites were judged to be the highest quality of any of the Voyager mission's.

The planet was another matter. It was the least photogenic major object in the solar system, very close to being a blue-green sphere, *period.* JPL's graphics wizards produced a succession of false-color, psychedelic, solarized-looking pictures. There were cloud bands after all, they decided. They also inferred the existence of a reddish haze overlaying the cooler tones.

This haze particularly commanded Sagan's attention. Khare, Edward Arakawa, and Paul Votaw bombarded a mixture of methane, hydrogen, and helium with energetic electrons such as are produced in Uranus's magnetic field. The result: "mysterious reddish Uranian gunk," reported a campus newspaper.

And what was that, exactly? It was easier to make tholins than to determine what exactly they were made of. Sagan likened the mystery to that of the precise composition of coal, still elusive after centuries of study. In one study, he and Khare found, however, that certain bacteria could metabolize tholins. They theorized that their "gunk" might have been the base of the primordial food chain, a literal manna from the heavens.

*   *   *

From 1986 on, Sagan had a new collaborator in grad student Christopher Chyba. Chyba was an American studying mathematical physics at Cambridge University. He switched fields and came to Cornell after Sagan sent him an encouraging letter. Much of his work with Sagan involved a notion that would have seemed crazy only a few years before: the role of comets in the origins of life.

By the early 1980s, some of the Miller-Urey-era ideas about the origins of life were running into trouble. Geological evidence challenged Urey's view that the early Earth had a methane-ammonia atmosphere. The most popular models supposed an atmosphere of nitrogen and carbon dioxide. A mixture of these gases (and water) does *not* produce any appreciable yield of organic molecules.

At the same time, it was becoming apparent that there are plenty of organic molecules in comets and meteorites. New analysis techniques showed, now unequivocally, that there were amino acids of extraterrestrial origin in meteorites. Comet spectra showed organic compounds.

In July 1986, Sagan proposed that Chyba attempt a quantitative analysis of the role of infalling organic compounds from comets and meteorites in the origin of life. It would be interesting to know whether the organic compounds on the early Earth were mostly synthesized on the Earth or came from elsewhere. This suggestion became the foundation of Chyba's doctoral work and a series of articles with Sagan.

The analysis was subtle because comet impacts can destroy organic compounds as well as deliver or create them. A large body hitting the Earth will produce so much heat as to destroy most or all the organic compounds it may contain. Conversely, the shock wave of an impact can synthesize organic compounds (as in Sagan's 1970 shock-synthesis of amino acids)—provided a suitable chemistry exists. A fine rain of meteoric dust can deliver substantial organic compounds as well. Chyba and Sagan tentatively concluded that extraterrestrial organics were likely to be comparable in quantities to those produced on Earth.

A survey of cratering statistics on the moon, Mars, and Mercury showed that all had suffered a "heavy bombardment" of asteroids and comets until about 3.5 billion years ago. (Barren Mercury, long bypassed by Sagan and by NASA, finally had relevance to the origins of life.) This finding implied that the Earth too had suffered the heavy bombardment.

The impact energy of early collisions would have vaporized the oceans and much rock as well. For a short time, the Earth would have had a searing-hot atmosphere of vaporized rock. That would have destroyed any existing organic compounds and any early life. If the Earth experienced several major impacts in its first billion years, it seemed possible that life had begun several times—and was exterminated several times (less one).

This picture challenged the steady upward progression of life implicit in nearly all "creation myths," scientific or otherwise. It was a vision of chaos, of randomness. Life on Earth was a Sisyphus who, after many setbacks to square one, finally made it to the top of the hill—and whose victory can be no more permanent than the lucky streak on which it was founded.

*   *   *

The comet studies led to another claim of the detection of extraterrestrial life. Sagan and Chyba attributed certain infrared spectral features of Halley's comet to grains of organic compounds. In 1988 Fred Hoyle (who like his friend Tommy Gold made a specialty of challenging the conventional wisdom) and N. C. Wickramasinghe reported that the infrared spectra of Halley's comet resembled that of freeze-dried bacteria or viruses. They modestly proposed that the comet was a living ball of germs.

Sagan and Chyba naturally argued that their analysis was simpler and therefore more likely to be correct. Hoyle and Wickramasinghe countered, surely with tongue in cheek, that their Cornell colleagues had fallen victim to the "strongly held cultural prejudice that there is no life outside the Earth."

Edward Teller

Follow-up study of the nuclear winter problem was subject to prejudices of its own. The foot-dragging was not just on the Soviet side. There were only a few American organizations with the talent and computers to attempt a credible three-dimensional model. Most had political reasons for not pursuing nuclear winter. NASA and the National Oceanic and Atmospheric Administration essentially forbade their employees from working on the subject. Some studies were initiated at the Defense Department's Los Alamos and Livermore labs, but these raised (at the very least) the appearance of a conflict of interest.

Livermore's Edward Teller had no more use for nuclear winter than Sagan did for Teller's pet cause, SDI. Writing in *Nature*, Teller called nuclear winter "dubious rather than robust. . . . Highly speculative theories of worldwide destruction—even of the end of life on earth—used as a call for a particular kind of political action serve neither the good reputation of science nor dispassionate political thought."

Teller's scientific criticisms provided grist for others who disagreed with Sagan's politics. "Nuclear winter isn't science," wrote Brad Sparks in Buckley's *National Review*. "It is propaganda. And the willingness of prominent men of science to debase themselves and their calling for the cheap thrills of political notoriety is a scandal."

However, the logic was often murky. Sparks objected that nuclear winter was nonsense because no such effect had followed Hiroshima and Nagasaki. He seemingly failed to appreciate the three-orders-of-magnitude difference in power between the first fission bombs and contemporary thermonuclear arsenals.

Edward Teller would not make *that* mistake. In the aforementioned *Nature* article, he conceded that "the *possibility* of nuclear winter has not been excluded." He in fact agreed with Sagan on one key point. Even if TTAPS had overestimated the cooling by a factor of 10, Teller wrote, it "could still lead to widespread failure of harvests and famine. . . . The amount of sufferings that would be produced today by the failure of a single year's harvest is horrifying to consider."

Teller's policy recommendations differed from Sagan's, though. Teller wanted to start stockpiling food.

Who's Afraid of Autumn?

All things considered, the freest research climate was to be found in the clear Colorado air of the National Center for Atmospheric Research. In 1986 NCAR's Starley Thompson and Stephen Schneider published a new, three-dimensional model of nuclear cooling. The NCAR study predicted cooling about one-third that of the most often cited TTAPS values. Typically, a 25° C decrease in TTAPS was downsized to an 8° C decrease in NCAR. "We intend to show," wrote Thompson and Schneider, "that on scientific grounds the global apocalyptic predictions of the initial nuclear winter hypothesis can now be relegated to a vanishingly low level of probability."

Why were the new figures so different?

The new model's authors were not "out to get" Sagan or TTAPS. Schneider participated in TTAPS's peer review. The NCAR study had been a long time in the works. A preliminary version of it had been presented at the Conference on the World After Nuclear War. That early study had been described as *supporting* TTAPS.

In all models, the cooling was a highly "nonlinear" effect. Small differences in the initial assumptions could lead to big differences in the predicted cooling. For instance, TTAPS had assumed that most of the smoke would be lofted in firestorm updrafts to the airy realm of cruising jetliners (between five and seven kilometers). Thompson and Schneider assumed that the smoke would mix evenly with the air. Since most of the air is near the ground, most of the smoke was near the ground in their model.

Both "smoke profiles," as they were called, were reasonable guesses. But because TTAPS's high smoke sat above the weather, and above the atmospheric layers responsible for most of the greenhouse effect, it lingered a long time and was effective in blocking the natural greenhouse effect. NCAR's low smoke rained out more quickly and did less damage to the greenhouse effect.

There were other instances where NCAR had adopted "reasonable" figures different from TTAPS's "reasonable" figures, causing the predictions to diverge. In one obvious respect, NCAR was clearly more realistic than TTAPS. Being three-dimensional, the NCAR model treated the continents and oceans close to the way they really existed. NCAR generally found that the oceanic cooling effect (seen in TTAPS's water planet) prevailed over coastal areas and would be felt within the deepest reaches of the continents. Evidently it would take a planet like Mars, without surface water, to experience the deep-freeze conditions of TTAPS's land-planet model.

The new study further underscored how seasonally dependent the cooling was. Should war take place during winter in the Northern Hemisphere (when the hemisphere is not getting much sunlight anyway), the effect would be much less.

With typical cooling about one-third that of TTAPS, Thompson and Schneider thought their predictions were better labeled "nuclear fall." Their study had a dramatic effect on press and public perceptions.

The general note was of relief. Nuclear Armageddon might not be the end of the world after all. TTAPS further became the victim of journalistic imperatives. There had always been a tendency for the press (and Sagan, and Sagan's critics) to focus on worst-case extremes: the cooling could be *as much as* 35° C. When the "story" became that maybe nuclear winter wasn't so bad, journalists flipped their comparatives. Reports of the NCAR study spoke of how the cooling could be *as little as* 5° C. Thompson and Schneider were themselves conscious of this effect. "In an attempt to contrast the most soothing of our statements with the most alarming of Carl Sagan's," they wrote, "some analysts misrepresent both of our positions."

Still, with the news that a new study had downgraded nuclear winter, it was easy for the general public to skim a few paragraphs and turn the page, relieved that *one* of the world's problems had vanished on its own.

Now that it appeared that TTAPS's science might be faulty, many of Sagan's political foes refused to believe that the faults had been honest ones. Buckley's *National Review* branded nuclear winter a case of "scientific lying" and "a fraud from the start." In a scorching 1986 piece for the *Wall Street Journal*, Russell Seitz wrote nuclear winter's obituary. "Cause of death: notorious lack of scientific integrity."

Seitz charged that the "worst-case effects had melted down from a year of arctic darkness to warmer temperatures than the cool months in Palm Beach!" He ridiculed computer modeling (no matter that NCAR was a digital result, too).

> Mere software has been advertised as scientific fact. . . . Nuclear winter never existed outside of a computer, except as a painting commissioned by a P.R. firm. What is being advertised is not science but a pernicious fantasy that strikes at the very foundations of crisis management, one that attempts to transform the Alliance doctrine of flexible response into a dangerous vision. . . . What more destabilizing fantasy than the equation of theater deterrence with a global *Götterdämmerung* could they dream of?

The juiciest part of the Seitz piece was damning quotes from several of the nation's most respected scientists. "It's an absolutely atrocious piece of science," Freeman Dyson was quoted, "but I quite despair of setting the public record straight. Who wants to be accused of being in favor of nuclear war?"

"You know, I really don't think (these) guys know what they're talking about" (Richard Feynman).

Cautioned not to use four-letter words in expressing his feelings about nuclear winter, Washington University's Jonathan Katz was quoted as saying, "Humbug is six."

"Nuclear winter is the worst example of the misrepresentation of science to the public in my memory" (MIT's George Rathjens).

With Alexandrov out of the picture, Seitz quoted an unnamed Russian scientist: "You guys are fools. You can't use mathematical models like these. . . . You're playing with toys." While he seemed to have no problem getting people to trash nuclear winter, Seitz implied that many other people weren't being more vocal "out of fear of being denounced as . . . closet Strangeloves."

*   *   *

In *A Path Where No Man Thought*, Sagan and Turco accused Seitz of invented quotations. While these quotes were obviously chosen to make Seitz's point, I found no evidence that Seitz put anti-TTAPS sentiments in anyone's mouth. At most Seitz might be said to have made people's complex feelings look simple (something all journalists tend to do from time to time).

Freeman Dyson is a case in point. Dyson was a longtime friend of Sagan's. According to the introduction to *A Path Where No Man Thought*, it was Dyson who urged Sagan to do a book on nuclear winter for general audiences. In a 1985 speech in Aberdeen, Scotland, Dyson said he took TTAPS seriously enough that he "spent a few weeks in 1985 trying to make nuclear winter go away. . . . I found, after two weeks of work, that I could not make nuclear winter go away. That is to say, I could not prove the theory wrong." Dyson went away from the experience understanding the theory better and judging it more likely to be true than he had initially.

But in the same speech Dyson *did* call nuclear winter "a sloppy piece of work, full of gaps and unjustified assumptions." He remarked that "nobody wants to be put in the position of saying that, after all, nuclear war may not be so bad."

The core complaint of most scientists who criticized TTAPS was not that it was demonstrably wrong but that its results were too preliminary to be used to formulate defense policy. The "gaps and unjustified assumptions" bothered many intelligent and open-minded people. "I really think they decided beforehand what the conclusion should be," Kathy Rages of NASA

Ames told me, "and then selected their assumptions to lead to this conclusion." As one of Sagan's grad students and a longtime coworker of Pollack's, Rages was closer to the principals than most critics. Her complaint was similar to that sometimes leveled at the Drake equation. When one is forced to estimate a string of multiplied (or exponentiated!) unknowns, it is easy for a bias toward a dramatic result to creep in.

For some, the most troubling "unjustified assumption" was the uniformity of the smoke pall. TTAPS (and NCAR, too) postulated that the smoke would be mixed evenly throughout the air of the Northern Hemisphere. This was another simplifying assumption. In reality, of course, the smoke initially would be concentrated near the burning cities. It would then diffuse. As that happened, the smoke would simultaneously begin to settle and rain out.

It was (and is) hard to be certain which effect would be faster. If the former, then the smoke would spread into an even pall before much of it rained out, and the TTAPS model might be a good approximation. But some climatologists believed that the smoke might rain out faster than it diffused. Temperature differences might create chaotic weather near the smoke-shrouded cities. The smoke cover would remain patchy, allowing sunlight to pass through the gaps and warm the Earth. If that were the case, TTAPS's model would be less reliable.

*   *   *

Sagan quickly rose to TTAPS's defense. He criticized NCAR's own gaps and assumptions point for point—even as he was claiming that NCAR *confirmed* TTAPS.

> In some commentary, these conclusions are said to make the climatic effects of nuclear winter nearly trivial. After all, who's afraid of autumn? In the first place, the difference between 10° C and 20 to 25° C is not a central issue. What matters is any temperature drop of more than a few degrees. These values are sufficiently close to one another to be mutually reinforcing. They are derived from the same physics. Both values represent extreme climatic changes. . . . There is a very real sense in which the "autumn" calculations confirm nuclear winter theory.

Defensive as this may sound, Sagan had a point. NCAR *did* confirm TTAPS's qualitative argument. In scientific terms, there would be no dishonor if an article establishing a new and important phenomenon were to overestimate its magnitude by a factor of 3—not given the uncertainties TTAPS had to work with. TTAPS's two models succeeded in bracketing the results of NCAR's 3D model (obviously, NCAR's cooling was *greater* than the water planet's almost nonexistent cooling and *less* than the land planet's).

NCAR challenged not so much TTAPS's science as the political edifice Sagan had constructed around TTAPS. Sagan's policy recommendations *did* depend sensitively on the magnitude of the cooling. The NCAR study's cooling undermined Sagan's talk of certain catastrophe for first-strike aggressors. If NCAR was right, nuclear cooling could no longer be regarded as a doomsday machine (where doom must above all be *certain*).

The very term "nuclear winter" worked against the kind of graceful retreat that is frequently necessary in science and politics. Sagan balked at "nuclear autumn." Thompson and Schneider said they had no problem with the continued use of "nuclear winter," citing "the extended definition of 'winter' as an event generally inimical to many forms of life." But George Rathjens and Ronald Siegel found these verbal gymnastics reminiscent of *Through the Looking Glass.* They quoted Carroll's Humpty-Dumpty: "When I use a word, it means just what I choose it to mean—neither more nor less."

Sagan continued to maintain that TTAPS's predictions were likely to be more accurate than NCAR's. His main concession to NCAR was to recast some of his arguments in the familiar (for Sagan) terms of needing to take seriously a small risk of a great catastrophe. "An argument can be made for worst-case thinking when the stakes are this high," Sagan wrote, "for precisely the same reason that military strategists routinely plan for the worst that a potential adversary is capable of." He admitted, "We have here a tension between the usual standards of scientific caution and the usual standards of scientific prudence."

Burning Forests

One point on which all were agreed was that more studies were needed. Sagan pressed for funding of relevant studies, and some were done.

Estimates of smoke production were always problematic. They could hardly be pulled from old data on nuclear tests done in the desert, the middle of the ocean, or underground. As a partial remedy, the U.S. and Canadian forest services agreed to set fire to stands of dead trees under conditions that would allow scientists to study what happened to the smoke. In August 1985, the Canadian forest service set ablaze 1,600 acres of dead trees near Chapleau, Ontario. The fire was big enough to create a mushroom cloud. The smoke rose four to six kilometers. That was seen as vindication for TTAPS's smoke profile.

Sagan was less successful in getting studies of the biological effects of nuclear winter. He envisioned large terraria and aquaria, each subjected to a different combination of cold, dark, smoke toxins, radioactivity, and ultraviolet radiation (such as would flood the Earth if bombs damaged the ozone layer). The results would help determine how the conditions would affect agriculture and the environment. The idea failed to interest the Defense Nuclear Agency or the weapons labs.

In 1987 Congress ordered a "comprehensive study" of nuclear war's climatic and biological consequences. By then, however, public opinion had turned against nuclear winter. The Defense Department dragged its feet. In 1988, the department turned in a report *one page long*. In response to complaints that the department had not complied with the intent of Congress, Secretary of Defense Caspar W. Weinberger said that "Nuclear Winter is a hypothesis whose science is not well understood by the scientific community. Assumptions and uncertainty abound in its predictions."

Nuremberg Trial

The Soviet rhetoric was quite different. In an August 18, 1986, TV speech Mikhail Gorbachev said:

> The explosion of even a small part of the existing nuclear arsenal would be a catastrophe, an irreversible catastrophe, and if someone still dares to make a first nuclear strike, he will doom himself to agonizing death, not even from a retaliatory strike, but from the consequences of the explosion of his own warheads.

Was this for real—or another "asymmetry of perception" deal? American pundits were split. The Soviets were willing to put their money where their mouth was. Gorbachev announced a unilateral halt on their nuclear testing. The ball was in America's court.

Both houses of Congress drafted bills to cut off funding for further U.S. nuclear tests. The Reagan administration continued to schedule tests, however. Sagan, and the liberal press, generally blamed this policy on the administration's continued support of the Strategic Defense Initiative. "The problem is the civilians in the White House," Sagan told one reporter. "The White House has been captured by extremists."

Some in Reagan's own party were almost as critical. James Schlesinger and Brent Scowcroft supported a moratorium on testing. Senator Mark Hatfield confessed, "I don't know what kind of a macho game plan we are engaged in."

*   *   *

Sagan was a celebrity guest on a Halley's comet–viewing cruise in the South Pacific. He brought along Annie and the Grinspoons. During the cruise, Lester mentioned that a friend of his was planning to protest the nuclear tests by trespassing at the Nevada Test Site. He would probably be arrested. Lester intended to go himself. He asked if Carl and Annie would want to participate.

Annie was all for going. Carl was less sure he wanted to get mixed up in it. He consented only to tag along as a "support person" for Annie and Lester. That meant he would make sure they were all right and promptly bail them out of jail.

"Trespassing on a nuclear test site" is neither so dramatic nor dangerous as it sounds. The test explosions vaporize a huge sphere of rock about 700 feet beneath the desert floor. Over time subsidence of the desert creates football field–sized craters marking where tests have occurred. The tests are designed so that no radiation is released on the surface, and only once—the "Banberry Event" in 1970—did a significant leak occur. One industrial lessee called the test site "probably the safest place in the whole United States."

The protesters collected at a place called Mercury, sixty-five miles northwest of Las Vegas. It is little more than a collection of trailers serving as base camp for the site. One may normally drive all the way to the test site's guard gate without being stopped. In the mid-1980s, protesters were a common and generally tolerated sight. It was, literally, tough to get arrested.

The demonstration went off about as planned. It did not get much media attention. This was not the first time there had been a protest, and the press wasn't crazy about sending cameras and talent to a remote and hot locale. Grinspoon and Druyan were arrested and put in a stifling hot police van (the temperature felt about 115° F). Carl came to their aid with a big bottle of Coca-Cola (also at about 115° F). The instant Carl broke the lid's twist-off seal, the bottle erupted, showering everyone with warm, sticky cola.

After this experience, Carl decided that he would be willing to be arrested. A new tactic was called for, though. He, Annie, and Lester decided that it might be easier to get media coverage of a *trial* than a protest. They planned a "Nuremberg trial." Carl would get arrested and be tried. He would take the stand and speak eloquently in his defense, advancing simple, devastating arguments that would win over the jury.

That was the idea, anyway. Sagan convinced McDonald's heiress Joan

Kroc to finance some of the organizational costs—for it was now a big project. Activist and former attorney general Ramsey Clarke agreed to defend them. Meeting with Carl and Annie, Clarke pulled a small leaflet out of his pocket. On it was printed the Bill of Rights. They liked the cut of his jib. Clarke spoke of calling a roster of expert witnesses: top military brass, nuclear activists, specialists in international law.

They set a date of September 30, 1986, for the protest. About 550 people showed up, many from the American Public Health Association. Sagan gave an off-the-cuff talk. In the middle of the speech, a test explosion went off. There was not so much as a rumble. A seismograph informed them of the test. Police moved in and arrested 139 people. Both Carl and Annie were booked for criminal trespass.

Sagan's arrest was still not the stuff of a media frenzy. It rated a paragraph in *Time* magazine—in the "Milestones" section under news of Marie Osmond's engagement. Trial was scheduled for January. Several days before the court date, the district attorney dropped all charges. Sagan was told it was because the government couldn't identify the people arrested. He volunteered to identify *himself*. The DA wasn't interested.

*   *   *

The Soviet Union was now irked that the United States was not following its lead. It announced that it would end its moratorium on testing, effective the next time the United States tested a nuclear device. Undeterred, the United States announced another test for February 5, 1987.

Sagan and Druyan planned another, bigger demonstration for that date. They convinced a host of notables to show up, among them Marvin Minsky, "Pentagon Papers" activist Daniel Ellsberg, and a substantial Hollywood contingent (Martin Sheen, Kris Kristofferson, Robert Blake). This time the administration demonstrated some media savvy of its own. The Energy Department detonated its bomb two days early, robbing the protest of its intended set piece.

The show went on. This time the media were there in force. The demonstration finally got its fifteen minutes of attention, albeit much of it at the *Entertainment Tonight* level of political analysis. Six members of Congress showed up and spoke in favor of the protest. Representative Patricia Schroeder of Colorado vowed not to let Reagan run a "Rambo foreign policy." However, Schroeder and the other congresspeople decamped before the arrests began.

Nye County police booked 438 people, a large number for a county with fewer than 18,000 residents. Sagan was arrested for the second time, Druyan for the third. Once again, the powers that be realized that nothing would be gained by prosecuting celebrities for acts of conscience. The charges against the Sagans and everyone else were dropped. There was no Nuremberg trial.

Reagan in the Kremlin

Late 1987 found Sagan in Moscow for the thirtieth anniversary of Sputnik. He again fell seriously ill and spent several days in the Kremlin Hospital. For a foreigner to be treated in the Kremlin was a rare distinction, so much so that one news organization tried to get Annie to take a spy camera inside. She refused.

Shklovskii's prediction aside, things were starting to change in the Soviet Union. In June 1988, Reagan met with Gorbachev in Moscow. During Reagan's visit, Gorbachev took Reagan on a walking tour of the Kremlin yard. He showed him the historic Czar Cannon, a monument of sixteenth-century Russian engineering. Using that as a segue to contemporary achievement, Gorbachev asked, "Why don't we send a mission to Mars?"

Reagan nodded warmly.

A piloted mission to Mars was to have been the swan song of the Soviet space program. Two coupled Energia boosters had been built. The boosters were to have been sent into low-Earth orbit, then nuclear propulsion would take them to Mars. After the fashion of Apollo, a lander would set down on the Martian surface. Humans would set foot on the red planet, collect samples of rock and soil, and return to Earth.

It would all be phenomenally expensive, more than the Soviets or any one nation could afford. Sagan's talk of a joint mission had been widely endorsed by the Soviet scientific establishment.

That evening, Reagan and Gorbachev attended a state dinner in the Kremlin. Gorbachev spotted physicist Roald Sagdeev and pulled him over to meet Reagan. "This is the man who is promoting this mission to Mars," he said. Gorbachev added, "You know who in America is doing the same, who is his closest friend?"

Reagan's eyes lighted up. Sagdeev was about to chime in and say that, yes, his good American friend General James Abrahamson favored a joint Mars mission.

Gorbachev triumphantly answered his own question: "Carl Sagan."

Sagdeev saw something click the wrong way in Reagan's expression. It was the end of the joint mission.

No one complains that Sagan's first publications were "wrong" by 150° K (270° F!). The point is, Sagan was *conceptually* right about Venus, and he was willing to revise his figures as new evidence demanded.

With nuclear winter, too, the TTAPS group was qualitatively right and quantitatively wrong in their first publication—and then they revised as new data became available. What makes nuclear winter *different* is that the error-correcting mechanism of science was played out in the political arena. The scaling back of nuclear winter had a political dimension quite unlike most scientific work.

The public still tends to regard science as a dispassionate affair in which scientists' hopes, preconceptions, and egos are irrelevant, and in which the "right answers" are already in the backs of the science books. Many therefore saw the downsizing of nuclear winter as a betrayal, rather than as scientific business as usual.

*   *   *

It is worth asking what we *want* from a politically engaged scientist. There are many who would say that the ideal "political scientist" is *a*political, a dispassionate dispenser of incontestable "facts." There *are* cases where the science is so well established that one can and should expect that. *Any* reasonable scientist must advise against funding a perpetual-motion machine; against setting pi equal to 3 by legislative mandate. But so much of the politically sensitive science concerning us today is a work in progress. It is likely to involve complex and chaotic feedback loops of technology and environment. Answers may come slowly, and reasonable minds may differ through political administrations.

Not many intelligent people are apolitical. We need to be sophisticated enough to accept that political scientists will have political agendas—and to examine especially critically any scientific claims (such as nuclear winter) that advance the scientists' own political views.

One possible reaction to nuclear winter is that Sagan should have delayed pressing his political case. It proved impossible to compress the process of scientific criticism and response into a four-day junket. Sagan was fighting the scientific battles of nuclear winter even as he was fighting the political battles. If nuclear winter had been "normal science," as Norman Horowitz might have said, the scientific debate would have been conducted out of the spotlight, and in the end, the scientists would have come out and told everyone the right answer. Then it might have been easier to wield such political leverage as was justified.

But Sagan believed that the urgency was justified by the nature of the problem: a world in which nuclear war might break out before the scientific uncertainties could be contained. There will inevitably be ongoing scientific investigations whose policy implications cannot be deferred. In that sense, nuclear winter is not so much the fluke it may appear. The real question is how we as a society should deal with doomsaying scientists of conscience. We hear gloomy predictions a lot.

With his sometimes unnerving insight, Sagan addressed this very point in a January 1990 speech to the American Association of Physics Teachers. Though the speech is about the parallel global warming controversy, it surely drew on Sagan's frustrations with nuclear winter.

Sagan said that we must acknowledge the necessity of steering a middle course between blanket denial and unbridled paranoia. It is absurd to believe *every* prediction of doom. It is ruinous to believe *none*. It must further be recognized that few scientific predictions are infinitely precise or infinitely certain. This must not in itself be taken as an excuse for failing to act. Sagan concluded that only the error-correcting mechanism of science is a valid guide in making policy. That generally takes time.

*   *   *

To this day, the "error bars" around nuclear winter (and *refutations* of nuclear winter) remain distressingly large. The best case is the agricultural one. Today's most widely adopted values for the magnitude of cooling following a baseline war are more than sufficient to cripple agriculture in the Northern Hemisphere. As Sagan and Turco argue in *A Path Where No Man Thought*, the world's population is in disequilibrium with the planet that supports it. Billions of people exist only because of modern agriculture and a global economy that transports foods, fuel, and spare parts around the world.

In the largest sense, nuclear winter can be read as an expression of Sagan's philosophy of risk. Denial is not just the name of a river in Africa, Sagan liked to say. Honed by natural selection, the denial of remote risks has been built into most people's makeup. Maybe we would be unable to function were we *too* aware of all the bad things that could happen. Ignoring risks does not make them go away, of course. Every now and then one of the risks we ignore kills someone. Individual tragedies scarcely budge the grand economy of natural selection. But we live in a unique age. For the first time in history, our technology is making it possible for things to go wrong that could wipe out the human species. Natural selection has not prepared us for the type of global risks that would suspend natural selection itself. Faced with such risks, a more global and so-called paranoid stance might properly apply.

Politically, the weakness of Sagan's nuclear winter crusade was that the science was more effective in underscoring what should have always been obvious—that we must do everything we possibly can to prevent a nuclear war—than in suggesting a means toward that end in a world ruled by alpha males. The science did not unequivocally endorse the disarmament plans Sagan championed. It was always possible to co-opt nuclear winter to the status quo, as the Reagan administration did.

Nevertheless, Sagan's talk of the end of the world *did* change thinking a good deal more than one strategist thought possible. It further seems to have confounded the pundits by having a more decisive effect in the Kremlin than in the Pentagon. By asking questions that no one else did, Sagan (and Turco, Toon, Ackerman, and Pollack) played a key role in the global team effort that led to the end of the cold war.

Pollack once confided to Sagan that his family had told him that, with nuclear winter, he had *finally* done something useful. According to Druyan, Sagan rated his efforts in preventing nuclear war as the body of work of which he was proudest.

With his global viewpoint, Sagan probably would be the first to point out that history is long and memories short. At moments in the history of warfare, the crossbow, dynamite, World War I, the atomic bomb, and the hydrogen bomb (exclusive of climatic effects) have been viewed as so horrific as to make future war unthinkable. Sooner than most imagined, people accepted apocalypse, were thinking and doing the unthinkable. In such melancholy history was to be found the roots of Sagan's advocacy—and of Shklovskii's cosmic pessimism.

Things That Go Bump in the Night

Or was Shklovskii wrong? Every now and then it looked that way—momentarily—as the Harvard META dish scanned the heavens. One day, the META software detected a powerful narrowband 1420 MHz burst among the spectrum of background noise.

When Sagan got the data, he noticed that the "signal" (?) was coming from the direction of the center of the Galaxy. The Earth is on the Galaxy's outskirts. Most of the Galaxy's stars (and most of its extraterrestrial civilizations?) cluster in a concentration at the center. Sagan dashed down a few quick calculations. He concluded that the chance of an earthbound source happening to be located in precisely that direction was less than 1 percent. A chill ran down his spine.

In due course Paul Horowitz turned the telescope back to where the "signal" had come from. It was gone. Whatever it was, it was never detected again.

There were other "candidate events," or "things that go bump in the night," as Sagan and Horowitz termed these narrowband spikes. Each was as tantalizing as the first.

You may wonder how momentary glitches could be even generally suggestive of an intelligent signal. There were several reasons. All radio telescope observations are subject to random noise. It was easy to show that the strongest "candidate events" were too strong to be mere noise. The "events" were narrowband, existing on a single frequency. Like a perfect right angle, a narrowband signal is held to be characteristically artificial. All known natural radio sources are broadband, occupying a wide range of radio frequencies. But for someone trying to send a message across the galaxy, a narrowband signal is far more energy efficient. There is no point broadcasting on *all* frequencies when one will suffice.

But why would the signal switch off just after it was observed? Sagan and Horowitz played with many ideas. Horowitz worried about processor errors. A cosmic ray may occasionally zap a memory chip, flipping a zero to a one. The same thing is liable to happen to a desktop PC every now and then. But the META software was specifically designed to look for anything unusual, flag it, and archive it. META's software filters were able to screen out most errors, but others might manage to jump through all the hoops and therefore seem to be significant. Reobservation would then fail because there was never a signal in the first place (and lightning, or rather a cosmic ray, is unlikely to strike the same bit twice).

There was or appeared to be one argument against this scenario. Sagan found that the five strongest events were close to the plane of the galaxy. Two of the five were in Sagittarius, the constellation whose teapot shape marks the direction of the center of the galaxy. That would fit in with the idea that they were true signals from extraterrestrials.

Thin gases between the stars play tricks on the propagation of radio waves, such as those produced by pulsars. The effect is called "scintillation." It is analogous to the way that the Earth's much thicker atmosphere causes stars to twinkle. Sagan realized that scintillation would similarly affect artificial radio signals. In particular, scintillation might occasionally amplify a faint signal above the threshold of detectability. The momentary amplification would be detectable—and then the signal would dip back to its normal level, too weak to be picked up. When the telescope was turned back to the location, it would likely find nothing.

*   *   *

Horowitz had originally intended to publish the META results with himself as sole author. Sagan offered so many ideas and questions after reading Horowitz's early drafts that the article became a collaboration. Horowitz found that collaborating with Sagan meant laying in ample supplies of fax paper. Carl Sagan telephoned, his family told Horowitz one evening. He left a message: *make sure the fax machine is turned on.*

Days, nights, and weekends, Horowitz's fax would start its shrill chattering . . . Sagan had a new draft. Horowitz would come home to find the machine buried in curly scrolls of paper. Gathering the paper up, he would spot the error light: out of paper. A fresh roll installed, more wordage would spew out.

Great Martian Chase

One thing the Massachusetts dish could *not* do was to probe far into the southern sky. In fact, virtually all SETI had been conducted from midnorthern latitudes. What if there was only *one* currently detectable signal in the sky, and it happened to be in the Southern Hemisphere? Sagan was concerned about that. At his urging, the Planetary Society raised $150,000 from members to set up a second dish in the Southern Hemisphere. A duplicate META receiver was installed at a ninety-eight-foot dish, thirty miles southeast of Buenos Aires at the Institute of Radioastronomy. On Columbus Day, 1990, the second META dish turned to the Southern Cross and began operation. Announced Sagan, "You would have to be made of wood not to be interested in knowing whether we're alone in the universe."

Not everyone shared that enthusiasm. Earlier that year, Rhode Island congressman Ronald Machtley moved to kill NASA's modest SETI funding. "We have no, and I repeat no scientific evidence that there is anything beyond our galaxy," Machtley told Congress. "If, in fact, there is a super-intelligent form of life out there, might it be easier just to listen and let them call us?" (This, of course, is what the people at NASA were intending to do!)

Machtley's bill was defeated, but in 1994 Nevada senator Richard Bryan succeeded in ending "the Great Martian Chase," as he called it. This did not affect privately funded efforts like META, but it did kick some of SETI's top talent out of NASA Ames. Jill Tarter, Frank Drake, and others set up shop nearby, in the nonprofit SETI Institute funded largely by the new money of Silicon Valley. Supporters included William R. Hewlett and David Packard; Intel's Gordon Moore; and Microsoft cofounder Paul Allen.

*   *   *

It was bad Martian-chasing season all around. In August 1993, NASA's billion-dollar Mars Observer spacecraft failed before it entered Mars orbit. It was the first Mars mission in seventeen years, and Sagan would not live to see another.

Despite such defeats, Sagan's influence at NASA was probably never greater than in the early 1990s. In 1992 Dan Goldin became NASA administrator with a mandate to revitalize the agency. Goldin relied on Sagan's advice extensively. Sagan was an early advocate of sending multiple, low-cost missions to Mars rather than betting everything on one expensive mission (the soundness of that advice was underscored by Observer's failure). Sagan galvanized the relatively moribund field of exobiology—or astrobiology as it is often called now. He convinced Goldin to draw plans for a NASA-funded astrobiology institute, a think tank that would explore such problems as how to search for life in what may be the ice-shackled oceans of Jupiter's moon Europa.

Ultimately, neither META dish found a repeatable signal. There is, Horowitz admits, a slightly "schizophrenic quality" to the 1993 article reporting the results. Horowitz was happy enough to say they had found nothing. Sagan insisted on giving a certain emphasis to the "things that go bump in the night." He plotted the events on a map of the galaxy, showing the provocative concentration near the galactic plane. The clustering was not strongly significant, being based on a few events and a somewhat arbitrary choice of threshold.

What *was* clear was that there were no strong, steady extraterrestrial signals of the type they were looking for. This time Sagan was more willing to explore the consequences of a negative result than he had been at Arecibo. If there were Type III supercivilizations anywhere in the universe, or Type II anywhere in our galactic neighborhood, META ought to have found them—no matter where they were in the sky.

For weaker and more plausible broadcasts, the search was far from definitive. A Type I civilization that managed to broadcast with a power equal to that of all the sunlight falling on its planet (by most standards, still a fantastic notion) would be detectable from only about 2,100 light-years away. In comparison, the "optimistic" Green Bank estimates had put the nearest civilizations anywhere from a few hundred to 10,000 light-years distant. Weaker signals would have to be closer yet. In that sense META had only scratched the surface.

Remodeling

In 1991 Annie gave birth to Carl's fifth and last child, Samuel Democritus Druyan Sagan. Carl had had a child in each of the last five decades of the twentieth century.

The new baby inspired a massive remodeling project. The couple decided that a house with a 200-foot sheer drop was not the best place to raise an inquisitive toddler. They chose to move the family into the lakeside home, the one that Carl had built with Linda. Then they would renovate Sphinx House as their offices.

They contacted about thirty architects. None seemed right. The Sagans hated "postmodern gewgaws," and the project of updating a retro/*faux* Egyptian temple seemed to bring out the postmodernism in architects. A friend of theirs in Cornell's architecture department recommended they talk to the husband-and-wife architectural team of Guillaume Jullian de la Fuente and Ann Pendleton-Jullian. Jullian de la Fuente, known as Jullian, was a classic modernist who had worked with Le Corbusier.

The architects proposed to cut new skylights and windows in the temple's solid walls. The contemporary house on the property had mushrooms growing in the showers. It was in such bad shape that the architects planned to demolish it and build an entirely new home, cantilevered like Aladdin's carpet, as Jullian put it, over the gorge. The Sagans approved the work, and it took the better part of three years to complete.

Sphinx House thereby became one of the world's more spectacular private offices. Carl called it the "Thinking House." The design was tailored to the Sagans' work habits. Carl liked to pace the floor as he thought and dictated, so the interior was kept clear of obstructions. On the west wall, a pivoting glass door opens perilously out into space, revealing a view of Lake Cayuga.

The property has a number of subtle gimmicks. When Ithaca's weather cooperates, a rhomboid of light on the floor marks the passing hours like a sundial. The light comes from a skylight painted yellow, red, and green to match the Sagans' Miró paintings. There is also an environmental kaleidoscope, a skylight painted Miró red, green, and yellow that reflects its hues chaotically in the bathroom mirrors. When finished, the house rated a photo feature in *Architectural Digest*. Jullian told the magazine that "Carl and Ann understand that architecture is as much about the fabrication of poetical facts as it is about building."

It was a place for work, not entertainment. There were family members and close friends who never saw the house's interior. These interior spaces were designed for cocoonlike privacy. Carl and Annie were spatially proximate yet would not see each other as they worked. There was a stereo but no TV, and a phone that almost never rang. Only one person had the number, and it was to be used only for emergencies.

Genealogy

Meanwhile, the children were raised in the lakeside home. Carl and Annie disavowed corporal punishment in favor of logic and love. The inevitable tantrums were tolerantly waited out, even in restaurants or other people's homes. Such behavior caused a few outsiders to suggest the kids could have used, well, if not a good slap then a stronger sense of discipline. This seems to have been Ted Turner's opinion. He once called Alexandra a brat, causing her parents to storm out of his house.

As a child living in a house with a big yard, Sasha (Alexandra's nickname) wanted pets. That was a problem because Annie had an allergy to fur. Mammals were out. Instead, they kept two Chinese box turtles, Beverly and Tiny.

Carl's grown sons each had unconventional careers. After high school, Jeremy went into the burgeoning software industry. He seemed to have inherited the musical talent latent in the Sagan line, for he wrote a popular program used by music composers. After achieving that success in the business world, he went back to Cornell in the mid-1990s to get a degree. While there, he saw his father more regularly than he had for most of his childhood.

To his father's alarm, Nick dropped out of school in Los Angeles, unsure what he wanted to do with his life. What turned out to be an epiphany was Linda's suggestion that he take a look at some videos of Patrick McGoohan's 1960s spy series, *The Prisoner*. The show convinced Nick that television writing did not necessarily have to be moronic. He enrolled in community college, then transferred to UCLA's competitive TV and film school.

One of the scripts that Nick wrote for a class assignment was so promising that a professor sent it to an agent. This led to a job writing for *Star Trek: The Next Generation*. Nick watched the first episode he wrote with Carl and Annie, half expecting his father to pick it apart. Carl found no fault, scientific or otherwise, repeatedly insisting the episode was brilliant.

Carl's relationship with his third set of in-laws was as seemingly outside the usual scheme of things as his third marriage itself. After Harry Druyan retired, he and Pearl moved up to Ithaca, right next door to Carl and Annie's home. For many, the prospect would be terrifying. But the Sagans happily had the Druyans over for dinner three times a week. After dinner, they would talk into the night, Carl sometimes comfortably ensconced in a window seat, his arm around his father-in-law.

*   *   *

By age fifty-seven, Sagan was in a retrospective mood. He and Annie hosted a "genealogical weekend" at their home. It was a small family reunion with a twist. No sooner had the guests assembled than Carl announced that he had brought them there for a purpose. They were going to solve a mystery.

Sagan produced a photocopy of his mother's birth certificate. It listed "Anne Cohen" as Rachel's mother. No one in the family had ever heard of this woman. Rachel's mother was, or had been supposed to be, Chaya Klein. Carl therefore wanted to know whether his mother had been born out of wedlock.

Sagan discussed his mother's possible illegitimacy as if it were a promising new scientific theory. There was evidence pro and con. One exhibit was Tobi Gruber's birth certificate. It listed Chaya Klein as mother. Then there was the murky character of Sagan's grandfather. If Leib Gruber had killed a man in Sasov, how chaste would he have been in the New World, an ocean away from his legal wife?

Two bits of evidence led the family to conclude that Rachel *was* Tobi's legitimate sister. In family photos, Rachel and Tobi looked extremely similar throughout their lives, implying that they were sisters and not just half sisters. Another point was the coincidence that the surname of the mystery woman, Cohen, was the maiden name of Chaya's mother. Sagan theorized that a doctor or functionary had asked, "Who is the mother?" Chaya, who couldn't have known much English, might have given *her* mother's name rather than her own.

National Academy

In 1992 Sagan and Druyan published their second fully collaborative book. *Shadows of Forgotten Ancestors* offered an evolutionary perspective on such human attributes as altruism and anger; fear of strangers and submission to authority. According to Druyan, it was probably Sagan's favorite book.

By 1992, Sagan had eighteen honorary doctorates and over sixty awards or medals. He had a Pulitzer and three Emmys; the John F. Kennedy Astronautics Award (1983), NASA Medals for Exceptional Scientific Achievement (1972) and Distinguished Public Service (1977 and 1981), and the Prix Galabert (1973); the Joseph Priestley Award (1975), the Glenn Seaborg Prize (1981), the Leo Szilard Award (1985), the Konstantin Tsiolkovsky Medal (1987), and the Oersted Medal (1990); the John Campbell, Jr., Memorial Award (1974) and the Arthur C. Clarke Award (1984); the Humanist of the Year Award (1981), the United Nations Environmental Programme Medal (1984), and the Honda Prize (1985). A high school wing (of Rahway High) and an asteroid were named after Sagan.

What Sagan *didn't* have was membership in the National Academy of Sciences. Signed into being by President Abraham Lincoln, the National Academy is America's most prestigious club for scientists. The academy has about 2,000 members, about seventy of them astronomers. Had you, in 1992, asked anyone, from a scientist to the neighborhood dry cleaner, to name the top living astronomers, it is a safe bet that (a) few could come up with anywhere near seventy names and (b) Carl Sagan would be among those they *would* name.

Of course, academy membership is not based on name recognition but on somewhat subjective measures of achievement. The academy has several means of nominating new members. In the most usual method, members of a particular discipline nominate scientists in their field. It is also possible for an academy member to organize a special nominating committee to sponsor a worthy scientist. This method is most often used when a scientist's work "falls between the cracks." That described Sagan, whose research bridged astronomy, biology, chemistry, and earth sciences, and whose career bridged research, popularization, and political activism.

Stanley Miller, then at the University of California, San Diego, organized a special committee to nominate Sagan. Without Sagan's knowledge, Miller approached most of Sagan's associates in the academy to sign the nominating petition.

A few refused. "I wouldn't do it because I didn't know anything that Carl had done that deserved that," Norman Horowitz said. "He never really *did* any science—he never discovered anything that's attached to his name." MIT's Bernard Burke had a similar reaction.

Nonetheless, Miller collected an impressive list of signatures, including a number of Nobel laureates. He submitted this petition along with a description of Sagan's scientific work to the academy. This put Sagan on a list of nominees for 1992 induction.

The academy organization screens the nominees, occasionally rejecting a candidate who seems unqualified. The names are then placed on a ballot mailed to all members of the academy. Members vote and return the ballots by mail. The sixty nominees who win the most votes (in the 1992 voting) are elected.

Sagan came in about fiftieth in the voting. Miller was a bit surprised at that lukewarm showing. Still, Sagan comfortably made the cut.

*   *   *

Academy bylaws allow newly elected members to be challenged at its meeting. This is a ritual formula akin to the wedding ceremony's "speak now or forever hold your peace." It is not expected to be invoked much. One academy member recalled only two successful challenges during the past twenty years, a period in which more than 1,000 scientists were inducted. Sagan was one of the two.

When there *is* a challenge, an open debate is held at the meeting. At the April 28 meeting, Sagan, (who was not present) was a polarizing force. Most of the astronomers (including Chandrasekhar) and many biologists supported him. But a few belittled even Sagan's work on Venus. Worse, many interpreted Sagan's candidacy as a referendum on whether popularizers should be admitted. This was exactly what Miller had hoped to avoid. (His petition hewed to Sagan's scientific achievements. He did *not* press the arguable but murkier case that Sagan's writing and TV work were worthy of consideration.)

One Nobel laureate got up and told of watching *Cosmos* with his young son. He felt it *was* relevant to consider Sagan's popularization career. Texas A&M chemist Albert Cotton took dead aim on the popularization issue. He judged popularization to be oversimplification—symptomatic of an inadequacy in *doing* science. There were nods of approval. Rosalyn Yalow, the Nobel-laureate medical physicist, shook her head, vowing, "Never, never." One foe said that the fact that Carl Sagan had even gotten on the ballot demonstrated how "dangerous" it was to allow open nominations. (" 'Dangerous,' like we were throwing bombs," says Miller.)

*   *   *

Some academy members have been admitted for achievements outside the scope of pure science. In a not entirely dissimilar case, Thomas Edison's nomination was contested. Like Sagan, Edison was more famous than most academy members of his day, and his opponents sniped that what he did wasn't science. (Edison got in.)

Academy rules dictate that a second vote be taken after the debate. This time, only those present at the meeting can vote, and the challenged nominee must be reconfirmed by a two-thirds majority. In this challenge vote, Sagan fell short. More than a third of his peers voted to keep him out.

For obvious reasons, no names are released to the press until the new members are confirmed. In 1992 someone leaked news of Sagan's turndown to the press. This changed a private rebuff into a public one. (At about the time the news got out, a poll of readers of *Parade* magazine voted Sagan the smartest man in America.)

*   *   *

There was one associate of Sagan's that Miller *hadn't* asked to sign the nominating petition: Lynn Margulis. Miller had heard the stories about that marriage. He thought it best not to ask. Margulis was present at the meeting. She was astonished at the narrow-mindedness of the people trying to deny

Carl admission. After the meeting, she sent Carl a letter describing the academy debate. She wrote that Albert Cotton's speech

> resonated with every small mind, ugly body, and verbal maladapt present, and that means half the membership. They are jealous of your communication skills, charm, good looks, and outspoken attitude, especially on nuclear winter. With such a high proportion of henpecked conformists I would guess that most probably don't like the three wives and five kids bit. In neo-Darwinian terms you are simply too fit. . . . In summary, you deserved election to the National Academy years ago and still do; it is the worst of human frailties that keeps you out: jealousy.

From the timing of the letter, Sagan suspected its contents. He handed it over to Annie, asking her to read it to him, omitting names. This she did. Carl wrote back to Lynn saying that, of all the letters of support he received, hers meant the most.

*   *   *

In an unusual act of restitution, the academy leadership gave Sagan their Public Welfare Medal in April 1994. Described as the highest award of the academy, it cited Sagan "for his distinguished contributions in the application of science to the public welfare. . . . His ability to capture the imagination of millions and to explain difficult concepts in understandable terms is a magnificent achievement."

Shortly before Sagan's death, the National Academy of Sciences organized a meeting on communicating science with the public. Sagan naturally was there. During a group discussion, biologist Jared Diamond remarked on the "disturbing paradox" that the scientists who communicated best with the public were often objects of scorn to their colleagues.

Sagan signaled that he wanted to speak.

The room fell silent. Diamond sensed everyone holding their breath. Sagan said that, yes, he had taken flak from his colleagues. But—and he paused, as if searching for the proper words—the disadvantages had not been serious. He said his piece and sat down, without mentioning the rejection.

Freak Accident

Sagan's unique approach to science worked because he was able to recruit and inspire talented people whose skills complemented his own.

One of these people was W. Reid Thompson. Thompson ran Sagan's lab on a day-to-day basis. Many of Sagan's most important articles on the chemistry of Titan, Triton, and the outer planets were done with Thompson (who often got first billing).

Thompson was a soft-spoken man from Kentucky. Trained as a chemist, he was drawn to the challenge of investigating the chemistry of the planets. True to his rural upbringing, Thompson believed that UFOs were extraterrestrial spaceships. In his disputations with Sagan on this point, Thompson held that the aliens were like our own anthropologists, furtively limiting contact to avoid threatening our culture.

In fall 1993, Thompson was diagnosed with lung cancer. This news came as a shock to Sagan and everyone in the lab. Thompson was just over forty, at the peak of his talents, and on the verge of yet-greater achievements. He was eagerly anticipating the Galileo data from Jupiter.

Thompson told friends he might lose one lung but had every expectation of beating the disease. These hopes were dashed when surgeons discovered that the cancer had metastasized. He had bone cancer as well. It was inoperable.

*   *   *

This was not the only tragedy in Sagan's immediate circle. Jim Pollack had chordoma, a rare form of spinal cancer. Sagan delegated Ray Reynolds of NASA Ames to inform him when it seemed Pollack was near death, so he could fly out to California to see him one last time. The plan failed. One June day in 1994, Pollack was wracked with pain but no worse than he had been. A few days later, he was dead at the age of fifty-five.

Sagan was profoundly affected. Seeing a grad student die was almost like losing a child, something counter to the normal scheme of things.

Sagan's own health could be worrisome. One winter day in the Ithaca airport parking lot, he slipped on a patch of ice. He fell and began bleeding profusely. He was taken to a hospital. The injury did not seem to be serious. Yet there was so much blood on his coat that he had to throw it away.

These bleeding problems were chronic. "Minor" injuries or "routine" surgery always seemed liable to escalate into something life-threatening. Lester Grinspoon convinced Sagan to get a battery of tests. The results were inconclusive. One bright note, given all the egg salad sandwiches, was that Sagan's aorta was in magnificent shape. There were more tests that could be done, but Sagan lost interest. The incident was put down to a freak accident.

Again with the Alien Abductions

One day Lester Grinspoon had sushi with Harvard psychiatrist John Mack. Mack mentioned that he was thinking of focusing on a new field of study: people who had been abducted by extraterrestrials. He wanted Grinspoon's reaction.

Grinspoon said it might be interesting because alien abduction was almost a new religion forming in our own time. It would be instructive to study the way these beliefs were being shaped and transmitted.

No, Mack said, you don't understand. These abductions really happened. He sketched the stories of several of the people who had been seeing him since about 1990. Mack said he had his doubts, too—at first.

"Wait until next time Carl's in town," Grinspoon told Mack. "You, and I, and Carl will sit down and have a talk."

John Mack had several things in common with Sagan. Mack won a Pulitzer Prize the year before Sagan did. It was for *A Prince of Our Disorder*, a biography of T. E. Lawrence (a figure who intrigued Sagan as well). Like Sagan, Mack was a liberal activist on environmental and antiwar issues. Unlike Sagan, Mack really believed that extraterrestrials were abducting humans. Also unlike Sagan, Mack had been granted tenure at Harvard.

The two-hour meeting was part conversation, part debate, and part "intervention." Sagan and Grinspoon had both taken high-risk career moves in their time, but they felt *this* was crazy. It would *ruin* Mack, they said.

Mack insisted on the heartfelt sincerity of his subjects. He was sure they could not be lying. Sagan and Grinspoon countered that Betty and Barney Hill had been equally compelling (making few points with Mack, who had no reason to disbelieve the Hills' story).

The discreet sexuality of the Hills' encounter had, in some of Mack's cases, taken on S&M overtones. The aliens were now inserting needles in genitals to remove eggs and sperm. They were breeding half-human, half-alien hybrids and piercing skin to insert "implants" suspected to be homing devices. Mack said that one abductee had managed to remove an implant from her head. It looked like a needle or wire.

Grinspoon suggested that Mack give Sagan the implant to have it analyzed. Mack wasn't willing to do that. As the meeting ended, Mack told Grinspoon, "Lester, the problem with you and Carl is, you're too Cartesian."

*   *   *

Mack eventually did take the "implant" to an MIT scientist for analysis. According to Mack, the tests determined it to be "an interestingly twisted fiber consisting of carbon, silicon, oxygen, no nitrogen, and traces of other elements." A nuclear biologist concluded it was not a natural biological formation but might be a manufactured fiber.

Sagan was wrong about one thing: alien abductions did not ruin Mack professionally. While much of Harvard was and is mortified at Mack's beliefs, academic tenure protects his ability to speak out freely. Mack's 1994 book *Abduction: Human Encounters with Aliens* became a best-seller, receiving favorable reviews in major newspapers and landing him on the talk-show circuit. Mack is, like Sagan, truly a man of his time. The unique thing about Mack is his blend of postmodernist philosophy with the cheesiest sort of pop mythology. When Mack considers whether the abductions are "real," he refuses to commit himself too deeply. This stance has met with equal approval on tabloid TV shows and at certain high-powered scholarly conferences.

*   *   *

It was experiences like that that led Carl to write *The Demon-Haunted World*, his manifesto against unreason. The book is dedicated to grandson Tonio. Carl sent Dorion the manuscript for comment. Dorion took issue with a passage where Carl dismissed those "standard postmodern texts, where anything can mean anything." He had a hunch, first of all, his father had not *read* any standard postmodern texts.

Dorion told his father that there was a big difference between the pseudoscience of supermarket tabloids and postmodern critiques of science. He felt Carl was too quick to assume the latter was merely a high-toned version of the former. Dorion wished Carl would extend the scope of his skepticism to the cultural underpinnings of science itself.

But Carl would have no postmodernism in his house or in his thinking. If he had not read the "standard texts," he was familiar enough with John Mack, who writes in *Abductions*:

> Terms like "abduction," "alien," "happening," and even "reality" itself, need redefinition lest subtle distinctions be lost. In this context, thinking of memory too literally as "true" or "false" may restrict what we can learn about human consciousness from the abduction experience I recount in the pages that follow.

Whether Mack accepts the implications of his own postmodernism is unclear. These caveats are for the most part confined to prefaces, like a Chippendale notch surmounting a more conventional edifice. To Sagan, this solipsism was the most puzzling and even threatening thing about Mack and a certain strain of contemporary thought. To *not care* whether extraterrestrial life was real was beyond Sagan's pale.

Karmic Boomerang

Contact, the movie, had spent a decade in the circles of development hell. Eventually Peter Guber left Warner Brothers to head Sony Pictures. *Contact* remained at Warner.

That meant it needed a new producer. Warner vice president Lucy Fisher studied the various candidates and decided that one of the company's new hires would be perfect: Lynda Obst. Fisher was unaware that Obst had originated the project.

Delighted at this "lovely karmic boomerang," Obst immediately secured Carl and Annie's active participation in the film. Then she began seeing about a new script, hiring James V. Hart and Michael Goldenberg as screenwriters. The biggest challenge was the ending. The novel ends on a clever twist that is too clever for the statistically average moviegoer. Many at Warner Brothers were sure that what the film needed was a *Close Encounters* ending. They wanted flying saucers to hover over the Earth and put on a spectacular light show. And maybe the people could be, well, *awestruck*. One of Goldenberg's scripts gave them just that.

The first choice for director was Steven Spielberg. Not only did it seem to be up his alley, but he had funded the META project. Spielberg, however, said no. Perhaps the script's ending—so similar to *Close Encounters*—gave him déjà vu.

They went to Robert Zemeckis. He thought the script was great "until the last page and a half. And then it had the sky open up and these angelic aliens putting on a light show and I said, 'That's just not going to work.'"

Next on the list was George Miller. Miller had done the *Mad Max* movies and was working on a film about a talking pig called *Babe*. He lived in Australia, didn't use an agent, and was hard to get in touch with. Within weeks Miller expressed interest. Obst decided that Carl and Annie would be the best deal closers. She flew them to Australia to meet with Miller, and he signed on. In 1993, the studio finally gave *Contact* the go-ahead.

*   *   *

Through Carl and Annie, Lester Grinspoon's son, David, met Lynda Obst, now divorced. David and Lynda dated for a while. About 1992, Carl was in Palo Alto for a scientific conference. He met David to go to dinner at the home of psychedelic chemist Sasha Shulgin. On the drive to dinner, Carl said he wanted to talk to Dave about his treatment of Lynda Obst. He pulled out a written list of things David had supposedly done wrong.

From Carl's point of view, this must have been a well-intentioned attempt to help two friends who happened to have been dating. From David's point of view, it was meddling. He told Carl that much of his information was wrong. Among Carl's theses was that David had rejected Obst because she was older. Age shouldn't matter, Carl said—pointing to his own marriage to Annie, who was much younger than he was.

When David got home from the conference, he wrote Carl and Annie an angry letter. "They flipped out," he says. He was thereafter out of their good graces.

When Sagan felt he had been wronged, he could be unyielding. The tales of "excommunications" are so numerous as to suggest that they were "part of a pattern," as David Grinspoon sees it. It would be difficult to overstate the dedication of Shirley Arden to Sagan's many projects over the years. She was out, over what started as a money dispute. Jon Lomberg was out. Even Lester Grinspoon had a falling-out with Carl. He couldn't believe the way Carl and Annie had treated his son.

"You were either in their fold or out of it," says David Grinspoon. "When you were in the fold, it was wonderful and exciting. But if you did or said the wrong thing, then you were out of it."

Sagan Versus Apple Computer

A hint of a querulous nature surfaced in Sagan's public battles with a corporation he thought had wronged him. Apple Computer was readying its Power PC line of desktop computers for release in 1994. In keeping with industry practice, each of three models was designated by a so-called code name: Piltdown Man, Carl Sagan, and Cold Fusion. The Sagan was the midrange model. The story was that Apple hoped to earn "billions and billions" from it.

Apple was not planning to *market* a Carl Sagan computer. The computer was to be sold as the Power Macintosh 7100/70. But the code names were leaked to the press, and Sagan found out about it via e-mail in 1993. He was upset. Product endorsements happened to be a hot button with him.

It's tough to say why. Sagan was the same man who had once had a warehouse full of unsold Cosmospheres. The best clue to his attitude (or at least the way he rationalized what he felt) is some comments in *The Demon-Haunted World*. There he argues with Sagan logic that the notion of buying something because a celebrity endorsed it is inherently absurd. Over the years Sagan had been offered, but had turned down, a number of endorsement contracts.

Sagan fired off a letter telling Apple to cease and desist. Apple responded, saying it would stop using his name.

Then in January 1994, the computer press reported, with evident amusement, that Apple had changed the code name of the computer in question to BHA. When asked what that meant, an engineer is alleged to have replied, "Butt-Head Astronomer."

Sagan sued Apple for libel. Apple's response was to deny that BHA stood for anything. They said the letters were chosen "randomly." (But the low-end Piltdown Man computer was also known as PDM, which did not look so random.) Industry columnists editorialized that it was an honor to have one's name so used. Apple had also appropriated the good names of Charles Lindbergh, George Gershwin, Aaron Copland, and Isaac Newton. Admittedly, those people were long dead—a good thing, too; Newton would have sued Apple's pants off.

In June 1994, Judge Lourdes G. Baird of the U.S. District Court ruled that Sagan, as a public figure, would have to meet a stringent standard of proof in any suit for libel. She added that, with BHA, Apple "was clearly attempting to retaliate in a humorous and satirical way."

In October, Baird dismissed the entire suit. She wrote archly that "there can be no question that the use of the figurative term 'Butt-Head' negates the impression that Defendant was seriously implying an assertion of fact. It strains reason to conclude that Defendant was attempting to criticize Plaintiff's reputation or competency as an astronomer. One does not seriously attack the expertise of a scientist using the undefined phrase 'butt-head.' "

*   *   *

At that time, "Butt-Head" most likely called to mind one of the adolescent principals of TV's *Beavis and Butthead*. That series, along with *The Simpsons*, was the subject of Sagan family controversy. Carl regarded both shows as symptoms of the "dumbing down" of America. The younger Sagans disagreed. Nick tried to convince his father that the shows were, for the most part, intelligently written programs whose protagonists were *not* being presented as role models—Lisa Simpson aside. Sasha, who was taken with *The Simpsons*, hit on the right tactic. She told her father that *he* had said that evidence was what counted. He should not make up his mind about *The Simpsons* until he had seen the show. Carl agreed to watch it. He liked it, admitted he was wrong, and began watching reruns every night after the news.

The "I Touched Carl Sagan" Contest

As the fall 1994 academic year began, the *Cornell Review* announced the "I Touched Carl Sagan Contest." A six-pack of beer and a free subscription were offered to the first undergraduate "actually making physical contact with Dr. Sagan."

> The "I Touched Carl Sagan" Contest is only open to undergraduate students studying at Cornell University, including students enrolled at other colleges and universities who are currently studying at Cornell, not directly affiliated with the astronomy major or the Building of Space Sciences. This means the contest is closed to:
> • Undergraduates employed in the Building of Space Sciences
> • All graduate students (who shouldn't be wasting time reading the *Review*, anyway)
> • Mrs. Sagan
> Written entries must be of at least 500 words and must be postmarked no later than April 8, 1995.

The *Review* was the conservative newspaper on campus. Famously liberal Sagan was a natural target. The gibe at what was held to be Sagan's Garbo-like inaccessibility hit home with students of all political stripes. "Flashing a name like Carl Sagan to incoming freshmen is a sort of a cruel hoax," explained David Curran, the *Review*'s production manager, who conceived the contest.

Yervant Terzian submitted a facetious entry, which was published under his own name and title. Cornell freshman Dae Young Lee had a friend snap his picture as Sagan unsuspectingly signed an autograph for him. This was judged inadequate proof as it did not appear to show Lee touching Sagan. The winner was declared to be another freshman, Joe Novak, who submitted a photograph of himself standing to the side of Sagan and tapping him on the back (so Novak claimed, though this was not visible in the photograph, either).

*   *   *

Matt T. Stover, a humor columnist for the *Cornell Daily News*, took the contest as an occasion to let Sagan have it with both barrels. Instead of an "I Touched Carl Sagan Contest," Stover suggested, they should try to run over Sagan with a car. Also taking him to task for the Apple lawsuit, Stover called Sagan "the most pompous man on campus" and "an arrogant

egghead who deserves to ranked with such degenerates as Butt-Head."
Stover wrote:

> He's a two-bit headcase with an ego the size of a supernova
> who shouldn't get even a cupfull [*sic*] of cooled-down spit
> for respect. . . . The man does nothing for Cornell but
> attract bad press and bad vibes. Remove him. He has
> become the epitome of what is wrong with the state of
> higher education: a lot of hot air with very little benefit.
> Let us not honor a man who is only able to talk to a camera,
> who claims to be a teacher but hides from real students,
> and who is now too old to care.

Birthday Party

While Stover's rant was too generic to hit home, it demonstrated the
equivocal nature of fame in a college environment. The article ran the same
week that Cornell organized a gala sixtieth birthday party for Sagan. Held
a month early, in October 1994, the party was a symposium reuniting
colleagues from throughout Sagan's career. The guest list included Philip
Morrison, Frank Drake, Bruce Murray, Jon Lomberg, Frank Press, Paul
Horowitz, Kip Thorne, James Randi, Richard Turco, Brian Toon, Christopher
Chyba, Joan Campbell, and many others. They flew in a twenty-one-year-
old student who had organized the "Carl Sagan Astronomy Club" in
Niamey, Niger. There were letters from many other friends who couldn't
attend, among them Al Gore and Arthur C. Clarke.

The symposium was also a family reunion. All of Sagan's children and
two of his three wives attended. (Linda, still estranged, did not. She was by
then a working TV writer in L.A. whose credits included several network
series.) Sagan spoke of how much it meant to him to see his family assembled there. Even Dorion found himself moved to tears by this.

Sagan received gifts ranging from a poem composed by an undergraduate who had read *Contact*, to the astronomy department's replica of a
classical Greek head of Aphrodite, to a slightly smaller but remarkably similar reproduction of Aphrodite from a Greek colleague who was out of
the loop on the former present. (Both were nods to Sagan's thesis work on
Venus and his interest in Ionian Greece.) Sagan managed to accept both
Aphrodites with aplomb.

The most unusual present was of Sagan's own devising. Since he already
had an asteroid named for *him*, he suggested that an appropriate gift would
be an asteroid named for his wife. Eleanor Helin, one of the most prolific

discovers of asteroids, officially christened near-Earth asteroid 4970 Asteroid Druyan. Helin talked up the property like a real estate agent. Asteroid Druyan was "very close in"—"large, bright and big"—"of the 17th magnitude but it would be a bright 15th in February." It was said to be about the size of Ithaca, or the same size as the asteroid that killed the dinosaurs. She hastened to add that both asteroids Druyan and Sagan were in "good stable orbits."

Conference Call

Around the time of the celebration, Annie noticed that a bruise on Carl's arm had been there for some weeks. She convinced him to get a checkup. He was in Austin when the results came in. "Is Carl in bed?" the doctor asked Annie.

No, he's traveling, Annie said.

The doctor was relieved to hear that. "The person with these blood tests couldn't possibly be on the road." It appeared that there had been a mix-up in the lab. But: "Please get retested right away."

Carl did. The second results came in while Carl and Annie were having a conference call with *Contact*'s producers. They were bad news.

He had *myelodysplasia*. Even the erudite Sagan had never heard of it. The doctor told him flatly that he would be dead in six months unless he got a bone marrow transplant.

The news came as a "grotesque joke," in Sagan's words. The dead-in-six-months remark sounded like a line from a TV movie. He felt fine, aside from a little light-headedness. When the doctor hung up, Carl and Annie switched back to the producers. They said not a word and continued the conference.

*   *   *

Myelodysplasia is known by several names, from the corporate-sounding acronym MDS (for Myelodysplastic Syndrome) to the coldly romantic "smoldering leukemia." It is a disease of the bone marrow, estimated to strike about 1 in 1,000 people over the age of fifty-five. In myelodysplasia, abnormal stem cells in the marrow crowd out the healthy cells needed to produce blood cells. The abnormal tissue produces ever-fewer red blood cells, creating fatigue and weakness. Lessened numbers of white blood cells compromise the body's ability to fight infections. There are also fewer of the platelets responsible for clotting blood. Cuts fail to heal; bruises linger.

In its early stages, the disease eludes diagnosis. The patient may be perpetually tired and "sickly," with no obvious or alarming symptoms. (Annie guesses that Carl's naturally high energy level delayed recognition that something was wrong.) Some die from myelodysplasia itself. In other cases the disease leads to leukemia.

Carl considered *not* having the bone marrow transplant, simply ignoring the disease. That is often done with very elderly patients and with those lacking adequate medical insurance. He tried to convince himself that a cure or a better treatment might be discovered if he could wait it out.

He did wait it out, for nearly the allotted six months. He did not tell colleagues of his condition. Most sensed that *something* was wrong. Carl looked gaunt. His characteristic vitality had departed.

Nonetheless, he maintained his workload. Sagan was in the midst of promoting *Pale Blue Dot*. There were only subtle concessions to his lagging energy. Speaking at UCLA on December 7, he seated himself in a large leather chair onstage for the question-and-answer period.

In January 1995, Sagan took part in a then-trendy digital forum. America Online users typed in questions so that Sagan could answer a few of them in maddeningly-slow-but-"real" time. (Dorion tried to contact him but couldn't get through.) There was a valedictory quality to some of the exchanges. One AOL subscriber bluntly asked, "Does it bother you that you will probably never get to know the answers to the most interesting questions about the universe?"

Sagan's reply echoed what he'd written in *The Cosmic Connection*—now in the past tense. "I've been privileged to live through the only time in human history we visited the other planets." Another wanted to know the one question he'd ask an alien. Sagan typed back, "What took you so long?"

Sagan's last Cornell class was Astronomy 490: A Seminar on Critical Thinking. Sagan never missed a class. Then one day, he informed Terzian that he was very sick and had to go to a hospital for treatment. Terzian took over the class.

On March 13, 1995, Cornell University announced that its most famous faculty member had taken a temporary medical leave. "I fully expect to be back at Cornell by next semester," Sagan said in a prepared statement.

The ominous tone of the announcement owed more to what *wasn't* being said than what was. Sagan had a "rare, curable bone marrow disease" he declined to identify, said Cornell News Service director Linda Grace-Kobas. "We don't have details on the illness, or what it is, or where he's going for treatment."

*   *   *

Sagan had decided to have the transplant. He was getting weaker each day; he was *not* destined to defy the odds.

He tapped his connections to find the best hospital for myelodysplasia:

Seattle's Fred Hutchinson Cancer Research Center (known as the "Hutch"). One of the center's doctors, E. Donnall Thomas, invented the bone marrow transplantation technique. This invention had won him the 1990 Nobel Prize in medicine, an indication of how new it all was. The Hutchinson Center's success rate with the disease is claimed to be "in the 40–50 percent range."

The chances for success depend a lot on age. They are best with young people. Unfortunately, myelodysplasia is a disease that affects older individuals. Until recently, the cut-off age for transplant was fifty-five, which ruled out *most* myelodysplasia patients. Sagan was told that, at sixty, he would probably be the oldest person ever to have the transplant. (The age limit has been rising and is sixty-five at this writing.)

Sagan needed a bone marrow donor. This had to be someone closely related to him—a child, parent, or sibling. Even then, six compatibility factors had to match. Ruling out his children, Carl had only one candidate: his sister.

Cari was then living in Charleston, West Virginia, where her husband, Bill Greene, worked for Union Carbide. She did not know her brother was sick. Carl called her long distance and stumbled trying to explain the situation. Annie got on the line and explained.

Before Cari could hear the whole story, she said, "You got it. Whatever it is—liver, lung—it's yours."

SEATTLE
1995–96

CARL AND CARI had seen relatively little of each other during the 1970s and 1980s. The bone marrow donation was a powerful bonding experience, forged in pain. First they took the compatibility tests; all six of the compatibility factors matched. Then Cari flew to Seattle.

Brother and sister had long and heartfelt conversations in the hospital. Someone raised the hypothetical question of how their parents would have reacted to a request to donate bone marrow. Both agreed that Samuel would have donated for any family member. Rachel, they felt, would have been selective. It would depend on who the family member was.

Biohazard

As with any organ donation, it was necessary to suppress Carl's immune system with drugs. These drugs caused nausea so severe that it had to be controlled with other drugs. Before the operation, Carl had to take seventy-two tablets of a toxic drug called bisulfan in order to destroy *all* his bone marrow, good cells and bad. The inscrutable protocol of hospitals dictated that this dismal act had to be done one chill Seattle morning at 2 A.M. The seventy-two tablets were in six complete packages of twelve, each package marked with dire instructions to dispose of the contents as a biohazard. Bisulfan cannot even be flushed down the drain for fear of wreaking envi-

ronmental havoc. This was the point of no return. The transplant would
have to work, or he would be dead.

Carl turned ghastly pale and lost all his hair to the drugs, shocking visitors who expected to see the Carl Sagan they knew from TV. ("Nice haircut,
Dad," four-year-old Sam said, rating a smile.)

The transplant was done on April 7, 1995. Cari underwent surgery in
order to extract healthy marrow and its precious stem cells from her bones.
The donated stem cells were then mixed with blood and injected into her
brother's system, much as in a simple blood transfusion. The Hutchinson
Center permits donors to watch the transfer. For Cari, this was a surprisingly moving experience.

Despite the relative simplicity of the transfusion, the course of treatment was excruciatingly painful. It was necessary to do bone marrow
aspirations—to dig into the hip bone and scoop out bone marrow for evalua-
tion. This grisly procedure was done under local anesthetic and sedatives.
Carl gallantly tried to tell Annie that it looked worse than it felt. The Hutch
allows patients to self-administer morphine derivatives and other painkillers. These drugs eased recuperation somewhat.

At an Easter service at New York's St. John the Divine Cathedral, 5,000
people prayed for the recovery of the man who was, with the possible exception of Madalyn Murray O'Hair, the nation's best-known atheist. Half a
world away, a Hindu priest held a vigil for Carl on the banks of the Ganges.

*   *   *

One day, Carl looked out of his hospital window and got a shock. There,
towering over the city, was the giant head of . . . *Dean Martin.*

Carl got on the phone to Lester Grinspoon in Boston. Despite attempts
to patch things up, there were still hurt feelings between Carl and Lester
over the Sagans' break with David Grinspoon. Lester reassured Carl that a
Dean Martin hallucination was within the scope of normal reactions to the
opiate painkillers he was taking.

If all goes well in a transplant, the transfused stem cells find their way to
the recipient's bone marrow. They take up residence and start producing
health-restoring red and white cells and platelets. Tests on the extracted tissue confirmed that that had indeed happened. Most of the white cells in
Sagan's blood had female (XX) chromosomes, meaning that they had been
produced by Cari's stem cells. Sagan joked that he kept waiting for Cari's
interests to assert themselves—to be seized with a desire to ride horses or
take in Broadway shows.

An Isolated Experiment

Back in Ithaca, at 8:37 A.M. on April 25, 1995, someone reported a fire in Cornell's Space Sciences Building. Firefighters arrived to find smoke roiling out of the building's ventilation system. The fumes' livid color and noxious odor hinted at something other than an ordinary blaze.

The crew broke two windows and extinguished the flames in about fifteen minutes. The fire was traced to the Laboratory for Planetary Studies. The lab's director was still recuperating in Seattle, of course, and no one had been in the lab at the time the fire broke out.

Many of the experiments in Sagan's lab sound bizarre to average folks. The tholin-streaked glass tubes have a disquieting appearance. When firefighters learned that they had possibly been exposed to unknown-organic-materials-such-as-might-exist-on-Jupiter, some became alarmed. The fire department ordered "hazardous material decontamination" of seventeen workers, their clothing, and equipment. The department promised to monitor the workers' health.

Investigators identified the source of the fire as an electrical failure in a laboratory fume hood. It was assumed that a researcher had accidentally left equipment on overnight. The major casualty was an experiment Bishun Khare was doing on the atmosphere of Jupiter. "It was an isolated experiment," Khare told a campus newspaper, "and layers of safety precautions were in place." The odor—described as "really noxious"—was believed to be from melted lab plastics, not Jovian smog.

Things quickly went back to normal, aside from the lingering odor. Over the following weeks, the Space Sciences Building came down with a case of sick building syndrome. "A lot of people in the department have been complaining of headaches, dizziness and sore throats since the fire," one astronomy grad student said. It was now claimed that the air in the building had always been bad, even before the fire: "It feels like you are breathing in dirt."

*   *   *

There were more serious worries than headaches and odors. W. Reid Thompson left a message with Cornell's department of environmental health and safety, asking its staff to investigate a possible health hazard in the Laboratory for Planetary Studies. The evidence was "anecdotal" but striking. Sagan's assistant, Eleanor York, had died of cancer a few years previously. Thompson now had a strangely virulent cancer (with no family history of such). Sagan had a disease that was not exactly a cancer but related to leukemia.

York's, Thompson's, and Sagan's offices formed a corner of the Space

Sciences Building. The other room in the corner was used for the Laboratory for Planetary Studies.

The causes of myelodysplasia are poorly known. It has been tentatively linked to prior chemotherapy or radiotherapy, hereditary factors, or exposure to benzene. Lester Grinspoon notes that Sagan had had many X rays over the years because of his other medical problems. Traces of benzene were reported in some of the experiments simulating planetary atmospheres. Even so, the benzene exposure, if any, was probably no greater than in any chemistry lab. Harder to dismiss outright were the tholins. It was possible to imagine that these raw building blocks of life might play havoc with someone's DNA.

Khare pointed out that *he* was the person most exposed to any chemicals in the lab, and he was in perfect health. The health department responded, however, by closing down Sagan's lab. Health inspectors interviewed building occupants, assembling a dossier of vague complaints. It was reiterated that the air in the building was "bad." The health department discovered that the building's air intake shaft was next to a parking lot and took in cars' exhaust fumes—"although not in harmful concentrations."

After doing everything it had the expertise or budget to do, the health department was unable to establish any health hazard in the Space Sciences Building. The matter was closed. "The lab doesn't have any cancerous chemicals," Khare told a campus newspaper. "I can live and sleep in the lab without any worry at all." Yet even Khare allowed that "the building as a whole does not get enough ventilation."

Pirates

In Seattle, Sagan's recuperation dragged on. The young children and in-laws had moved to Seattle for the duration. Five weeks after the transplant, Carl was well enough to be released from the hospital and join his family in the Four Seasons Hotel. He remained weak, tethered by an umbilical cord of daily treatments to the Hutch.

Weeks passed, then months. The children were growing. Sam (who looked remarkably like photos of Carl at his age) went through a phase where he was intrigued by pirates. Carl tried to talk his son into choosing more ethical role models. It was to no avail. Carl concluded that there was something biologically hard-wired in the fascination. Sam also liked soldiers.

Sagan could not, and did not, stay idle for long. Requests for speaking engagements and interviews were pouring in, encouraged by Sagan's optimism that a full recovery was imminent. As his strength grew, he began granting interviews. "Sagan Likes Seattle, But Not Lattes," was one local newspaper's scoop.

He was working on *Contact*, too. Jody Foster, cast for the film's lead, flew up to Seattle to meet with Carl and Annie. In L.A., a speakerphone was set on a desk for story meetings. Sagan was the voice in the box, the sick kid who never came to school.

Then suddenly Sagan was off and running. On August 2 he gave his first speech since the transplant: a keynote address to the Pacific Rim Transtech Conference in Seattle.

Two days later, he was in San Diego for a symposium with Colin Powell and Henry Kissinger.

On September 22, he was in De Kalb, Illinois, to pick up his twenty-second honorary degree.

On September 25, he was in San Francisco to give a keynote address at the State of the World Forum (with Mikhail Gorbachev, George Bush, Margaret Thatcher, Ted Turner, Jane Goodall, and Richard Leakey).

On October 18, Sagan presided at a naturalization ceremony for sixty-seven new American citizens at the Tompkins County, New York, court-house. Very much his old self, Sagan refused to pledge allegiance to Old Glory, objected to the mention of God in the Oath of Allegiance, and proposed that, instead of pledging to flags, citizens vow "to question everything my leaders tell me."

"I've been very, very lucky," Sagan told his hometown newspaper. "All signs are positive." There was reason to be optimistic. Sagan was looking better. His hair was growing back, and he had regained lost weight. He returned to his lab, now cleaned up, and supervised ongoing work on the atmospheres of Titan and Triton. He pored over the Galileo data streaming in from Jupiter. He worked on an article titled "On the Rarity of Long-Lived, Non-Spacefaring Galactic Civilizations" and contemplated another proposing that the Tharsis region of Mars was the relic of a vast impact that had blown off much of the planet's water. He corrected galleys for *The Demon-Haunted World* and worked on a collection of essays, *Billions and Billions*, and a second novel. The novel was a romance inspired by the serendipitous way he and Annie had met.

Sagan was feeling his oats enough to conclude his legal battles with Apple Computer. After dismissal of the libel suit, he had filed another suit over Apple's original use of his name without permission. That too had been rejected, and an appeal filed, virtually from the plaintiff's deathbed. In November 1995, an out-of-court settlement was announced. Terms were not disclosed. Apple's director of patents and trademarks, Paul D. Carmichael, made the conciliatory statement that "Apple has always had great respect for Dr. Sagan. It was never Apple's intention to cause Dr. Sagan or his family any embarrassment or concern." The Power Mac 7100 was reported to be selling briskly in Cornell's Campus Store.

Zeno's Paradox

The same month, Sagan received a sternly worded letter from Francis Ford Coppola. It was now Coppola's contention that when he had okayed Sagan's writing of the *Contact* novel, he had still expected to share any profits. Coppola therefore demanded his share of the money that Warner Brothers had paid Sagan.

But it was Sagan's understanding that Coppola had explicitly waived any rights to *Contact*. Supporting this was the fact that Coppola had never asked for a piece of the novel's highly publicized $2-million advance. Sagan composed a letter saying Coppola's claim was without merit. He posed twenty or more questions regarding the claim. Neither Coppola nor his attorneys answered this letter.

Meanwhile the *Contact* film was progressing slowly. Sagan was well enough to meet with the staff in person. At one point, *Contact* was supposed to have been ready for a Christmas 1996 release. But in October 1995, the sets had yet to be built and Miller was still tinkering with script and budget. Miller did not shy away from Sagan's science-versus-religion theme; in fact he thought the pope should figure in the film. There were more labored attempts to fashion an ending as flashy as the one in *Close Encounters*—only not quite identical with it.

Obst nervously reminded Miller of the need to move forward. Annie likened the situation to Zeno's Paradox: "You know, you're always going a fraction of the way you have to go, so theoretically you never actually get there."

Then one day Warner Brothers fired Miller. It looked as if the film might not get made at all.

Obst conferred with the Sagans. They had invested two years in the project with Miller. "We sort of knew," Obst said, "we'd never be that intimate with a director again."

Obst went back to Robert Zemeckis. This time she told him he could end the film any way he wanted. Zemeckis agreed to do it.

This was a stunning save. Zemeckis's *Forrest Gump* had been the biggest-grossing film of 1994 and swept the Oscars. "To quote Carl Sagan," Zemeckis told a journalist, "the mathematical probability that I would ever make a movie like *Gump* again is pretty nil."

Postcard from the Titanic

In December Carl went in for a follow-up test in Rochester, New York. The doctors found what they had hoped not to find. The chemotherapy hadn't knocked out all the diseased bone marrow cells. A new, burgeoning population of diseased cells was again crowding out the healthy cells. It was back to square one—or minus one, for there was less room for hope now.

The family returned to Seattle on December 22. Carl and Annie met with doctors on Christmas Eve. More tests were run, and they confirmed the condition. The *Ithaca Journal* quoted Annie: "We are expecting a complete cure. . . . I really feel very hopeful and lucky that he is in such good shape. . . . Doctors are very upbeat."

During these cheerless holidays, Carl wrote one of his most compelling short pieces. With more emotional candor than the press releases, he faced his impending mortality. "The world is so exquisite," Carl wrote, "with so much love and moral depth, that there is no reason to deceive ourselves with pretty stories for which there's little good evidence. Far better, it seems to me, in our vulnerability, is to look Death in the eye and to be grateful every day for the brief but magnificent opportunity that life provides."

Carl mentioned that he kept a memento mori next to his shaving mirror: a framed postcard mailed from the *Titanic* the day before it went down. "Dear Friend," read the handwritten message. "Just a line to show that I am alive & kicking and going grand. It's a treat."

*   *   *

The doctors at the Hutch were not giving up yet. They determined that the diseased cells in Carl's body lacked a certain enzyme. This would make the cells vulnerable to two chemotherapy drugs that had *not* been tried in the first round of treatment.

They gave Carl three rounds of the new medicines, hoping that the third would be the charm. Even after the first of the treatments, they couldn't find any of the diseased cells. Cari again generously went through the unpleasant procedure of donating marrow for a second transplant.

Meanwhile, the children were put in schools in Seattle. They acquired new pets suited to the soggy climate: snails. The children devised names for each mollusk (one was "Cornell Junior") and kept them in miniature terraria. Occasionally they released them for exercise, a perilous venture that often necessitated a search for stragglers. Evenings the Sagan family would order a green salad with no dressing from their hotel's room service. It was the snails' dinner. (When journalists pressed Sagan for a description of what an extraterrestrial being would look like, he would counter: "If you'd never seen one, how could you imagine something like a snail?")

At the end of this recuperation Carl was, to all appearances, back to where he was before the test in Rochester.

*   *   *

The Demon-Haunted World hit the bookstores. Magician James Randi, who read the galleys, noted in the completed book "many instances where Carl had strengthened his language, upgraded and fortified his adjectives, and in general hardened his language. I had the chilling thought that perhaps he felt this might be his last statement about the pseudoscience, crackpots, frauds, and quacks that he so resented."

Sagan's "hardened language" is his alone, more humane than the garden-variety debunker's.

> Have I ever heard a skeptic wax superior and contemptu-
> ous? Certainly. I've even sometimes heard, to my retro-
> spective dismay, that unpleasant tone in my own
> voice. . . . And, it must be said, some scientists and dedi-
> cated skeptics apply this tool as a blunt instrument, with
> little finesse. . . . All of us cherish our beliefs. They are, to a
> degree, self-defining. When someone comes along who
> challenges our belief system as insufficiently well-based—
> or who, like Socrates, merely asks embarrassing questions
> that we haven't thought of, or demonstrates that we've
> swept key underlying assumptions under the rug—it
> becomes much more than a search for knowledge. It feels
> like a personal assault.

This empathy for those holding the very beliefs the book attacks was characteristic of Sagan.

*   *   *

After the second transplant, Sagan felt well enough to collaborate with Christopher Chyba on a new explanation of the early faint sun paradox, involving an organic haze not unlike that found on Titan.

Sagan also had enough energy to give Robert Zemeckis a hard time. Zemeckis had not done serious science fiction before and questioned whether *Contact* should be a special effects–driven blockbuster. Maybe the movie should be Ellie's story, more "down to earth."

Sagan was protective, not only of scientific accuracy but of making sure there was a lot of science in the movie. Sagan gave the production artists pep talks (encouraging them to make their sketches as impressive as possi-ble, so Zemeckis would use the art) and gave the cast a slide lecture on the history of astronomy. He worried that Zemeckis's approach was "like doing a movie of the Lewis and Clark expedition and setting it in Seinfeld's apartment."

X Rays

In May 1996, W. Reid Thompson died from cancer. At the memorial service, Carl somberly told Christopher Chyba to take care of himself. He had lost Jim Pollack and now Reid, and he did not want to lose anyone else.

That summer, the now-familiar catastrophe repeated itself. This time, "routine" tests at a Syracuse hospital showed that Carl's disease was flaring up yet again. By early July, he was back in Seattle for the third time. Officially, the objective was a "complete cure" so that he could return to Cornell for the fall semester. "He's going to be getting more treatment but of what nature we don't know," a Cornell spokesman said.

The treatment Sagan would be getting was a desperate gamble. Since the first two treatments had failed to eradicate the diseased marrow, the third would have to be more rigorous to offer any hope of succeeding. Sagan's physicians proposed whole-body X-radiation.

Like some nightmare version of his own experiments, Sagan's entire body would be exposed to a primordial blast of radiation. The cancer risk would be immense. Such treatment is thinkable only for those who have no prospect of survival otherwise.

Sagan consented to the treatment. It was done, followed by a third transplant of Cari's stem cells. Afterward, tests indicated that *all* the bone marrow cells in his body were genetically derived from Cari's donated tissue. There were apparently none of Carl's own marrow cells left, healthy or otherwise.

This was the best result that could be hoped for. The diseased cells had demonstrated their ability to burgeon from practically nothing at frightening speed. Detection of *any* of Carl's own cells would be worrisome. On the other hand, having none of one's own stem cells was itself a virtual death sentence, shrinking life expectancy to a few years.

Martian Meteorite

The first day Sagan was out of the hospital, it looked as if he might live to see proof of extraterrestrial life, after all.

Strange rumors had been leaking out of NASA. It was said that some scientists had found fossils in a meteorite that came from Mars. When the news media got wind of the story, it forced NASA's hand. The NASA group made an announcement, however premature. They had found microscopic structures in meteorite ALH84001,0, one of the rare meteorites believed to have been knocked off Mars.

To most of the public, it was news that we had Mars rocks here on Earth. The Martian origin of the rock was the one part of the story generally accepted by space scientists. Writing of the Martian meteorites two years earlier, Sagan prophetically remarked that there had been no reports of microbes in them—"so far."

Within a hour of hearing about the meteorite findings, Richard Berendzen got on the phone to Dan Goldin's office at NASA. "I think this ought to be renamed the Sagan Rock," he told Goldin. ALH84001,0 was a candidate for a name change. But of course no one knew whether the claims would pan out, and the team working on the meteorite might have their own ideas. The rock was not renamed.

For almost the first time since the space age began, Sagan had to watch from the sidelines as someone *else* had a shot at proving there was life beyond the Earth. (He reviewed the NASA team's article for *Science* and green-lighted it.) At a Cornell astronomy department meeting on the findings, an obviously ailing Sagan spoke of the reports with guarded enthusiasm. He was old enough to remember the previous meteoritic "fossil" controversy. In one of his last essays, Sagan cautioned that "the evidence for life on Mars is not yet extraordinary enough." He permitted himself to add that the discovery "opens up the entire field of Martian exobiology" (as if, for Sagan, it was ever closed!).

*   *   *

For a few moments, the rock was so much in the news that President Clinton gave a news conference on it. Zemeckis watched the conference, then got on the phone to Sagan. "Did you see what Clinton just said?" he asked. "I swear to God it was like it was scripted for this movie. When he said the line 'We will continue to listen closely to what it has to say,' I almost died. I stood there with my mouth hanging open."

Zemeckis had used digital effects to put a succession of dead presidents into *Forrest Gump*. The Clinton speech convinced him to use similar techniques in *Contact*. This mandated some juggling. In Sagan's novel, the U.S. president is a woman. George Miller had pictured Linda Hunt in the role. Zemeckis had wanted Sidney Poitier. Instead, he analyzed the lighting and camera angle in Clinton's TV speech (which took place in the rose garden) and duplicated it for an indoor movie set. Unlike the situation in *Gump*, Clinton's remarks were fitting enough to be used verbatim.

Like *Forrest Gump*, *Contact* drew complaints from those who thought it compromised the veracity of the electronic news media. A White House attorney sent Zemeckis a letter saying the use of Clinton's image was "fundamentally unfair." The *American Spectator*'s Mark Steyn noted that the president had given an interview on MTV in which he fielded questions about his underwear. "He's lucky," said Steyn, "Zemeckis didn't decide to make Attack of the Killer BVDs."

Death

Sagan had now, by turns, been deathly ill for two years. In the period from March 1995 through his death, he spent about thirteen of twenty-two months in Seattle. The very month before his death, Carl's health rallied yet again.

In early November Sagan returned to Ithaca. He had no hair; his skin was the hue of rice paper. "Medical tests point toward a complete recovery," reported the *Ithaca Journal*. "I've been tremendously lucky," Carl said. "The signs look very good now. But with the nature of this disease, it's wise to wait a couple of years to determine if you're really in the clear."

Cornell announced that Sagan was to take over a class (Astronomy 202: Our Home in the Solar System) the next semester. The *Cornell Daily Sun* ran a photo of Sagan—shockingly gaunt, though with hair—and captioned it "Ready to Teach."

The extended Sagan clan gathered for Thanksgiving dinner in Ithaca. It was by general consent the best family Thanksgiving ever. Carl's presence was something to be thankful for, the more precious for the realization it might be Carl's last Thanksgiving holiday. But who could say? He had dodged the bullet yet again.

Sagan settled back to work in his home office. Almost immediately, something was not well. One night in early December, he could scarcely bring himself to taste a favorite meal. After that, eating was a mechanical exercise, done in a dogged struggle to preserve life.

In his last weeks, Sagan met with Dan Goldin at NASA headquarters to discuss future space missions and visited the *Contact* set. "As sick as he was, he was sending us notes on last-minute rewrites," Zemeckis recalled.

One of Sagan's last public appearances was on ABC's *Nightline*, on December 4. The producers arranged for NASA chief Dan Goldin and astronomer Richard Berendzen to be interviewed on NASA's planetary missions. Shortly before the show, a producer called Berendzen and said that Sagan had agreed to be on the show. They had invited Sagan, too, as they always did on space-themed shows. Usually he declined.

"Then what you ought to do," Berendzen insisted, "is *just* interview Sagan. Cancel me and Goldin."

The producer said, "We already have."

Sagan appeared by hook-up from his home in Ithaca. For most viewers, his appearance was a shock. The old Sagan had vanished, leaving only his grin. Ted Koppel asked the inevitable question about Sagan's health. Sagan spoke briefly of his illness and treatment; talked of having turned the corner.

*   *   *

Sagan was scheduled to give a speech for the 1996 National Science Teachers' Association in San Francisco. He had originally committed to give a speech at the 1995 meeting. That had been canceled for health reasons, and Sagan had promised the association's William Aldridge to make the 1996 meeting.

Sagan made plans to see Frank Drake while he was in San Francisco. While Drake was waiting for Sagan to arrive at the restaurant, he idly watched a waiter help a stooped, elderly man shuffle slowly through the restaurant. With a shock, Drake realized the "old man" was Carl.

Carl was upbeat. Even so, Drake was privately amazed that he would be giving lectures in that condition.

After the second talk, Carl barely made it back to his hotel room with Annie's help. He was deathly weak. He had possibly caught a bug on the plane. They called the Hutch for advice. The doctors thought he should fly directly to Seattle for observation.

Annie had to phone the children and tell them that they would not be coming home. They had to go to Seattle again. Hanukkah would be postponed. Sasha was then thirteen, old enough to know what this meant.

The situation quickly worsened in Seattle. An X ray showed an intractable pneumonia. As far as the physicians could tell, it wasn't caused by a virus, bacterium, or fungus. The doctors' best guess was that the pneumonia was a reaction to the past summer's radiation treatment.

They prescribed steroids. The drugs worsened Carl's suffering and didn't appear to help much. He dictated a letter to Vice President Al Gore saying he would not be able to attend an upcoming White House meeting on the future of the space program.

*   *   *

There was a portentous chill in the doctors' speech and body language. Eyes were averted, throats were cleared. Annie realized she was losing Carl.

The children were flown in from Ithaca. Annie got on the phone to Lynda Obst. "He's going very quickly and I need you," she said. Lynda took the first plane from Los Angeles.

When Lynda arrived, Carl looked even less like himself. He was on a respirator. That and general weakness made it difficult to speak. He was lucid, however, and pulled himself together for what he knew would be his children's last memory of him. The sight of Sasha particularly cheered him. Sasha spent the night sitting up with Carl. He and Annie had decided that would be an appropriate form of leave-taking. "Beautiful, beautiful Sasha," Carl told her. "You are not only beautiful, but you also have enormous gorgeousness."

Not among the visitors to Sagan's bedside was Lester Grinspoon. One way or another, the reconciliation that both must have wanted never happened. Sagan's stubborn pride convinced him that he had been wronged. Grinspoon felt he could not fly to Seattle under the circumstances. Thus Carl's sense of personal honor kept him from saying good-bye to the man who was his best and most loyal friend.

*   *   *

The psychological boost of seeing the children manifested itself on the hospital monitors. Annie pointed that out to the doctors. They identified it as "Indian summer." The rally before the end.

"This is a deathwatch," Carl announced to Annie at one point. "I'm going to die."

"No," she said. "You're going to beat this, just as you have before when it looked hopeless."

"Well, we'll see who's right about this one."

*   *   *

Sagan had married well. As he left the world, he had the undivided attention he had always desired. To Annie, even the heat emanating from his fevered skin was welcome proof that he was still with her. She kissed him and rubbed her face against his, to make an indelible memory of the moment. "What a wonderfully lived life," she said, gripping his hand tightly. Over and over she repeated: "With pride and joy in our love, I let you go. Without fear. June 1. June 1. For keeps."

Carl Sagan died of pneumonia early in the morning of December 20, 1996. Annie and Lynda wrote the press release announcing the death and sent it out. As they were walking out of the hospital, they saw that the story was already being covered on CNN.

AFTERWORD

CORNELL HELD TWO large memorial services for Sagan, one December 23 in its Johnson Museum of Art and a second on February 3 in Bailey Hall. After the December service, Sagan was buried at Ithaca's Lakeview Cemetery in the company of his parents and the grand neoclassic monuments of Cornell's founders.

Annie received bags of mail after Carl's death. A lot of it told essentially the same story: an unknown postdoc sent a preprint to twenty astronomers, hoping to get a response. Only one took the time to write back. It was Sagan, the busiest of them all. A note from Al Gore said, "It is appropriate that the man who wrote the Encyclopedia Britannica entry on 'Life' should have taught us all so much about living."

The Planetary Society's Web site permitted people to post comments in a Sagan tribute. The participants were remarkably cosmopolitan. "I was very sorry to hear about the demise of Mr. Carl Sagan, whom most of us from the United Arab Emirates hold in great esteem," wrote one. People who never met Sagan said they were brought to tears: "I pulled my truck over to the side of the road and wept when I heard the news." For some, Sagan's influence was like that of a pop psychologist or motivational speaker. "I only truly started to be who I am after being exposed to Carl Sagan," wrote one person. A surprising number spoke of the hope that Sagan was in a better place. "I am somehow torn between embracing his views and hoping that his soul will rest in God's peace," wrote a California high school teacher. "I believe that God believed in Carl Sagan—and still does," stated a planetarium director from Fort Worth.

There were also memorial services in New York City and Pasadena. Linda Salzman attended the Pasadena memorial. After the Pasadena service, a few friends quietly toasted Sagan. The most visibly affected of all was the stolid Bruce Murray, who, sipping his brandy, could barely hold back the tears.

*   *   *

Three days after Sagan's body had been laid to rest, Francis Ford Coppola filed suit against Sagan's estate and Warner Brothers. Coppola charged that Sagan had violated the contract for the old TV movie idea from the 1970s. Coppola asked for $250,000 in compensatory damages and for the film to be canceled.

Lynda Obst called Coppola "a nut—you can quote me on that." Ultimately, a Los Angeles County Superior Court judge more or less agreed. In a four-hour deposition, Gentry Lee traced the complex origins of *Contact* and showed how little the Coppola discussions had influenced the plot. The judge threw out the suit on the grounds that no contract existed and Coppola had waited too long to file a claim.

The Coppola suit had scarcely been settled when Random House sued the Sagan estate. The publisher, which had just been bought by the German media conglomerate Bertelsmann AG, demanded return of $1.2 million in advances plus interest, for an undelivered book.

Sagan's will was primarily in favor of his wife and minor children. It provided for $40,000 in college money for grandson Tonio. Dorion and Jeremy are to receive a relatively modest bequest of about $50,000 each, payable after the death of Carl's widow. Annie is only a decade older than Carl's first two sons and comes from a family known for longevity.

*   *   *

On the Fourth of July, 1997, the Mars Pathfinder bounced and safely unfurled its metallic petals in Chryse Planitia, not too far from the relic Viking 1. Its cameras sent back panoramas of rocks, sand dunes, and a Martian sky whose hue was now likened to that of butterscotch. After it was clear that Pathfinder was a success, NASA renamed the craft the Sagan Memorial Station.

The name scarcely took. After the christening, JPL and the press mostly reverted to calling it the Mars Pathfinder. By any name, the mission's instruments changed the scientific view of Mars. Lacking an eloquent interpreter, its findings remain poorly known to the public.

Pathfinder found sedimentary rocks, among them several that appear to be conglomerates—masses of round pebbles cemented together. Conglomerate is a rock of rivers, canyons, and deltas. It is not the work of a geological moment. Pebbles are carved and polished slowly by flowing rivers or lapping shores. In another epoch, the pebbles get washed into sand, silt, and clay and cemented together. At a still later time, the conglomerate may be eroded and carried downstream. All this presumably had to have happened for Pathfinder to ramble across exposed conglomerates.

Conglomerates on Mars bespeak not apocalyptic floods of melted permafrost but lazy rivers and lakes. Recent orbiter photos of Mars show what appear to be the boundaries of these extinct lakes—and possibly an ancient Martian ocean in the northern hemisphere. The most radical feature of the new antediluvian Mars, which few dared to propose before, is *rain*. It's hard to explain conglomerates without conceding precipitation and the mythopoetic Mars of Sagan. Mars was once a planet of balmy temperatures, pattering rain, innumerable rivulets, and mighty rivers. This, at least, is the picture now espoused by many card-carrying geologists.

*   *   *

The Martian meteorite controversy is fading away much like the similar claims of the early 1960s. At this writing, support for the "nanofossils" is pretty much limited to the NASA team that reported them—and to Gil Levin. Levin hailed the meteorite findings as confirmation that his Viking experiment had found life on Mars. Levin theorized that NASA was downplaying the evidence for fear of offending the American public, whose Bibles said nothing of Martian microbes. Norman Horowitz was resolutely *un*convinced, both about Martian fossils and about Levin's talk of a theological cover-up.

Sagan's hypothesis about the META events being extraterrestrial signals amplified by scintillation now seems to have been convincingly refuted. Jill Tarter reobserved the positions of the META candidate events using a receiver a couple of orders of magnitude more powerful than META had. If Sagan's idea were right, Tarter's receiver should have picked up the presumed steady signals throughout the cycle of amplification and deamplification. It found nothing. Tarter's present opinion echoes Paul Horowitz's: that the "things that go bump in the night" are most likely to be rare processor failures.

*   *   *

After Sagan's death, the Laboratory for Planetary Studies was quietly dismantled. The tubes of tholins and gases were cautiously disposed of, the rooms converted to office space and a conference room. That the lab presented a health hazard was never proved, but this issue may have been a factor in Cornell's decision not to perpetuate a laboratory where so much pacesetting work was done.

Today Sagan's scientific legacy is most keenly felt at NASA's new Astrobiology Institute at Ames Research Center and in the striking number of his students now continuing his search for extraterrestrial life. Most visible are Steven Squyres and Christopher Chyba. Squyres, now a Cornell professor, heads the NASA team planning a Martian sample return mission currently slated for 2003. The mission is to dig deep into the Martian surface and shoot rock samples back to Earth, to be examined for (among other things) organic chemistry, fossils, or even extant life.

Chyba, who holds the Carl Sagan chair at the SETI Institute, heads a NASA panel planning a Europa orbiter. Europa is the current "hero" of the astrobiology community. Physical considerations imply that the cracked, icy surface revealed by Voyager must liquefy some distance underground. If it *is* liquid water that is the indispensable prerequisite for life, Europa is a logical next place to look.

This subterranean ocean would be inky black. The Earth's own oceans hold creatures and (more to the point) ecosystems that exist without sunlight. However, the Earth's abyssal communities use oxygen, which ultimately comes from photosynthetic life at the surface.

Europa's oceans are still only an appealing conjecture. Exobiology has been stung by appealing conjectures before. The primary mission of the Europa orbiter (also scheduled for 2003) is to determine whether an ocean exists. If so, biological missions would surely follow. "The whole program," Chyba said, "is carrying Carl's torch."

*   *   *

In the months after his death, Sagan was also an omnipresent figure in pop culture. The film of *Contact*, dedicated "For Carl," was released in July 1997. In a publicist's nightmare, it came out a week after *Men in Black*, another "alien" movie better fitting the commercial mold. Obst, sounding much like Sagan himself, told the press, "I'll be disappointed in America if it can only think of aliens as green monsters that objectify our xenophobia."

Linda Salzman attended the *Contact* premiere at Annie's invitation—a rapprochement that probably couldn't have happened while Carl was alive. The film contains a number of retrospective allusions to Sagan's life. One that might be missed is a sign in a mob scene: a picture of Jesus inscribed with the message that shocked Bloomington's Sunday diners in the summer of 1952.

Middle-brow critics loved *Contact* but worried that the general public wouldn't be smart enough to get it. High-brow critics hated the movie and feared it was the sort of thing that Middle America would eat up. *Contact* thus got two thumbs up from Siskel and Ebert, while a panel of *Village Voice* critics dished it as the worst movie of the summer. Unusual for a science-fiction film, *Contact* was popular with women. In mid-August 1997, it was projected to gross $105 million for a profit of $15 million.

*   *   *

Sagan also figured in prime-time TV to a degree unusual for a scientist living or dead. He was seemingly on the verge of a posthumous metamorphosis like Machiavelli's, from flesh-and-blood reality to a stock character of popular fiction.

The writers of *The X-Files* wrote Sagan into the 1997 season finale. Ironically, Agent Mulder is presented as a man who has spent his career trying unsuccessfully to prove that extraterrestrial life exists. Then he comes across a frozen alien and witnesses its autopsy. Scully informs him that the frozen alien has been a Defense Department hoax. Mulder is crushed. He tearfully pops a tape into his VCR. The screen fills with a young Carl Sagan and Philip Morrison discoursing on extraterrestrial life. This is in fact public-domain NASA footage of the 1972 "Life Beyond the Earth" conference at Boston University, discovered by the producers.

Sagan also made it into *Dark Skies*, a series that was, if not exactly a rip-off of the *X-Files*, intended to tap into the same audience. A turtlenecked actor did an unintentionally funny impression of the young Sagan. Federal agents detained this Sagan in order to show him some living aliens they had in a vault. Viewers were asked to believe that Sagan spent the rest of his career promoting extraterrestrial life while preserving the government's secret—for reasons of national security, of course.

*   *   *

At the dawn of a new millennium, it seems that an overarching theme of intellectual life in the twentieth century has been the absence of absolutes. In the physical sciences this theme was epitomized by those two uncannily evocative words "relativity" and "uncertainty." In the humanities, it led to the postmodern criticism Sagan found so distasteful.

Nowhere is the absence of privileged frames of reference more inescapable than in astronomy. In the past century, the scale of the known universe has increased by orders of magnitude, proportionately diminishing the importance of the human race. We are not at the center of the cosmic scheme; the center, if it exists, is remote and unknowable. Even our small world's distinction as the only known habitat of life seems fated to be surrendered sooner or later.

Meanwhile, science has failed to find anything like a humanistic meaning to it all. "The more the universe seems comprehensible," said physicist

Steven Weinberg, "the more it also seems pointless." A universe where we are infinitely unimportant and where the answers to the questions we really care about either do not exist or are forever inaccessible to us sounds like a Kafka story. But this is the universe we live in.

To a public discomforted by such a universe, Sagan was a signal figure. Extraterrestrial life appeals as the one truly mythic entity still permitted by the empiricist tradition that has denuded the woods of dragons and devils, satyrs and yeti. Desire to believe in such ambivalent beings transcends all known cultures and ages. It is not likely to be extinguished by a couple of centuries of science.

In that regard, Sagan can be seen as a prophet. Yet, in his failures to find aliens, Sagan came to represent a distinctly *un*prophetlike intellectual honesty. He was willing to accept the world's ambiguity, the questions that must go unanswered in our time.

Sagan's philosophy was not original (only a perversely idiosyncratic philosophy can be that). He recognized his sympathy with Democritus, the first recorded Western thinker to ponder the meaninglessness of things. Democritus's philosophy was not pessimistic. He was the "laughing philosopher," asserting that it was possible to be happy in a "meaningless" universe. This simple humanism was the public Sagan's underlying message, too, transmitted to millions who never entirely followed Sagan's scientific exposition but sensed something comforting in the tone of his voice. To a degree that not all of his fellow scientists realized, Sagan helped reconcile our culture to the science it embraces yet ever mistrusts.

*   *   *

Even in death, Sagan has become a recurring presence in the dreams of those close to him. Dorion had a dream in which he spotted a man sitting on a bench. He did not recognize the man until he heard his voice: it was his father. They had made up, come to the understanding they never achieved in life. Carl got up to leave. Suddenly, Dorion was a small child again, hugging his father's legs. He looked up, and Carl was gone. His legs had transformed into the trunks of two giant trees, rising into the sky. They were (Dorion realized upon waking) two of the four trees from a childhood bedtime story, the trees whose significance would be made clear later.

In one of Nick's dreams, he found himself at the lakeside home in Ithaca, attending a funeral service for his father. In the midst of the milling crowd, Nick spotted Carl himself, alive and well. As they spoke, the impossibility of this meeting dawned on Nick. "You can't be here," he protested. "You don't believe in life after death." In the face of that irrefutable logic, Carl graciously dissolved; the dream ended.

Notes

This book is based primarily on interviews conducted between February 1997 and February 1999. In these notes, published sources are abbreviated as follows:

> Sagan's books: title and year *[Pale Blue Dot 1994]*. Sagan's scientific papers: year (and letter where necessary) for papers where Sagan was sole author [1961b]; authors and year for group publications [Sagan and Pollack 1966a]. Standard bibliographic format may clip off Sagan's name when he is one of a large group of coauthors, as in many of the NASA planetary mission publications. Other publications: author and year [Thomas 1963] or (mainly for material in popular magazines and newspapers) the full reference (*Time*, June 26, 1939).

See bibliography for full references.

Foreword

xiii   Carl was still young enough to ride piggyback; reassured by mother: *Billions and Billions* 1997, 180.

A DAY THAT POWERFULLY INFLUENCED MY THINKING: ibid., 180.

A PERFECT FUTURE MADE POSSIBLE BY SCIENCE: *The Demon-Haunted World* 1996, xiii.

xiv   THE FREAK SHOWS BOAST NO OVERPOWERING MONSTERS: *Time*, June 26, 1939, 10.

Rides, nude shows: ibid., 10, 12.

CREDERE! OBBEDIRE! COMBATTERE!: ibid., 12.

$200 cars, "I have seen the future" button: Gelernter 1995, 34.

ROCKET FLIGHT IS AT PRESENT IMPOSSIBLE: Gelernter 1995, 155.

xv   BEYOND THAT THEY KNOW NOTHING: *Life* magazine quoted in ibid., 166.
A WOMAN'S HAT, RAZOR, CAN OPENER: *Time,* September 30, 1939, 59.

xvi   [Carl had] CLARITY OF PURPOSE; he would be too old to go to the moon or Mars:
Lu Nahemow, interview.
SAGAN DESPERATELY WANTS TO FIND LIFE SOMEPLACE: Cooper 1976a, 83.

Brooklyn 1934–48

3   Gruber killed a man in hand-to-hand combat: Ann Druyan, interview.
Gruber carried passengers across river: ibid.

4   Gruber was disguised in women's clothing: Dorion Sagan, personal communi-
cation.
[CHAYA HAD] VALVULAR DISEASE OF HEART; Grubers lived at 230 East Seventh
Street: "List or Manifest of Alien Passengers for the U.S. Immigration Officer at
Port of Arrival" for the *Batavia.*
Clara died of cardiac failure due to chronic endocarditis: State of New York
Certificate and Record of Death for Annie Gruber, supplied by Brian Neil
Burg. It is unclear whether "Annie" was a clerical mistake or another name that
Chaya/Clara went by. The address and father's and mother's name confirm that
this is Chaya's death certificate.
Tobi in orphanage, Rachel on eastbound ship: Druyan, interview.
Rachel in care of Leib's sisters in Austria: Dorion Sagan, personal communication.
Rachel's "lice head" nickname: ibid. She refused to accept Rosie as mother:
Cari Greene, interview.

5   IN MODERN HEBREW: Thomas 1963, 185.
Samuel was about five, George about seventeen: Greene, interview.
Samuel wanted to be pharmacist: Greene, interview. Spent two years at
Columbia: Swift 1990, 216.
Samuel beat students who could afford to lose money at pool: Samuel Sagan
told this to Carl's friend Timothy Ferris (interview.)
"Red" and "Lucky" were Samuel's nicknames: Dorion Sagan, personal
communication.
Samuel and Rachel never tired of each other: Greene, interview.
IT'S FINE: Nick Sagan, interview.
[RACHEL WAS] SCREAMER: Lu Nahemow, interview.
People saved Rachel's letters: Greene, interview.
Rachel's competitiveness; reaction to red-haired half niece: Dorion Sagan, per-
sonal communication.

6   Samuel was less passionate though more compassionate: Greene, interview.
[SAMUEL WAS] MENSCH: David Grinspoon, interview.
Samuel worked as usher: Sheff 1991, 88. Then at New York Girls' and Women's
Coat Company: Greene, interview.
Sagan family never wanted for coats: ibid.
Samuel and Rachel lived at Bay Thirty-seventh Street: ibid. Then on Bay
Parkway: Druyan, interview. No one in the family is now certain of the exact
addresses. Druyan's impression was that both Brooklyn apartments were
on Bay Parkway, one at 8614 Bay Parkway. As an adult, Sagan once visited the
Bay Parkway apartment with Annie and introduced himself to the then-current
tenants.

6   Description of Bensonhurst: *New York City Guide* (New York: Random House, 1939), 470.
Broiled fish, spinach, pudding: Greene, interview.
Rachel's habit of thrift; European money: Nahemow, interview.
Carl did not walk until thirteen months: letter, Rachel Sagan to Cari and Bill Greene, February 10, 1971, in possession of Cari Greene.
[RACHEL] FOLLOWED PRESCRIPTIONS ON CHILDHOOD NUTRITION: *The Demon-Haunted World* 1996, 359.

7   Carl's fight, Schechter's drugstore: ibid., xi.
Carl's dual nature: See Thomas 1963, 185–86.
Carl and Samuel followed Yankees, not Dodgers: Greene, interview.
Writing numbers 1 to 1,000: *The Demon-Haunted World* 1996, xii–xiii.
Carl's stamp collection: Druyan, interview.
I COULD SEE THEM AT WHATEVER TIME: Cooper 1976a, 70.
JUST SMALL HOVERING LAMPS?: *Cosmos* 1980, 168.

8   *Superman* comic books: Greene, interview.
Carl devoured Burroughs titles: *The Cosmic Connection* 1973, 101.
[CARL LIKED] THE HURTLING MOONS OF BARSOOM: ibid., 102.
Fantasia, mythology, classical music: Greene, interview; Sweeney 1982.
Prehistoric animals: Thomas 1963, 185.
Carl learned to identify constellations: Greene, interview.
Carl's mythology speech; special school suggested: ibid.

9   Carl skipped grades: Steele 1987, 22.
Carl tried to transport himself to Mars: Golden and Stoler 1980, 66.
Zatara anecdote: *The Demon-Haunted World* 1996, 14–15.
YES, BUT HOW WILL YOU MAKE A LIVING?: Goodell 1977, 167; *The Cosmic Connection* 1973, vii; Greene, interview; Baur 1975, 30.
Carl proposed name Carol: Greene, interview. (As an adult, Carol goes by the nickname "Cari.")
Carol's tricycle accident: ibid.
Rachel didn't like unattractive women: ibid.
Rachel dressed and made up her face: *The Demon-Haunted World* 1996, xii.
Dyed hair blond: Greene, interview. Used cold cream: Nick Sagan, interview.

10   Beer in bathroom story: Dorion Sagan, personal communication.
I AM SANE BECAUSE OF MY FATHER: Greene, interview.
Mushrooms and onions: Dorion Sagan, personal communication. Dorion says Carl may been in his *teens* when he found out about the switch.
Rachel replaced canary: Greene, interview. This happened after the family had moved to Rahway, New Jersey.
Carl invited black friend to dinner: Nahemow, interview.
THERE ARE PEOPLE FIGHTING OUT THERE: *The Demon-Haunted World* 1996, xii.
Nazis exterminated Sasov's Jews: Brian Neil Burg, interview.

Rahway 1948–51

11   Sagan family's 1948 move to Rahway: Swift 1990, 210.
[RAHWAY] HAS INTERESTED LANDSCAPE ARTISTS BECAUSE OF VISTAS: in the WPA guide *New Jersey* (New York: Hastings House, 1939), 484–85.

11   Sagans lived at 576 Bryant Street: Cari Greene, interview.
      Dogs, summer camp, Dumont TV: ibid. Jersey shore: Lu Nahemow, interview.
12   Conway's Concentration Camp: Swift 1990, 211.
      [CARL] WASTED A LOT OF TIME [IN HIGH SCHOOL]: Thomas 1963, 186.
      Carl read *Astounding Science Fiction*: Steele 1987, 20.
      THE CHALLENGE OF THE GREAT SPACES BETWEEN THE WORLDS: Clarke 1951.
      TURNING POINT: see Sagan's "In Praise of Arthur C. Clarke." *Planetary Report*,
      May–June, 1983, 3.
      Scientist-popularizers: *The Demon-Haunted World* 1996, 336. Willy Ley:
      Thomas 1963, 185.
      THERE APPEARS TO BE LIFE ON THE PLANET MARS: quoted in *Pale Blue Dot*
      1994, 239.
13   Carl was skeptical of religion: Swift 1990, 216.
      Hebrew school teacher's "trick": Clarise Samuels in "Tribute to Carl Sagan"
      1996–97.
      GIRLS WANT BOYS: Nahemow, interview.
      Chemistry set story: ibid.
14   Goose cake story: Greene, interview.
      Samuel wanted Carl to go into garment business: Nahemow, interview.
      Rachel hoped Carl would be pianist: ibid.
      Carl played piano beautifully: ibid.
      Home movie of Carl's piano performance: Greene, interview.
      Carl's Carnegie Hall performance: Ann Druyan, interview.
      Few colleges would take sixteen-year-old; Rachel opposed Carl's choice of col-
      lege: Nahemow, interview.
15   [CARL WAS VOTED] MOST LIKELY TO SUCCEED: Goodell 1977, 170.
      ASTRONOMY RESEARCH IS CARL'S MAIN AIM: "Carl Sagan: A Cosmic Celebrity"
      1996.
      Knights of Columbus essay; Carl wasn't permitted to be valedictorian: Druyan,
      interview.

Chicago 1951–60

16   WE'D ALL READ SCIENCE FICTION: Ronald Blum, interview.
      IT WAS LIKE MOVING FROM A DESERT TO THE GARDEN OF EDEN: Swift 1990, 217.
      Greek playwrights, architecture, Freud: Steele 1987, 22.
      A B.A. IN NOTHING: ibid., 22 WHICH SERVES YOU FOR ABSOLUTELY NOTHING:
      Goodell 1977, 167.
      Sagan did best work from 10 P.M. to 5 A.M.: Thomas 1963, 195–96.
      MY TIME IS WORTH MORE THAN THAT: Blum, interview.
17   Astronomy club, basketball team: Cari Greene, interview.
      [SAGAN] HAD NO VISIBLE MUSCULATURE . . . IRRELEVANT TO HIM: Blum, inter-
      view. KNOWN FOR THE SHARPNESS OF HIS ELBOWS: Leon Wanerman, quoted in
      "Carl Sagan: A Cosmic Celebrity" 1996.
      HE ARGUED PROPOSITIONS: Blum, interview.
      Rachel disapproved of non-Jewish girlfriend: Greene, interview.
      UNCLES OF GIRL FRIENDS: Goodell 1977, 167.
      THERE I HAVE MY SNEAKERS ON: ibid., 168. Sagan said this happened on spring

break. Seymour Abrahamson remembers the first meeting as being during the Christmas break and says they saw each other again on spring break.

18   Muller was five foot three: *Current Biography* 1947, 460.

Muller was a dedicated communist until the day he died: Sagan told this to Antonio Lazcano (interview) in those words or close to them.

Two grad students had nervous breakdowns: Seymour Abrahamson, interview.

DOESN'T HE KNOW HIS WEEKENDS AREN'T SACRED?: ibid.

Dinner, offer to work in Muller's lab: ibid.

That summer and the next: Sagan's curriculum vitae lists his position as "Research Assistant in Genetics" for 1952–53.

19   OH, HE WASN'T VERY GOOD: Abrahamson, interview.

EXTRAORDINARY . . . I DON'T SUPPOSE: Thomas 1963, 188. A slightly different telling of the incident is in *Cosmos*, 29–30.

20   Sagan learned lesson of scientific caution: Thomas 1963, 188.

THE CRITICAL EVENT: Swift 1990, 212.

CARL WAS A REAL PAIN IN THE ASS: Abrahamson, interview.

Sagan really "believed" in UFOs, went looking for them: ibid.

NOT A SINGLE ADULT I KNEW WAS PREOCCUPIED WITH UFOs: *The Demon-Haunted World* 1996, 67.

21   IF THE UNIDENTIFIED AERIAL OBJECTS SOBRIQUETED "FLYING SAUCERS": Document No. 711.5/8-352, August 3, 1952, National Archives.

UNDER THE CIRCUMSTANCES OF A PURELY HYPOTHETICAL SITUATION: letter of August 27, 1952, by Grace B. Ruckh, obtained from National Archives.

"Jesus Christ is extraterrestrial" story: Abrahamson, interview.

21–22   "Fermi question" story: See Jones 1985. The basic story is repeated throughout the SETI literature, generally at second or greater hand. Many accounts (including Sagan 1963 and my own *Prisoner's Dilemma* [New York: Doubleday, 1992]) say or imply that the conversation(s) took place during the Manhattan Project. Eric Jones of Los Alamos contacted several living witnesses, to which the above discussion is greatly indebted. He was able to narrow down the date to summer 1950.

22   *New Yorker* cartoon: drawn by Alan Dunn, it appeared in the May 20, 1950, issue on p. 20. Dunn did a number of alien-themed cartoons for the magazine, some of which are reproduced in Sagan's *Other Worlds* 1975.

EDWARD, WHAT DO YOU THINK?: Teller's recollection in Jones 1985, 7.

[CONVERSATION] HAD NOTHING TO DO WITH ASTRONOMY OR WITH EXTRATERRESTRIAL BEINGS: ibid., 7–8.

FAMOUS AND POSSIBLY EVEN APOCRYPHAL QUESTION: Newman and Sagan 1981, 293. As this indicates, Sagan was not sure this much-told tale was true.

23   Urey biography: Sagan 1981.

I DON'T LIKE ROCKS: Sagan 1981, 348.

24   Calvin's 1951 experiment: Garrison, Morrison, Hamilton, et al. 1951.

BEILSTEIN: See, for instance, Thomas 1963, 248.

25   Sagan told Miller that audience didn't appreciate work's significance: Stanley Miller, interview.

[SIGHT OF THESIS] WAS LIKE A PLUNGE INTO AN ICE BATH: Thomas 1963, 189.

26   Physics difficult, Sagan's true interests elsewhere: Blum, interview; Peter Meyer, quoted in Golden and Stoler 1980, 66.

IT IS DIFFICULT . . . TO ESCAPE THE CONCLUSION: Sagan 1957, 53.

THE CYTOPLASM MAY SELECT THE INSTRUMENTS: ibid., 54.

26   I HAD ONLY A VAGUE IDEA: Thomas 1963, 190.

26–27   Kuiper and Urey feud: Christopher Chyba, interview.

30        $2,000 Nash-Hudson: Letter, Carl Sagan to Lynn Alexander, dated July 4, 1956, in Lynn Margulis's papers.

          Los Angeles trip: Letter, Carl Sagan to Lynn Alexander, dated July 18, 1956, in Lynn Margulis's papers.

30   Meeting, Eckhart Hall: Lynn Margulis, personal communication.

31   Anthills and dandelions: *Current Biography* 1982, 373.

          Diaries, plays in the basement: ibid.

          Near South Side tenements; razors in garters: Wolkomir 1985, 52.

          Lynn rammed hand through window: Sharon Kleitman, interview.

          Oppenheimer visit: Margulis and Sagan 1997, 10–18.

32   Wanted babies; would make a scientific team: Letter, Carl Sagan to Lynn Alexander, dated July 11, 1956, in Lynn Margulis's papers.

          "NOSE IN A BOOK"; drove car into village: Lynn Margulis, interview.

          Forget marriage; continue to date: Letter, Carl Sagan to Lynn Alexander, dated September 3, 1956, in Lynn Margulis's papers.

          Relationship on; asking for another chance: Letters, Carl Sagan to Lynn Alexander, dated September 12, 1956, and October 4, 1956, in Lynn Margulis's papers.

          Rachel's reaction to Leone's nervous breakdown: Lynn Margulis, interview.

33   Tape-recording: Margulis 1998, 16.

          Sagan encountered anti-Semitism: Goodell 1977, 169.

          I SPENT ALL MORNING GOING DOOR TO DOOR: ibid.

          THERE WAS A KIND OF VIEW: Achenbach 1996, C2.

34   FRIVOLOUS QUESTIONS FROM PEOPLE: Wali 1991, 19.

          Students crossed to other side of street; Sagan took other stairway: Wali 1991, 7, 6.

          Chandra said Sagan should have worn a suit and tie: Margulis, personal communication.

          Chandra colloquium story: Wali 1991, 6.

          Sagan was impressed by Kuiper's order-of-magnitude estimates: Thomas 1963, 191.

35   MARS' DARK SPOTS HELD TO BE LAVA: *New York Times*, December 29, 1956.

          I'VE BEEN FOLLOWING YOUR CAREER: Goodell 1977, 173.

          Leading scientist called Sagan once a day: Philleo Nash made this claim (admitting it might be "folklore") in Thomas 1963, 191. This would most likely refer to Muller or Lederberg, or possibly just to Sagan's reputation for hobnobbing with scientists of that caliber.

          THE CREATION OF LIFE AND THE UNIVERSE: the lecture series is mentioned in many articles; the title comes from Sagan's December 1961 curriculum vitae, in the papers of Joshua Lederberg.

          SAGAN'S CIRCUS: Golden and Stoler 1980, 66.

          Gamow gave a talk: Ann Druyan, interview.

          Alexanders' feelings about Carl: Margulis, personal communication.

          Rachel's complaints about Lynn: Lu Nahemow, interview.

          Rachel complained about breasts in *National Geographic*: Dorion Sagan, personal communication.

36   FROM A BACHELOR TO A MRS.: Margulis 1998, 16.

36   Sagans' addresses in Madison: Lederberg letter to Sagan, February 16, 1959, and Sagan letter to Lederberg, November 29, 1959, both in Lederberg's papers. Lederberg's reaction to *War of the Worlds* broadcast: Lederberg 1987.

THAT BACTERIA HAVE A SEX LIFE OF A SORT: *Time*, November 10, 1958.

Tutored Lederberg, aware of the irony: see Goodell 1977, 169.

37   Chocolate bar wager: Golden and Stoler 1980, 66.

THE SOVIET UNION NO LONGER IS A PEASANT COUNTRY: *Newsweek*, October 21, 1957, 34.

IN RED TRIUMPH—OVER NEARLY ALL OF THE INHABITED EARTH: *Time*, October 14, 1957.

BY ALL ODDS THE MOST IMPORTANT JOB: *Newsweek*, October 21, 1957, 32.

Trip to Mars in a "coma": ibid., 37.

38   Calculation about H-bomb on moon: Lederberg 1987.

I AM DEEPLY CONCERNED OVER THE INCIPIENT DESPOILMENT: Lederberg n.d. ("Cosmic Microbiology") in Lederberg's papers.

THE FIRST ROCKET PERHAPS CARRYING CASUAL DIRT: ibid. The mention of pigment refers to speculation that the Soviets might crash a pigment-filled satellite to make a visible mark on the moon. Otherwise, Western skeptics might doubt that the Soviets had reached the moon.

Lynn fainted while pipetting amoebas; concluded she must be pregnant: Wolkomir 1985, 52.

Sagan's scholarships and fellowships: Sagan's December 1961 curriculum vitae, in Lederberg's papers.

Sagans' finances; job paid Sagan $3 an hour: letter, Sagan to Lederberg, March 7, 1959, and Sagan's December 1961 curriculum vitae, both in ibid.

38–39   Origin of name Dorion: Dorion Sagan, personal communication.

39   Kuiper's students in great demand: Steele 1987, 22.

A NASA CONTRACT TO DO SOME SPADEWORK: this letter is reproduced in Levinthal n.d. as Attachment 1.

THIS REALLY IS A SUBSTANTIAL JOB: letter of March 25, 1959, reproduced in Levinthal n.d. as Attachment 2.

40   I SORT OF GLIDED EFFORTLESSLY: Swift 1990, 213.

[THE IDEA] MUST NOT BE DISMISSED: Sullivan 1964, 137.

Gause's mention of canned foods, antibiotics: letter, Sagan to Lederberg, November 29, 1959, in Lederberg's papers.

41   Sagan's Ph.D. thesis: University of Chicago, 1960.

EVERYTHING ON VENUS IS DRIPPING WET: quoted in Sagan 1961b, 849.

42   Botanist, mineralogist, petroleum geologist, or deep-sea diver: ibid.

An emotional basis for disbelief in high temperatures: Sagan 1970, 116.

43   Sagan knew French from high school: Greene, interview.

Kuiper advised Sagan to go to Berkeley: letter, Sagan to Lederberg, February 8, 1960, in Lederberg's papers.

Sagan forgot to mention the spectrophotometer: Margulis, personal communication.

THE ONLY ASTRONOMER: Goodell 1977, 168.

43–44   FOR A LONG WHILE HE HAD BEEN COMPLETELY DEVOTED TO VENUS: Thomas 1963, 206.

44   Life on Jupiter was mentioned in Sagan's article: Sagan 1961a, 189.

LOOK, I'M TALKING ABOUT ORGANIC MOLECULES: Goodell 1977, 173.

Berkeley 1960–63

45   Sagan insisted on teaching: Golden and Stoler 1980, 68.

Sagan spoke of "global warming" in early 1960s: Ronald Blum, interview.

46   [NOBEL PRIZE ENABLED LEDERBERG] TO STAY IN A NON-REPUTABLE GAME: Ezell and Ezell 1984, 58.

MY PRINCIPAL CRITICISM: letter, Harold Urey to Sagan, December 17, 1959, in Harold Urey's papers, Mandeville Special Collections Library, University of California, San Diego.

VIRTUALLY CONCLUSIVE EVIDENCE FOR "VEGETATION": letter of March 24, 1959, to G. F. Schilling, reproduced in Levinthal n.d., as Attachment 2.

SURELY ONE OF THE MOST . . . ALL THE PROJECTED SPACE FLIGHTS: Miller and Urey 1959, 251.

47   Kellogg recognized Sagan's writing ability: Thomas 1963, 203–4.

THE EVIDENCE TAKEN AS A WHOLE: *The Atmospheres of Mars and Venus* 1961, 35.

Carl and Lynn's reactions to son Dorion's scream: Blum, interview.

Winston Churchill comment: Lynn Margulis, personal communication.

Carl jealous of children: Sagan, Dorion 1997.

A TORTURE CHAMBER SHARED WITH CHILDREN: Margulis, personal communication.

Lynn put off separation until Jeremy old enough to walk: ibid.

48   Aeolosphere model: Öpik 1961.

VERY STIMULATING AND IMAGINATIVE ARTICLE: ibid., 2819. He refers to Sagan 1961b.

49   Sagan visited lab, kibitzed: Elliott Levinthal, interview.

INCOMPETENT WITH HIS HANDS: Timothy Ferris, interview.

Wolf Trap description: see Ezell and Ezell 1984, 67–68, which includes a photograph.

DAZZLED . . . AS A NEWLY MINTED PH.D.: *Pale Blue Dot* 1994, 208.

Apollo scientific goals: document, signed "Carl Sagan" and dated May 8, 1962, in Urey's papers.

49–50   THERE ARE CERTAIN TIMES: Thomas 1963, 194.

50   THE READER MAY SEEK TO CONSIGN: Cocconi and Morrison 1959, 184.

Struve's reaction to Cocconi and Morrison article: Drake and Sobel 1992, 2.

50–51   IN A WAY WE'RE LIKE DOROTHY: *Saturday Evening Post*, February 10, 1962, 28.

51   Oriental Institute; fundamentalist religion: Swift 1990, 57.

Navy electronics courses better than Cornell's: Drake and Sobel 1992, 13.

WHAT I FELT WAS NOT A NORMAL EMOTION: ibid., 19.

Drake's hair was white by age thirty: ibid., 19.

52   Loaded gun: ibid., 214.

[SAGAN] KNEW MORE ABOUT BIOLOGY: ibid., 47.

JOHN C. LILLY: ibid., 47.

53   Only eleven people invited: Swift 1990, 60.

Lederberg dubious about SETI: ibid., 213; Drake and Sobel 1992, 47.

Struve didn't introduce wife: Drake and Sobel 1992, 31.

Pearman looked as British as he sounded: ibid., 53.

54   [LILLY] DIDN'T LOOK AT ALL LIKE THE KIND OF MAN: ibid.

Taboo subjects of fear and love: Thomas 1963, 128.

Lilly's experimental philosophy: see, for instance, Lilly 1997, opposite p. 87.

54   Atchley background: Dana Atchley III, personal communication. See also Atchley III's Web site, "Next Exit" at http://www.nextexit.com.

Murmur as Drake wrote equation: Drake and Sobel 1992, 54.

56   Dolphin catches ring on penis: Lilly 1966, 76.

56–57   Military applications of dolphins; Lilly wondered if dolphins were pacifists: Sullivan 1964, 248–49.

57   Notification of Calvin's Nobel Prize: Melvin Calvin's 1963 recollection in Thomas 1963, 42–43, differs in some minor details from Frank Drake's (interview and Drake and Sobel 1992). I have favored Calvin's account.

Nobel Prize legitimized conference: Drake and Sobel 1992, 59.

Group at conference got drunk on champagne: Baur 1975, 31.

WITH ELVAR'S PERMISSION: Thomas 1963.

58   Morrison armed second bomb: Drake and Sobel 1992, 62.

Catastrophe ideas: ibid.

59   It would be necessary to hear a two-way conversation: Calvin in Swift 1990, 130.

TO THE VALUE OF L: Drake and Sobel 1992, 64.

Description of coin: Thomas 1963, 144. John Lilly (interview) says he found the coin and pointed it out to Calvin.

New club members, Haldane comment: *The Cosmic Connection* 1973, 168.

59–60   Drake's puzzle: Drake and Sobel 1992, 167–68.

60   Feynman response: Drake, interview; also ibid., 169.

61   Oliver's martini glass reply: Drake and Sobel 1992, 169.

WE BELIEVE THAT WHEREVER THIS METEORITE ORIGINATED: quoted in Sullivan 1964, 127.

BEAUTIFUL LITTLE BUTTONS; CRUD: Urey 1962, 626, 628.

Investigators named species after themselves: see Sullivan 1964, 135.

62   ANDERS IS STILL ARGUING: letter, Urey to Sagan, July 11, 1962, in Urey's papers.

Fitch and Anders's identification of ragweed pollen: see Sullivan 1964, 143.

Bacteria would leave residue of opposite-handed compounds: Letter, Sagan to Nagy, April 28, 1964, in Urey's papers.

63   Suggestion impressed Urey: see letter, Urey to Sagan, May 5, 1964, in ibid.

THAT AN ARTICLE ON METEORITES APPEARED: Sullivan 1964, 133.

Sagan and Lederberg encouraged endosymbiosis work: Margulis, personal communication; Ann Druyan, interview. See also letter, Carl Sagan to Lynn Sagan, January 10, 1966, in Lynn Margulis's papers.

64   "Art film" establishment; phone call to Lynn: Letter, Sagan to Lynn Sagan, August 12, 1962, in Lynn Margulis's papers.

64–65   May 8, 1962, content of discussion: unpublished "Summary of a Discussion on Exobiology with Professor A. A. Imshenetsky of the Soviet Academy of Sciences," in Lederberg's papers. Background of discussion: *The Cosmic Connection* 1973, 95–97.

65   Notified Lederberg: letter, Sagan to Lederberg, May 15, 1962, in Lederberg's papers. Sagan also mentions the formaldehyde and steam method in Thomas 1963, 200.

64–66   Story about Imshenetsky and "translator"; CIA: *The Cosmic Connection* 1973, 95–99.

66   Sterilization standards; Wolf Vishniac; Imshenetsky was ill: Sagan, Levinthal, and Lederberg 1968, 1191.
ISN'T THAT THE FELLOW WHO WAS WITH US IN LOS ANGELES?: *The Cosmic Connection* 1973, 99.
Sagan believed there was more to life than science; open to new experiences: Sagan (as "Mr. X":) in Grinspoon 1971, 110. (Identification of Sagan as "Mr. X": Lester Grinspoon, interview.)
Volkswagen shadows: Grinspoon 1971, 110.
Landscape changed colors: ibid., 110–11.

67   Man on Sandeman bottle: ibid., 111. (Sagan identifies Sandeman as sherry, but it is actually a port.)
Sagan may have contemplated focus on biology: Joshua Lederberg, interview.
Lynn tried to discourage press interviews: Blum, interview.
Sagan on 1961 CBS news show: Sagan's December 1961 curriculum vitae, in Lederberg's papers.
CARL HAS CREATED A NEW FIELD: Thomas 1963, 192.

68   Assumed Harvard post in February 1963: ibid., 195.
STANFORD WAS A PRETTY LOOSE SHIP: Levinthal, interview.
Nagged Sagan to do his share: Stanley Miller, interview.
Collaborative work: Sagan and Miller 1961.
Ponnamperuma committed to getting preconceived results: Ruth Mariner, interview, and Miller, interview.
Ponnamperuma briefed lab on Sagan: Mariner, interview.
Sagan made Mariner nervous: ibid.

69   PHOTOSYNTHESIS WITHOUT LIFE: Ponnamperuma, Sagan, and Mariner 1963, 225.
70   *Nature* articles: ibid. and Ponnamperuma, Mariner, and Sagan 1963.
Work was clouded with ambiguities: Miller, interview.
CARL, YOU ARE A BEAUTIFUL PERSON: Letter, Lynn Sagan to Carl Sagan, January 7, 1963, in Lynn Margulis's papers.
Offer to move to Massachusetts, reaction: Lynn Margulis, interview.

Cambridge 1963–68

71   Wanted a wife, not a roommate: Letter, Carl Sagan to Leone Alexander, undated (c. March 1963), in Lynn Margulis's papers.
Lynn was very happy in anticipation of leaving: Lynn Margulis, personal communication.
Sagan's old car, turtlenecks: Richard Berendzen, interview.
MEETING CARL FOR THE FIRST TIME: Philleo Nash, quoted in Thomas 1963, 191.

72   [SAGAN'S] BASS VOICE (I HEARD IT IN THE WOMB): Sagan, Dorion 1997.
HE BROUGHT TO THE CLASS THREE INGREDIENTS: Berendzen, interview.
I FEEL THAT I'M REMARKABLY LUCKY: Thomas 1963, 189–90.
SNOB: Cari Greene, interview. (She adds that Carl wasn't a snob later in life, owing to the influence of his third wife, Ann Druyan.)
HE IS TOO QUICK: Thomas 1963, 186.

73   Sagan did not wear a watch: Ridpath 1974, 37.
Sagan missed meeting with the Vishniacs: Helen Vishniac, personal communication.
Sagan revealed findings in "introductions": Ray Reynolds, interview.

73   [SAGAN REGARDED] MOST PEOPLE [AS INTELLECTUAL INFERIORS]: Margulis, personal communication.

YOU KNOW, ORR, WE'RE HEARING THIS PROPOSAL: Sagan's words as recalled by Elliott Levinthal, interview.

[SAGAN'S] EXTRAORDINARY SELF-CENTEREDNESS: Margulis, personal communication.

74   IF THE ODDS OF PROBABILITY: Thomas 1963, 210–11.

Whipple tried to steer Sagan into areas with more certain results: Fred Whipple, interview.

With other professors, the doctoral time would drag on: Berendzen, interview.

75   THE PROJECTS OF THE SPACE CADETS: Sullivan 1964, 234.

OTHER CIVILIZATIONS, AEONS MORE ADVANCED: ibid., 238.

75–76   Sagan's article on interstellar rockets: Sagan 1963.

75   AS HE MIGHT . . . FOR A NEW SPORTS CAR: Thomas 1963, 210.

BONUS ADVENTURE: ibid., 208.

76   IT IS NOT OUT OF THE QUESTION THAT ARTIFACTS: Sagan 1963, 497.

Shklovskii had pen in hand, about to begin chapter on interstellar travel: Sagan 1985, 3.

77–78   Biographical data on Shklovskii: ibid. and Shklovsky 1991. (Shklovskii's name has also been transliterated as "Shklovsky." I favor the spelling Sagan used.)

77   Siberian railroad job, magazine article: Drake and Sobel 1992, 96–97.

Shklovskii considered studies of Crab Nebula his best work: Shklovsky 1991, 110.

78   BECAUSE THE SONS OF BITCHES: Frank Drake, interview.

Shklovskii promised book, hoped to get past censors: Shklovsky 1991, 249.

50,000-copy first printing of Shklovskii's book sold out: ibid., 251.

Oparin ripped up letter and returned it to Shklovskii: ibid., 251.

[SAGAN COULD] MAKE ANY ADDITIONS HE WISHED TO THE AMERICAN EDITION: ibid., 251.

79   AN ELEGANTLY PRODUCED, FAT VOLUME: ibid., 251–52.

I HAVE NO GRIEVANCE: ibid., 252.

Nuclear holocaust likely while capitalism exists: *Intelligent Life in the Universe* 1966, 437.

Aliens without navels: Dorion Sagan (personal communication) heard this description from his mother. Jon Lomberg (interview) confirms that Sagan wrote unpublished science fiction early in his career.

I VISUALIZED HIM AS AN ELDERLY PERSON: Asimov 1980, 302.

Two people more intelligent than Asimov: ibid., 302.

80   Sagan asked Asimov to rewrite introduction: ibid., 306–7.

IT'S NOT AS IF WE HAD PAID ADMISSION: see Sagan's "In Praise of Arthur C. Clarke" *Planetary Report*, May-June 1983, 3.

Divorce was nonnegotiable: Margulis, personal communication.

Carl's Franklin Street residence: Lester Grinspoon, interview.

81   [CARL] WENT THROUGH THE ROOF: Margulis, interview.

I WAS UNABLE TO DO WHAT 10,000: Margulis, personal communication.

Both Carl and Lynn had dates at New Year's party: David Layzer, interview.

Carl went into therapy, helped somewhat: Lu Nahemow, interview.

Talk about marriage's failure: ibid.

PROBLEM OF THE ORIGIN OF THE NUCLEATED CELL: Wolkomir 1985, 78.

81   Fifteen journals rejected Lynn's article: *Current Biography* 1992, 375.
      Carl wrote name as Lynn Sagan Margulis: Margulis, interview.

82   Two of Lilly's dolphins in *Flipper*: Thomas 1963, 140; 144.
      CARL, THIS IS ELVAR: *The Cosmic Connection* 1973, 169.
      WAS IT IN CONTEXT?: ibid., 171.

83   Dolphin suicide: Drake and Sobel 1992, 58.
      THE REALLY CRITICAL SCIENTIFIC TESTS: *The Cosmic Connection* 1973, 175.

84   Sagan tried to get Howe into bed: John Lilly, interview.
      Sagan introduced Howe to Bateson: *The Cosmic Connection* 1973, 174.
      Experiment living with dolphin: Lilly 1966, 250–300.
      A DOLPHIN IS MORE LIKE A SHADOW: ibid., 266.
      I HAVE FOUND THAT DURING THE DAY: ibid., 273.
      Dolphin car: ibid., 273.
      REACH SOME SORT OF ORGASM: ibid., 274.
      Dolphin sexually aroused; Sagan's game with dolphin: *The Cosmic Connection* 1973; 174–75.

85   Peter in *Flipper* movie: Thomas 1963, 140. Peter was one of several dolphins used in the production of the 1963 motion picture, *Flipper*, which inspired the TV series.
      TO SEE ITS EFFECTS ON DOLPHINS: Lilly 1997, 123.
      Sagan's reasoning about dangers of LSD: Sagan (as "Mr. X") in Grinspoon 1971, 116.
      Sagan attended lectures on sexual freedom: Clark Chapman, interview.
      [LINDA SALZMAN WAS] EXTRAORDINARILY ATTRACTIVE: Asimov 1980, 391.
      Wind-tossed hair; 1960s fashions: Robert Keiser, interview.
      That Linda wasn't a scientist was a welcome change: so suggests David Grinspoon (interview).
      Description of Linda's art: Keiser, interview.
      Carl nursed Linda during illness: Greene, interview.

86   [LINDA WAS] QUITE OBVIOUSLY IN LOVE WITH CARL: Asimov 1980, 391.
      [MARINER] MAY ANSWER LONG STANDING QUESTIONS ABOUT THE "CANALS": Ezell and Ezell 1984, 76.

87   AS A MEMBER OF A GENERATION THAT ORSON WELLES SCARED: *New York Times*, July 30, 1965.
      [NEW DATA ON MARS] SEEM TO REFUTE THE THESIS: *New York Times*, July 30, 1965.
      Sagan recalled Johnson quote: Ferris 1973, 26. Sagan's recollection was not word-for-word accurate but quite good considering the time interval.

88   Pollack spoke slowly: Cuzzi 1994, 1606; Bruce Hassell, interview.
      If you couldn't explain an idea to Pollack . . . : Cuzzi 1994, 1608.
      Pollack spotted fatal errors: Brian Toon, interview.
      NINETY DEGREES OFF FROM EVERYTHING YOU THOUGHT OF: ibid.
      Recruitment pitches during Pollack's oral examinations: Bill Gile, interview.
      Pollack was gay, adored by women: ibid., Bruce Hassell, interview.
      [Carl's] lobotomized gay relative kept secret: Dorion Sagan, personal communication.
      [CARL] TURNED TO EMOTIONAL ICE: ibid.
      Linda unknowingly fell in with lesbian crowd: ibid.

88   Sagan was angry over health service's refusal to treat Bill: Gile, interview. This incident took place at Cornell.

Carl lectured Dorion about gay classmate: Dorion Sagan, personal communication.

89   Dark-area regeneration model for Mars: Pollack and Sagan 1967c.

Both the biological and the dust models: Pollack, Greenberg, and Sagan 1967, 823.

Mariner-like photography could not detect life on Earth: Kilston, Drummond, and Sagan 1966.

Explanation of Martian "canals": Sagan and Pollack 1966.

90   In 1966 Sagan published twenty-four articles and abstracts: Sagan's curriculum vitae, Cornell University.

[Sagan's] habit of extrapolating adventurously: Ridpath 1974, 37.

The probability of our meeting: Sagan 1985b, 3.

Fifty percent of what Shklovskii does is brilliant: Sagan 1985b, 3.

91   Shternberg Institute press conference: *Intelligent Life in the Universe* 1966, 395; Shklovsky 1991, 253; Drake and Sobel 1992, 102–4.

One just cannot read: letter, Harold Urey to Sagan, dated June 29, 1966, in Harold Urey's papers, Mandeville Special Collections Library, University of California, San Diego.

Here is a body of literature whose ratio: *Communication with Extraterrestrial Intelligence (CETI)* 1973, 364.

92   Fourteen printings of *Intelligent Life in the Universe*: Baur 1975, 28.

Group of 1950s investigators believed in UFOs: William K. Hartmann in *UFO's—A Scientific Debate* 1972, 17.

93   "Spoofing": ibid., 292; *The Demon-Haunted World* 1996, 86–87.

Excision of phrase "the Director": *UFO's—A Scientific Debate* 1972, 288.

Sagan saw UFO: the most complete description is in ibid., 272–73; also see *Broca's Brain* 1979, 66.

94   Jaded ex-preppies shrieking and crying with laughter: Roberts 1980, 30.

The state where this trial took place has been identified as Kansas, Arkansas, and Nebraska. Sagan's account in *Intelligent Life in the Universe* 1966 asserts the defendant was born in Nebraska.

94–95 UFO trial: *Intelligent Life in the Universe* 1966, 16–18.

96   Horowitz compared to fox terrier: Cooper 1980, 126.

Antarctica was a paradise next to Mars: Norman Horowitz, interview.

97   300° F sterilization temperature: Ezell and Ezell 1984, 104.

An analogy that has been useful: Sagan, Levinthal, and Lederberg 1968, 1195. In Thomas 1963, Sagan attributes the matches analogy to microbiologist John Phillips.

98   Sagan's political views: Berendzen, interview.

Sagan resigned in protest from air force board: Ann Druyan in Terzian and Bilson 1997, 166.

Sagan was visiting lecturer at Tuskegee, 1963–72: Sagan's curriculum vitae.

Sagan met Grinspoon during debate at party: Lester Grinspoon, interview.

99   When you're a kid: David Grinspoon, interview.

Sagan's bedtime stories about black holes: Sagan, Dorion 1997; Collins 1985.

Four trees in a line: Sagan, Dorion 1997.

99   Grinspoon wanted to assemble scientific case against marijuana: Lester Grinspoon, interview.

        Washington diary on hemp: Grinspoon 1971, 12.

100   Queen Victoria prescribed cannabis: Grinspoon and Bakalar 1997, 4.

        Sagan was the opposite of pot-smoker stereotype: Lester Grinspoon, interview. Grinspoon didn't try marijuana himself, anticipating testimony: Lester Grinspoon, interview.

101   THE FOLLOWING BIOGRAPHY IS APPROXIMATELY ACCURATE: Grinspoon 1971, 109–10. Identification of Sagan as "Mr. X": Lester Grinspoon, interview. Grinspoon says Sagan's account was written well in advance of the book's publication, perhaps around 1968. Sagan actually turned thirty-seven the year the book was published; the age was changed. He was remarried by the time the book appeared.

        MY HIGH IS ALWAYS REFLECTIVE, PEACEABLE: Sagan (as "Mr. X") in Grinspoon 1971, 116.

        I WOULD GUESS THIS IS A SIGNAL-TO-NOISE PROBLEM: ibid., 111.

        INFORMATION-THEORETICAL: ibid., 111.

        Yellow and red words: ibid., 112.

102   WHEN CANNABIS IS LEGALIZED: ibid., 116.

        While high, Sagan appreciated counterpoint, Tanguy works: ibid., 112.

        CANNABIS ALSO ENHANCES THE ENJOYMENT OF SEX: ibid.

        Cannabis used to enhance Sagan's swim: Lester Grinspoon, interview.

        Beach resembling Tanguy painting: Grinspoon 1971, 112.

        I DO NOT CONSIDER MYSELF A RELIGIOUS PERSON IN THE USUAL SENSE: ibid., 113.

103   I HAVE MADE A CONSCIOUS EFFORT: ibid., 115–16. Grinspoon does not recall the "very bizarre" idea. (One that might qualify is floating life on Jupiter.)

        Sagan got many of best ideas while using marijuana: Lester Grinspoon, interview.

        YOU'VE GOT TO GIVE THAT TO ME: ibid.

        Ginsberg credited marijuana: see Grinspoon 1971. Sondheim: see Merle Secrest's *Stephen Sondheim: A Life* (New York: Knopf, 1998).

        Shower anecdote, use of ideas in Sagan's lectures and books: Grinspoon 1971, 114.

104   Sagan excused himself to record thoughts: David Grinspoon, interview.

        I HAD A VERY ACCURATE SENSE: Grinspoon 1971, 115.

        LISTEN CLOSELY, YOU SONOFABITCH: Grinspoon, 1971, 115.

        YOU DIRTY HARVARD JEW!: Lester Grinspoon, interview.

105   Sagan was upset at *New York Times* piece: ibid.

        Cannabis remains were weighted down with ashtray: ibid.

        [SAGAN WAS SCIENTIFIC COMMUNITY'S] COLLECTIVE UNCONSCIOUS: Cooper 1976a, 44.

        IN CONSULTATION WITH THE AUTHOR: *National Geographic*, December 1967, 833.

105–6   Sagan's meeting with Kubrick, Clarke: *The Cosmic Connection* 1973, 181–84.

106   Not showing aliens in *2001*: Roberts 1980, 22; also Jon Lomberg, interview (running out of money story).

        Dancer in tights with polka dots: *The Cosmic Connection* 1973, 182.

        Sagan refused to be interviewed: Asimov 1980, 394–95.

        Lloyd's of London story: Roberts 1980, 22; *The Cosmic Connection* 1973, 184.

106 THERE WAS A SORT OF A RUMBLE: Berendzen, interview.
Empty set of experimental objects: see Lederberg 1987.

106–7 CERTAIN BIOLOGISTS (SOME OF THEM NOW EX-BIOLOGISTS ...): Simpson 1964, 774.

107 [EXOBIOLOGY'S] SPECULATIONS CANNOT BE CONFIRMED: Gelman 1977, 52.
Layzer friendly with Carl and Lynn; kids played together: Layzer, interview.
Size of Harvard's astronomy department; wait for tenure: ibid.
Sagan's interest in MIT: letter, Urey to Bruno Rossi, March 8, 1967, in Urey's papers.

108 WHAT WILL IT PROFIT THIS COUNTRY: Ezell and Ezell 1984, 117.
[GOLD] WEARS HIS RENOWN AS CORRECTLY: *Current Biography* 1966, 134.
IN CHOOSING A HYPOTHESIS: *Ithaca Journal,* August 19, 1996.

109 Gold said he didn't have the money to hire Sagan: Corson in Terzian and Bilson 1997, 141–42.
YOU WON'T REGRET IT: Thomas Gold, interview.
Treman State Park was as beautiful as a national park: Sagan in Terzian and Bilson 1997, 142.

110 Sagan believed sources might be extraterrestrial signals: *The Cosmic Connection* 1973, 260.
Drake bought $30 Sears antenna: Drake and Sobel 1992, 86–87.

111 Linda's ultimatum: Lester Grinspoon, interview.
[SAGAN WAS] INTENSELY JEWISH CHARACTER: Ronald Blum, interview.
Fans didn't know Sagan was Jewish: Clarise Samuels, personal communication.
Sagan wanted rabbi to mention big bang: Asimov 1980, 457.
Wedding reception at Grinspoons' house: Lester Grinspoon, interview.
Rachel anecdote: Asimov 1980, 457–58.

112 Asked if SDS a reason for denial: Lester Grinspoon, interview.
Layzer suspected of voting against Sagan's tenure; denied: Gelman 1977, 52; Layzer, interview and personal communication.
Whipple debated whether to tell Sagan; Babette's reasoning: Fred Whipple, interview.

Ithaca 1968–76

114 [ITHACA IS] CENTRALLY ISOLATED ... A LOT OF PEOPLE ... IF I DIDN'T: Brown 1978.
ITHACA, THANKFULLY, ISN'T IN THE SNOWBELT: "Cornell University," brochure issued by Office of Publication Services, Cornell, 1987.
Carl and Linda's address: Cornell faculty directory.
COMFORTABLE MODERN furnishings from Bloomingdale's: Bill Gile, interview.
Cupboards full: Robert Keiser, interview.
[STOVES AND DISHWASHERS WERE] FOREIGN OBJECTS: ibid.
Veal roast and chocolate cake: letter, Rachel Sagan to Cari Greene, November 30, 1969, in possession of Cari Greene.
Chocolate-chip cookie crumbs: Keiser, interview.

114–15 IF I'D ORDERED THESE IN A RESTAURANT: ibid.

115 IT FLEW: ibid.
Asimov got tipsy on Linda's punch: Nick Sagan, interview.
[SAGAN] LIKES TO WALK IN THE FLOWER GARDEN: Brown 1978, 2.

115 Sagan got students jobs at NASA; origins of life research: Chyba 1997b, 6.

NO ONE WAS BORN WITH FOURIER TRANSFORMS: Emily Haynes in "Tribute to Carl Sagan" 1996–97.

116 IF A SCIENTIST IDENTIFIES HIS SELF-ESTEEM: Thomas 1963, 210.

Multiple hypotheses make it easier to discard wrong ideas: Cooper 1976a, 64.

Tyson's visit to Cornell: Neil deGrasse Tyson, personal communication.

Sagan could resume conversations: Antonio Lazcano, interview.

Kuiper's influence on Sagan: Thomas 1963, 191. Sagan's impromptu calculations: Len Tyler, interview; Lazcano, interview.

WHEN IT CAME TO THE MATHEMATICS: William I. Newman, interview.

117 HE WAS SOMEONE WHO HAD MORE IDEAS THAN HE COULD POSSIBLY HANDLE: Tokasz 1996; see also Chyba 1997b, 6.

[SAGAN] WOULD TAKE YOUR NEW RESULT: David Grinspoon, interview.

Pollack's method of moving items on his desk: Gile, interview.

SOME PEOPLE HAVE A TENDENCY: Steele 1987, 22.

Assumed editorship of *Icarus* January 1, 1969: letter, Sagan to Harold Urey, December 14, 1968, filed with Harold Urey's papers, Mandeville Special Collections Library, University of California, San Diego.

Sagan liked being editor, assembling tables of contents: McDonough 1996, 10.

Classroom humor discussion: James B. Marshall in the "Tribute to Carl Sagan" 1996–97.

118 WHEN PEOPLE FIRST MEET HIM: Thomas 1963, 193.

Fictional map of Mars: Owen B. Toon in Terzian and Bilson 1997, 51–52.

118–19 Sagan and Drake's visit to Timothy Leary: Frank Drake, interview.

119 Asked him to convince Carl to be captain: Lester Grinspoon, interview.

A drift away from science: *UFO's—A Scientific Debate* 1972, xiii.

SDS suspected Soter of being an FBI agent: Rink 1996.

119–20 Rink's visit to Sagan home: ibid.

120 Tear gas incident: Seymour Abrahamson, interview.

Carl and Linda left for London: letter, Rachel Sagan to Cari and Bill Greene, March 19, 1969; in possession of Cari Greene.

121 Trip to "barn"/holding facility: Gile, interview.

Pollack drove Volvo: Robert Keiser, interview.

Kameny; Pollack's security check: Gile, interview; Frank Kameny, interview.

122 WHERE WE ARE PROFOUNDLY IGNORANT: Duff 1994, 43.

[SAGAN WAS] PARANOID: Lester Grinspoon, interview.

If you're not a little paranoid . . . : *UFO's—A Scientific Debate* 1972, 274.

122–23 THE EXISTENCE OF LIFE ON THE MOON: Compton 1989, 45.

123 LIKE WITCHES: ibid.

FINE, BUT HE WILL HAVE TO EAT IT *ON THE MOON*: Duff 1994, 39.

THE ABSURDITY OF THE EFFORTS: *New York Times,* July 13, 1969.

SUPPOSE SOMETHING GOES WRONG: Elliott Levinthal, interview.

NASA ruled quarantine could be suspended for emergency: Duff 1994, 43.

124 Astronauts refused to go along with quarantine: Levinthal, interview.

MAYBE IT'S SURE TO 99%: *Time,* June 13, 1969, 78.

NASA received letters on Crichton's *The Andromeda Strain*: Duff 1994, 39.

125 Astronauts isolated for twenty-one days before flight: ibid., 40.

Esophagus problem dated to Carl's adolescence: Ann Druyan, interview.

Carl's achalasia: Lester Grinspoon, interview.

125 Carl had modified Heller myotomy: Druyan, interview.

    Asimovs visited Carl in hospital: Asimov 1980, 493–94.

    Grinspoon saw X ray: Lester Grinspoon, interview.

    Carl needed ten to eleven units of blood: ibid.

    Carl's paranoia about hospital; nurse could barely lift him: ibid.

126 Linda looked in on Carl occasionally: ibid.

    Grinspoon saved Carl's life: Jon Lomberg, interview; ibid.

    Carl insisted on clearing doctors' orders with Grinspoon: Lester Grinspoon, interview.

    THERE WERE THESE TWO STRANGELY GARBED FIGURES, AS IN A DREAM: Bruning 1994.

    Quarantine procedures: for an overview of the quarantine, see Duff 1994.

127 Cockroach story: attributed to NASA's Robin Brett in ibid., 42.

    [QUARANTINE WAS A] SHAM . . . THE PUBLIC NEEDS TO BE COMFORTED: *Time*, June 13, 1969, 78.

    Photographing Sagan's scars: Lester Grinspoon, interview.

    [ARMSTRONG'S BOOTS SANK] MAYBE AN EIGHTH OF AN INCH: Duff 1994, 41.

    Sagan wanted to view microphotographs with Gold: Thomas Gold, interview.

128 [LUNAR SAMPLE WAS] DEAD AS DOORNAIL: Duff 1994, 43.

    PROBABLY THE QUARANTINE WAS A DAMN GOOD IDEA: ibid., 42.

    [UREY SAID UFOS WERE] REAL: letter, Donald Menzel to Urey, July 31, 1969, in Urey's papers.

129 Linda tried to talk Carl out of meeting: Timothy Ferris, interview.

    Astrology symposium wasn't necessarily a bad idea: *UFO's—A Scientific Debate* 1972, xiii.

    Threat to report Sagan to Spiro Agnew: *Broca's Brain* 1979, 70 (paperback edition).

    McDonald background: see obituary in the *New York Times*, June 16, 1971.

    Signal and noise in UFO sightings: *UFO's—A Scientific Debate* 1972, 53.

129–30 Flying saucer with rivets story: Philip Morrison, interview.

130 McDonald did not believe Hills' story: Lester Grinspoon, interview.

    THE ABSOLUTE TERROR [IN BARNEY HILL'S VOICE]: *The Demon-Haunted World* 1996, 103.

131 I HAD SEEN PHOTOGRAPHS THAT HE HAD TAKEN: Fuller 1996, 173.

    IF YOU DON'T KNOW WHERE YOU ARE: ibid., 50.

    [HILL'S STORY WAS] DREAM: *The Demon-Haunted World* 1996, 104.

    I AM ENOUGH OF A REALIST: *UFO's—A Scientific Debate* 1972, 53.

132 I THINK IT IS PRETTY CLEAR: ibid., 272.

    Well-known UFO sighting could be *folie à deux*: ibid., 238–39.

    McDonald's suicide: *New York Times*, June 16, 1971.

133–34 Design of plaque: Drake, interview.

134 Figures looked more Caucasian on etched plaque: *The Cosmic Connection* 1973, 26–27.

    Reproductions of plaque: ibid., 21.

    Caretaker called plaque pornography: Drake and Sobel 1992, 179.

    A FAMILY NEWSPAPER MUST UPHOLD COMMUNITY STANDARDS: *The Cosmic Connection* 1973, 24.

    Catholic Review recommended praying hands: ibid., 26.

135 I MUST SAY I WAS SHOCKED: ibid., 25.

135   Nudes and Map Tell About Earth to Other Worlds: ibid., 26.
      In retrospect, we may have judged: ibid., 24.
      Nigerian newspaper: Drake, interview.
      Hello. We're from Orange County: *The Cosmic Connection* 1973, 26.
      Cesarean delivery of Nicholas Sagan: Nick Sagan, interview.
      Explanation of name: ibid.

136   As the hard-hats say: letter, Rachel Sagan to Cari Greene, September 18,
      1970, in possession of Cari Greene.
      Nicholas Sagan's first word; red and cold birth memory: Nick Sagan, interview.
      See also *The Dragons of Eden* 1977, 156 (paperback edition), where Carl won-
      ders whether this is a true birth memory.
      [Sagan was] guiding spirit [of Viking]: Ferris 1977, 62.

137   Sagan insisted that site selection be documented: Ezell and Ezell 1984, 285.
      Sagan's analysis of mission's goals: ibid., 279.
      A crashed lander is not very useful: ibid., 286.

138   Remark about thinking side of brain: Ray Reynolds, interview. (Reynolds pre-
      ferred to leave the MIT scientist unnamed.)
      Disneyland, Brooklyn Bridge, JFK shooting: Herbert Friedman in Shklovsky
      1991, 20–24.
      Buying shoes: Drake, interview.
      Pornographic playing cards: Lomberg, interview. See also description of "Vay-
      gay" in *Contact* 1985.
      In your country this slogan is offensive: Drake and Sobel 1992, 100.
      How's that—Rich?: Shklovsky 1991, 252.

138–39 Royalties story: Drake and Sobel 1992, 100.

139   Shklovskii used theory in lectures to nonscientists: Herbert Friedman in
      Shklovsky 1991, 18.
      [Space stations] weren't just a joke: ibid., 250.
      Saving NASA $200 million: *The Cosmic Connection* 1973, 108.

140   You will shortly be called upon: ibid., viii.
      Planetarium show, points on stars: Drake and Sobel 1992, 101.

141   Kardashev's objection to "philosophers": Shklovsky 1991, 256.
      The main thing is not to look: ibid., 258.

142   Orchards, laser telephone link at Byurakan: Dyson 1971, 130.
      Ambartsumian resembled Smokey the Bear: Drake and Sobel 1992, 109. Those
      wanting to judge the resemblance are referred to Phylis Morrison's photograph
      of Ambartsumian in *Communication with Extraterrestrial Intelligence (CETI)*
      1973, opposite p. xxii.
      Bypassing Soviet customs: Drake 1976, 24.
      Russians feared stenotype machine was Xerox machine: Drake and Sobel
      1992, 111.
      Morrisons' luggage woes: Philip and Phylis Morrison, interview; Drake 1976, 24.
      Informal dress: see photos in *Communication with Extraterrestrial Intelligence
      (CETI)* 1973, after p. xxii.
      Minsky brought Frisbees: Drake and Sobel 1992, 109.

143   Sunspot theory: Philip Morrison, interview; McDonough 1996, 11; Sagan
      1985b, 3; Dyson 1971, 137. Morrison doesn't remember, and none of the pub-
      lished sources give, the name of the scientist with the sunspot theory.

143   [AMBARTSUMIAN WAS] SLIGHTLY SKEPTICAL OF THE CONDENSATION THEORY: *Communication with Extraterrestrial Intelligence (CETI)* 1973, 28.
        THE DISINTEGRATION OF SUPERDENSE BODIES: ibid., 29.

144   G STAR CHAUVINISM: ibid., 37.
        STATISTICAL CALCULATION: ibid., 39.

145   IN ORDER TO DISPLAY THE DIFFERENCE: ibid., 65.
        PROFESSOR CRICK AND I ARE PLAYING DIFFERENT CARD GAMES: ibid., 66.
        THIS, TO ME, SPEAKS RATHER PERSUASIVELY: ibid., 57.
        Drake formula was an "entertainment": *UFO's—A Scientific Debate* 1972, 267.

146   IF THERE IS ANYTHING MORE TO BE SAID: *Communication with Extraterrestrial Intelligence (CETI)* 1973, 146.
        ACADEMICIAN AMBARTSUMIAN WHO INSISTED: ibid., 146.
        I HAVE NOT THE SLIGHTEST IDEA: ibid., 77–78.

147   Intelligence is synonymous with language: ibid., 91.
        Sophistication of !Kung campfire tales: ibid., 92.

147–48 McNeill's dispute over Drake equation: ibid., 115.

148   IF SOMEONE MANAGED WITH GREAT DIFFICULTY: ibid., 117.
        IF YOU SAW THEM FROM A DISTANCE: Swift 1990, 83.
        Gold and octopus eyes: *Communication with Extraterrestrial Intelligence (CETI)* 1973, 121–22.

149   Stent's "Golden Age": ibid., 154–58.
        FAUSTIAN . . . WILL TO POWER: ibid., 155–57.
        GALACTIC POLYNESIAN ARCHIPELAGO: ibid., 158.
        SOFT APOCALYPSE . . . A FEW ACADEMICS: ibid., 159.
        THE HORRIFYING GOLDEN AGE OF DOCTOR STENT: ibid., 160.
        A SENTIMENTAL ATTACHMENT: ibid., 160.
        I WILL SIMPLY HAVE TO PLAY POKER WITH YOU: ibid., 161.

150   Between 1 part in 10 and 1 part in 1 million: ibid., 161.
        VERY LARGE AND POWERFUL MACHINES: ibid., 162.
        I BELIEVE HUGE CHANGE: ibid., 163.
        [WORLD'S PROBLEMS COULD BE HANDLED] BY AN AGGRESSIVE TECHNOLOGICAL EXPANSION: ibid., 163.

151   IF WE ASSUMED A PESSIMISTIC SCENARIO: ibid., 166.
        I THEREFORE RAISE THE POSSIBILITY: Sagan 1973c, 350–51.

152   Shklovskii advocated Andromeda search: Thomas 1963, 86.
        ANTIQUE COMMUNICATION MODES: Sagan 1973c, 350.
        THE BEST SEARCH MODE: *Communication with Extraterrestrial Intelligence (CETI)* 1973, 212.
        IT SEEMS TO ME THAT WE SHOULD WATCH OUT: ibid., 215.

153   IF A LION COULD TALK: Wittgenstein, quoted in a *New York Times* editorial, "Beware the Cow in E.T.'s Barn," December 28, 1982.
        EARTH PRIME: *Communication with Extraterrestrial Intelligence (CETI)* 1973, 320.
        Panovkin doubted mathematics is universal: ibid., 341.
        THE CONFIDENCE THAT I KNOW MATHEMATICIANS AND NATURAL SCIENTISTS HAVE: ibid., 346.
        A VERY RICH THREE-DIMENSIONAL, MOVING, CAREFULLY SCALED CINEMA: ibid., 349.
        THE PICTURE WOULD BE DISTORTED: ibid., 322–24.

153   Morrison and Dyson "deciphered" Armenian alphabet: Philip Morrison, interview.

154   AND YOU DOUBT THE POSSIBILITY: Shklovsky 1991, 255. This incident occurred in 1964, not during the better-known 1971 Byurakan conference co-organized by Sagan.

Drake wanted plans for tachyon telescope: *Communication with Extraterrestrial Intelligence (CETI)* 1973, 340.

[UNDERSTANDING ET MESSAGE WOULD BE] A DISCIPLINE RATHER THAN A HEADLINE: ibid., 339.

155   UNLESS MY READING OF HISTORY IS RADICALLY WRONG: ibid., 343.

WAS A TYRANT IN LIFE: ibid., 343.

A PSEUDO OR SCIENTIFIC RELIGION: ibid., 344.

BECAUSE THEY REFLECT OPINIONS: ibid., 344.

TO AN INTELLIGENT AND GOOD PERSON: Shklovsky 1991, 259.

Melancholy as conference ended: see ibid., 260.

156   A MODERN VERSION OF THE PURSUIT OF THE GOLDEN FLEECE: *Mars and the Mind of Man* 1973, 34.

I THINK THE OBSERVATIONS WILL HAVE TO BECOME: ibid., 23.

THE MOST ADVANCED SOCIETY . . . A MONUMENT TO A MARS: ibid., 24.

Mars was like tennis ball without the seams: *A Path Where No Man Thought* 1990, 456.

Joke about sending craft to Venus: Ezell and Ezell 1984, 290.

Observing the moons of Mars was not such a bad idea: Steve Mencinsky in "Tribute to Carl Sagan" 1996–97; *The Cosmic Connection* 1973, 109.

157   Image enhancement story; "diseased potato": *The Cosmic Connection* 1973, 110.

158   IF IT WERE NOT MARS: Ezell and Ezell 1984, 292–93.

Lederberg turned ashen; emotional confrontation: Cooper 1976a, 60.

159   Nick Sagan read road, airport signs: Nick Sagan, interview.

Alphabet book story: ibid.

Sagan's temporary residences: Cornell faculty directories list Sagan's address as 507 The Parkway in 1972; 330 The Parkway in 1973; 14 Fairview Heights in 1974.

Linda painted cabinets and Formica: Keiser, interview.

MY IDEA OF HEAVEN: Ferris 1977, 63.

Dolphin in lagoon: *The Cosmic Connection* 1973, 168.

160   Khare made helium balloons for kids: Nick Sagan, interview.

Production of sulfur-containing amino acids: Sagan and Khare 1971.

Synthetic proteins from light: Steele 1987, 24.

161   Article on early faint sun paradox: Sagan and Mullen 1972a.

162   Starting in 1972, Margulis worked on Gaia hypothesis: Lynn Margulis, personal communication.

Lynn saw absence of life on Mars as confirming Gaia: Margulis 1998, 116.

163   Lederberg's conference call with Viking landing site group: Ezell and Ezell 1984, 302.

164   Microenvironments article: Lederberg and Sagan 1962.

Sagan's long winter theory: Sagan 1971.

165   TWELVE THOUSAND YEARS AGO MAY HAVE BEEN A TIME ON MARS: *The Cosmic Connection* 1973.

165	Add water to find life on Mars: Sagan 1971, 513–14.
	Article on ultraviolet radiation: Sagan and Pollack 1974.
166	WHEN I TOTAL UP THE PROS AND CONS: Ezell and Ezell 1984, 309.
	[SAGAN'S OPPOSITION WAS] OUT OF CHARACTER: Joshua Lederberg, interview.
	Lederberg complained to Fletcher: Ezell and Ezell 1984, 304.
	IT'S NOT THAT DIFFERENT: ibid., 308.
	Deliberation on landing sites: see ibid., 309–15.
167	ROSE BOWL SIZE HAZARDS: James Martin quoted in Ezell and Ezell 1986, 14.
	Sagan doubted value of photos in avoiding hazards: Ezell and Ezell 1984, 321.
	Radar "feels" boulders a meter across or less: Ezell and Ezell 1986, 14; also, G. Leonard Tyler, interview.
	Martian "quicksand" would be similar to Gold's idea about lunar dust: Ezell and Ezell 1984, 320–21.
168	Martin was hired because he looked like a contractor: Ferris 1977, 58.
	Martin was the General Leslie Groves of Viking: this is Timothy Ferris's apt analogy (interview).
	DER FÜHRER, GREAT WHITE CHIEF: Ferris 1977, 60. PRUSSIAN GENERAL: Ezell and Ezell 1984, xi.
	Two volumes on things that might go wrong with Viking: Ferris 1977, 60.
	Martin's plan for nuclear war: ibid.
	Tyler's report on November 4, 1974: Ezell and Ezell 1984, 322.
169	Pariisky looked like Bob Newhart: Drake and Sobel 1992, 105; see photograph in *Communication with Extraterrestrial Intelligence (CETI)* 1973, after p. xxii.
	Pariisky's "signals": Drake and Sobel 1992, 105–6.
169–70	Bora Bora story: Drake, interview.
171	YOU KNOW, I'VE HAD THE STRANGEST LETTER: Fred Whipple, interview.
	Urey blocked Harvard tenure: ibid; David Layzer, interview and personal communication.
	Whipple expected opposition within Harvard: Layzer, personal communication.
	"Thermodynamic Equilibria" article: Lippincott, Eck, Dayhoff, and Sagan 1967.
172	THIS ARTICLE ILLUSTRATES TO ME: letter, Urey to Bruno Rossi, March 8, 1967, in Urey's papers.
	"Nitrogen Oxides on Mars" article: Sagan, Hanst, and Young 1965.
	A TYPICAL VALUE FOR THE ABUNDANCE OF NO_2: ibid., 73.
172–73	SAGAN HAS DASHED ALL OVER THE FIELD OF THE PLANETS: letter, Urey to Rossi, March 8, 1967, in Urey's papers.
173	YOU EMBARRASS ME ENORMOUSLY: letter, Urey to Sagan, September 17, 1973, in ibid.
	I'VE THOUGHT AS CAREFULLY AS I CAN: letter, Sagan to Urey, October 2, 1973, in ibid.
	Sagan's early faint sun paradox work may have impressed Urey: Stanley Miller, interview.
174	Sagan was six foot two and 190 pounds: *Current Biography* 1970, 372.
	Sagan got better looking as he entered middle age: Lu Nahemow, interview.
	Sagan tried a mustache: Lomberg, interview.
	[SAGAN LOOKED] LIKE A COLOMBIAN NOVELIST: Baur 1975, 28.
	[SAGAN AS] GUATEMALAN POET: Yaukey 1996a, 7A.
	[SAGAN WAS] BORED BY THE COMPANY OF SCIENTISTS: Cooper 1976a, 44.
	Porsche 914: Baur 1975, 32.

174   Wanted BARSOOM: *The Cosmic Connection* 1973, 114.

175   [Sagan called] exobiology's most energetic and articulate spokesman: *Time*, December 13, 1971, 50–52.

Is the scientific method changing: Ferris 1973, 30.

[Discovery of ET life as] mind-expanding experience: ibid., 26.

176   So while not at all taking away from the ecstasy: ibid., 30.

Even today, there are moments: *The Cosmic Connection* 1973, vii–viii.

177   Too down to Mars: Lomberg, interview.

Meeting of Sagan and Lomberg: ibid.

I want that guy: Goodell 1977, 171.

He was passionate about astronomy: Johnny Carson, personal communication.

177–78   Sagan launched into a cosmological crash course for adults: Baur 1975, 26.

178   Twenty printings, over 500,000 copies of *The Cosmic Connection*: Moss 1980, 25.

I can see you've never waited for the Long Island Railroad: *Broca's Brain* 1979 (paperback edition), 64.

What am *I* doing here?: Gil Levin, interview.

It captured his speaking style perfectly: Phil Karn in "Tribute to Carl Sagan" 1996–97.

You know, if I went to every meeting: Goodell 1977, 174.

And what are you going to do, Mr. Big Carl Sagan?: Lomberg, interview.

179   Vishniac had limited arm mobility; didn't take survival course: Norman Horowitz, interview.

Mounts Baldr and Thor: The irony of the locale names is pointed out in DiGregorio 1997, 125.

The first person since Giordano Bruno: Sagan 1974d, 397–98.

180   Gold considers himself responsible for Vishniac's death: Thomas Gold, interview.

What do *you* say?: Cooper 1976b, 54.

1 in 50 chance: ibid., 53.

Oyama put odds at 50 percent: Cooper 1980, 126.

[Horowitz put odds at] not quite zero: Cooper 1980, 99.

I'm an honest-to-God, card-carrying geologist: Ferris 1977, 63. This was said three weeks after the Viking landing.

Sagan put odds at 50 percent; made polar bear wager: Chapman 1997, 6.

181   A dumbed-down *Cosmic Connection*: Goodell 1977, 165.

Crystophages, petrophages: *Time*, July 5, 1976, 90.

181–82   Murray's appearance on camera: this description is based on a 1981 edition of ABC's *Nightline* in which Murray and Sagan appeared.

182   [Sagan and Murray were] like an odd pair of siblings joined at their navels: Terzian and Bilson 1997, 36.

I think it's because we human beings: Cooper 1976a, 83.

Murray couldn't understand Sagan's preoccupation with life: Ferris 1977, 63.

I keep having this recurring fantasy: Cooper 1976b, 48.

Lederberg doubted nocturnal life: ibid.

183   A silicon-based giraffe: PBS *Nova* series "The Search for Life," 1976.

183 I DON'T THINK THE ENGINEERS ARE WALLOWING IN IGNORANCE: Cooper 1976b, 48.

One geologist admired Mutch for not shooting Sagan: ibid., 47.

184 Test with snake, chameleon, and tortoises; group photo: ibid.

185 Sagan stayed in Ferris's apartment; Ferris received invitations: Ferris, interview.

Guests at Ephron's apartment: Druyan, interview.

Druyan biographical background: Druyan, interview.

Druyan's novel: Druyan 1977b.

Carl was sprawled on floor, laughing; conversation topics; Druyan, interview.

Carl's shirtsleeves were rolled up, had warm smile: Druyan 1997, 10.

186 Sagan understood message content: Drake, interview.

Tears and sighs: Drake in *Murmurs of Earth* 1978, 65.

HI in Morse code: Drake and Sobel 1992, 184. The first ten bits were all 0 ("dot"). *H* is four dots, and *I* is two dots. In real Morse code, there is a slight gap between letters, absent in the Arecibo transmission. You could just as well parse it *IH* or *III*.

187 Soviets planned to search for ET signals: Thomas 1963, 86.

Troitsky observed Andromeda with fifty-foot dish: *Communication with Extraterrestrial Intelligence (CETI)* 1973, 257.

LET'S DO IT: Drake and Sobel 1992, 148.

Cordes watched Watergate hearings: James Cordes, interview.

188 IT WAS A BIG TRIP: Drake, interview.

Sagan and Drake were awakened at 4 A.M.; Drake drove, Sagan ate garlic bread: Drake 1976, 24.

189 Sagan's body language: Drake, interview.

100 hours in observation: Drake and Sobel 1992, 151.

ALL WE SAW WERE LEVEL, FLAT SPECTRA: Drake, interview.

IT WAS AN ACTUAL FEELING OF DEPRESSION: Cooper 1976b, 46.

A BRIEF RUN ON THE NIGHT OF MARCH 24/25: Drake and Sagan 1975.

190 THE MORE YOU THINK ABOUT IT, THE LESS IT MEANS: Newman, interview.

IF THERE WERE ONCE COCKEYED OPTIMISTS: Drake 1976, 26.

Humans are probably the only intelligent species in the local group of galaxies: Herbert Friedman in Shklovsky 1991, 19.

191 *Voprosy Filosofii* article: Shklovskii 1976.

Sagan uses ET arguments with Shklovskii: Sagan 1985b, 18.

Sagans in new house for 1975–76 academic year: Cornell faculty directory.

Glass galaxy, Asimov's reaction: Lomberg, interview.

Parents as opposites: Nick Sagan, interview.

192 A DADDY AND A HOST: Cooper 1976a.

I'M PAN!: Ferris, interview.

The Count of Monte Cristo, Superman: Nick Sagan, interview.

Nick's art resembled Tassili frescoes: *Other Worlds* 1975, 118–19.

Ping-Pong: Nick Sagan, interview.

"Babe" Ruth story; Dorion apologizes to Rachel: letter, Rachel Sagan to Cari Greene, April 29, 1969, in possession of Cari Greene.

193 THE QUEEN IS A VERY DANGEROUS PIECE: Nick Sagan, interview.

Boys spied on parents: David Grinspoon, interview.

[VIKING LAUNCH WAS] A SCREWED-UP MESS: COOPER 1976A, 44.

193   Lederberg pessimistic before launch: Cooper 1980, 107.

193–94   "WHAT IF IT BLOWS UP?": Cooper 1976a, 40–43.

194   Hydrogen and helium abundances in Jupiter's atmosphere: Elliot, Wasserman, Veverka, et al. 1974.

        WE CAN IMAGINE ORGANISMS: *Intelligent Life in the Universe* 1966, 329.

195   "A Meeting with Medusa" story: Clarke 1978.

        Chapman's line about floating life, Sagan's reaction: Clark Chapman, interview.

196   THE DISTINCTION BETWEEN HUNTING AND MATING: Sagan and Salpeter 1976, 747.

Pasadena 1976

197–223 Viking mission: For dates and events—and in many cases people's words, thoughts, and motivations—this chapter is deeply indebted to Ezell and Ezell 1984 and Cooper 1980, both written at or near the time of the mission.

197   WHY CAN'T I HAVE BOTH?: Lester Grinspoon, interview.

        Carl and Linda's passion cooled; bickering in Pasadena: David Grinspoon, interview. Monopoly game: Ann Druyan, interview.

        Sagans were in Pasadena in mid-June: letter, Sagan to Harold Urey, June 14, 1976, in Harold Urey's papers, University of California, San Diego.

        IN A CERTAIN SENSE I SPENT A YEAR ON MARS: *Pale Blue Dot* 1994, xvi.

198   Sagan became member of Cornell geology department: see Sagan's curriculum vitae and Ferris 1997, 63. His title was Member, Graduate Field of Geological Sciences.

        Trilobite story: Thomas Mutch in the Viking Lander Imaging Team 1978 [*The Martian Landscape*], 25.

        Mars simulations; Martin as "Ted Baxter": Ferris 1977, 60.

        Satchel labeled "Embassy of Mars": ibid., 62.

        Use of Sagan's quotes: Christopher Chyba, interview.

        I DON'T THINK WITH COMPLETE SINCERITY: Timothy Ferris, interview.

        YOU AT CALTECH LIVE ON THE SIDE OF PESSIMISM: Terzian and Bilson 1997, 36.

198–99   CARL IS A GREAT ONE FOR POSING A QUESTION: Gelman 1977, 51.

199   TO KEEP POSSIBILITIES ALIVE: ibid.

        CARL SERVES AN IMPORTANT FUNCTION: Cooper 1976a, 44.

        CARL'S THE GREATEST MENACE SINCE THE BLACK PLAGUE: Cooper 1976b, 47.

        HE'S CHARMING, HE'S BRIGHT: Cooper 1976a, 43.

        New Yorker profile made Sagan almost angry enough to sue: Ferris, interview. Sagan's chocolate milkshake for breakfast: Ferris 1977, 62.

200   Reaction to first orbital photos from Viking 1: Ezell and Ezell 1986, 331.

        Sagan wanted good photos and radar: Martin 1986, 12.

        Landing sites that looked good in photos did not look good in radar: ibid., 11.

201   "Carl Sagan rule": Ezell and Ezell 1984, 339–40.

        CARL, WE HAVE A *REAL* SPACECRAFT: Elliott Levinthal (reconstruction of Martin's and Sagan's comments), personal communication.

        Sagan wanted to postpone the Viking landing: Ezell and Ezell 1984, 361.

        Martin concerned about Bicentennial coverage: ibid., 357.

        NASA's press release; TV anchors had time to cancel flights: ibid., 336.

202   23–12 straw vote: ibid., 343–44.

        Hole through the planet: ibid., 346.

        COSMIC ICE HOCKEY: ibid., 346.

202 Sagan suggested interns to count craters: Biemann 1977, 15.

203 Angie Dickinson was rumored to be coming to party: Don Davis, interview. Martian cartoons at JPL: Cooper 1980, 121.

Delay of eighteen minutes, eighteen seconds in receiving Viking's signal: Ezell and Ezell 1984, xi.

IT'S ON MARS, ONE WAY OR ANOTHER: Ferris 1977, 56.

TOUCHDOWN, WE HAVE TOUCHDOWN: Martin 1986, 10.

HERE'S WHAT APPEARS TO BE THE FIRST PICTURE COMING IN: ABC news coverage, collection of Museum of Television and Radio.

Planning of first two photographs of Mars: See Ezell and Ezell 1984, 380.

204 YOU WOULD HAVE BELIEVED THAT ALL THE PEOPLE: ibid., 330.

Sagan was never so glad to see a rivet: Cooper 1980, 117.

THERE WAS NOT A HINT OF LIFE: ibid., 121.

Sagan's TV appearances: Ferris 1977, 63.

205 [SEARCH FOR] SPOOR: Mutch, Binder, Huck, et al. 1976, 800.

Sagan taped photos together; Sagan and Ferris sat with them wrapped around their heads: Ferris, interview; Ferris 1977, 58.

BRING FULL CONCENTRATION TO IT: Ferris 1977, 58.

"Chicken tracks" on Mars: Biemann 1977, 42.

"Martian graffiti" reports: Ferris 1977, 58. B reminded Sagan of Barsoom: *Cosmos* 1980, 122.

Sagan's dream of being on Mars: Ferris 1977, 62.

206 UNDEFINABLE PESSIMISM: The Viking Lander Imaging Team 1978 [*The Martian Landscape*], 29.

THE RULES OF THE GAME: Ferris 1977, 63.

WE WERE REASONABLY LUCKY: ibid.

IT WAS HARD WORK AND PERSEVERANCE: ibid.

LOOK, I HAVE THIS COIN: ibid.

IT'S YOUR COIN!: ibid.

IF I WERE AN ORGANISM: ibid.

207 LOOK AT THAT SKY: Ezell and Ezell 1984, 383.

Ron Levin turned monitors back; Martin scolded: DiGregorio 1997, 140.

208 THE SORT OF BOOS GIVEN TO JIM POLLACK'S PRONOUNCEMENT: Ezell and Ezell 1984, 383. This source has Sagan saying "*Jerry* Pollack," which must be a misquote.

National Enquirer prediction of pink sky on Mars: Biemann 1977, 140. The same article also predicted that Viking would find ruins of ancient civilizations (maybe the famous Cydonia "face"?).

A REAL ANSEL ADAMS PICTURE: Cooper 1980, 119.

YOU CAN'T LOOK AT THAT PICTURE: ibid.

[SAGAN] WOULD PROBABLY SAY THAT WE *STILL* HAVEN'T EXPLORED: Chapman 1997, 6.

Oyama's appearance: see photo in DiGregorio 1997, 151; also in Biemann 1977.

209 [SAGAN] WAS SMART ENOUGH TO TURN DOWN [LEVIN'S JOB OFFER]: Gil Levin, interview.

Biology team wondered why Horowitz participated: Ezell and Ezell 1984, 412. Horowitz offered to eat Mars dust: Norman Horowitz, interview (to which Horowitz added, "I don't know whether I'd do it now!"—not because of microbes but the soil's active chemistry).

210   No opportunity for calibration tests until after launch: Cooper 1980, 102–3.
       Biemann's dress: see photos (taken by Biemann's teenage son) in Biemann 1977.
211   Martian soil was like soil in Los Angeles backyards: Scott, quoted in *Los Angeles Times*, July 30, 1976.
       [LEVIN EXPERIMENT'S] SUPER CURVE: Biemann 1977, 59.
212   IMPORTANT, UNIQUE, AND EXCITING THINGS: Cooper 1980, 125.
       A FAIRLY HIGH LEVEL OF RADIOACTIVITY: Ezell and Ezell 1984, 401.
       VERY MUCH LIKE BIOLOGICAL ACTIVITY . . . MAY IN FACT MIMIC: *Newsweek*, August 9, 1976, 63.
213   "Death gasp" hypothesis: Cooper 1980, 145.
       YOUR SUPEROXIDE, OR WHATEVER IT IS: ibid., 140–41.
       Sagan in Washington, D.C., missed excitement: ibid., 152.
       YOU COULD HAVE KNOCKED ME OVER: ibid., 150.
214   I WANT TO EMPHASIZE THAT IF THIS WERE NORMAL SCIENCE: Ezell and Ezell 1984, 403.
       Horowitz was worried about Sagan's spirits: Cooper 1980, 157–58.
       IF IT TURNS OUT THAT THESE SIGNALS ARE *NOT* BIOLOGICAL: ibid., 157.
       THE ONLY INSTRUMENT I KNOW: ibid., 141.
215   Dust storms on Mars would distribute organics: Ezell and Ezell 1984, 409.
216   IN HARSH CONDITIONS, WHAT COULD BE MORE EFFICIENT: Cooper 1980, 168.
       YOU HAVE TO ENDOW YOUR BUGS: ibid., 169.
       100 to 1,000 bacteria: Ezell and Ezell 1984, 406.
217   [LANDING SITE'S] BLANDNESS . . . IF THERE AREN'T FAR MORE EXCITING AREAS: *U.S. News and World Report*, August 30, 1976, 52–53.
       "Fish hook" appearance of curve: Biemann 1977, 69.
217–18 Levin suggested microbes were dead: DiGregorio 1997, 160.
218   Margulis's views on experiments; Levin's results were "trash": Levin, interview.
       Sagan wanted site where temperature rises above freezing: Biemann 1977, 88.
       THAT'S GOTTA BE THE PLACE!: Cooper 1980, 183.
       DO YOU CALL 155-FOOT-HIGH SAND DUNES: Ezell and Ezell 1984, 354–55.
       IF THAT'S UTOPIA . . . : Ferris 1977, 63.
       THE NEXT TIME I WANT YOU TO FIND A LANDING SITE: Biemann 1977, 135.
219   [LEVIN'S RESULT WAS] MIND-BOGGLING: Cooper 1980, 196.
       THAT'S THE BALL GAME: Ezell and Ezell 1984, 408.
220   THE HUMMERS: Biemann 1977, 5.
       SUBROCK SAMPLE: Cooper 1980, 206–9.
       Rock "categories": ibid., 207.
221   IS IT CONCEIVABLE: ibid., 211.
       SAY SOME OF THESE BUGS: ibid., 213.
221–22 Horowitz and Levin's objection to "hard-shell bug" theory: ibid., 214–15.
223   SIMILAR CALCULATIONS OF ORGANISM SPACING: Sagan 1976b.
       Horowitz posted Sagan's face on his door: Cooper 1980, 215.

Ithaca 1977–78

224   Witch anecdote: Ann Druyan, interview.
224–25 Problems with foot-deep dig: Cooper 1980; Ezell and Ezell 1984.
226   IT'S AS IF THE MARTIANS: Ferris 1977, 65.

226   BIOLOGISTS HAVE NOT REACHED ANY FINAL CONCLUSIONS: Cooper 1980, 238.

227   I AM, RELUCTANTLY, (. . .) CARBON CHAUVINIST: *Cosmos* 1980, 126.
         Horowitz reinterpreted his control's "negative" as a "positive": Horowitz
         1977, 61.

227–28   Article on Martian dust storm particles: Toon, Pollack, and Sagan 1977.

228   Horowitz's results with clays: Cooper 1980, 241.

229   GIL, THAT'S RIDICULOUS: DiGregorio 1997, 195.
         IT REALLY LOOKS LIKE YOU'VE GOT SOMETHING: Levin, interview.
         Levin, Sagan, Pieri collaboration, one-sigma difference: ibid., DiGregorio
         1997, 179–90.

230   Levin disappointed that Sagan disagreed with him: Horowitz, interview.
         Lee read works of Faulkner, Dostoyevsky, Camus: Grimwood 1996.
         Lee's appearance: see photos in Biemann 1977.
         HERE WE HAD BROUGHT MARS RIGHT INTO PEOPLE'S BACKYARDS: Holt 1981.
         Lee approached Sagan with business idea: Gentry Lee, personal communica-
         tion.

231   Andorfer's ideas for TV hosts: Cook 1980, 23.
         THEY SAID GREAT THINGS: ibid., 25.
         Sagan and Lee hired Malone in March 1977: Lee, personal communication.
         Would Lee be interested in working for them?: Jon Lomberg, interview.

231–48   Voyager record: *Murmurs of Earth* 1978, to which this discussion is indebted, is
         a detailed account of the record's making in the principals' own words.

233   Fell in love instantly: Sweeney 1982.
         Feared she was falling in love: Obst, interview.
         Sagan directed words to Druyan: Lester Grinspoon, interview.
         Russian Tea Room conversation: Druyan, interview.

233–34   Idea to ask John Lennon to choose music: Timothy Ferris, interview.

234   MAKING THE RECORD . . . BECAME AN ODDLY PRACTICAL WAY: Druyan 1977a, 12.
         LACK OF HISTORICAL DETERMINISM IN THE DETAILS: Sagan in *Murmurs of Earth*
         1978, 5.
         Sagan's piano lessons; liked rock, reggae: Druyan, interview.
         "Hey, Mr. Tambourine Man": Lomberg, interview.

235   [MUSIC TO EXPRESS] COSMIC LONELINESS: Sagan in *Murmurs of Earth* 1978, 20.
         NOW, LET'S SEE IF I GOT THIS STRAIGHT: Sagan quoting Williams in ibid., 18.
         Search for "Jaat Kahan Ho": ibid., 19–20.
         Sagan's telegram to Russian colleague: Druyan, interview. Druyan does not
         recall who the colleague was.

235–36   "Moscow Nights" story: Sagan in *Murmurs of Earth* 1978, 21.

236   Sagan thought Berry song was awful: Ferris, interview.

237   ["JOHNNY B. GOODE" AS] TRAVELING MUSIC: Druyan audio interview on *Contact*
         Web site, http://www.contact-themovie.com, 1997.

237–38   Morrison and Heinlein's comments about pictures: Jon Lomberg in *Murmurs
         of Earth* 1978, 77.

238   Charles Eames's refusal: Lomberg, interview.
         Picture books were consulted: Lomberg in *Murmurs of Earth* 1978, 75.

239   Perfect humans or "real people": Frank Drake, interview; Drake and Sobel
         1992, 187–88.

240   [NASA] HAD SOME NERVE SENDING A LITTLE GIRL: Druyan in *Murmurs of Earth*
         1978, 152.

240   [SOLDIER'S] HORRIBLY CHEERFUL AND THOUGHTLESS [VOICE]: ibid.
         Record should not have negative images: Sagan in *Murmurs of Earth* 1978, 40.

241   Recording of kiss: Druyan in ibid., 157.

242   Question about postponing launch: Sagan in ibid., 24.
         "FLOWING STREAMS". . . BECAUSE IT IS A MEDITATION: Druyan 1977a, 13.
         I GOT BACK TO MY ROOM AND FOUND A MESSAGE: Druyan 1997, 11.

243   I JUST WANT TO MAKE SURE: Druyan, interview.
         Obst wanted to know when Carl was going to tell his wife: Obst, interview.
         MY DEAR FRIENDS IN OUTER SPACE: *Murmurs of Earth* 1978, 251.

244   . . . AND GOOD LUCK: Samuel Ramsay Nichol quoted in ibid.
         Sagan wasn't aware of Waldheim's Nazi past: Timothy Ferris (interview)
         pointed out this irony.

245   Druyan was hooked up to Honeywell computer, data recorded: Druyan audio
         interview on *Contact* Web site, http://www.contact-themovie.com, 1997.
         Data sounded like a string of firecrackers: Druyan in *Murmurs of Earth* 1978,
         158.

246   "Danny Boy" story: Sagan in ibid., 32.
         Questions about art, religion: ibid., 34–35.
         THERE'S A *LITTLE* PROBLEM: Lomberg, interview.
         Humans who take their clothes off turn to stone: Drake and Sobel 1992, 188.
         Memo about pregnant women being erotic: Lomberg, interview.
         Carl and Annie's Circle Line tour, NASA worries, plans to inform others:
         Druyan, interview.

247   Lomberg suggested cutting music; Ferris refused: Ferris, interview.
         Bruce Springsteen was cutting a record: ibid.
         TO THE MAKERS OF MUSIC: Sagan in *Murmurs of Earth* 1978, 40; also ibid.

248   Inspector rejected record; band drowned out press conference: Ferris, inter-
         view.
         Estimates of record's lifetime: Sagan in *Murmurs of Earth* 1978, 233–34.

249   Plan to tell Linda at Cape Cod: Lester Grinspoon, interview.
         List of assets on yellow pad: ibid.
         Carl phoned Annie; Ferris's reaction: Druyan, interview; Ferris, interview.
         Ferris's and Druyan's engagement presents to be returned: Lester Grinspoon,
         interview.
         Wanted another child: ibid.
         Linda and Annie were in tears at launch: Ferris, interview.

250   DON'T THINK I'M GOING TO DO SOMETHING: Nick Sagan, interview.
         ARE YOU SURE SHE FEELS THE SAME WAY ABOUT YOU?: Lomberg, interview.
         Samuel and Rachel took title on condo in August 1977: letter, Rachel and
         Samuel Sagan to Cari Greene, June 27, 1977, in possession of Cari Greene.
         I HOPE IT'S ANNIE DRUYAN: Druyan, interview.
         DEEDS, MY FRIEND, NOT WORDS: ibid.
         I WAS ALWAYS IN A STATE OF NORMAL AMBIVALENCE: Obst, interview.
         I THINK ANNIE FEARED FOR CARL: ibid.

251   Slaterville Springs home: Druyan, interview.
         Sagan's Hodgkin's disease diagnosis; doctors' change of mind: ibid.
         Sagan was surprised at sales of *The Dragons of Eden*: Ferris, interview.
         Sales figures for *The Dragons of Eden*: McDowell 1981. The royalty amount is

estimated from sales of 200,000 hardcover copies at $8.95 list price and standard publishing terms.

252   Two dozen drafts of the typical Sagan book: Druyan, interview.
Sagan liked Swinburne, Melville: ibid. Also Blake, Shakespeare, Aztec poetry: Antonio Lazcano, interview.
WHEN I TRY TO EXPRESS AN EMOTION IN PROSE: Roberts 1980, 30.
IT IS ALWAYS RAINING: *Cosmos* 1980, 96.
IN THE HISTORY OF THE WORLD: *Comet* 1985 (with Ann Druyan), 14.
WITH HIS ARTIFICIAL NOSE: ibid., 33.

253   Annie conceived book titles: Druyan, interview.
"The Alien and the Skeptic" title: Yaukey 1994, 12A.
WHO ARE YOU?: *The Dragons of Eden* 1977, 180 (paperback edition).
Sagan's exchange with President Carter: Sagan, "On the Prehistory of the Planetary Society," *Planetary Report,* January–February 1986, 5.

254   [WAS PULITZER AWARDED] FOR FICTION OR NONFICTION?: the source of this story (not Horowitz) asked to remain anonymous. When I asked Horowitz to confirm it, he laughed and said he didn't remember it—but neither did he feel certain that it *didn't* happen. Hence the qualification as part of the Sagan folklore.
IT'S DISMAYING FOR PEOPLE LIKE US: Holzman 1984, 17.
TOTALLY NONTHREATENING ENVIRONMENT [AT NEW JERSEY ELEMENTARY SCHOOL]: ibid.

Los Angeles 1978–81

255   Carl and Annie rented orange house on Sierra Bonita Avenue: Ann Druyan, interview.
Rachel pleaded for friends to make nonkosher foods: Cari Greene, interview.

255–56 Schedule of assets a point of contention: Lester Grinspoon, interview.

256   Linda thought of moving to New York; California divorce laws: Nick Sagan, interview.
WHAT IT'S BEEN LIKE ON *COSMOS*: Cook 1980, 26.
DO YOU LIKE CHILDREN?: Dorion Sagan, personal communication.
HE MURDERED MY HUSBAND: Druyan, interview.
Everyone was asked for ideas: ibid.

257   Malone annoyed with claim of sexist title: ibid.
Malone thought series came first, book could be delayed: Rink 1996.
Malone was overcharged for table; money raised for *Cosmos* was used for station's general expenses: Crook and Epstein 1982.

258   Concerns about spaceship; dandelion seed: Jon Lomberg, interview.
Sagan wanted to see the Pleiades: ibid.
THE TOUGHEST SCHEDULE I'VE EVER HAD: Roberts 1980, 24.
I DON'T LIKE THE ACTING PART: Brown 1978, 2.
[SAGAN NEEDED] A LITTLE LIGHT MAKEUP: Birkhoff 1979.
Sagan went through customs with "Rosetta stone": Christopher Chyba, interview.

259   [CARL] TOOK EVERY SINGLE ONE OF HER ARGUMENTS: Lynda Obst, interview.
Terzian ignored sabbatical limit: Yervant Terzian, interview.

259   I'VE NEVER BEEN OVER BUDGET: Crook 1982.

Arco approved extra funds without seeing the show: Druyan, interview.

TAKE CARE: *The Demon-Haunted World* 1996, 203.

[SAGAN WAS A] GAUNTER, MORE SOMBER INDIVIDUAL: Rink 1996.

260   [SAGAN ACTED] LIKE A PETULANT CHILD: ibid.

Carl refused to let Jeremy stay with him: Lynn Margulis, personal communication, and Dorion Sagan, personal communication.

Effects sequences were not delivered: Timothy Ferris, interview.

[SAGAN'S] PERPETUAL EXPRESSION OF AWE-STRUCK REVERENCE: *Newsweek*, October 6, 1980, 75.

A LOT OF CARL: Richard Berendzen (quoting comments at premiere), interview.

YOU DON'T WANT A DIRECTOR MAD AT YOU: Lomberg, interview.

Malone never spoke with Sagan or Druyan again: Druyan, interview.

261   IF WE GET A HIGH RATING: *Newsweek*, October 6, 1980, 75.

KCET had to fight off women: Rink 1996.

Turtlenecks, pets, son named Sagan, etc.: "Tribute to Carl Sagan" 1996–97.

Cosmos was popular with two-year-olds: Sweeney 1982.

Robbie anecdote: Nyasia A. Maire in "Tribute to Carl Sagan" 1996–97.

Cosmos shown in class; schoolmate's comment: Nick Sagan, interview.

[SAGAN'S VOICE WAS] SIMULTANEOUSLY NASAL AND THROATY: Roberts 1980, 25.

262   [SAGAN WAS] JUST PLAIN SNOTTY: O'Malley 1981, 95.

[*Cosmos*'S OVERSEAS SALES] WERE ACTUALLY QUITE GOOD: Crook and Epstein 1982.

Analysis of KCET's financial problems: ibid.; Crook 1982.

$1.3 million in royalties for *Cosmos* (book): estimated from sales of 452,000 copies at cover price of $19.95, assuming standard contract terms.

263   Colleagues couldn't do business with Sagan in restaurants: Frank Drake, interview.

Sagan sat facing the wall in restaurants: Paul Horowitz, interview.

LOOK, BECKY . . . THERE MUST BE HUNDREDS AND HUNDREDS: Gary Larson, *The Far Side Gallery* (Kansas City: Andrews and McMeel, 1984). I'm indebted to Doug Steckel for pointing out this cartoon.

BILLIONS UPON BILLIONS OF STARS: *Cosmos* 1980, 5.

I NEVER SAID IT. HONEST: *Billions and Billions* 1997, 3.

PAROCHIAL ASTRONOMERS, UNAPPRECIATIVE: Chapman 1997, 6–7.

JOYCE BROTHERS OF ASTRONOMY: Achenbach 1996. (Dr. Brothers is a Cornell almuna!)

Complaint about Sagan traveling too much: Ferris, interview.

MANY OF HIS PEERS TREATED HIM LIKE SHIT: Stewart Brand, interview.

263–64   I DON'T KNOW WHETHER YOU HAVE TO SELL SCIENCE: Gelman 1977, 47. Horowitz's views have moderated considerably since then. He told me (interview): "[Sagan's] great contribution was in convincing the public that science is interesting, and especially space science. He did that with such consummate artistry, and without cheating in any way on facts."

264   A SCIENTIST WHO DEVOTES HIS LIFE: Diamond 1997.

Sagan was in love (with science) and wanted to express it: Druyan, interview.

Sagan talked about choosing between research and popularization: Chapman, interview.

265   Martian channels article: Wallace and Sagan 1979.
266   IN A WAY, I GREW UP WITH TITAN: *Pale Blue Dot* 1994, 106.
       Possibility of balmy temperatures, life on Titan: *Cosmos* 1980, 162.
       Chemists annoyed at term "tholin": Steele 1987, 24.
       WE CLAIM TO HAVE BOTTLED THE CLOUDS OF TITAN: ibid.
266–67 WHEN I REMEMBER UREY THE MAN: Sagan 1981, 351–52.
267   YOU KNOW, I THINK I DO: Obst, interview.
       IT WAS THE TOUGHEST THING I HAVE EVER DONE: Svetkey 1997, 22.
       DOING *COSMOS*-TYPE EFFECTS ON A LARGE SCREEN: Sweeney 1982.
       113-page treatment for *Contact: Los Angeles Times,* May 11, 1997. But Svetkey
       1997 says the treatment was 60 pages.
       A VERY, VERY LARGE SUM [FOR MOVIE DEAL]: Smith 1981.
       WE ARE PROUD TO BE ASSOCIATED WITH CARL SAGAN: Obst 1996, photo opposite
       p. 114.
268   Outline for novel sent to nine publishing houses, date: McDowell 1981.
       [RANDOM HOUSE WAS] QUITE RESENTFUL: ibid.
       WE HAD A GENTLEMANLY BUT NOT ESPECIALLY FRIENDLY GET-TOGETHER: ibid.
       IT'S SAGAN'S POSITION . . . IT GOES BACK: ibid.
       Contradictory accounts of bidding: ibid.
       $2 million, biggest sum: Smith 1981.
       Lee got 15 percent: Gentry Lee, personal communication.
269   Permission from Coppola: Puig 1997, 27.
       WHAT'S THE WORST THING THAT COULD HAPPEN?: Collins 1985.
270   ANYTHING THAT DOES NOT TEACH SCIENCE IS NOT WORTH DOING: Sagan quoted
       in Broad 1982.
       Waldenbooks buyer turned away: *Time,* December 14, 1981, 68.
       23 percent interest on bank loan: ibid.
       THE ECONOMY IS SUCH THAT ESTABLISHED BUSINESSES: Broad 1982.
270–71 BUSINESSMEN ARE A SPECIAL BREED: ibid.
271   [ET CONTACT] COULD HAVE A DRAMATIC EFFECT ON HUMAN AFFAIRS: "Beware
       the Cow in E.T.'s Barn," editorial in the *New York Times,* December 28, 1982.
       WHAT IF THESE HIGH-TECH ALIENS ARE UNPLEASANT: ibid.
       EVEN IF HUMAN BEINGS WERE A FAMOUS INTERSTELLAR DELICACY: Sagan, "If
       Extraterrestrials Do Exist: Not to Worry," letter to the editor in the *New York
       Times,* January 30, 1983.
272   Tipler's account of *Science* rejection: Tipler 1981, 289.
       Sagan treated Tipler article fairly: William I. Newman, interview.
       I FEEL AS IF I HAVE BECOME INVOLVED: Tipler 1981, 289.
       Tipler contacted Proxmire: Newman, interview.
       [POSTPONE STUDY FOR] A FEW MILLION LIGHT-YEARS: Drake and Sobel 1992,
       192.
       IF WE INTERCEPT MESSAGES SENT FROM THEM: ibid.; Frank Drake, interview.
273   [AMENDMENT FORBIDDING NASA FROM SPENDING] TO SUPPORT THE DEFINITION
       AND DEVELOPMENT OF TECHNIQUES: Drake and Sobel 1992, 195.
       Sagan's meeting with Senator Proxmire: Newman, interview; Salisbury 1986, 9.
       I COULD SEE A LIGHT GOING ON UPSTAIRS: Newman, interview.
       Von Neumann machines: See Tipler 1980. However, none of the first-person
       sources in Eric Jones's meticulously researched 1985 article on the history of
       the Fermi question mentions von Neumann machines. Von Neumann was a

consultant at Los Alamos during this period, and he was working on his theory of self-reproducing automata. The two ideas may have been linked in later retellings and elaborations.

273   A STEP IN THE DIRECTION OF A VON NEUMANN MACHINE: Tipler 1980, 276.

274   We are like ants, unable to comprehend advanced engineering: Sagan 1973c. Enigmatic astrophysical phenomena could be artificial: Sagan 1974b.
THE PERFECT ZOO: Ball 1973, 348–49.

275   NOW THE SIRENS HAVE A STILL MORE FATAL WEAPON: Kafka quoted in *Contact* 1985 (paperback edition), 40.
WE REPRESENT A WIDE VARIETY OF OPINION: Sagan 1982.

277   "ROME WAS NOT BUILT IN A DAY": Newman and Sagan 1981, 296.
A STRONG COMMITMENT TO TERRITORIALITY: Newman and Sagan 1981, 295.

278   STAR WARS [ARE UNLIKELY]: Newman and Sagan 1981, 319.
FOR A GUY WILLING, IN A MILLISECOND: Newman, interview. (Among the film's sins, in Sagan's view, was the stranger-than-Proxmire use of "parsec" as unit of speed!)
NOT TO WORRY: Newman, interview.
Linda changed her mind about divorce settlement: Lester Grinspoon, interview.
Wedding at Hotel Bel-Air: Druyan, interview.
Makeovers at wedding: Cari Greene, interview.
Grinspoon was best man: Lester Grinspoon, interview.
Lynda Obst helped select wedding dress: Obst, interview.
Rachel made sure beautiful niece was not at wedding: Dorion Sagan, personal communication.

279   Toast about Annie's "improvement" of Carl: Greene, interview.

Ithaca 1981–95

280   Sagans' house said to be originally a tomb: Ross 1981.
Sagans' house said to be originally a power plant: See Terzian and Bilson 1997, 156.
Sagans' house built in 1890: Viladas 1994, 72. Built in 1925: Ross 1981.
Sagans' house was physicist's sculpture studio: Terzian and Bilson 1997, 156.
I'VE LOST MY IDENTITY TO THIS BUILDING: Ross 1981.

281   HIS SECURITY PROBLEMS AT CORNELL: Vitkauskas 1986a.
Alpha Sigma Phi Christmas lights prank: Stover 1994. Students of urban legends will note parallels to such tales as "The Red Velvet Cake" (where an average person asks for something expected to be free, is told it will cost an exorbitant amount, and wreaks ingenious Yuletide revenge).
INTERMINABLE CLOSE-UPS OF ME LOOKING AWED: Collins 1985.
ON A PERSONAL LEVEL, [CARL] WAS POSITIVELY HANDICAPPED BY HIS EGO: Dorion Sagan, personal communication.

282   Carl sent back orders in restaurants: Jon Lomberg, interview. Sent to three delis for sandwich: Jill Tarter, interview. Salad dressing story: David Grinspoon, interview.
KING CARL: Tarter, personal communication.
A CROCK . . . MEANS YOU KNOW WHAT YOU'RE AFTER: Timothy Ferris, interview.
Carl did not suffer fools gladly: Ann Druyan, interview.

282   HE HAD A TAKE NO PRISONERS APPROACH TO LIFE: Lynda Obst, interview.
         CARL HAD A JEKYLL AND HYDE PERSONALITY: Tobias Owen, personal communi-
         cation.
         Carl was not subject to depression: Druyan (interview) says she never saw him
         depressed in twenty years of marriage. Ferris (interview) told me he once saw
         Carl depressed, after a dispiriting NASA meeting and airline delays.
         [ANNIE MADE CARL A] COMPLETE PERSON: Cari Greene, interview. THE BEST
         POSSIBLE VERSION OF HIMSELF: Obst, interview.
         ANNIE WAS AWARE OF THE EFFECT: ibid.
         Carl stopped wearing leather jacket: Sagan in Terzian and Bilson 1997, 157–58.
         Ethical questions at dinner table: Druyan, interview.
283   Carl changed views on women, gays: Dorion Sagan, personal communication.
         [MORAL QUESTION OF] EATING ANIMALS AND JAILING CHIMPANZEES: *The Demon-
         Haunted World* 1996, 259.
         Logic was more infuriating than screaming: Druyan, interview.
         [CARL WAS] NOT AN ALPHA MALE: ibid.
         Lynn had refused to provide Annie's degree of attention: Lynn Margulis, per-
         sonal communication.
         WHAT DO WE THINK ABOUT THAT?: Mendenhall 1992.
         Carl wanted to participate in "girl talk": Obst, interview.
         Pinstripe suit story: Richard Berendzen, interview.
         Lee wanted out of Carl Sagan Productions: Gentry Lee, personal communica-
         tion.
284   Carl was generous about expense of Annie's dress: Druyan, interview.
         Annie's birthday cruise: ibid.
         Cornell students surprised at Carl's girth: Michael Leavy, interview.
         Annie's comment about "exercise": Lomberg, interview.
         Carl fell off treadmill: Lester Grinspoon, interview.
         Carl was not handyman and disliked clothes shopping: Druyan, interview.
285   Carl's reading tastes, *Lawrence of Arabia*: Lomberg, interview.
         Godfather I and *II*; *Brideshead Revisited, All in the Family, Hill Street Blues*:
         Druyan, interview. *L.A. Law: TV Guide*, October 10, 1992, 5.
         Carl's collection of letters and prints: Druyan, interview.
         Carl was the most demanding patron: Davis in "Tribute to Carl Sagan"
         1996–97.
         Carl received hate mail, death threats: Christopher Chyba, interview.
         "Fissured Ceramics" file: Druyan, interview.
285–86   Letter writers' inventions; shower head, dental fillings: *The Cosmic Connection*
         1973, 77.
286   IMAGES WILL POP INTO MY HEAD: *The Demon-Haunted World* 1996, 194.
         Nick saw himself as "Switzerland": Nick Sagan, interview.
         Nick played Dungeons and Dragons, computer games: ibid. *Heavy Metal:*
         Lomberg, interview.
         Carl and Nick saw family counselor: Nick Sagan, interview.
         TO THE ONLY TRUE DAUGHTER-IN-LAW: Ann Druyan, interview.
         DON'T WORRY, DARLING: Ann Druyan, interview.
286–87   Rachel's death: Cari Greene, interview.
287   Parents were calling Carl's name: *The Demon-Haunted World* 1996, 104.

287   Theory about Rachel's influence on Carl's career: Nick Sagan, interview; Dorion Sagan, personal communication.
Alexandra born November 1982: Druyan, interview.
WHERE IS CARL SAGAN'S OFFICE?: Terzian and Trimble, 1997.
HIGH-POWERED FACULTY MEMBERS: Cornell University brochure, 1987.
WORDS OF COSMOS WOULD BE ECHOING: Vitkauskas 1986a; Mitchell 1990.
I FEEL THAT HE SHOULD BE ACCESSIBLE: Mitchell 1990.

288   MANY PEOPLE DO NOT REALIZE: ibid.
Grad students were asked whether they ever saw Sagan: Chyba 1997b, 6.
Toon could catch Sagan in elevators: Brian Toon, interview.
HE WAS UNFAILINGLY SCRUPULOUS ABOUT AUTHORSHIP: Chyba 1997b, 6.

289   Sagan's organizations: see Sagan's curriculum vitae, Cornell University.
[SAGAN WAS] A VERY PROGRESSIVE MILLIONAIRE: Shklovsky 1991, 252.
[CARL AND ANNIE] WOULD HOLD COURT ON THE TOP FLOOR: Dorion Sagan, personal communication.
Carl and Nick's capital punishment debates: Nick Sagan, interview.

290   Sagan vetoed name with "cosmos": Salisbury 1986, 6.
Paul Newman's contribution; Gene Roddenberry letter: ibid., 9.
Sagan could quote membership numbers: Ferris, interview.
Sagan's preparation for speeches: Druyan, interview.
Jacket, cuffs: Hilary Hopkins in "Tribute to Carl Sagan" 1996–97.

291   WHOSE NEED IS GREATEST?: ibid.
YOU'VE DEBUNKED EVERYTHING: Christopher Todd in ibid. With slight variations, the question and answer came up more than once. See also Terzian and Bilson 1997, 160.
[SAGAN'S CV WAS] KIND OF A WORK OF ART FOR HIM: Ferris, interview.
Sagan accepted award so kids could visit science museum: Bill Gile, interview.

291–92 Grinspoon's denial studies; meetings with experts: Lester Grinspoon, interview.

292   *Nucleus* series: ibid.; Lomberg, interview.
ABC as Moscow Broadcasting Company: Druyan, interview.
THE CENTRAL THESIS OF NUCLEAR WINTER: *A Path Where No Man Thought*, 1990, 21–22.

293   Dilbert cubicles: This is Ames planetary scientist Kathy Rages's apt description (interview).

294   Pollack worried about getting security clearance: Gile, interview.
Pollack's boyfriend worked at Ames, died from AIDS: ibid.
Line outside Pollack's door: David Grinspoon, interview.
Pollack walked around car; reason: Toon, interview.
Pollack liked rarely performed operas: Cuzzi 1994, 1608.
Workstation was named Tosca: ibid.
Pollack saw and was impressed by meteor crater: Gile, interview. Gile cannot date this trip any more precisely than the early 1970s. Conceivably it was during Pollack's 1970 move to the West Coast.
Sagan linked nuclear winter to Mariner 9: *The Cold and the Dark* 1984, 3–5.

294–95 Two 1976 articles on volcanoes: Pollack, Toon, Sagan, et al. 1976a and 1976b.

295   Asteroid as cause for dinosaur extinction: Alvarez, Alvarez, Asaro, and Michel 1980.

296   NUCLEAR WAR'S DUST WOULD COOL THE EARTH A LITTLE: *Cosmos*, 322.
Crutzen and Birks's conclusions: Crutzen and Birks 1982.

298 TWO WEEKS AGO, SOME NUT: *A Path Where No Man Thought* 1990, 462.

Review meeting conceived as a way of circumventing NASA's restrictions: Toon, interview.

$40,000 cut in Ames group's research funds, replaced by internal funds: *A Path Where No Man Thought* 1990, 462.

Rationale about needing Soviets on peer review panel: ibid., 135–36. "Alexandrov" is also spelled "Aleksandrov."

299 Alexandrov background: Revkin 1986; ibid., 136.

299–300 Sagan's botched appendectomy: Yaukey 1995.

Grinspoon flew in, found Annie taking good care of Carl: Lester Grinspoon, interview.

Carl had jejunal interposition, later was white as napkin: Druyan, interview.

300 FELLOWS, CAN YOU GIVE ME A BREAK HERE?: ibid. Coming to during an operation is, of course, all but unheard of. Druyan says the surgeon, David From, said it was the only time he had seen such a thing in his career.

IS ANNIE OKAY?: ibid.

Sagan's brush with death made him value time more: Tarter, interview.

[ANNIE MADE] HUGE MISTAKE: Druyan, interview.

Anti-SDI petition: Garwin and Sagan 1983.

301 YOU SPELLED "CISLUNAR" WRONG!: Druyan, interview.

Sagan's $4-million book contract: "Random House Sues Sagan Estate," Associated Press, March 27, 1998.

[TURCO WAS] EXHAUSTED BY THE PACE CARL HAD SET: Terzian and Bilson 1997, 242.

WE ARE, OF COURSE, KEENLY AWARE: *A Path Where No Man Thought* 1990, 464.

305 Soviet computer was 500 times slower than Cray: Revkin 1986, 35, which says that "an atmospheric model that Alexandrov ran on the Cray-1A in six minutes would have taken 48 hours on a BESM-6."

306 YOU ARE OUT OF YOUR MINDS!: Druyan, interview.

Sagan avoided jobs, social relationships, that compromised his freedom to speak out: Chyba, interview.

Sagan's reason for turning down Reagan invitations: Druyan, interview.

YOU WOULDN'T BELIEVE HOW OFTEN THOSE GUYS: ibid.

Rumor of Reagan administration opposing *Nucleus*: Lomberg, interview.

Message to Wald about KAL downed: Druyan, interview.

307 NASA pressured Pollack, Toon, Ackerman not to attend: *A Path Where No Man Thought* 1990, 465.

IT IS THE HALLOWEEN PRECEDING 1984: *The Cold and the Dark* 1984, 3.

THE MOST IMPORTANT RESEARCH FINDINGS: ibid., xxi.

THE TURNING POINT IN THE AFFAIRS OF HUMANKIND: ibid., xx.

WE SEE THAT NO MILITARY: ibid., 151–52.

HOW COULD THAT BE?: ibid., 89.

308 THIS WOULD CAUSE THE MOUNTAIN SNOW: ibid., 100.

A QUANTUM JUMP IN DETAIL: Smith 1984, 31.

IT'S WHAT THE COMPUTER TELLS US: *A Path Where No Man Thought* 1990, 138.

309 ACTUAL TEMPERATURE DECREASES: Turco, Toon, Ackerman, et al. 1983, 1286.

310 TEMPERATURES GENERALLY APPLY TO THE INTERIOR: ibid.

Cooling was more than triple that for coastal regions: A "70 percent smaller" decrease means the coastal cooling would be 30 percent (100 minus 70) of the land-planet model's. The model thus overstates coastal cooling by 100/30 or over three times.

310 OUR ESTIMATES OF THE PHYSICAL AND CHEMICAL IMPACTS: Turco, Toon, Ackerman, et al. 1983, 1290.

311 WEAPONS OF MASS DESTRUCTION: Sagan and Newman 1983, 120.

312 THERE IS A REAL DANGER: Sagan 1983, 292.

313 THE POSSIBILITY OF THE EXTINCTION: Ehrlich, Harte, Harwell, et al. 1983, 1299.
IF YOU BELIEVE THE THREAT OF THE END OF THE WORLD: Turco in Terzian and Bilson 1997, 243.
THE CHERNOBYL AND CHALLENGER DISASTERS: Sagan 1996, 167.

314 THE INCIDENCE OF ARMED ROBBERY: *A Path Where No Man Thought* 1990, 145–46.
[REDUCING NUCLEAR ARSENAL] HAS BEEN AT THE TOP OF HIS LIST: *ABC News Viewpoint: The Nuclear Dilemma* (1983). Collection of the Museum of Television and Radio, New York and Beverly Hills, California.

315 THE REALITY IS MUCH WORSE THAN . . . MOVIE: ibid.
[TV MOVIE WAS] A VERY SIMPLE-MINDED NOTION OF THE NUCLEAR PROBLEM: ibid.
MAYBE THE WHOLE WORLD: ibid.
Hoboken a nuclear-free zone: *New York Times*, September 27, 1984.
Ann Arbor rejects measure: ibid., November 8, 1984.
Brown University suicide pills: ibid., October 4, 1984. Colorado University: ibid., November 2, 1984.
Columbia University course: ibid., November 26, 1984.
Symposium on psychological aspects of nuclear winter: see Grinspoon 1986.
Teenagers' worries: *New York Times*, December 1, 1985.
Falwell's Armageddon ideology: ibid., October 24, 1984.
Editorial doubts Reagan's statements: ibid., October 25, 1984.

316 Sagan briefed heads of state in Canada, Mexico, Argentina, etc.: Druyan in Terzian and Bilson 1997, 166.
Officials hid behind a one-way mirror: Sheff 1991, 84.
Strategist thought it a mistake to publish threshold: *A Path Where No Man Thought* 1990, 339.
Military officers were more open than civilian appointees: Sheff 1991, 84.

317 ASYMMETRY OF PERCEPTION: *A Path Where No Man Thought* 1990, 149.
KGB Road Show: Paul Gallagher, "New KGB Road Show Plays in U.S. Senate," *New Solidarity*, December 16, 1983.
THE NUCLEAR WINTER LIE WAS GIVEN WIDE CURRENCY: Carol White, "CFR Journal Confirms Nuclear Winter Hoax," ibid., July 14, 1986.

318 Reaction to Sagan's briefing: Terzian and Bilson 1997, 166; Druyan, interview.
Surikov's comments: *A Path Where No Man Thought* 1990, 369–70.
Gorbachev saw himself as implementing Sagan's foreign policy: Druyan, interview.
Sagdeev credited Sagan with ending cold war: Sagan, Dorion 1997.

318–19 A GREAT MANY REPUTABLE SCIENTISTS: *New York Times*, February 12, 1985.

319 WE ARE PERSUADED THAT A NUCLEAR WAR: *A Path Where No Man Thought* 1990, 378.
YOU WOULD HAVE TO BE REALLY LOONY TUNES: Dickenson 1985.
SAGAN GAVE A PERFORMANCE SO ARROGANT: Buckley 1985.

319   Shklovskii's embolism, stroke, call to Frank Press: Shklovsky 1991, 29.
           WE ARE ALL DIMINISHED BY HIS DEATH: Sagan 1985b, 18.
           Nothing could change in the next fifty years: Shklovsky 1991, 28.

319–20   Saber-tooth analogy: Sagan 1985b, 18.

320   [ALEXANDROV'S CLIMATE MODEL WAS] A VERY WEAK PIECE OF WORK: Smith 1984, 31.
           [ALEXANDROV WAS] NOT PERMITTED DIRECT OR INDIRECT ACCESS: *A Path Where No Man Thought* 1990, 139.
           Soviet military technology was reverse-engineered from American technology: See *Fortune*, November 25, 1985, 120, which cites a 1985 Pentagon report claiming that 5 percent of all Soviet military research projects were inspired by Western technology.

321   IT IS HARD TO TELL THE DIFFERENCE: Revkin 1986, 38.
           [ALEXANDROV WAS] SULLEN AND GRAY-LOOKING: Ron Santoni quoted in ibid., 39.

322   Alexandrov's last sighting: ibid.
           [ALEXANDROV] WAS A GUY WHO DISAPPEARED A LOT: Toon, interview.
           VLADIMIR HAD A PROMISING CAREER: *A Path Where No Man Thought* 1990, 141.
           Sagan theorized Soviets decided Alexandrov had not defected: ibid., 142.

323   Alexandrov bought VCR; *Doctor Zhivago* and Jane Fonda tapes: Revkin 1986, 36–38.
           Alexandrov was silenced lest he reveal Soviet planning: Rich 1985.
           HE PRIDED HIMSELF ON WHAT HE KNEW: Revkin 1986, 43.
           Someone tried to log on to computer from Moscow: ibid.
           Dorion's son was named for "Tonio Krueger": Lynn Margulis, personal communication.
           Grandchild story: Sagan in Cornell University video of the sixtieth anniversary banquet, 1994.

324   Carl complained about *Microcosmos* title: Sagan, Dorion 1997.
           I NEVER FELT CLOSE ENOUGH TO HIM: Dorion Sagan, personal communication.
           Carl visited Dorion after attack: Druyan, interview.
           Fear of Godhead splintering; Carl's reply: Sagan, Dorion 1997.
           Dorion's letter; conversation about "giving up": Dorion Sagan, personal communication.

325   WE HAVE A DREAM: Collins 1985.
           Sagan used Tarter's personal life for novel: Tarter, interview.

326   INFINITELY ADVANCED CIVILIZATION: Thorne in Terzian and Bilson 1997, 122.
           Hawking comment about tourists from the future: ibid., 131.
           CHRONOLOGY PROTECTION CONJECTURE: Hawking 1992.

327   Guber hired Gentry Lee as coproducer: Lee, personal communication.
           Native American astronaut: Svetkey 1997, 22.
           I THOUGHT IT [TEENAGE CHARACTER] LENT A TREMENDOUS ELEMENT TO THE PICTURE: ibid., 23.

327–28   META history: Horowitz, interview; see also Terzian and Bilson 1997, 112–20.

328   I KNEW YOU'D DO THAT: Paul Horowitz, interview.
           MARRY THE WOMAN: ibid.

329   7,000 images of Uranus: Smith, Soderblom, Beebe, et al. 1986.
           MYSTERIOUS REDDISH URANIAN GUNK: Meredith 1988, 5.
           Coal analogy: ibid.
           Bacteria metabolize tholins: Stoker, Boston, Mancinelli, et al. 1990.

329–30   Origins of Chyba's research: Chyba, interview.
331   STRONGLY HELD CULTURAL PREJUDICE: Hoyle and Wickramasinghe 1988.
         [NUCLEAR WINTER WAS] DUBIOUS RATHER THAN ROBUST. . . . HIGHLY SPECULA-
         TIVE THEORIES: Teller 1984, 624.
         NUCLEAR WINTER ISN'T SCIENCE: Brad Sparke, "The Scandal of Nuclear Win-
         ter," *National Review*, November 15, 1985.
         THE POSSIBILITY OF NUCLEAR WINTER HAS NOT BEEN EXCLUDED: Teller 1984,
         624.
322   NCAR model: Thompson and Schneider 1986.
332   WE INTEND TO SHOW: ibid., 983.
333   IN AN ATTEMPT TO CONTRAST: *A Path Where No Man Thought* 1990, 321.
         [NUCLEAR WINTER WAS] SCIENTIFIC LYING: Jeffrey Hart, "The Death of Truth,"
         National Review, November 7, 1986.
         [NUCLEAR WINTER WAS] A FRAUD FROM THE START: "Reichstag Fire II" (editorial),
         ibid., December 19, 1986.
         CAUSE OF DEATH [OF NUCLEAR WINTER]: Seitz 1986.
         WORST-CASE EFFECTS [OF NUCLEAR WINTER]: ibid.
333–34   IT'S AN ABSOLUTELY ATROCIOUS PIECE OF SCIENCE: ibid.
334   YOU KNOW, I REALLY DON'T THINK: ibid.
         HUMBUG IS SIX: ibid.
         NUCLEAR WINTER IS THE WORST EXAMPLE: ibid.
         YOU GUYS ARE FOOLS: ibid.
         OUT OF FEAR OF BEING DENOUNCED: ibid.
         Seitz invented quotations: *A Path Where No Man Thought* 1990, 313.
         Dyson encouraged Sagan to do popular book: ibid., xxi.
         [DYSON] SPENT A FEW WEEKS: Dyson 1988, 262.
         [NUCLEAR WINTER WAS] A SLOPPY PIECE OF WORK: ibid., 259.
         I REALLY THINK THEY DECIDED BEFOREHAND: Rages, interview.
335   Uniformity of smoke questions: see, for instance, Singer 1984.
         IN SOME COMMENTARY, THESE CONCLUSIONS: *A Path Where No Man Thought*
         1990, 35.
336   THE EXTENDED DEFINITION OF "WINTER": *Foreign Affairs*, fall 1986, 178n.
         WHEN I USE A WORD: quoted in ibid., 169n.
         AN ARGUMENT CAN BE MADE FOR WORST-CASE THINKING: Sagan 1986, 167.
337   Sagan's idea for terraria and aquaria experiments: *A Path Where No Man
         Thought* 1990, 328–29.
         NUCLEAR WINTER IS A HYPOTHESIS: letter, Caspar Weinberger to Timothy E.
         Wirth, October 13, 1987, quoted in ibid., 378.
         THE EXPLOSION OF EVEN A SMALL PART: ibid., 183.
         THE PROBLEM IS THE CIVILIANS: Vitkauskas 1986a,
338   I DON'T KNOW WHAT KIND OF A MACHO GAME PLAN: Hammer 1987.
         Background information on Nevada Test Site: ibid. and Simon 1998.
         [NEVADA TEST SITE WAS] PROBABLY THE SAFEST PLACE IN THE WHOLE UNITED
         STATES: George Mueller, quoted in Simon 1998, 17.
         Idea for protest; Coca-Cola bottle erupted: Druyan, interview.
         NUREMBERG TRIAL: Lester Grinspoon, interview.
339   Joan Kroc financed planning of protest: ibid.
         Ramsey Clarke's leaflet with Bill of Rights: Druyan, interview.

339   Clarke planned to call expert witnesses: "Nevada Charges Against Sagan, Druyan Dropped," *Ithaca Journal,* January 20, 1987.
550 attended protest, 139 arrested: Vitkauskas 1986.
Paragraph on Carl's arrest in *Time:* October 13, 1986, 76.
Government said it couldn't identify people arrested: Lester Grinspoon, interview.
[REAGAN'S] RAMBO FOREIGN POLICY: "Sagan Among 438 Protesters Arrested," *Ithaca Journal,* February 6, 1987.

340   Carl was in Kremlin Hospital; Annie was approached about spy camera: Druyan, interview.
Reagan and Gorbachev story: Sagdeev in Terzian and Bilson 1997, 32. A slightly different version of the dialogue appears in Sagdeev 1994.
Details of Mars mission: Sagdeev in Terzian and Bilson 1997, 32.

341   [CORNELL'S INVESTMENT IN SOUTH AFRICA WAS] A CONTINUING SOURCE OF PERSONAL EMBARRASSMENT: Sagan, letter to the *Cornell Daily Sun,* January 26, 1989.
Abortion rally: Hovis 1989.
37-million circulation of *Parade*: Terzian and Bilson 1997, 209.

342   [PULL COPIES OF *PARADE*] OUT OF THE GARAGE: *Billions and Billions* 1997, 178.
WELL, YOU KNOW, A FORCE MORE POWERFUL: Sagan gives this example in *Other Worlds* 1975, 151.
Sagan knew the New Testament better than most ministers: Obst, interview.

343   Horowitz sent the *Demon-Haunted World* to grandson: Norman Horowitz, interview.
TIBETAN BUDDHISM WOULD HAVE TO CHANGE: *The Demon-Haunted World* 1996, 278.
Cost of Mars mission would be less than savings-and-loan bailout: Hoversten 1990.
MARS IS SOMEWHAT THE SAME DISTANCE: Slansky and Radlauer 1992, 119–20.
Afterward, a press secretary said that Quayle "obviously knows there's no water flowing in the canals now."
9,000 images of Neptune: Smith, Soderblom, Banfield, et. al. 1989, 1422.
WHAT WE KNOW WOULDN'T FILL A LEMUR'S FIST: *Broca's Brain* 1979, 157.

344   [TRITON WAS] RIFE WITH COLOR: Cooper 1990, 77.
[PHOTO OF SOLAR SYSTEM] MIGHT HELP IN THE CONTINUING PROCESS: *Pale Blue Dot* 1994, 6.

344–45 THE AGGREGATE OF OUR JOY: ibid., 8.

345   Chuck Berry photo story: Druyan, interview.
TTAPS II article: Turco, Toon, Ackerman, et al. 1990.
Prediction of oil field fires: see Seitz 1997.

346   Venus surface temperature of 600° K, plus or minus 50°: Sagan 1961.
750° K/640° K for bright and dark sides of Venus: Sagan 1962b.
580° K estimate for Venus: Walker and Sagan 1966. 700° K: Sagan 1967a.
750° K: Sagan and Pollack 1969a.

347   Urgency was justified by possibility of war: this theme runs throughout *A Path Where No Man Thought* 1990.

348   Sagan's Physics Teachers speech: Sagan 1990.

349   Reaction of Pollack's family to his nuclear winter work: Toon, Cuzzi, and Sagan 1995, 231.

349   Sagan was proudest of nuclear war work: Druyan, interview.

Chill ran down Sagan's spine: *Pale Blue Dot* 1994, 360.

350   THINGS THAT GO BUMP IN THE NIGHT: Paul Horowitz in Terzian and Bilson 1997, 112.

Five strongest events near plane of galaxy: see *Pale Blue Dot* 1994, 360, which reproduces a diagram from *Sky and Telescope*.

Scintillation theory: Cordes, Lazio, and Sagan 1997.

351   Fax machine stories: Paul Horowitz, interview.

YOU WOULD HAVE TO BE MADE OF WOOD: Siegel 1990.

WE HAVE NO, AND I REPEAT NO SCIENTIFIC EVIDENCE: Drake and Sobel 1992, 196.

THE GREAT MARTIAN CHASE: news bulletin issued by Senator Richard Bryan, September 22, 1993.

352   Sagan's influence with Goldin: See Broad 1998.

SCHIZOPHRENIC QUALITY [TO 1993 ARTICLE]: Paul Horowitz, interview.

Sagan had a child in each of the last five decades of the twentieth century: Sheff 1991, 88.

353   [SAGANS HATED] POSTMODERN GEWGAWS: Viladas 1994, 72.

Mushrooms in shower: Druyan, interview.

CARL AND ANN UNDERSTAND THAT ARCHITECTURE: Viladas 1994, 147.

Family members were not invited to Sagans' "Thinking House": Margulis, personal communication.

Phone was used only for emergencies: Druyan, interview.

354   Child-rearing; Ted Turner incident: Dorion Sagan, personal communication.

Turtles as pets: Druyan, interview.

Jeremy inherited father's musical talent: Lazcano, interview.

The Prisoner, Nick's job writing for *Star Trek*: Nick Sagan, interview.

Nick watched *Star Trek* episode with Carl; Carl's reaction: Ann Druyan, interview.

Carl with arm around Harry Druyan: Druyan, interview.

355   Family mystery story: Brian Neil Burg and Rosalie Burg, interview.

Sagan's awards: curriculum vitae, Cornell University.

356   I WOULDN'T DO IT BECAUSE I DIDN'T KNOW ANYTHING: Norman Horowitz, interview.

Burke's views on Sagan's nomination: Bernard Burke, interview.

356–57 Sagan's nomination: Stanley Miller, interview.

357   Two successful challenges in twenty years: Diamond 1997.

Debate on Sagan's science: letter, Lynn Margulis to Carl Sagan, dated "May ?, 1992," in Lynn Margulis's papers.

Nobel laureate watched *Cosmos* with son: Miller, interview.

Cotton, Yalow reactions: letter, Lynn Margulis to Carl Sagan, dated "May 7, 1992," in Lynn Margulis's papers.

"DANGEROUS" LIKE WE WERE THOWING BOMBS: Miller, interview.

Miller didn't ask Margulis; she supported Sagan: Miller, interview; Margulis, interview.

358   RESONATED WITH EVERY SMALL MIND: letter, Lynn Margulis to Carl Sagan, dated "May ?, 1992," in Lynn Margulis's papers.

Lynn's letter meant the most: letter, Carl Sagan to Lynn Margulis, June 3, 1992, in Lynn Margulis's papers.

358   [SAGAN WAS CITED] FOR HIS DISTINGUISHED CONTRIBUTIONS: *Pale Blue Dot*
1994, 429.
DISTURBING PARADOX [ABOUT POPULARIZERS' TREATMENT BY OTHER SCIENTISTS]:
Diamond 1997.

359   Thompson's belief in UFOs: Chyba, interview; Sagan 1996, 3.
Sagan planned to see Pollack one last time: Ray Reynolds, interview.
Sagan's slip on ice, tests, aorta: Lester Grinspoon, interview.

360   WAIT UNTIL NEXT TIME CARL'S IN TOWN: ibid.
Sagan and Grinspoon's confrontation with Mack, alien implant: ibid.
LESTER, THE PROBLEM WITH YOU AND CARL: ibid.
[ALIEN IMPLANT WAS] AN INTERESTINGLY TWISTED FIBER: Mack 1994, 27.

361   Dorion's reaction to Sagan's dismissal of "postmodern texts": Sagan, Dorion
1997.
TERMS LIKE "ABDUCTION," "ALIEN," "HAPPENING": Mack 1998, xiii.

362   LOVELY KARMIC BOOMERANG: Svetkey 1997, 23.
Close Encounters ending for *Contact*: ibid., 23.
[ZEMECKIS LIKED SCRIPT] UNTIL THE LAST PAGE AND A HALF: ibid., 24.

363   THEY FLIPPED OUT: David Grinspoon, interview.
Arden, Lomberg were "out": Dorion Sagan, personal communication.
YOU WERE EITHER IN THEIR FOLD OR OUT OF IT: David Grinspoon, interview.
Sagan's attitude about product endorsements: *The Demon-Haunted World*
1996, 208.

364   Endorsement contracts turned down: Druyan, interview.
[APPLE] WAS CLEARLY ATTEMPTING TO RETALIATE: *Ithaca Journal*, June 30, 1994.
THERE CAN BE NO QUESTION THAT THE USE: Littman 1994.
Debate about *Beavis and Butthead, The Simpsons*: Nick Sagan, interview.
Beavis and Butthead is mentioned (unfavorably) in *The Demon-Haunted World*
1996, 26.
Sasha convinced Carl to watch *The Simpsons*: Obst, interview.

365   THE "I TOUCHED CARL SAGAN" CONTEST: *Cornell Review*, issues of 1994–95
academic year.
FLASHING A NAME LIKE CARL SAGAN: ibid., November 3, 1994. The statement
actually occurs in an unidentified newspaper clipping that is reproduced in the
Review.
Terzian's entry: ibid., November 3, 1994.
Lee, Novak entries: ibid., issues of 1994–95 academic year.
[STOVER CALLED SAGAN] THE MOST POMPOUS MAN ON CAMPUS: Stover 1994.

366   Linda's network TV credits: Nick Sagan, interview.
Dorion moved to tears: Chandler 1994.
Sagan accepted both gifts with aplomb: videotape of banquet shot by Cornell,
1994.

367   [ASTEROID DRUYAN WAS] VERY CLOSE IN: ibid., Bernard 1994, 7.
IS CARL IN BED?: Achenbach 1996.
PLEASE GET RETESTED RIGHT AWAY: *Billions and Billions* 1997, 216.
[CARL'S DIAGNOSIS WAS] GROTESQUE JOKE: ibid.

368   Carl's energy level delayed diagnosis: Druyan, interview.
Carl used a leather chair at UCLA: Pete Riley in "Tribute to Carl Sagan"
1996–97.
Dorion tried to contact father via AOL: Dorion Sagan, personal communication.

368   Does it bother you that you will probably never get to know the answers: @times Auditorium, America Online, January 23, 1995.
Terzian took over Sagan's last class: Yervant Terzian, interview.
I fully expect to be back at Cornell: Tokasz 1995.
[Sagan had a] Rare, curable bone marrow disease: ibid.

369   [Hutchinson Center's success rate is] In the 40–50 percent range: Fred Hutchinson Center Web site.
You got it. whatever it is: *Billions and Billions* 1997, 217.

Seattle 1995–96

370–82   Carl's illness, treatment, death: see especially Carl and Annie's accounts in *Billions and Billions* 1997, 214–28.

370   Discussion of Sam and Rachel: Cari Greene, interview.

371   Nice haircut, dad: *Billions and Billions* 1997, 218.
Viewing transfusion was emotional experience for Cari: Greene, interview.
Marrow aspirations looked worse than they felt: Ann Druyan, interview.
Dean Martin hallucination: Lester Grinspoon, interview.
Carl's joke about Cari's interests in horses, plays: *Billions and Billions* 1997, 218–19.

372   Fire in lab: Stern 1995.
Researcher left equipment on: Thomas Gold, interview.
It was an isolated experiment: Stern 1995.
A lot of people in the department . . . it feels like you are breathing in dirt: Merrill 1995.
Thompson left message with health service: Denise Weldon, interview.

373   Causes of myelodysplasia: Fred Hutchinson Cancer Research Center Web site 1997.
Sagan had many X rays: Grinspoon, interview.
Traces of benzene were reported: see, for instance, Thompson, Henry, Khare, et al. 1987, 15087.
Tholins suspected as carcinogens: Druyan (interview) and Dorion (Sagan, Dorion 1997) expressed concern at this possibility.
Although [cars' exhaust fumes were] not in harmful concentrations: Merrill 1995.
The lab doesn't have any cancerous chemicals: ibid.
Sam's interest in pirates and soldiers was "biological": Christopher Chyba, interview.

374   Sagan Likes Seattle, But Not Lattes: Godden 1995.
Speakerphone at story meetings: Don Davis, interview.
Sagan's travel, speaking engagements: Sagan's curriculum vitae, Cornell University.
[Citizens should vow] To question everything my leaders tell me: Crawford 1995.
I've been very, very lucky: Yaukey 1995.
Sagan's idea about the Tharsis region of Mars: William I. Newman, interview.
Sagan worked on second novel: Druyan, interview.

374–75   Apple has always had great respect for Dr. Sagan: Lehrer 1995.

375   Sagan's letter to Coppola, questions not answered: Druyan, interview.

Miller wanted pope to be character in film: Svetkey 1997, 23.

Obst pressed Miller to move forward: Druyan, interview.

YOU KNOW, YOU'RE ALWAYS GOING A FRACTION OF THE WAY: Svetkey 1997, 23–24.

WE SORT OF KNEW: Lynda Obst, interview.

TO QUOTE CARL SAGAN, THE MATHEMATICAL PROBABILITY: Svetkey 1997, 24.

376   WE ARE EXPECTING A COMPLETE CURE: Kohn 1997.

THE WORLD IS SO EXQUISITE: *Billions and Billions* 1997, 215.

DEAR FRIEND, JUST A LINE: ibid.

Children kept snails as pets: ibid.

Green salad was snails' dinner: ibid.

377   MANY INSTANCES WHERE CARL HAD STRENGTHENED HIS LANGUAGE: "Tribute to Carl Sagan" 1997–97.

HAVE I EVER HEARD A SKEPTIC WAX SUPERIOR: *The Demon-Haunted World,* 1996, 297.

New early faint sun paradox study: Sagan and Chyba 1997.

378   [ZEMECKIS'S APPROACH WAS] LIKE DOING A MOVIE OF THE LEWIS AND CLARK: Jon Lomberg, interview.

Carl told Chyba to take care of himself: Chyba 1997b, 6.

COMPLETE CURE . . . HE'S GOING TO BE GETTING MORE TREATMENT: *Ithaca Journal,* July 3, 1996.

News about Mars hit the first day Carl was out of the hospital: "Carl Sagan: A Cosmic Celebrity" 1996.

379   [NO REPORTS OF MICROBES IN MARTIAN METEORITES] SO FAR: *Pale Blue Dot* 1994, 242.

I THINK THIS OUGHT TO RENAMED: Richard Berendzen, interview.

Sagan reviewed *Science* article: Lynn Margulis, personal communication.

THE EVIDENCE FOR LIFE ON MARS: *Billions and Billions* 1997, 49.

DID YOU SEE WHAT CLINTON JUST SAID?: Druyan, interview.

I SWEAR TO GOD IT WAS LIKE IT WAS SCRIPTED FOR THIS MOVIE: Svetkey 1997, 27.

Casting choices for *Contact* film: ibid.

[USE OF CLINTON'S IMAGE WAS] FUNDAMENTALLY UNFAIR: Steyn 1997, 44.

380   HE'S LUCKY ZEMECKIS DIDN'T DECIDE TO MAKE: ibid., 45.

Carl's skin was color of rice paper: Ferris 1997, 55.

MEDICAL TESTS POINT TOWARD A COMPLETE RECOVERY: Yaukey 1996.

[SAGAN WAS] READY TO TEACH: Guifre 1996.

Best Thanksgiving ever: Greene, interview; *Billions and Billions* 1997, 227.

Sagan met with Goldin: Broad 1998.

AS SICK AS HE WAS, HE WAS SENDING US NOTES: Svetkey 1997, 27.

380–81 *Nightline* story: Berendzen, interview.

381   Only Sagan's grin was recognizable: Jill Tarter, interview.

Drake realized the "old man" was Sagan: Frank Drake, interview.

Call to children: Druyan 1997, 10.

HE'S GOING VERY QUICKLY: Lynda Obst, interview.

382   Sasha sat up with father as form of leave-taking: ibid.

BEAUTIFUL, BEAUTIFUL SASHA: Druyan 1997, 10.

Grinspoon and Sagan did not have chance to say good-bye: Lester Grinspoon, interview.

382   THIS IS A DEATHWATCH: ibid., 10.

Annie kissed and rubbed Carl's face to create a memory: ibid., 11.

WHAT A WONDERFULLY LIVED LIFE: held hand tightly: Obst, interview. WITH PRIDE AND JOY IN OUR LOVE . . . : Druyan 1997, 11.

Sagan's death was covered on CNN as they left building: Obst, interview.

Afterword

383   Mail after death: Ann Druyan, interview; Timothy Ferris, interview.

IT IS APPROPRIATE THAT THE MAN: Gore 1996.

I WAS VERY SORRY TO HEAR ABOUT THE DEMISE: Ayadh Farooq in "Tribute to Carl Sagan" 1997–97.

I PULLED MY TRUCK OVER TO THE SIDE: Pete and Allie Dwyer in ibid.

I ONLY TRULY STARTED TO BE WHO I AM: coyote@purplenet.net in ibid.

383–84   I AM SOMEHOW TORN BETWEEN EMBRACING HIS VIEWS: Dave Schlom in ibid.

384   I BELIEVE THAT GOD BELIEVED IN CARL SAGAN: Larry Sessions in ibid.

Murray's reaction to Sagan's death: Jon Lomberg, interview.

Coppola filed suit, asked for $250,000 in damages: Puig 1997, 27.

[COPPOLA WAS] A NUT—YOU CAN QUOTE ME ON THAT: Svetkey 1997, 27.

Judge threw out lawsuit: Bates 1998.

Random House suit: Associated Press, March 27, 1998.

Terms of Sagan's will: Lynn Margulis and Dorion Sagan personal communication.

385   NASA minimized Martian life evidence for religious reasons: DiGregorio 1997, 303–6.

Horowitz doubted fossils, religious motive: Norman Horowitz, interview.

Tarter's reobservations and scintillation theory: Jill Tarter, interview.

386   Use of oxygen by abyssal life: I thank Lynn Margulis for this clarification (personal communication).

THE WHOLE PROGRAM IS CARRYING CARL'S TORCH: Broad 1998.

I'LL BE DISAPPOINTED IN AMERICA: Svetkey 1997, 27.

Linda at premiere; probably wouldn't have attended prior to Carl's death: Cari Greene, interview.

387–88   THE MORE THE UNIVERSE SEEMS COMPREHENSIBLE: Weinberg in *The First Three Minutes* (New York: Basic Books, 1977).

388   Dorion's dream: Sagan, Dorion 1997.

Nick's dream: Nick Sagan, interview.

Bibliography

An exhaustive list of everything written by or about Carl Sagan would make a book in itself. I have attempted to provide what readers are most likely to find useful: a complete list of Sagan's books; a selective list of his scientific articles; and other sources cited in the notes.

Books by Sagan

1961. With William W. Kellogg. *The Atmospheres of Mars and Venus*. Washington, D.C.: National Academy of Sciences–National Research Council.

1966. With I. S. Shklovskii. *Intelligent Life in the Universe*. San Francisco: Holden-Day.

———. With Jonathan Leonard. *Planets*. New York: Time-Life Science Library.

1970. *Planetary Exploration*. Eugene, Oreg.: Oregon State System of Higher Education.

1971, ed. With K. Y. Kondratyev and M. Rycroft. *Space Research XI*. Berlin: Akademie Verlag.

———, ed. With Tobias C. Owen and Harlan J. Smith. *Planetary Atmospheres*. Proceedings of International Astronomical Union Symposium No. 40. Dordrecht, Holland: D. Reidel.

1972, ed. With Thornton Page. *UFOs—A Scientific Debate*. Ithaca, N.Y., and London: Cornell University Press. (A revised edition was published by W. W. Norton, New York, in 1974.)

1973. *The Cosmic Connection: An Extraterrestrial Perspective*. New York: Doubleday.

———, ed. *Communication with Extraterrestrial Intelligence (CETI)*. Cambridge, Mass.: MIT Press.

———. With Richard Berendzen, Ashley Montagu, Philip Morrison, Krista Stendahl, and George Wald. *Life Beyond Earth and the Mind of Man*. Washington: U.S. Government Printing Office.

————. With Ray Bradbury, Arthur C. Clarke, Bruce Murray, and Walter Sullivan. *Mars and the Mind of Man.* New York: Harper and Row.

1975. *Other Worlds.* New York: Bantam Books.

1977. *The Dragons of Eden: Speculations on the Evolution of Human Intelligence.* New York: Random House.

————. With Philip Morrison, et al. *The Search for Extraterrestrial Intelligence.* Washington: U.S. Government Printing Office.

1978. With F. D. Drake, Ann Druyan, Timothy Ferris, Jon Lomberg, and Linda Salzman Sagan. *Murmurs of Earth: The Voyager Interstellar Record.* New York: Random House.

1979. *Broca's Brain: Reflections on the Romance of Science.* New York: Random House.

1980. *Cosmos.* New York: Random House.

1984. With Paul R. Ehrlich, Donald Kennedy, and Walter Orr Roberts. *The Cold and the Dark: The World After Nuclear War.* New York: W. W. Norton.

1985. *Contact.* New York: Simon and Schuster.

————. With Ann Druyan. *Comet.* New York: Random House.

1990. With Richard Turco. *A Path Where No Man Thought: Nuclear Winter and the End of the Arms Race.* New York: Random House.

1992. With Ann Druyan. *Shadows of Forgotten Ancestors: A Search for Who We Are.* New York: Random House.

1994. *Pale Blue Dot: A Vision of the Human Future in Space.* New York: Random House.

1996. *The Demon-Haunted World: Science as a Candle in the Dark.* New York: Random House.

1997. *Billions and Billions: Thoughts on Life and Death at the Brink of the Millennium.* New York: Random House.

Sagan's Scientific Articles

Sagan's career defied many of the usual standards of scientific discourse. This highly selective list, chosen from approximately 500 articles and abstracts, can only suggest the breadth of his interests. I have chosen articles not only for their scientific "importance," as that word is generally understood, but also for their importance in the history of space exploration and in the history of thought relating to life beyond the Earth. Much of Sagan's most characteristic work falls under the latter headings.

Also included here are Sagan's scientific petitions and memorial pieces on colleagues, when these have been used as sources.

1957

1957. "Radiation and the Origin of the Gene." *Evolution* 11:40.

1960

1960a. "Biological Contamination of the Moon." *Proceedings of the National Academy of Sciences* 46:396–402.

1960b. "Indigenous Organic Matter on the Moon." *Proceedings of the National Academy of Sciences* 46:393–96.

1960c. "The Radiation Balance of Venus." Pasadena: *Jet Propulsion Laboratory Technical Report No. 32–34.*

1961

1961a. "On the Origin and Planetary Distribution of Life." *Radiation Research* 15:174–92.

1961b. "The Planet Venus." *Science* 133:849.

Sagan and Miller, S. L. 1961. "Molecular Synthesis in Simulated Reducing Planetary Atmospheres." *Astronomical Journal* 65:499. (Abstract.)

1962

1962a. "Is the Martian Blue Haze Produced by Solar Protons?" *Icarus* 1:70.

1962b. "Structure of the Lower Atmosphere of Venus." *Icarus* 1:151.

1962c. "Summary of a Discussion with Erdtman on Organized Elements in Carbonaceous Chondrites." *Science* 137:626.

Lederberg, Joshua, and Sagan. 1962. "Microenvironments for Life on Mars." *Proceedings of the National Academy of Sciences* 48:1473–75.

1963

1963. "Direct Contact Among Galactic Civilizations by Relativistic Interstellar Spaceflight." *Planetary and Space Science* 11:485.

Packer, E.; Scher, S.; and Sagan. 1963. "Biological Contamination of Mars: II. Cold and Aridity as Constraints on the Survival of Terrestrial Microorganisms in Simulated Martian Environments." *Icarus* 2:293.

Ponnamperuma, Cyril; Mariner, Ruth; and Sagan. 1963. "Formation of Adenosine by Ultra-violet Irradiation of a Solution of Adenine and Ribose." *Nature* 198:1199.

Ponnamperuma, Cyril; Sagan; and Mariner, Ruth. 1963. "Synthesis of Adenosine Triphosphate under Possible Primitive Earth Conditions." *Nature* 199:222.

1965

1965. "Is the Early Evolution of Life Related to the Development of the Earth's Core?" *Nature* 206:448.

Pollack, James B., and Sagan. 1965a. "The Infrared Limb Darkening of Venus." *Journal of Geophysical Research* 70:4403.

———. 1965b. "The Microwave Phase Effect of Venus." *Icarus* 4:62.

———. 1965c. "Polarization of Thermal Emission from Venus." *Astrophysical Journal* 141:1161.

Sagan and Coleman, S. 1965. "Spacecraft Sterilization Standards and Contamination of Mars." *Astronautics and Aeronautics* 3:22.

Sagan; Hanst, Philip L.; and Young, Andrew T. 1965. "Nitrogen Oxides on Mars." *Planetary and Space Science* 13:73–88.

Swan, Paul R., and Sagan. 1965. "Martian Landing Sites for the Voyager Mission." *Journal of Spacecraft and Rockets* 2:18–25.

1966

1966a. Nine chapters, some with coauthors. In *Biology and the Exploration of Mars.* Edited by C. S. Pittendrigh, W. Vishniac, and J. P. T. Pearman. Washington, D.C.: National Academy of Sciences.

1966b. "Mariner IV Observations and the Possibility of Iron Oxides on the Martian Surface." *Icarus* 5:102.

1966c. "The Photometric Properties of Mercury." *Astrophysical Journal* 144:1218.

Kilston, Steven D.; Drummond, Robert R.; and Sagan. 1966. "A Search for Life on Earth at Kilometer Resolution." *Icarus* 5:79–98.

Sagan and Pollack, James B. 1966. "On the Nature of the Canals of Mars." *Nature* 212:117.

Sagan and Walker, Russell G. 1966. "The Infrared Delectability of Dyson Civilizations." *Astrophysical Journal* 144:1216.

Walker, Russell G., and Sagan. 1966. "The Ionospheric Model of the Venus Microwave Emission: An Obituary." *Icarus* 5:105.

1967

1967a. "An Estimate of the Surface Temperature of Venus Independent of Passive Microwave Radiometry." *Astrophysical Journal* 149:731. Erratum in *Astrophysical Journal* 152:1119.

1967b. "Life on the Surface of Venus?" *Nature* 216:1198.

Lippincott, Ellis R.; Eck, Richard V.; Dayhoff, Margaret O.; and Sagan. 1967. "Thermodynamic Equilibria in Planetary Atmospheres." *Astrophysical Journal* 147:753.

Morowitz, Harold, and Sagan. 1967. "Life in the Clouds of Venus?" *Nature* 215:1259.

Pollack, James B.; Greenberg, Edward H.; and Sagan. 1967. "A Statistical Analysis of the Martian Wave of Darkening and Related Phenomena." *Planetary and Space Science* 15:817.

Pollack, James B., and Sagan. 1967a. "An Analysis of the Mariner 2 Microwave Observations of Venus." *Astrophysical Journal* 150:327.

———. 1967b. "A Critical Test of the Electrical Discharge Model of the Venus Microwave Emission." *Astrophysical Journal* 150:699.

———. 1967c. "Secular Changes and Dark-Area Regeneration on Mars." *Icarus* 6:434.

Sagan; Lippincott, E. R.; Dayhoff, M. O.; and Eck, R. 1967. "Organic Molecules and the Coloration of Jupiter." *Nature* 213:273.

Sagan and Morrison, D. 1967. "The Microwave Phase Effect of Mercury." *Astrophysical Journal* 150:1105.

Sagan and Pollack, J. B. 1967. "Anisotropic Nonconservative Scattering and the Clouds of Venus." *Journal of Geophysical Research* 72:469.

Sagan; Pollack, James B.; and Goldstein, Richard M. 1967. "Radar Doppler Spectroscopy of Mars. I. Elevation Differences Between Bright and Dark Areas." *Astronomical Journal* 72:20–34.

Sagan and Veverka, Joseph. 1967. "Martian Ionosphere: A Component Due to Solar Protons." *Science* 158:110.

1968

1968. "Jovian Atmosphere: Near-Ultraviolet Absorption Features." *Science* 159:448.

Pollack, James B., and Sagan. 1968. "The Case for Ice Clouds on Venus." *Journal of Geophysical Research* 73:5943.

Sagan; Levinthal, Elliott C.; and Lederberg, Joshua. 1968. "Contamination of Mars." *Science* 159:1191.

Sagan and Pollack, James B. 1968. "Elevation Differences on Mars." *Journal of Geophysical Research* 73:1373.

1969

1969. "Gray and Nongray Planetary Atmospheres: Structure, Convective Instability, and Greenhouse Effect." *Icarus* 10:290.

Campbell, Malcolm J.; O'Leary, Brian T.; and Sagan. 1969. "Moon: Two New Mascon Basins." *Science* 164:1273.

Chapman, C. R.; Pollack, J. B.; and Sagan. 1969. "An Analysis of the Mariner-4 Cratering Statistics." *Astronomical Journal* 74:1039–48.

Sagan; O'Leary, B. T.; and Campbell, M. J. 1969. "Lunar and Planetary Mass Concentrations." *Science* 165:651.

Sagan and Pollack, James B. 1969a. "On the Structure of the Venus Atmosphere." *Icarus* 10:274.

———. 1969b. "Windblown Dust on Mars." *Nature* 223:791.

1970

1970a. "The Trouble With Venus." In *Planetary Atmospheres*. Proceedings of the International Astronomical Union Symposium No. 40. Edited by Sagan, Harlan J. Smith, and Tobias C. Owen. Amsterdam: D. Reidel.

Bar-Nun, A; Bar-Nun, B.; Bauer, S. H.; and Sagan. 1970a. "Amino Acid Synthesis in Simulated Primitive Environments." *Science* 170:1000.

————. 1970b. "Shock Synthesis of Amino Acids in Simulated Primitive Environments." *Science* 168:470.

Masursky, H.; Batson, R.; Borgeson, W.; et al. 1970. "Television Experiment for Mariner Mars 1971." *Icarus* 12:10.

1971

1971. "The Long Winter Model of Martian Biology: A Speculation." *Icarus* 15:511.

Gierasch, Peter, and Sagan. 1971. "A Preliminary Assessment of Martian Wind Regimes." *Icarus* 14:312.

Khare, Bishun N., and Sagan. 1971. "Synthesis of Cystine in Simulated Primitive Conditions." *Nature* 232:577.

Sagan and Khare, Bishun N. 1971. "Long-Wavelength Ultraviolet Photoproduction of Amino Acids on the Primitive Earth." *Science* 173:417–20.

Sagan; Veverka, Joseph; and Gierasch, Peter. 1971. "Observational Consequences of Martian Wind Regimes." *Icarus* 15:253.

Sagan and Wallace, David. 1971. "A Search for Life on Earth at 100 Meter Resolution." *Icarus* 15:515.

1972

1972. "Interstellar Organic Chemistry." *Nature* 238:77.

Masursky, Harold; Batson, R. M.; McCauley, J. F.; et al. 1972. "Mariner 9 Television Reconnaissance of Mars and Its Satellites: Preliminary Results." *Science* 175:294.

Mutch, T. A.; Binder, A. B.; Huck, F. O.; et al. 1972. "Imaging Experiment: The Viking Mars Lander." *Icarus* 16:92.

Owen, Tobias, and Sagan. 1972. "Minor Constituents in Planetary Atmospheres: Ultraviolet Spectroscopy from the Orbiting Astronomical Observatory." *Icarus* 16:557.

Pollack, J. B.; Veverka, J.; Noland, M.; et al. 1972. "Mariner 9 Television Observations of Phobos and Deimos." *Icarus* 17:394.

Sagan; Belton, M. J. S.; et al. 1972. "Quantitative Imaging of the Outer Planets and their Satellites." In *Grand Tour Outer Planet Missions*. Washington, D.C.: NASA.

Sagan and Mullen, George. 1972a. "Earth and Mars: Evolution of Atmospheres and Surface Temperatures." *Science* 177:52.

————. 1972b. "The Jupiter Greenhouse." *Icarus* 16:397–400.

Sagan; Veverka, Joseph; Fox, Paul; et al. 1972. "Variable Features on Mars: Preliminary Mariner 9 Television Results." *Icarus* 17:346.

Veverka, J.; Elliot, J.; Sagan; et al. 1972. "Jupiter Occultation of Beta Scorpii: Are the Flashes Time-symmetric?" *Nature* 240:344.

1973

1973a. "The Greenhouse of Titan." *Icarus* 18:649.

1973b. "Landing on Mars." *Nature* 244:61.

1973c. "On the Detectivity of Advanced Galactic Civilizations." *Icarus* 19:350.

Drake, F. D., and Sagan. 1973. "Interstellar Radio Communication and the Frequency Selection Problem." *Nature* 245:257.

Houck, J. R.; Pollack, James B.; Sagan; et al. 1973. "High Altitude Infrared Spectroscopic Evidence for Bound Water on Mars." *Icarus* 18:470.

Khare, B. N., and Sagan. 1973. "Red Clouds in Reducing Atmospheres." *Icarus* 20:311.

Sagan; Toon, O. B.; and Gierasch, P. J. 1973. "Climatic Change on Mars." *Science* 181:1045.

Sagan and Young, Andrew T. 1973. "Solar Neutrinos, Martian Rivers, and Praesepe." *Nature* 243:459.

1974

1974a. "Frictional and Stream Velocities in Sandstorms." *Journal of Geophysical Research* 79:2147.

1974b. "An Introduction to the Problem of Cosmic Communication." In *Cosmic Communication*. Edited by C. Ponnamperuma and A. G. W. Cameron. Boston: Houghton-Mifflin.

1974c. "Obituary: Gerard Peter Kuiper (1905–1973)." *Icarus* 22:117–18.

1974d. "Wolf Vladimir Vishniac: An Obituary." *Icarus* 22:397–98.

Elliot, J. L.; Wasserman, L. H.; Veverka, J.; et al. 1974. "The Occultation of Beta Scorpii by Jupiter: II. The Hydrogen-Helium Abundance in the Jovian Atmosphere." *Astrophysics Journal* 190:719–29.

Sagan and Pollack, James B. 1974. "Differential Transmission of Sunlight on Mars: Biological Implications." *Icarus* 21:490.

Sagan; Veverka, J.; et al. 1974. "The Occultation of β Scorpii by Jupiter: I. The Structure of the Jovian Atmosphere." *Astrophysics Journal* 79:73.

Sagan; Veverka, Joseph; Wasserman, Lawrence; et al. 1974. "Jovian Atmosphere: Structure and Composition Between the Turbopause and the Mesopause." *Science* 184:901.

Veverka, Joseph: Noland, Michael; Sagan; et al. 1974. "A Mariner 9 Atlas of the Moons of Mars." *Icarus* 23:206.

Veverka, J.; Sagan; Quam, Lynn; et al. 1974. "Variable Features on Mars III: Comparison of Mariner 1969 and Mariner 1971 Photography." *Icarus* 21:317.

1975

1975a. "Hot Hydrogen in Prebiological and Interstellar Chemistry." *Science* 188:72.

1975b. "Windblown Dust on Venus." *Journal of Atmospheric Science* 32:1079.

Drake, F. D., and Sagan. 1975. "Search for Signals from Extraterrestrial Life." *Arecibo Observatory Quarterly Report.*

Khare, B. N., and Sagan. 1975. "Cyclic Octatomic Sulfur: A Possible Infrared and Visible Chromophore in the Clouds of Jupiter." *Science* 189:722.

Sagan and Bagnold, R. A. 1975. "Fluid Transport on Earth and Aeolian Transport on Mars." *Icarus* 26:209.

1976

1976a. "Erosion and the Rocks of Venus." *Nature* 261:31.

1976b. "If There Are Any, Could There Be Many?" *Nature* 264:497.

Mutch, Thomas A.; Binder, Alan B.; Huck, Friedrich O.; et al. 1976. "The Surface of Mars: The View from the Viking 1 Lander." *Science* 193:791.

Mutch, T. A.; Grenander, S. U.; Jones, K. L.; et al. 1976. "The Surface of Mars: The View from the Viking 2 Lander." *Science* 194:1277.

Pollack, James B.; Toon, O. B.; Sagan; et al. 1976a. "Stratospheric Aerosols and Climatic Change." *Nature* 263:551–55.

———. 1976b. "Volcanic Explosions and Climatic Change: A Theoretical Assessment." *Journal of Geophysical Research* 81:1071.

Sagan and Lederberg, Joshua. 1976. "The Prospects for Life on Mars: A Pre-Viking Assessment." *Icarus* 28:291.

Sagan and Salpeter, E. E. 1976. "Particles, Environments, and Possible Ecologies in the Jovian Atmosphere." *Astrophysical Journal Supplement* 32:737.

1977

1977. "Reducing Greenhouses and the Temperature History of Earth and Mars." *Nature* 269:224.

Elliot, J. L.; French, R. G.; Dunham, E.; et al. 1977. "Occultation of ϵ Geminorum by Mars: Evidence for Atmospheric Tides?" *Science* 195:485.

Isaacman, Richard, and Sagan. 1977. "Computer Simulations of Planetary Accretion Dynamics: Sensitivity to Initial Conditions." *Icarus* 31:510.

Khare, B. N., and Sagan. 1977. "On the Temperature Dependence of Possible S_8 Infrared Bands in Planetary Atmospheres." *Icarus* 30:231.

Levinthal, Elliott, C.; Jones, Kenneth L.; Fox, Paul; and Sagan. 1977. "Lander Imaging as a Detector of Life on Mars." *Journal of Geophysical Research* 82:4468.

Toon, Owen B.; Pollack, James B.; and Sagan. 1977. "Physical Properties of the Particles Composing the Martian Dust Storm of 1971–1972." *Icarus* 30:663.

1978

1978. "Eavesdropping on Galactic Civilizations." *Science* 202:374.

Khare, B. N.; Sagan; Bandurski, Eric L.; and Nagy, Bartholomew. 1978. "Ultraviolet-Photoproduced Organic Solids Synthesized Under Simulated Jovian Conditions: Molecular Analysis." *Science* 199:1199.

Newman, William I., and Sagan. 1978. "Five Micron Limb-Darkening and the Structure of the Jovian Atmosphere." *Icarus* 36:223.

Veverka, J.; Thomas, P.; and Sagan. 1978. "On the Nature and Visibility of Crater-Associated Streaks on Mars." *Icarus* 36:147–52.

1979

1979. "Sulphur Flows on Io." *Nature* 280:750.

Johnson, T. V.; Cook, A. F., II; Sagan; and Soderblom, L. A. 1979. "Volcanic Resurfacing Rates and Implications for Volatiles on Io." *Nature* 280:746–50.

Sagan and Khare, B. N. 1979. "Tholins: Organic Chemistry of Interstellar Grains and Gas." *Nature* 277:102–7. Erratum in *Nature* 282:536.

Sagan; Toon, O. B.; and Pollack, J. B. 1979. "Anthropogenic Albedeo Changes and the Earth's Climate." *Science* 206:1363.

Smith, Bradford A.; Soderblom, Laurence A.; Beebe, Reta; et al. 1979. "The Galilean Satellites and Jupiter: Voyager 2 Imaging Science Results." *Science* 206:927–50.

Smith, Bradford A.; Soderblom, Laurence A.; Johnson, Torrence V.; et al. 1979. "The Jupiter System Through the Eyes of Voyager 1." *Science* 204:951–72.

Wallace, David, and Sagan. 1979. "Evaporation of Ice in Planetary Atmospheres: Ice-Covered Rivers on Mars." *Icarus* 39:385–400.

1981

1981. "Harold Clayton Urey: 1893–1981." *Icarus* 48:348–52.

Khare, B. N.; Sagan; Zumberge, John E.; et al. 1981. "Organic Solids Produced by Electrical Discharge in Reducing Atmospheres: Tholin Molecular Analysis." *Icarus* 48:209–97.

Newman, William I., and Sagan. 1981. "Galactic Civilizations: Population Dynamics and Interstellar Diffusion." *Icarus* 46:293–327.

Smith, Bradford A.; Soderblom, Laurence; Beebe, Reta; et al. 1981. "Encounter with Saturn: Voyager 1 Imaging Science Results." *Science* 212:163–91.

Sromovsky, Lawrence A.; Suomi, Verner E.; Pollack, James B.; et al. 1981. "Implications of Titan's North-South Brightness Asymmetry." *Nature* 292:698–702.

1982

1982. "Extraterrestrial Intelligence: An International Petition." *Science* 218:426.

Sagan and Dermott, Stanley F. 1982. "The Tide in the Seas of Titan." *Nature* 300:731–33.

Smith, Bradford A.; Soderblom, Laurence; Batson, Raymond; et al. 1982. "A New Look at the Saturn System: The Voyager 2 Images." *Science* 215:504–37.

1983

1983. "Nuclear War and Climatic Catastrophe: Some Policy Implications." *Foreign Affairs* 62:257–92.

Ehrlich, Paul R.; Harte, John; Harwell, Mark A.; et al. 1983. "Long-term Biological Consequences of Nuclear War." *Science* 222:1293.

Garwin, Richard, and Sagan. 1983. "Ban Weapons from Space, Scientists Ask." *Science 83*, June, 17.

Sagan and Newman, W. I. 1983. "The Solipsist Approach to Extraterrestrial Intelligence". *Quarterly Journal of the Royal Astronomical Society* 24:113.

Squyres, Steven W., and Sagan. 1983. "Albedeo Asymmetry of Iapetus." *Nature* 303:782.

Turco, R. P.; Toon, O. B.; Ackerman, T. P.; et al. 1983. "Nuclear Winter: Global Consequences of Multiple Nuclear Explosions." *Science* 222:1283.

1984

Khare, B. N.; Sagan; Arakawa, E. T.; et al. 1984. "Optical Constants of Organic Tholins Produced in a Simulated Titanian Atmosphere: From Soft X-Ray to Microwave Frequencies." *Icarus* 60:127–37.

Pieri, D. C.; Baloga, S. M.; Nelson, R. M.; and Sagan. 1984. "Sulfur Flows of Ra Patera, Io." *Icarus* 60:685–700.

Sagan and Thompson, W. Reid. 1984a. "Production and Condensation of Organic Gases in the Atmosphere of Titan." *Icarus* 59:133–61.

———. 1984b. "Titan: Far Infrared and Microwave Remote Sensing of Methane Clouds and Organic Haze." *Icarus* 60:236.

Squyres, Steven W.; Buratti, Bonnie; Veverka, Joseph; and Sagan. 1984. "Voyager Photometry of Iapetus." *Icarus* 59:426–35.

1985

1985a. "On Minimizing the Consequences of Nuclear War." *Nature* 317:485–88.

1985b. "I. S. Shklovskii, 1916–1985." *Planetary Report*, May–June, 3, 18.

1986

1986. "Comment and Correspondence: The Nuclear Winter Debate." *Foreign Affairs*, fall, 163–68.

Khare, Bishun N.; Sagan; Ogino, Hiroshi; et al. 1986. "Amino Acids Derived from Titan Tholins." *Icarus* 68:176–84.

Smith, B. A.; Soderblom, L. A.; Beebe, R.; et al. 1986. "Voyager 2 in the Uranian System: Imaging Science Results." *Science* 233:43–64.

1987

Chyba, Christopher, and Sagan. 1987a. "Cometary Organics But No Evidence for Bacteria." *Nature* 329:208.

———. 1987b. "Infrared Emission by Organic Grains in the Coma of Comet Halley." *Nature* 330:350–53.

Khare, B. N.; Sagan; Thompson, W. R.; et al. 1987. "Solid Hydrocarbon Aerosols Produced in Simulated Uranian and Neptunian Stratospheres." *Journal of Geophysical Research* 92:15067–82.

Thompson, W. Reid; Henry, Todd; Khare, B. N.; et al. 1987. "Light Hydrocarbons from Plasma Discharge in H_2-He-CH_4: First Results and Uranian Auroral Chemistry." *Journal of Geophysical Research* 92:15,083–92.

1988

Chyba, Christopher, and Sagan. 1988. "Cometary Organic Matter Still a Contentious Issue." *Nature* 332:592.

1989

Chyba, Christopher F.; Sagan; and Mumma, Michael J. 1989. "The Heliocentric Evolution of Cometary Infrared Spectra: Results from an Organic Grain Model." *Icarus* 79:362–81.

Sagan; Chyba, C.; and Squyres, S. W. 1989. "Depth to Unoxidized Material in the Martian Regolith." *Lunar and Planetary Science* 20:157.

Smith, B. A.; Soderblom, L. A.; Banfield, D.; et al. 1989. "Voyager 2 at Neptune: Imaging Science Results." *Science* 246:1422–49.

1990

1990. "Croesus and Cassandra: Policy Response to Global Warming." *American Journal of Physics* 58:721–30.

Chyba, Christopher F.; Thomas, Paul J.; Brookshaw, Leigh; and Sagan. 1990. "Cometary Delivery of Organic Molecules to the Early Earth." *Science* 249:366–73.

Sagan and Chyba, Christopher. 1990. "Triton's Streaks as Windblown Dust." *Nature* 346:546–48.

Stoker, C. R.; Boston, P. J.; Mancinelli, R. L.; et al. 1990. "Microbial Metabolism of Tholin." *Icarus* 85:241–56.

Thompson, W. Reid, and Sagan. 1990. "Color and Chemistry on Triton." *Science* 250:415–18.

Turco, R. P.; Toon, O. B.; Ackerman, T. P.; et al. 1990. "Climate and Smoke: An Appraisal of Nuclear Winter." *Science* 247:166–76.

1991

1991. "Kuwaiti Fires and Nuclear Winter." *Science* 254:1434.

1992

Chyba, Christopher, and Sagan. 1992. "Endogenous Production, Exogenous Delivery, and Impact-Shock Synthesis of Organic Molecules: An Inventory for the Origins of Life." *Nature* 355:125–32.

McDonald, Gene D.; Thompson, W. Reid; and Sagan. 1992. "Radiation Chemistry in the Jovian Stratosphere: Laboratory Simulations." *Icarus* 99:131–42.

Sagan; Thompson, W. Reid; and Khare, Bishun N. 1992. "Titan: A Laboratory for Prebiological Organic Chemistry." *Accounts of Chemical Research* 25:286–82.

1993

Horowitz, Paul, and Sagan. 1993. "Five Years of Project META: An All-Sky Narrow-Band Radio Search for Extraterrestrial Signals." *Astrophysical Journal* 415:218–35.

Sagan; Thompson, W. Reid; Carlson, Robert; et al. 1993. "A Search for Life on Earth from the Galileo Spacecraft." *Nature* 365:715–21.

Sagan and Turco, R. P. 1993. "Nuclear Winter in the Post-Cold-War Era." *Journal of Peace Research* 30:369–73.

1994

Sagan and Ostro, Steven J. 1994a. "Dangers of Asteroid Deflection." *Nature* 368:501.
———. 1994b. "Long-Range Consequences of Interplanetary Collisions." *Issues in Science and Technology* 10:67–72.
Sagan and Pollack, James B. 1994. "Planetary Engineering." *Eos,* November 1, 198.
Thompson, W. Reid; McDonald, Gene D.; and Sagan. 1994. "The Titan Haze Revisited: Magnetospheric Energy Sources and Quantitative Tholin Yields." *Icarus* 112:376–81.
Wilson, Peter D.; Sagan; and Thompson, W. Reid. 1994. "The Organic Surface of 5145 Pholus: Constraints Set by Scattering Theory." *Icarus* 107:288–303.

1995

Dermott, Stanley F., and Sagan. 1995. "Tidal Effects of Disconnected Hydrocarbon Seas on Titan." *Nature* 374:238–40.
Toon, Brian; Cuzzi, Jeff; and Sagan. 1995. "In Memoriam: James B. Pollack (1938–1994)." *Icarus* 113:227–31.

1996

1996. "In Memoriam: Thompson, W. Reid (1952–1996). *Icarus* 132:2–3.

1997

Cordes, James M.; Lazio, T. Joseph W.; and Sagan. 1997. "Scintillation-Induced Intermittency in SETI." *Astrophysical Journal* 487:782–808.
Sagan and Chyba, Christopher. 1997. "The Early Faint Sun Paradox: Organic Shielding of Ultraviolet-Labile Greenhouse Gases." *Science* 276:1217–21.
Wilson, Peter D., and Sagan. 1997. "Nature and Source of Organic Matter in the Shoemaker-Levy 9 Jovian Impact Blemishes." *Icarus* 129:207–16.

1998

Ostro, S. J., and Sagan. 1998. "Cosmic Collisions and Galactic Civilizations." *Astronomy and Geophysics* 39:22–24.

Other Sources

Here are all other cited sources in which Sagan was not an author. They include biographic, news, or general scientific works pertaining to Sagan, his close associates, and his scientific milieu, and key scientific articles that influenced Sagan.

Achenbach, Joel. 1996. "The Final Frontier?" *Washington Post,* May 30.
Alvarez, Luis W.; Alvarez, Walter; Asaro, Frank; and Michel, Helen V. 1980. "Extraterrestrial Cause for the Cretaceous-Tertiary Extinction." *Science* 208:1095.
Asimov, Isaac. 1980. *In Joy Still Felt: The Autobiography of Isaac Asimov, 1954–1978.* Garden City: Doubleday.
Ball, John A. 1973. "The Zoo Hypothesis." *Icarus* 19:347–49.
Bates, James. 1998. "Judge Dismisses Coppola 'Contact' Suit." *Los Angeles Times,* February 14.
Baur, Stuart. 1975. "Kneedeep in the Cosmic Overwhelm with Carl Sagan." *New York Magazine,* September, 26–32.
Biemann, Hans-Peter. 1977. *The Vikings of '76.* Cambridge, Mass.: Hans-Peter Biemann.
Birkhoff, Ruth. 1979. "PBS Launches Life Quest in the Cosmos." *Los Angeles Times,* February 25.
Bernard, Larry. 1994. "Two-Day Symposium Marks Carl Sagan's 60th Birthday." *Cornell Chronicle,* October 20.

Broad, William J. 1982. "A Star Fades for Entrepreneur Sagan." *Science* 215:149.

———. 1998. "Even in Death, Carl Sagan's Influence Is Still Cosmic." *New York Times,* December 1.

Brown, Jane. 1978. "Carl Sagan: Ithaca's Very Own Down to Earth Science Evangelist." *Saturday Ithaca Journal Magazine,* September 30, 1–2.

Bruning, Fred. 1994. "Remembering One Small Step on Eagle's Wings." *Newsday,* July 19.

Buckley, William F., Jr. 1985. "Perle's Reasoning Destroys Sagan's Arrogant Testimony." *Atlanta Journal and Constitution,* April 19.

"Carl Sagan: A Cosmic Celebrity." 1996. A&E *Biography* series. (Most notable for vintage clips of Sagan's TV interviews.)

Chandler, David. 1994. "Sagan's 60 Years of Cosmic Wonder." *Boston Globe,* December 19.

Chapman, Clark R. 1997. "Carl Sagan: An Appreciation." *Sky and Telescope,* March, 6–7.

Chyba, Christopher. 1997a. "Carl Sagan (1934–1996)." *Eos* 78:167.

———. 1997b. "Carl Sagan, Teacher." *Planetary Report,* May–June, 4–7.

Clarke, Arthur C. 1951. *Interplanetary Flight.* New York: Harper and Row.

———. 1978. "A Meeting with Medusa." In *Aliens.* Edited by Ben Bova. New York: St. Martin's Press.

Cocconi, Giuseppe, and Morrison, Philip. 1959. "Searching for Interstellar Communications." *Nature* 184:844.

Cohen, Daniel. 1987. *Carl Sagan: Superstar Scientist.* New York: Dodd, Mead. (Written for a juvenile readership, this is the only biography in book form that appeared during Sagan's lifetime.)

Collins, Glenn. 1985. "The Sagans: Fiction and Fact Back to Back." *New York Times,* September 30.

Compton, William David. 1989. *Where No Man Has Gone Before: A History of Apollo Lunar Exploration Missions.* Washington, D.C.: NASA.

Condon, Edward U. 1969. *Scientific Study of Unidentified Flying Objects.* New York: Dutton.

Cook, Bruce. 1980. "Carl Sagan's Guided Tour of the Universe." *American Film,* June, 22–27.

Cooper, Henry S. F., Jr. 1976a. "A Resonance with Something Alive—I." *New Yorker,* June 21, 39–83.

———. 1976b. "A Resonance with Something Alive—II." *New Yorker,* June 28, 30–61.

———. 1980. *The Search for Life on Mars: Evolution of an Idea.* New York: Holt, Rinehart and Winston. (Based on the *New Yorker* articles.)

———. 1990. "Annals of Space: The Planetary Community." *New Yorker,* June 18, 73–90.

Crawford, Franklin. 1995. "New Citizens Reach for Stars . . . and Stripes." *Ithaca Journal,* October 19.

Crook, David. 1982. "Cosmic Debt Symbol of KCET's Woes." *Los Angeles Times,* March 1.

Crook, David, and Epstein, Andrew. 1982. "Catch 28 or Where Has All the Money Gone?" *Los Angeles Times,* February 28.

Crutzen, Paul J., and Birks, John W. 1982. "The Atmosphere After a Nuclear War: Twilight at Noon." *Ambio* 11:114–25.

Cuzzi, Jeffrey N. 1994. "James B. Pollack, 1938–1994." *Bulletin of the American Astronomical Society* 26: 1607–8.

Diamond, Jared. 1997. "Kinship with the Stars." *Discover,* May, 44.

Dickenson, James R. 1985. "Sagan, Defense Official Clash on Nuclear Winter." *Washington Post,* March 15.

DiGregorio, Barry E., with Gilbert W. Levin and Patricia Ann Straat. 1997. *Mars: The Living Planet.* Berkeley: Frog. (Claims Viking found life on Mars and NASA is keeping the fact secret.)

Drake, Frank. 1976. "On Hands and Knees in Search of Elysium." *Technology Review.* June, 22–29.

Drake, Frank, and Sobel, Dava. 1992. *Is Anyone Out There? The Scientific Search for Extraterrestrial Intelligence.* New York: Delacorte Press.

Druyan, Ann. 1977a. "Earth's Greatest Hits." *New York Times Magazine,* September 4.

———. 1977b. *A Famous Broken Heart.* New York: Stonehill.

———. 1997. "A Love Story." *Parade,* June 1, 10–11.

Duff, Brian. 1994. "The Great Lunar Quarantine." *Air and Space/Smithsonian,* February–March, 38–43.

Dyson, Freeman. 1971. "Letter from Armenia." *New Yorker,* November 6, 126–37.

———. 1988. *Infinite in all Directions.* New York: Harper. (Chapter 15 presents Dyson's thoughts on nuclear winter.)

Ezell, Edward Clinton, and Ezell, Linda Neuman. 1984. *On Mars: Exploration of the Red Planet, 1958–1978.* Washington, D.C.: NASA.

———. 1986. "Crisis over Chryse." *Planetary Report,* July–August, 10–14.

Ferris, Timothy. 1973. "Life on Other Planets? A Conversation with Carl Sagan of the Mars Mariner Project." *Rolling Stone,* June 7, 26–30.

———. 1977. "The Odyssey and the Ecstasy: The Vikings' Search for Life on Mars." *Rolling Stone,* April 7, 56–65.

———. 1997. "Is This the End?" *New Yorker,* January 27, 44–55.

Fred Hutchinson Cancer Research Center. 1997. Web site, http://www.fhcrc.org/.

Fuller, John. 1966. *The Interrupted Journey.* New York: Dial Press.

Garrison, W. M.; Morrison, D. C.; Hamilton, J. G.; et al. 1951. "Reduction of Carbon Dioxide in Aqueous Solutions by Ionizing Radiation." *Science* 114:416–18.

Gelernter, David. 1995. *1939: The Lost World of the Fair.* New York: Free Press.

Gelman, David, with Sharon Begley, Dewey Gram, et al. 1977. "Seeking Other Worlds." *Newsweek,* August 15, 46–53.

Giufre, Stacy. 1996. "Sagan Returns to Campus." *Cornell Daily Sun,* November 11.

Godden, Jean. 1995. "Sagan Likes Seattle, But Not Lattes." *Seattle Times,* July 28.

Golden, Frederic, and Peter Stoler. 1980. "The Cosmic Explainer." Time, October 20, 62–69.

Goodell, Rae. 1977. *The Visible Scientists.* Boston: Little, Brown.

Gore, Al. 1996. "From the Vice President." *Ithaca Journal,* December 21.

Grimwood, Jon Courtenay. 1996. "Gentry Lee Interview." *Guardian,* c. November 11.

Grinspoon, Lester. 1971. *Marihuana Reconsidered.* Cambridge, Mass.: Harvard University Press.

———, ed. 1986. *The Long Darkness: Psychological and Moral Perspectives on Nuclear Winter.* New Haven: Yale University Press.

Grinspoon, Lester, and Bakalar, James B. 1997. *Marihuana: The Forbidden Medicine.* New Haven and London: Yale University Press.

Hammer, Joshua. 1987. "Life at the Nevada Atomic-Test Site." *Newsday,* April 19.

Hawking, S. W. 1992. "The Chronology Protection Conjecture." *Physics Review D.* 47:603–11.

Holt, Patricia. 1981. "Carl Sagan Is Partner in Cosmos Store, A New LA Publishing Venture." *Publishers Weekly,* July 31, 30.

Holzman, David. 1984. "Whose Brain Is It, Anyway?" *Washington Post Magazine,* February 12.

Horowitz, Norman. 1977. "The Search for Life on Mars." *Scientific American,* November, 52–61.

———. 1986. *To Utopia and Back: The Search for Life in the Solar System.* New York: W. H. Freeman.

Horowitz, Paul, and Hill, Winfield. 1989. *The Art of Electronics.* 2nd ed. Cambridge: Cambridge University Press.

Hoversten, Paul. 1990. "Sagan Calls on Bush, Gorbachev to Discuss Manned Mars Mission." *Ithaca Journal,* May 1.

Hovis, Kathy. 1989. "Abortion Rally draws 2,200 to Arts Quad." *Ithaca Journal,* March 6.

Hoyle, F., and Wickramasinghe, N. C. 1988. "Cometary Organics." *Nature* 331:123–24.

"Is There Life on Mars—or Beyond?" 1971. *Time,* December 13, 50–52.

Jones, Eric M. 1985. *"Where Is Everybody?": An Account of Fermi's Question.* Los Alamos, N. M.: Los Alamos National Laboratory.

Kardashev, N. S. 1964. "Transmission of Information by Extraterrestrial Civilizations." *Astrononicheskii Zh.* 41:282. English translation in *Soviet Astronomy—A. J.* 8:217.

Kohn, Brian. 1995. "More Treatment Scheduled for Cornell's Sagan." *Ithaca Journal,* December 27.

Lederberg, Joshua. 1987. "Sputnik, 1957–1987." *Scientist,* October 5.

Lehrer, Eli. 1995. "Carl Sagan Settles Dispute with Apple." *Cornell Daily Sun,* November 20.

Levinthal, Elliott. n.d. [1980 or after]. *Cytochemical Studies of Planetary Microorganisms: Explorations in Exobiology.* Palo Alto: Stanford University.

Lilly, John C. 1966. "Sexual Behavior of the Bottlenose Dolphin." In *Brain and Behavior,* Vol. 3, edited by R. A. Gorski and R. E. Whalens, 72–76. Los Angeles: University of California Press.

———. 1997. *The Scientist: A Metaphysical Autobiography.* Berkeley: Ronin.

Littman, Bill. 1994. "Sagan Lawsuit Ends in Acquittal for Apple." *Cornell Daily Sun,* October 14.

Mack, John. 1994. *Abduction: Human Encounters With Aliens.* New York: Scribner.

Margulis, Lynn. 1998. *Symbiotic Planet.* New York: Basic Books.

Margulis, Lynn, and Dorion Sagan. 1997. *Slanted Truths.* New York: Copernicus.

"Mars' Dark Spots Held to Be Lava." 1956. *New York Times,* December 29.

Martin, James S., Jr. 1986. "Viking: Reflections After Ten Years." *Planetary Report,* July–August, 10–13.

McDonough, Tom. 1996. "Star-Stuff." *Skeptic* 4, 10

McDowell, Edwin. 1981. "Sagan Sells First Novel to Simon & Schuster." *New York Times,* January 13.

Mendenhall, Preston. 1992. "Carl Sagan and Ann Druyan Bring Science to the Masses." *Cornell Daily Sun,* October 5.

Meredith, Dennis. 1988. "Astronomers Reproduce Alien Worlds Under Glass." *Cornell Chronicle,* July 21.

Merrill, Nancy. 1995. "String of Illnesses Provokes Investigation of Sagan's Lab." *Cornell Daily Sun,* May 4.

Miller, Stanley L., and Harold C. Urey. 1959. "Organic Compound Synthesis on the Primitive Earth." *Science,* 130:245–51.

Mitchell, Margaret. 1990. "Sagan to Teach Introductory Class." *Cornell Daily Sun*, April 17.

Morris, M. S., and Thorne, K. S. 1988. "Wormholes in Spacetime and Their Use for Interstellar Travel: A Tool for Teaching General Relativity." *American Journal of Physics* 56:395–412.

Moss, Robert F. 1980. "The Scientist Superstar." *Saturday Review*, August 24–25.

Obst, Lynda. 1996. *Hello, He Lied—and Other Truths from the Hollywood Trenches.* Boston: Little, Brown.

O'Malley, William J. 1981. "Carl Sagan's Gospel of Scientism." *America*, February 7, 95.

Öpik, E. J. 1961. "The Aeolosphere and Atmosphere of Venus." *Journal of Geophysical Research* 66:2807–19.

Puig, Claudia. 1997. "Deep Space $250,000." *Los Angeles Times*, January 26.

"Random House Sues Sagan Estate." 1998. Associated Press, March 27.

"Readers Pick America's Smartest People." 1992. *Parade*, January 5, 13.

Revkin, Andrew C. 1986. "Why Is This Top Soviet Scientist Missing?" *Science Digest*, July 32–43. (An account of Alexandrov's disappearance.)

Rich, Vera. 1985. "Nuclear Winter Expert Vanishes Without Trace." *Nature* 316:3.

Ridpath, Ian. 1974. "A Man Whose Time Has Come." *New Scientist*, July 4, 36–37.

Rink, Deane. 1996. "Encounters with Authors: Carl Sagan." Web page, http://www.pavucina.sk/mirrors/www.samizdat.com/encount2.html.

Roberts, David. 1980. "Carl Sagan's Cosmos." *Horizon*, October 22–30.

Ross, Don. 1981. "Sphinx House." *Ithaca Journal*, June 3. (A feature on the home Sagan later bought.)

Sagan, Dorion. 1997. "Partial Closure." *Whole Earth*, summer, 34–37.

Sagdeev, Roald. 1994. *The Making of a Soviet Scientist.* New York: John Wiley.

Salisbury, David F. 1986. "The Planetary Society: A Short History." *Planetary Report*, January–February, 3–11.

Schell, Jonathan. 1982. *The Fate of the Earth.* New York: Knopf.

Seitz, Russell. 1986. "The Melting of 'Nuclear Winter.'" *Wall Street Journal*, November 5.

———. 1997. "An Incomplete Obituary." *Forbes*, February 10, 123.

Sheff, David. 1991. "Playboy Interview: Carl Sagan." *Playboy*, December, 69–88, 239.

Shklovskii, I. S. 1976. "Could Intelligent Life in the Universe be Unique?" *Voprosy Filosofii* 95:80–93. (In Russian.)

Shklovsky, Iosif. 1991. *Five Billion Vodka Bottles to the Moon: Tales of a Soviet Scientist.* Translated by Mary Fleming Zirin and Harold Zirin. New York: W. W. Norton. (A tragicomic memoir that Shklovskii dared not publish while alive.)

Siegel, Lee. 1990. "Extraterrestrial Search Moves to Southern Skies." *Ithaca Journal*, October 18.

Simon, Stephanie. 1998. "Marketing a Nuclear Wasteland." *Los Angeles Times*, February 4.

Simpson, George Gaylord. 1964. "The Nonprevalance of Humanoids." *Science* 143:769–75. (An early critique of exobiology.)

Singer, S. Fred. 1984. "Is the 'Nuclear Winter' real?" *Nature* 310:625.

Slansky, Paul, and Steve Radlauer. 1992. "Airhead Apparent." *Esquire*, August, 117–24.

Smith, R. Jeffrey. 1984. "Nuclear Winter Attracts Additional Scrutiny." *Science* 225:30–33.

Smith, Wendy. 1981. "S & S Pays $2-Million for Carl Sagan Novel, in Outline." *Publishers Weekly*, January 23, 17.

Steele, William. 1987. "Sagan's Universe." *Cornell Alumni News*, March, 20–25.

Stern, Seth. 1995. "Fire Damages Sagan's Labs in Space Sciences Building." *Cornell Daily Sun*, April 26.

Steyn, Mark. 1997. "Boy Martian: Contact Had Reason to Exploit the President from Mars." *American Spectator,* September, 44–45.

Stover, Matt T. 1994. "Happy Birthday, Mr. Sagan." *Cornell Daily Sun,* October 14.

Sullivan, Walter. 1964. *We Are Not Alone: The Search for Intelligent Life on Other Worlds.* New York: McGraw-Hill.

Svetkey, Benjamin. 1997. "Making Contact a Long Time Ago, Carl Sagan Looked Toward Hollywood and Asked the Cosmic Question, Is There Intelligent Life Out There?" *Entertainment Weekly,* July 18, 20–27.

Sweeney, Louise. 1982. "Carl Sagan: Reviving Our Sense of Wonder." *Christian Science Monitor,* June 3.

Swift, David W. 1990. *The SETI Pioneers: Scientists Talk About Their Search for Extraterrestrial Intelligence.* Tucson: University of Arizona Press.

Teller, Edward. 1984. "Widespread After-effects of Nuclear War." *Nature* 310:621–24.

Terzian, Yervant, and Elizabeth Bilson, eds. 1997. *Carl Sagan's Universe.* New York: Cambridge University Press.

Terzian, Yervant, and Trimble, Virginia. 1997. "Carl Sagan (1934–1996)." (Privately circulated obituary.)

Thomas, Shirley. 1963. *Men of Space.* Vol. 6. Philadelphia: Chilton Books. (The chapter on Sagan is the best early biography extant.)

Thompson, Starley L., and Schneider, Stephen H. 1986. "Nuclear Winter Reappraised." *Foreign Affairs,* summer, 981–1005.

Tipler, Frank J. 1980. "Extraterrestrial Intelligent Beings Do Not Exist." *Quarterly Journal of the Royal Astronomical Society* 21:267–81.

———. 1981. "Additional Remarks on Extraterrestrial Intelligence." *Quarterly Journal of the Royal Astronomical Society* 22:279–92.

Tokasz, Jay. 1995. "Sagan Takes Temporary Medical Leave from CU." *Ithaca Journal,* March 13.

———. 1996. "Charisma Gave Sagan Hero Status." *Ithaca Journal,* December 21.

"Tribute to Carl Sagan." 1996–97. The Planetary Society Web site, http://www.planetary.org/society-sagan-tribute-1.html.

Urey, Harold C. 1962. "Lifelike Forms in Meteorites." *Science* 137:623–28.

The Viking Lander Imaging Team. 1978. *The Martian Landscape.* Washington, D.C.: NASA. (Credited to the imaging team [which included Sagan], but there is no indication that he wrote any of the text. The main historical essay is written in engaging first-person by Thomas Mutch.)

Viladas, Pilar. 1994. "Of Architecture and Astronomy: Capturing the Sky in Carl Sagan's Ithaca, New York, Study." *Architectural Digest,* July, 72–77+.

Vitkauskas, Dina. 1986a. "Carl Sagan: A Scientific Celebrity or Celebrated Scientist?" *Cornell Daily Sun,* November 19.

———. 1986b. "Carl Sagan's New Roles: Protester and Activist." *Cornell Daily Sun,* November 18.

Wali, Kameshwar C. 1991. *Chandra: A Biography of S. Chandrasekhar.* Chicago and London: University of Chicago Press.

Wolkomir, Richard. 1985. "The Wizard of Ooze." *Omni,* January, 48–52, 78. (A profile of Lynn Margulis.)

Yaukey, John. 1994. "Sagan at 60." *Ithaca Journal,* October 8.

———. 1995. "Sagan's Lucky Stars." *Ithaca Journal,* September 12.

———. 1996a. "Astronomical Ambassador Dies." *Ithaca Journal,* December 21.

———. 1996b. "Sagan Returns to CU Ready to Teach." *Ithaca Journal,* November 8.

Acknowledgments

SAGAN'S FAMILY AND friends cooperated generously with this project during a time of personal loss. Ann Druyan was instrumental in locating Carl's far-flung friends, relatives, and colleagues. She, Lynn Margulis, Dorion Sagan, Lester Grinspoon, and Gentry Lee were each kind enough to look at the manuscript and offer comments. The result is far more accurate and complete for their efforts. (I of course accept responsibility for any errors that remain.) Cari Sagan Greene, Joshua Lederberg, Jon Lomberg, Paul Horowitz, Stanley Miller, and Yervant Terzian each directed me to relevant people, letters, archives, and/or publications. Brian Neil Burg and Rosalie Barnett Burg shared their research of the Sagan genealogy and family history.

Particular thanks also go to Seymour Abrahamson, Philip Bailey, Richard Berendzen, Klaus and Hans Biemann, Elizabeth M. Bilson, Ronald Blum, Stewart Brand, John Brockman, Bernard Burke, Johnny Carson, Clark Chapman, Christopher Chyba, James M. Cordes, Jeff Cuzzi, Don Davis, Frank Drake, Michael Eidel, Timothy Ferris, Terry Fonville, Bill Frucht, Joan Gephart, Bill Gile, Joan Glashow, Thomas Gold, David Grinspoon, Bruce Hassell, Norman Horowitz, Larry Hussar, Eric Jones, Frank Kameny, Robert Keiser, Sharon Kleitman, David Layzer, Antonio Lazcano, T. Joseph W. Lazio, Gilbert Levin, Elliott C. Levinthal, John C. Lilly, Ruth Mariner, Katinka Matson, Marilyn Mellows, Virginia Messinger, Philip and Phylis Morrison, Lu Nahemow, William I. Newman, Lynda

Obst, Tobias Owen, William Patrick, Pat Podufalski, Kathy Rages, Hunter Rawlings III, Ray Reynolds, Jeremy Sagan, Nick Sagan, Edwin E. Salpeter, Clarise Samuels, David Sobel, Steven Soter, Doug Steckel, Jill Tarter, Marilyn Taylor, Brian Toon, Len Tyler, Neil Tyson, Helen S. Vishniac, William J. Walsh, Andrew Weir, Denise Weldon, and Fred Whipple.

Index

Abduction: Human Encounters with Aliens (Mack), 361

abortion
  Pat Robertson on, 341–42
  Sagan and Druyan article on, 341

Abrahamson, General James, 340

Abrahamson, Seymour, 17–20
  introduces Sagan to Hermann Muller, 18
  as roommate of Sagan, 20

Ackerman, Diane, 343–44

Ackerman, Thomas, 296, 345

ACLU (American Civil Liberties Union), 289

active biology experiments. *See* life-detecting tests

activism. *See* nuclear activism

adenosine triphosphate (ATP)
  attempts to synthesize, 68–70
  firefly experiment and, 70
  photosynthesis without life and, 69

advanced civilizations
  duration of, 149–50
  Kardashev theories on, 151
  Sagan on numbers of, 149–50
  Shklovskii on duration of, 148

aeolosphere model of Venus's atmosphere (Opik), 48

aerosols, atmospheric effect of, 295

Agel, Jerome, 140, 181

The Air War in Indochina, 140

Alexander, Leone, 31
  arranging Lynn and Carl's wedding, 35
  Sagan's comments to about attempted reconciliation with Lynn, 71

Alexander, Lynn. *See* Margulis, Lynn

Alexander, Martin, 127

Alexander, Morris, 35

Alexandrov, Vladimir
  The Conference on the World After Nuclear War and, 307–8
  credibility questioned, 317
  disappearance of, 320–23
  effect of disappearance on Sagan, 322
  on need for three-dimensional model to test TTAPS conclusions, 304
  political suspicions regarding, 320–21, 323
  Sagan's relationship to, 304–5
  as Soviet expert on climate modeling, 299

alien communication. *See also* ET messages; META project
  deciphering, 58–59
  Drake's brainteaser and, 60–61
  possibility of understanding, 153–54
  work with dolphins as model for, 82–85

aliens
  conjectures on physical appearance of, 148
  Hill abduction incident, 130–32

aliens (*cont'd*)
　Mack abduction theories, 360–62
　on possibility of hostility of, 271
Allen, Paul, 351
Allen, Robert, 297
Alvarez, Luis, 295
Alvarez, Walter, 295
Ambartsumian, Viktor
　co-chair with Sagan at Byurakan, 141–42
　on condensation theory, 143–44
American Civil Liberties Union (ACLU), 289
American Heritage Dictionary, 289
Ames Research Center
　budget cuts due to work on nuclear warfare,
　　298
　Sagan's scientific legacy and, 386
　study on effects of nuclear warfare, 293,
　　296
　TTAPS article and, 301–2
amino acids, 159–60
ammonia, 161
Anders, Edward
　comments on back contamination, 123
　views on meteorite controversy, 62, 63
Andorfer, Greg, 230–31
The Andromeda Strain (Crichton), 124
Apollo program, 49–50
　back contamination controversy and, 121–24
　bacteria found on strengthens quarantine
　　argument, 128
　Sagan's work on, 49–50
Apple computer, Sagan lawsuit, 363–64, 374–75
Arakawa, E. T.
　as major collaborator with Sagan, 288–89
　work with Uranus photos, 329
ARCO, backs PBS space series, 231
Arden, Shirley
　helps with *Cosmos*, 255
　money dispute with Sagan, 363
Arecibo radar dish
　Newman on failure of search with, 190
　searching for extragalactic signals with, 187
　sending radio message to extraterrestials,
　　186
Armageddon ideology (Falwell), 315
Armour Research Foundation of Chicago, 38
arms control, 311. *See also* nuclear activism
Armstrong, Neil, 126
Arnold, Kenneth, 20
artificial intelligence (Winograd), 150
Art of Electronics, The (Paul Horowitz), 327–28
Asimov, Gertrude, 125
Asimov, Isaac
　article in *Fantasy and Science Fiction*, 79–80

article on appearance of aliens, 148
　comments on Lomberg's model galaxy, 191
　first meeting with Sagan, 79–80
　mentions Sagan's Jovian life-forms in *Fantasy and Science Fiction*, 194–95
　on Sagan's relationship with Linda Salzman,
　　86
　The Universe, 86
　Visions of the Universe, 269
　visits Sagan in hospital, 125
　visits Sagan's Ithaca home, 115
　witness at Sagan's wedding to Linda Salzman, 111–12
　work on Voyager time capsule, 232
asteroids
　Alvarez theory on extinction of dinosaurs
　　and, 295
　Helin names asteroid for Druyan, 366–67
Astounding Science Fiction, 12
astrobiology. *See* exobiology
Astronomy for Everybody (Newcomb), 12
Atchley, Dana, 52–54
"The Atmosphere After a Nuclear War: Twilight at Noon" (Crutzen and Birks), 296
The Atmospheres of Mars and Venus (Sagan and Kellogg), 46–47
ATP. *See* adenosine triphosphate (ATP)
Atwood, Kimball C., 41
awards, Sagan's, 355–56

back contamination. *See also* quarantine policy
　discredited by Apollo 11, 126–27
　NASA's quarantine policy and, 124–25
　opposition to Sagan regarding, 123–24
　Sagan's position regarding, 122
Baird, Judge Lourdes G., 364
Ball, John A., 274
Bateson, Gregory, 84–85
Beatles, 236
Beavis and Butthead, 364
Bell, Jocelyn, 110
Berendzen, Richard
　on Carl and Annie's matching attire, 283
　on comments at Harvard regarding Sagan's
　　public career, 106
　Mars meteorite and, 379
Bernal, J. D., 81
Bernstein, Robert, 268
Berry, Chuck
　with Annie Druyan at Voyager wrap-up
　　party, 345
　music selection for Voyager time capsule and,
　　237
Biemann, Klaus

gas chromatography/mass spectrometer experiment, 210–11

Viking 1 test shows absence of organic compounds in Mars sample, 215–16

Viking 2 test repeats finding of Viking 1 test, 219

Billions and Billions (Sagan), 263, 374

"Biological Contamination of the Moon" (Sagan), 41

Birks, John, 296

Blake, Robert, 339

Blue Book files, 92–94, 128

Blum, Ronald
conversation with Sagan on effect of carbon dioxide, 45
on Sagan's Jewish character, 111
at University of Chicago with Sagan, 16

Bok, Bart, 107

Bonestell, Chesley
art style contrasted with that of Lomberg, 177
paintings in Sagan collection, 285

Boriakoff, Valentin, 247

Brand, Stewart, 263

Brown, Robert E., 235

Bruno, Giordano, 179

Bryan, Senator Richard, 351

Buckley, William F.
comparing Sagan's arrogance to his own, 319
The Day After panel discussion and, 314–315
response to nuclear winter controversy, 316–17

Bug River, 3

Burgess, Eric, 133

Burke, Bernard
on advanced civilization theories, 149
non-support of Sagan's nomination to National Academy of Sciences, 356

Burroughs, Edgar Rice
influence on young Carl, 9
Martian map of, 118
science fiction novels of, 8

Bussard ramjet, 75

Byurakan meeting, 140–43
conjectures on appearance of aliens, 148
Drake's equation at, 143
Hubel on evolution of intelligent life, 144–46
Lee on evolution of technology, 147
lifetime of advanced civilizations debated, 149–50
Morrison on social consequences of an ET message, 154–55
numbers of advanced civilizations projected, 150–52
participants at, 141
Sagan and Crick debate probability of extraterrestrial life, 144–46
understanding extraterrestrial communication, 153–54

Calderon, Maria, 32

Calvin, Melvin
on Drake's equation, 56, 57, 59
experiments on chemical evolution, 24
gifting Green Bank participants, 59
Green Bank meeting and, 52–54
Nobel Prize of, 57
on Viking molecular analysis, 137
work on organic chemistry of meteorites, 61

Cameron, A. G. W., 232

Cameron, Roy
collecting soil samples in Antarctica, 96
reports sterile soil in Antarctica, 179

Campbell, Boyd, 254

Campbell, Joan, 343

canals, Martian, 89–90

carbon dioxide
Kuiper identifies on Mars, 28
Martian polar caps composed of, 87
Sagan on buildup in Earth's atmosphere, 45

Cari. *See* Sagan, Carol Mae

Carl Sagan Productions
Cosmos Store and, 269–71
Lee backs out, 283–84

Carson, Johnny
Sagan appearance on *Tonight Show*, 177–78
Tonight Show monologue on color images from Mars, 208

Carson, Rachel, 12

Carter, President Jimmy
meeting with Sagan, 253
Voyager time capsule message of, 244

Casani, John, 231–32

catastrophe theory (Shklovskii and Krasovsky), 76

Cavett, Dick
narrates film made by Linda Salzman, 192
Sagan appearance on his show, 178

CETI (Communication with Extraterrestrial Intelligence), 53. *See also* SETI (Search for Extraterrestrial Intelligence)

Chaffee, Douglas, 105

Chandrasekhar, Subrahmanyan
contrasted with Kuiper, 33

Chandrasekhar, Subrahmanyan (*cont'd*)
  mathematical prowess of, 116
  Sagan takes classes with, 34
  supports Sagan nomination to National
    Academy of Sciences, 357
  theory on LGM pulses, 110
Chapman, Clark
  on effect Sagan's fame had on colleagues,
    263
  response to a Sagan question, 195
  as Sagan student, 74
  on Sagan's estimate of probability of life on
    Mars, 180
  on time conflict in Sagan between research
    and popularization, 264
  wins bet with Sagan regarding macrobes on
    Mars, 208
chemical evolution, theories of, 24–25
chloroplasts (Ris), 63
Chou Wen Chung, 242
Chyba, Christopher
  collaborates with Sagan on faint sun para-
    dox, 377
  Europa orbiter project and, 386
  on Sagan's scrupulousness as an author, 288
  works with Sagan on role of comets in ori-
    gins of life, 329
civilizations. *See* advanced civilizations
Clarke, Arthur C.
  consultation with Sagan on 2001: A Space
    Odyssey, 105–6
  influence on young Carl, 12
  Interplanetary Flight, 12
  "A Meeting with Medusa," 194–95
  with Sagan at 1964 World's Fair, 80
  sixtieth birthday greetings for Sagan, 366
Clarke, Ramsey, 339
climate, effects of nuclear war on, 296
"Climate in Smoke" (Turco, Toon, Ackerman,
    Pollack, and Sagan), 345
Clinton, President William J.
  comments on Mars meteorite, 379
  in *Contact* film, 379
Cocconi, Giuseppe, 50
Cohen, Anne, 355
The Cold and the Dark, 306
colors of giant planets, theories about, 266
Comet (Sagan), 325
comets
  creation myths and, 330
  Halley's comet, 330–31
  Sagan's work on role in origins of life, 329
Committee for Scientific Investigation of
    Claims of the Paranormal (CSICOP), 290

Committee on Space Research (COSPAR), 66
communication. *See* alien communication; in-
    terspecies communication
Communication with Extraterrestrial Intelli-
    gence (CETI), 53. *See also* SETI (Search
    for Extraterrestrial Intelligence)
*Communication with Extraterrestrial Intelli-
    gence (CETI)* (Sagan), 142
condensation theory, 143–44
Condon, Edward, 36
  directs investigation of Project Blue Book,
    92–94
  report on Blue Book files, 128
The Conference on the World After Nuclear
    War NASA pressures Pollack, Toon, and
    Ackerman not to attend, 307
  Scrivner and Allen organize, 297
  TTAPS article presented in preliminary
    form, 306
The Conquest of Space (Ley and von Braun),
    285
Conrad, Pete, 128
Consumers Union, 289
Contact book version (Sagan)
  on best-seller list, 325
  Sagan's Jewish background reflected in, 111
Contact film version (Sagan)
  Coppola-Sagan legal dispute over, 269, 375,
    384
  inspiration and idea for, 267
  Lynda Obst as producer, 362
  Miller replaced by Zemeckis as director, 375
  released, 386
  reviews of, 387
  Sagan working on after bone-marrow trans-
    plant, 374
  Sagan's lack of control over, 327
contamination. *See* back contamination; for-
    ward contamination
Cooper, Henry S. F. Jr.
  on conversation between Sagan and chil-
    dren, 193–94
  critical article on Sagan, 199
Coppola, Francis Ford
  controversy with Sagan over Contact, 375
  files suit against Sagan and Warner Bros.,
    384
  negotiations with Sagan over Contact, 269
Cordes, James, 187
Cornel Review, 365
Cornell University
  description of, 113
  Gold recruits Sagan, 108–9
  grants tenure to Sagan (1970), 117

Sagan attracting students to, 287
Sagan memorial services at, 383
Sagan sabbatical to complete *Cosmos*, 259
Sagan's influence on faculty at, 288
student unrest at, 120
Corson, Dale, 109
Cosmic Connection, The (Sagan), 174
   promoted by appearance on *Tonight Show*, 178
   Sagan's statement of his manifest destiny in, 176
Cosmos book version (Sagan)
   success of, 262
   time demands of, 257
Cosmos Store
   as forerunner of Nature Company, 270
   liquidation of, 270–71
   products of, 269–70
   Sagan partnership with Lee in, 269
Cosmos TV series
   begins production, 255
   cartographic accuracy on, 258
   criticisms of, 260
   establishes Sagan's fame, 262–63
   overbudget and overschedule, 259
   Sagan conflict with Malone over, 256–57
   Sagan's schedule on, 258
   shooting locations for, 258
   special effects of, 257–60
   success of, 261
COSPAR (Committee on Space Research), 66
Cotton, Albert, 357
"Could Intelligent Life in the Universe Be Unique?" (Shklovskii), 191
creation myths, 330
Crichton, Michael, 124
Crick, Francis, 144–46
Crutzen, Paul, 296
CSICOP (Committee for Scientific Investigation of Claims of the Paranormal), 290
CTA-102 (radio emissions), 91
Cyvertson, Clarence, 297–98

Dalai Lama, 14th, 343
Dark Skies TV series, 387
David Duncan Professor of Astronomy and Space Sciences, 117
Davis, Arthur Vining, 231
Davis, Don, 285
Davis Foundation, 231
The Day After symposium, 314–15
De Vaucouleurs, Gerard, 28–29
Deimos
   photos of, 156–157

Shklovskii theory regarding, 139
DeLauer, Richard, 316
Democritus, 388
The Demon-Haunted World (Sagan), 282–83, 361, 377
Dermott, Stanley, 288
deuterium, 23
Diamond, Jared, 358
dinosaur extinction theories, 295
Dollfus, Audouin, 28, 43
dolphins, 56–57, 59, 82–85
"doomsday machine," 314
doppler radar spectroscopy, 89
The Double Helix (Watson), 144
The Dragons of Eden (Sagan), 251
   criticisms of, 254
   Davis paints cover of, 285
   wins Pulitzer Prize, 253–54
Drake, Frank, 153
   adventure with Sagan in Bora Bora, 169–70
   choosing career in astronomy, 51
   collaborates with Sagan on message for Pioneer 10, 133–34
   collaborating with Sagan at Arecibo, 188–90
   Drake's equation and, 54–56
   early life of, 51
   Green Bank meeting and, 52–54
   LGM pulses and, 110
   meets with Sagan week before Sagan dies, 381
   moves to SETI Institute, 351
   "Ozma" search for intelligent life and, 50–51
   participant of UFO symposium, 131
   personality of, 51–52
   prime number scheme of, 59–61, 153
   sending radio message to extraterrestials, 186
   statistical support for Kardashev's theories, 152
   visits Leary with Sagan, 118
   work on Voyager time capsule, 231–33, 247
Drake's equation
   debated at Byurakan, 144–46
   presented at Green Banks meeting, 55–58
Druyan, Ann
   abortion article with Sagan, 341
   activism of, 289, 338–40
   asteroid named for her, 366–67
   breaks the news of her relationship with Sagan, 246–47
   collaborates with Sagan on his writing, 253
   engagement to Sagan, 242–43
   falling in love with Sagan, 233
   first meeting with Sagan, 185

Druyan, Ann (*cont'd*)
    gives birth to Samuel Democritus Druyan
      Sagan, 352
    marriage to Sagan, 278
    personal and professional partnership with
      Sagan, 283
    positive effects on Sagan's personality,
      282–84
    produces TV special on Neptune, 345
    pros and cons on Sagan's arrogance and, 282
    receiving mail after Sagan's death, 383
    with Sagan at his death, 381–82
    with Sagan at hospital in Syracuse, 299–300
    Sagan's will and, 384
    Shadows of Forgotten Ancestors, 355
    viewing Viking 1 photos, 204–5
    work on *Contact*, 267
    work on *Cosmos*, 257
    work on *Nucleus* series, 291–92
    work on Voyager time capsule, 232, 240–41,
      245
Druyan, Harry (Annie's father)
    moves to Ithaca, 354
    reaction to Carl and Annie's relationship,
      250
Druyan, Pearl, 354
dust storms, Martian (Sagan and Pollack), 156
Dyson, Freeman
    criticisms of nuclear winter theory, 334
    Order of the Dolphin and, 59

Eames, Charles, 238
early faint sun paradox, 161–63, 377
"Earth and Mars: Evolution of Atmospheres
    and Surface Temperatures" (Sagan and
    Mullen), 161–63
    comparing greenhouse effect on Earth with
      those of Mars and Venus, 162–63
    as explanation of "early faint sun paradox,"
      161
    on role of greenhouse effect in developing
      Earth's atmosphere, 161–62
Earth prime theory (Ranovkin), 153
Eckelmann, Herman, 233
Eddington, Sir Arthur, 12
Edison, Thomas, 357
Ellsberg, Daniel, 339
Elvar (dolphin), 82–85
Ephron, Nora, 185
Erdtman, Gunnar, 62
ET messages, 154–155. *See also* alien commu-
    nication
eugenics, 18
Europa orbiter project, 386

Evolution, 26
exobiology
    as dubious field of scientific study, 45–47
    Lederberg coins term, 46
    Lederberg heads panel on, 39
    Mariner 4 undermines theories of life on
      Mars, 86–87
    Miller-Urey experiment and, 25
    pros and cons at Harvard, 106–7
    Sagan revives, 352
    Shneour on Sagan's work in, 67–68
extinction theories, dinosaurs, 295
"Extraterrestrial Beings Do Not Exist"
    (Tipler), 272
extraterrestrial communication. *See* alien com-
    munication
extraterrestrial life. *See also* SETI (Search for
    Extraterrestrial Intelligence)
    Byurakan conference on, 140–43
    Fermi's famous question about, 22
    Horowitz interest in, 96
    Icarus and, 117
    Kuiper theories about life on Mars, 27–30
    Lederberg's interest in, 36–37
    Mariner 4 undermines theories of life on
      Mars, 86–87
    Muller's interest in, 20
    Murray and Horowitz criticize search for
      life on Mars, 155–56
    mythic nature of search for, 388
    possibility of life on Mars, 163–65, 180
    Sagan and Crick debate probability of,
      144–46
    Sagan's theory of religious figures and, 21
    Shklovskii's interest in, 76
    speculation about life on Jupiter, 43–44
    Teller on probability of, 22
    Tipler opposition to theories on, 272

faint sun paradox. *See* early faint sun paradox
Falwell, Jerry, 315
A Famous Broken Heart (Druyan), 185
The Fate of the Earth (Schell), 312
Federation of American Scientists, 289
Fehsenfeld, Fred, 296
Fermi, Enrico
    famous question about extraterrestrial life,
      22
    Sagan's response to the Fermi question, 276
    at University of Chicago, 14
Ferris, Timothy
    conversations with Sagan, 175–76
    finishing details for Voyager time capsule,
      247–48

inspects Viking 1 photos with Sagan, 204–5
pros and cons on Sagan's arrogance and, 282
reaction to Carl and Annie's relationship, 249
Sagan as frequent visitor to Ferris's New York apartment, 185
on Sagan's curricula vitae, 291
on Sagan's need for public adulation, 264
work on Voyager time capsule, 232–33, 240, 243–45
Feynmann, Richard
    criticisms of nuclear winter theory, 334
    response to Drake's brainteaser, 60
Fisher, R. A., 276
Fitch, Frank, 62
Fletcher, James C., 166
Foreign Affairs, 312
forward contamination, 122. *See also* planetary contamination
fossils, Mars meteorite, 378–79
Foster, Jody, 374
Fred Hutchinson Cancer Research Center, 369
Frutkin, Arnold, 242

Gaia hypothesis (Margulis), 162–63
"Galactic Civilizations: Population Dynamics and Interstellar Diffusion" (Newman and Sagan), 276
Gamow, George, 12, 35
Garwin, Richard, 292
gas chromatography/mass spectrometer (GCMS), 210–11
Gause, G. F., 40
gay rights, 120–21
Gedda, Nicolai, 235
genetic studies
    of Lederberg, 36
    of Muller, 18–19
Gierasch, Peter, 117
Gile, Bill
    decorating Sagan's Ithaca home, 114
    relationship with James Pollack, 88
    Sagan's concern about Gile's gay rights activism, 120–21
    visits meteor crater with Pollack, 294
Ginsberg, Allen, 103
global warming, 45
Gluck, David, 192
Gold, Thomas, 48
    on advanced civilization theories, 150
    conjectures on appearance of aliens, 148
    Gold's box and Viking 1 life-detection experiments, 214

personality of, 108
recruits Sagan to come to Cornell University, 108–9
speaks on formation of solar systems, 143
theories about depth of lunar dust, 127–28
theory on LGM pulses, 110
on Vishniac's death, 180
visits to Sagan's Ithaca home, 115
Golden Age theory of Stent, 148–49
Goldenberg, Michael, 362
Goldin, Dan
    conversation with Sagan in last weeks of life, 380
    Mars meteorite and, 379
    as NASA administrator, 352
Gorbachev, Mikhail
    announces unilateral halt to Soviet nuclear testing, 337
    discusses joint Mars meeting with Reagan, 340
    Sagan's role in Soviet disarmament and, 318
Gore, Al
    letter to Ann Druyan after Sagan's death, 383
    sixtieth birthday greetings for Sagan, 366
Gradison, Wendy, 233, 238
"Great Books" program, 16
Green Bank meeting
    Drake equation and, 54–56
    participants of, 52–54
greenhouse effect
    applied by Sagan and Mullen to Earth's evolution, 161–63
    confirmed by Pioneer Venus, 265
    Gaia hypothesis and, 162–63
    as model for Venus's atmosphere, 48
    Pollack thesis on, 88
    role of ammonia in development of Earth's atmosphere, 161
    Sagan on effects of carbon dioxide on, 45
    in Sagan's "Physical Studies of Planets," 41
Grinspoon, David
    falling out with Sagan, 362–63
    on Sagan as teacher, 117
Grinspoon, Lester, 98–100
    alien abduction conversation with Mack and Sagan, 360
    assistance to Sagan in hospital, 125–26
    best man at Sagan's wedding to Ann Druyan, 278
    best man at Sagan's wedding to Linda Salzman, 111–12
    failure to attend Sagan's death, 382
    falling out with Sagan, 363, 371

Grinspoon, Lester, 98–100 (*cont'd*)
first meeting and friendship with Sagan, 98–99
on Hill alien abduction controversy, 130–32
Leary's correspondence with, 119
nuclear activism of, 291–92, 338–40
photographs Sagan's post-surgery scars, 127
present at Linda and Carl's divorce arrangement, 249
on psychiatric aspects of UFOs, 132
on psychological aspects of nuclear winter, 315
research on marijuana, 99–100
on Sagan being passed over at Harvard, 112
on Sagan's attraction to Ann Druyan, 233
visits Sagan in hospital in Syracuse, 299
Gruber, Clara
emigrates to the New World, 3–4
heart disease of, 4
Gruber, Leib, 4
emigrates to the New World, 3–4
genealogical conjectures about, 355
influence on young Carl, 4
remarriage to Rose Klinghofer, 4
Gruber, Rachel Molly. *See* Sagan, Rachel
Gruber, Rose, 4
Guber, Peter
Contact movie and, 267, 326
Obst takes job with, 259
Gustafero, Angelo, 297–98

Haldane, J. B. S.
chemical evolution theories and, 24
dinner with Lederberg, 37–38
Order of the Dolphin and, 59
young Carl's reading of, 12
Halley's comet, 330–31
Hart, James V., 362
Harvard University
Leary effect on attitudes at, 100
offers Sagan position, 67
pros and cons at Harvard on exobiology, 107
Sagan's decision to leave, 107, 112
Hatfield, Senator Mark, 338
Hawking, Stephen, 326
Heinlein, Robert, 232
Helin, Eleanor, 366–67
Hewlett, William R., 351
Hill, Betty and Barney, 130–32
Hoagland, Richard, 133
Horowitz, Norman
attitudes on religion, 343
criticism of search for life on Mars, 155–56

criticizes Sagan as popularizer of science, 263–64
first meeting with Sagan, 30
interest in extraterrestrial life, 96
on Martian meteorites, 385
non-support of Sagan's nomination to National Academy of Sciences, 356
on possibility of life on Jupiter, 195
on possibility of life on Mars, 164, 180
reports sterile soil in Antarctica, 179
Viking life-detection test, design of, 209–10
Viking life-detection test, positive results from, 213–14
Viking life-detection test, retesting, 216–18, 219, 222–23, 226
Horowitz, Paul
The Art of Electronics, 327–28
collaboration with Sagan on META results, 350–51
Project META and, 327–28
Tarter's work supports his findings, 385
Howe, Margaret, 84–85
Hoyle, Fred
collaborates with N. C. Wickramasinghe on theory about Haley's comet, 330–31
theories about water on Venus, 41
Hubel, David, 143, 146
Hunt, Lee, 296
Huxley, Julian, 12
Hynek, J. Allen, 131

Icarus
known for articles on extraterrestrial life, 117
Sagan as editor of, 117
Sagan relinquishes editorship of, 255
imaging team, Viking project, 136
Imshenetsky, Alexander, 64–66
"Indigenous Organic Matter on the Moon" (Sagan), 41
intelligent life, evolution of, 143, 144–46
Intelligent Life in the Universe (Shklovskii and Sagan)
reviews of and comments on, 91–92
Sagan's rework of "Universe-Life-Intelligence," 78–79
Interplanetary Flight (Clarke), 12
Interrupted Journey, The (Hill), 130
interspecies communication, 83–85
interstellar diffusion model (Newman and Sagan), 276–78
interstellar travel
in *Contact*, 325
Hawking on, 326

Sagan-Purcell controversy over, 74–76
Thorne and Morris paper on, 326
"The Ionospheric Model of the Venus Microwave Emission: An Obituary" (Sagan and Walker), 89–90
Iovine, Jimmy, 241
ITEK camera, 182–84
Ithaca, 113–14
Iwasaki, Kazuaki, 269

Jagger, Bianca, 259
Jeans, Sir James, 12
Jullian de la Fuente, Guillaume, 353
Jupiter
    gaseous structure of, 194
    Sagan and Salpeter collaborate on article on, 195–96
    Sagan speculations about life on, 43–44
    Voyager returns photos of Jupiter and its moons, 258–59
    Voyager reveals moons of ice, 265

Kahn, Herman, 314
Kameny, Frank, 121
Kardashev, Nikolai
    international conference on extraterrestrial intelligence, 140–43
    theories of supercivilizations, 151
Katz, Jonathan, 334
KCET
    Cosmos TV series on, 256–57
    financial difficulties stemming from *Cosmos*, 262
Kellogg, William W., 46–47
Kennedy, President John F., 49
Kerkar, Surshri Kesar Bai, 242
Khare, Bishun
    attracted from Harvard to Cornell by Sagan, 117
    collaboration with Sagan, 159–60, 288
    fire in Sagan's lab and, 372
    lab as health hazard and, 373
    work on colors of giant planets, 266
    work with Uranus photos, 329
Kiess, C. C., 172
Kissinger, Henry
    The Day After panel discussion and, 314–15
    response to nuclear winter controversy, 316–17
    Sagan at symposium with, 374
Kistiakowsky, George, 292
Klein, Chaya, 355
Klein, Harold
    on probability of life on Mars, 180

reporting results of Mars life-detecting tests, 212
    on Sagan's optimism, 198–99
Klinghofer, Rose. *See* Gruber, Rose
Konopinski, Emil, 22
Koppel, Ted
    moderates *The Day After* panel discussion, 314–15
    questioning Sagan about his illness, 381
Krasovsky, Valerian, 76
Kristofferson, Kris, 339
Kroc, Joan, 338–39
Kuan P'ing-Hu, 242
Kubrick, Stanley, 105–6
Kuiper, Gerald, 26–30
    compared with Chandrasekhar, 33
    dispute with Urey, 27
    encourages Sagan to take Miller fellowship at Berkeley, 43
    identifying carbon dioxide on Mars, 28
    media controversy involving Sagan, 35
    NASA and, 39
    "order-of-magnitude estimating," 34
    Sagan spends summer (1956) working with, 27
    Sagan's work on colors of giant planets and, 266
    theories about lichens on Mars, 29–30
    theories about Martian life, 27–30
    theories about Martian polar caps, 28
!Kung Bushmen of Kalahari, 147
Kuznetzov, Y. I., 153

Laboratory for Planetary Studies, Cornell, 109
    dismantled after Sagan's death, 385–86
    work on tholins at, 266
lawsuits
    Coppola-Sagan legal dispute over *Contact*, 269, 375, 384
    Random House vs. Sagan, 384
    Sagan divorce with Linda Salzman, 255–56
    Sagan vs. Apple computer, 363–64
Layzer, David
    criticism of exobiology, 107
    on rumors of why Sagan was passed over at Harvard, 112
Leary, Timothy, 118–19
    at California State Medical Facility, 118
    conversation with Sagan and Drake on cosmic Noah's ark, 118–19
    effect on attitudes at Harvard, 100
Lederberg, Joshua
    coins term *exobiology*, 46
    collaboration with Sagan, 36–37

Lederberg, Joshua (*cont'd*)
  concern for planetary contamination, 38, 123, 158
  defends possibility of life on Mars, 163–65
  dinner with Haldane, 37–38
  exchanging quips with Sagan, 178
  genetic work of, 36
  heading panel on exobiology, 39
  interest in extraterrestrial life, 36–37
  Nobel Prize of, 37
  nominates Sagan for Miller fellowship at Berkeley, 43
  as part of Viking active biology team, 137
  recommending Sagan to NASA, 39–40
  Science article on Soviet Martian probes, 97
  on Viking landing sites, 165–66, 206
  work on "life detectors," 49
Lee, B. Gentry
  argues for northern landing site for Viking 2, 206–7
  collaborates with Sagan on idea for *Contact* movie, 267
  decides to leave Carl Sagan Productions, 283–84
  on first photos of Mars from Viking 1, 203–4
  payment for role in *Contact*, 268
  promotes TV series with Sagan, 230–31
  role in Carl Sagan Productions and Cosmos Store, 269–71
  testifies in Coppola suit, 384
  work on *Contact*, 327
Lee, Richard
  on evolution of technology, 147
  inspects Viking 1 photos, 205
  role at Byurakan meeting, 141
Leighton, Robert
  computes changes in Mars axis of rotation, 165
  concludes Mars polar caps are carbon dioxide, 87
Lennon, John, 233–34
Leonov, General Alexei, 318
Levin, Gil
  on Biemann experiment, 216
  defense of theory of life on Mars, 225–26, 228
  identifying color changes in Mars rocks, 228–30
  on Martian meteorites, 385
  Sagan backs out of collaboration with, 229–30
  Viking life-detection test of, 209
  Viking life-detection test of, early results, 211–12

Viking life-detection test of, retesting, 216–18, 219
Levinthal, Elliott
  on back contamination, 123
  on Sagan's role in selecting Viking 1 landing site, 201
  Science article on Soviet Mars probes, 97
  on Viking imaging team, 136
  working on "life detectors," 49
Ley, Willy, 12, 285
LGM pulses, 110, 134
lichens, Mars, 29–30
life-detecting tests, Viking project
  Biemann, retesting, 219
  Biemann's result, 215–16
  Horowitz design for, 209–10
  Horowitz, retesting, 216–18
  Horowitz's positive results, 213–14
  Klein on results of, 212
  Levin, retesting, 216–18, 219
  Levin's design for, 209
  Levin's result, 211–12
  Margulis's criticism of, 218
  Martin on results of, 212
  Ponnamperuma reviews, 218
  Sagan considers test inconclusive, 226–28
"life detectors," 48–49
  Calvin on, 137
  Gold's box and, 214
  Lederberg's work on, 49
  Levinthal and, 49
Lilly, John C., 52–53
  dolphin research facility in St. Thomas, 82–85
  experimentation with LSD-25, 84–85
  on fraction of planets with life that develop intelligent life (Drake's equation), 56–57
  Green Bank meeting and, 52–54
  total-immersion approach to interspecies communication, 83–85
Lisenbaum, Etta, 5
Literary Volunteers of America, 289
Lomax, Alan, 236
Lomberg, Jon
  as astronomical artist, 176–77
  designs galaxy model for Sagan's home, 191
  falling out with Sagan, 363
  friendship with Sagan, 177
  on Malone's relationship with Sagan, 260
  reaction to Carl and Linda's divorce, 250
  work on *Cosmos*, 257–58
  work on Voyager time capsule, 232, 238–39

"Long-Term Biological Consequences of Nuclear Wars" (Sagan and others), 312–13
Long-Term Worldwide Effects of Multiple Nuclear-Weapon Detonations, 296
Loper, James, 262
Lovelock, James E., 162–63
Lowell, Percival
  Kuiper apprenticeship with, 26
  theories about Martian life, 27, 29
LSD-25, 84–85
Lucas, George, 257
lunar dust and rocks, 126–28
Lyons, John, 308
Lysenko, Trofim, 17–20

Machtley, Ronald, 351
Mack, John
  Abduction: Human Encounters with Aliens, 360
  A Prince of Our Disorder, 360
  Sagan's criticism of, 361–62
MacLean, Paul, 254
macrobes, 208
macromutation, 19
Magazine of Fantasy and Science Fiction, 79–80
maghemite theories, Mars (Oyama), 225
Malone, Adrian
  British producer of BBC specials, 231
  conflict with Sagan over *Cosmos*, 256–57
  early departure from *Cosmos* production, 260
Malone, Thomas, 307
Manhattan project, 58
Manson, Charles, 118
Margulis, Lynn
  anthropological fieldwork of, 32
  attempted reconciliation with Sagan, 70–71
  birth of Dorion Solomon Sagan, 38–39
  birth of Jeremy Ethan Sagan, 47
  breakup of marriage with Sagan, 63–64
  co-author with Dorion of *Microcosmos*, 324
  confronts Sagan about his relationship with Jeremy, 260
  criticism of Levin's Viking 1 life-detection tests, 218
  dating Sagan, 30–33
  divorces Sagan, 80–81
  family background of, 31
  fighting with Sagan, 31–32
  graduate studies of, 36
  interest in writing, 31
  letter of support to Sagan after National Academy of Sciences incident, 357–58
  marriage to Sagan, 35–36
  relationship to Rachel Sagan, 32
  rules out life on Mars, 164
  on Sagan's need for public adulation, 264
  schooling of, 31
  serial enodsymbiosis theory of, 63, 81
  troubled marriage of, 47
  work advancing Gaia hypothesis, 162–63
Margulis, Thomas, 81
Marihuana Reconsidered (Grinspoon), 100
marijuana
  Grinspoon research on, 99–100
  numinous quality of Sagan's experience with, 102–3
  Sagan's anonymous article on, 100–102
  Sagan's techniques for recalling drug-induced insights, 104
  Sagan's use for scientific work, 103–5
Mariner 9
  confirms Sagan/Pollack theory of dust storms on Mar, 156
  photos of Deimos and Phobos, 156–57
  surface photos and speculation about water, 158
Mariner projects
  Mariner 2, 47–48
  Mariner 4, 86–87
  Mariner 6 and 7, 121
  Mariner 9, 139, 156–57, 158
Mariner, Ruth, 68–70
Mars
  assumptions about atmospheric nitrogen, 28–29
  assumptions about water on, 28–29
  Chaffee conception of life on, 105
  experiments to determine presence of microbes, 208
  first photos from Viking 1, 203–6
  identifying carbon dioxide on Mars, 28
  joint U.S.-Soviet mission, 343
  Kuiper theories about lichens on, 29–30
  Leighton and Murray work on axis of rotation of, 165
  Mariner 4 undermines theories of life on, 86–87
  Mariner 9 photos after dust settles, 157–58
  Mariner 9 photos confirm Sagan's dust storm theory, 156
  Mars Observer fails, 351
  Murray and Horowitz criticize search for life on, 155–56
  polar caps composed of carbon dioxide, 87
  possibility of life on, 163–65, 180

Mars (*cont'd*)

Sagan considers life-detection tests inconclusive, 226–28

Sagan-Pollack collaboration on canals, 89–90

Sagan-Pollack collaboration on seasonal changes, 87–89, 89–90

Soviet probes to, 97–98

theories about life on, 27–30

viewed by radar, 167

Viking 1 color images, 207–8

Viking project supports case for running water on Mars, 200

Mars Observer, 351

Mars Pathfinder

evidence of water, rivers, and rain on Mars, 385

renamed Sagan Memorial Station, 384

Martian meteorite, 378–79, 385

Martin, Jim

creating team drills for Viking project members, 198

on results of Mars life-detecting tests, 212

on Viking 2 landing site, 218

as Viking project leader, 168

Massachusetts Institute of Technology (MIT), 107

Masursky, Hal

on possibility of water channels on Mars, 158

role in selecting Viking 1 landing site, 202

McDonald, Gene, 289

McDonald, James E.

discredited professionally, 132

reaction to Hill alien abduction claims, 130

on UFOs, 129

McDonough, Tom, 327

McNamara, Robert, 314–15

McNeil, William

criticism of mathematics as universal language, 153

criticism of pseudo or scientific religion, 155

debates Sagan on validity of Drake's equation, 147–48

media, perils of

Jupiter controversy, 44

Kuiper-Sagan mixup, 34–35

"A Meeting with Medusa" (Clarke), 194–195

memorial services, 383, 384

Menzel, Donald

Blue Book files and, 128

as full professor at Harvard, 107

participant of UFO symposium, 131

theories about water on Venus, 41

Meredith, Scott, 268, 301

META project

Horowitz throws switch for, 328

inconclusiveness of, 352

promising signals of, 349–50

Sagan gets Spielberg to fund, 328

Sagan's collaboration with Horowitz on, 349–50

Sagan's promotion of, 327

scope of SETI search with, 328

second META dish set up in Southern Hemisphere, 351

"SETI in a suitcase," 327

Tarter continues work on, 385

meteor craters, 294

meteorite controversy. *See also* Martian meteorite

Nagy study of Orgueil meteorite, 61

pollen theories and, 61–62

Meudon Observatory, 43

microbes, Mars, 208–11

Microcosmos (Margulis and Dorion Sagan), 324

microwave energy, 42

Miller, George, 362, 375

Miller, Stanley, 23

puts Sagan forward for nomination to National Academy of Sciences, 356

Sagan's collaborations with, 68

unaware of Urey's critical stance on Sagan, 173

Miller Research Fellow at Berkeley, 43

Miller-Urey experiment, 24–25

as basis for work on ATP, 68

chemical evolution and, 24

effect on Sagan, 25

as foundation for work on tholins, 266, 329

as support for life-suitability criteria of Drake's equation, 56

Minsky, Marvin, 79

on advanced civilization theories, 149–50

conjectures on appearance of aliens, 148

nuclear activism of, 339

MIT (Massachusetts Institute of Technology), 107

Mitchelson, Marvin, 255

Moore, Gordon, 351

Moran, William, 296

Morris, Mike, 326

Morrison, David, 74

Morrison, Philip, 50

on advanced civilization theories, 150

arms control and, 311

on average lifetime of communicating civilizations (Drake's equation), 58

defense of Sagan's speculative approach to science, 199

on dolphin intelligence, 57

on fraction of stars having planets (Drake's equation), 55

Green Bank meeting and, 52–54

on *Intelligent Life in the Universe,* 91

participant of UFO symposium, 131

Powers of Ten, 238

prepares with Sagan for UFO symposium, 129–30

presentation on social consequences of an ET message, 154–55

suggests that advanced civilizations may not communicate, 151

work on Voyager time capsule, 232

Morton, Dean James, 343

Mothers Embracing Nuclear Disarmament, 289

Mullen, George, 161

Muller, Hermann, 17–20

comparing Sagan's thoroughness with, 259

genetics studies of, 18–19

meeting with Sagan, 18

mutation theory of, 18

perfectionism of, 18

Murphy, Fred, 138–39

Murray, Bruce

attends memorial services for Sagan, 384

computes changes in Mars axis of rotation, 165

concludes Mars polar caps are carbon dioxide, 87

controversy with Sagan over life on Mars, 181–82

critical of Sagan's speculative methodology, 198–99

criticism of search for life on Mars, 155–56

founded Planetary Society with Sagan, 290

on probability of life on Mars, 180

theory about canals on Mars, 158

work on Mariner 4 mission, 86

music selection, Voyager time capsule, 235

mutation theory (Muller), 18

Mutch, Thomas

on color images of Mars, 207

concern for testing ITEK camera prior to use on Viking projects, 183–84

heading imaging team of Viking project, 136

on pessimism surrounding Viking 2, 206

support for Lederberg on Viking landing spot, 166

Nagy, Bartholomew, 61–63

Nahemow, Lu

conversation about Sagan's divorce, 81

as potential bride for Sagan, 13

NASA

Apollo program and, 49–50

beginning of Sagan's association with, 39–40

bio-satellite project of, 73

blocks work on nuclear winter, 331

cuts Ames budget over nuclear winter work, 298

Mariner program and, 47–48

objection to nudity in Voyager time capsule, 246

political pressure on Ames group over nuclear winter studies, 297, 307

quarantine policy of, 121–25

reviewing Voyager time capsule contents, 245–46

rumors about fossils on Martian meteorite, 378–79

Sagan consulting with, 39–40

Sagan work on Mariner projects, 47–48

Sagan's influence at, 352

terminating Sagan's consulting job with, 108

Voyager funding cut off by Congress, 108

Voyager time capsule and, 244

NASA Ames Research Center. *See* Ames Research Center

National Academy of Sciences

awards Sagan with Public Welfare Medal, 358

meeting on climatic effects of nuclear war, 296

Miller puts Sagan forward for nomination, 356

Sagan nomination voted down, 357

National Book Awards, 289

National Center for Atmospheric Research (NCAR). *See* NCAR study

National Geographic (December, 1967), 105

National Oceanic and Atmospheric Administration, 331

National Organization to Reform Marijuana Legislation, 289

National Research Council, 296

National Review, 333

National Women's Hall of Fame, 289

Nature Company, 270

Nature Conservatory, 289

NCAR study
  Sagan's counterargument to, 335–36
  study counters findings of TTAPS, 332
  three-dimensional modeling of nuclear winter theory, 332
Neptune
  Druyan produces TV special on, 345
  Sagan's interest in, 344
  Voyager photos from, 343–44
Neuman machines, 273
neutron stars, 134
Newcomb, Simon, 12, 326
Newman, Paul, 290
Newman, William I.
  article with Sagan on nuclear dilemma, 311
  on failure of Arecibo radar search, 190
  "Galactic Civilizations: Population Dynamics and Interstellar Diffusion," 276
  on Sagan's mathematical disinclination, 116
  on Sagan's response to Tipler article, 272
Nick. *See* Sagan, Nicholas Julian Zapata
Nightline, 381
Nixon, Richard, 126
nuclear activism
  celebrities and, 339
  of Lester Grinspoon, 291–92, 338–40
  Sagan's participation in, 338–340
nuclear testing
  Gorbachev and, 337
  Reagan and, 337–38
nuclear warfare, 293, 296, 298
nuclear winter controversy, 292–93
  conservatives response to, 316–17
  effect on public awareness, 315
  follow-up studies, 336–37
  NCAR study, 333
  politics and, 336
  reaction of scientific community to, 334–35
  Sagan organizes peer review for Ames study on, 298
  summing it up, 346–49
  Teller and others criticize Sagan theory, 331
  TTAPS article and, 301–2
  TTAPS revised article, 345–46
"Nuclear Winter: Global Consequences of Multiple Nuclear Explosions" (Turco, Toon, Ackerman, Pollack, Sagan), 305
Nucleus TV series, 291–92, 306

Obst, Lynda
  on Carl and Annie's relationship, 250
  collaborates on idea for *Contact* movie, 267
  on *Contact*, 386
  on Coppola suit, 384
  dating David Grinspoon, 362–63
  friendship with Annie Druyan, 233
  helps Annie with wedding dress selection, 278
  on intimacy with George Miller, 375
  present at death of Sagan, 381–82
  as producer on *Contact* film, 362
  pros and cons on Sagan's arrogance and, 282
  Voyager party of, 259
O'Hair, Madalyn Murray, 371
Oliver, Bernard
  Byurakan meeting and, 155
  Green Bank meeting and, 52–54
  solving Drake's brainteaser, 60–61
O'Malley, William J., 262
"On the Rarity of Long-Lived, Non-Spacefaring Galactic Civilizations" (Sagan), 374
O'Neill, Tip, 246
Ono, Yoko, 233
Oparin, Aleksandr, 24
Opik, Ernst
  aeolosphere model of Venus's atmosphere, 48
  theories about life on Mars, 29
Oppenheimer, J. Robert
  arms control and, 311
  Lynn Margulis visits, 31
Oppenheimer, Kitty, 32
"order-of-magnitude estimating" (Kuiper), 34
Order of the Dolphin, 57, 59
Orgel, Leslie
  as member of Viking molecular analysis team, 137
  supports Drake's equation, 147–48
  work on Voyager time capsule, 232
origin of life
  chemical evolution theories and, 24–25
  Sagan and Chyba research on role of comets in, 329
Oro, Juan, 212
Other Worlds (Sagan), 180–81
Outer Space Committee, UN, 241–42
Owen, Tobias, 282
Oyama, Vance
  gas-exchange experiment for detecting microbes on Mars, 208–9, 211–12, 217, 219
  on probability of life on Mars, 180
  theories about presence of maghemite on Mars, 225
"Ozma" search for intelligent life, 50–51

Page, Thornton, 128–29
Pale Blue Dot (Sagan), 368

Parckard, David, 351
Pariisky, Yury, 169
A Path Where No Man Thought (Sagan and Turco), 334, 345, 348
Pauling, Linus, 30
Pearman, J. Peter, 52–54
Pendleton-Jullian, Ann, 353
Pennybacker, Reverend Albert, 342
Penzo, Paul, 248
Perle, Richard N., 319
Persky, Alan D.
    on psychiatric aspects of UFOs, 132
    on risks and benefits of SETI, 155
Pesek, Rudolf, 141
Phobos
    photos of, 157
    Shklovskii theory regarding, 139
"Physical Studies of Planets" (Sagan), 41
Picture of Dorian Gray, The (Wilde), 38–39
Pieri, Dave
    as major collaborator with Sagan, 288
    Sagan and Pieri evaluate Levin's theory of color changes in Mars rocks, 229
Pioneer 10, 132–34
Pioneer plagues
    compared with Voyager time capsule, 248
    controversy concerning, 134–35
    as greeting for extraterrestrials, 132
    Linda Sagan's artwork for, 134
    Sagan and Drake collaboration on, 133–34
Pioneer Venus, 265
Planetary Atmospheres (Sagan), 140
planetary contamination. *See also* quarantine policy
    backward contamination, 121–27
    concern for, 38
    forward contamination, 122
    Lederberg and Sagan on, 40
    Mariner 9 and, 158
    Soviets and, 40
    sterilization of planetary probes and, 64
Planetary Exploration (Sagan), 140
Planetary Society
    funding META, 351
    lobbying power of, 290
    Sagan as founder of, 290
planets. *See specific planets*
Planets (Sagan), 194–195
The Planets (Urey), 27
Platt, J. R., 154
politics and science, 346–49
Pollack, James
    attracted from Harvard to Cornell by Sagan, 117
    cancels talk on nuclear winter work, 297–98
    correcting color in images from Mars, 207–8
    doctoral thesis of, 88
    ending collaboration with Sagan, 137–38
    modeling effect of dust created by nuclear war, 296
    modeling effect of volcanoes, 294–95
    personal characteristics of, 88, 293–94
    relationship with Bill Gile, 88
    as Sagan student, 74
    Sagan's concern about Pollack's gay rights activism, 120–21
    on seasonal changes on Mars, 87–89
    spinal cancer of, 359
    supports research on nuclear winter, 293
    on Viking imaging team, 136
    work on dinosaur extinction theory, 295
pollen theories (meteorites), 61–62
Ponnamperuma, Cyril
    attempts to synthesize ATP, 68–70
    reviews results of Viking life-detection tests, 218
    work compared with work of Khare and Sagan, 160
Popper, Karl, 275
popularization of science
    criticism of Sagan and, 263–64
    Sagan's defense, 264
Potter, Jerry, 323
Powell, Colin, 374
Powers of Ten (Morrison), 238
Press, Frank, 297, 320
prime number scheme (Drake), 59–61
A Prince of Our Disorder (Mack), 360
"Production of Amino Acids from Gaseous Mixtures Using Ultraviolet Light" patent, 160
"Production of Organic Molecules in Planetary Atmospheres: A Preliminary Report" (Sagan), 41
Proxmire, William
    "golden fleece" award to SETI, 272
    Sagan contact with, 273
Public Welfare Medal, 358
Pulitzer Prize, *The Dragons of Eden*, 253–54
pulsars, 134
Purcell, Edward, 74–76

quarantine policy. *See also* back contamination; planetary contamination
    abandoned after Apollo 11, 128
    astronauts' opposition to, 124
    bacteria found on Apollo and, 128

quarantine policy (*cont'd*)
  as comedy of errors following Apollo 11 return, 126–27
  influence of Crichton's book on, 124
  NASA introduces new policy, 124–25
Quayle, Dan, 343

radar
  Arecibo radar dish, 187
  doppler radar spectroscopy, 89
  used for Viking landing site selection, 167–68
"Radiation and the Origin of the Gene" (Sagan), 26
"The Radiation Balance of Venus" (Sagan), 41
radio telescopes, 50–51
Rages, Kathy, 334–335
Rahway High School, 12
Rahway home, 11
Ramjet, Bussard, 75
Randi, James, 377
Random House
  negotiations with, 268
  postmortem suit against Sagan estate, 384
Ranovkin, B. I.
  Earth prime theory of, 153
  presentation on understanding extraterrestrial communication, 153–54
Rathjens, George, 334
Reagan, Nancy, 305–6
Reagan, Ronald
  continues nuclear testing, 337–38
  discusses joint Mars project with Gorbachev, 340
  on Falwell's Armageddon ideology, 315
  invitations to Sagan to visit White House and, 305–6
  speech on SDI, 300
  words echoing Sagan's nuclear winter fears, 318–19
Rees, Martin, 275
religion
  Armageddon ideology of Falwell, 315
  Norman Horowitz attitudes on, 343
  Sagan on religious creationist belief, 80
  Sagan's early relationship to, 13
  Sagan's theory of extraterrestrial beings in, 21
  Sagan's views on, 342–43
Reynolds, Orr, 73
Ridpath, Ian, 90
Rink, Deane
  cofounder of Cornell SDS, 119
  conflict with Sagan while working on Cosmos, 259–60

conversation with Sagan on immorality of Vietnam War, 120
Ris, Hans, 63
Robertson, Pat, 341–42
Roddenberry, Gene, 290
Rolling Stone, 175–76
Rossi, Bruno, 171–72
Rotblat, Joseph, 297
Ryle, Sir Martin, 271

Sagan, Alexandra Rachel Druyan
  birth of, 287
  childhood behavior of, 354
  convinces Carl to watch *The Simpsons*, 364
  present at father's death, 382
Sagan, Carl Edward, personal characteristics
  appropriates ideas of others, 73
  art collecting, 285
  brashness of, 71
  casualness about appointments, 73
  charisma of, 73, 174–75
  early fascination with numbers, 7
  early interest in astronomy, 7–8
  early relationship to religion, 13
  humor of, 71, 117–18
  impressive memory of, 116
  interest in ethics, 282–83
  interest in piano, 14
  interest in UFOs and extraterrestrial life, 20–23, 45–47
  Jewish characteristics of, 111
  lack of inclination to mathematics, 116
  need for attention, 47
  optimism of, 198–99
  paranoid attitudes of, 122, 126
  personal charm of, 72
  preference for theories, 116
  pros and cons on Sagan's arrogance, 72–73, 281–82
  reaction to fame, 262–63
  reading and entertainment preferences of, 285
  relationship to his children, 99, 284, 323–24
  role as activist, 284, 289–91, 311, 341
  romantic relationship with Ann Druyan, 284
  sense of destiny, 72, 175–76
  stamp collecting of, 7, 285
  turning against friends, 363
Sagan, Carl Edward, principal biographical events
  birth of, 6
  Brooklyn home of, 6
  early schooling of, 7–9
  attending Rahway High School, 12

Rahway home of, 12

Knights of Columbus essay contest, 15

University of Chicago, undergraduate studies, 16–17

University of Chicago, A.B. degree, 25

dating Lynn Alexander, 30–33

marriage to Lynn Alexander, 35–36

birth of Dorion Solomon Sagan, 38–39

University of Chicago, Ph.D. in astronomy and astrophysics, 43

Miller Research Fellow at Berkeley, 45

birth of Jeremy Ethan Sagan, 47

marital problems with Lynn, 47

separation from Lynn, 63–64

Harvard, professor of astronomy, 67

attempted reconciliation with Lynn, 70–71

divorces Lynn, 80–81

Harvard, tenure problems at, 107

marriage to Linda Salzman, 111–112

Sagan leaves Cambridge, 112

Cornell, life in Ithaca, 113–115

admitted to Massachusetts General Hospital, 125–26

Cornell grants tenure to Sagan, 117

birth of Nicholas Julian Zapata Sagan, 135–36

Carl and Linda move into new house in Ithaca, 191

domestic difficulties with Linda, 197

year in Pasadena, 197

meets Ann Druyan, 233

proposal of marriage to Ann Druyan, 242–43

requests divorce from Linda, 249

moves into Slaterville Springs home with Annie, 251

wins Pulitzer Prize for *The Dragons of Eden*, 253–54

moves to Los Angeles to work on Cosmos, 255

divorce proceedings with Linda, 255–56

marriage to Ann Druyan, 278

death of Sagan's father, 259

Sphinx house in Ithaca, 280–81

birth of Alexandra Rachel Druyan Sagan, 287

death of Sagan's mother, 287

Sagan's near death in Syracuse hospital, 299

birth of Samuel Democritus Druyan Sagan, 352

sixtieth birthday party, 366–67

diagnosed with myelodysplasia, 367

death of, 380–82

will of, 384

Sagan, Carl Edward, views of

on abortion, 341

on apartheid in South Africa, 341

on arms race and dangers of nuclear war, 292–93

on capital punishment, 289

on death, 376

on extraterrestrial communication, 153

on extraterrestrial life, 56, 180–81, 220–22

on gay rights, 88–89, 120–21

global warming, 45

on Lily's dolphin experiments, 83, 84–85

on LSD-25, 85

on marijuana, 66–67

on meteorite controversy, 62–63

on mystic revelation, 175–76

on not identifying with one's theories, 116

on nuclear arms, 311–14

on parenting, 191–93

on peer envy, 264

on philosophy, 388

on piloted space travel, 49

on planetary contamination, 122, 158

on postmodernism, 361–362

on predestination, 259

on product endorsements, 363–64

on religion, 80, 342–43

on robotic exploration of solar system, 136

on teaching, 72, 115–18

on violence, 240

on war, 98, 120

Sagan, Carl Edward, writings of

anonymous writings on marijuana, 100–102

article in *Foreign Affairs* on nuclear warfare, 312

article with Newman on nuclear dilemma, 311

articles on Martian seasonal darkening, 89–90

The Atmospheres of Mars and Venus, 46–47

Billions and Billions, 374

"Climate in Smoke," 345

collaborating with Annie on abortion article, 341

Comet, 325

Communication with Extraterrestrial Intelligence (CETI), 142

Contact, 325

The Cosmic Connection, 174

The Demon-Haunted World, 282–83, 361, 377

The Dragons of Eden, 251

"Earth and Mars: Evolution of Atmospheres and Surface Temperatures," 161–63

Sagan, Carl Edward, writings of (*cont'd*)
  essay on life on Mars, 379
  feature on Mars for *National Geographic,*
    105
  "Galactic Civilizations: Population Dynam-
    ics and Interstellar Diffusion," 276
  "Indigenous Organic matter on the Moon,"
    41
  Intelligent Life in the Universe, 78–79, 91–92
  on interstellar travel, 74–76
  "Life" entry in *Encyclopaedia Britannica,*
    140
  "Long-Term Biological Consequences of
    Nuclear Wars," 312–13
  major collaborators and, 288–89
  "Nitrogen Oxides on Mars," 172
  "On the Rarity of Long-Lived, Non-Space-
    faring Galactic Civilizations," 374
  Other Worlds, 181
  Pale Blue Dot, 368
  A Path Where No Man Thought, 334, 345,
    348
  "Physical Studies of Planets," 41
  Planetary Exploration, 139, 140
  preface to *Visions of the Universe,* 269
  "Production of Organic Molecules in Plane-
    tary Atmospheres: A Preliminary Re-
    port," 41
  "Radiation and the Origin of the Gene," 26
  Saturday Review article on flying saucers,
    105
  Science article on Soviet Mars probes, 97
  Shadows of Forgotten Ancestors, 355
  Space Research, 140
  "The Ionospheric Model of the Venus Mi-
    crowave Emission: An Obituary," 89–90
  "The Radiation Balance of Venus," 41
  writing style of, 251–52
  writing techniques and approach of, 252–53
Sagan, Carol Mae
  birth of, 9
  bonding with Sagan during his illness, 370
  Carl and Cari visit Rachel in hospital,
    286–87
  donates bone marrow for Carl's operations,
    369, 376
Sagan, Dorion Solomon
  birth of, 38–39
  birth of Tonio Jerome Sagan, 323
  Carl as father to, 47, 323–24
  at Carl's sixtieth birthday party, 366
  co-author with Lynn Margulis of *Microcos-
    mos,* 324
  dream of Carl after Carl's death, 388

father's reaction to relationship with gay class-
    mate, 88–89
  on his father's egotism, 281–82
  on his father's manner of speaking, 71–72
  on his father's social activism, 289
  interactions with Carl, 192–93, 284
  recalling childhood stories told by father,
    99
  response to *The Demon-Haunted World,* 361
  Sagan's will and, 384
Sagan, Jeremy Ethan
  birth of, 47
  career in software industry, 354
  difficulties in relationship with Carl, 260
  interactions with Carl, 192–93, 284
  Sagan's will and, 384
Sagan, Linda. *See* Salzman, Linda
Sagan, Louis, 5
Sagan, Lynn. *See* Margulis, Lynn
Sagan Memorial Station, 384
Sagan, Nicholas Julian Zapata, 135–36
  argument with Carl over popular TV shows,
    364
  Carl and Linda's divorce and, 247, 249–50
  debates Carl on capital punishment, 289
  dreams of Carl after Carl's death, 388
  early childhood memories of, 136
  interactions with Carl, 191–92, 284
  maintains good terms with both Annie and
    Linda, 286
  precocious intellect of, 159
  reaction of classmates to *Cosmos,* 261
  script writing for *Star Trek,* 354
  speaking on Voyager time capsule, 245
  verbal ability of, 136
Sagan, Rachel
  birth and early life of, 4
  on Carl and Lynn's marriage, 35–36
  death of, 286–87
  genealogical conjectures about, 355
  influence on Carl's career, 287
  marriage of, 5
  on Nicholas Julian Zapata's name, 136
  personality of, 5, 10
  pride in Carl's achievements, 13–14
  putting Carl in his place, 178
  relationship with daughter Carol, 9
  relationship with Linda Salzman, 114–15
  relationship with Lynn Margulis, 32–33
  relationship with Ann Druyan, 278
  religious nature of, 13
  run-in with Asimov, 111
Sagan, Samuel
  agnostic belief of, 13

birthplace of, 5
death of, 259
finances of, 11
marriage of, 5
move to Rahway, 11
nicknames, 5
personality of, 6, 10
reaction to Carl and Linda's divorce, 250
struggles with lung cancer, 255
Sagan, Samuel Democritus Druyan
birth of, 352
Sagan's parenting of, 373
Sagan, Tonio Jerome
birth of, 323
Sagan dedicates book to, 361
Sagan's will and, 384
Sakharov, Andrey
relocation of during WWII, 77
on risks and benefits of SETI, 155
Salpeter, Edwin E., 195–96
Salzman, Linda
attends memorial services for Sagan, 384
creates artwork for message for Pioneer 10,
134
divorce proceeding with Sagan, 255–56
domestic difficulties with Sagan, 197
filmmaking at Ithaca, 191–92
gives birth to Nicholas Julian Zapata Sagan,
135–36
home decorating by, 159
housekeeping in Ithaca, 114–15
impending divorce, 246–47
marriage to Sagan, 111–12
rapprochement with Ann Druyan at *Contact*
premiere, 386
reaction to Carl and Annie's relationship,
251
reaction to divorce request, 249
relationship with Bill Gile, 88
during Sagan illness, 125–26
Sagan's relationship with, 85–86
work on Voyager time capsule, 232, 239, 244
Sasha. *See* Sagan, Alexandra Rachel Druyan
Sasov
extermination of Jewish population of, 10
Gruber ancestral home, 3
Saturday Review, 105
Saturn, 266
Schell, Jonathan, 312
Schlesinger, James, 337
Schneider, Stephen, 332–33
Scientific Study of Unidentified Flying Objects,
93
Scowcroft, Brent

The Day After panel discussion and, 314–15
opposition to nuclear testing, 338
Scrivner, Robert W., 297
seasonal changes on Mars, 87–89
Seitz, Russell, 333
serial enodsymbiosis theory (Margulis), 63
SETI Institute, 351
SETI (Search for Extraterrestrial Intelligence), 53
as basis for movie *Contact*, 267
hostile aliens and, 271
influence of Drake's brainteaser on, 61
limits and possibilities discussed at Byurakan, 151–52
META project and, 327–28, 349–51
Newman and Sagan modeling for speed of
space colonization, 276–278
"Ozma" search for intelligent life and, 50–51
political opposition to, 351
popularized by *Cosmos*, 271
Sagan petitions for international coopera-
tion on, 275
Sakharov and Persky on risks and benefits
of, 155
Senator Proxmire's criticism of, 272
Shklovskii doubts regarding, 319–20
Shklovskii's cosmic miracles argument and,
274
Tipler opposition to, 272
using Arecibo radar dish for, 187–90
Shadows of Forgotten Ancestors (Sagan and
Druyan), 355
Shakhashiri, Amahl, 233
Shapley, Harlow, 14
Sheen, Martin, 339
Sheour, Elie, 67–68
Shklovskii, I. S. (Iosiff Shmuelovich)
background of, 77
catastrophe theory of, 76
collaboration with Sagan, 78–79
comic miracles argument of, 274
Communist views of, 79
"Could Intelligent Life in the Universe Be
Unique?", 191
death of, 319–20
effect of Arecibo SETI study on, 190–91,
320
Intelligent Life in the Universe, 78–79
on lifetime of advanced civilizations, 148
Order of the Dolphin and, 59
on radio emissions from CTA-102, 91
signs Sagan's SETI petition, 275–76
supports Kardashev's theories of supercivilizations, 152

Shklovskii, I. S. (Iosiff Shmuelovich) (*cont'd*)
  theories about Martian moons, 139
  "Universe-Life-Intelligence," 78
  visits U.S., 138–39
Sholomitsky, Evgeny, 91
Shternberg Institute, Moscow University, 77, 91
Sidlin, Murry, 235
Simon and Schuster, 268
Simon, Benjamin, 130
Simpsons, The, 364
Simpson, George Gaylor
  criticism of exobiology, 106–7
  uses Kiess theories to support arguments against search for life on Mars, 172
Sinton bands, 30
Sinton, William M., 30, 46, 87
Sisler, Frederick, 61
Smithsonian Astrophysical Observatory, 67
Smithsonian Institution, 289
Soderblom, Laurence, 289
Soffen, Gerald, 44
  on Biemann experiment, 215, 219
  on Levin's theory of color changes in Mars rocks, 229
  on Sagan's humor, 118
solar systems, formation of (Gold), 143
Sondheim, Stephen, 103
Soter, Steven
  helps with *Cosmos,* 255
  SDS and, 119
  works with Sagan and Druyan on *Nucleus* series, 291–92
Soviet Central Committee, 318
Soviets
  Gorbachev announces unilateral halt to Soviet nuclear testing, 337
  Martian probes of, 97–98
  music selection for Voyager time capsule and, 235–36
  planetary contamination and, 40
  Sagan's role in Soviet disarmament policy, 317–18
  Sputnik and, 37–38
  technique for sterilization of planetary probes, 64
  U.S.-Soviet cooperation in space, 319
  Venera 1, 48
  Veneras 11 and 12, 265
Space Research (Sagan), 140
space travel. *See* interstellar travel
Sparks, Brad, 331
Sphinx House, 352–53
Spiegel, Laurie, 240

Spielberg, Steven
  funding for Project META, 327–28
  turns down *Contact* job, 362
Sputnik, 37–38, 49
Squyres, Steven
  as major collaborator with Sagan, 288
  work on Mars samples, 386
Stanford University School of Medicine, 68–70
Star Wars, 257
Star Wars. *See* Strategic Defense Initiative (SDI)
Stent, Gunther
  Golden Age theory of, 148–49
  on Lynn Margulis's research, 63
sterile soil theory (Horowitz and Cameron), 96
sterilization of planetary probes. *See* planetary contamination
Steyn, Mark, 380
Stover, Matt T., 365–66
Straat, Patricia
  defense of theory of life on Mars, 226
  works with Levin on Viking biology tests, 225
Strategic Defense Initiative (SDI)
  Sagan speaks to Congress on, 319
  Sagan's opposition to, 300–301
Struve, Otto
  as director, National Radio Astronomy Observatory, 50
  on fraction of stars having planets (Drake's equation), 55
  Green Bank meeting and, 52–54
Students for Democratic Society (SDS), 119
Su Shu Huang, 52–54, 55
Sullivan, Walter
  participant of UFO symposium, 131
  We Are Not Alone, 86
supercivilizations. *See* advanced civilizations
Surikov, Major General Boris Trofimovich, 318

Tambora volcano, 294–95
Tarter, Jill
  as character model for Sagan novel, 325
  continues work on META project after Sagan's death, 385
  moves to SETI Institute, 351
  pros and cons on Sagan's arrogance and, 282
  role on Project META, 327
teaching
  Sagan at Harvard, 72
  Sagan's influence at Cornell, 115–18
technology, evolution of, 147
Teller, Edward
  on probability of extraterrestrial life, 22

on Sagan's nuclear winter theories, 331
at University of Chicago, 14
Terzian, Yervant
on accessibility of Sagan, 287–88
ignores Sagan's exceeding two year sabbatical limit, 259
participates with *Cornel Review* spoof, 365
tholins, 266, 329
Thomas, E. Donnall, 369
Thomas, Lewis, 307
Thomas, Shirley, 74
Thompson, Starley, 332–33
Thompson, W. Reid
death of, 378
lung cancer of, 359
as major collaborator with Sagan, 289
Sagan's lab as health hazard and, 372
Thorne, Kip
Sagan requests his feedback on *Contact*, 325–26
"Wormholes in spacetime and their use for interstellar travel," 326
Tipler, Frank
article published in *Quarterly Journal of the Royal Astronomical Society*, 273
contacts Senator Proxmire about SETI, 272
"Extraterrestrial Beings Do Not Exist" article, 272
feud with Sagan, 311
Titan, 266
Today Show, 178
Tonight Show
Carson monologue on color images from Mars, 208
Sagan's appearances on, 177–78
Toon, Owen Brian, 288
modeling effect of dust created by nuclear war, 296
research on nuclear winter, 293
studies dinosaur extinction theory with Pollack and Turco, 295
Toulmin, Steven, 232
Triton, 344
triune brain theory (MacLean), 254
Troitsky, V. S., 187
Truly, Richard, 344
TTAPS article
attacked for lack of integrity, 333
complexity of findings in, 308–10
conclusions of, 302–03
criticisms of, 303–04
models used in, 302
preliminary presentation of, 306
reaction of scientific community to, 334–35

Sagan's defense of, 335–36
Sagan's politics and, 310
TTAPS II and, 345–46
Turco, Toon, Ackerman, Pollack and Sagan collaborate on, 301
Turco, Richard
coins term "nuclear winter," 305
modeling effect of dust created by nuclear war, 296
A Path Where No Man Thought, 334, 345, 348
research on nuclear winter, 293
on weakness of Alexandrov's model, 320
work on dinosaur extinction theory, 295
work on effect of aerosols on atmosphere, 295
Turner, Ted, 354
Two Ball Games (Linda Sagan and David Gluck), 192
2001: A Space Odyssey, Sagan's consultation on, 105–6
Tyler, G. Leonard
radar view of Mars conflicts with photos, 168
radar views of Mars, 167
role in selecting Viking 1 landing site, 202
Type I, II, III civilizations (Kardashev), 151–52
Tyson, Neil deGrasse, 116

UFOs
psychiatric aspects of, 132
Sagan participates in Project Blue Book, 92–94
Sagan testifies as expert witness relative to UFO scam, 94–95
Sagan's interest in, 20–23
Sagan's sighting of supposed UFO, 93
symposium on, 128–130, 131
UFOs—A Scientific Debate (Sagan), 132, 140
unfalsifiable hypothesis (Popper), 275
United Nations
Outer Space Committee of, 241–42
participation in Voyager time capsule, 241–42, 243–45
The Universe (Asimov), 86
"Universe-Life-Intelligence" (Shklovskii), 78
University of Chicago
awards Sagan Ph.D. in astronomy and astrophysics, 43
"Great Books" program of, 16
Sagan's A.B. degree from, 25
Sagan's application to, 14–15
Sagan's physics major at, 26
Uranus, 329
Urey, Harold Clayton, 23–25
on absence of water on Venus, 41

Urey, Harold Clayton (*cont'd*)
  arms control and, 311
  Blue Book files and, 128
  changes his stance on Sagan, 173
  commenting on Sagan's interest in exobiology, 46
  criticism of Sagan undermines his employment at MIT, 171
  criticism of Sagan undermines his tenure at Harvard, 171
  death of and Sagan's obituary in *Icarus*, 266–67
  dispute with Kuiper, 27
  on *Intelligent Life in the Universe*, 91
  Manhattan project and, 23
  meeting with Sagan, 23
  as member of Viking molecular analysis team, 137
  meteorite controversy and, 61–63
  Miller-Urey experiment and, 24–25
  Nobel Prize for discovering deuterium, 23
  The Planets, 27
  at University of Chicago, 14
U.S. Congress, 244
U.S. News and World Reprt, 217
U.S.-Soviet Mars mission, 343

Velikhov, Yevgeny P.
  The Conference on the World After Nuclear War and, 307
  Sagan meeting with regarding nuclear winter work at Ames, 299
Venera 1, 48
Venera 11 and 12, 265
Venus
  greenhouse effect and, 48, 162–63
  microwave energy and temperature of, 42
  Sagan's greenhouse theory about, 41–43
  theories about water on Venus, 41–42
Veverka, Joseph
  attracted from Harvard to Cornell by Sagan, 117
  as major collaborator with Sagan, 288
  receives Mariner 9 photos with Sagan, 156–57
Viking 1
  color images of Mars, 207–8
  controversy over results of life-detecting tests, 212–13
  debate over landing site for, 202
  early results from life-detecting tests, 211–12
  experiments to determine presence of microbes, 208–11

ongoing experimentation and controversy about life-detection experiments, 216–18
  photos from surface of Mars, 203–6
  touchdown, 203
Viking 2
  biology experiments of, 218, 219–21
  controversy over results of life-detecting tests, 221–23
  debate over northern landing site, 206–7
  landing site of, 218
  Levin, Oyama, Horowitz repeat experiments of Viking 1, 218
Viking project, 136–38
  comparing photos and radar views of Mars, 166–67
  controversy over results of life-detecting tests, 227–28
  count down, 193–94
  first photos of Mars, 203–6
  life-detection tests continue until equipment fails, 224–26
  Jim Martin drills for project members, 198
  Martin as project leader of, 168
  pessimism surrounding Viking 2, 206
  photos from orbit reveal problems with landing site, 200–201
  project teams for, 136–37
  Sagan and Lederberg debate landing site, 165–66
  Sagan arguing for a design to detect widest range of possible organisms, 181
  Sagan as guiding spirit of, 136
  Sagan considers life-detection tests inconclusive, 226–28
  Sagan role in landing site selection for, 137
  Sagan role in making speculative hypotheses for biology experiments, 220–22
  Sagan work on cameras and, 182–84
  support case for running water on Mars, 200
  Viking 1 touchdown, 203
Vishniac, Roman, 49
Vishniac, Wolf
  death of, 179
  as member of Viking active biology team, 137
  Sagan's casualness about appointments and, 73
  work on back contamination, 122
  work on "life detectors," 49
Visions of the Universe (Asimov), 269
volcanoes, 294–95
von Braun, Wernher, 285
von Karman, Theodore, 37

von Neumann, John, 273
Votaw, Paul, 329
Voyager program. *See also* Voyager time capsule
  abandoned, 108
  new Voyager mission planned 1972, 159–60
  passing Saturn, 266
  returning photographic images of Jupiter and its moons, 258–59
  reveals Jupiter's moons of ice, 265
  Sagan works on time capsule for, 231–33
  Voyager 2 launch date, 248
Voyager time capsule
  compared with Pioneer plaques, 248
  finishing details for, 247–48
  human portrait on, 239
  participants in, 231–32
  protecting, 248
  representing human languages on, 241–45
  Sagan projects lifetime of, 248
  sound essay on, 240–41
  technical difficulties of, 247
  UN participation and UN protocol, 241–42, 243–45
  work on music selection for, 233–37
  work on photo album for, 237–39

Waldheim, U.N. Secretary General Kurt
  gives message for inclusion on Voyager time capsule, 244
  Voyager time capsule and, 242
Walker, G. Russel, 89–90
Wallace, David, 265
water
  impossibility of water on Mars, 86
  Mariner 9 raises questions about water on Mars, 158
  Mars and, 28–29
  Mars Pathfinder evidence for running water on Mars, 385
  Venus and, 41
  Viking supports case for running water on Mars, 200
Watson, James, 144
We Are Not Alone (Sullivan), 86
Weinberg, Steven, 388

Whipple, Babette, 112
Whipple, Fred
  changing stance on Sagan's full professorship at Harvard, 107
  discloses reason for Harvard tenure problem to Sagan, 171
  on rumors of why Sagan was passed over at Harvard, 112
  Sagan's opportunity to work with, 67
  theories about water on Venus, 41
The Whole Earth Catalog, 175
Wickramasinghe, N. C., 330–31
Wiesel, Elie, 314–15
Williams, Martin, 235
Williamson, Marianne, 259
Wilson, Peter
  as major collaborator with Sagan, 289
  on Sagan's ethics, 282
Winograd, Terry, 150
"Wormholes in spacetime and their use for interstellar travel" (Thorne and Morris), 326
Wright-Patterson Air Force Base, 93

X-Files, The 387

Yalow, Rosalyn, 357
Yerkes observatory, 14, 33
York, Eleanor, 372
York, Herbert, 22
Young, A. Thomas
  bet with Soffen regarding life on Mars, 215, 219
  Viking landing site selection and, 137

Zemeckis, Robert
  Forrest Gump techniques applied to *Contact,* 380
  initially turns down *Contact* job, 362
  replaces George Miller as director, 375
  Sagan presses him for scientific accuracy on *Contact,* 377–78
  Sagan sending notes about *Contact* while on deathbed, 380
  uses images and speech of Clinton in *Contact,* 379